The **Rough G**

Korea

written and researched by

Norbert Paxton

www.roughguides.com

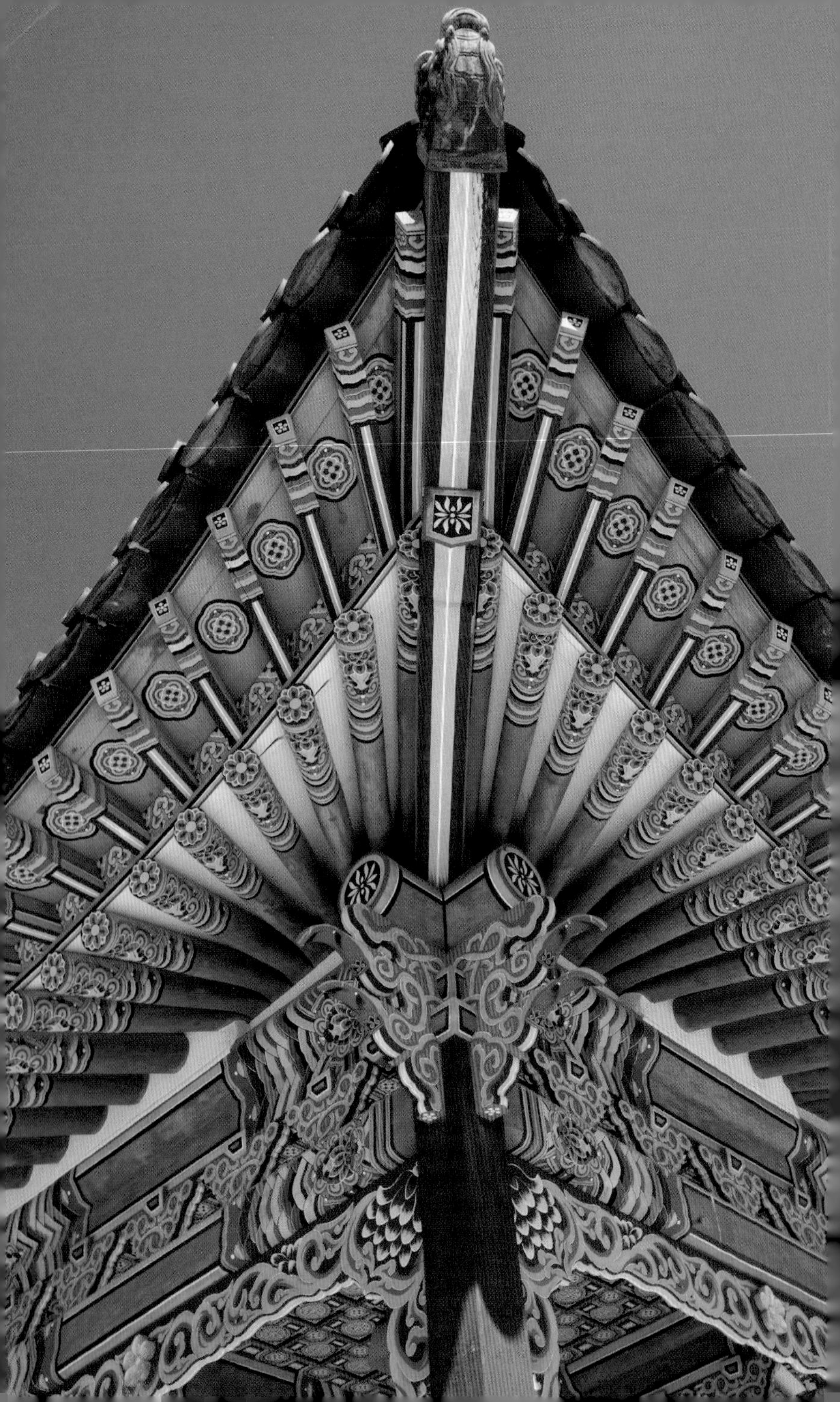

Contents

◀◀ Beomeosa temple, Busan ◀ Changdeokgung palace, Seoul

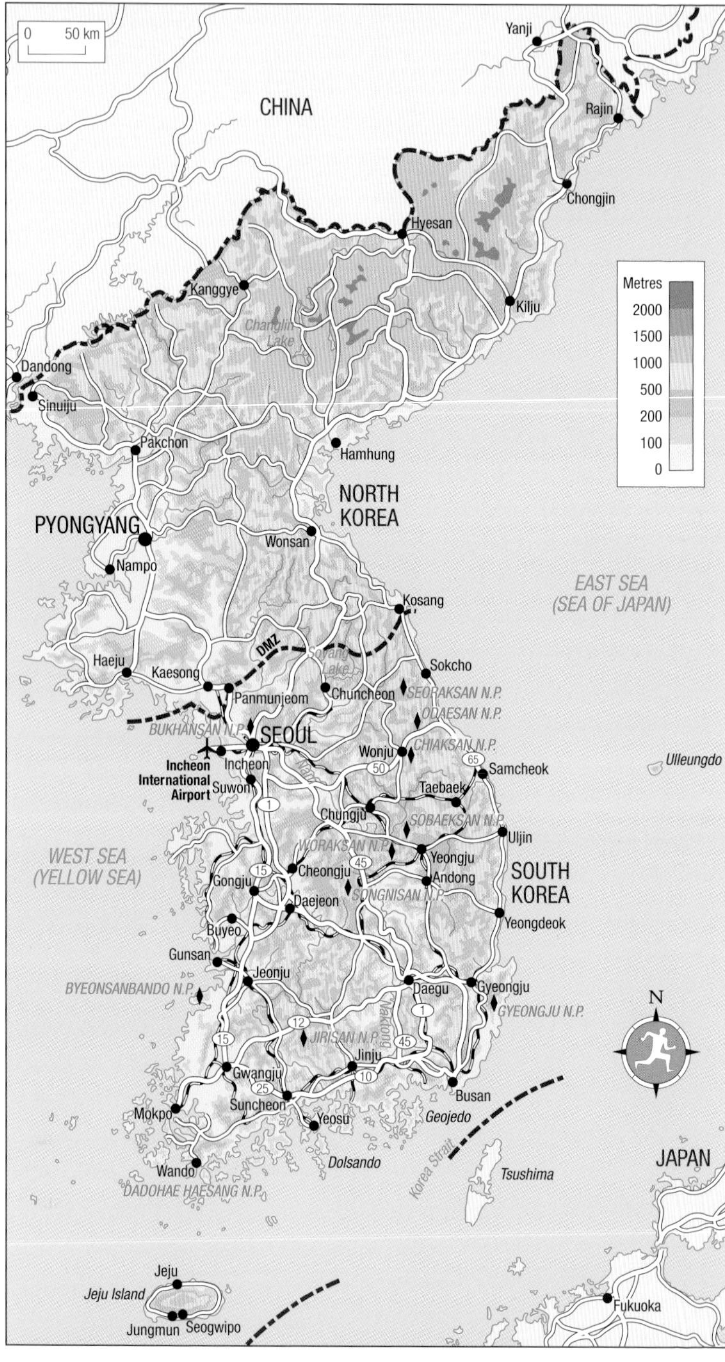

0 50 km
CHINA
Yanji
Rajin
Chongjin
Hyesan
Kanggye
Changjin Lake
Kilju
Metres
2000
1500
1000
500
200
100
0
Dandong
Sinuiju
Pakchon
Hamhung
NORTH KOREA
PYONGYANG
Wonsan
Nampo
EAST SEA (SEA OF JAPAN)
Kosang
DMZ
Soyang Lake
Haeju
Kaesong
Sokcho
Panmunjeom
Chuncheon
SEORAKSAN N.P.
ODAESAN N.P.
BUKHANSAN N.P.
SEOUL
CHIAKSAN N.P.
Wonju
Samcheok
Ulleungdo
Incheon International Airport
Incheon
Suwon
Taebaek
Chungju
SOBAEKSAN N.P.
Uljin
WEST SEA (YELLOW SEA)
WORAKSAN N.P.
Yeongju
Cheongju
Andong
SOUTH KOREA
Gongju
SONGNISAN N.P.
Daejeon
Yeongdeok
Buyeo
Gunsan
Jeonju
BYEONSANBANDO N.P.
Daegu
Gyeongju
GYEONGJU N.P.
N
JIRISAN N.P.
Nakdong
Jinju
Gwangju
Busan
Suncheon
Mokpo
Yeosu
Geojedo
Korea Strait
Wando
Dolsando
Tsushima
JAPAN
DADOHAE HAESANG N.P.
Jeju
Jeju Island
Jungmun
Seogwipo
Fukuoka

Introduction to

Korea

The Korean peninsula is a tantalizingly unexplored slice of East Asia – a pine-clad land of mountains, misty archipelagos and rice paddies of emerald green, studded with urban pockets of incomparable *joie de vivre*. While its troubled history has made Korea's very existence nothing short of miraculous, amazingly its traditions and customs have largely survived intact – and for visitors, this highly distinctive culture is an absolute joy to dive into.

Having gone their separate ways in 1953 after the catastrophic **Korean War** – essentially a civil war, but one largely brought about by external forces, which left millions dead and flattened almost the whole peninsula – the two Koreas are now separated by the spiky twin frontiers of the Demilitarized Zone. **North Korea** has armed itself to the teeth since 1953, stagnated in its pursuit of a local brand of **Communism** and become one of the least accessible countries in the world. Unbelievably, many foreigners seem to expect something similar of **South Korea**, which shows just how well kept a secret this fascinating place really is: beyond the glittering city of Seoul, *gimchi*, dog meat and *taekwondo*, little is known about the country in the outside world (and in actual fact, one of those four has largely gone the way of the dodo anyway).

Fact file

• The Korean peninsula is split in two by the 4km-wide Demilitarized Zone (DMZ), sharing borders with China and – for about 20km, south of Vladivostok – Russia. These frontiers form a northern boundary with **North Korea** – the "Democratic People's Republic of Korea" – whose population of around 24 million live in an area half the size of the United Kingdom. Slightly smaller **South Korea**, also known as the "Republic of Korea", has a population of 49 million, making it the world's 26th most populous country.

• Ethnic Koreans dominate the populations of both countries, making them two of the most **ethnically homogenous** societies on earth. Before splitting, both were traditionally Buddhist nations – though deeply steeped in Confucianism and shamanistic ritual. Since then the North has followed Juche, a local brand of Communism, while in the South Christianity has become the most popular religion.

• Before the Japanese occupation in 1910, the Silla, Goryeo and Joseon dynasties were ruled over by an unbroken run of **116 monarchs**, dating back to 57 BC.

• The economies of South and North Korea were almost equal in size until the mid-1970s. The "Economic Miracle" that followed in the South has propelled it to the cusp of the world's top ten economies, while the North languishes just above 100th place.

After the war, the South gradually embraced democracy and has since gone on to become a powerful and dynamic economy. Its **cities** are a pulsating feast of eye-searing neon, feverish activity and round-the-clock business. Here you can shop till you drop at markets that never close, feast on eye-wateringly spicy food, get giddy on a bottle or two of *soju*, then sweat out the day's exertions at a night-time sauna. However, set foot outside the urban centres and your mere presence will cause quite a stir – in the remote **rural areas** life continues much as it did before the "Economic Miracle" of the 1970s, and pockets of **islands** exist where no foreigner has ever set foot.

And for all its newfound prosperity, the South remains a land steeped in **tradition**. Before being abruptly

▲ Ceremonial guard, Gyeongbokgung, Seoul

▲ Woljeongsa temple, Odaesan National Park

choked off by the Japanese occupation in 1910, an unbroken line of more than one hundred kings existed for almost two thousand years – their grassy burial mounds have yielded thousands of golden relics – and even the capital, Seoul, has a number of **palaces** dating back to the fourteenth century. The wooden *hanok* housing of decades gone by may have largely given way to

The creation of hangeul

One thing that will strike you on a trip around Korea is **hangeul**, the peninsula's distinctive, almost Tetris-like alphabet. Amazingly, this was a royal creation, having been the brainchild of **King Sejong** in the 1440s. Most of this creative king's subjects were unable to read the Chinese script used across the land at the time, so he devised a system that would be easier for ordinary people to learn. Sejong was forced to do much of his work in secret, as the plan did not go down well with the *yangban* – Confucian scholars who were even more powerful than the royalty at the time. As the only truly educated members of society, the *yangban* argued fiercely against the change in an effort to maintain their monopoly over knowledge.

Hangeul experienced periodic bursts of popularity, but was almost erased entirely by the Japanese during their occupation of the peninsula (1910–45). However, it's now the **official writing system** in both North and South Korea, as well as a small autonomous Korean pocket in the Chinese province of Jilin; it's also used in Bau-Bau, a small town in Indonesia.

The alphabet, while it appears complex, is surprisingly **easy to learn**, and demonstrating that you can read even a handful of simple words will generate gasps of admiration across Korea. Just a few hours of hard study should suffice – to get started, turn to the table of characters on p.392.

rows of apartment blocks, but these traditional dwellings can still be found in places, and you'll never be more than a walk away from an immaculately painted **Buddhist temple**. Meanwhile, Confucian-style formal ceremonies continue to play an important part in local life, and some mountains still even host shamanistic rituals.

As for the **Korean people** themselves, they are a real delight: fiercely proud, and with a character almost as spicy as their food, they're markedly eager to please foreigners who come to live or holiday in their country. Within hours of arriving, you may well find yourself with new friends in tow, racing up a mountainside, lunching over a delicious barbequed *galbi*, throwing back *makkeolli* until dawn, or singing the night away at a *noraebang*. Few travellers leave without tales of the kindness of Korean strangers, and all of them wonder why the country isn't a more popular stop on the international travel circuit.

Where to go

▲ Rice wine

Korea is still something of an unknown territory, and more than half of all its visitors get no further than **Seoul**. One of the largest and most technically advanced cities in the world, the capital regularly confounds expectations by proving itself steeped in history. Here, fourteenth-century palaces, imperial gardens, teeming markets and secluded tearooms continue to exude charm among a maze of skyscrapers and shopping malls. From Seoul, anywhere in the country is reachable within a day, but the best day-trip by far is to the **DMZ**, the strip of land that separates the two Koreas from coast to coast.

Gyeonggi, the province that surrounds Seoul, is a largely unappealing area dissected by the roads and railways that snake their way into the capital, but two of its cities certainly deserve a visit: **Suwon**, home to a wonderful UNESCO-listed fortress dating from the late eighteenth century; and cosmopolitan **Incheon**, where you can eat some of the best food in the country before making your way to the **islands** of the West Sea. By contrast,

▲ Jeongbang waterfall, Seogwipu, Jeju Island

▲ Hongdae, Seoul

the neighbouring province of **Gangwon** is unspoilt and stuffed full of attractions – in addition to a number of national parks, of which craggy **Seoraksan** is the most visited, you can head to the unspoilt beaches and colossal caves that surround the small city of **Samcheok**, or peek inside a genuine American warship and North Korean submarine north of the sleepy fishing village of **Jeongdongjin**.

Stretching down from Gangwon to the South Sea lie the markedly traditional **Gyeongsang** provinces, home to some of the peninsula's most popular attractions. Foremost among these is gorgeous **Gyeongju**; capital of the Silla dynasty for almost a thousand years, and extremely laid-back by Korean standards, it's spotted with the grassy burial tombs of the many kings and queens who ruled here. There's enough in the surrounding area to fill at least a week of sightseeing – most notable are **Namsan**, a small mountain area peppered with trails, tombs and some intriguing Buddhas, and the sumptuously decorated **Bulguksa** temple, another sight on the UNESCO World Heritage list. Although less picturesque as a town, **Andong** is almost as relaxed as Gyeongju, and a superb base from which to access **Dosan Seowon**, a remote Confucian academy, and the charmingly dusty village of **Hahoe**, a functioning showcase of traditional Korean life. The region's

▲ Playing Go outside Jongmyo shrine, Seoul

The Taegeukki

South Korea's national flag – the *Taegeukki* – is one of the most distinctive around, and is heavily imbued with philsophical meaning. The design itself has changed a little since its first unveiling in the 1880s, though its fundamental elements remain the same: a red-and-blue circle surrounded by four black trigams, all set on a white background. The puritanical connotations of the white are obvious, whereas the circle and trigrams offer greater food for thought. The four trigams make up half of the eight used in the *I Ching*, an ancient Chinese book of divination. Each can represent a number of different concepts: moving clockwise from the top-left of the flag, these may be read as spring, winter, summer and autumn; heaven, moon, earth and sun; father, son, mother and daughter; as well as many more besides.

The circle is split into the "Yin–Yang" shape, its two halves representing opposites such as light and dark, male and female, day and night. Though coincidental, connections with the divided Korean peninsula are easy to find, with two opposing halves forming part of the same whole – the red half is even on top.

▲ Dancers, Korean Folk Village, Suwon

rustic charm is actually best appreciated offshore on the windswept island of **Ulleungdo**, an extinct volcanic cone that rises precipitously from the East Sea, and where tiny fishing settlements cling barnacle-like to its coast. Thrills with a more urban flavour can be had in **Busan**, Korea's second city, which has an atmosphere markedly different from Seoul; as well as the most raucous nightlife outside the capital, it has the best fish market in the country, and a number of excellent beaches on its fringes.

Even more characterful are the **Jeolla** provinces, which make up the southwest of the peninsula. Left to stagnate by the government while Korea's economy kicked into gear, they have long played the role of the renegade, though this energy is now being rechannelled. Violent political protests took place in regional capital **Gwangju** as recently as 1980, though the city

Titles and transliteration

The Korean peninsula is split into the **Republic of Korea** (South Korea) and the **Democratic People's Republic of Korea** (North Korea). Most of this book is about the former, which is referred to throughout as "Korea"; this is how locals refer to their nation when talking to outsiders, though in Korean they use the term "*Hanguk*". North Korea has, where necessary, been referred to as such, or as "the DPRK"; North Koreans' own word for both country and peninsula is "*Choson*".

Also note that a uniform system of transliteration is used throughout this book. It's the best and most recent one, but as older generations have been schooled with different systems you may well spot a few varieties of the same word on your travels – see the Language section on p.389 for more information.

▶ Pyongyang, North Korea

has reinvented itself to become one of the artiest and most business-savvy in the land. **Jeonju** has a similar feel, plus a delightful district of traditional *hanok* housing, and is justly famed for its wonderful, flavoursome cuisine. Earthy **Mokpo** is the hub for ferry trips to a mind-boggling number of **West Sea islands**, dotted with fishing communities where life has changed little in decades, while inland there are a number of excellent national parks.

The **Chungcheong** provinces at the centre of the country are bypassed by many travellers, but this is a shame, as they contain some fine sights. The old Baekje capitals of **Gongju** and **Buyeo** provide glimpses of a dynasty long dead, **Daecheon beach** hosts a rumbustious annual mud festival that may well be Korea's most enjoyable event, and there are temples galore – the gigantic golden Buddha at **Beopjusa** is surrounded by 1000m-high peaks, while the meandering trails and vivid colour schemes at **Guinsa** make it the most visually stimulating temple in the land.

Lying within a ferry ride of the mainland's southern shore is the island of **Jeju**, a popular honeymoon destination for Koreans. While it's undoubtedly

▶ Shoes outside Jogyesa temple, Seoul

a touristy place, it has its remote stretches and anyone who has climbed the volcanic cone of **Hallasan**, walked through the lava tubes of **Manjanggul** or watched the sun go down from **Yakcheonsa** temple will tell you the trip is more than worthwhile.

And finally, of course, there's **North Korea**. A visit to one of the world's most feared and most fascinating countries will instantly earn you kudos – even experienced travellers routinely put the DPRK at the top of their "most interesting" list. Visits don't come cheap and can only be made as part of a guided tour, but the country's inaccessibility brings an epic quality to its few officially sanctioned sights.

When to go

Korea's year is split into **four distinct seasons**. **Spring** generally lasts from April to June, and is one of the best times to visit: flowers are in bloom, and a frothy cloak of cherry blossom washes a brief wave of pinkish white from south to north. Locals head for the hills, making use of the country's many national parks, and the effects of the change in weather can also be seen in a number of interesting festivals.

Korea's **summer**, on the other hand, can be unbearably muggy, and you may find yourself leaping from one air-conditioned sanctuary to the next. You'll wonder how Koreans can persist with their uniformly fiery food at this time, and you'll certainly be grateful for the ubiquitous water fountains. It's best to avoid the **monsoon** season: more than half of the country's annual rain falls from early July to late August. In a neat reversal of history, Japan and China protect Korea from most of the area's typhoons, but one or two manage to get through the gap each year.

▲ Deogyusan National Park

The very best time of the year to visit is **autumn** (Sept–Nov), when temperatures are mild, rainfall is generally low and festivals are easy to come across. Korea's mountains erupt in a magnificent array of

Buyeo, Chungcheong

reds, yellows and oranges, and locals flock to national parks to picnic under their fiery canopies. T-shirt weather can continue long into October, though you're likely to need some extra layers by then.

The Korean **winter** is long and cold, with the effects of the Siberian weather system more pronounced the further north you go. However, travel at this time is far from impossible – public transport services continue undaunted, underfloor *ondol* heating systems are cranked up, and the lack of rain creates photogenic contrasts between powdery snow, crisp blue skies, off-black pine trees and the earthy yellow of dead grass.

Average monthly temperatures and rainfall

	Jan	Feb	Mar	Apr	May	Jun	Jul	Aug	Sep	Oct	Nov	Dec
BUSAN												
Max/Min(ºC)	6/-2	7/-1	12/3	17/8	21/13	24/17	27/22	29/23	26/18	21/12	15/6	9/1
Max/Min (ºF)	43/28	45/30	54/38	63/47	70/55	75/63	81/71	84/73	79/64	70/54	59/43	48/34
Rainfall	43	36	69	140	132	201	295	130	173	74	41	31
JEJU CITY												
Max/Min (ºC)	10/5	12/6	15/8	19/10	23/14	26/18	28/23	29/24	27/20	23/14	17/8	13/6
Max/Min (ºF)	50/41	54/43	59/46	66/50	73/57	79/64	82/73	84/75	80/68	73/57	63/46	55/43
Rainfall	84	89	94	176	171	205	356	243	184	95	93	82
PYONGYANG												
Max/Min (ºC)	-3/-13	1/-10	7/-4	16/3	22/9	26/15	29/20	29/20	24/14	18/6	9/-2	0/-10
Max/Min (ºF)	27/7	34/14	45/25	61/37	71/48	79/59	84/68	84/68	75/57	64/43	48/28	32/14
Rainfall	15	11	25	46	67	76	237	228	112	45	41	21
SEOUL												
Max/Min (ºC)	0/-9	3/-7	8/-2	17/5	22/11	27/16	29/21	31/22	26/15	19/7	11/0	3/-7
Max/Min (ºF)	32/16	37/19	46/28	63/41	72/52	81/61	84/70	88/72	79/59	66/45	52/32	37/19
Rainfall	31	20	38	76	81	130	376	267	119	41	46	25

things not to miss

It's not possible to see everything that Korea has to offer on a short trip – and we don't suggest you try. What follows is a selective taste of the peninsula's highlights: fascinating museums, spectacular buildings and a few ways simply to indulge yourself. They're arranged in five colour-coded categories, which you can browse through to find the very best things to see and experience. All highlights have a page reference to take you straight into the Guide, where you can find out more.

01 Insadong tearooms Page **112** • Tea may have ceded ground to coffee across the nation, but Seoul's traditional Insadong district still has dozens of secluded places serving traditional brews.

02 Udo Page **307** • This bucolic, beach-frirged island, its narrow lanes lined with gorgeous walls of hand-stacked stone, is the ideal spot for a cycle ride.

03 Huwon Page **87** • Relax by the lake as kings once did at this secluded "Secret Garden", which nestles at the back of a UNESCO-listed palace in central Seoul.

04 Jeonju hanok village Page **254** • Here you can sleep in a traditional wooden *hanok* house heated from underneath by gentle flames, in one of Korea's most agreeable cities.

05 Boryeong Mud Festival Page **267** • Korea's dirtiest, most enjoyable festival takes place each July on the west coast – don't forget your soap.

06 Makkeolli Page **47** • Get drunk the local way with this milky rice wine, which has undergone a huge surge in popularity of late.

07 Teddy Bear Museum Page **314** • The epitome of kitsch, most notable for its diorama room portraying twentieth-century events such as teddies tearing down the Berlin Wall, landing on the moon and going down with the *Titanic*.

08 Guinsa Page **291** • The most distinctive temple complex in the country, Guinsa's paths wind snake-like routes up a tight, remote valley in Korea's heartland.

09 Yakcheonsa Page **315** • Large, splendid temple on the southern coast of Jeju Island, and almost unique among Korean temples in that it faces the sea – pop along for sundown and evening prayers.

10 Dosan Seowon Page **178** • The wonderfully unspoilt countryside surrounding the city of Andong is studded with gems, and this former Confucian academy is one of the best.

11 Flower ssambap Page **42** • A feast of leaves, roots and shoots, topped with dozens of edible flowers – simply heavenly when swallowed down with barbecued duck.

12 West Sea Islands Page **242** • Over three thousand islands are sprinkled like confetti around Korea's western coast – pick up a map in Mokpo, get on a ferry and lose track of time.

13 Dongdaemun Market Page **92** • A 24-hour market in a city that never sleeps, Dongdaemun is a Seoul institution, with sights and smells redolent of decades gone by.

14 Naejangsan National Park Page **249** • Shaped like a soft volcano, this national park's ring of peaks provide the country's most mesmerising displays of autumn foliage.

15 The DMZ Page **140** • Take a step inside the 4km-wide Demilitarized Zone separating North and South Korea: the world's frostiest remnant of the Cold War.

16 Buamdong Page **111** • Seoul's latest "secret" area is a quiet maze of roads tucked away behind the royal palaces. Here you'll find elegant restaurants and cafés – and very few tourists.

17 Noraebang Page **96** • A near-mandatory part of a Korean night out is a trip to a "singing room", the local take on Japan's karaoke bars.

18 Galbi see *Korean cuisine* colour section • A fire at the centre of your table and a plate of raw meat to fling onto it – could this be the world's most fun-to-eat dish?

19 Gongsanseong Page **275** • Overlooking the river in sleepy Gongju, the walls of this fortress follow an almost caldera-like course; in the middle you'll find dreamy pavilions and walking paths.

20 Jeongdongjin Page **162** • Korea's most surreal village has a train station on the beach, a ship-hotel atop a cliff, an American warship and a North Korean spy submarine.

21 Gyeongju Page **185** • The former capital of Silla is the most traditional city in Korea, and should be on every visitor's itinerary.

22 Socialist realist art Page **330** • That which has become ironic in Eastern Europe remains iconic in the DPRK, with colourful murals found all across the country – send one home on a postcard.

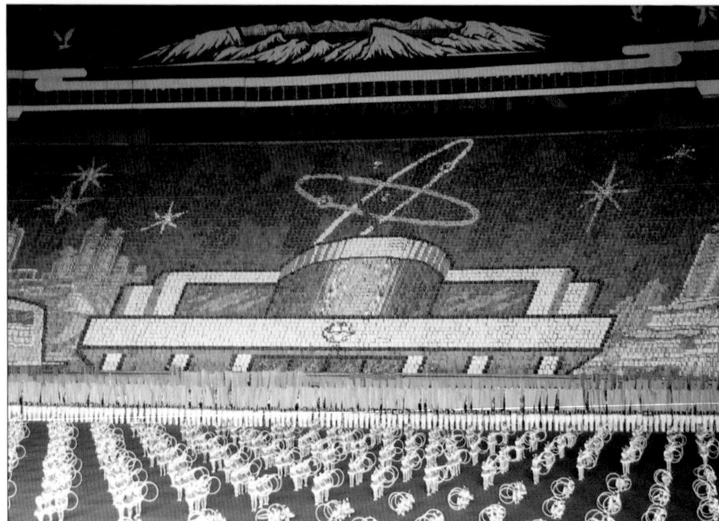

23 Arirang Mass Games Page **341** • Performers outnumber spectators at this feast of synchronized dance, one of the biggest and most spectacular events you're likely to see.

24 Paekdusan Page **353** • The legendary birthplace of the Korean nation, this dormant volcano – the highest peak on the peninsula – rises up through the Chinese-North Korean border, its crater lake a preternatural blue when not frozen over.

25 Pyongyang Page **340** • The world's least-visited capital – a rhapsody of brutalist architecture and red *hangeul* slogans extolling the virtues of the government and its leaders – proudly proffers its subway system on its list of attractions.

Basics

Basics

Getting there

With no way to travel to Korea by road or rail, the vast majority of travellers arrive at the gleaming Incheon international airport; often referred to as "Seoul Incheon" on international departure boards, this offshore beast handles a large and ever-increasing number of international flights. The only other way in is by sea – there are services from both China and Japan.

Korean Air and Asiana are the two big Korean **airlines**, operating direct flights from a number of destinations around the world. Seoul increasingly features as a stopover on round-the-world trips, and the country is well served by dozens of international carriers. **Fares** increase for travel in the summer months and at Christmas time. A **departure tax** applies when leaving Korea, but will almost certainly be factored in to your ticket price.

Incheon itself is served by a number of Chinese **ferry** ports, and there are services from several destinations in Japan to Busan. Those arriving by ferry will be rewarded with a pretty introduction to the country – the Korean coastline around Incheon melts into countless islands, though the port area itself has been ravaged by industry, as have some nearby islands. Yet more interesting would be to arrive by **train** through North Korea, but though the country's relationship with the outside world has so far prevented Seoul-bound trains from making the journey from Beijing, lines across the demilitarized zone dividing the Koreas (the DMZ) have been upgraded in anticipation of a political thaw on the peninsula – keep your eyes peeled.

Flights from the UK and Ireland

Korean Air and Asiana have **direct** connections from London Heathrow to Incheon – Korean Air has a daily service, while Asiana has five per week. The journey takes eleven hours, with fares costing around £600; this can sail over £800 during summer and at Christmas, when it's common for all flights to be fully booked weeks in advance. You can save money by taking an indirect flight, with prices often dipping below £400 during low season; good options include Finnair via Helsinki, Qatar Airways via Doha, Aeroflot via Moscow and Emirates via Dubai. It's also worth checking deals with KLM and Air France, whose routes are as close to direct as possible.

There are no direct flights to Korea from **Ireland** so you'll have to transfer in the UK or in mainland Europe.

Flights from the US and Canada

If you are coming from the **US** you have a number of options available to you: there are direct flights to Incheon from New York, Dallas, Las Vegas, Los Angeles, San Francisco, Detroit, Seattle, Chicago, Atlanta, Washington and Honolulu; carriers include Delta and United, as well as Asiana and Korean Air. Sample low season fares are $1400 from New York (a journey of around 14hr), $1200 from Chicago (14hr) and $1150 from Los Angeles (13hr). In all cases you may save up to a couple of hundred dollars by transferring – San Francisco and Seattle are popular hubs. Fares on many routes can almost double during summer and Christmas time.

Korean Air has direct flights from Incheon from two **Canadian** cities, Vancouver and Toronto, but these can be very expensive when demand is high (over Can$3000). Again, you're likely to save money by taking an

Unless explicitly stated, this Basics section is referring to South Korea, calling that country "Korea" as the locals do. For North Korea travel basics, see pp.323–332.

Six steps to a better kind of travel

At Rough Guides we are passionately committed to travel. We feel strongly that only through travelling do we truly come to understand the world we live in and the people we share it with – plus tourism has brought a great deal of **benefit** to developing economies around the world over the last few decades. But the extraordinary growth in tourism has also damaged some places irreparably, and of course **climate change** is exacerbated by most forms of transport, especially flying. This means that now more than ever it's important to **travel thoughtfully** and **responsibly**, with respect for the cultures you're visiting – not only to derive the most benefit from your trip but also to preserve the best bits of the planet for everyone to enjoy. At Rough Guides we feel there are six main areas in which you can make a difference:

- Consider what you're contributing to the **local economy**, and how much the services you use do the same, whether it's through employing local workers and guides or sourcing locally grown produce and local services.
- Consider the **environment** on holiday as well as at home. Water is scarce in many developing destinations, and the biodiversity of local flora and fauna can be adversely affected by tourism. Try to patronize businesses that take account of this.
- Travel with a purpose, not just to tick off experiences. Consider **spending longer** in a place, and getting to know it and its people.
- Give thought to how often you **fly**. Try to avoid short hops by air and more harmful night flights.
- Consider **alternatives to flying**, travelling instead by bus, train, boat and even by bike or on foot where possible.
- Make your trips "**climate neutral**" via a reputable carbon-offset scheme. All Rough Guide flights are offset, and every year we donate money to a variety of charities devoted to combating the effects of climate change.

indirect flight, in which case Can$1700 would be a typical low season fare from both cities.

Flights from Australia, New Zealand and South Africa

From **Australia**, the only three cities with direct connections to Korea are Sydney (10hr), twice per day; Brisbane (9hr), five times per week; and Melbourne (11hr) three times per week. There are sometimes direct flights from Cairns during the Korean winter. The number of Koreans going to Australia means that bargain flights are few and far between, but Qantas usually prices its direct services competitively – return fares start at around Aus$1500, while the Korean carriers may ask for almost double that. It's worth checking around for indirect flights via a Southeast Asian hub; prices can often drop close to Aus$1000. Likewise, if travelling from **New Zealand** – keep your fingers crossed for a NZ$1400 fare, but assume you'll pay around NZ$1900. There are also direct flights from Auckland (12hr), and a few from Christchurch.

At the time of writing, there were no direct flights from **South Africa**.

Flights from Japan and China

If you're travelling from elsewhere in Asia – particularly from **Japan** or **China**'s eastern seaboard – it may be worth checking for a connection to another Korean international airport. In decreasing order of importance, these include Busan's Gimhae airport, Jeju, Daegu and Gwangju; those at Yangyang (near Sokcho) and Cheongju are also equipped to handle international flights, though don't always get the opportunity. There's also a handy, and extremely regular, connection between Seoul's Gimpo airport and Tokyo Haneda, both of which are closer to the

centre of their respective capitals than the larger hubs, Incheon and Narita.

Trains

Despite the fact that South Korea is part of the Eurasian landmass, and technically connected to the rest of it by rail, the DMZ and North Korean red tape means that the country is currently **inaccessible by land**. This may well change – two old lines across the DMZ have been renovated and 2007 saw trains rumble across the border as part of a peace ceremony. However, overnight trains from Beijing to Seoul station remain a distant prospect. Until then, surface-based access from the continent takes the form of **ferries** from Japan or China, possibly via a ride on the Trans-Siberian Railway (see box below). Note that if you're heading to or from China or Japan, you can make use of a **combined rail and ferry ticket** that gives substantial discounts on what you'd pay separately – see Ⓦwww.korail.com for details.

Ferries

There are several **ferry routes** from **China**'s eastern coast, almost all of which head to Incheon's international termini. All vessels have numerous classes of comfort, with one-way prices starting at around 700 RMB. The most popular connections are Dalian and Qingdao, and Tianjin's port in Tanggu, which is most convenient if you're heading to or from Beijing. See the box below for more on these routes.

Services from **Japan** depart from Fukuoka and Shimonoseki to Busan (see p.207), and arrive reasonably close to Busan train station, so you can be heading to other Korean destinations in no time. Fukuoka is by far the better choice, since there are, in fact, two different services to and from Korea – one a regular ferry, departing Fukuoka every day except Sunday (6hr; ¥9000), or a faster jetfoil with at least five services per day (3hr; ¥13,000; Ⓦwww.jrbeetle.co.jp).

Airlines, agents and operators

Airlines

Aeroflot Ⓦwww.aeroflot.ru.
Air Canada Ⓦwww.aircanada.com.

The Trans-Siberian train, and ferries from China

Although you can't actually reach Korea by train, if you're coming from or via Europe you may wish to consider one of the world's best overland trips – a **train-ride across Russia** and **China**. There are three main routes from Moscow, the main one a week-long, 9288km journey ending in Vladivostok on the East Sea. The Trans-Manchurian and Trans-Mongolian are slightly shorter rides ending in Beijing. The most popular cities to stop at – other than the termini of Moscow, Vladivostok and Beijing – are Irkutsk, next to beautiful Lake Baikal in Russian Siberia, and Ulaan Baatar, the idiosyncratic capital of Mongolia. Prices vary massively depending upon where you start and stop, and whether you go through a tour agency or not; for more information go to Ⓦwww.seat61.com. To complete the overland journey to Korea, you'll have to continue by ferry from China's eastern seaboard.

Chinese ports	Departure days and times	Journey times
Dalian	Mon, Wed & Fri 3.30pm	17hr
Dandong	Tues, Thurs & Sun 3pm	16hr
Lianyungang	Mon 11pm, Thurs 1pm	24hr
Qingdao	Mon, Wed & Fri 4pm	15hr
Qinhuangdao	Wed & Sun 1pm	23hr
Shidao	Tues, Thurs & Sun at 6pm	14hr
Tanggu (Tianjin)	Thurs & Sun 11am	24hr
Weihai	Tues, Thurs & Sun 6pm	14hr
Yantai	Mon, Wed & Fri 5pm	14hr
Yingkou	Mon & Thurs 11am	24hr

Air China Ⓦ www.air-china.co.uk, Ⓦ www.airchina.com.cn.
Air France Ⓦ www.airfrance.com.
All Nippon Airways (ANA) Ⓦ www.anaskyweb.com.
American Airlines Ⓦ www.aa.com.
Asiana Airlines Ⓦ www.flyasiana.com.
British Airways Ⓦ www.ba.com.
Cathay Pacific Ⓦ www.cathaypacific.com.
Delta Ⓦ www.delta.com.
Emirates Ⓦ www.emirates.com.
Finnair Ⓦ www.finnair.com.
JAL (Japan Air Lines) Ⓦ www.ar.jal.com.
KLM (Royal Dutch Airlines) Ⓦ www.klm.com.
Korean Air Ⓦ www.koreanair.com.
Lufthansa Ⓦ www.lufthansa.com.
Qantas Ⓦ www.qantas.com.
Qatar Airways Ⓦ www.qatarairways.com.
Singapore Airlines Ⓦ www.singaporeair.com.
United Airlines Ⓦ www.united.com.
US Airways Ⓦ www.usair.com.

Agents and operators

ebookers Ⓦ www.ebookers.com. Low fares on an extensive selection of scheduled flights and package deals.
North South Travel Ⓦ www.northsouthtravel.co.uk. Friendly, competitive travel agency, offering discounted fares worldwide. Profits are used to support projects in the developing world, especially the promotion of sustainable tourism.
STA Travel Ⓦ www.statravel.com. Worldwide specialists in independent travel; also student IDs, travel insurance, car rental, rail passes, and more. Good discounts for students and under-26s.
Trailfinders Ⓦ www.trailfinders.com. One of the best-informed and most efficient agents for independent travellers.

Local tour operators

Aju Tours Ⓦ www.ajutours.co.kr. A few interesting additions to the regular Seoul tours and DMZ trips, including birdwatching, oriental health or a tour of shamanistic sites.
Grace Travel Ⓦ www.triptokorea.com. A user-friendly website – click on "Customised Tours", select your time window, then choose from a range of interesting options.
Rye Tour Ⓦ www.ryetour.com. In addition to a few Korea-only itineraries, they also offer week-long tours which combine Seoul and Busan with Beijing, Shanghai or Tokyo.
TIK Tour Service Ⓦ www.tiktourservice.com. Offers affordable tours including skiing holidays, temple tours and trips around Jeju Island.

Getting around

Travelling around the country is simple – even if the train won't take you where you want to go, there's almost always a bus that will; should you have a choice, it's usually faster but more expensive to take the train. Travel prices are also reasonable by international standards, even if you choose to hop on one of the surprisingly numerous domestic flights. Korea is surrounded by islands, and should you take a ferry to one of these, it may well be the most pleasurable part of your visit. All cities have comprehensive (if slightly incomprehensible) bus networks, and many now have subway lines. Taxis are remarkably good value, and can even be feasible modes of transport from city to city.

Wherever you are, it's wise to avoid **peak travel seasons** if possible. During the two biggest holidays (Seollal and Chuseok; see p.57) it can often feel as if the whole country is on the move, as people rush to their home towns and back again – there's gridlock on the roads, it's hard to find a seat on trains or buses, and many shops and businesses (including some hotels) close down. Weekend or rush-hour train tickets can also be hard to come by throughout the year. For **travel information**, it's best to ask at a

Distance in kilometres

	Sokcho	Jeonju	Gyeongju	Chuncheon	Daegu	Daejeon	Gwangju	Busan	Seoul
Seoul	239	221	347	89	283	155	231	385	–
Busan	431	325	71	431	128	253	249	–	385
Gwangju	488	105	289	401	222	178	–	249	231
Daejeon	361	97	211	257	149	–	178	253	155
Daegu	385	295	68	288	–	149	222	128	283
Chuncheon	176	303	339	–	288	257	401	431	89
Gyeongju	359	325	–	339	68	211	289	71	347
Jeonju	382	–	325	303	295	97	105	325	221
Sokcho	–	382	359	176	385	361	488	431	239

tourist office, or call the English-speaking information line on ⓣ1330 (you'll need to add an area code if dialling from a mobile phone or abroad – see p.58).

By plane

For such a small country, Korea is surprisingly well served by **domestic flights**. The two national carriers, Korean Air and Asiana, have near-identical services – with near-identical fares – linking over a dozen airports across the nation, with the two main hubs being Gimpo in Seoul, and the holiday hotspot of Jeju Island. However, the country is so well covered by train and bus that only a trip to Jeju would see the average traveller need to use a domestic flight. Prices are reasonable – almost always between W60,000 and W100,000 – which is hardly surprising given that few trips take longer than an hour. Don't forget your **passport**, as you're likely to need it for identification purposes.

By ferry

With several thousand islands sprinkled around Korea's western and southern shores, no trip to Korea would be complete without a **ferry ride**. Several towns and cities have connections, though the main ports of entry to Korea's offshore kingdom are Incheon, Mokpo, Wando, Yeosu and Busan, all of which embrace sizeable island communities. The choice from Mokpo, in particular, is incredible – some travellers have inadvertently made trailblazers of themselves, finding their way onto islands that had never seen a foreign face. Popular **Jeju Island** is quite the opposite, and although the vast majority of Koreans travel here by plane, it has ferry connections to a number of southcoast mainland cities (see p.300 for details). Fares, on the whole, are reasonable – short hops may cost as little as W5000, but for return fares to outlying islands such as Jeju, Hongdo, Ulleungdo or Dokdo you'll probably have to shell out at least ten times that. Only tickets to these destinations will be in much danger of selling out, and even then, only in high season; at these times, it's best to head to a Korean travel agent.

By rail

A fleet of excellent **trains** ply the mainland provinces – sleek, affordable and punctual to a fault. There are two main lines, both starting in Seoul; these split in Daejeon, heading to Daegu and Busan to the southeast and Mokpo to the southwest. The highest of four main classes of train is the **KTX** – these high-speed machines entered service in 2004, and occasionally reach speeds of over 300km per hour. The Gyeongbu line runs from Seoul to

Moving on from Incheon Airport

Connections to Seoul from Incheon Airport are good; see p.69 for more details. There are also express buses that dash from the airport to all of the country's major cities at pleasingly regular intervals. Wherever you're going, useful signs help point the way, or you can ask at the information desk to find the most suitable route.

Busan and connects the cities in around two hours (W51,800). The KTX has taken over from the previous lord of the tracks, the **Saemaeul**; though slower (Seoul to Busan takes over four hours), travelling on this class cuts KTX costs by around a third (W39,300 Seoul to Busan), and the greater legroom usually makes for a more comfortable journey. A third cheaper again is the network's third class of train, the **Mugunghwa**, which was forced to cede most of its schedule space to the KTX – a good thing, since the Seoul to Busan journey (W26,500) is now a haul of nearly six hours. Last of all are the dirt-cheap **commuter class** trains, which largely cater for rural communities and Seoul's satellite cities – only a handful of lines use them, and you're unlikely to see or need one. All non-commuter trains have **toilets**, and folk pushing trolleys of beer, peanuts, chocolate and *gimbap* for sale down the carriages with almost disturbing frequency. For fare and schedule information, check ⓦwww.korail.com.

Tickets

Almost all stations have English-language signs where necessary, and schedules can also be checked online. When buying your **tickets**, the bigger stations have special lanes for foreigners, though it doesn't really matter which one you use, as the ticketing system is computerized and buying one is easy. Simply state your destination and the class you require, and the cashier will swing a computer screen in your direction, showing the price and seat availability. If she's pointing at a zero and looking apologetic, you'll probably need another train; additional allocations of standing tickets are available on non-KTX classes once all seats are sold out, and with these you'll be able to use any empty ones that become available. You'll be given a carriage and seat number: take your seat and not someone else's, otherwise it throws the seating system into disarray and may cause a domino-run of disgruntled passengers. As trains are far less numerous than buses, they're far more likely to sell out quickly – on holidays or weekends, you'll need fortune on your side to walk into a station and find KTX tickets for the main routes. **Advance reservations** are highly recommended – tickets for all classes go on sale a month ahead of travel, and can be bought at any station. Also, quite sensibly, a **return ticket** costs the same as two single ones.

Subway trains

Six Korean cities now have **underground** networks – Busan, Daegu, Daejeon and Gwangju have independent systems, while Incheon's lines are linked to the marauding Seoul network; all are continuing to grow, and new networks are likely to be born in other cities. Prices start at about W1000 for a short hop (or from one end to the other on the single lines in Daejeon and Gwangju), and increase with distance in the bigger cities, though even the full run through Seoul from Soyosan to Cheonan – about one-third of the country, and one of the longest metro routes in the world at three hours plus – will only set you back W3100. Signs are dual-language, and station maps easy to read.

By bus

There are a staggering number of **long-distance buses** in Korea – during rush hour, some scheduled services can run as often as every two minutes, with all departing on time. They come in two types – express (고속; *gosok*) and intercity (시외; *si-oe*, pronounced "shee-way"). Although the express services are more expensive and tend to be used for longer journeys, they are likely to run in tandem with intercity buses on many routes; allied to this, the two bus types use **separate stations** in most cities, and even the locals don't always know which one to go to, or which one they'll be arriving at – very frustrating, though some cities are starting to see sense and group both into one building (Gwangju, for example). Some cities have even more than two, so all in all it pays to keep a loose schedule when using buses, even more so if the highways are full.

Longer journeys are broken at **service stations**, housing fast-food bars and snack shops, resonating to the sound of the "throat" (a Korean word for warbly grandmother techno; see p.383) tapes on sale outside. You typically get fifteen minutes to make your purchases and use the **toilets** (there aren't any on the buses), but many a traveller has come a cropper after exiting the building to be confronted by forty near-identical vehicles, of which half-a-dozen may be heading to the same destination – your bus won't wait for you, so make sure that you know where it's parked.

Buses are so frequent that it's rare for them to sell out, though the last service of the day between major cities tends to be quite full. This can be surprisingly early: many services make their last trips at 7pm, though some have overnight connections. **Prices** are reasonable and usually lower than the trains, with intercity services slightly cheaper than express if the two coexist – Seoul to Busan is around W25,000 (5hr) on the former, W35,000 (4hr 30min) on the latter. Journeys take longer than the fastest trains, and are more prone to delays. Tickets are often checked at the start of the journey, but also at the end, so if possible try to avoid losing your ticket, lest the driver refuse to release you from his bus (which does happen).

City buses

With little English language on the signs or vehicles, Korea's **city bus** networks can be more than a little confusing for the first-time visitor, and some of Seoul's route numbers look more like postcodes. Once you are familiar with a route, city buses can be a good way of getting around – they're pleasingly frequent, and very affordable at around W1000 per ride. Throw your money into the collection box next to the driver; change will be spat out just below – make sure that you've an ample supply of coins or W1000 notes with you, as higher-value bills are unlikely to be accepted (though foreigners in such situations may be waved on with a grin). The bigger cities have started to avoid these problems by introducing **pre-paid cards**; these work out cheaper per journey than paying by cash, and some are also valid on subway networks or longer-distance buses. They last for as long as you have credit, and can be topped up in increments of W1000 at kiosks or ticket booths.

By car or motorbike

There are good reasons for the relative reluctance of travellers to **hire a car** in Korea. The main one is the country's excellent public transport infrastructure, another the threat posed by Korean drivers. Korean **road fatality rates** are often cited as the highest in the world, with most estimates putting the figures above 30 per 100,000 people per year – five times higher than the UK, for example. If you do decide to drive, you will inevitably get snarled up in the traffic that blights the cities and highways, with exceptions being Jeju Island and rural Gangwon province in the northeast, where the roads are relatively calm and traffic-free.

To hire a car you will need an international driving licence, and to be at least 21 years of age. Rental offices can be found at all airports and many train stations, as well as around the cities. Prices usually start at W45,000 per day, though as insurance is compulsory, you should budget on a little extra. Vehicles usually drive on the right-handside of the road (though not all the time; the pavement can be just as popular in some city areas).

Taxis

Korean **taxis** are pleasingly cheap for a developed country, and in any city you shouldn't have to wait long to spot one. Look for cars with illuminated blocks on top, usually something resembling a plastic pyramid. Those whose blocks aren't illuminated are taken or on call; others can be **waved down** from the roadside, though to make sure of being understood you'll have to do it the Korean way – arm out, palm to the ground, fingers dangling underneath. As few drivers speak English, it's a good idea to have your destination **written down**, if possible – even the cheapest motels should have business cards with their address on. **Rates** will vary slightly from city to city, though they should start at under W2500 – over short distances, cab rides may work out cheaper than taking buses if you're in a group. All taxis are **metered** and though dishonesty is rarely an issue, when you start moving, check that the numbers are doing likewise. The only time that you may have to negotiate a fee is if you're using a *chong-al* – or "bullet" – taxi. Piloted by death-wish drivers, these hover like vultures around train and bus stations when tickets have sold out, or daily services have finished. Rides in such vehicles are not recommended for those of a nervous disposition, while others may find it quite a thrill.

Motorbikes

You'll be hard pushed to find two-wheeled vehicles above 125cc in the country, as the vast majority of Oriental superbikes are exported for use in Europe or America. Despite this, though, a sizeable number of expats still don leather during their Korean stint. One good place to hunt for information or cycle partners is **Yongsan Motorcycle Club**, whose website (ⓦwww.roaddragons.com) features a calendar of forthcoming trips and events.

Cycling

There are nowhere near as many **bikes** on the roads of Korea as there are in other Asian countries, the chief reason being that Korean roads are dangerous places to be whatever vehicle you're in or on. Not that you're much safer away from the street; cars regularly glide along the pavements looking for a place to park, and half of the country's road fatalities are **pedestrians** – an unusually high proportion. There are, however, a few pleasant areas to cycle along rural roads; particular recommendations are the sparsely populated provinces of Gangwon and Jeju Island. Rides circumnavigating the latter take three or four days at a steady pace, and are becoming more and more commonplace. Those confined to a city will usually be able to go for a ride on a riverbank, with bikes available for hire at the most popular places; details have been included in this guide where appropriate.

Hitching

Foreigners who attempt to cover long distances by **hitching rides** in Korea

Korean addresses

First, the good news – almost all Korean road signs are dual-language, spelling the Korean *hangeul* out in Roman characters. The bad news is that there are very few street signs – most streets don't even have names. Instead, addresses point to a numbered section of a **dong** (city district), which until recently were doled out in chronological order when the buildings were made. The year 2010 saw the Korean government slapping new road signs all over the country, with addresses listed by their position on a road rather than their relative age, but it'll be a while before these new addresses find common use.

As you can imagine, this patchwork system leads to all sorts of problems; it's common for hotels and restaurants to include a small map on their business cards. With this in mind, almost all of the accommodation listed in this guidebook is either mapped or easy to find. The local tourist office may be able to contact hotels and get them to fax you through a map, or you could take your chances in a taxi. Drivers will know the location of each city *dong*, but not necessarily the exact road or address, so don't worry if they pull in at a police station – it's quite common for cabbies to consult police maps for exact directions.

Despite the general confusion, addresses fit into a very rigid system; unlike the Western world, components are usually listed from largest to smallest when writing an address. The country is split into nine 도 – *do*, or provinces. In these you'll find cities (시; – *si*, pronounced shee), towns (읍; – *eup*) and villages (리; – *ri* or – *li*), with the larger cities split into a number of 구 – *gu*, or wards. The number of – *gu* will vary with the city's size – Seoul, for example, has 25 such sections – and these are further subdivided into 동 – *dong* districts. Large roads are signified by a 로 (– *no*, – *ro* or – *lo*) suffix, with the very meatiest divided into numbered 가 – *ga* sections. Smaller roads come with a 길 – *gil* suffix; anything else will be a number in its local – *dong* city section, which is itself part of a larger – *gu*. Therefore Tapgol Park in *Seoul-si* sits at the end of *Insadonggil* in *Insadong*, part of *Jongnogu*, at the confluence of *Samillo* and *Jongno 2-ga*. Happy hunting!

generally have a hard time of things. Even with your destination on a handwritten sign, and even after having confirmed to the smiling driver where it is that you want to go, you're likely to be dropped at the nearest bus or train station. After all, to Koreans, this is the only sensible way to travel if you don't have a vehicle of your own – hitching is almost unheard of as a money-saving device. **Short-distance** rides are a different proposition altogether; although the scope of Korea's public transport system means that you'd be very unfortunate to find yourself stuck without a bus or train, it can happen, and in such circumstances hitching a ride can be as easy as flagging down the first car that you see. Of course, accepting lifts with strangers isn't devoid of risk anywhere on earth, but if you're ever determined to give it a try, there can be few easier and safer places to do it than the Korean countryside.

Online travel resources

Incheon International Airport Ⓦ www.airport.or.kr. Information on flights into and out of Korea's main airport.
Korail Ⓦ www.korail.com. Information on train times and passes, including discounted combined train and ferry tickets to Japan.
Seoul Metropolitan Rapid Transport (SMRT) Ⓦ www.smrt.co.kr. Timetables, and a useful best-route subway map.
Tour2Korea Ⓦ english.tour2korea.com. Good for bus connections between major cities, with cursory information on trains and ferries.

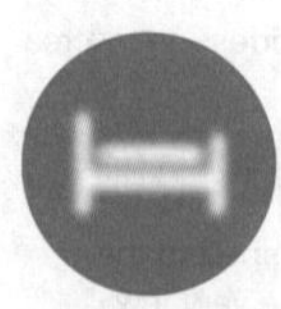

Accommodation

Accommodation is likely to swallow up a large chunk of your travel budget, especially for those who favour Western-style luxuries, but for adventurous travellers there are ways to keep costs to a minimum. Finding a place is less likely to be a problem – Korea has an incredible number of places to stay, and one would be forgiven for thinking that there are actually more beds than there are people in the country. Do note, however, that most of these are on the cheaper side – only a few places around the country have top-drawer hotel facilities.

Luxury hotels can be found in all cities and major tourist areas, as well as a number of specially dedicated tourist hotels, though with space at such a premium, rooms are generally on the small side. Dropping down the price scale, budget travellers can choose from thousands of motels and guesthouses – many of which have nicer rooms than the dedicated tourist hotels at far lower prices – or even sleep in a *jjimjilbang* (a Korean sauna; see p.38). At these levels, there's so much choice that reservations are almost unheard of. English is spoken to varying degrees in all top hotels, but elsewhere it

Accommodation price codes

The accommodation listed in this book has been categorized into one of nine **price codes**, as set out below. These represent the cost of the **cheapest** room in **high season**; in the case of dorms in hostels, we give the price of a bed in won.

❶ W20,000 and under
❷ W21,000–30,000
❸ W31,000–40,000
❹ W41,000–60,000
❺ W61,000–100,000
❻ W101,000–150,000
❼ W151,000–250,000
❽ W251,000–400,000
❾ W401,000 and over

pays to know a few keywords in Korean (or to have good miming skills).

Hotels

The big **hotel** chains have dipped their toes into the Korean market, and there's at least one five-star option in every major city. You're most likely to pay full rack rates in July or August, though high-season at national parks and ski resorts will be autumn and winter respectively. Standards are high, by and large, though even at the top end it's hard to find rooms of a decent size.

Korean hotels are split by **class**; from top to bottom, these are super deluxe, deluxe, first-class, second-class and third-class. Categories are marked by a plaque at the front showing a number of flowers – five for superdeluxe down to one for third-class. Many **tourist hotels** were built as Korea was getting rich in the 1980s, and now offer questionable value; stained carpets, tiny bathrooms and curious smells have become the norm, and few have staff with English language skills. Indeed, some of the most recently built motels offer better rooms, and at much lower prices. Most hotels have "Western" or "Korean" rooms; there are no beds in the latter (the sandwich of blankets on a heated *ondol* floor represents the traditional Korean way to sleep), and prices for both are about the same.

When booking, bear in mind that the 10 percent **tax** levied on hotel rooms is not always factored into the quoted prices; in higher-end establishments, you're also likely to be hit with an additional 10 percent service charge.

Motels

Bearing little resemblance to their American counterparts, **motels** (모텔) are absolutely all over the place – in any urban centre, you should never be more than a walk from the nearest one. Most offer fairly uniform en-suite doubles for W30,000–50,000, and standard facilities include shampoo and shower gel, hairdryers, televisions, a water fountain and free cans of beer, coffee or "vitamin juice". Extortion of foreigners is extremely rare, and you shouldn't be afraid to haggle the price down if you're travelling alone, especially outside summer.

Korean motels won't appeal to everybody, as they're generally used as a much-needed source of privacy by young couples (or those who need to keep their relationship secret). A few would be more honestly described as "love hotels" – pink neon and Cinderella turrets are the most obvious giveaways, while the interior may feature heart-shaped beds, condom machines and more mirrors than you can shake a stick at. That said, the majority of establishments are quite tame, any seaminess is kept behind closed doors, and even for lone women most make acceptable places to stay – indeed, those that can put up with the decor will find them Korea's best-value accommodation option. The motels that have gone up since the turn of the century, in particular, often have cleaner rooms than the average tourist hotel, typically featuring huge flatscreen TVs and internet-ready computer terminals.

Guesthouses

Yeogwan (여관) are older, smaller, less polished versions of motels. Slightly cheaper, but often a little grubby, they once formed the backbone of Korea's budget travel accommodation, and can still be found in teams around bus and train stations. With whole streets full of them, it's easy to hunt around for the best deal – a double room usually costs W20,000–35,000, though prices are higher in Seoul, and tend to rise in high season. Single rooms do not exist, but almost all have en-suite bathrooms.

Minbak rooms (민박) are usually rented-out parts of a residential property, and are less likely to have private bathrooms. These are most commonly found on islands and by popular beaches or national parks, and though the prices are comparable to *yeogwan* rates for much of the year they can quadruple if there's enough demand – summer is peak season for the beaches and islands, spring and autumn for the parks.

Even cheaper rooms can be found at a **yeoinsuk** (여인숙) – around W10,000 per night. Slowly disappearing, these are a noisier, more spartan variation of the *yeogwan*, invariably found in older areas of town, with rooms containing nothing more than a couple of blankets, a television and a heated linoleum *ondol* floor to sleep on.

Such wipe-clean minimalism generally makes for clean rooms, though some have a cockroach problem, and the communal toilets and showers can be quite off-putting.

Hostels

Aside from a smattering of backpacker dens in Seoul, Korean **hostels** differ greatly from those that Western travellers might be used to – created for and primarily used by the nation's youth, the atmosphere is more boarding school than Bohemian. Generally found in the countryside, most hostels are large, well-appointed places with private rooms of various sizes, and a few dormitories; dorm beds go for W15,000–20,000, and private rooms for W35,000 and up.

Camping and mountain huts

Most national parks have at least one **campsite** to cater for the swarms of Korean hikers who spend their weekends in the mountains. Most are free, but those that charge (typically under W5000) have excellent toilet and shower facilities. Jirisan and Seoraksan, two of the largest parks, have well-signposted **shelters** or **huts** dotted around the hiking trails; these cost under W8000 per person, though they may only open from summer until autumn, and you're advised to book ahead – check the national park website at ⓦenglish.knps.or.kr. At both campsites and shelters, drinking water should always be available, and though simple snacks may also be on offer, it's best to bring your own food.

Templestay and hanok guesthouses

If you're looking for a more traditional experience, you could try staying at a **temple**. Though temples with sufficient room are pretty much obliged to take in needy travellers for the night, many offer interesting, prearranged programmes for around W50,000 per night, some with the capacity for English-language translation – see ⓦeng.templestay.com for more details. There's usually meditation, grounds-sweeping, a tea ceremony and a meal or two on the agenda, but be prepared for spartan sleeping arrangements and a pre-dawn wake-up call. If you're after something traditional but without the routine, try hunting down a **hanok** – these are traditional Korean buildings, replete with wooden frames, sliding doors and a woodfired underfloor heating system. Few such buildings cater for travellers, though some can be found at the traditional villages scattered around the country (Hahoe near Andong is the best; see p.178), and there are dedicated districts in Seoul (see box, p.74) and Jeonju (p.254). Many include tea ceremonies and other activities such as *gimchi*-making in the cost.

Staying at a jjimjilbang

For travellers willing to take the plunge and bare all in front of curious strangers, saunas (known locally as **jjimjilbang**; 찜질방) are some of the cheapest and most uniquely Korean places to get a night's sleep. Almost entirely devoid of the seedy reputations that may dog similar facilities abroad, *jjimjilbang* are large, round-the-clock establishments primarily used by families escaping their homes for the night, businessmen who've worked or partied beyond their last trains, or teenage groups having a safe night out together. They can be found in any Korean city, typically costing W5000–8000, and consist of a shower and pool area, a sauna or steam room, and a large playschool-style quiet room or two for communal napping; most also have snack bars and internet terminals. Upon entry, guests are given a locker key and matching T-shirts and shorts to change into – outside clothes are not allowed to be worn inside the complex, though it's OK to wear underwear beneath your robe. All must be sacrificed on entry to the pools, which are segregated by gender. The common rooms are uniformly clean but vary in style; some have TVs and hi-tech recliner chairs, others invite you to roll out a mini-mattress, but all will have a floorful of snoring Koreans.

Online accommodation resources

Ⓦ **www.asiarooms.com** An excellent discount site with interesting reviews of the hotel rooms on offer.
Ⓦ **eng.templestay.com** Information on the various templestay programmes around the country.
Ⓦ **english.knps.or.kr** Korea National Park Service site detailing available shelters.
Ⓦ **www.hostelworld.com** Good listings of Seoul's budget accommodation, and a few more choices from around the country.
Ⓦ **www.hotelwide.com** See just how much you're saving by comparing quotes with rack rates.
Ⓦ **innostel.visitseoulnet** City-sponsored site featuring a range of cheap accommodation in Seoul, all at places deemed suitable for foreigners.
Ⓦ **www.khrc.com** Website for the Korea Hotel Reservation Centre, worth a look for occasional special deals.
Ⓦ **www.koreahotels.net** A well-presented site with a wealth of choice.

Food and drink

Korean cuisine deserves greater international attention. A thrillingly spicy mishmash of simple but invariably healthy ingredients, it's prepared with consummate attention, then doled out in hearty portions at more restaurants than you could possibly count – even if every single person in the country suddenly decided to go out for dinner simultaneously, there would probably still be some free tables. Most are open from early morning until late at night, and a full 24 hours a day in many cases. You can usually find a restaurant to suit your budget, and there will always be an affordable option close by, a fact attested to by the great number of foreigners that live here quite happily for weeks, months or even years on end without doing a single bit of cooking for themselves.

Though Korean cuisine is one of the most distinctive around, few Westerners arrive with knowledge of anything other than **gimchi** (김치; fermented vegetables) and **dog meat**. To say that the former is ubiquitous is a severe understatement, as it's served as a side dish with pretty much everything you order (for more information about popular Korean dishes see the *Korean cuisine* colour section), but rest assured that the latter will not be part of your diet unless you go to a dedicated restaurant (see p.43). One common problem for visitors is the **spice** level of the food, an issue that has given Korea one of the world's highest rates of stomach cancer. It's not so much the spiciness of the individual dishes that causes problems (British travellers trained on curry, for example, rarely have any problems adjusting to Korean spice) but the fact that there's little respite from it – red pepper paste (*gochujang*; 고추장) is a component of almost every meal. Another common complaint by foreign visitors is the lack of attention paid to **vegetarians**, as such folk are extremely rare in Korea. Despite the high vegetable content of many meals, almost all have at least a little meat, and very few are cooked in meat-free environments. Most resort to asking for *bibimbap* without the meat, eating *ramyeon* (라면; instant noodles), or poking the bits of ham out of *gimbap* with a chopstick.

When eating with locals, it's polite to observe Korean **culinary etiquette** (see p.51 for a few pointers). Many meals are eaten with flattened stainless-steel **chopsticks**; those unable to use them may have to rely on a combination of fork and spoon, as knives are rarely used.

Korean eating establishments are hard to pigeonhole. The lines between bar, restaurant, snack-shop and even home are often blurry to say the least, and some places cover all bases: in provincial towns, you may well see children tucked up for the night under empty tables. The more traditional eateries will see diners sitting on floor-cushions, their legs folded under low tables in a modified lotus position that can play merry hell on Western knees and ankles. Many dishes are for **sharing**, a fantastic arrangement that fosters togetherness and increases mealtime variety, though this has adverse implications for single travellers – Koreans don't like to eat alone, and are likely to fret about those who do. One other point worth mentioning is the incredible number of foodstuffs that are claimed to be "good for **sexual stamina**"; at times it feels as if food is an augmenter of male potency first, and a necessary means of sustenance second. Raw fish and dog meat, in particular, are said to be good for this.

For more on Korea's **culinary curiosities**, see p.105.

Korean staples

The following are available around the country, and few will cost more than W5000. Many meals involve **rice** in various forms: one that proves a hit with many foreigners is **bibimbap**, a mixture of shoots, leaves and vegetables on a bed of rice, flecked with meat, then topped with an egg and spicy *gochujang* pepper sauce. The dish can cost as little as W3500, though there are sometimes a few varieties to choose from. See the *Korean cuisine* colour section for more details on this classic dish. Other dishes to be served on a bed of rice include beef (*bulgogi deop-bap*; 불고기덮밥), highly spicy squid (*ojingeo deop-bap*; 오징어덮밥) or *donkasseu* (돈까스), a breaded pork cutlet dish imported from Japan that's particularly popular with those who want to avoid spice. Also fulfilling this need are rolls of **gimbap** (김밥): *gim* means laver seaweed, *bap* means rice, and the former is rolled around the latter, which itself surrounds strips of egg, ham and pickled radish; the resulting tube is then cut into segments with a sharp knife to make the

Fast food chains

Such is the pace at which Koreans live their lives that many find it impossible to spare time for a leisurely meal, so it should come as no surprise that their city streets are packed with **fast food outlets**. Korean fast food is something of a misnomer: fast it may well be, but in general the local offerings are far healthier than their Western equivalents – you could eat them every day and never get fat. One slight problem for travellers is that few of these cheap places are used to dealing with foreigners, so don't expect English-language menus or service; you'll find a menu reader on pp.398–401. Below is a selection of the outlets you're most likely to come across in cities across the nation.

Bongchu Jjimdak (봉추찜닭) *Jjimdak* is steamed chicken, mixed with potatoes and other vegetables in a delicious, aromatic stew. A W22,000 serving – one chicken – should be enough for two, and be sure to don one of the bibs provided, as there's bound to be some splashback.

Gimbap Cheonguk (김밥천국) In Korean street-space terms, this ubiquitous orange-fronted franchise is rivalled only by internet bars and the more prominent convenience store chains. The concept is pretty miraculous – almost all basic Korean meals are served here for around W5000 per dish, and despite the variety on offer you'll usually be eating within minutes of sitting down. They also do *gimbap* from W1500, and these can be made to go: perfect if you're off on a hike. Other similar chains include *Gimbap Nara* and *Jongno Gimbap*; in major cities, you'll never be more than a short walk from one.

Isaac Toast (이삭토스트) Toast, but not as you know it. The Korean variety is made on a huge hot-plate – first your perfectly square bread will be fried and smeared with kiwi jam, then joined by perfect squares of spam and/or fried egg (or even a burger, dish chopstick-friendly. The basic dish is filling and only costs W1000 or so, but for a little more you'll usually have a variety of fillings to choose from, including tuna (*chamchi*; 참치), minced beef (*sogogi*; 소고기), processed cheese (*chi-jeu*; 치즈) and *gimchi*.

Noodles are also used as a base in many dishes, and one of the cheapest dishes to eat – a bowl of **ramyeon** can go for just W2000. This is a block of instant noodles boiled up in a spicy red pepper soup, and usually mixed in with an egg and some onion. For double the price you can have dumplings (*mandu*; 만두), rice-cake (*ddeok*; 떡) or processed cheese thrown in. Those travelling in the sticky Korean summer will find it hard to throw back a bowl of hot, spicy soup; a better choice may be **naengmyeon** (냉면), bowls of grey buckwheat noodles served with a boiled egg and vegetable slices in a cold soup (though still spicy – this is Korea, after all).

Soups are also available without noodles. The names of these dishes usually end with *-tang* (탕) or *-guk* (국), though special mention must be made of the spicy **jjigae** broths (찌개). These are bargain meals that cost W3500 and up, and come with rice and a range of vegetable side dishes; the red pepper broth contains chopped-up vegetables, as well as a choice of tofu (*sundubu*; 순두부), tuna, soybean paste (*doenjang*; 된장) or *gimchi*. Many foreigners find themselves going for the more familiar **dumpling** (*mandu*) options; again, these can cost as little as W1000 for a dish, and you can have them with meat (*gogi*) or *gimchi* fillings. Most are steamed, though it's sometimes possible to have them flash-fried.

All of the above can be found at **fast food chains** around the country; see the box below for details.

Restaurant food

The traditional Korean **restaurant** is filled with low tables; diners are required to remove their footwear and sit on floor-cushions. There are a number of rules of restaurant **etiquette** (see p.51) but a substantial amount of custom also surrounds the food itself; while what often appears to be a culinary free-for-all can draw

for those to whom the word "cholesterol" means nothing), and the whole lot injected with two sauces, one spicy and one brown. No, it's not healthy, but it makes a tasty breakfast; prices start at W1500.

Kim Ga Ne (김家네) A slightly more upmarket version of *Gimbap Cheonguk* (see above), serving more or less the same things with a few snazzy "fusion" additions. Most branches have their menu on the walls in pictorial form, handy if you don't speak Korean. Dishes W3000–7000.

Lotteria (롯데리아) Unlike the similarly omnipresent *McDonald's* outlets, at least this is a Korean burger chain: witness the delicious *bulgogi* burger (W4500), made with marinated beef (at least in theory), or the meatless *gimchi* variety, served between two slabs of rice rather than a bun.

Paris Baguette (파리바게뜨) & **Tous Les Jours** (뚜레쥬르) A pair of near-identical bakery chains, whose offerings may satisfy if you need a breakfast devoid of spice or rice; many branches are also able to whip up a passable coffee. Baked goods start at around W1500, but note that even the savoury-looking ones are usually extremely sugary. You'll find branches all over the place; harder to spot is *Paris Croissant*, a slightly more upmarket version.

Sinpo Woori Mandoo (신포우리만두) A good selection of cheap dumplings (*mandu*), as well as a few Korean staple meals, and a few from Japan. Meals from W3000 to W8000.

Yu Ga Ne (유가네) This chain serves tasty barbecued meat, cooked at your table by an apron-wearing attendant. Unlike most barbecue joints, there are dishes for those dining alone, such as the delectable *dakgalbi beokkeumbap*, which is something like a chicken kebab fried up with rice. W10,000 should be enough to get a bellyful.

gasps from foreign observers (eat the meal; boil off the soup; throw in some rice to fry up with the scraps; add some noodles), Korea's great on conformity, and you may well provoke chuckles of derision by performing actions that you deem quite sensible – it's best just to follow the Korean lead.

Restaurant meals usually consist of communal servings of **meat** or **fish** around which are placed a bewildering assortment of **side dishes** (*banchan*; 반찬). Often, these are the best part of the meal – a range of fish, meat, vegetables and steamed egg broth, they're included in the price of the meal, and there may be as many as twenty on the table; when your favourite is finished, waitresses will scoot around with a free refill. Two of the most popular meat dishes are *galbi* and *samgyeopsal*, which are almost always cooked by the diners themselves in the centre of the table. **Galbi** is rib-meat, most often beef (*so-galbi*; 소갈비) but sometimes pork (*dwaeji-galbi*; 돼지갈비) see the *Korean cuisine* colour section for more details. **Samgyeopsal** (삼겹살) is strips of rather fatty pork belly. Prices vary but figure on around W7000 per portion for beef and a little less for pork; a minimum of two diners is usually required. Better for single travellers may be the **hanjeongsik** (한정식); this is a traditional Korean banquet meal centred on a bowl of rice and a spicy *jjigae* stew, which are surrounded by side dishes – a full belly of healthy, lovingly prepared food can be yours for just W6000 or so. **Ssambap** (쌈밥) meals are similarly good-value collections of rice and vegetable side dishes, though here the array is far greater – often filling the whole table – and is supposed to be wrapped up in leaves before it enters the mouth; figure on W8000 per person, and a total failure to clear everything that's in front of you.

Snack food

Though the most common variety of Korean **snack food** is *gimbap* there are many more options available. One is a dish called **ddeokbokki** (떡볶이), a mix of rice-cake and processed fish boiled up in a highly spicy red-pepper sauce; this typically costs around W2000 per portion, and is doled out in bowls by street vendors and small roadside booths. The same places usually serve **twigim** (튀김), which are flash-fried pieces of squid, potato, seaweed-covered noodle-roll or stuffed chilli pepper, to name but a few ingredients. The price varies but is usually around W3000 for six pieces – choose from the display, and they'll be refried in front of you. You can have the resulting dish smothered in *ddeokbokki* sauce for no extra charge – delicious.

Convenience stores are usually good places to grab some food, as all sell sandwiches, rolls and triangles of *gimbap*, and instant noodles; boiling water will always be available for the latter, as well as a bench or table to eat it from, an activity that will mark you as an honorary Korean. A less appealing practice, but one that will endear

Royal cuisine

Being such an important part of daily Korean life, it's inevitable that food should wend its way into traditional events. The hundredth day of a child's life is marked with a feast of colourful rice-cake, while a simpler variety is served in a soup (*ddeokguk*) to celebrate Lunar New Year. More interesting by far, however, is **royal court cuisine**: a remnant of the Joseon dynasty, which ruled over the Korean peninsula from 1392 to 1910, this was once served to Korean rulers and associated nobility. The exact ingredients and styles vary and go by several different names, but usually rice, soup and a charcoal-fired casserole form the centre of the banquets, and are then surrounded by a team of perfectly prepared dishes; twelve was once the royal number of dishes and banned to the peasant class, but now anyone can indulge as long as they have the money. The aim of the combination is to harmonize culinary opposites such as spicy and mild, solid and liquid, rough and smooth; a balance of colour and texture is thereby achieved – the Yin-Yang principle in edible form.

Some of the best places to try this kind of food are *Korea House* (p.108) and *Baru* in Seoul (p.107), or *Naedang* in Busan (p.214).

Dog meat

Korea's consumption of **dog meat** (*gae-gogi;* 개고기) became global knowledge when the country hosted the 1988 Olympics, at which time the government kowtowed to Western mores and attempted to sweep the issue under the carpet.

Today, eating dog meat amounts to a shameful national secret. Foreigners looking for it on the menu or in their hamburgers are likely to be relieved, as it's almost nowhere to be seen. Should the issue be raised, even with a Korean you know well, they'll probably laugh and tell you that they don't eat dog, and that the practice only takes place behind closed doors, if at all.

That said, and though it's true that few young people consume dog, the soup *yeongyangtang*, for one, is still popular with older Koreans due to its purported health-giving properties, and can be hunted down in specialist restaurants.

Any fears of Koreans chowing down on an Alsatian or Border Collie should be quelled; almost all dog meat comes from a scraggly mongrel breed colloquially known as the *ddong-gae (*똥개*)*, or "shit-dog", an animal named for its tendency to eat whatever it finds on the floor. Even so, the poor conditions that the animals are often kept in, and the continuing – and occasionally verified – stories of dogs being clubbed to death to tenderize the meat, are good reasons to avoid this kind of meal. For those who wish to know, it's a slightly stringy meat somewhere between duck and beef in texture, and is generally agreed to taste better than it smells.

you to Koreans more than anything else can, is the eating of **beonddegi** 번데기 – boiled silkworm larvae.

You'll find **ice cream** in any convenience store, where prices can be as low as W500; if you want to keep your selection as Korean as possible, go for green tea, melon, or red-bean paste flavours. An even more distinctively local variety, available from specialist snack bars, is *patbingsu* (팥빙수), a strange concoction of fruit, cream, shaved ice and red-bean paste. Also keep an eye out in colder months for a **hoddeok** (호떡) stand – these press out little fried pancakes of rice-mix filled with brown sugar and cinnamon for just W500 per piece, and are extremely popular with foreigners.

Seafood, markets and mountain food

Some Korean eating places exude an essence little changed for decades. Raw fish stalls around the coast, city-centre marketplaces and mountain restaurants are your best options for that traditional feeling.

Korean **seafood** is a bit of a maze for most foreigners, and much more expensive than other meals, though it's worth persevering. Some is served raw, while other dishes are boiled up in a spicy soup. Jagalchi market in Busan deserves a special mention (see p.213 for seafood listings), but in small coastal villages – particularly on the islands of the West and South seas – there's little other industry to speak of; battered fishing flotillas yo-yo in and out with the tide, and you may be able to buy fish literally straight off the boat. This may seem as fresh as seafood can possibly be, but baby octopus is often served live (*sannakji*; 산낙지), its severed tentacles still squirming as they head down your throat. Be warned: several people die each year when their prey decides to make a last futile stab at survival with its suckers, so you may wish to wait until it has stopped moving, or at least kill the nerves with a few powerful bites. A far simpler choice is *hoe deop-bap* (회덮밥), a widely available dish similar to *bibimbap*, but with sliced raw fish in place of egg and meat. A halfway house in excitement terms is *jogae-gui* (조개구이), a shellfish barbecue – the unfortunate creatures are grilled in front of you, and W35,000 will buy enough of them to fill two people.

Korean **markets** offer similar opportunities for culinary exploration. Here you're also likely to spot seafood on sale, along with fruits, vegetables, grilled or boiled meats and an assortment of snacks. Many options have been detailed under "Snack food" (see opposite), but one favourite almost unique to the market is *sundae* (순대), a kind of sausage made with intestinal lining and noodles (see box, p.105). Sokcho on the Gangwon coast is the best place to sample this.

Korea's wonderful **national parks** feature some splendid eating opportunities surrounding the main entrances. One of the most popular hiker dishes is *sanchae bibimbap* (산채 비빔밥), a variety of the Korean staple made with roots, shoots and vegetables from the surrounding countryside – knowing that everything is sourced locally somehow makes the dish taste better. Most popular, though, are *pajeon* (파전); locals may refer to these as "Korean pizza", but they're more similar to a savoury pancake. They usually contain strips of spring onion and seafood (*haemul*; 해물) *pajeon*, though other varieties are available; it's usually washed down with a bowl or three of *dongdongju*, a milky rice wine.

International cuisine

While many visitors fall head over heels for Korean food, it's not to everybody's taste, and after a while the near-permanent spicy tang of red-pepper paste can wear down even the most tolerant taste buds. One problem concerns **breakfast**, which, to most Koreans, is simply another time-window for the intake of *gimchi* and rice. This is too heavy for many Westerners, but though a fry-up or smörgåsbord will be hard to find outside the major hotels, you may find some solace in the buns, cakes and pastries of major bakery chains such as *Tous Les Jours* and *Paris Baguette* (see box, pp.40–41), or the mayonnaise-heavy sandwiches of the convenience stores.

International food is getting easier to come by in Korea, though only Seoul can be said to have a truly cosmopolitan range (and a thinly spread one, at that). **American-style fast food**, however, can be found pretty much everywhere – *McDonald's* and *Burger King* are joined by *Lotteria*, a local chain, and there are also a great number of fried chicken joints scattered around. Traditional **Japanese food** has made serious inroads into the Korean scene, and the obligatory red lanterns of *izakaya*-style bar-restaurants are especially easy to spot in student areas. **Italian food** has long been popular with Koreans, who have added their own twists to pizzas and pasta – almost every single meal will be served with a small tub of pickled gherkin, an addition that locals assume to be *de rigueur* in the restaurants of Napoli or Palermo. **Chinese restaurants** are equally numerous, though unfortunately they're no more authentic than their counterparts in Western countries, even in the many cases where the restaurateurs themselves are Chinese. One recommendation, however, is *beokkeumbap* – fried rice mixed with cubes of ham and vegetable, topped with a fried egg and black bean sauce, and served with deliciously spicy seafood broth; the whole thing will cost about W5000, and is, therefore, a great way to fill up on the cheap.

Drink

A sweet potato wine named **soju** (소주) is the national drink – a cheap, clear Korean version of vodka that you'll either love or hate (or love, then hate the next morning) – but there's a pleasing variety of grog to choose from. The country also has a wealth of excellent tea on offer, though coffee is increasingly winning the urban caffeine battles.

Alcoholic drinks

Though the imbibing of *soju* is *de rigueur* at restaurants of an evening, most people do their serious drinking in bars and "*hofs*". There are a quite incredible number of both in the cities, though the majority can be surprisingly empty, even at weekends – you may wonder how most of them stay in business. **Hofs**, pronounced more like "hop", are bright, booth-filled places serving **beer** (*maekju*; 맥주) by the bucketload. The main beers are Cass, OB and Hite; prices are more or less the same for each, starting at about W2500 for a 500cc glass. Quite fascinating are the three- or five-litre plastic jugs of draught beer (*saeng-maekju*; 생맥주), which often come billowing dry ice and illuminated with flashing lights. The downside of such places is that customers are pretty much obliged to eat as well as drink; you'll be given free snacks, but customers are expected to order something from the menu.

Bars are almost invariably dark, neon-strewn dens; unlike in *hofs*, customers are not usually expected to eat and tend to take roost in an extensive cocktail menu; beer will still be available, in draught or bottled form. Each city has one or more main "going-out" district,

Get drunk the local way

Though Koreans largely favour beer and imported drinks, the country has more than a few superb **local hooches**, many of which go down very well indeed with the few foreigners lucky enough to learn about them.

Baekseju (백세주) A nutty, whisky-coloured concoction, about the same strength as wine. Its name means "one-hundred-year alcohol", on account of healthy ingredients including ginseng and medicinal herbs. Surely the tastiest path towards becoming a centenarian, *baekseju* is available at convenience stores (W3600) and many barbecue houses (W6000 or so), though bar-restaurant chain *Baekseju Maeul* is the most entertaining place to get your first hit.

Bokbunjaju (복분자주) Made with black raspberries, this sweet, fruity drink is similar to sugary, low-grade port. Available at all convenience stores (W6500), though if you're on a mountain hike in late summer you may be lucky enough to try some freshly made: it's sold by farmers at makeshift stalls.

Dongdongju (동동주) Very similar to *makkeolli*, *dongdongju* is a little heavier taste-wise, and since it can only be served fresh you'll have to head to a specialist place for a try. The restaurants most likely to have *dongdongju* are those also serving savoury pancakes known as *pajeon*; usually rustic affairs decked out with Korean bric-a-brac and serving *dongdongju* in large wooden bowls (W8000) to be doled out into smaller versions of the same. A word of warning: many foreigners have "hit the wall" on their first dabble, suddenly finding themsevels floored by this deceptively quaffable drink.

Maehwasu (매화수) Similar to *baekseju* in colour, strength and price, this is made with the blossom of the *maesil*, a type of Korean plum, and some bottles come with said fruit steeping inside.

Makkeolli (막걸리) Usually around 8 percent alcohol by volume, this milky rice wine was seen as granddad fuel for years, but a recent shift back towards Korean tradition has seen its popularity go through the roof. The stuff is now sold in upscale bars, and preliminary attempts have been made towards its marketing abroad. Interestingly, although it's the most expensive of Korea's alcohols to make, it's actually the cheapest to buy, since its centuries-old heritage has afforded it tax-exempt status. W1500 in a convenience store, W3000 in a barbecue house.

Soju (소주) The national drink, for better or worse. Locals refer to it as "Korean vodka", but it's only half the strength – a good thing too, as it's usually fired down in staccato shots over barbecued meat. It's traditionally made with sweet potato, but these days most companies go for cheaper, chemical concoctions: the resultant taste puts many foreigners off, but some find themselves near-addicted within days of arrival. W1500 from a convenience store, W3000 at a restaurant.

with the most raucous to be found outside the rear entrances of the **universities** (which maintain a veneer of respectability by keeping their main entrances free of such revelry). Most cities have at least one resident **expat bar**; these are usually the best places for foreigners to meet fellow *waeguk-in* or new Korean friends. Often surrounded with tables and chairs for customer use, convenience stores are equally great places to meet new mates, and actually the best hunting grounds for local drinks. They also sell bottles of foreign wine for W7000 and up, though special mention must be made of a local variety named Jinro House Wine: this curiously pink liquid, which may or may not be derived from grapes, costs about W2000 per bottle and can only be described as "comedy wine" as it tends to give people the giggles.

Tea and coffee

Tea is big business in Korea. Unfortunately, most of the drinking takes place at home or work, though Insadong in Seoul has dozens of interesting tearooms (see box, p.112), and there are some gems outside national parks

Korean tea varieties

Daechu-cha 대추차 Jujube tea
Gukhwa-cha 국화차 Chrysanthemum tea
Gyepi-cha 계피차 Cinnamon tea
Ggulsam cha 꿀삼차 Honey ginseng tea
Insam-cha 인삼차 Ginseng tea
Ma-cha 마차 Wild herb tea
Maesil-cha 매실차 Plum tea
Nok-cha 녹차 Green tea
Omija-cha 오미자차 Five Flavours tea
Saenggang-cha 생강차 Ginger tea
Yak-cha 약차 Medicinal herb tea
Yuja-cha 유자차 Citron tea
Yulmu-cha 율무차 "Job's Tears" tea

and in Jeonju's *hanok* district (p.254). Green tea is by far the most popular, though if you find your way to a specialist tearoom, do take the opportunity to try something more special (see box opposite for suggestions).

Korea is now a bona fide coffee nation. **Café culture** has found its way into the lives of Korean youth, and even in smaller towns you shouldn't have to look too far to find somewhere to sate your caffeine cravings. In addition to coffee, modern cafés usually serve delicious **green tea latte**, with some of the more adventurous throwing in ginseng or sweet potato varieties for good measure. Though certainly not for purists, worth mentioning are the cans and cartons of coffee on sale in convenience stores, and the three-in-one instant mixes that pop up all over the place, including most motel rooms.

The media

Korean media has come a long way since bursting out of the dictatorial straitjacket of the 1970s and 1980s, but most of it remains inaccessible to anyone not versed in Korean.

Newspapers and magazines

The two big English-language **newspapers** are the *Korea Times* (Ⓦwww.koreatimes.co.kr) and *Korean Herald* (Ⓦwww.koreanherald.co.kr), near-identical dailies with near-identical addictions to news agency output and dull business statistics. This said, both have decent listings sections in their weekend editions, which detail events around the country, as well as the goings-on in Seoul's restaurant, film and club scenes. The *International Herald Tribune* is pretty easy to track down in top hotels, with copies containing the eight-page *Joongang Daily* (Ⓦjoongangdaily.joins.com), an interesting local news supplement. You should also be able to hunt down the previous week's *Time*, *Newsweek* or *Economist* in most Korean cities – try the larger bookstores, or the book section of a large department store. An interesting source of information is *Ohmy News* (Ⓦenglish.ohmynews.com), a large online compendium of articles written by members of the public that has long been a quirky bee in the bonnet of local politicians and "proper" journalists.

Television

Korean **television** is a gaudy feast of madcap game shows and soppy period dramas, and there are few more accessible windows into the true nature of local society. **Arirang** (Ⓦwww.arirang.co.kr) is a 24-hour English-language television network based in Seoul, which promotes the country with occasionally interesting documentaries, and has regular news bulletins. Arirang TV is free-to-air throughout much of the world, and though not free in Korea itself, it comes as part of most cable packages.

Festivals

On even a short trip around the country you're more than likely to stumble across a special event of some sort. Many are religious in nature, with Buddhist celebrations supplemented by Confucian and even animist events. Most festivals are concentrated around spring and autumn, but there are many spread throughout the year. If you're heading to one, don't be shy – the locals love to see foreigners joining in with traditional Korean events, and those who dare to get stuck in may finish the day with a whole troupe of new friends.

Though there are some crackers on the calendar, it must be said that a fair number of **Korean festivals** are brazenly commercial, making no bones about being held to "promote the salted seafood industry", for example. Other festivals can be rather odd, including those dedicated to agricultural utensils, clean peppers and the "Joy of Rolled Laver" – you'll easily be able to spot the duds. The most interesting events are highlighted below, though bear in mind that celebrations for two of the big national festivals – **Seollal**, the Lunar New Year, and a Korean version of Thanksgiving named **Chuseok** – are family affairs that generally take place behind closed doors. Details on these and other Korean national holidays can be found on p.57, while festivals in Seoul are covered on p.118 and in Busan on p.207.

April–June

Cherry blossom festivals Usually early April. Heralding the arrival of spring, soft blossom wafts through the air across the country, a cue for all good Koreans to lay down blankets at parks or riverbanks, barbeque some meat and throw back the *soju*.

Jeonju International Film Festival ⓦ www.jiff.or.kr. Last week of April. Smaller and more underground than the biggie in Busan, JIFF focuses on the arty, independent side of the movie industry (p.252).

Buddha's Birthday Late May. A public holiday during which temples across the land are adorned with colourful paper lanterns; there's an even more vibrant night parade in Seoul.

International Mime Festival ⓦ www.mimefestival.com. May. Held in the Gangwonese capital of Chuncheon, this foreigner-friendly event is a showcase of soundless talent (p.148).

Dano Usually June. A shamanist festival held on the fifth day of the fifth lunar month, featuring circus acts, *ssireum* wrestling, mask dramas and a whole lot more. The city of Gangneung (p.159) is host to the biggest displays.

July–August

Boryeong Mud Festival ⓦ www.mudfestival.or.kr. Late July. This annual expat favourite pulls mud-happy hordes to Daecheon Beach (p.267) for all kinds of muck-related fun.

International Puppet Festival Aug. Puppets and their masters come from around the world to flaunt their skills in Chuncheon (p.148), a city in Gangwon province.

Firefly Festival Aug. Glow worms are the tiny stars of the show at this modest night-time event, which takes place over a weekend near Muju (p.259). One unexpected treat is the chance to don a firefly costume.

September–November

Gwangju Biennale ⓦ gb.or.kr. Sept–Nov. A wide-ranging, two-month-long festival of contemporary art, the biennale usually takes place on alternate autumns, though it has also been held in spring.

Andong Mask Dance Festival ⓦ www.maskdance.com. Late Sept or early Oct. Legend has it that if a person fails to attend a mask festival in their lifetime, they cannot get into heaven, so if you're in Korea in the autumn you might as well have a crack at salvation by participating in one of the country's most popular events – a week of anonymous dancing, performed by the best troupes in the land (p.178).

Pusan International Film Festival ⓦ www.piff.org. Usually Oct. One of Asia's biggest such events, PIFF draws in big-shots and hangers-on for a week of cinematic fun (see p.207).

Baekje Festival ⓦ www.baekje.org. Early Oct. This annual event commemorating the Baekje dynasty is held each year in the old Baekje capitals of Gongju (see p.274) and Buyeo (p.272).

World Martial Arts Festival Usually Oct. A week-long series of international fisticuff action, held each year in Chungju.

Gimchi Festival Late Oct. In Gwangju. You'll be able to see, smell and taste dozens of varieties of the spicy stuff, and there's even a *gimchi*-making contest for foreigners keen to show off.

Pepero Day Nov 11. A crass marketing ploy, but amusing nonetheless – like Pocky, their Japanese cousins, Pepero are thin sticks of chocolate-coated biscuit, and on the date when it looks as if four of them are standing together, millions of Koreans say "I love you" by giving a box to their sweethearts, friends, parents or pets.

Sports and outdoor activities

The 1988 Seoul Olympics did much to thrust Korea into the international spotlight, a trick repeated with the even more successful 2002 FIFA World Cup, an event co-hosted with Japan. But sport here is less about watching than doing, a fact evident in the well-trodden trails of the national parks, and the svelte proportions of the average Korean.

The most popular activity is **hiking**, which is the national pastime owing to the country's abundance of mountains and national parks – see the *Hiking in Korea* colour section for more details.

Spectator sports

The two most popular spectator sports in the country are **football** and **baseball**. Koreans tend to follow one or the other, though football has been in the ascendancy of late, particularly with females and the younger generations. Those looking for something authentically Korean should try to hunt down a *ssireum* wrestling tournament.

Football

Soccer, or *chuk-gu* (축구), became the most popular sport in the country following its co-hosting of the World Cup in 2002. The ten gleaming new *gyeonggi-jang* built for the tournament were swiftly moved into by teams from the national K-League (see opposite), but the high attendances that the tournament spawned dropped sharply as spectators realized that their local boys weren't really better than Argentina – rows of empty seats mean that you'll always be able to get a ticket at the door, with prices generally around W10,000. The championship trophy usually sits in or around Seoul: Suwon, Seongnam and FC Seoul have achieved domestic and international success, though Pohang and Jeonbuk have also won titles recently. Suwon and Daejeon are said to have the rowdiest fans. Other teams are listed below, though note that most teams operate as American-style "franchises" that can move lock, stock and barrel to more profitable locations at the drop of a hat. A few locals have escaped the K-League for more lucrative pastures, and Koreans are immensely proud of their sporting diaspora; as a foreigner you're very likely to be quizzed about players such as Park Ji-sung, who made it to Manchester United via Holland.

K-League teams

Busan I'Park Asiad Main Stadium, Busan

Chunnam Dragons Gwangyang Stadium, Gwangyang

Daegu FC World Cup Stadium, Daegu

Daejeon Citizen World Cup Stadium, Daejeon

FC Seoul World Cup Stadium, Seoul

Gangwon FC 2 main bases: Gangneung and Chuncheon

Gwangju FC Guus Hiddink Stadium, Gwangju

Gwangju Phoenix Guus Hiddink Stadium, Gwangju

Gyeongnam FC Civil Stadium, Changwon

Incheon United Munhak Stadium, Incheon
Jeju United FC World Cup Stadium, Seogwipo
Jeonbuk Motors World Cup Stadium, Jeonju
Pohang Steelers Steelyard Stadium, Pohang
Seongnam Chunma Seongnam Stadium, Seongnam
Suwon Bluewings Big Bird Stadium, Suwon
Ulsan Tigers Munsu Cup Stadium, Ulsan

Baseball

Until 2002, **baseball** (*yagu*; 야구) was the spectator sport of choice. Though its popularity has waned, you'll see a lot of games on Korean television, or can attend a professional game at one of the *yagu-jang* listed below; seasons run from April to October, with a break at the height of summer. Though the fielding, in particular, isn't quite up to the level that American fans will be used to (and neither is the ballpark atmosphere), several Korean players have made their way into the Major League, including pitchers Kim Byung-hyun and Park Chan-ho. Since the turn of the century, the Unicorns, Lions and Wyverns have ruled the roost, though the Giants also deserve a mention thanks to their noisy support. Bear in mind that the team names listed below are subject to regular change, thanks to the franchise system.

Korean baseball teams

Doosan Bears Jamsil Baseball Stadium, Seoul
Hanhwa Eagles Baseball Stadium, Daejeon
Hyundai Unicorns Baseball Stadium, Suwon
LG Twins Jamsil Baseball Stadium, Seoul
Lotte Giants Sajik Baseball Stadium, Busan
Nexen Heroes Mokdong Baseball Stadium, Seoul
Samsung Lions Baseball Stadium, Daegu
SK Wyverns Munhak Baseball Stadium, Incheon

Ssireum

Though inevitably compared to *sumo*, this Korean form of wrestling (씨름) bears more resemblance to Mongolian styles – the wrestlers are chunky, rather than gargantuan, and they rely on grabs and throws, rather than slaps and pushes. As with *sumo*, the object of the wrestlers is to force their opponents to the floor, but in **ssireum** the fights start with both fighters interlocked. The sport is markedly less popular than its Japanese counterpart; few Koreans will be able to point you in the right direction if you wish to see a tournament, and even if you hunt one down the atmosphere will usually be low-key. The best place to catch a fight will be as part of a traditional festival, notably the early summer Dano in Gangneung (see p.159).

Participatory sports

In addition to being a nation of compulsive hikers (see the *Hiking in Korea* colour section), all Koreans are taught at school to exercise as a matter of course. Martial arts are among the nation's most famed exports, but Western activities such as golf and skiing have caught on in recent decades.

Martial arts

Most Korean martial arts are variations of those that originated in China or Japan. *Taekwondo* (태권도) is the best known – developed in Tang-dynasty China, it was given a Korean twist during the Three Kingdoms period, going on to become one of the country's most famed exports, and an Olympic sport to boot. The predominantly kick-based style is taught at schools, and forms the backbone of compulsory military service for the nation's men. There are dozens of less common local styles to choose from; these include *hapkido* (합기도), better known in the West as *aikido*, its Japanese counterpart; and *geomdo* (검도), a form in which participants get to bonk each other with wooden poles and likewise known to the world as *kendo*. See p.120 for information about *taekwondo* classes in Seoul.

Golf

The success of professional Korean golfers, mainly females such as LPGA champ Park Se-ri, has tempted many into taking up the game. Over a hundred **courses** dot the country, mainly surrounding Seoul or on Jeju Island; most are members-only clubs, however, and those that aren't are pretty dear – the fact that Korean golfers often go to Japan to save money says it all. If you come in with clubs, don't forget to **declare** them on arrival at the airport. Tourist offices will have information about nearby courses, though the average traveller will have to stick to the **driving ranges** dotted around the cities – scan the urban horizon for tower blocks topped by a large green net.

Skiing

With sub-zero winters and mountainous terrain, it's hardly surprising that **skiing** is big business in Korea, a country that came agonizingly close to being selected as the host of the 2010 and 2014 Winter Olympics. Non-Olympians looking to ski or snowboard in Korea should have few problems – there are a number of resorts, mainly in the northern provinces of Gyeonggi and Gangwon (see p.125); most of these have ample accommodation facilities, though prices soar in the ski season (usually Dec–Feb). Clothes and ski equipment are available for hire, and many resorts have English-speaking instructors; **prices** vary from place to place, but expect lift passes to cost around W60,000 per day, with ski or snowboard rental another W30,000 on top of that.

Football and rugby

Football is played across the country by young males, mostly in the form of kick-abouts that would gladly absorb a foreign player or two. The best places to look are riverside flood plains, often wide enough to accommodate the odd pitch, or university campuses. There's also the **foreigners' football league**, a highly competitive affair; ask at your local expat bar for details, or try your luck on ⓦssflkorea.com.

Culture and etiquette

You may have mastered the art of the polite bow, worked out how to use the tricky steel chopsticks, and learnt a few words of the Korean language, but beware, you may upset new friends by accepting gifts with your hand in the wrong place. While even seasoned expats receive heartfelt congratulations for getting the easy bits right (some are even surprised when foreigners are able to use Korean money), there are still innumerable ways to offend the locals, and unfortunately it's the things that are hardest to guess that are most likely to see you come a cropper.

Korea is often said to be the world's most **Confucian** nation, such values having been instilled for over a thousand years across several dynasties (see p.371). Elements of Confucianism still linger on today – it's still basically true that anyone older, richer or more important than you (or just male as opposed to female) is simply "better" and deserving of more respect, a fact that becomes sorely clear to many working in Korea. Perhaps most evident to foreigners will be what amounts to a national obsession with **age** – you're likely to be asked how old you are soon after your first meeting with any Korean, and any similarity of birth years is likely to be greeted with a genuine whoop of delight (note that Koreans count years differently from Westerners – children are already 1 when they're born, and gain another digit at Lunar New Year, meaning that those born on December 31 are technically two years old the next day). Women have traditionally been treated as inferior to men, and expected to ditch their job as soon as they give birth to their first child; however, recent years have shown a marked shift towards gender equality, with males more forgiving in the home and females more assertive in the workplace. **Foreigners** are largely exempt from the code of conduct that would be required of both parties following their knowledge of age, employment and background, and little is expected of them in such terms, but this does have its drawbacks – in such an ethnically homogenous society, those that aren't Korean will always remain "outsiders", even if they speak the language fluently or have actually spent their whole lives in the country. Meanwhile, foreigners with Korean blood will be expected to behave as a local would, even if they can't speak a word of the language.

Conduct

The East Asian concept of "face" is very important in Korea, and known here as **gibun**; the main goal is to avoid the **embarrassment** of self or others. Great lengths are taken to smooth out awkward situations, and foreigners getting unnecessarily angry are unlikely to invoke much sympathy. This occasionally happens as the result of an embarrassed smile, the traditional Korean retort to an uncomfortable question or incident; remember that they're not laughing at you (even if they've just dropped something on your head), merely trying to show empathy or move the topic onto safer ground. Foreigners may also see Koreans as disrespectful: nobody's going to thank you for holding open a door, and you're unlikely to get an apology if bumped into (which is almost inevitable on the subway). **Dressing well** has long been important, but though pretty much anything goes for local girls these days, foreign women may be assumed to be brazen hussies (or Russian prostitutes) if they wear revealing clothing.

Meeting and greeting

Foreigners will see Koreans **bowing** all the time, even during telephone conversations. Though doing likewise will do much to endear you to locals, don't go overboard – a full, right-angled bow would only be appropriate for meeting royalty (and the monarchy ended in 1910). Generally, a short bow with eyes closed and the head directed downwards will do just fine, but it's best to observe the Koreans themselves, and the action will become quite natural after a short time; many visitors find themselves inadvertently maintaining the habit long after they've left. **Attracting attention** is also done differently here – you beckon with fingers fluttering beneath a downward-facing palm, rather than with your index fingers protruding hook-like from an upturned one.

Koreans are great lovers of **business cards**, which are exchanged in all meetings that have even a whiff of commerce about them. The humble rectangles garner far greater respect than they do in the West, and folding or stuffing one into a pocket or wallet is a huge *faux pas* – accept your card with profuse thanks, leave it on the table for the duration of the meeting, and file it away with respect (a card-holder is an essential purchase for anyone here on business). Also note that it's seen as incredibly rude to write someone's name in red ink – this colour is reserved for names of those who have died, a practice that most Koreans seem to think goes on all around the world.

If you're lucky enough to be invited to a Korean home, try to bring a **gift** – fruit, chocolates and flowers go down well. The offering is likely to be refused at first, and probably on the second attempt too – persevere and it will eventually be accepted with thanks. The manner of receiving is also important – the receiving hand should be held from underneath by the non-receiving one, the distance up or down the arm dependent on exactly how polite you want to be. This will only come with experience and will not be expected of most foreigners, but you will be expected to take your **shoes off** once inside the house or apartment, so try to ensure that your socks are clean and hole-free.

Dining

Korea's Confucian legacy can often be a great boon to foreigners, as it has long been customary for hosts (usually "betters") to **pay** – many English teachers get taken out for regular slap-up meals by their bosses, and don't have to pay a dime. Koreans also tend to make a big show of trying to pay, with the bill passing rapidly from hand to hand until the right person coughs up. Nowadays things are changing slowly – "going Dutch" is increasingly common where it would once have been unthinkable – but there are still innumerable codes of conduct; Koreans will usually guide foreigners through the various dos and don'ts. Many surround the use of **chopsticks** – don't use these to point or to pick your teeth, and try not to spear food with them unless your skills are really poor. It's also bad form, as natural as it may seem, to leave your chopsticks in the bowl: this is said to resemble incense sticks used after a death, but to most Koreans it just looks wrong (just as many Westerners obey unwritten and seemingly meaningless rules governing cutlery positions). Just leave the sticks balanced on the rim of the bowl.

Many Korean meals are group affairs, and this has given rise to a number of rules surrounding who **serves the food** from the communal trays to the individual ones – it's usually the youngest woman at the table. Foreign women finding themselves in this position will be able to mop up a great deal of respect by performing the duty, though as there are particular ways to serve each kind of food, it's probably best to watch first. The **serving of drinks** is a little less formal, though again the minutiae of recommended conduct could fill a small book – basically, you should never refill your own cup or glass, and should endeavour to keep topped up those belonging to others. The position of the hands is important – watch to see how the Koreans are doing it (both the pourer and the recipient), and you'll be increasing your "face" value in no time.

One big no-no is to **blow your nose** during the meal – preposterously unfair, given the spice level of pretty much every Korean dish. Should you need to do so, make your excuses and head to the toilets. It's also proper form to wait for the **head of the table** – the one who is paying, in other words – to sit down first, as well as to allow them to be the first to stand at the end of the meal. The latter can be quite tricky, as many Korean restaurants are sit-on-the-floor affairs that play havoc on the knees and backs of foreigners unaccustomed to the practice.

All in all, Koreans will tolerate anything viewed as a "mistake" on the part of the foreigner, and offer great encouragement to those who are at least attempting to get things right. This can sometimes go a little too far – you're likely to be praised for your chopstick-handling abilities however long you've been around, and it's almost impossible to avoid the Korean Catch-22: locals love to ask foreigners questions during a meal, but anyone stopping to answer will likely fail to keep pace with the fast-eating Koreans, who will then assume that your dish is not disappearing quickly because you don't like it.

Travel essentials

Costs

Some people come to Korea expecting it to be a budget destination on a par with the Southeast Asian countries, while others arrive with expectations of Japanese-style levels. The latter is closer to the truth – those staying at five-star hotels and eating at Western-style restaurants will spend almost as much as they would in other developed countries, though there are numerous ways for budget travellers to make their trip a cheap one. Your biggest outlay is likely to be **accommodation** – Seoul has some grand places to stay for W400,000 and up, though most cities have dedicated tourist hotels for around W100,000. Though they're not to everyone's taste, motels usually make acceptable places to stay; costing around W30,000 (or often double that in Seoul). The capital does, however, have a few backpacker hostels with dorms for around W20,000, while real scrimpers can stay at a *jjimjilbang* (see p.38) for a few bucks.

Because the country is small, **transport** is unlikely to make too much of a dent in your wallet – even a high-speed KTX train from

Seoul in the northwest to Busan in the southeast will only set you back W52,000, and you can cut that in half by taking a slower service. Inner-city transport is also good value, with most journeys costing W1000 or so, and **admission charges** to temples, museums and the like are similarly unlikely to cause your wallet discomfort.

By staying in motels or guesthouses and eating at reasonably cheap restaurants, you should be able to survive easily on a daily budget of W40,000, or even half this if seriously pushed. After you've added in transport costs and a few entry tickets, a realistic daily figure may be W60,000.

Tipping plays almost no part in Korean transactions – try not to leave unwanted change in the hands of a cashier, lest they feel forced to abandon their duties and chase you down the street with it. Exceptions are tourist hotels, most of which tack a 10 percent service charge onto the room bill; these are also among the few places in the country to omit **tax** – levied at 10 percent – from their quoted prices.

Crime and personal safety

Korea is a country in which you're far more likely to see someone running towards you with a dropped wallet than away with a stolen one – tales abound about travellers who have left a valuable possession on a restaurant table or park bench and returned hours later to find it in the same place. Though you'd be very unlucky to fall victim to a crime, it's prudent to take a few simple precautions. The country has an awful **road safety** record, the gruesome statistics heightened by the number of vehicles that use pavements as shortcuts or parking spaces. Caution should also be exercised around any **street fights** that you may have the misfortune to come across – since Korean men practise *taekwondo* to a fairly high level during their compulsory national service, Korea is not a great place to get caught in a scuffle.

Electricity

The electrical **current** runs at 220v, 60Hz throughout the country, and requires European-style plugs with two round pins, though some older buildings, including many *yeogwan* and *yeoinsuk*, may still take flat-pinned plugs at 110v.

Entry requirements

Citizens of almost any Western nation can enter Korea visa-free with an onward ticket, though the duration of the permit varies. Most West European nationals qualify for a three-month visa exemption, as do citizens of New Zealand and Australia; Italians and Portuguese are allowed sixty days, Americans and South Africans just thirty, and Canadians a full six months. If you need more than this, apply before entering Korea. **Overstaying** your visa will result in a large fine (up to W500,000 per day), with exceptions only being made in emergencies such as illness or loss of passport. Getting a new passport is time-consuming and troublesome, though the process will be simplified if your passport has been registered with your embassy in Seoul, or if you can prove your existence with a birth certificate or copy of your old passport.

Work visas

Work visas, valid for one year and extendable for at least one more, can be applied for before or after entering Korea. Applications can take up to a month to be processed by Korean embassies, but once inside the country it can take as little as a week. Your **employer** will do all the hard work with the authorities, then provide you with a visa confirmation slip; the visa must be picked up outside Korea (the nearest consulate is in Fukuoka, Japan; visas here can be issued on the day of application). Visas with the same employer can be extended without leaving Korea. An **alien card** must be applied for at the local immigration office within 90 days of arrival – again, this is usually taken care of by the employer. Work visas are forfeited on leaving Korea, though re-entry visas can be applied for at your provincial immigration office, W30,000 for single entry, W50,000 for multiple. Australians, Canadians and New Zealanders can apply for a **working holiday** visa at their local South Korean embassy.

South Korean embassies and consulates abroad

Australia ⓦ www.korea.org.au.
Canada ⓦ www.koreanconsulate.on.ca.
China ⓦ www.koreanembassy.cn.
Ireland ⓦ southkorea.visahq.com/embassy/Ireland/.
Japan ⓦ south-korea.visahq.com/embassy/Japan/.
New Zealand ⓦ www.koreanembassy.org.nz.
Singapore ⓦ www.koreaembassy.org.sg.
South Africa ⓦ south-korea.visahq.com/embassy/South-Africa/.
UK ⓦ www.koreanembassy.org.uk.
USA ⓦ www.koreaembassyusa.org.

Gay and lesbian travellers

Despite Goryeo-era evidence suggesting that undisguised homosexuality was common in Royal and Buddhist circles, the **gay scene** in today's Korea forms a small, alienated section of society. Indeed, many locals genuinely seem to believe that Korean homosexuality simply does not exist, regarding it instead as a "foreign disease" that instantly gives people AIDS. The prevalent Confucian attitudes, together with the lack of a decent gay scene, have been the bane of many a queer expat's life in the country. For Korean homosexuals, the problems are more serious – although the law makes no explicit reference to the legality of sexual intercourse between adults of the same sex, this is less a tacit nod of consent than a refusal of officialdom to discuss such matters, and gay activities may be punishable as sexual harassment, or even, shockingly, "mutual rape" if it takes place in the military. In the early 1990s, the first few gay and lesbian websites were cracked down on by a government that, during the course of the subsequent appeal, made it clear that human rights did not fully apply to homosexuals – all the more reason for the "different people" (*iban-in*), already fearful of losing their jobs, friends and family, to lock themselves firmly in the closet.

Korean society is, however, becoming more liberal. With more and more high-profile homosexuals coming out, a critical mass has been reached, and younger generations are markedly less prejudiced against – and more willing to discuss – the pink issue. Gay clubs, bars and saunas, while still generally low-key outside "Homo Hill" in Seoul's Itaewon district, can be found in every major city, and lobbyists have been making inroads into the Korean parliament. Still the only pride event in the country, the **Korean Queer Culture Festival** takes place over a fortnight in early June at locations across Seoul. See p.118 for more on the festival, and p.116 for gay venues in Seoul.

Gay information sources

Buddy ⓦ buddy79.com. A popular gay and lesbian lifestyle magazine; you have to sign up before using the site.
Chingusai ⓦ chingusai.net. Loosely meaning "Among Friends", *Chingusai*'s trailblazing magazine is available at many gay bars in the capital. Mainly in Korean, but with some English-language information.
Happy & Safe Most useful for its gay scene city maps, you may come across the odd copy of this little guide on your way around Seoul's bars.
Utopia Asia ⓦ www.utopia-asia.com. Useful information about bars, clubs and saunas, much of which goes into their book, *The Utopia Guide to Japan, Korea and Taiwan*.

Health

South Korea is pretty high in the world rankings as far as **healthcare** goes, and there are no compulsory vaccinations or diseases worth getting too worried about. Hospitals are clean and well staffed, and most doctors can speak English, so the main health concerns for foreign travellers are likely to be financial – without adequate insurance cover, a large bill may rub salt into your healing wounds if you end up in hospital (see opposite). Though no **vaccinations** are legally required, get medical advice ahead of your trip, particularly regarding Hepatitis A and B, typhoid and Japanese B Encephalitis (which are all rare in Korea but it's better to err on the side of caution), and make sure you're up to date with the usual boosters. It's also wise to bring along any medicines that you might need, especially for drugs that need to be prescribed – bring a copy of your prescription, as well as the generic name of the drug in question, as brand names may vary from country to country.

Despite the swarms of mosquitoes that blanket the country in warmer months, **malaria** is not prevalent in Korea. However, infected mosquitoes breed in the DMZ, so those planning to hang around the rural north of the Gyeonggi or Gangwon provinces should take extra precautions to prevent getting bitten. All travellers should get up-to-date malarial advice from their GP before arriving in Korea, and wherever you are in the country during the monsoon season in late summer, it's also a good idea to slap on some repellent before going out.

Drinking Korean **tap water** is a bad idea, and with free drinking fountains in every restaurant, hotel, supermarket, police station, department store and PC bar in the country, there really should be no need. Water is also sold at train and bus stations – around W700 for a small bottle. Restaurant food will almost always be prepared and cooked adequately, and all necessary precautions taken with raw fish.

In an **emergency**, you should first try to ask a local to call for an ambulance. Should you need to do so yourself, the number is ⓣ119, though it's possible that no English-speaker will be available to take your call. Alternatively, try the tourist information line on ⓣ1330 (see p.59). If you're in a major city and the problem isn't life-threatening, the local tourist office should be able to point you towards the most suitable doctor or hospital. Once there, you may find it surprisingly hard to get information about what's wrong with you – as in much of East Asia, patients are expected to trust doctors to do their jobs properly, and any sign that this trust is not in place results in a loss of face for the practitioner.

For minor complaints or medical advice, there are **pharmacies** all over the place, usually distinguished by the Korean character "*yak*" (약) at the entrance, though English-speakers are few and far between. Travellers can also visit a practitioner of **oriental medicine**, who uses acupuncture and pressure-point massage, among other techniques, to combat the problems that Western medicine cannot reach. If you have Korean friends, ask around for a personal recommendation in order to find a reputable practitioner.

Insurance

The price of hospital treatment in Korea can be quite high so it's advisable to take out a decent **travel insurance** policy before you go. Bear in mind that most policies exclude "dangerous activities"; this term may well cover activities as seemingly benign as hiking or skiing, and if you plan to bungee or raft you'll probably be paying a premium. Keep the emergency number of your insurance company handy in the event of an accident and, as in any country, if you have anything stolen make sure to obtain a copy of the police report, as you will need this to make a claim.

Internet

You should have no problem getting online in South Korea, possibly the most connected nation on the planet. It's a national addiction – **PC rooms** (PC-방; pronounced "*pishi-bang*") are everywhere; look around any urban area and you'll see one. These noisy, air-conditioned shrines to the latest computing equipment hide behind neon-lit street signs (the PC in Roman characters; the *bang*, meaning room, in Korean text), and despite their ubiquity can be full to the brim with gamers – you're likely to be the only one checking your mail. These cafés have charged the same price since the dawn of the internet age: an almost uniform W1000 per hour, with a one-hour minimum charge (though it's far more expensive in hotels, and usually free in post offices). Most will have snacks and instant noodles for sale behind the counter – customers need occasional nutrition – and some will offer you a free tea or coffee when you sit down, topping you up every few hours.

Wi-fi access is becoming ever more common, with many cafés allowing customers to use their connection for free. *Tom N' Toms* and *Ti-amo* are generally the best chains for this (though the coffee at the former is pretty poor); *Starbucks* will only let you on if you have a Korean ID number. You may also be able to get online at your accommodation, though ironically the cheaper places are better: most modern motels have free-to-use terminals inside the rooms, while hotels generally charge extortionate rates of over W20,000 per day.

Laundry

Almost all tourist hotels provide a **laundry** service, and some of the Seoul backpacker hostels will wash your smalls for free, but with public laundries so thin on the ground those staying elsewhere may have to resort to a spot of DIY cleaning. All motels have 24-hour hot water, as well as soap, body lotion and/or shampoo in the bathrooms, and in the winter clothes dry in no time on the heated *ondol* floors. Summer is a different story, with the humidity making it very hard to dry clothes in a hurry.

Mail

The Korean postal system is cheap and trustworthy, and there are **post offices** in even the smallest town. Most are open Monday to Friday from 9am to 6pm; all should be able to handle international mail, and the larger ones offer free internet access. The main problem facing many travellers is the relative dearth of **postcards** for sale, though if you do track some down postal rates are cheap, at around W400 per card. Letters will cost a little more, though as with **parcels** the tariff will vary depending on their destination – the largest box you can send (20kg) will cost about W150,000 to mail to the UK or USA, though this price drops to about W50,000 if you post via **surface mail**, a process that can take up to three months. All post offices have the necessary boxes for sale, and will even do your packing for a small fee. Alternatively, international courier chains such as UPS and FedEx can also ship from Korea.

Maps

Free maps – many of which are available in English – can be picked up at any tourist office or higher-end hotel, as well as most travel terminals. The main drawback with them is that distances and exact street patterns are hard to gauge, though it's a complaint the powers that be are slowly taking on board. Excellent **national park** maps, drawn to scale, cost W1000 from the ticket booths.

Money

The **Korean currency** is the won (W), which comes in notes of W1000, W5000, W10,000 and W50,000, and coins of W10, W50, W100 and W500. At the time of writing the **exchange rate** was approximately W1750 to £1, W1550 to €1, and W1050 to US$1.

ATMs are everywhere in Korea, not only in banks (*eunhaeng*) but 24-hour convenience stores such as *Family Mart*, *7-Eleven* or *LG25*. Most machines are capable of dealing with foreign cards, and those that do are usually able to switch to English-language mode. Smaller towns may not have such facilities – stock up on cash in larger cities.

Foreign **credit cards** are being accepted in more and more hotels, restaurants and shops. It shouldn't be too hard to **exchange** foreign notes or travellers' cheques for Korean cash; banks are all over the place, and the only likely problem when dealing in dollars, pounds or euros is time – some places simply won't have exchanged money before, forcing staff to consult the procedure manual.

Opening hours and public holidays

Korea is one of the world's truest 24-hour societies – **opening hours** are such that almost everything you need is likely to be available when you require it. Most shops and almost all restaurants are open daily, often until late, as are tourist information offices. A quite incredible number of establishments are open 24/7, including convenience stores, saunas, internet cafés and some of the busier shops and restaurants. Post offices (Mon–Fri 9am–6pm) and banks (Mon–Fri 9.30am–4pm) keep more sensible hours.

Until recently, the country was one of the few in the world to have a **six-day working week**; though this has been officially altered to five, the changes haven't filtered through to all workers, and Korea's place at the top of the world's "average hours worked per year" table has not been affected. The number of **national holidays** has fallen, however, in an attempt to make up the slack, and as most of the country's population are forced to take their holiday at the same times, there can be chaos on the roads and rails. Three of the biggest holidays – Lunar New Year, Buddha's birthday and *Chuseok* – are based on the lunar calendar, and have no fixed dates. See below for further details on national holidays and festivals.

Phones

Living in one of the world's most important fonts of **mobile phone** technology, Koreans may deem passé what qualifies as cutting-edge elsewhere. Getting hold of a phone while you're in the country is easy – there are 24-hour rental booths at Incheon Airport. If you're going to be in Korea for a while, you may care to buy a secondhand mobile phone – these can be as cheap as W15,000, and the pace of change means that even high-quality units may be available for knock-down prices; the best places to look are shopping districts, electrical stores or underground malls – just look for a glassed-off bank of phones. After purchase you'll need to register with a major service provider – KTF and SK Telecom are two of the biggest chains, and so ubiquitous that

Korean public holidays

Sinjeong (New Year's Day) Jan 1. Seoul celebrates New Year in much the same fashion as Western countries, with huge crowds gathering around City Hall.

Seollal (Lunar New Year) Usually early Feb. One of the most important holidays on the calendar, Lunar New Year sees Koreans flock to their home towns for a three-day holiday of relaxed celebration, and many businesses close up.

Independence Movement Day March 1.

Children's Day May 5. Koreans make an even bigger fuss over their kids than usual on this national holiday – expect parks, zoos and amusement parks to be jam-packed.

Memorial Day June 6. Little more than a day off for most Koreans, this day honours those who fell in battle, and is best observed in the National Cemetery (see p.248).

Constitution Day July 17.

Independence Day Aug 15. The country becomes a sea of Korean flags on this holiday celebrating the end of Japanese rule in 1945.

Chuseok Late Sept or early Oct. One of the biggest events in the Korean calendar is this three-day national holiday, similar to Thanksgiving; families head to their home towns to venerate their ancestors in low-key ceremonies, and eat a special crescent-shaped rice-cake.

National Foundation Day Oct 3. Celebrates the 2333 BC birth of Dangun, the legendary founder of the Korean nation. Shamanist celebrations take place at shrines around Seoul, with the most important on Inwangsan mountain.

Christmas Day Dec 25. Every evening looks like Christmas in neon-drenched Seoul, but on this occasion Santa Haraboji (Grandpa Santa) finally arrives.

the nearest store is likely to be within walking distance. Registration is free (bring your passport), and you can top up pay-as-you-go accounts in increments of W10,000. Despite the prevalence of mobile phones, you'll still see **payphones** on every major street; these ageing units only take coins, so you'll have to pump in change at a furious pace to avoid the deafening squawks that signal the end of your call-time.

Korea's **international dialling code** is ⓣ82. When dialling from abroad, omit the initial zero from the area codes. Area codes are given throughout this Guide.

Photography

Photography is a national obsession in Korea – at tourist sights around the country, locals feed their cameras as they would hungry pets. Most **internet cafés** are kitted out for the transfer of digital images from memory cards.

A mountainous country with four distinct seasons, pulsating cities and a temple around every corner, Korea should keep your camera-finger busy; if you want a personal shot, few locals will mind being photographed, though of course it's polite to ask first. One serious no-no is to go snap-happy on a tour of the DMZ (see p.140) – this can, and has, landed tourists in trouble. You may also see temple-keepers and monks poised at the ready to admonish would-be photographers of sacrosanct areas.

Shopping

Most visitors who want to splash their cash do so in **Seoul**, which has some fantastic shopping opportunities, including the trinket shops on Insadonggil, the underground EXPO mall, the brand-name flagship stores in Apgujeong, and the colossal markets of Dongdaemun and Namdaemun; see "Shopping" in Seoul on p.121 for more information.

Studying in Korea

Korea has long been a popular place for the study of **martial arts**, while the country's ever-stronger ties with global business are also prompting many to gain a competitive advantage by studying the Korean language. It's also one of the world's great **archery** hotbeds, though courses here are not for amateurs and teachers demand substantial time and effort from their charges.

Language

Courses at the institutes run by many of the larger **universities** vary in terms of price, study time, skill level and accommodation. Most of the year-long courses are in Seoul and start in March – apply in good time. There's a good list at ⓦenglish.visitkorea.or.kr, while information on study visas and how to apply for them can be found on the Ministry of Education's website (ⓦwww.studyinkorea.go.kr). There are **private institutes** dotted around Seoul and other major cities – ⓦenglish.seoul.go.kr has a list of safe recommendations in the capital, while other official city websites are the best places to look for institutes elsewhere.

If you're working in Korea, you may not have time for intensive study; if so, it's worth looking into the **government-funded courses** run by a few major cities, some of which are so cheap that their price is barely an issue. Many people opt for an even higher degree of informality and take language lessons from friends or colleagues, but with so few English speakers around, just living in Korea can be all the practice you need.

Martial arts classes

Finding classes for the most popular styles (including **taekwondo**, *hapkido* and *geomdo*) isn't hard, but very few classes cater for foreigners – it's best to go hunting on the expat circuit. The obvious exception is Seoul; here, popular introductory *taekwondo* courses take place at Gyeonghuigung palace. Those looking for something more advanced should seek advice from their home country's own *taekwondo* federation.

Buddhist teachings

Many **temples** offer teaching and templestay programmes for around W50,000 per night – a wonderful opportunity to see the "Land of Morning Calm" at its most serene (as long as you can stand the early mornings). Some temples are able to provide English-language instruction, and some not – see ⓦeng.templestay.com for more details.

Time

The Korean peninsula shares a **time zone** with Japan – one hour ahead of China, nine hours ahead of Greenwich Mean Time, seven hours ahead of South Africa, fourteen hours ahead of Eastern Standard Time in the US or Montreal in Canada, and one hour behind Sydney. Daylight Saving hours are not observed, so though noon in London will be 9pm in Seoul for much of the year, the difference drops to eight hours during British Summer Time.

Tourist information

The Korean tourist authorities churn out a commendable number of English-language maps, pamphlets and books, most of which are handed out at **information booths** – you'll be able to find one in every city, usually outside the train or bus stations. Not all of these are staffed with an English-speaker, but you'll be able to get 24-hour assistance and advice on the dedicated **tourist information line** – dial ⓣ1330 and you'll be put through to helpful call-centre staff who speak a number of languages and can advise on transport, sights, accommodation, theatre ticket prices and much more. If calling from a mobile phone or abroad, you'll also need to put in a regional prefix – to reach Seoul, for example, dial ⓣ02/1330. The official **Korean tourist website** (ⓦenglish.visitkorea.or.kr) is quite useful, and most cities and provinces have sites of their own.

Travelling with children

Korea is a country with high standards of **health and hygiene**, low levels of crime and plenty to see and do – bringing children of any age should pose no special problems. **Changing facilities** are most common in Seoul – department stores are good places to head – though few restaurants have highchairs, and baby food labelled in English is almost non-existent. A few hotels provide a **babysitting service**, though those in need can ask their concierge for a newspaper with babysitter adverts. Every city has cinemas, theme parks and a zoo or two to keep children amused; Everland (p.133) and Seoul Land (p.102) are the two most popular escapes from Seoul, while there are a number of interesting museums in the capital itself. Note that some of the restaurants listed in this guide – especially those serving *galbi*, a self-barbecued meat – have hot-plates or charcoal in the centre of the table, which poses an obvious danger to little hands, and in a country where it's perfectly normal for cars to drive on the pavements, you may want to exercise a little more caution than normal when walking around town.

Travellers with disabilities

Despite its First World status, Korea can be filed under "developing countries" as far as **disabled accessibility** is concerned, and with rushing traffic and crowded streets, it's never going to be the easiest destination to get around. Until recently, very little attention was paid to those with disabilities, but things are changing. Streets are being made more wheelchair-friendly, and many subway and train stations have been fitted with lifts. Almost all motels and tourist hotels have these, too, though occasionally you'll come across an entrance that hasn't been built with wheelchairs in mind. Some museums and tourist attractions will be able to provide a helper if necessary, but wherever you are, willing Koreans will jump at the chance to help travellers in obvious need of assistance.

Working in Korea

There are two main types of foreigner in Korea: English teachers and American soldiers. Other jobs are hard to come by, though today's Korea is becoming ever more prominent in global business, with the resulting foreign contingent gradually permeating Seoul's army of suits. It's still fairly easy to land a teaching job, though to do this legally a degree certificate is nigh-on essential; wages are good, and Korea is a popular port of call for those wishing to pay off their student loan quickly while seeing a bit of the world. The cost of living, though rising, is still below that in most English-speaking countries.

With the number of **teaching jobs** on offer, it's quite possible to handpick a city or province of your choice. Seoul is an obvious target and the easiest place from which to escape into Western pleasures if necessary, though note that a hefty proportion of positions listed as being in the capital are actually in uninteresting satellite cities such as Bundang, Anyang or Ilsan, all a long journey from central Seoul – try to find the nearest subway station to your prospective position on a map if possible. Those who head to provincial cities such as Daejeon, Mokpo or Busan generally seem to have a better time of things, and emerge with a truer appreciation of the country, as well as better Korean language skills. There are also those who arrive with a specific purpose in mind – surfers dig Jeju and the east coast, for example, while others choose to immerse themselves in the culture by staying in the smallest possible town.

For details of **Korean language courses**, see p.58.

Teaching English

Uncomplicated entry requirements, low tax and decent pay cheques make Korea one of the most popular stops on the **English-teaching** circuit. Demand for native speakers is high and still growing; English-teaching qualifications are far from essential, and all that is usually required is a degree certificate, and a copy of your passport – many people have been taken on by a Korean school without so much as a telephone interview. Most new entrants start off by teaching kids at a language school (*hagwon*). Some of the bigger companies are ECC, YBM and Pagoda, and most pay around W2,000,000 per month, though even for people doing the same job at the same school this may vary depending on nationality and gender – Canadian women usually get the most, British gents the least. After a year or two, many teachers are sick of kids and puny holiday allowances (typically less than two weeks per year), and make their way to a university teaching post; pay is usually lower and responsibilities higher than at a *hagwon*, though the holiday allowances (as much as five months per year) are hard to resist. Most teachers give their bank balance a nudge in the right direction by offering **private lessons** on the side – an illegal practice, but largely tolerated unless you start organizing them for others. To land a full-time job from outside Korea you'll have to go online, and it's still the best option if you're already in Korea – popular sites include Dave's ESL Café (Ⓦwww.eslcafe.com), ESL Hub (Ⓦwww.eslhub.com) and HiTeacher (Ⓦhiteacher.com), though a thorough web search will yield more.

One of the most regular *hagwon*-related **complaints** is the long hours many teachers have to work – figure on up to 30 per week. This may include Saturdays, or be spread quite liberally across the day from 9am to 9pm – try to find jobs with "no split shift" if possible. Questionable school policies also come in for stick; for example, teachers are often expected to be present at the school for show even if they have no lessons on. Real scare stories are ten-a-penny, too – every teacher knows an unfortunate fellow-foreigner whose school suddenly closed, the manager having ridden off into the sunset with a pay cheque or two. This said, most schools are reputable; you can typically expect them to organize **free accommodation**, and to do the legwork with your **visa** application. Some countries operate Working Holiday visa schemes with Korea, but others will need a full working visa to be legally employed; those unable to collect this in their home country are usually given a plane ticket and directions for a quick visa-run to Japan (the closest embassy is in Fukuoka).

Guide

Guide

South Korea

North Korea

1

Seoul

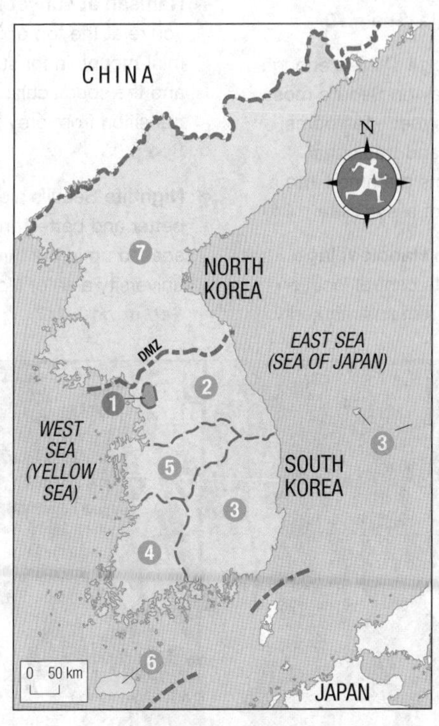
CHINA
N
7
NORTH
KOREA
DMZ
EAST SEA
(SEA OF JAPAN)
1
2
WEST
SEA
(YELLOW
SEA)
3
5
SOUTH
KOREA
3
4
6
0 50 km
JAPAN

CHAPTER 1 Highlights

* **Hanok guesthouses** Stay a night in a *hanok* – a wooden building kept warm in the winter by underfloor fires – an authentically Korean experience. See p.74
* **Confucian palaces** Five beautiful palaces remain from Seoul's time as capital of the Joseon dynasty, each with its own merits. See p.79
* **Insadonggil** There's enough to fill a day on Seoul's most popular street – tearooms, galleries and traditional restaurants crammed into a network of alleys. See p.84
* **Bukchon Hanok Village** Despite its central location, this area remains markedly traditional and filled with wooden *hanok* housing. See p.85
* **Dongdaemun** Head to this huge market, which never sleeps and is at its most atmospheric around midnight, for an assault on the senses. See p.92
* **Namsan at sunset** Make sure you're at the top of Seoul's mini-mountain for sunset and the spectacular city's transition from grey to neon. See p.93
* **Nightlife** Seoul's nightlife gets better and better, and is best soaked up in the throbbing university area of Hongdae. See pp.113–117

▲ Changing of the guards outside Gyeongbokgung

1

Seoul

The Korean capital of **SEOUL** (서울) is an assault on the senses. Even small streets find themselves quite alive with frenzied activity by day and searing neon after sunset, while eardrums are set pounding by clamouring shop assistants and the nighttime thump of a thousand karaoke rooms. Restaurants serving Korea's delectably spicy national dishes lure you in with their amazing aromas and tastes while doing minimal damage to your figure (or wallet), and for tactile bliss, the hot pools and ice rooms of the ubiquitous *jjimjilbang* bathhouses have no equal. With over twenty million souls packed sardine-like into a metropolitan area smaller than Luxembourg, this is one of the most densely populated places on the planet, but for all its nonstop consumption, Seoul is also a place of considerable tradition and history. **Joseon-dynasty palaces**, displayed like medals in the centre of the city, proclaim its status as a seat of regal power from as far back as 1392; the tiled roofs of wooden *hanok* houses gently fish-scale their way towards the ash-coloured granite crags of **Bukhansan**, the world's most-visited national park; the ancient songs and dances of farmhands and court performers are still clashed out in a whirligig of sound and colour along the street of Insadonggil. A city with a hyper-efficient transport system, a negligible crime rate, locals eager to please foreign guests and an almost astonishing wealth of locally produced modern art: it's little wonder that so many visitors come away so impressed.

Top of most tourists' agendas are the half-a-dozen sumptuous **palaces** dating from the late fourteenth century that surround the city centre; these include **Gyeongbokgung** and **Changdeokgung**, together with the nearby ancestral shrine of **Jongmyo**. Situated in the middle is **Insadong**; by far the most popular part of the city with tourists, its warren of tight streets is littered with traditional restaurants, quaint tearooms, art galleries and trinket shops, and makes for a great wander. **Samcheongdong** and **Bukchon Hanok Village** are two areas offering similar delights, though with fewer tourists. The amount of art on display in all three areas can come as quite a surprise – contemporary Korean work receives a fraction of the international press devoted to art from Japan or China, but is just as creative. Also offering a modern-day fusion of Korea old and new are the colossal markets of **Dongdaemun** and **Namdaemun**, in whose sprawling reaches you'll find anything from pig intestines to clip-on ties. The more modern facets of the city can be seen in the shoppers' paradise of **Myeongdong** or achingly fashionable **Apgujeong**, while the number of American soldiers hanging out in cosmopolitan **Itaewon** hint at Seoul's proximity to North Korea – it's even possible to take a day-trip to the border.

To get a sense of what makes Seoul so unique, however, you'll need to do more than tick off the sights. To truly appreciate the subtle facets of this distinctive society,

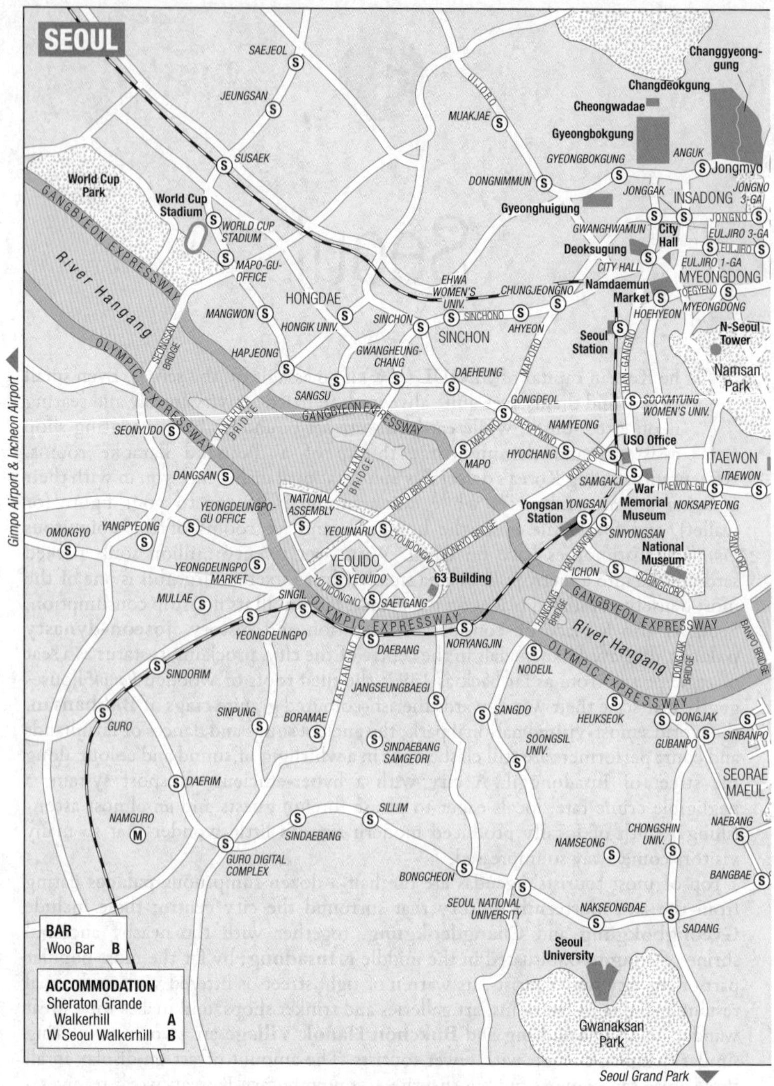

take a leap of faith into the local cuisine, follow the Korean lead on a wild night (and early morning) out, and spend a decent amount of time simply walking the streets.

Some history

Contrary to the expectations of many a visitor, Seoul possesses a long and interesting past; after first rising to prominence at the beginning of the **Three Kingdoms** period, it was then ruled over by almost every major power in Korean history. In 18 AD, then named Wiryeseong, it became the first capital of the **Baekje** kingdom (see box, p.271); the exact location is believed to be a site just east of present-day Seoul, but this was to change several times. The kings and clans

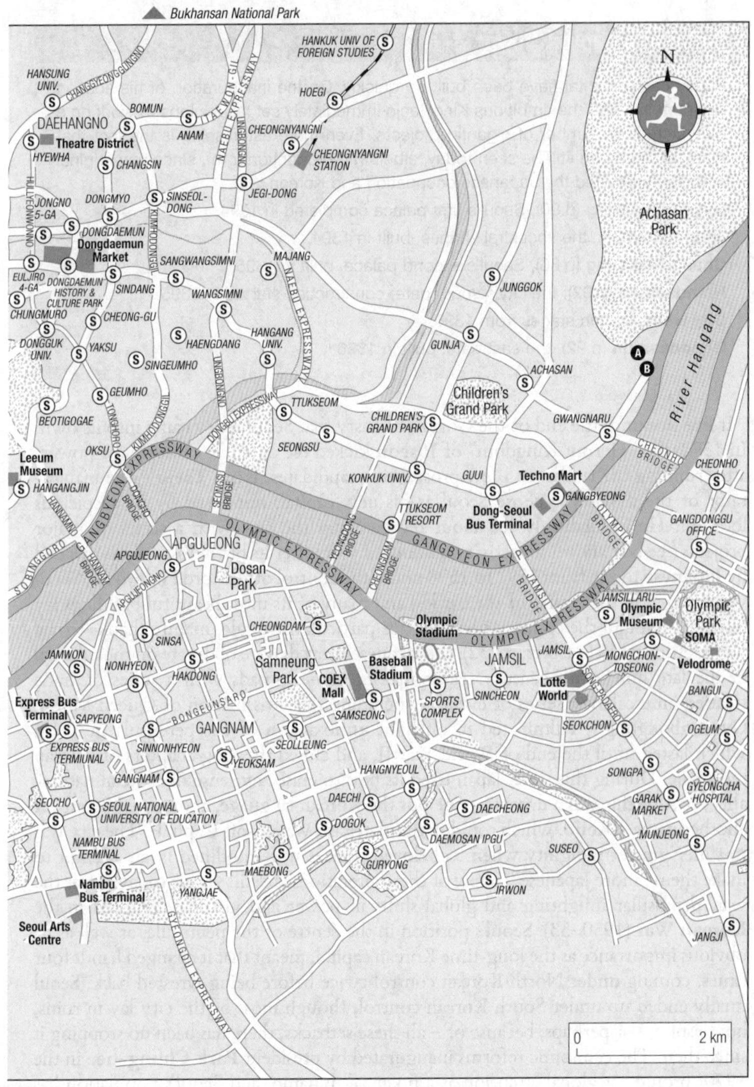

were forced far south to Gongju in 475, having been squeezed out by the rival **Goguryeo** kingdom; less than a century later, the city completed a Three Kingdoms clean-sweep when King Jinheung expanded the domain of his **Silla** kingdom (see box, p.173) far to the north, absorbing Seoul – then known as Hanseong – on the way. By 668, Silla forces held control of the whole peninsula, but having chosen Gyeongju as their capital, Seoul faded into the background. In the tenth century, Silla was usurped by the nascent **Goryeo** kingdom – they chose Kaesong, in modern-day North Korea, as the seat of their power, though Seoul was close enough to become an important trading hub, and soon earned yet another name, Namgyeong, meaning "Southern Capital".

Building a capital

Rarely can a capital have been built so quickly. On the inauguration of his Joseon kingdom in 1392, the ambitious King Taejo immediately set his minions to work on a truly incredible number of gigantic projects. Even more astonishing is the fact that many of them can still be seen today, albeit in reproduction form, since few original structures survived the Japanese occupation and Korean War.

Gyeongbokgung (p.80), Seoul's first palace completed in 1394.

Jongmyo (p.88), the ancestral shrines, built in 1394.

Changdeokgung (p.86), Seoul's second palace, built in 1395.

Namdaemun (p.92), the city's south gate; construction started in 1395.

City walls, built in stages from 1396.

Dongdaemun (p.92), the east gate, built in 1396.

It was not until the end of the Goryeo dynasty that Seoul really came into its own. In 1392, the "Hermit Kingdom" of **Joseon** kicked off over five centuries of power; after running the rule over a few prospective candidates, **King Taejo** – the inaugurator of the dynasty – chose Seoul as his new capital, impressed by its auspicious location. He immediately set about reorganizing the city with a series of major projects (see box above). Exactly two hundred years after its birth, Joseon was invaded by **Japanese** forces from 1592 to 1598 under the control of warlord Hideyoshi; Seoul was pillaged in the course of the battles, and many of its most beautiful buildings lay in ruins. Though the country survived this particular struggle, mainly thanks to the heroic Admiral Yi (see box, p.232), the Japanese proved more obdurate on their return in the late nineteenth century. After making tame inroads with a series of trade treaties, an escalating series of events – including the assassination of Queen Min in Gyeongbokgung – culminated in outright **annexation** of the peninsula in 1910, which lasted until the end of World War II, and closed the long chapters of Korean regal rule. During this time, Japan tried its best to erase any sense of Korean nationality; part of this was a drive to wipe out the Korean language, and earned Seoul yet another name – **Keijo**, which roughly translates as "Walled-off Capital". The city was to suffer greater indignity when its beloved palaces were modified in an attempt to make them "more Japanese"; a few of these alterations are still visible today. After the war, peninsular infighting and global shifts in power and ideology resulted in the **Korean War** (1950–53). Seoul's position in the centre of the peninsula, as well as its obvious importance as the long-time Korean capital, meant that it changed hands four times, coming under North Korean control twice before being wrested back. Seoul finally ended up under South Korean control, though most of the city lay in ruins, but despite – or perhaps, because of – all these setbacks, there has been no stopping it since then. The economic reforms inaugurated by president **Park Chung-hee** in the 1970s brought it global attention as a financial dynamo, and Seoul's population has ballooned to over ten million, more than double this if the whole metropolitan area is taken into account.

Arrival

The vast majority of international planes to Korea touch down at **Incheon International Airport** (인천 공항), which sits in curvy, chrome-and-glass splendour on an island about 50km west of central Seoul. With this distance easy to cover on public transport, Seoul is the first and last Korean city that most foreign visitors see. Arriving from elsewhere in the country, your choices will mainly be bus or train, although there is a domestic airport, Gimpo; the **bus** system is the more comprehensive, and its services usually cheaper, though **trains** arrive at more convenient locations in the centre of Seoul, their services more impervious to the heavy traffic.

By plane

Most people take the **bus** from **Incheon Airport** to Seoul; there are direct buses to all parts of the city, the journey taking anything from 45min to 1hr 20min depending upon the destination. These buses start at around W10,000, while more expensive limousine buses head straight to many of the top hotels (W15,000).

Moving on from Seoul

By train

Most destinations are served from **Seoul station**, which is located fairly centrally on subway lines 1 and 4. However, those who want to head to cities to the southwest of the country (such as Gwangju, Mokpo and Yeosu) have to head instead to **Yongsan station** (also on lines 1 and 4) just north of the river. Trains to and from the areas east of Seoul (Chuncheon, Wonju, Gangneung) depart from **Cheongnyangni station** to the east of the centre, and also on subway line 1. Trains from Cheongnyangni tend to be slow services, but from Yongsan and Seoul station you're likely to have a choice of **train classes**, which vary in speed and price – for more information, see p.32.

By bus

Despite the excellent punctuality and frequency of the buses heading out of Seoul, it's usually far easier to depart by train if possible as the **bus system** is rather confusing. The **express bus terminal** (which sits on top of a subway station of the same name, served by lines 3, 7 and 9) has connections to most destinations around the country, but is badly signed and made up of three different terminals – in general, the Gongbu side serves areas to the southeast of Seoul, and the Honam building across the way serves the southwest, while a smaller terminal has buses to more local destinations in Gyeonggi province. The main launching point for intercity buses is **Dong-Seoul terminal** to the east of town (subway line 2), though some destinations will require you to go to the **Nambu terminal** two stations south of the express terminal on line 3. A detailed rundown of destinations served by each terminal can be found on pp.123–124, though it's best to check at a tourist information office for the latest, or call the English-speaking information line on ⓣ1330.

By subway

So vast is Seoul's underground network that it's actually possible – and, in some cases, advisable – to reach some surrounding destinations by subway. **Incheon** lies just over an hour away from central Seoul at the western end of line 1, with ticket prices (W1900) much cheaper than buses heading the same way. **Suwon** is an hour away from central Seoul – slower than the trains, but a fraction of the price (W1600). It's also connected to Seoul by line 1, though on a separate branch line to the one heading to Incheon – check the destination on the front of the train. Suwon-bound trains often head to **Cheonan** (a mere two hours south of the capital) and beyond, though these are only for the most budget-conscious travellers.

By plane

Most domestic flights leave from **Gimpo airport**, 20km west of central Seoul on subway line 5 and the A'REX line, and also accessible by bus from all around the capital.

The A'REX **train line** heads direct to Seoul station via **Gimpo airport** (김포 공항), the terminus for most domestic flights. The A'REX has connections to several Seoul subway lines, but the poorly designed airport trains are actually slower than the buses, and head to far fewer destinations. Also note that there are two classes of train: an "express" train (40min) costing W14,000, and more regular subway-like "commuter" trains costing less than W4000, but only taking slightly longer to complete the journey (50min).

Alternatively you can take a **taxi** from Incheon Airport to central Seoul (around 30min; W75,000); the black "deluxe" taxis are more costly. From Gimpo it's around half that price.

By train

There are three major **train** stations in Seoul, all of them large and modern – most services arrive at either Seoul (서울역) or Yongsan (용산역) stations, both in the city centre, but those coming from Gangwon province will arrive at Cheongnyangni (청량리) station a short way to the east. All the stations lie on subway line 1, while Seoul station is also on line 4 – as is Sinyongsan subway station, almost literally across the road from Yongsan.

By bus

When travelling from other Korean cities by **bus**, you have a choice of Seoul terminals to choose from: most head to either the express bus terminal (고속 버스 터미널) on the south side of the river (subway lines 3, 7 and 9), or Dong-Seoul terminal (동서울 버스 터미널) to the east of town on line 2.

Information

Seoul is dotted with **information booths**, all of which dole out maps of the city, can advise on accommodation and help out with any transportation enquiries. The largest and most info-packed is the main **KTO office** (daily 9am–8pm; ⓣ02/729-9497), which fills the basement level of a tall tower that overlooks the Chonggyecheon, a stream just south of Jonggak subway station – take exit five, cross the bridge and turn right. Other useful information points include those in Seoul station, Itaewon subway station, City Hall and Myeongdong, as well as three on and around Insadonggil. Wherever you are in Korea, you can also make use of a supremely useful **dedicated foreigners' helpline** (see p.59) – just dial ⓣ1330 (with area code if calling from a mobile phone or abroad).

Orientation

Seoul is colossal, its metropolitan area stretching far and wide in a confusion of concrete and cleaved in two by the **Han**, a wide river crossed by many bridges. But despite its size, a very definite city centre – just small enough to be traversed by foot – has been in place north of the Han River since the late fourteenth century, and bounded by the five **grand palaces**. Sitting in the middle of these is **Insadong**, Seoul's tourist hub. A short walk north are **Samcheongdong** and **Bukchon Hanok Village**, two quirky zones that offer similar pleasures – though less touristed – to Insadong. This whole area is hemmed in to the north by the muscular granite peaks of **Bukhansan**, a wonderful backdrop to **Gyeongbokgung** and **Changdeokgung**, the most northerly – and popular – of the five palaces.

Seoul on the web

10 Magazine Ⓦ www.10magazine.asia. A fun publication with good listings sections for Seoul and other Korean cities.

Eloquence Ⓦ www.eloquence.co.kr. Stylish magazine that focuses on upper-class Seoul society.

Marmot's Hole Ⓦ www.rjkoehler.com. This personal blog of long-time expat Robert Koehler is full of interesting, extremely informative snippets about Seoul's culture and history.

Roboseyo Ⓦ roboseyo.blogspot.com. Expat blog that takes an often offbeat view of Seoul society.

Seoul Ⓦ www.seoulselection.com. City-sponsored magazine that's usually much more interesting than its name may suggest.

Seoul Eats Ⓦ www.seouleats.com. Food blog with an admirable selection of restaurant reviews.

The Seoul Times Ⓦ www.theseoultimes.com. Though the news itself is stale to say the least, the site has good job listings and is a useful place to hunt for flatmates.

Visit Seoul Ⓦ www.visitseoul.net. Much improved in recent years, this is the official tourist site of Seoul's city government.

Zen Kimchi Ⓦ www.zenkimchi.com. Another food blog, with a slightly more user-friendly interface than *Seoul Eats*.

South of Insadong are the busy parallel roads of Jongno and Euljiro, two of Seoul's most important thoroughfares. These sit either side of **Cheonggyecheon**, a recently gentrified stream that lies beneath street level. A walk east along this stream will bring you to **Dongdaemun**, once the eastern gate to the city, but now a traffic-heavy focal point of the colossal 24-hour market that blankets the area. Walking west instead to Cheonggyecheon's "source" – the point at which the subterranean stream becomes open-air – will land you near **City Hall**; surrounded by skyscrapers, it's flanked on one side by **Deoksugung** – another of the five palaces – and on the other by a maze of five-star hotels. These segue into **Myeongdong**, the busiest shopping area in the country, packed with clothes stores and restaurants. Just west of Myeongdong is **Namdaemun** – a market almost as big as Dongdaemun, and similarly named after a city gate – while heading south will bring you to the slopes of **Namsan**, Seoul's very own mountain, which affords fantastic views of the city centre and beyond.

South of Namsan is **Itaewon**, long the hub of foreign activity in the city; a curious mix of the sleazy and the cosmopolitan, it's home to some of Seoul's best restaurants, bars and clubs, but also most of its brothels. However, even Itaewon's nightlife is nothing compared with that found in happening **Hongdae**. This is a university area west of central Seoul, and possesses by far the most rocking nightlife in the country, a neon-drenched maze of hip-hop clubs, live music venues and trendy subterranean bars.

A number of important city districts lie south of the Han River. Starting in the west is the islet of **Yeouido**, Seoul's main centre of business and politics, and a rather uninteresting place. Further east are **Gangnam**, a shop- and restaurant-filled south-bank alternative to Myeongdong, and ultra-trendy **Apgujeong**, filled with boutiques and some of the best restaurants in the city. The **COEX Mall**, a gigantic underground shopping complex, is also in the south, as is the **Jamsil** area – home to **Lotte World**, one of the country's most popular theme parks – and **Olympic Park**, where Seoul's Summer Games were held in 1988.

City transport

With Seoul's hectic streets making car hire almost tantamount to suicide, and bicycle riding even more so, it's lucky that the city is covered by a cheap, clean and highly comprehensive **public transport** system – the subway network is one of the best developed in the world, not least because of the sheer number of workers it has to speed from A to B. Buses dash around the city every which way, and even taxis are cheap enough to be viable for many routes. If you're staying in the city for more than a few days, invest in a **T-money transport card** (see box below), which saves you not only money but also time waiting in ticket queues.

Busy roads and noxious emissions mean that **walking** through Seoul is rarely pleasurable, though Insadonggil is closed to traffic on Sundays; the shopping district of Myeongdong and club-heavy Hongdae are so swamped with people that vehicles tend to avoid these areas; and there are innumerable malls and underground shopping arcades. Riding a **bike** is only really advisable on a specially designed route along the river; see p.100 for further details.

The subway

With nine lines and counting, and over three hundred stations, Seoul's **subway system** (see the colour map at the end of this book) is one of the most comprehensive on earth – in the area bounded by the circular 2 line, you'll never be more than a short walk or taxi ride from the nearest station, while line 1 runs for a whole third of the country's length, stretching well over 100km from Soyosan in the north to Sinchang in the south. It's also possible to get to Suwon (p.129), Cheonan (p.283) or Incheon (p.133) by subway, and a special extension line connects the network to Incheon Airport; see box, p.69 for more. **Fares** are reasonable, starting at W1000 for rides of less than 10km, and very rarely costing more than W2000. **Ticket purchase** has become slightly trickier since station staff were laid off en masse in 2009; unless you've invested in a transport card (highly recommended; see box below), you'll have to buy a single-use card (W2000; refundable) from a machine; though the operating system is a little curious, you should get there in the end. Bafflingly, each card requires a deposit of W500, retrievable from machines outside the turnstiles when you've completed your journey. The subway system itself is very user-friendly: **network maps** are conveniently located around the stations, which are easily navigable with multilanguage signs. You'll find maps of the surrounding area on walls near the station exits, though be warned that north only faces upwards a quarter of the time, since each map is oriented to the direction that it happens to be facing. Running from around 5.30am to midnight (slightly earlier on weekends), trains are extremely frequent but are packed to bursting at rush hour, and often livened up by hawkers selling anything from hand cream to folk music.

Transport cards

T-money or **U-Pass transport cards** are sold for a refundable W3000 at all subway stations and some street-level kiosks. After loading them with credit (easiest at machines in the subway station), you'll save W100 on each subway or bus journey, and any remaining balance can be refunded at the end of your stay. These cards make it possible to switch at no extra cost from bus to subway – or vice versa – should you need to; you'll otherwise need two separate tickets. In addition, you can use them to pay **taxi fares**, make **phone calls** from most streetside booths, and even pay your bill at **convenience stores**.

Buses

In comparison with the almost idiot-proof subway system, Seoul's **bus network** often proves too complicated for foreign guests – English-language signage is rare, and some of the route numbers would look more at home in a telephone directory (for instance, the #9009-1 to City Hall). The buses are split into four coloured categories – **blue** buses travel long distances along major arterial roads, **green** buses are for shorter hops, **red** ones travel to the suburbs and **yellow** ones use tight loop routes. These are marked on the side and the rear by a capital letter – B for blue, R for red and so on. **Fares** start at W1000 for blue and green, W1500 for red and W550 for yellow buses, increasing on longer journeys; cash is still accepted on the bus, but see box opposite for details about travel cards. For more on routes go to Ⓦbus.seoul.go.kr, or call the tourist information line on Ⓣ1330 (see p.59).

Taxis

As in every Korean city, Seoul's taxis are **cheap** and ubiquitous. A W2400 fare covers the first 2km, and goes up in W100 increments every 144m – given that bus and subway fares start at W1000, it often works out almost as cheap for groups of three or four to travel short distances by cab rather than public transport. Note that a twenty percent **surcharge** is added between midnight and 4am. There are also deluxe *mobeom* cabs, which are black with a yellow stripe; these usually congregate around expensive hotels, charging W4500 for the first 3km and W200 for each additional 164m. You should never have to wait long for a cab. Drivers do not expect tips, but it's also unlikely that they'll speak any **English** – having your destination written in *hangeul* is the easiest way to get the information across, though drivers are able to phone interpreters for no extra charge.

Accommodation

Seoul has by far the best range of **accommodation** in the country, with everything from five-star hotels to cheap hostels. Those seeking high-quality accommodation have a wealth of places to choose from, particularly around Myeongdong and City Hall on the north of the river, and Gangnam to the south. At the lower end of the price spectrum are Seoul's ballooning number of **backpacker guesthouses**. One interesting option, popular with foreign travellers, is to stay in **traditional wooden guesthouses** north of Anguk station in the **palace district**.

At around the same price, though different in character, **motels** form a cheap alternative to official tourist hotels, sometimes having rooms of comparable size and quality; note that two of the most popular nightlife areas – Itaewon and Hongdae – have a shockingly poor range of motel accommodation. It's hard to book motels in advance, except for those listed on the excellent **Innostel** website (Ⓦinnostel.visitseoul.net), which also features an ever-growing number of **cheap hotels**.

Insadong

Despite **Insadong**'s status as a tourist magnet, accommodation here is firmly in the cheap to mid-range bracket – the nearest places with decent tourist facilities are around **City Hall**.

Traditional guesthouses in the palace district

In the surprisingly tranquil city sector north of Anguk subway station lie some of Seoul's most interesting places to stay – here you can spend the night in traditional Korean housing known as **hanok**. Highly beautiful, these are wooden buildings with tiled roofs, set around a dirt courtyard – a style that once blanketed the nation, but rarely seen in today's high-rise Korea. The generally bed-less rooms – you'll be sleeping Korean-style in a sandwich of blankets – are kept deliberately rustic and heated in the winter with the underfloor *ondol* system; all, however, provide modern-day indoor toilets and internet access.

The following places are marked on the "Palace district" **map**, p.79, and within walking distance of Anguk subway station (line 3).

Anguk Guesthouse Angukdong ⓣ02/736-8304, ⓦwww.anguk-house.com. There are just five rooms at this tiny guesthouse, where breakfast is included. The owner speaks excellent English and is full of information about the area; though his place is tucked away down some small side-alleys, the website has good directions. ❺

Bukchon Guesthouse Gyedong ⓣ02/743-8530, ⓦwww.bukchon72.com. Simple, comfortable rooms set around a pleasingly authentic courtyard, within easy walking distance of two palaces and Insadonggil. The friendly owners will even pick you up from Anguk subway station if you phone ahead; if you feel like walking, take exit three and continue straight up the main road, then take the first left, and the guesthouse will be on your left after five minutes or so. ❹

Rakkojae Gyedong ⓣ02/742-3410, ⓦwww.rkj.co.kr. The most authentic of the bunch, character-wise. Not only is the *hanok* a 1870s original, but the owners serve traditional food for dinner: a little like a Japanese *ryokan*. Studded with maple and pine trees, the courtyard is divine, featuring precious few concessions to the modern day; it's best appreciated at night, when soft light pours through the paper doors. ❼

Seoul Guesthouse Gyedong ⓣ02/745-0057, ⓦwww.seoul110.com. Seoul by name but not by nature. For somewhere so close to the centre, the atmosphere here is astonishingly rural – they even grow crops in the garden. There are no beds, though the simple rooms do come with wi-fi connections. ❹

Tea Guesthouse Bukchon Hanok Village ⓣ02/3675-9877, ⓦwww.teaguesthouse.com. More expensive than most other traditional guesthouses in the area, but *Tea*'s owners put in a lot of effort to introduce Korean traditions to their guests – if there are enough people around, you may find yourself making (and eating) *gimchi* or *pajeon*. The owners also have an endearing habit of chalking up information, such as the day's weather, on a tiny blackboard. ❺

The following places are marked on the "Insadong" **map**, p.83. The three most useful **subway stations** are Anguk, Jonggak and Jongno 3-ga. For details of backpacker guesthouses in the area, see p.77.

Doulos Gwangsudong ⓣ02/2266-2244, ⓦwww.douloshotel.com. Excellent value, comfy rooms, friendly staff and a convenient location...this mid-range hotel ticks all the boxes, even if it's a little tricky to find: take a few steps south of Jongno and you should be able to make out its sign. There's usually a W20,000 discount if you book online. ❺

Hotel Saerim Gwanhundong ⓣ02/739-3377. Whatever its titular claims, this is a motel through and through. Some rooms have huge TVs and internet, making it extremely good value for the area. ❹

Sheel Jongnodong ⓣ02/466-3330. Like the better-known *Jelly* (see p.77), this is something of a "high-end" motel, its rooms filled with all sorts of interesting quirks. Lace curtains billow from the ceilings, projectors screen computer or TV output over entire walls, and some bathrooms are decked out in the style of a sauna. ❺

Sunbee Gwanhundong ⓣ02/730-3451. Tucked into a side street near Insadonggil, rooms here are moderately sized, quirkily designed and good value; all have internet and large TVs, and staff will bring you free toast in the morning. ❹

Tomgi Nagwondong ⓣ02/742-6660. Rooms at this pleasantly seedy love motel are excellent value for the area, and come in a variety of fresh styles, some of which include whirlpool baths. Just choose from the panel at reception: those not illuminated are taken (or just "busy"). ❹

City Hall

There are a number of five-star hotels around Seoul Plaza and **City Hall**, near Deoksugung palace; it's also convenient for the Myeongdong shopping area. The places below are within walking distance of City Hall or Euljiro 1-ga subway stations, and are marked on the "Business district" **map**, p.90.

Koreana Hotel Taepyeongno ⓣ02/2171-7000, ⓦwww.koreanahotel.com. Half the price of some of its competitors, but with similar rooms and service standards. It's worth paying a little extra for the larger "Prestige" rooms – try to nab one from the eleventh to the fifteenth floors, which have been renovated. ❼

Lotte Hotel Euljiro ⓣ02/771-1000, ⓦwww.lottehotel.co.kr. Like others in the chain, the *Lotte* sits on top of a busy shopping mall. The hotel has two wings – the older one, though cheaper, is truly dire, with rooms no better than the average motel. Those in the new wing are far bigger and better value. ❾

Metro Hotel Euljiro 2-ga ⓣ02/752-1112, ⓦwww.metrohotel.co.kr. A modern, squeaky-clean hotel away from the bustling Myeongdong main roads, where the staff are friendly and breakfast is included. Rooms are fresh and have free internet connections, though views are generally poor – ask to see a few. Come out of Euljiro 1-ga subway station, turn right off the main road then right again. ❺

Millennium Seoul Hilton Namdaemunno ⓣ02/753-7788, ⓦwww.hilton.co.kr. Up on the Namsan slopes above Seoul station, this top hotel is a regular on the international conference circuit. Views are excellent whichever side of the building you end up staying in, and the on-site restaurants nothing short of superb. In addition, Seoul's best wine bar, *Naos Nova* (p.115), is just up the road. ❽

The Plaza City Hall ⓣ02/771-2200, ⓦwww.hoteltheplaza.com. Directly facing City Hall and adjacent to Deoksugung, you could hardly wish for a more central location. In addition, a thorough overhaul in 2010 made its interior one of the most attractive in the city, with immaculate rooms and superb on-site restaurants. Try to grab a north-facing upper-floor room for some wonderfully Manhattanesque views. ❾

Westin Chosun Sogongdong ⓣ02/771-0500, ⓦwww.echosunhotel.com. Serious effort has been put into making this the most appealing hotel in central Seoul – an energetic group of knowledgeable staff preside over rooms that eschew the typical Korean concrete blockiness for splashes of lime, plush carpets and curved sofas. Even the bathrooms are graced with modern art, and a free mobile phone will be yours for the duration of your stay. Prices often fall to W250,000 off-season. ❾

Myeongdong

Myeongdong, Seoul's busy shopping area, has a wide range of accommodation, from flophouses to five-star. The following places are marked on the "Business district" **map**, p.90.

Astoria Hotel Namhakdong ⓣ02/2268-7111; Chungmuro station. Set away from the bustle of central Myeongdong (though still on a main road), the gently decaying *Astoria* has acceptable rooms devoid of frills; try to nab one with a view of Namsan to the south. ❻

Ibis Ambassador Myeongdong ⓣ02/3454-1101, ⓦwww.ibishotel.com; Euljiro 1-ga station. Mid-range hotel right in the centre of Myeongdong, with clean and presentable rooms. Staff make a concerted effort, and are particularly adept at dispensing advice to those fresh off the plane: handy, since the airport bus stops right outside. ❼

Pacific Hotel Namsandong ⓣ02/752-5101; Myeongdong station. Excellent value when off-season discounts kick in, this hotel tries its best to look like a five-star, with a wide range of services including a tailor and bakery. Some rooms have views of Namsan or central Myeongdong. ❼

Sejong Hotel Chungmuro ⓣ02/773-6000, ⓦwww.sejong.co.kr; Myeongdong station. This large, expensive Myeongdong landmark seems to attract most of the city's Japanese tourists, and is extremely busy for much of the year. Rooms are perfectly adequate, and some have great views of Namsan and its tower. Access to the hotel is easy, since there's an airport limousine bus stop right outside the entrance. ❽

Seoul Royal Hotel Myeongdong ⓣ02/756-1112, ⓦwww.seoulroyal.co.kr; Euljiro 3-ga station. Golden hues and comfy beds make rooms rather appealing at this towering hotel, which rises near the cathedral at the centre of Myeongdong's sprawling shopping district. Rooms are cosy, the grill and buffet bars on the 21st floor are great, and there are free shuttle buses to and from the airport. ❼

The Shilla Namsandong ⓣ02/2233-3310, ⓦwww.shilla.net; Dongguk University station. Tucked away in a quiet area on the eastern access road to Namsan, this hotel is characterized by the traditional style of its rooms and exterior. The lobby and restaurants are a luscious shade of brown, as if they've been dunked in tea, though the common areas can often be a little busy – this is one of Seoul's most popular conference venues. The rooms are five-star quality, if a little overpriced, and feature genuine Joseon-era antiques. ❾

Itaewon

Given the area's popularity with foreigners, there are surprisingly few places to stay in **Itaewon**. All the places reviewed below are a short walk from Itaewon subway station, and are marked on the "Itaewon" **map**, p.94.

Grand Hyatt Hannamdong ⓣ02/797-1234, ⓦwww.seoul.grand.hyatt.com. A favourite of visiting dignitaries, this is one of Seoul's top hotels in more ways than one – perched on a hill overlooking Itaewon, almost every room has a fantastic view through floor-to-ceiling windows. There's a fitness centre, an ice rink and squash courts, as well as swimming pools, indoors and out. ❽

Hotel D'Oro Hannamdong ⓣ02/749-6525. Highly recommended mid-range establishment on Itaewon's main drag, and rare value for money in a notoriously poor area for accommodation. Free wi-fi and minibar, and standards of service more akin to a hotel. ❻

Hamilton Hotel Itaewondong ⓣ02/794-0171, ⓦwww.hamilton.co.kr. More of an Itaewon landmark than a decent place to stay, but countless foreigners do regardless. Despite dated rooms and patchy service, this remains the only real high-end option on the strip, and guests can make use of an outdoor pool in warmer months. ❼

IP Boutique Hannamdong ⓣ02/3702-8000, ⓦwww.ipboutiquehotel.com. Korea's first genuine stab at the boutique hotel concept, though sadly a little flawed. Rooms are individually decorated, with different colour schemes for each floor, and are mercifully a lot better than the nightmarish lobby: something like a giant handbag with a few swing-chairs and medieval statues. ❼

Gangnam

There are a great number of places to stay in the **Gangnam** station area, mostly lining Bongeunsaro, the road 1km north of Gangnam subway station, though there are a few motels closer to the station exits. The following places are marked on the "Southern Seoul" **map**, p.98.

COEX InterContinental COEX complex ⓣ02/3452-2500, ⓦwww.seoul.intercontinental.com; Samseong station. One of a pair sitting at opposite ends of the COEX mall, this is newer and marginally less expensive than the *Grand*, and though also slightly less inviting has high service standards and admirable restaurants. ❾

Ellui Cheongdamdong ⓣ02/574-3535, ⓦwww.ellui.com; Apgujeong station. Despite being near the centre of Seoul's most affluent and stylish area, this hotel has a pleasing 1970s style. Some rooms overlook the Hangang, and these are the ones to aim for. ❼

Grand InterContinental COEX complex ⓣ02/555-5656, ⓦwww.seoul.intercontinental.com; Samseong station. Designed with exceptional attention to detail, this hotel belies its age with regular overhauls. Rooms are fresh and tastefully decorated in pleasing tones, with modern furniture. Some of the city's best restaurants can be found on the lower floors (see pp.109–110), and guests have access to a gym and indoor swimming pool. ❾

Imperial Palace Nonhyeondong ⓣ02/3440-8000, ⓦwww.imperialpalace.co.kr; Hakdong station. One of the most eye-catching hotels in all Korea. Don't be fooled by the cheesy stylings of the lobby; rooms are almost unbearably opulent, filled with antique lamps, oil paintings and other mementoes of the owner's (evidently numerous) trips abroad. Best are the

Backpacker guesthouses

Seoul is the only city in Korea to have a good range of **backpacker accommodation**. There are a couple of places in and around **Insadong**, and **Daehangno** has long had a few good cheapies, but these days most backpackers stay close to the hectic nightlife of the **Hongdae** area. All of the following have private rooms available for around W35,000; motel rooms are larger and better value, but for some the chance to meet fellow travellers is adequate compensation.

Ann Guesthouse Seogyodong ⓣ070/8279-0835, ⓦwww.annguesthouse.co.kr; Hongik University station. See "Hongdae" map, p.95. Terrific location, peering over Hongdae subway station. Despite being in the centre of Seoul nightlife, it's a quiet and relaxed place, presided over by a friendly couple. If it's full, there's another decent hostel (*Hongdae Guesthouse*) in the same building. Free laundry service. Dorms W20,000.

Banana Backpackers Angukdong ⓣ02/3672-1972, ⓦwww.bananabackpackers.com; Anguk station. See "Insadong" map, p.83. One of the oldest hostels in the city, this is an easy walk from Insadonggil; it has free internet, laundry and cooking facilities, and a common area that's great for making mates. There's bread and jam to tuck into in the morning, as well as free tea and coffee throughout the day. Take exit four from the subway station, head straight past the palace and turn left, then right at the crossroads; if it's full, there's a sister hostel around the corner. Dorms W20,000.

Bong House Daehangno ⓣ02/6080-3346, ⓦwww.bonghouse.net; Hyehwa station. See "Northern Seoul" map, p.111. Sprightly owner Bong tries his best to make guests feel at home – the free can of beer on arrival is an especially nice touch. Dorms (W17,000) are simple but do the job, while anyone staying a while can negotiate a similar daily rate for private rooms. The surrounding area is a pleasing slice of retro Seoul.

Daewon Inn Gyeongbokgung Yeok-ap ⓣ02/735-7891; Gyeongbokgung station. See "Palace district" map, p.79. In a prime location just west of Gyeongbokgung – take exit four from the station – this is one of Seoul's longest serving backpacker guesthouses, and though a little long in the tooth still makes an agreeable place to stay. Rooms are clustered around a small courtyard. Dorms W19,000.

Golden Pond Guesthouse Daehangno ⓣ02/741-5621, ⓦwww.goldenpond.co.kr; Hyehwa station. See "Northern Seoul" map, p.111. Highly popular with Western backpackers and people seeking work in Seoul, this is the cleanest and most secure guesthouse in the area; it's small and very often full. Dorm beds go for as little as W17,000, and drop by a couple of thousand if you stay for more than a night.

Grape Garden House Seogyodong ⓣ010/4278-9808, ⓦwww.grapegardenhouse.com; Hongik University station. See "Hongdae" map, p.95. In the heart of the Hongdae nightlife area, this new place is something of a party spot: there are regular barbecues on the outside patio, and shindigs on the balcony almost every night. Don't expect to do too much sightseeing if you stay here. Dorms W17,000.

Inside Daehangno ⓣ02/3672-1120, ⓦguesthouseinsideseoul.com; Hyehwa station. See "Northern Seoul" map, p.111. A great place to stay in studenty Daehangno. The owners try as hard as possible to please their guests, even down to laying out computer games when the weather's bad. Dorms are colourfully decorated and cheap at W17,000.

duplex rooms, which allow you to bathe upstairs before climbing down to bed. The only weak point is its rather uninteresting location. ❽

Jelly Hotel Yeoksamdong ⓣ02/553-4737, ⓦwww.jellyhotel.com; Yeoksam station. A hip and extremely interesting love hotel that has achieved cult status with young Seoulites, some of whom come to couple up (a "rest" is half the price of a night's stay), others to party with a group of friends. The hotel is possibly home to the most idiosyncratic rooms in the city – some contain pool tables, jacuzzis or karaoke systems. ❺

Novotel Ambassador Yeoksamdong ⓣ02/567-1101, ⓦwww.ambatel.com; Sinnonhyeon station. More of a base for business travellers than tourists, rooms here are accordingly more practical than aesthetically pleasing. There's a health club on site, as well as a buffet restaurant, and the friendly staff will be more than happy to give travel advice. ❽

Park Hyatt COEX ⓣ02/2016-1234, ⓦseoul.park.hyatt.com; Samseong station. First things first: this is Seoul's best hotel. Designed in its entirety by Japanese firm Super Potato, its class is evident by the time you've entered the lobby, which is actually on the top floor. Rooms employ an almost Zen-like use of space, and the hewed-granite bathrooms were voted "Asia's best place to be naked" by *Time* magazine. Staff are experts at making themselves available only when needed, and anyone on a repeat visit will find their preferred room temperature, TV channels and light level all ready and waiting. Bliss. ❾

Ritz-Carlton Yeoksamdong ⓣ02/3451-8000, ⓦwww.ritzcarltonseoul.com; Sinnonhyeon station. Service here is as professional as you'd expect from the chain, and no effort has been spared to make this one of Seoul's top hotels. The on-site bakery and restaurants are excellent (including a leafy outdoor area for warmer months), and though the rooms aren't terribly spacious, there are wonderful views from those that face north. ❾

Riviera Cheongdamdong ⓣ02/541-3111, ⓦwww.riviera.co.kr; Apgujeong station. Very convenient for Apgujeong's classy shopping strip. Although the twelve-lane road outside is a conduit for traffic rampaging over the Han, rooms are so quiet that you'll barely notice. Ask to be placed in the newer building, which has bigger and airier rooms than those in the old block; some doubles have great views over the river. ❽

Tea Tree Garosugil ⓣ02/542-9954; Sinsa station. Small, boutique-style hotel that's very good value for a south-of-the-river establishment, especially given its location on fashionable Garosugil. Some ground-floor rooms come with cute mini-gardens, which are ideal places to drain a coffee. ❺

Apgujeong

Apgujeong, Seoul's fashion capital, has surprisingly few places to stay, and those that exist tend to be overpriced. The following place is marked on the "Southern Seoul" **map**, p.98.

Popgreen Sinsadong ⓣ02/5446-6237; Apgujeong station. For years a favourite with first-time visitors to Seoul, this hotel is on trendy Apgujeongno, a mere stroll from dozens of brand-name showrooms. Rooms are a little small, though, and note that many have bathrooms that are visible from the bedroom: better not share with someone you don't know intimately. ❻

Gwanjangdong

Though these interconnected hotels are among the best in the country, they're inconveniently located far to the east of town, in a nondescript area near **Gwangnaru** subway station on line 5. From here a cab will cost W2000, or there are free shuttle buses every twenty minutes. Both establishments are marked on the "Seoul" **map**, pp.66–67.

Sheraton Grande Walkerhill Gwanjangdong ⓣ02/455-5000, ⓦwww.sheratonwalkerhill.co.kr. With scented, plush-carpeted corridors and muted-tone rooms, it's not as showy as the *W* next door, and the views are rarely as good, but it's immaculately designed nonetheless. There are some wonderful restaurants within the complex (you can also use those in the *W*), and the hotel contains the most expensive rooms in the country – up to a colossal W15,000,000 per night. ❾

W Seoul Walkerhill Gwanjangdong ⓣ02/465-2222, ⓦwww.starwoodhotels.com/whotels. The *W* is the most distinctive hotel in Korea. With artfully designed furniture in the rooms, neon gym rings in the elevators, sharp-suited staff and a loungey beat pulsing through the lobby, every inch of it is achingly trendy – not to everyone's tastes. Particularly popular with Korean honeymooners, rooms range in style – many have their own whirlpool and views over the river – while there's also a gym, a juice bar and a great swimming pool. On-site restaurants are excellent, as is the *Woo Bar* (see p.117), where the city's *nouveau riche* come to slurp $15 cocktails. ❾

The palace district

The area of central Seoul bounded by the five **grand palaces** is by far the most interesting in the city. During the Joseon dynasty, which ruled over the Korean peninsula from 1392 to 1910, each of the palaces at one time served as the country's seat of power, and no visit to Seoul would be complete without a visit to at least one or two. By far the most visited is **Gyeongbokgung**, the oldest of the group, though nearby **Changdeokgung** is the only one to have been added to UNESCO's World Heritage list. Literally a stone's throw away across a perimeter wall is **Changgyeonggung**, which probably has the most interesting history of the five, as well as the most natural setting, while further south are the smaller pair of **Gyeonghuigung** and **Deoksugung** (see p.91 for details on these two). Note that the suffix *-gung* means palace, and once it's removed you're left with the two-syllable name of the complex.

While visits to only one or two of the palaces should suffice, there's much more to see in the area, from the trinkets and teashops on **Insadonggil** to the more laid-back areas of **Samcheongdong** and **Bukchon Hanok Village**, the former studded with galleries, the latter with traditional *hanok* buildings. Also in the area, just north of Gyeongbokgung, is **Cheongwadae**, the official residence of the Korean president.

One popular **itinerary** is to start the day at Gyeongbokgung and take in the on-site museums before heading to Insadonggil for a traditional Korean meal and a cup of tea; energy thus restored, you can then visit one or two nearby galleries and shop at the stalls, or the nearby palace of Changdeokgung, before taking a well-earned rest at Tapgol Park.

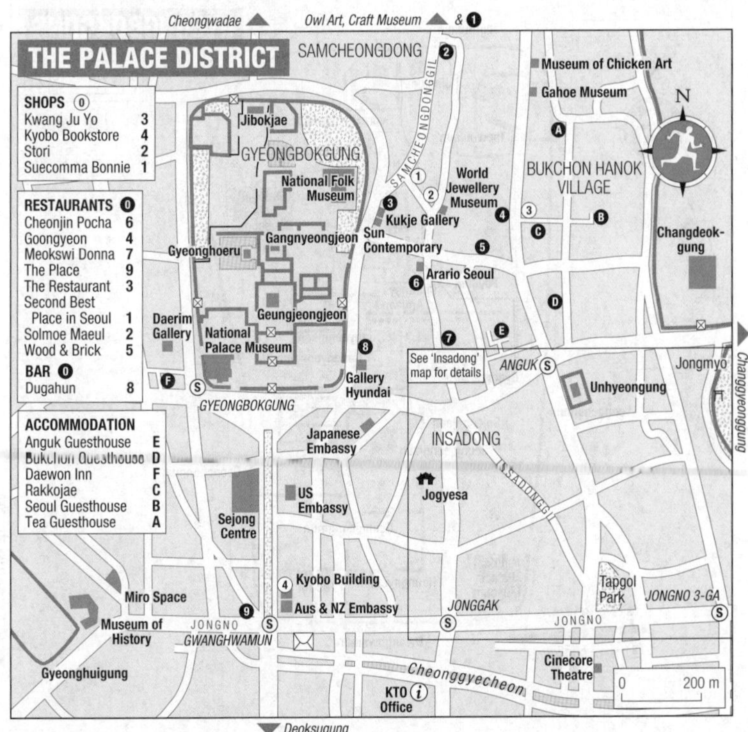

Gyeongbokgung

The glorious palace of **Gyeongbokgung** (경복궁; daily: March–Oct 9am–5pm; Nov–Feb 9am–4pm; W3000) is, with good reason, the most popular tourist sight in the city, and a focal point of the country as a whole. The place is absorbing, and the chance to stroll the dusty paths between its delicate tile-roofed buildings is one of the most enjoyable experiences Seoul has to offer. Gyeongbokgung was ground zero for Seoul's emergence as a place of power, having been built to house the royal family of the embryonic **Joseon dynasty**, shortly after they transferred their capital here in 1392. The complex has witnessed fires, repeated destruction and even a royal assassination (see box opposite and "History", p.364), but careful reconstruction means that the regal atmosphere of old is still palpable, aided no end by the suitably majestic crags of Bugaksan to the north. A large historical complex with excellent on-site **museums**, it can easily eat up the best part of a day.

To **get to** Gyeongbokgung, take subway line 3 to the station of the same name (exit five); alternatively, it's an easy walk from Insadonggil (p.84). Try to time your visit to coincide with the colourful **changing of the guard** ceremony, which takes place outside the main entrance at 11am, 2pm and 3.30pm daily except Monday. There are free English-language **tours** of the grounds at 11am, 1.30pm and 3.30pm, although the complex has information boards all over the place, and most visitors choose to go it alone.

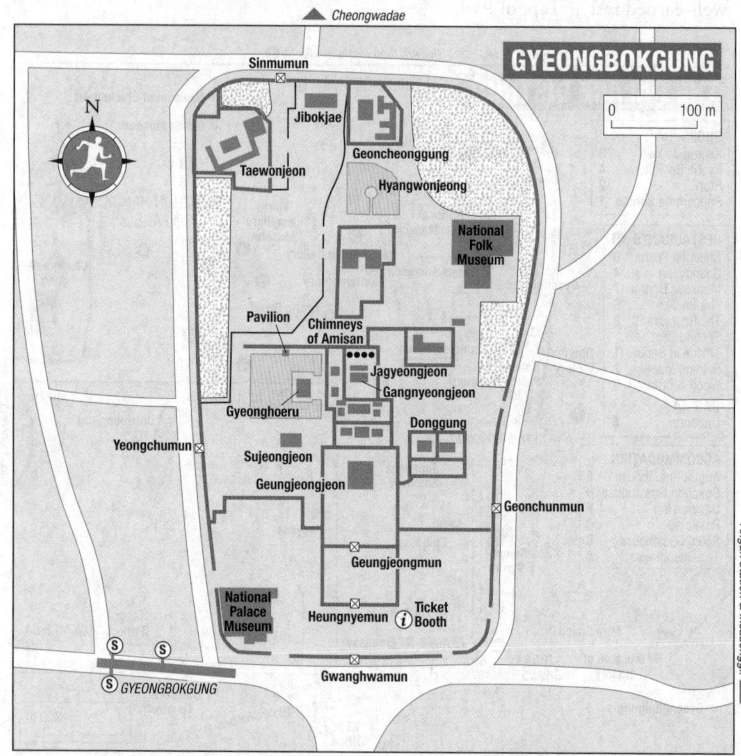

A history of Gyeongbokgung

Gyeongbokgung's construction was ordered by **King Taejo** in 1394, and the "Palace of Shining Happiness" held the regal throne for over two hundred years. At its peak, the palace housed over four hundred buildings within its vaguely rectangular perimeter walls, but most were burned down during the Japanese invasions in the 1590s. However, though few Koreans will admit to it, the invaders were not directly to blame – the arsonists were actually a group of local slaves, angered by their living and working conditions. The palace was only rebuilt following the coronation of child-king **Gojong** in 1863, but the Japanese were to invade again shortly afterwards, forcibly opening up Korea to foreign trade, and slowly ratcheting up their standing on the peninsula.

In 1895 **Empress Myeongseong**, one of Gojong's wives and an obstacle to the Japanese – who refer to her as "Queen Min" – was assassinated in the Gyeongbokgung grounds, a shady tale told in countless movies and soap operas, and a precursor to the full-scale Japanese annexation of Korea in 1910. During the occupation, which ended with World War II in 1945, the Japanese used Gyeongbokgung for police interrogation and torture, and made numerous changes to the building in an apparent effort to destroy Korean pride. The front gate, Gwanghwamun, was moved to the east of the complex, destroying the north–south geometric principles followed during the palace's creation, while a Japanese command post was built in the sacred first courtyard in a shape identical to the Japanese written character for "sun" (日). One interesting suggestion – and one certainly not beyond the scope of Japanese thinking at that time – is that Bukhansan mountain to the north resembled the character for "big" (大) and City Hall to the south that of "root" (本), thereby emblazoning Seoul's most prominent points with the three characters that made up the name of the Empire of the Rising Sun (大日本).

The palace

Most visitors will start their tour at Gwanghwamun (광화문), the palace's southern gate. Entering through the first courtyard you'll see **Geunjeongjeon** (근정전), the palace's former throne room, looming ahead. Despite being the largest wooden structure in the country, this two-level construction remains surprisingly graceful, the corners of its gently sloping roof home to lines of tiny guardian figurines. The central path leading up to the building was once used only by the king, but the best views of its interior are actually from the sides – from here you'll see the golden dragons on the hall ceiling, as well as the throne itself, backed by its traditional folding screen.

After Geunjeongjeon you can take one of a number of routes around the complex. To the east of the throne room are the buildings that once housed **crown princes**, deliberately placed here to give these regal pups the day's first light, while behind is **Gangnyeongjeon** (강녕전), the former living quarters of the king and queen, furnished with replica furniture. Also worth seeking out is **Jagyeongjeon** (자경전), a building backed by a beautiful stone wall, and chimneys decorated with animal figures. West of the throne room is **Gyeonghoeru** (경회루), a colossal pavilion looking out over a tranquil **lotus pond** that was a favourite with artists in regal times, and remains so today. The pond was used both for leisure and as a ready source of water for the fires that regularly broke out around the palace (an unfortunate by-product of heating buildings with burning wood or charcoal under the floor), while the pavilion itself was once a place for banquets and civil service examinations. North of the throne room, and right at the back of the complex, are a few buildings constructed in 1888 during the rule of King Gojong to house books and works of art. These structures were designed in the Chinese style that was the height of fashion at the time, and are markedly different from any other structures around the palace.

National Folk Museum

Inside the palace complex is the **National Folk Museum** (국립 민속 박물관; March–Oct Mon & Wed–Fri 9am–6pm, Sat & Sun 9am–7pm; Nov–Feb Mon & Wed–Fri 9am–5pm, Sat & Sun 9am–7pm; same ticket as the palace). Although huge, there's only one level, stuffed with dioramas and explanations of Korean ways of life long since gone, from old fishing and farming practices to clothing worn during the Three Kingdoms era. The free **folk performances** outside the museum (March–Oct Sat 3pm; occasionally also Sun 2pm) are well worth watching.

National Palace Museum

At the far southwest of the palace grounds is the **National Palace Museum** (국립 고궁 박물관; Tues–Fri 9am–6pm, Sat & Sun 9am–7pm; same ticket as the palace) – take exit five from Gyeongbokgung subway station. The star of the show here is a **folding screen** which would have once been placed behind the imperial throne, and features the sun, moon and five peaks painted onto a dark blue background, symbolically positioning the seated kings at the nexus of heaven and earth. It's a glorious, deep piece of art that deserves to be better known. Other items in the fascinating display include a jade book belonging to King Taejo, paraphernalia relating to ancestral rites, and some of the wooden dragons taken from the temple eaves, whose size and detail can be better appreciated when seen up close. Equally meticulous is a map of the heavens engraved onto a stone slab in 1395.

Cheongwadae

What the White House is to Washington, **Cheongwadae** (청와대) is to Seoul. Sitting directly behind Gyeongbokgung and surrounded by mountains, this official presidential residence is named the "Blue House" on account of the colour of its roof tiles. In Joseon times, blue roofs were reserved for kings, but the office of the president is the nearest modern-day equivalent to regal rule. The road

Hiking Bugaksan, Seoul's forbidden mountain

Rising up directly behind Cheongwadae is **Bugaksan** (북악산), one of the most significant mountains in Seoul. It provides some of the most glorious possible views of the capital, but was off-limits for decades thanks to the rather important building nestling on its southern slopes. These protective measures were not without foundation, as in 1968 Bugaksan was the scene of an **assassination attempt**: a squad of North Korean commandos descended from the mountain with the intention of assassinating then-president **Park Chung-hee**.

You can now follow in their dubious footsteps, since the mountain was finally reopened to the public in 2006. The **hiking route** (9am–5pm, last entrance 3pm) across Bugaksan is 3.8km long, and on the way you'll see remnants of Seoul's fortress wall, which once circled what was then a much smaller city. The route can be accessed from either its eastern or western sides, though neither are near subway stations. The western entrance is the easier to get to – take bus #1020 from exit 2 of Gwanghwamun subway station, get off at Buamdong, and head for the oriental gate 100m back up the road. You'll have to register at the entrance (either one is OK) – bring your **passport**, or some other form of identification.

that borders the palace is open for public access, but don't venture too close to the entrance as it's understandably a high-security area. In 1968, a group of 31 North Korean soldiers were apprehended here during an attempt to assassinate then-President Park Chung-hee; while you're unlikely to be accused of doing the same, if you loiter or stray too close you may well be questioned. Free **tours** (Tues–Fri 10am, 11am, 2pm & 3pm) of the opulent palace grounds are available; book online in advance at Ⓦenglish.president.go.kr, and remember your passport.

Insadong

The undisputed hub of Korea's tourist scene, **INSADONG** (인사동) is a city district whose tight lattice of streets is full to the brim with art galleries, shops, tearooms and traditional restaurants – you could quite happily spend most of the day here. The appeal of the area lies in simply strolling around and taking it all in – most of the commerce is pleasingly traditional, not only at the restaurants, but also in the galleries, which display a fusion of old and contemporary styles very much in keeping with the atmosphere of the place. Should such delights bring out your artistic muse, there are numerous shops selling paints, brushes and handmade paper. Details of the most interesting **galleries** can be found in the box on p.84, the area's best **restaurants** on p.107, and a selection of **tearooms** in the box on p.112.

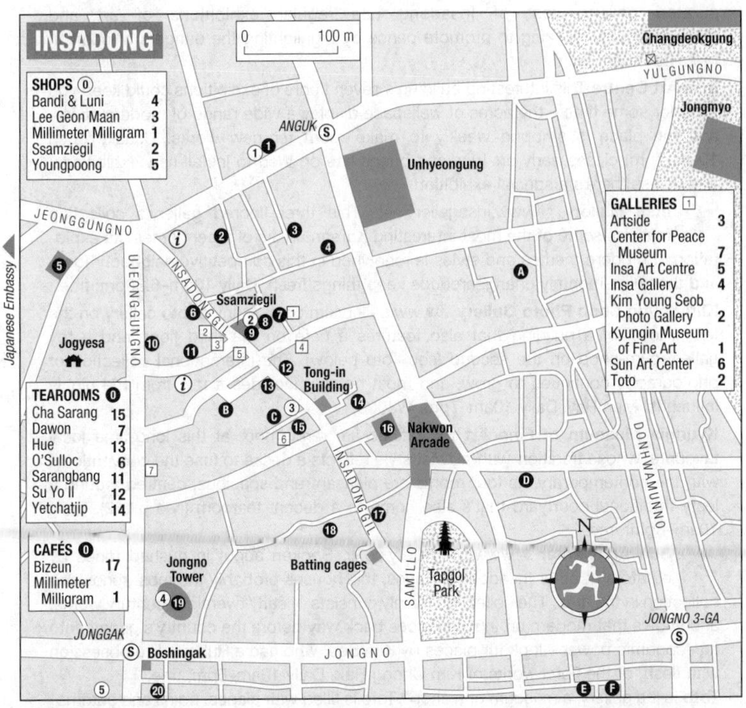

ACCOMMODATION				RESTAURANTS						BARS	
Banana Backpackers	A	Sheel	E	Arirang Garden	18	Baru	10	Min's Club	4	Baekseju Maeul	20
Doulos	F	Sunbee	C	Baekseju Maeul	20	Gogung	9	Sagwa Namu	3	Starmoon	16
Hotel Saerim	B	Tomgi	D	Bärlin	5	Janchijip	8	Top Cloud	19	Story of the Blue Star	2

Insadonggil

Insadong's action is centred on **Insadonggil** (인사동길), the area's main street, which despite being cramped and people-packed is still open to traffic – be careful when walking here, as Korean taxis tend to be a law unto themselves. The one exception is Sunday, when the street is closed to vehicles; unless the weather's bad, you'll are likely to see music and dance performances or a traditional parade. At the northern end of the street – take exit six from Anguk station, walk up the main street for a few minutes and then turn left – there are a couple of **tourist information** booths, as well as the interesting **Ssamziegil** building, a spiralling complex of trendy trinket shops (see p.122) with a rooftop market. Tiny side

Insadong art galleries

There are hundreds of galleries on and around Insadonggil; below are some of the most interesting. The following places are marked on the "Insadong" map, p.83.

Artside ⓦwww.artside.org. With a sister gallery in Beijing, Artside is one of two galleries in Seoul (the other is Arario in Samcheongdong, see p.86) that regularly exhibit work from China's increasingly interesting contemporary art scene. Exhibitions change every month or so. Daily 10am–6.30pm; free unless there's a special exhibition.

Center for Peace Museum ⓦwww.peacemuseum.or.kr. This unassuming but well-curated gallery west of Insadong has regular exhibitions of art and photography, all seeking to promote peace by highlighting the dangers of conflict. Mon–Sat 10am–5pm.

Insa Art Centre This interesting building's seven floors of exhibitions could keep you busy for some time – the acres of wallspace display a wide range of modern styles, and the place is stripped weekly to make room for new works. Usually open 10am–7pm; closes early on Tues and opens late on Wed to install new exhibitions; free unless there's a special exhibition.

Insa Gallery ⓦwww.insagallery.net. This three-floored gallery's collection features some of the most interesting Korean artists of recent times. Its exploration of modern themes and styles is renowned in this competitive neighbourhood, and the twice-monthly changearounds keep things fresh. Daily 10am–6.30pm; free.

Kim Young Seob Photo Gallery ⓦwww.gallerykim.com. A tiny photo gallery on the fourth level of a building that also features a café on the third floor, and a toy gallery-cum-shop on the second (see Toto below). The international collection of photographs continues to grow, and most notably includes a few from the highly influential Man Ray. Daily 10am–7pm; W3000.

Kyungin Museum of Fine Art Exhibitions are rarely poor at this long-time local favourite, whose tradition-with-a-twist style reflects a desire to fuse the conventional with the contemporary. Its four rooms are pleasant and spacious, centred around a leafy traditional courtyard that's also home to a decent tearoom (see p.112). Daily 10am–6pm; free.

Sun Art Center ⓦwww.sungallery.co.kr. Spoken about in hushed tones by curators at other Insadong galleries, this houses probably the most renowned collection in the area. The collection mainly consists of early twentieth-century works, and shows that modern art in Korea goes back way before the country's growth into an economic power – look for pieces by Kim Sou, who had a Rubens-like obsession with flesh, or the floral works of Kim Chong Hak. Daily 10am–6pm; free.

Toto Is it a gallery, a museum or a shop? Toto is filled with planes, trains and automobiles, as well as action figures that wear their underpants on the outside. Some pieces are rare, but there are cheaper ones to take away as quirky souvenirs. Daily 10am–6pm; W1000.

streets branch off Insadonggil as you head south along the road, most of which are lined with traditional Korean restaurants. Continuing south, the street segues into the more Westernized buildings of "regular" Seoul; look out for the *Starbucks* on the southern reaches of the road, which was the scene of traditionalist protests when it opened – it made a slight concession by having its name spelt in *hangeul*. Insadonggil finishes at small **Tapgol Park** (탑골 공원), where a huge, stunning Joseon-era **stone pagoda** grandly titled "National Treasure Number Two" sits resplendent inside. Sadly, though, its beauty is marred by the ugly glass box that has been placed around it for protection.

Around Insadonggil

East of Insadonggil, and very close to Anguk subway station – take exit four – is the tiny palace of **Unhyeongung** (운현궁; Tues–Sun 9am–7pm; W700). Having never been an official royal residence, it doesn't qualify as one of Seoul's "big five" palaces; accordingly, it's less showy than the others, but the relative lack of people makes it a pleasant place to visit – the bare wood and paper doors would provide the perfect setting for a Japanese *anime*. Though he never lived here, King Gojong married the ill-fated Princess Myeongseong in Unhyeongung, and it was also the centre of neo-Confucian thought during the Joseon period, which sought to base civil progress on merit rather than lineage (see p.179 for information on Yi Toegye, one of the main instigators). Near the north end of Insadonggil, on the west side, is **Jogyesa** (조계사), the only major temple in the centre of Seoul. Created in 1910 and hemmed in by large buildings, it has neither history nor beauty to its credit, but for visitors with little time in the country it may represent the only chance to see a Korean temple of such size. The best times to visit are on Buddha's birthday (see p.47) and the Lotus Lantern festival.

Further west still, and on the way to Gyeongbokgung, is the **Japanese embassy** (일본 대사관). This may not sound like a tourist sight, but each Wednesday at noon an ever-decreasing number of elderly Korean women come to stage a **protest** – these are the "**comfort women**" who were forced into sexual slavery during the Japanese occupation (see p.365), and are still awaiting compensation, or even an apology. "Say you're sorry!" and "You know you did wrong!" are the most popular chants, and it's not just the *ajummas* doing the shouting – though their numbers dwindle from year to year, they're being supplemented by younger protesters whose demonstrations are likely to continue until Tokyo issues an official apology – still some way off, it seems.

North of Anguk station

North of Anguk subway station, and between the palaces of Gyeongbokgung and Changdeokgung, lie **Samcheongdong** (삼청동) and **Bukchon Hanok Village** (북촌 한옥 마을), two of the city's most characterful areas. Like Insadong, Samcheongdong is crammed with quirky restaurants, cafés and galleries (see p.86). Though most of the area remains charming and relaxed, one particular street has become rather popular; heading off from Gyeongbokgun's northeastern corner, and a five-minute walk from the palace's eastern exit, **Samcheongdonggil** has an almost European air to it, its side streets snaking uphill in a manner reminiscent of Naples or Lisbon. A few of the cafés and galleries spill over into **Bukchon Hanok Village**, an area characterized by the prevalence of traditional wooden **hanok buildings** – these once covered the whole country, but most were torn down during Korea's economic revolution and replaced with row upon row of fifteen-storey blocks. The city council spared this area the wrecking ball, and as a result

Museums and art galleries north of Anguk station

As in Insadong, there are whole squads of galleries (all free) in the area north of Anguk station, supplemented by some quirky museums. The following (all Tues–Sun 10am–6pm) are particularly interesting, and are marked on the "Palace district" map, p.79.

Museums

Chicken Art Museum Impressionism, Art Deco, Bauhaus... chicken art. Focusing solely on the latter school of creation, this museum proves highly popular with international visitors. The greatest surprise is finding out how many countries have produced artists obsessed with the humble chicken. W5000.

Gahoe Museum Housed in one of the area's many *hanok* abodes (see p.74), the folk art here is suitably traditional. The friendly curators also offer regular hands-on craft programmes. W3000.

Owl Art & Craft Museum The result of its founder's quirky (and slightly scary) obsession, this small museum is stuffed to the gills with anything and everything pertaining to owls. There's a small tearoom-cum-café in which you can buy strigiform trinkets. W5000.

World Jewellery Museum With a name that's as coldly descriptive as they come, it may come as a surprise that this museum is the most rewarding in the area, with the pieces on display offering great subtlety and variety. W5000.

Galleries

Arario Seoul Ⓦwww.ararioseoul.com. With a sister gallery in Beijing (as well as one in Cheonan; see p.283) Arario is often a great place to check out the latest offerings from the highly interesting art scene over the Yellow Sea.

Gallery Hyundai Ⓦwww.galleryhyundai.com. This large gallery possesses the most esteemed collection in the area; in existence since the 1960s, it's Korea's longest-running commercial gallery. The focus has long been on artists born before 1930, but there's an ever-increasing emphasis on newer trends.

Kukje Gallery Ⓦwww.kukjegallery.com. The Kukje is one of the most important players in the area, actively promoting Korean artists abroad, and hauling a wide, well-selected range of exhibits into its own space, near the palace side of Samcheongdonggil. It's surrounded by excellent cafés and restaurants – including one adjoining the gallery (see p.106)

Sun Contemporary Ⓦwww.sungallery.co.kr. The contemporary side of the excellent Sun Art Center in Insadong (see box, p.84), this gallery's collection is equally well put together, and occupies a few floors in a building near trendy Samcheongdonggil. To get to other floors, you'll have to go through what looks like a fire escape from the entry room.

there's some delightful walking to be done among its quiet lanes, where tiny restaurants, tearooms and comic book shops line the streets, and children play games on mini arcade machines, creating a pleasant air of indifference hard to find in the capital; a few of the buildings have even been converted into guesthouses (see box, p.74).

Changdeokgung

While Gyeongbokgung plays to the crowd, its smaller neighbour **Changdeokgung** (창덕궁; Tues–Sun; English-language tours 11.30am, 1.30pm & 3.30pm; 80min; W3000; independent tours April–Oct Thurs 9.15am–6.30pm; W15,000) is the choice of palace connoisseurs. Completed in 1412 and home to royalty as recently as 1910, this is the best-preserved palace in Seoul, and has been put on UNESCO's list of World Heritage sites. Entry here is regulated to a far greater degree than the other palaces, and for most of the week you'll have no option but to join a **tour**. Though the information is interesting, you really can't beat the freedom of exploring the palace by yourself; to do this you will need to come on a Thursday from April to October, and pay more.

The suitably impressive **throne room** is without doubt the most regal-looking of any Seoul palace – light from outside is filtered through paper doors and windows, bathing in a dim glow the elaborate wooden beam structure, as well as the throne and its folding-screen backdrop. From here you'll be led past a number of buildings pertaining to the various kings that used the palace, some of which still have the original furniture inside. One building even contains vehicles used by **King Sunjong**, the Daimler and Cadillac looking more than a little incongruous in their palatial setting. Sunjong was the last ruler of the Joseon dynasty, and held the throne from 1907 until his country's annexation by the Japanese in 1910; his lineage still continues today, though claims are contested, and the "royals" have no regal rights, claims or titles. Further on you'll come to **Nakseondae**. Built during the reign of King Heonjong (ruled 1834–49), the building's Qing-style latticed doors and arched pavilion reveal Heonjong's taste for foreign cultures; without the paint and decoration typical of Korean palace buildings, the colours of the bare wood are ignited during sunset. Look out for the circular sliding door inside – *Star Trek* in a Korean palace.

The **entrance** to Changdeokgung is a short walk from Anguk subway station – take exit three, walk up the main road, and it's on your left.

Huwon

Changdeokgung's highlight is **Huwon** (후원), the "Secret Garden". Approached on a suitably mysterious path, the garden is concealed by an arch of leaves. In the centre of the garden is a **lotus pond**, one of Seoul's most-photographed sights, and alive with colourful flowers in late June or early July. A small building overlooking the pond served as a library and study room, and the tiny gates blocking the entrance path were used as an interesting checking mechanism by the king – needing to crouch to pass through, he'd be reminded of his duty to be humble. This is the last stop on the tour, and most visitors take the opportunity to relax here awhile before exiting the complex.

Changgyeonggung and Jongmyo

Though not as heralded as its neighbouring palaces, **Changgyeonggung** provides one of Seoul's best-value days out – a W1000 ticket buys access not just to the palace, but also to the UNESCO-listed shrine of **Jongmyo**. These two sights are connected by footbridge, and can be seen in either order, while Changgyeonggung's entrance is harder to get to, starting here is recommended as it means that you'll wade into Jongmyo Park, one of Seoul's most chracterful areas, on exiting the shrine. The Changgyeonggung entrance is awkwardly located on the east side of the complex, and a confusing fifteen-minute walk from Hyehwa, the nearest subway station; it's usually better to take a bus from Anguk station – #150 and #171 are the most frequent. It's also possible to walk here from Changdeokgung or Insadonggil; allow twenty to thirty minutes. The Jongmyo entrance is far easier to find: it's a short walk east down the main road from Jongno 3-ga subway station – exit eleven is best.

The murder of Crown Prince Sado

In 1762, a sinister event occurred in the grounds of Changgyeonggung, one whose story is, for some reason, omitted from the information boards that dot the palace grounds – a **royal murder**. A young prince named **Sado** was heir to the throne of **King Yeongjo**, but had been born mentally ill, with a rather unfortunate habit of killing people unnecessarily. Fearing dire consequences if the nation's power were placed into his son's hands, Yeongjo escorted Sado to Seonninmun, a gate on the eastern side of the palace, and ordered him to climb into a rice casket; his son obeyed, was locked in, and starved to death. Sado's wife, Hyegyong, held the secret until after Yeongjo's death in 1776, at which point she spilled the beans in a book, *Hanjungnok* (published in English as *The Memoirs of Lady Hyegyong*). Sado's son **Jeongjo** became king on the death of Yeongjo, and built Hwaseong fortress in Suwon (see p.131) to house his father's remains. Jeongjo went on to become one of Korea's most respected rulers.

Changgyeonggung

Separated from Changdeokgung to the west by a perimeter wall, **Changgyeonggung** (창경궁; Wed–Mon 9am–5pm; free tours 11.30am & 4pm) tends to split visitors into two camps – those who marvel at its history and the relatively natural beauty of its interior, which is far greener than Seoul's other palaces, and those who feel that there's a little less to see.

King Sejong built Changgyeonggung in 1418 as a resting place for his father, the recently abdicated King Taejong. At its peak the palace had a far greater number of buildings than are visible today, but these were to suffer badly from fires and during the Japanese invasions. Almost the whole of the complex burned down in the Japanese attacks of 1592, and then again during a devastating inferno in 1830, two events that sandwiched the murder of a crown prince by his father (see box above). When the Japanese returned in 1907, they turned much of the palace into Korea's first **amusement park**, and included a botanical garden, kindergarten and zoo, as well as a museum – the red brick exterior and pointed steel roof were very much in keeping with the Japanese style of the time, and pictures of this can still be seen around the palace entrance. The building and zoo themselves were tolerated for nearly a century before finally being ripped down in 1983, whereas the **botanical garden** still remains today.

Considering its turbulent history, the palace is a markedly relaxed place to wander around. The buildings themselves are nowhere near as polished as those in the Gyeongbok or Changdeok palaces, which helps accentuate their validity; the history of each structure is chronicled on information boards. Be sure to look for **Myeongjeongjeon**, the oldest main hall of any of Seoul's palaces – it was built in 1616, and somehow escaped the fires that followed. From here, a number of paths wind their way to a pond at the north of the complex, many of which are highly beautiful, with some full of scent from herbs planted along the way. Near the pond are a couple of **herb gardens**, while also visible are the white-painted lattices of the Japanese-built botanical garden. Those who still have energy after their palace sightseeing can head to the far southwest of the complex, where a footbridge crosses over to Jongmyo shrine.

Jongmyo

Along with the palace of Gyeongbokgung, the construction of **Jongmyo shrine** (종묘; Wed–Mon: March–Oct 9am–5pm; Nov–Feb 9am–4.30pm) was on King Taejo's manifesto as he kicked off the Joseon dynasty in 1392. He decreed that dead kings and queens would be honoured here in true Confucian style, with a series of ancestral rites. These ceremonies were performed five times a year, once each season, with an extra one on the winter solstice, when the ruling king would pay his respects to those who died before him by bowing profusely, and explaining pertinent national issues to their **spirit tablets**. These wooden blocks, in which deceased royalty were believed to reside, are still stored in large wooden buildings that were said to be the biggest in Asia at the time of their construction. Jeongjeon was the first, but such was the length of the Joseon dynasty that another building – Yeongnyeongjeon – had to be added. Though the courtyards are open – take the opportunity to walk on the raised paths that were once reserved for kings – the buildings themselves remain locked for most of the year. The one exception to this is on the first Sunday in May, which is the day of **Jongmyo Daeje** (see p.118), a long, solemn ceremony (9am–3pm) followed by traditional court dances – an absolute must-see.

On exiting the shrine from the main entrance, you'll find yourself in **Jongmyo Park**, one of the most atmospheric areas in Seoul – on warm days it's full of old men selling calligraphy, drinking *soju* and playing *baduk* (a Korean board game similar to Go). Find a spot to sit, close your eyes and listen to the wooden clack of a thousand game pieces.

Cheonggyecheon

Until recently, **Cheonggyecheon** (청계천) was a mucky stream running under an elevated highway, but in 2003 the Mayor of Seoul decided to ditch the road and beautify the creek – this controversial project saw heads rolling on corruption charges, grumbles from local businesses and protests from environmentalists, but since completion in 2005 it has been looked upon as a resounding success. Both the stream and the walkways that flank it are below street level, and on descending you'll notice that Seoul's ceaseless cacophony has been diluted and largely replaced by the sound of rushing water. Heading west, you'll pass a series of features, including fountains, sculpture and stepping stones, before coming to an abrupt halt at a curious piece of modern art that some locals have described as an elongated red-and-blue dog turd.

The business district

Looking north from Gwanghwamun, one can see little but cascading palace roofs and the mountains beyond. Turn south again and the contrast is almost unbelievably stark. Looming up are the ranked masses of high-rise blocks that announce Seoul's main **business district**, its walkways teeming with black-suited businessfolk. However, there's more to the area than one might expect – two **palaces**, a few major **museums** and **art galleries**, and one of Seoul's most charming roads. In addition, the country's largest **market** and most popular **shopping district** lie within this area, as does **Namsan**, a small mountain in the very centre of the capital.

At the western edge of the business district is **Gyeonghuigung**, Seoul's "forgotten" palace, which has an excellent history museum just outside its main gate. A stroll east along the quiet, tree-lined road of Jeongdonggil will bring you to a second palace, **Deoksugung**, which boasts a superb art museum. East again is **Myeongdong**, the country's premier shopping district, followed and counterbalanced by the sprawling arcades of **Dongdaemun** market.

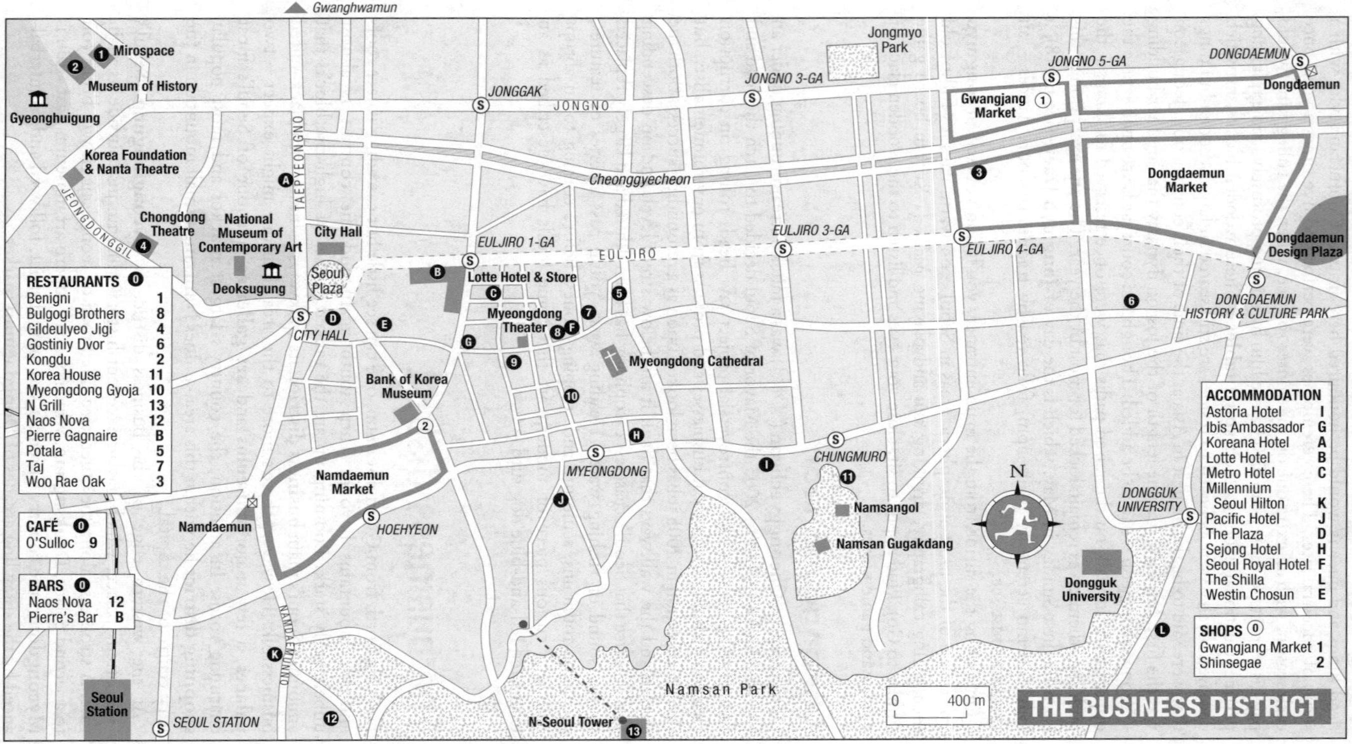

THE BUSINESS DISTRICT

RESTAURANTS

Benigni	1
Bulgogi Brothers	8
Gildeulyeo Jigi	4
Gostiniy Dvor	6
Kongdu	2
Korea House	11
Myeongdong Gyoja	10
N Grill	13
Naos Nova	12
Pierre Gagnaire	B
Potala	5
Taj	7
Woo Rae Oak	3

CAFÉ

O'Sulloc	9

BARS

Naos Nova	12
Pierre's Bar	B

ACCOMMODATION

Astoria Hotel	I
Ibis Ambassador	G
Koreana Hotel	A
Lotte Hotel	B
Metro Hotel	C
Millennium Seoul Hilton	K
Pacific Hotel	J
The Plaza	D
Sejong Hotel	H
Seoul Royal Hotel	F
The Shilla	L
Westin Chosun	E

SHOPS

Gwangjang Market	1
Shinsegae	2

Gwanghwamun
Mirospace
Museum of History
Gyeonghuigung
Korea Foundation & Nanta Theatre
JEONGDONGGIL
Chongdong Theatre
National Museum of Contemporary Art
Deoksugung
City Hall
Seoul Plaza
TAEPYEONGNO
CITY HALL
JONGGAK
JONGNO
JONGNO 3-GA
Jongmyo Park
JONGNO 5-GA
DONGDAEMUN
Dongdaemun
Gwangjang Market
Cheonggyecheon
Dongdaemun Market
EULJIRO 1-GA
EULJIRO
EULJIRO 3-GA
EULJIRO 4-GA
Dongdaemun Design Plaza
DONGDAEMUN HISTORY & CULTURE PARK
Lotte Hotel & Store
Myeongdong Theater
Myeongdong Cathedral
Bank of Korea Museum
Namdaemun Market
Namdaemun
HOEHYEON
MYEONGDONG
CHUNGMURO
Namsangol
Namsan Gugakdang
DONGGUK UNIVERSITY
Dongguk University
NAMDAEMUNNO
Namsan Park
N-Seoul Tower
Seoul Station
SEOUL STATION
N
0 400 m

Gyeonghuigung

The most anonymous and least visited of Seoul's Five Grand Palaces (even locals who work in the area may struggle to point you towards it) is **Gyeonghuigung** (경희궁; Tues–Sun 9am–6pm; free), which was built in 1616. Lonely and a little forlorn, it's a pretty place nonetheless, and may be the palace for you if crowds, souvenir shops and camera-dodging aren't to your liking. Unlike other palaces, you'll be able to enter the throne room – bare but for the throne, but worth a look – before scrambling up to the halls of the upper level, which are backed with grass and rock.

The Museum of History

You might want to make your trip to **Gyeonghuigung** to coincide with a visit to the **Museum of History** (서울 역사 박물관; Tues–Fri 9am–10pm, Sat & Sun 10am–7pm; W700), a large building adjacent to the palace, and resembling for all intents and purposes a leisure centre. The permanent exhibition on the third floor focuses on Joseon-era Seoul. Here you find lacquered boxes with mother-of-pearl inlay, porcelain bowls and vases thrown in gentle shapes, and silk gowns with embroidered leaves and dragons; you may be surprised by how much of what appears to be quintessentially Japanese design actually started in Korea, or at least passed through here first on its way from China. There's a café on the first floor. On exiting the museum look out for a strange piece of art across the road – a black metal statue of a man perpetually hammering, a mute reminder to folk from the nearby business district that life's not all about work.

Jeongdonggil

Running between the palaces of Gyeonghuigung and Deoksugung is **Jeongdonggil** (정동길), a quiet, shaded road that's a world removed from the bustle of the City Hall area. You may notice a near-total lack of couples on this road, as Seoulites have long held the superstition that those who walk here will soon break up. Along this road is the large, modern **Seoul Museum of Art** (서울 시립 미술관; Tues–Sun 10am–10pm; W700); it's well worth popping in for a look at what is almost always a fresh, high-quality exhibition of art from around the world. Continuing further up the road, you'll find a few restaurants and cafés, as well as **Chongdong Theatre**, which puts on regular *pansori* performances (see p.258). There's also an array of underground **shopping arcades** in and around City Hall station – one heads towards Myeongdong, while another heads east for a number of kilometres under the main road of Euljiro.

Deoksugung

Its small size, central location and easy access – take exit two from City Hall subway station – ensure that **Deoksugung** (덕수궁; Tues–Sun 9am–8pm; W1000) is often very busy. This was the last of Seoul's Famous Five palaces to be built, and it became the country's seat of power almost by default when the Japanese destroyed Gyeongbokgung (p.81) in 1592, and then again when King Gojong fled here after the assassination of his wife Myeongsong in 1895. Not quite as splendid as the other palaces, Deoksugung is overlooked by the tall grey towers of the City Hall business and embassy area, and includes a couple of Western-style buildings, dating back to when the "Hermit Kingdom" in the latter part of the Joseon dynasty was being forcibly opened up to trade. These neoclassical structures remain the most notable on the complex. At the end of a gorgeous rose garden is Seokjojeon, which was designed by an English

Dongdaemun and Namdaemun: market madness

Between them, the colossal markets of **Dongdaemun** (동대문 시장) and **Namdaemun** (남대문 시장) could quite conceivably feed, and maybe even clothe, the world. Both are deservedly high on most visitors' list of sights to tick off in Seoul. Namdaemun literally means "big south door", and Dongdaemun "big east door", referring to the **Great Gates** that once marked the city perimeter; like the palace of Gyeongbokgung and Jongmyo shrine, these were built in the 1390s under the rule of **King Taejo** as a means of glorifying and protecting his embryonic Joseon dynasty. Both gates have undergone extensive repairs, but although Dongdaemun still stands in imperial splendour today, surrounded by spiralling traffic day and night, an arson attack in February 2008 saw Namdaemun savaged by fire.

Dongdaemun market is the largest in the country, spread out, open-air and indoors, in various locations around the prettified Cheonggyecheon creek (see p.89). It would be impossible to list the whole range of things on sale here – you'll find yourself walking past anything from herbs to *hanbok* or paper lanterns to knock-off clothing, usually on sale for reasonable prices. Though each section of the market has its own opening and closing time, the complex as a whole simply never closes, so at least part of it will be open whenever you decide to come. Nighttime is when the market is at its most atmospheric, with clothes stores pumping out music into the street at ear-splitting volume, and the air filled with the smell of freshly made food sizzling at street-side stalls. Though some of the dishes on offer are utterly unrecognizable to many foreign visitors, it pays to be adventurous. One segment particularly popular with foreigners is **Gwangjang market** (광장 시장), a particularly salty offshoot of Dongdaemun to the northwest, and one of Seoul's most idiosyncratic places to eat in the evening – just look for something tasty and point. During the day, it's also the best place in Seoul to buy **secondhand clothes** (see p.121).

Smaller and more compact than Dongdaemun, you'll find essentially the same goods at **Namdaemun market**, which stretches out between City Hall and Seoul station. It's best accessed through Hoehyeon subway station (exits five or six), while Dongdaemun market's spine road runs between Dongdaemun and Dongdaemun Stadium stations.

architect and built by the Japanese in 1910; the first Western-style building in the country, it was actually used as the royal home for a short time. The second structure, completed in 1938, was designed and built by the Japanese; inside you'll find the **National Museum for Contemporary Art** (덕수궁 미술관; same times as the palace; W3000), whose exhibits are usually quality works from local artists, more often than not blending elements of traditional and modern Korean styles.

There are English-language **tours** of the palace at 10.30am on weekdays and 1.40pm on weekends, and traditional **changing of the guard** ceremonies take place outside the main entrance at 11am, 2pm and 3.30pm (Tues–Sun).

Myeongdong

With a justifiable claim to being the most popular shopping area in the country, **Myeongdong** (명동) is a dense lattice of streets that runs from the east–west thoroughfare of Euljiro to the northern slopes of Namsan peak. Though visitors to the area are primarily concerned with shopping or eating (see pp.107–108 for restaurants), there are a couple of sights in the area that are worth a glance while you're here. Most central is the large **Myeongdong Cathedral** (명동 성당); completed in 1898, it was Korea's first large Christian place of worship, and remains the symbol of the country's ever-growing Catholic community. It wouldn't win any prizes for design in Europe, but in Seoul the towering spire and red brick walls are appealingly incongruous. Nearby is the **Bank of Korea Museum** (한국 은행 화폐금융 박물관; Tues–Sun 10am–5pm; free), though the notes and coins on display are less interesting than the building itself, which was designed and built by the Japanese in the first years of their occupation. A little tricky to find, the museum is best accessed by walking south down the main road from exit seven of Euljiro 1-ga subway station.

East of central Myeongdong is **Namsangol** (남산골), a small display village filled with traditional *hanok* buildings; though a much more interesting and entertaining folk village can be found just south of Seoul (see p.132), this is a more than acceptable solution for those with little time. Take exit three from Chungmuro subway station, and walk away from the main road.

Namsan Park

South of Myeongdong station the roads rise up, eventually coming to a stop at the feet of **Namsan** (남산), Seoul's resident mountain. There are spectacular **views** of the city from the 265m-high peak, and yet more from the characteristic **N-Seoul Tower,** which sits at the summit. Namsan once marked the natural boundary of a city that has long since swelled over the edges and across the river – some sections of the city wall can still be seen on the mountain, as can the remains of **fire beacons** that formed part of a national communication system during the Joseon period. These were used to relay warnings across the land – one flame lit meant that all was well, while up to five were lit to signify varying degrees of unrest; the message was repeated along chains of beacons that stretched across the peninsula. Namsan's own are located just above the upper terminal of a **cable car** (daily 10am–11pm; W5000 one-way, W6500 return) that carries most visitors up to the summit. The base is an uphill slog south of Myeongdong: leave the subway station through exit three, keep going up and you can't miss it. The mountain is also accessible on the yellow **buses** (W550) that ply local route #2 – catch them outside exit four of Chungmuro station – or you could even **walk** up in under an hour from Seoul station.

N-Seoul Tower

The **N-Seoul Tower** (N-서울 타워; daily 10am–11pm; W7000; Ⓦwww.nseoultower.com) sits proudly on Namsan's crown, newly renovated and recently renamed ("Seoul Tower" clearly wasn't trendy enough). Inside there's a viewing platform and a pricey restaurant. For many, the views from the tower's base are good enough, and coming here to see the **sunset** is recommended – the grey mass of daytime Seoul turns in no time into a pulsating neon spectacle.

Itaewon

One of Seoul's most famed quarters, **Itaewon** (이태원) is something of an enigma. It has, for years, been popular with American soldiers, thanks to the major military base situated nearby. Expat businessmen and visiting foreigners have followed suit, and until English teachers started pouring into Korea by the planeload it was one of the only places in the country in which you could buy "Western" items such as leather jackets, deodorant, tampons or Hershey's Kisses. While it remains a great place to shop for cheap tailored suits and shoes, Itaewon's popularity also made it a byword for transactions of a more sexual nature – **hostess bars** sprung up all over the place, particularly south of the *Hamilton*, a hotel that marks the centre of

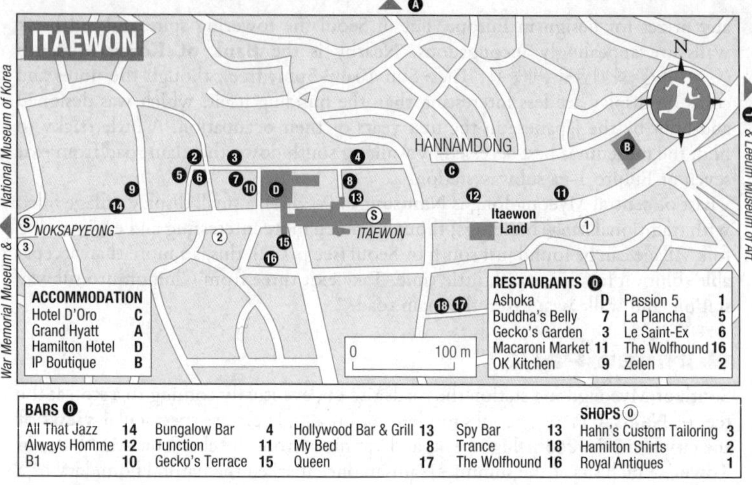

the area (see p.76), on the affectionately named "Hooker Hill". Times are changing, however. Most Western goods are available in cities across the country, and the gradual withdrawal of American troops has coincided with the opening of an ever more cosmopolitan array of restaurants (see pp.108–109), possibly the hippest in the city outside ultra-fashionable Apgujeong. The area is also heaving with clubbers on weekends, and from Hooker Hill also sprouts "Homo Hill", Seoul's only real gay area. For more details on Itaewon's bars and clubs, see p.115, and p.116 for more on Seoul's gay scene.

The War Memorial Museum

To the west of central Itaewon is the **War Memorial Museum** (전쟁 기념관; Tues–Sun 9.30am–5.30pm; W3000), a huge venue that charts the history of Korean warfare from ancient stones and arrows to more modern machinery. You don't even need a ticket to see the larger sights, as the museum's park-like periphery is riddled with B-52 bombers and other flying machines; with some, you'll be able to clamber up ladders to cockpit windows for a look inside. Before entering the main building itself, look for the names written on the outer wall: these are the names of every known member of Allied forces who died in the Korean War, and the list seems to go on forever. This is particularly heart-wrenching when you consider the fact that a far greater number of people, unmarked here, died on the Chinese and North Korean side. After all this, the main hall itself is a little disappointing, but you'll find plenty of exhibits and video displays relaying (incredibly one-sided) information about the **Korean War**; see Contexts, pp.365–367, for an account of the conflict. To get to the museum, take exit twelve from Samgakji subway station, or walk downhill from Itaewon.

The Leeum Museum of Art

Those with less pugnacious tastes can head east of Itaewon to the excellent **Leeum Museum of Art** (리움 미술관; Tues–Sun 10.30am–6pm; W10,000; Ⓦwww.leeum.org), which is not so much a museum as one of the most esteemed galleries in the country. It's split into several halls, each with a distinctive and original design; one, built in black concrete, was designed by acclaimed Dutch architect

Rem Koolhaas, who has since busied himself on the fantastic CCTV headquarters in Beijing. The museum hosts the occasional special exhibition of world-famous artists past and present – works from such luminaries as Mark Rothko and Damien Hirst have been displayed here. It's within walking distance from Itaewon, about fifteen minutes east of the subway station, but access is slightly faster from exit one of Hangangjin station.

National Museum of Korea

The huge **National Museum of Korea** (국립 중앙 박물관; Tues, Thurs & Fri 9am–6pm, Wed & Sat 9am–9pm, Sun 9am–7pm; W2000) is a Seoul must-see for anyone interested in history. It houses over eleven thousand artefacts, including an incredible 94 official National Treasures, but only a fraction of these will be on show at any one time. Among the many rooms on the ground level are exhibitions from the **Three Kingdoms** period (see Contexts, pp.359–360), which showcase the incredible skill of the artisans during that time – gold, silver and bronze have been cast into ornate shapes, the highlight being a fifth-century crown and belt set that once belonged to a Silla king. Moving up a floor the focus shifts to paintings, calligraphy and wooden art, and there's usually a colossal **Buddhist scroll** or two, over 10m high; some were hung behind the Buddha statue in temples' main halls, while others were used for such purposes as praying for rain. The museum owns quite a few, but due to the fragility of the material, they're put on a rota system and displays are changed regularly. The uppermost floor contains countless metal sculptures and a beautiful assortment of pots – some of these are over a thousand years old, though look as if they were made yesterday. From this floor you'll also get the best view of the museum's pride and joy, a ten-storey stone **pagoda** that sits in the main museum hall on the ground level and stretches almost all the way to the top floor. It's in remarkable condition for something that was taken apart by the Japanese in 1907, hauled overseas then all the way back some years later; from on high, you'll be able to appreciate more fully its true size, and the difficulties this must have posed for the people who built it. The museum is best accessed from Ichon subway station – take exit two and walk up the main road for a few minutes.

Hongdae

Just west of the city centre lies Seoul's greatest concentration of **universities**, but this is no place to be bookish – as with most

A banging good time

University areas are a good place to get a grip on the "**bang**" culture that pervades modern Korean life. The term is a suffix meaning "room", and is attached to all sorts of places where locals – and occasional foreigners – like to have fun. Below are a few of the most popular:

DVD-bang Imagine a small room with wipe-clean sofas, tissue paper on hand and a large television for movies – if it sounds a little sleazy, you'd be absolutely right. Though people do occasionally come to appreciate plot, cinematography or Oscar-winning performances, these places are more often used by couples looking for a cheap bit of privacy – going in by yourself, or with a person of the same sex, would draw some baffled looks. Figure on around W11,000 per movie.

Jjimjilbang Popular with families, teenagers and the occasional budget-minded traveller, these steam rooms have sauna rooms, a range of hot and cold pools, and often services from massage treatments to internet booths. Though they might sound dodgy, the reality is somewhat tamer; most are open all night, making them an incredibly cheap way to get a night's sleep – prices tend to be around W6000. See the box on p.38 for more information.

Noraebang These "singing rooms", found all over the country, even outside national park entrances, are wildly popular with people of all ages; if you have Korean friends, they're bound to invite you, as *noraebang* are usually *sam-cha* in a Korean night out – the "third step" after a meal and drinks. You don't sing in front of a crowd, but in a small room with your friends, where you'll find sofas, a TV, books full of songs to choose from and a couple of maracas or tambourines to play. Foreigners are usually intimidated at first, but after a few drinks it can be tough to get the microphone out of people's hands. Figure on around W15,000 per hour between the group.

PC-bang Even more ubiquitous in Korea are places to get online, which cost an almost uniform W1000 per hour. Despite the prevalence of such places, they're often packed full of gamers, and incredibly noisy – you're likely to be the only one sending emails. See p.123 for more information.

academic areas around the country, it's characterized less by what students do during the day than what they get up to at night, and streets are stuffed to the gills with **bars**, nightclubs, karaoke rooms and cheap restaurants. Though there are precious few tourist sights as such, it's possibly the best place in the land to get an understanding of what really makes Korea tick.

Hongdae (홍대) is one of the edgiest districts in the whole country, teeming with young and trendy people at almost every hour. The area only truly comes into its own after dark, its hundreds of bars and clubs buzzing with activity every night of the week (see p.114). During the daytime, it's fun to explore the streets lined with small shops selling stylish and secondhand clothing, and there are quirky cafés on every corner.

Hongdae university itself specializes in the **arts**, a fact that'll be most evident in **Nolita Park** (놀이터 공원) – actually a triangular wedge of ground with almost no greenery – which plays host to anything and everything from punk-rock bands to choreographed street dance. On weekends there's an interesting **flea market** at which local students sell handmade jewellery and other trinkets.

East of Hongdae, and just one subway station away on line 2, is **Sinchon**, which offers many of the same delights as Hongdae and is fast becoming just as busy.

South of the river

Before Seoul outgrew its boundaries and spread over most of the northwest of the country, the city's southern perimeter ran through Namsan, north of the river. Accordingly, the capital's historical sights become sparser on the south side of the Han River; still, to appreciate just how life ticks along in this fine city you'd do well to spend some time here. Each district has its own particular flavour and breed of Seoulite – **Yeouido** has its mass of suits, **Gangnam** its fun-seekers and fashionistas. You can also visit regal burial mounds, shop at gigantic malls or upscale boutiques, or head to a couple of huge theme parks.

Yeouido

You'd do well to banish any romantic visions before arriving at **YEOUIDO** (여의도) island. Meaning something akin to "useless land", it finally underwent development during Park Chung-hee's economic reforms in the 1970s, and is now one of South Korea's most important **business districts**, not to mention the home of its National Assembly and the 63 Building, formerly the tallest structure in the land. However, as Yeouido is manifestly a place to work, rather than live or go out, it has some of the quietest roads in the city. In fact, most of the northern fringe has been turned into a **riverside park**, which is a popular weekend picnicking place for Seoul families. This band of **semi-parkland** proves particularly popular on weekends and warm evenings. **Bike riding** is the most popular activity, though it's also possible to take a **riverboat trip** or a dip in a couple of **open-air swimming pools**; see the box on p.100 for more information.

63 Building

A short walk south of Wonhyo bridge is the **63 Building** (63 빌딩), one of the largest and most notable of Seoul's innumerable towers. A distinctive golden monolith 249m high, it was the tallest structure in Asia when completed in 1985. The sixtieth-floor **observation deck** (daily 10am–11pm; W7000) provides predictably good views of Seoul, and is actually at the top of the building; the other three floors from the building's name are basement levels. Down in the basement you'll find **Seaworld** (daily 10am–10pm; W12,000), an **aquarium** that's home to over twenty thousand sea creatures (there's also a reptile hall), and quite popular with young ones. The same can be said of the **Imax cinema** (daily 10am–8pm; W8000), though both this and the aquarium are somewhat dated.

The Full Gospel Church

Yeouido is also home to the almost sinfully ugly **Full Gospel Church** (순복음 교회), by some measures the largest church on earth – it has a membership exceeding one million. Obviously, not all of them pop along for prayers at the same time, but to meet the needs of Seoul's huge Protestant population there are no fewer than seven separate Sunday services, translated into sixteen languages in a dedicated foreigners section. This is quite a trip, whatever your denomination, since most Sunday services see more than ten thousand people pack into the building, creating something of a football crowd atmosphere on the way in. On occasion half of the congregation ends up in tears, as Korean pastors have a habit of ratcheting up the rhetoric to better exploit the national tendency towards melodrama.

Gangnam

Meaning "South of the River", **Gangnam** (강남) is the name for a huge swathe of land south of the Hangang, and an all-encompassing term for several distinct city

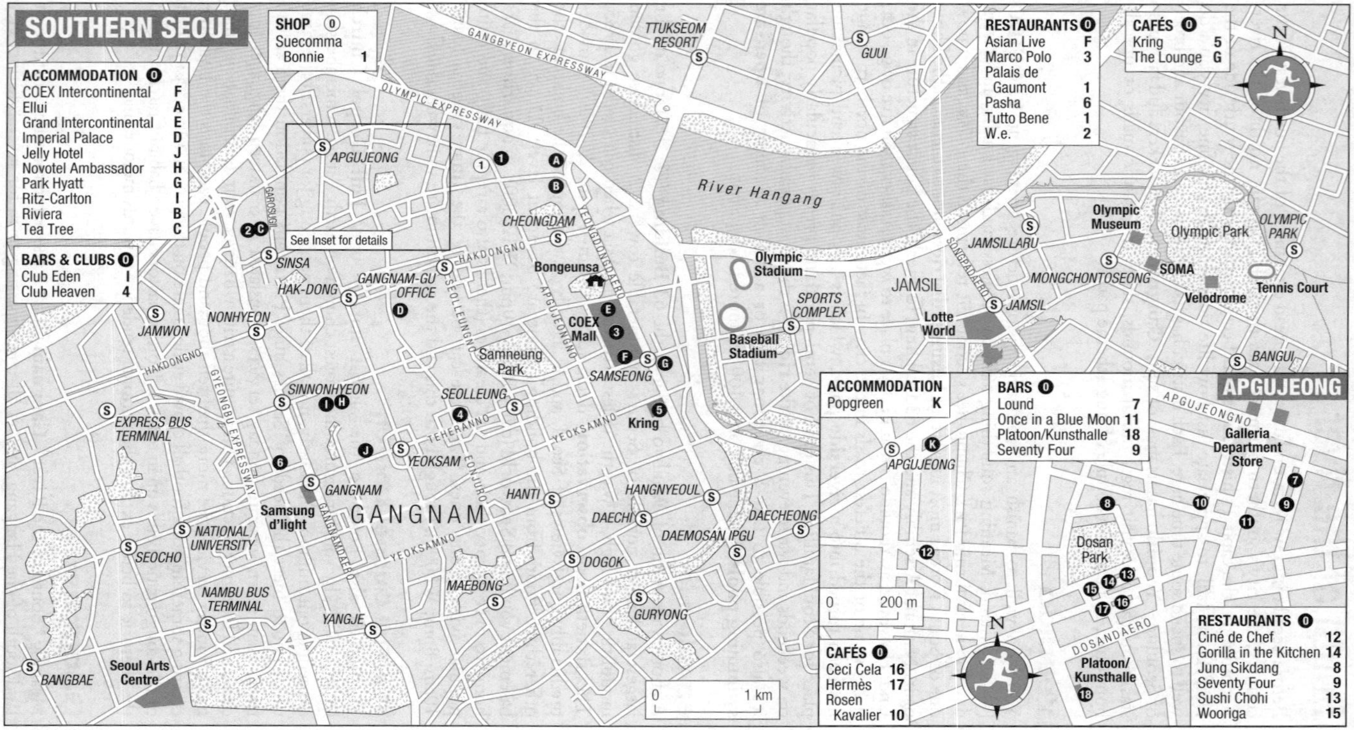

SOUTHERN SEOUL

SHOP ⓪	
Suecomma Bonnie	1

ACCOMMODATION ⓿	
COEX Intercontinental	F
Ellui	A
Grand Intercontinental	E
Imperial Palace	D
Jelly Hotel	J
Novotel Ambassador	H
Park Hyatt	G
Ritz-Carlton	I
Riviera	B
Tea Tree	C

BARS & CLUBS ⓿	
Club Eden	I
Club Heaven	4

RESTAURANTS ⓿	
Asian Live	F
Marco Polo	3
Palais de Gaumont	1
Pasha	6
Tutto Bene	1
W.e.	2

CAFÉS ⓿	
Kring	5
The Lounge	G

N

GANGBYEON EXPRESSWAY
OLYMPIC EXPRESSWAY
TTUKSEOM RESORT
GUUI
River Hangang
APGUJEONG
See Inset for details
GAROSUGIL
CHEONGDAM
SINSA
HAKDONGNO
Bongeunsa
YEONGDONGDAERO
GANGNAM-GU OFFICE
HAK-DONG
NONHYEON
JAMWON
SEOLLEUNGNO
APGUJEONGNO
COEX Mall
Samneung Park
SAMSEONG
HAKDONGNO
GYEONGBU EXPRESSWAY
SINNONHYEON
SEOLLEUNG
TEHERANNO
YEOKSAMNO
Kring
EXPRESS BUS TERMINAL
YEOKSAM
EONJURO
GANGNAM
HANTI
HANGNYEOUL
Samsung d'light
GANGNAM
GANGNAMDAERO
DAECHI
DAECHEONG
NATIONAL UNIVERSITY
SEOCHO
DAEMOSAN IPGU
YEOKSAMNO
DOGOK
MAEBONG
NAMBU BUS TERMINAL
GURYONG
YANGJE
BANGBAE
Seoul Arts Centre
0 1 km
Olympic Stadium
Baseball Stadium
SPORTS COMPLEX
JAMSIL
Lotte World
SONGPADAERO
JAMSIL
JAMSILLARU
MONGCHONTOSEONG
Olympic Museum
Olympic Park
OLYMPIC PARK
SOMA
Velodrome
Tennis Court
BANGUI

APGUJEONG

ACCOMMODATION	
Popgreen	K

BARS ⓿	
Lound	7
Once in a Blue Moon	11
Platoon/Kunsthalle	18
Seventy Four	9

CAFÉS ⓿	
Ceci Cela	16
Hermès	17
Rosen Kavalier	10

RESTAURANTS ⓿	
Ciné de Chef	12
Gorilla in the Kitchen	14
Jung Sikdang	8
Seventy Four	9
Sushi Chohi	13
Wooriga	15

APGUJEONGNO
Galleria Department Store
APGUJEONG
Dosan Park
DOSANDAERO
Platoon/ Kunsthalle
0 200 m
N

districts. Though primarily a commercial zone, this wide area contains a number of interesting sights: **Bongeunsa** is Seoul's most enchanting major temple, while just down the road are the **royal tombs** in **Samneung Park**, the grassy resting place of a few dynastic kings and queens. Moving into the modern day there's **COEX**, a huge underground shopping mall, and **Lotte World**, a colossal theme park.

The Gangnam station area has precious little in the way of sights. The single exception is **Samsung d'light** (daily 9am–9pm; free); a showroom of sorts for electronic goodies produced by Samsung, Korea's largest company. It's the place to come if you want a sneak preview of the gadgets that will be racing around the world in the near future. The complex connects directly to exit 4 of Gangnam station.

Apgujeong

Seoulites refer to **Apgujeong** (압구정) as "Korea's Beverly Hills", and the comparison is not far off the mark – if Louis Vuitton bags are your thing, look no further. Clothing boutiques, chic restaurants and European-style outdoor cafés line streets frequented by a disproportionate number of Seoul's young and beautiful, but note that their good looks may not be entirely natural – this is also Korea's plastic surgery capital, and clinics are ubiquitous. Though there are no real sights as such, Apgujeong is one of the most interesting places in Korea to sit down with a skinny latte and people-watch.

The best cafés and restaurants (see p.117 for details) huddle in a pleasantly relaxed, leafy area outside the main entrance to **Dosan Park** (도산 공원). Heading further north, past the clothes shops and plastic surgeons, you'll eventually come out onto **Apgujeongno**, the area's main road, which features the most exclusive clothes shops and department stores in Korea (see p.121).

Garosugil

West of Dosan Park, though actually far closer to exit 8 of Sinsa station (turn left after 200m), there's **Garosugil**, a particularly trendy street studded with hip cafés and sharp designer boutiques. Its name literally means "tree-lined street", bestowed on account of the roadside lines of gorgeous ginkgo trees, whose spectacular golden fall foliage makes this a superb place to stroll in Seoul's all-too-short autumn.

The Samneung burial mounds

During the Three Kingdoms period and beyond, deceased Korean royalty were buried in highly distinctive **grass mounds**. While these are easy to find in the relatively small former Silla capital Gyeongju (p.185), or the even tinier Baekje capitals of Gongju (p.274) and Buyeo (p.272), Seoul has a few of its own. The easiest to reach are in **Samneung Park** (삼릉 공원; Tues–Sun 6am–4.30pm; W1000), just to the north of Seolleung subway station – take exit eight and walk straight up the road for a few minutes. The park's name means "Three Mounds" in reference to the number that it holds. One was for **King Seongjong** (ruled 1469–94), an esteemed leader who – rarely, for that time – invited political opponents to have a say in national government. Two of his sons went on to rule – **Yeonsangun** (ruled 1494–1506) undid much of his father's hard work in a system of revenge-driven purges, and was overthrown to leave his half-brother **Jungjong** (ruled 1506–44) in control. Jungjong's mound can also be found on the complex, as can one created to house one of Seongjong's wives.

For all the history, it's the prettiness of the park itself that appeals to many visitors, a green refuge from grey Seoul crisscrossed by gorgeous **wooded pathways**. The area is popular with employees from nearby offices, many of

Making the most of the Hangang

The banks of the **Hangang** are a hive of activity: at any time of day or night, you'll see locals riding their **bikes**, jogging, or puffing and panting on **exercise equipment**. Summertime will provide another peek into Korean culture, since locals flock to the riverbanks for **picnics** – the air can be heavy with the scent of *gimchi* and barbecued meat, and the fact that there's usually a lot of *soju* being knocked back makes this a great place to make new friends. However, the river also opens up a whole raft of other possibilities.

Coffee and cocktails Six bridges – and counting – now have stylish cafés at their northern and southern ends, providing great views of the river and the teeming bridge traffic. They're a little tricky to get to, and are best approached by taxi or the river paths themselves; all are open daily from 10am to around 2am, making them equally good spots for an evening cocktail. The Dongjak and Hannam bridges are particularly recommended, since they provide great views of the Banpo bridge fountain shows (see below).

Cycling The Hangang is the most popular spot for **cycling** in Seoul, and a scoot along the grassy riverbanks constitutes one of the city's most pleasurable and picturesque activities. The main route runs for a whopping **21km** between **World Cup Stadium** to the west (see p.120), and **Olympic Park** in the east (see opposite). **Rental booths** (generally 9am–sunset) have been around for years, with the main ones just north of Yeouinaru station (W3000 per hour, W6000 for a tandem; kids' bikes also available).

Fountain shows Banpo bridge, located between the Seobinggo and Express Bus Terminal subway stations, plays host to eye-catching, ten-minute-long fountain shows from April to October. Moving jets of water burst from the bridge at noon, 2pm, 4pm, 8pm and 9pm (with more shows on weekends); the nighttime shows are particularly recommended, since the fountains are illuminated in eye-catching colours.

River cruises Evening cruises along the Hangang are quite enchanting, with the most popular routes running from Yeouido's north bank. Schedules change by the day and there's next to no English-language information, so it's best to ask at a tourist office. Hour-long round-trips cost W11,000, or W14,000 including live music or a magic show; special dinnertime services including a buffet meal are also available, and cost W55,000.

Swimming Seven open-air swimming pools (June–Aug 9am–8pm; W5000) have opened up along the Hangang, with those on Yeouido easiest to reach for foreign visitors. Note that they may be closed during bad weather.

whom come here during their lunch break to munch a sandwich or go for a jog. Its early opening times mean that you'll be able to visit at daybreak, which can be a rather atmospheric experience, dew sitting on the grass and the nearby buildings occluded by morning mist.

COEX Mall

This large underground **shopping mall** is a popular place for tourists to spend a rainy day. The mass of shops, restaurants and wall-to-wall people can be quite bewildering, but there are a couple of tourist attractions, too; the **Kimchi Museum** (Mon–Fri 10am–5pm, Sat & Sun 1–5pm; W3000), the only facility in the land dedicated to this national dish (see the *Korean cuisine* colour section), and worth a poke around. The **COEX Aquarium** (daily 10am–8pm; W16,500) sees far more visitors and has been designed with flair – this must be the only aquarium in the world to use toilets as goldfish tanks, though mercifully there are normal facilities for public use. Sharks, manta rays and colourful shoals are on display. Other activities within the mall include a pool hall, a board game café and a multiscreen cinema, while a couple of five-star hotels (see p.76) house some of Seoul's best restaurants (pp.109–110).

Bongeunsa

Sitting directly across from the north face of COEX is **Bongeunsa** (봉은사), the most appealing major temple in Seoul. Despite an incongruous location amidst a plethora of skyscrapers, this is a fairly decent rendition of a Korean temple; like Jogyesa, its uglier sibling to the north of the river (see p.85), it's affiliated to the **Jogye sect**, the largest Buddhist denomination in Korea. There has been a temple here since the late eighth century, but assorted fires and invasions mean that all of its buildings are of fairly recent vintage; still, it's worth peeking at its gorgeous main hall and clutch of small, appealing outer buildings. See Contexts, p.370 for more on Buddhism in Korea.

Lotte World

This local version of Disneyland is incredibly popular – the complex receives over five million tourists per year, and it's hard to find a Korean child, or even an adult, who hasn't been here at some point. While it may not be quite what some are looking for on their visit to Korea, **Lotte World** (롯데 월드; daily 9.30am–11pm; day-tickets W37,000 adults, W28,000 children, less after 4pm; Ⓦwww.lotteworld.com) can be a lot of fun, particularly for those travelling with children. It comprises two theme parks: indoor Lotte World Adventure and outdoor Magic Island, the latter in the middle of a lake and accessed by monorail from the former. Also within the complex is a bowling alley (9am–midnight; W3000 plus shoe rental), an overpriced ice rink (10am–9pm; W12,000 plus skate rental), and a large swimming pool (Mon–Fri noon–7pm, Sat & Sun noon–8pm; W8000). The complex is an easy walk from Jamsil subway station; you'll see signs pointing the way from the ticket gates.

Olympic Park

The large **Olympic Park** (올림픽 공원; 24hr; free), built for the **1988 Summer Olympics** (see p.102), remains a popular picnicking place for Seoul families, and hosts a regular assortment of festivals – you're likely to see one if you turn up on a weekend. Near the eastern entrance to the park – take subway line 5 to Olympic Park – you'll see a number of facilities that remain from the games, including a couple of gymnasiums and the indoor swimming pool, though very few are actually open for public use – there's a general air of decay about the place but this is part of the appeal. On the way into the park, you'll pass by buildings and sculptures displaying the rather Stalinist themes that were in vogue in 1980s Seoul – some of this would look quite at home in Pyongyang, and those with interests in art and architecture may find the area quite absorbing. The park itself is crisscrossed by a great number of paths, but it's best to stick to the south where the main concentration of sights are. The main ones are **SOMA** (Tues–Sun 10am–8pm; W3000), an excellent modern art gallery, and the **Olympic Museum** (Tues–Sun 10am–5pm; W3000), which may appeal to sports buffs – there's a collection of Olympic torches from various games, as well as an exhibit showing just how terrifying Olympic mascots have been through the years (Atlanta's "Izzy" and Barcelona's "Cobi", the cubist Catalan sheepdog, being just two examples).

Seoul Grand Park area

Seven subway stops south of the Han River on line 4 is **Seoul Grand Park** (서울대공원; daily 9.30am–9pm; Ⓦgrandpark.seoul.go.kr), one of the largest expanses of greenery in Seoul, and one of the best places to take children for a fun

The 1988 Summer Olympics

Seoul's hosting of the **Olympic Games** in 1988 was a tremendous success, bringing pride not just to the city, but to the whole nation. In fact, it did much to make Korea the country that it is today, and has even been credited with bringing democracy to the nation. President **Park Chung-hee** had been first to toy with the idea of bidding for the games in the 1970s, seemingly wishing to win international approval for his authoritarian running of the country; he was assassinated in 1979, but the bid went ahead. However, large-scale protests against the government in the years running up to the games brought a hitherto unprecedented level of international scrutiny, and direct elections took place in 1987.

The games themselves were no less interesting, and produced several moments which have become part of sporting folklore. The USA's **Greg Louganis** managed to win a second consecutive gold medal in the 3m springboard dive after an incredible comeback; after bloodying the pool by walloping his head on the dive-board, he somehow followed with a perfect dive that was enough to propel him into first place. A lesser-known tale is that of Canadian sailor **Lawrence Lemieux**, who sacrificed a probable medal to race to the aid of two Singaporean competitors who had been thrown into the water in treacherous conditions. However, the Games' defining moment came in the final of the men's 100m, where **Ben Johnson**, also from Canada, sped to the line in a world record time of 9.79 seconds; once he'd finally slowed down enough for the drugs testing unit to catch up with him, he was revealed to have tested positive for steroid use, and the gold went instead to Carl Lewis of the USA.

day out. The highlight is its **zoo** (9am–6pm; W3000); home to animals from around the world, it puts on special dolphin shows (W1500) at least four times per day, as well as other animal performances. In 2005, six elephants escaped during one of these events, and were only caught hours later after trashing a restaurant and wading through a nearby resident's garden; needless to say, security has been tightened, and a repeat pachyderm performance is unlikely. To get to Seoul Grand Park, take exit two from the subway station of the same name. The entrance is just fifteen minutes' walk away and well signed, or you can take a tram train (W800) or a chairlift (W4500).

Other attractions in the park area are **Seoul Land** (서울 랜드; daily 9am–6pm, later in peak season; entry to area W16,000, day-pass for rides W30,000; ⓦeng.seoulland.co.kr), a large amusement park with an abundance of rollercoasters and spinning rides, and the **National Museum of Contemporary Art** (March–Oct Tues–Fri 10am–6pm, Sat & Sun 10am–9pm; Nov–Feb Tues–Fri 10am–5pm, Sat & Sun 10am–8pm; W1000), an excellent collection of works by some of the biggest movers and shakers in the Korea modern art scene.

Bukhansan National Park

Few major cities can claim to have a national park right on their doorstep, but looming over central Seoul, and forming a natural northern boundary to the city, are the peaks of **BUKHANSAN NATIONAL PARK** (북한산 국립 공원), spears and spines of off-white granite that burst out of the undulating pine forests. Despite the park's relatively small size at just 80 square kilometres, its proximity to one of earth's most populated cities makes it the **world's most visited** national park, drawing in upwards of five million visitors per year. While an undeniably

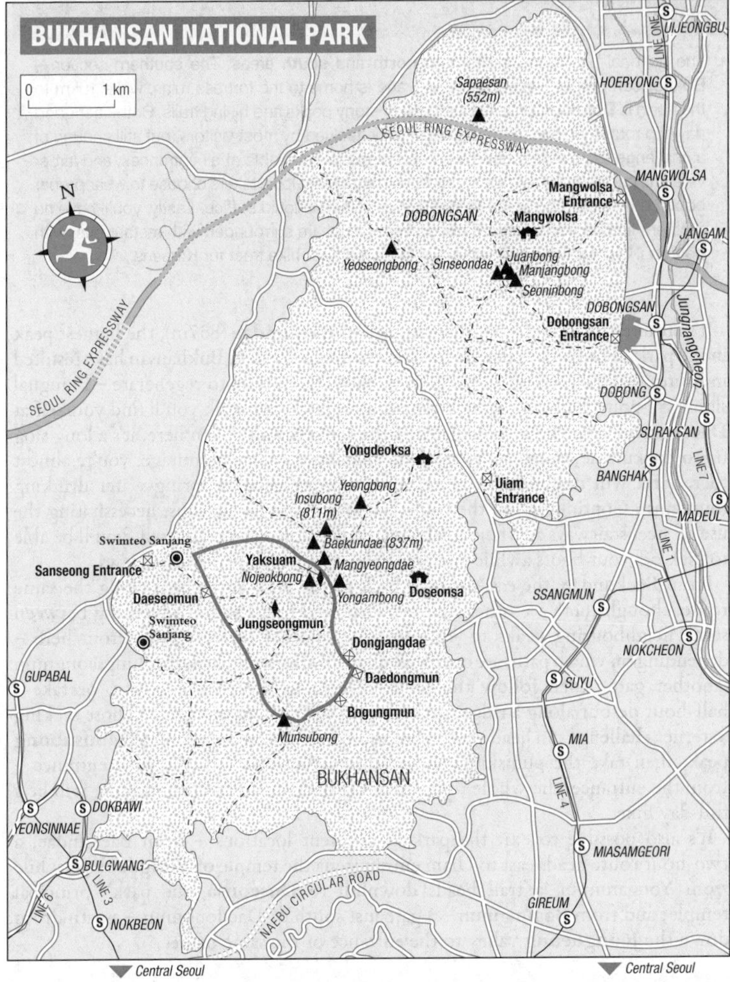

beautiful place, its popularity means that trails are often very busy indeed – especially so on warm weekends – and some can be as crowded as shopping mall aisles, hikers literally having to queue up to reach the peaks.

Southern Bukhansan

The southern half of Bukhansan is best accessed through **Sanseong**, an entry point on the western side of the park. To reach this, head first to Gupabal station on subway line 3 (20min from Gyeongbokgung), and walk from exit one to the small bus stop. From here, bus #704 (10min; W900) makes the run to the park entrance; get off when everyone else does. On the short walk to the clutch of restaurants that surround the entrance, you'll see the park's principal peaks soaring above; unless you're visiting on a weekend, the hustle and bustle of downtown Seoul will already feel a world away.

Park practicalities

The national park can be split into **north** and **south** areas. The southern section – **Bukhansan** proper – overlooks Seoul and is home to the fortress ruins, while 10km to the north is **Dobongsan**, a similar maze of stony peaks and hiking trails. Both offer good day-trip routes which are easy enough to be tackled by most visitors, but still enough of a challenge to provide a good workout; **maps** are available at all entrances, and larger versions can be seen at various points en route. Most local hikers choose to wear proper boots, but unless it's rainy a sturdy pair of trainers should suffice. Lastly, you'll have no problem finding a meal after a hike: all entrances are surrounded with restaurants, with **pajeon** (파전; a savoury pancake) the favoured post-hike treat for Koreans.

It's around two hours from the entrance to **Baekundae** (837m), the highest peak in the park, though note that the masses tramping through Bukhansan have resulted in routes being closed off in rotation to allow them time to regenerate – bilingual signs will point the way. Around ten minutes into your walk you'll find yourself at **Daeseomun**, one of the main gates of the fortress wall. From here, it's a long slog up to Baekundae; once you've reached **Yaksuam**, a lofty hermitage, you're almost there (and will doubtless be grateful for the presence of spring-water drinking fountains). Continuing on, the route becomes more precipitous, necessitating the use of steel stairways and fences. Having finally scaled the peak itself, you'll be able to kick off your boots awhile and enjoy the wonderful, panoramic views.

From Baekundae, the easiest route back to the park entrance is along the same route, though there are other options. One trail heads south, squeezing between some neighbouring peaks to Yongammun, another fortress gate. From here – depending on which paths are open – you can head downhill towards Jungseongmun (another gate), then follow the pretty stream to the park entrance, or take a half-hour detour along a ridge further south to Daedongmun gate. Those seeking a sterner challenge can head yet further southwest of Daedongmun to **Munsubong** peak, then take the punishing up-and-down route back to the park entrance – from the entrance, the whole round-trip via Baekundae and Munsubong will be a full-day hike.

It's also possible to exit the park at different locations – from Baekundae, a two-hour route heads east to Uiam entrance via the temple of **Yongdeoksa**; while from Yongammun, a trail heads downhill to **Doseonsa**, the park's principal temple; and from Bogungmun – a gate just south of Daedongmun – a path drops down the **Jeongneung** valley to the entrance of the same name.

Northern Bukhansan

The scenery in the **Dobongsan** area is much the same as around Baekundae to the south – trees, intriguing rock formations and wonderful views at every turn – though the hiking options are less numerous. Most choose to scale the main peak (740m) on a C-shaped route that curls uphill and down between **Mangwolsa** and **Dobongsan**, two subway stations on line 1 (each around 30min from Jongno 3-ga). It's hard to say which direction is better, but most head from Dobongsan. From this station, cross the main road, then go left along the perimeter of a dense network of ramshackle snack bars, then right up the main road. Whichever way you go, it takes just over two hours up to the gathering of peaks at the top; like Baeundae to the south of the park, the upper reaches of the trail are patches of bare rock, and you'll be grateful for the steel ropes on which you can haul yourself up or down. Coming back down, you can take a rest at **Mangwolsa**, a small but rather beautiful temple originally built here in 639, before heading back into

Seoul. Mangwolsa roughly translates as "Moon-viewing temple", and was likely used for such purposes by the kings of the Joseon period.

Eating

Food in Seoul is cheap by international standards and invariably excellent, while the number of **restaurants** is nothing short of astonishing – there's almost one on every corner, and many more in between. Korean food has a well-deserved reputation as one of the spiciest around; those looking for something a little blander can stick to the ever-growing choice of restaurants serving global cuisine, or breakfast at one of the many **bakeries** strewn around the city (note, however, that Korean bread is rather sweet for many foreigners' tastes). Restaurants are usually open whenever you're likely to require food, and some are 24hr; if you do get stuck, head for one of Seoul's seemingly infinite number of **convenience stores** – large chains include 7-Eleven, Mini Stop and Buy the Way – which sell drinks and fast food. All have hot water for instant noodles and small tables outside for eating; partaking in this highly Korean activity will endear you to any passing locals. For something even more authentic, head to one of Seoul's many **markets**, those at Dongdaemun and Namdaemun being the most popular. Also note that the consumption of food and drink have long been entwined in Korea; many **bars**, including some of those listed from pp.114–117, serve meals every bit as good as you'd find in a restaurant.

Culinary curiosities

While even "regular" Korean food may be alien to most visitors, there are a few edibles that deserve special attention. And if you're curious about dog, see p.43.

Baem soju 뱀소주 Not strictly a food, but interesting nonetheless – this is regular *soju* with a snake (*baem*) marinating in the bottle, which is said to be extremely healthy, especially for the back muscles. Though many may feel that the bottles would make wonderful souvenirs, particularly with the larger serpents inside, international customs officials aren't too fond of you taking them.

Beonddegi 번데기 When it gets cold, stalls selling this local delicacy – silkworm larvae – set up on pavements and riverbanks across the country. You'll smell them before you see them – the acrid stench of these mites boiled up in a broth is so disgusting that it may well breach international law. The treat is also served as bar snacks in many *hofs*, bursting in the mouth to release a grimy juice – perfect drinking game material.

Dak-pal 닭발 So you've learnt the word for "chicken" in Korean (*dak*), spotted it on the menu and ordered a dish. Unfortunately, with this particular meal the suffix means "foot", and that's just what you get – dozens of sauced-up chicken feet on a plate, with not an ounce of meat in sight.

Pojangmacha 포장마차 Plastic chairs to sit on, tables littered with *soju* bottles, and a cackling *ajumma* serving you food that's still half-alive – these are the delights of the *pojangmacha*, ramshackle seafood dens that congregate on many a Korean street. They're usually distinguishable by their orange, tent-like covering; one good area to find them in Seoul is outside exits three to six of Jongno 3-ga subway station. Just watch out for the octopus tentacles – every year, people die of suffocation when their still-wriggling prey makes a last bid for freedom.

Sundae 순대 Absolutely nothing to do with ice cream, but rather a sausage made with intestinal lining and stuffed with clear noodles – head to the nearest market to try some.

Restaurants

Seoul's excellent choice of **restaurants** is growing more cosmopolitan with each passing year. They run the full gamut from super-polished establishments in five-star hotels to local **snack bars** where stomachs can be filled for just W1000; even in the cheapest places, you may be surprised by the quality of the food. With much of the national cuisine alien to most foreign guests, it may be easier to head for the **food courts** in department stores and shopping malls, where you can see plastic versions of the available dishes. Also popular are snack chains serving basic Korean staples – see the box on pp.40–41 for more.

Many parts of Seoul have their own particular culinary flavour. Most popular with tourists are the streets around **Insadonggil**, where restaurants almost exclusively serve traditional Korean food in an equally fitting atmosphere. Then there's cosmopolitan **Itaewon**, where local restaurants are outnumbered by those serving Indian, Japanese, Thai or Italian food, among others. Student areas such as **Hongdae** and **Daehangno** are filled with cheap places, while **Gangnam** is also popular with local youth, and trendy **Apgujeong** with the fashionistas.

Most restaurants serve all day from early until late, but some of the more upscale establishments open for lunch and dinner only – details have been given in the reviews below where appropriate.

North of Anguk station: the palace district

The following places are marked on the "Palace district" **map**, p.111, and best accessed via Anguk subway station.

Cheonjin Pocha 천진 포차 Sogyeokdong. Almost permanently packed, this small, steamy place is so popular that you may have to take a number and wait outside while the Chinese chef doles out portion after portion of his famed Tianjin dumplings. Around W4000 per meal.

Goongyeon 궁연 Gahoedong ⓣ02/3673-1104, ⓦwww.goongyeon.com. Food literally fit for a king: the head chef at this restaurant is the only person schooled in the art of Korean court cuisine, and has been handed the singularly unromantic title of National Intangible Cultural Asset #38. The immaculately designed set menus showcase a subtlety and balance largely lost in modern Korean cuisine, and cost W28,000–130,000: a small price for what may well be the best food in Seoul. In warmer months, you can eat in the garden area outside.

Meokswi Donna 먹쉬돈나 Angukdong. In Korea, when places get popular, they get really popular – there's often a queue of people outside this plain-looking restaurant waiting to get their teeth around some *deokbokki*. This rice-cake smothered in a red-hot sauce is available all over the country, but *Meokswi* was the first place to experiment with ingredients such as seafood, cheese and *bulgogi*. Dishes W3000 and up.

The Place Sinmunno. Swanky Western-oriented place popular with staff from the local banks and embassies. Pasta meals go from W8000, while the mini pizzas (W5000) are good for something light. Waffles and cakes are available for dessert, and there are plenty of coffees to choose from.

The Restaurant Sogyeokdong ⓣ02/735-8441. Connected to the excellent Kukje Gallery (see p.86), and within easy walking distance of Gyeongbokgung, this Italian restaurant is perfectly placed for when you're sightseeing in the area. Pasta dishes start at W15,000, while for visitors just needing a snack there are desserts and baked goods on offer – the tiramisu is heavenly – as well as good coffee.

Second Best Place in Seoul Samcheongdong. A rarity on cosmopolitan and fast-changing Samcheongdonggil, in that it has not only been here for decades, but serves traditional food. The menu is short, with an assortment of Korean teas and snacks. Best is the *patjuk* (W4000), something like a viscous red bean fondue containing all manner of ingredients from cinnamon to chestnut chunks.

Solmoe Maeul 솔뫼 마을 Samcheongdong. A surefire contender for the "Best Side Dishes in Seoul" award, should it ever come into being – you'll be in danger of filling up before the main course arrives. Traditional Korean sets (*jeongsik*) go from W18,000 per person, while *ssambap* meals (consisting of side dishes, with leaves to wrap them in) are only marginally smaller and cost W8000. Try to nab a window table if you don't fancy sitting Korean-style on the floor. It's on the second floor, overlooking Samcheongdonggil.

Wood & Brick Gahoedong. This classy restaurant-cum-deli dishes out scrumptious Italian food from W20,000 a dish, with an excellent wine menu and in-house bakery and deli counter. Lunch sets go for W35,000 and up, and typically feature pasta or grilled meat, as well as a choice of cake.

Insadong

The following places are marked on the "Insadong" **map**, p.83; all are within walking distance of Anguk, Jonggak and Jongno 3-ga stations.

Arirang Garden Insadong. Traditional courtyard restaurant set back from Insadonggil, and illuminated in the evenings by fairy lights. The beef *galbi* sets (W24,000) are colossal and will feed two, with a similar pork option for just W11,000. Single diners can try a *jjigae* stew (W5000), which comes with rice and a few side dishes.

Bärlin Susongdong ⓣ02/722-5622, ⓦwww.baerlin.co.kr. Those hankering for a bit of *bratwurst* or *sauerkraut* should hunt down this upmarket German restaurant in the Somerset complex. Schnitzels come in three different styles (all around W27,000), the raw beef tartare on rye is delectable (W25,000) and there's herring on the menu – extremely rare in Korea.

Baru 바루 Gyeonjidong ⓣ02/2031-2081, ⓦwww.baru.or.kr. Overlooking Jogyesa temple, this is quite simply one of the best places to eat in Seoul, particularly for vegetarians. The huge set meals are consummately prepared approximations of Buddhist temple food, and the balance of colour, texture, shape and taste is beyond reproach. Mung-bean pancakes, acorn jelly, sweet pumpkin tofu and sticky rice with ginkgo nuts are among the dozens of items that may appear on your table. Sets W25,000–50,000; lunch noon–1.30pm or 1.30–3pm, dinner 6–9pm.

Gogung 고궁 Gwanhundong ⓣ02/736-3211. Next to a gallery in the basement of the Ssamziegil complex, the decor here is accordingly quirky, with walls festooned with threads and tie-dye. The food is traditional Korean – best is the *Jeonju bibimbap* (W10,000), a tasty regional take on the Korean staple.

Janchijip 잔치집 Gwanhundong. Tucked away behind Ssamziegil, this rambling den is a real jack of Insadong trades – here you can devour traditional Korean food (such as the savoury *pajeon* pancakes; W7000), sup traditional teas (W5000) or get drunk the traditional way with delicious *dongdongju*, a ginseng-infused rice wine.

Min's Club Gyeongundong ⓣ02/733-2966. This restaurant is a little piece of history. Named after Queen Min (see p.81), it was built in the 1930s to house one of her descendants. While the place may look traditionally Korean, this was actually one of the country's earliest "modern" structures, and the first to have a flushing indoor toilet. The menu is largely French, though Korean dishes such as barbecued beef and pumpkin congee also make an appearance; figure on around W50,000 per head. In addition, the wine list one of the best in Seoul. Noon–2.30pm & 6–11.30pm.

Sagwa Namu 사과나무 Insadong. Something different in traditional Insadong: this cosy hideaway serves plates of tasty bangers and mash, which you can eat in the courtyard under the apple trees the place is named after. Portions (W13,000) are on the small side, but so tasty you won't be grumbling.

Top Cloud Jongno Tower ⓣ02/2230-3000, ⓦwww.topcloud.co.kr. Though the tower itself is only 24 storeys high, this restaurant contrives to be on the 33rd floor – it's hoisted high on a barricade of steel. The views are tremendous, of course, and are almost equalled by the largely French food; the duck dishes are particularly recommended, as is tiramisu for dessert. Lunch noon–2.30pm (sets from W50,000), dinner 6–10pm (from W72,000).

The business district

The following places are marked on the "Business district" **map**, p.90.

Benigni Sinmunno 2-ga ⓣ02/3210-3351; Gwanghwamun station. A classy Italian restaurant on the ground floor of the Mirospace complex. The menu concentrates on Tuscan specialities, including pasta and risotto dishes (W14,000–16,000), as well as assorted steaks for around double the price; another highlight is the baked sea bass with fennel.

Bulgogi Brothers Myeongdong ⓣ02/319-3351; Myeongdong station. The barbecuing of raw meat at your table is a quintessential Korean experience, but new arrivals can find it hard to jump straight in at the deep end. This elegant venue is the easiest place to learn the ropes, and the meat is always of exceptional quality. Around W30,000 per person, including side dishes and drinks.

Gildeulyeo Jigi 길들여지기 Joongdong ⓣ02/319-7083; City Hall station. The name is a quote from the Korean translation of *The Little Prince*, and the decoration here is accordingly esoteric. Diners often call in on their way out of Chongdong Theatre (see p.118) underneath, to feast on spaghetti or grilled meat. Alternatively, the salmon with herb pepper sauce is particularly recommended. Mains from W20,000.

Gostiniy Dvor Daehogil ⓣ02/2275-7501; Dongdaemun History & Culture Park station.

By far the best restaurant in Dongdaemun's curious little Russiatown. Its owners are Uzbek but the food is typically Russian, including meaty mains (W10,000), filling soups (W6000) and delicious salads (W5000). The total lack of any sort of Korean atmosphere (and Korean people) can come as quite a surprise if you've been in Seoul a while: the restaurant's furniture, crockery and decoration are quite unique, and the Russian beer (W5,000) goes down nicely.

Kongdu 콩두 Seoul Museum of History ⓣ02/722-0272; Gwanghwamun station. On the ground floor of the history museum (p.91), this high-end restaurant prides itself on neo-Korean cuisine: basic ingredients with a modern twist, such as fish with pumpkin sauce or tofu ice cream. Come in the evening to sample some of their home-made *makkeolli* (see p.45).

Korea House Toegyero ⓣ02/2266-9101, ⓦwww.koreahouse.or.kr; Chungmuro station. Exquisite is not the word – meals here have been modelled on the court cuisine enjoyed by the kings of the Joseon dynasty. Dinner sets go for W68,000 and up (lunch ones are smaller and cheaper), and are made up of at least fifteen separate components, usually including broiled eel, ginseng in honey, grilled sliced beef and a royal hotpot. For W50,000 extra you'll be able to enjoy a performance of traditional song and dance after dinner. Reservations recommended. Lunch noon–2pm; dinner 5.30–7pm & 7.20–8.50pm.

Myeongdong Gyoja 명동교자 Myeongdong ⓣ02/776-5348; Myeongdong station. Everything's W6000 at this wildly popular restaurant, which is often full to the brim with hungry visitors jostling to try some of the famous meat dumplings. Noodle dishes are also available.

N Grill Namsan ⓣ02/3455-929, ⓦwww.nseoultower.net. Expensive steakhouse perched atop the N-Seoul Tower (see p.93). You won't get much change from W100,000 per person, but the steaks are top-class, and there are few better views of Seoul.

Pierre Gagnaire à Seoul Euljiro ⓣ02/317-7181, ⓦwww.pierregagnaire.co.kr; Euljiro 1-ga station. Molecular gastronomy hits Seoul: the unique creations of Michelin-starred French megachef Pierre Gagnaire are tickling tastebuds atop the otherwise awful *Lotte Hotel*. The menu has a discernable Korean twist, with ingredients such as ginger, sesame leaves and "five-flavoured" *omija* berries letting off little flavour bombs. Lunch menu W130,000, dinner W180,000 and up; reservations essential. Noon–3pm & 5–11pm.

Potala Myeongdong; Euljiro 1-ga station. Run by a Nepali–Korean couple and just downhill from the cathedral, this charmingly decorated second-floor restaurant serves simple specialities from Nepal, Tibet and India. Prices are incredibly reasonable; go in a small group and you should get change from W10,000 per head. One highly recommended dish is the *samosa chat* – three large samosas served with chopped green onion, chickpeas, curry sauce and sour cream (W7000).

Taj Myeongdong ⓣ02/776-0677; Euljiro 1-ga station. The best Indian restaurant in Seoul, according to many an expat. You'll be paying far more than you would for Korean food, but dishes are well made and absolutely delicious. Curries start at W17,000 and dinner sets are around double that, though from noon to 3pm on weekdays there are bargain lunch deals for just W10,000.

Woo Rae Oak 우래옥 Jugyodong ⓣ02/2265-0151; Euljiro 4-ga station. This meat-house and its elegant, hotel lobby-like atrium have been here since 1946: only one year less than South Korea itself. The customer base seems to have changed little in decades, and the sight of septuagenarians munching away in their Sunday best is rather charming. Most are here for the meat (W20,000 or so per head), though they also serve superb *naengmyeon*, cold buckwheat noodles similar to Japanese *soba* (W9000).

Itaewon

The following places are marked on the "Itaewon" **map**, p.94, and with the exception of *Passion 5* are best accessed via Itaewon subway station.

Ashoka Itaewondong ⓣ02/792-0117. On the third floor of the *Hamilton Hotel*, capturing the feel of an English curry house perfectly, this has long been a favourite with hungry expats. Tandoori meals are still the Rajasthani owner's pride and joy, but local competition has seen renewed effort put into all the dishes. There's also a daily buffet lunch (W15,000).

Buddha's Belly Itaewondong ⓣ02/796-9330. All of your favourite Thai dishes from green curry and *pad thai* to chicken coconut soup (all around W14,000) are lovingly prepared at this spick-and-span restaurant, and served in a wonderfully laid-back atmosphere – the comfy seating will tempt you to linger for a glass of wine or two.

Gecko's Garden Itaewondong ⓣ02/790-0540. Not to be confused with *Gecko's Terrace*, an expat bar just down the way, this rambling restaurant is fenced off from Itaewon by a line of trees, and feels a world removed from smoky Seoul. The silver bistro tables impart a vaguely European air to the courtyard and the menu follows suit with pastas and risottos (from W17,000), while on weekends chefs will grill your choice of meat on an open barbecue.

Macaroni Market Hannamdong ⓣ02/749-9181. This swanky second-floor Italian restaurant has all bases covered. In the morning, try something from the deli counter, and wash it down with a latte. Coming for lunch? Head to a windowside table for a sandwich or salad. Dinner? Move a little further around and order a pasta or steak (W15,000–30,000), served with bread, olive oil and balsamic vinegar. The popping of wine corks heralds the arrival of evening, and diners who fancy a dance can head to *Function*, an adjoining bar (see p.115).

OK Kitchen Itaewondong ⓣ02/797-6420. All of the veggies and most of the meat used in this restaurant come from the Okinawan chef's own patch of farmland, located far away near the North Korean border. A mix of French, Japanese and Korean dishes, menus change both with the season and the whim of the chef: in the mornings, he can often be seen at Noryangjin fish market. Three-course lunch sets are a bargain at W20,000, while mains cost around the same for dinner. Noon–3pm & 5–9pm.

Passion 5 Hannamdong ⓣ02/2071-9505; Hangangjin station. Precious few places in Seoul can whip up a decent Eggs Benedict, which makes this venue a valuable addition to Itaewon's culinary scene. Salads, pasta and an international range of coffees are also on the menu, with prices around W15,000 per person. The restaurant sits atop a superb bakery, from where customers are welcome to carry up a few treats for dessert.

La Plancha Itaewondong ⓣ02/790-0063. There's meat, meat and more meat on the menu at this Spanish restaurant, whose walls have been painted a pretty Andalucian pink. Beefy *combos* are W16,000 per person, while the same amount will buy four plates of tapas. It's located at the western end of the restaurant-filled road that runs behind the *Hamilton Hotel*.

Le Saint-Ex Itaewondong ⓣ02/795-2465. Check out the blackboard for the daily specials at this French bistro; they generally include steaks (W27,000) and hearty salads. Teasingly set out near the exit, the desserts are hard to resist, and there's a good wine list. Lunch noon–3pm; dinner 6pm–midnight (last orders 9.30pm).

The Wolfhound Itaewondong ⓣ02/749-7971, ⓦwolfhoundpub.com. This may be an Irish pub, but it's also notable for an authentic selection of pub grub, including burgers, fish and chips and shepherd's pie. Best, however, are the fried breakfasts, which cost from W9000 including a tea or coffee.

Zelen Itaewondong ⓣ02/749-0600. Bulgarian cuisine is one of the culinary world's best kept secrets, taking hearty meat and veg dishes from the Slavic lands to the West, and fusing them with kebabs and breads from the Turkic east; all the meals in this Bulgarian restaurant are well prepared, though best may be the gigantic "couple" *shashlik* kebab (W34,000).

Hongdae

The following places are marked on the "Hongdae" **map**, p.95, and best accessed via Sangsu subway station.

Jopok Deokbokki 조폭 떡볶이 Seogyodong. A dish of rice-cakes in spicy sauce, *deokbokki* is available at street-stands all across the city, though this small sit-down restaurant is by far the most famous venue, since its staff are rumoured to be connected to the local mafia (*jopok*). Whether fact or fib, the food's pretty good, especially if you have a few refried treats (*twigim*) thrown on top: just point at what you'd like. W2000 for four *twigim*.

Oyori Seogyodong ⓣ02/332-5525. One has to admire the thinking behind this restaurant, which not only gives employment to single mothers from other Asian countries, but uses the profit to send their children to kindergarten. The various nationalities working here take it in turns to enrich the menu, which contains Malaysian stir-fries, Japanese noodles, Burmese curry and Russian desserts. Benevolence aside, the food is excellent, and the setting surprisingly stylish thanks to connections with a local art society.

Samgeori Pocha 삼거리포차 Seogyodong. Nights out in Hongdae usually end late, meaning that this rustic raw fish restaurant can be heaving with drunken students at 6am: it's an integral part of the nightlife scene, and one of the most atmospheric places to be of a weekend. Having a drop of *soju* for Dutch courage makes it easier to handle the house speciality, *sannakji* (W15,000, feeds two) – chopped-up baby octopus that, while not exactly alive, is still writhing on your plate when served.

Gangnam

The following places are marked on the "Southern Seoul" **map**, p.98.

Asian Live COEX complex ⓣ02/3130-8620; Samseong station. Despite the rather tacky-sounding name, this is one of the city's top hotel restaurants, sitting pretty on the second floor of the *COEX InterContinental* (p.76). The kitchens are visible from many tables, so you get to see the chefs whipping up invariably excellent Indian,

Chinese, Japanese or Korean food – set meals are usually the best value, starting at around W70,000 per person. 11.30am–2.30pm & 5.30–10pm.

Marco Polo COEX complex ⓣ02/559-7620; Samseong station. Seoul's top restaurant – in a literal sense, at least, sitting as it does on the 52nd floor of the World Trade Center rising from the center of COEX. It's split into two halves: one serving Mediterranean cuisine and one Chinese, with prices slightly cheaper at the former. Either way, you'll be paying about W40,000 for lunch, and double that for dinner. Views are, of course, superb. 11.30am–1am; Sun11.30am–11.30pm.

Palais de Gaumont Cheongdamdong ⓣ02/546-8877. A firm favourite with local fashionistas, this may well be the most visually appealing restaurant in the country. Gigantic angled mirrors reflect the light of a dozen large chandeliers, while floor-to-ceiling windows bring the outdoor maple trees into the fray. The food is superbly crafted Parisian fare, though it doesn't come cheap – set meals start at W100,000 per head. Noon–3pm & 6–10pm.

Pasha Seochodong ⓣ02/593-8484; Gangnam station. Style and substance mix perfectly at this Turkish kebab house, whose attractive interior sets it apart from its dowdier counterparts in Itaewon. The meals (generally W15,000) are filling, with the familiar *doner* and *köfte* dishes supplemented by more unusual fish meals. *Pide* – a kind of Turkish pizza – is best washed down with sour *ayran* yoghurt.

Tutto Bene Cheongdamdong ⓣ02/546-1489. Connected by walkway to *Palais de Gaumont*, and under the same ownership, this serves Italian dishes and is slightly cheaper than its neighbour. The setting is utterly gorgeous, its Orient Express-like wooden panelling offset by amber and honey-yellow lighting, and the scent of freshly cut flowers mingling with the creations of the chef. Pasta dishes are most popullar (from W25,000), but don't overlook the seafood menu – sourced from remote islands off Korea's west coast, the oysters are superb.

Apgujeong

The following places are marked on the "Southern Seoul" **map**, p.98, and just about within walking distance (or a W3000 taxi ride) of Apgujeong subway station.

Ciné de Chef Sinsadong ⓣ02/3446-0541. Immaculate Italian restaurant in the bowels of the CGV cinema complex. The place is only really for couples, since dinner sets (from W70,000 per head, and usually including soup, a steak or pasta dish and dessert) include tickets to a private movie theatre, featuring just thirty comfy chairs laid out in couple formation; here you can watch the latest Hollywood blockbuster over a bottle of wine.

Gorilla in the Kitchen Sinsadong ⓣ02/3442-1688. Glass and chrome interior, all-white furniture and surgical-uniformed waitresses – this place has an air of arty European about it, but the calorie listings will serve as a reminder that you are, indeed, in waistline-conscious Apgujeong. The food is innovative and delicious, with temptations including turkey steak with berry sauce, rice-covered tofu salad in sesame dressing, and peppered chicken breast on black rice, but prices aren't extortionate, and lunch sets go for as low as W27,000.

Jung Sikdang 정식당 Sinsadong ⓣ02/517-4654, ⓦwww.jungsikdang.com. Another purveyor of neo-Korean cuisine, this restaurant had to relocate in 2009 due to an escalation in popularity. Korean ingredients are prepared with French techniques and a few non-native herbs and veggies, and the result is rather mouthwatering: the prawn salad is recommended, served with melon balls on wafer-thin lime jelly. Figure on at least W60,000 per head for a meal. Noon–4pm & 6pm–late; Sun lunch only.

Seventy Four Cheongdamdong ⓣ02/542-7412. As well as being one of Seoul's best cocktail bars, this rambling venue serves up excellent brunches and light meals (from W20,000). Come early to grab a window seat, and watch bag-laden shoppers trooping up and down one of the most fashionable streets in the country.

Sushi Chohi Sinsadong ⓣ02/545-8422. Sushi fans will be in their element at this pine-lined restaurant, overlooking Dosan Park. Absolutely no concessions are made regarding the fish or its preparation: the blades and chopping boards cost upwards of $1000 each, while each fish is selected from the best possible place, whether it be southwestern Korea or northern Japan. The head chef speaks English, and if you're seated at the main bar he will be happy to discourse on the merits of each creature as he performs his magic upon them. Sets from W50,000.

Wooriga 우리가 Sinsadong ⓣ02/3442-2288. Some meals are presented so beautifully that it seems a sin to destroy them, and that's certainly the case at this sparsely decorated neo-Korean hideaway. Whether you're here for lunch (sets from W40,000) or dinner (from W100,000), each dish is served as a work of art, and even the sweets and *omija* tea (see p.46) to finish provide gentle flavour explosions. Superb. Reservations only.

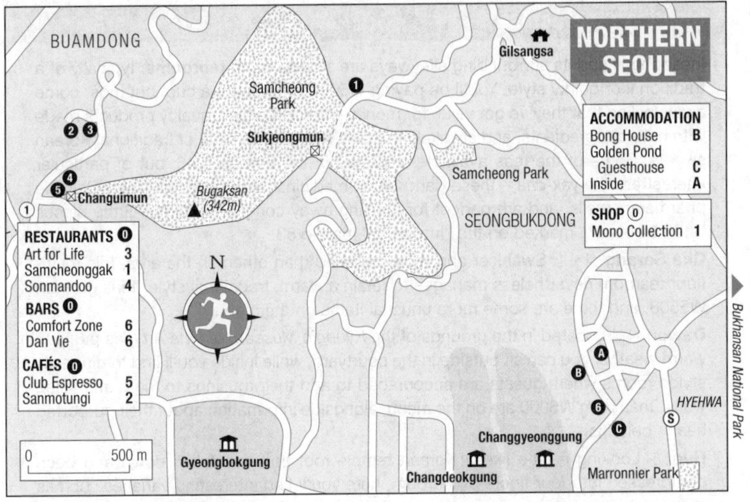

Northern Seoul

The following places are marked on the "Northern Seoul" **map**, p.111. None is particularly close to a subway station; see p.72 and p.123 for travel information.

Art for Life Buamdong ⓣ02/3217-9364. The hustle and bustle of Seoul feels very far away at this artsy, out-of-the-way lair. Authentic pizza and pasta meals start at W20,000 and Saturday evenings feature live jazz from some of Seoul's top musicians.

Samcheonggak 삼청각 Seongbukdong ⓣ02/765-3700. This mountainside venue was once a *gisaeng* house of some repute, and used by luminaries such as president Park Chung-hee as a secluded place of pleasure. It has since been converted into a traditionally styled restaurant serving a take on Korean royal cuisine, and still hosts occasional shows of traditional song and dance. Set meals W50,000–150,000.

Sonmandoo 손만두 Buamdong ⓣ02/379-2648. Dumplings known as *mandu* are a cheap Korean staple, but unlike the regular processed fare, the handmade versions made here are utterly delectable, filled with chunks of quality beef, radish, shiitake mushrooms and the like. The setting is just as pleasant, a minimalist space with mountain views. Dishes from W10,000.

Cafés and tearooms

There are a number of major café chains knocking around, including *Pascucci*, *Starbucks* and *The Coffee Bean & Tea Leaf*. In theory, all have **wi-fi access**, but you may need a Korean ID number to get online; with no such identity restrictions and power sockets aplenty, branches of *Tom & Toms* are best for the internet-hungry and open 24hr, though the coffee itself is poor. Far more interesting for the visitor are the thousands of privately run ventures, which reach heights of quirky individuality around **Hongdae** and **Samcheongdong**. Prices tend to be W3000–5000 per cup, though you can usually double this south of the river. There are also a number of cafés on the bridges crossing the **Hangang** itself; see p.100 for more information. Opening hours for cafés are generally 9am to 11pm.

The degree to which coffee has replaced tea, the former national drink, is somewhat surprising, but there are a number of wonderful **tearooms** on and around Insadonggil; see the box on p.112 for more details.

Insadong tearooms

Insadonggil and its surrounding alleyways are studded with **tearooms**, typically of a traditional or quirky style. You'll be paying W5000 or more for a cup, but most come away feeling that they've got value for money – these are high-quality products made with natural ingredients, and are likely to come with a small plate of traditional Korean sweets. Some of the teas available are listed in the box on p.46, but of particular interest are the *yak-cha* – these dark, bitter, medicinal teas taste just like a Chinese pharmacy smells, and are perfect for chasing away coughs or colds. All the places listed below are marked on the "Insadong" map, p.83.

Cha Sarang 차사랑 Swankier and more polished than others in the area, this multi-floor tearoom nevertheless manages to retain a warm, traditional style. Teas go from W5500, and there are some more unusual items on the menu.

Dawon 다원 Located in the grounds of the *Kyungin Museum of Fine Art* (see p.84). In warm weather you can sit outside in the courtyard, while inside you'll find traditionally styled rooms where guests are encouraged to add their musings to the graffiti-filled walls. Teas from W6000 are on the menu, alongside information about their purported health benefits.

Hue 휴 Looking a little like a Korean temple roof that has fallen down and been compressed into four floors of tearoom, here you'll find interesting varieties such as medicinal herb and pomegranate, as well as a number of fruit juices and shakes. There's a great view from the fifth-floor terrace.

Sarangbang 사랑방 On the second floor of an unassuming building west of Insadonggil, this small tearoom is run by a Korean man and his Japanese wife, a friendly pair who are full of local information and money-saving tips.

Su Yo Il 수요일 Built in a similar style to *Cha Sarang* across the road, though here the opportunity to see and be seen on the balconies overlooking Insadonggil push prices a little higher. Also on offer are Earl Grey, Darjeeling and other teas that may be more familiar to Westerners.

Yetchatjip 옛찻집 Though a little hard to find, this small upstairs tearoom is quite simply one of the most pleasurable places in Seoul. The comfy, soft-lit setting is agreeable enough, but add to this a team of amiable finches who happily chirp their way from wall to wall, occasionally stopping by to tilt a curious head at the guests. The tea's not bad, either.

Insadong

The following places are marked on the "Insadong" **map**, p.83, and are both accessible from Anguk station.

Bizeun 비즌 Insadong. Waffles and ice cream are the regular snacks in Korean cafés, but here you'll be able to chow down on something more traditional: sweet rice-cakes, known as *ddeok*, which come in a wonderful kaleidoscope of colours, with flavours running the gamut from pumpkin to black sesame.

Millimeter Milligram Angukdong. Also known as *MMMG*, Millimeter Milligram are a local design team producing arty stationery, postcards and other such items. This is the best place to buy their products – even the cup your coffee's served in will be available for sale.

The business district

The following place is marked on the "Business district" **map**, p.90, and is accessible from Euljiro 1-ga subway station.

O'Sulloc Myeongdong ⓣ02/774-5460. *O'Sulloc* is Korea's largest producer of green tea, but don't let that fool you into thinking that people come to their flagship tearoom to drink the stuff. Instead, this is a café and dessert bar *par excellence*, with the precious leaves blended into tiramisu, ice cream, lattes and chocolates (all W5000 or so). There's another branch on Insadonggil.

Hongdae

The following places are marked on the "Hongdae" **map**, p.95, and accessible from Sangsu subway station.

Bau House Seogyodong. Koreans are more famed abroad for eating dogs than owning them, but this café should show where the balance lies these days. Over a dozen cuddly pooches are on hand to greet customers, who are encouraged to bring their own dogs along. The coffee's good too, but in such a bizarre atmosphere you may barely notice the taste.

Cafe aA Seogyodong. Several things set this place apart from the regular Korean café. For a start, there's the huge, church-like front door, and a ceiling at least three times higher than the national average. Most notable, however, is a range of chairs imported from Europe; the upstairs floor functions as a sort of furniture museum, featuring examples from luminaries such as Jean Prouvé and Salvador Dalí. Art aside, the coffee is excellent, as are the cakes.

Southern Seoul

The following places are marked on the "Southern Seoul" **map**, p.98, and, apart from *W.e*, are accessible from Samseong subway station.

Kring Daechidong. This superbly designed artistic complex features a space-age café, where there's a pay-what-you-like policy for the uniformly excellent coffees.

The Lounge Daechidong. Sitting atop the *Park Hyatt* (p.78) alongside the infinity pool, this is a superb place for a coffee or light snack. Better still are a range of smoothies designed by David Beckham's nutritionist, Patricia Teixeira: well worth the W15,000 splurge.

W.e. Off Garosugil; Sinsa station. At last, a place willing to shun the American café norms and inject a rare bit of Korean culture. Here you can take your pick of quirky lattes such as ginseng, sweet pumpkin or green tea; those who fancy a little something extra can go for black sesame pudding, or delicious pancakes known as *hoddeok*, filled with cinnamon and burnt brown sugar, and served with Haagen-Dazs ice cream.

Apgujeong

The following places are marked on the "Southern Seoul" **map**, p.98, and are all accessible from Apgujeong subway station.

Ceci Cela Sinsadong. An Apgujeong institution, this is always full of young, fashionable females somehow keeping their waistlines intact while chowing down on waffles, panini or slabs of cheesecake. Coffees and vitamin juices are also available, as are thick milkshakes.

Hermès Sinsadong. The Hermès flagship store has a café discreetly tucked away on the basement level, and W10,000 will be enough to get you coffee. All cutlery, cups and glasses – plus the tables and chairs – are Hermès originals, and a fair proportion of the customers are local celebs. There's no cheaper way to buy your way into high society, but dress smartly.

Rosen Kavalier Sinsadong. Decked out like a 1930s Viennese café, right down to the waiter's starched shirt and the delicious cakes, *Rosen's* refined atmosphere is further enhanced by the melodies humming across from the classical music shop next door.

Northern Seoul

The following places are marked on the "Northern Seoul" **map**, p.111.

Club Espresso Buamdong. If you're living in Seoul, this is where to buy your beans. The range of single-plantation java is huge and truly global, from Zambian Munama Ndola to Brazilian Santo Antonio, and the pine interior is a pleasant place to compare and contrast a few samples.

Sanmotungi 산모퉁이 Buamdong. Made famous by its use as a set in Korean drama *The Coffee Prince*, this remote coffee house is worth a visit for the fresh air and mountain views from its upper level.

Nightlife and entertainment

Koreans love going out, whether it's with family, colleagues, social acquaintances or old study friends, making Seoul a truly 24-hour city – day and night, it simply hums with life. Those wanting to drink or dance can choose from myriad **bars** and **clubs**, with each area of Seoul having its own particular flavour. The city also has a thriving **theatre** scene that's surprisingly accessible to foreign visitors.

Bars and clubs

Clubs pumping out techno, trance and hip-hop to wiggling masses; loungey subterranean lairs filled with hookah smoke and philosophical conversation; noisy

A real Korean night out

The "proper" Korean night out has long followed the same format, one that entwines food, drink and entertainment. The venue for stage one (*il-cha*) is the **restaurant**, where a **meal** is chased down with copious shots of *soju*. This is followed by stage two (*i-cha*), a visit to a **bar**; here beers are followed with snacks (usually large dishes intended for groups). Those still able to walk then continue to stage three (*sam-cha*), the **entertainment** component of the night, which usually involves a trip to a *noraebang* room for a sing-along (see p.96), and yet more drinks. Stages four, five and beyond certainly exist, but few participants have ever remembered them clearly.

joints serving up live jazz and rock; neon-tinged cocktail bars in the bowels of five-star hotels. After a lengthy gestation, Seoul's nightlife scene is finally wide open, and the drinkers themselves are becoming ever more liberal. It wasn't so long ago that drinking in Seoul was pretty much a male-only affair, taking place in restaurants or at a **"hof"**, the ubiquitous faux-Western bars that are still winning the battle for street-space, but are increasingly being looked over in favour of more genuinely Western ideas imported from overseas. That said, there are some more local elements that can be factored into a night out: Korean friends are likely to drag you before long into a **noraebang** singing room to belt out your favourite songs amid a cacophony of castanets, while couples can end the night cuddled up at a DVD room (see p.96). Summer sees most of the city's convenience stores surround themselves with plastic tables and chairs; a cheap and popular way to start a night out.

Most of the action is concentrated into just a few areas. Of these, **Hongdae** is by far the busiest, its streets lined with bars, clubs and restaurants, and full every day of the week from early evening on. Towards midnight the crowds are swelled further by Seoul's clubbers, who get on the last subway services of the day to Hongdae, party all night, then slink off home at dawn. Almost as busy at the weekend is **Itaewon**, which has some of the best bars, clubs and restaurants in the capital. Its traditional popularity with American soldiers from the nearby base (though a mass military pull-out has long been mooted) has resulted in a mass of "sexy bars" (expensive venues where the bar-girls wear bikinis, hot-pants and the like, and the customers pay for their company) and brothels, many lining "Hooker Hill". The side street leading from this ("Homo Hill") has become the most popular **gay** area in the whole country, with some excellent bars. Also worth mentioning are **Sinchon**, one subway station from Hongdae and full of bars; studenty **Daehangno**, which is busy every evening (though most flee the area for home or Hongdae as midnight approaches); as well as a few relaxing places to wine and dine in **Samcheongdong**. South of the river, **Gangnam** has a couple of good bars (though is mainly an eating area), as does nearby **Apgujeong**.

For a rundown of the best **local tipples**, see p.45.

The palace district

The bar below is marked on the "Palace district" **map**, p.79.

Dugahun 두가헌 Sagandong; Anguk station. A charmingly characteristic venue to fall into for a glass of wine, set as it is in a revamped *hanok* building. Their selection runs the gamut from under W70,000 to well over W1,000,000 per bottle, augmented by fine European cuisine from the kitchens. Some of the views disappoint, so choose your table carefully.

Insadong

The following places are marked on the "Insadong" **map**, p.83.

Baekseju Maeul 백세주마을 Jongno; Jonggak station. This bar-restaurant prides itself on *baekseju* (see p.45), and serves local food to go with it. It's owned by Guksundang, Korea's biggest producer of alcoholic drinks, and the creator of all the *baekseju* you'll see in the convenience stores – here they serve a "draught" (ie, recently made) version of the drink, which tastes that much better.

Story of the Blue Star 푸른별주막 Insadong; Anguk station. Though technically a restaurant serving earthy food from rural Gangwon province, this *hanok* venue really comes alive in the evening, serving a variety of superb *makkeolli*: the rice wine is flavoured with ingredients such as green tea, pine needles and mugwort. You'll need to order at least one dish.

The business district

The following places are marked on the "Business district" **map**, p.90.

Naos Nova Huamdong; Seoul station. Seoul is slowly learning the ropes of the wine world, but this achingly cool bar-restaurant has already summited Grape Mountain. No fewer than three hundred varieties of wine can be imbibed here, all selected by a sommelier burdened by several international prizes. Good wine needs good food to go with it, and the menu here is largely Italian, with a few local elements sneaking in.

Pierre's Bar Jongno; Euljiro 1-ga station. Adjoining the superb *Pierre Gagnaire* restaurant (see p.108) at the top of the *Lotte Hotel*, this stylish bar is a firm favourite with international businessmen. Despite the modern, opulent surroundings, and the sky-high food prices next door, drinks are surprisingly cheap – W15,000 or so for a cocktail, and less than that for a glass of beer.

Itaewon

The following places are marked on the "Itaewon" **map**, p.94, and are within walking distance of Itaewon subway station.

B1 Underground club with a decent sound system, and usually DJs that know how to make the most of it. With lounge areas and snazzy decor, it's far classier than most dance venues in the area – at the beginning of the night, at least.

Bungalow Bar There are drinking options aplenty in this loungey, multilevel bar – sup sangria on the swing-seats, drink martinis in the sand pit, have a romantic glass of wine on a candlelit table or kick back with a beer on the outdoor terrace. The cocktails, however, are best avoided.

Function Taking up the rear of *Macaroni Market* restaurant (p.109), this is the most upscale drinking venue in Itaewon: no soldiers or microskirt-wearing teens, but plenty of sharply dressed young locals. Try one of the house cocktails.

Gecko's Terrace Unlike most Itaewon bars, *Gecko's* is busy every night. A lively mix of Koreans and foreigners, it's popular with people who don't feel like dancing, or those filling up on cheap beer before a night on the tiles – local draught beer is just W2500, and pints of Guinness reasonable for Korea at W8000.

Hollywood Bar and Grill An American-style bar that shows Premier League football, Major League baseball or any other sport coverage in demand from Seoul's expats. At quieter times, it's a pleasant place for a game of pool or darts, while during major sporting events you'll be lucky to find standing room.

Spy Bar Located on the basement level of a building that also houses the *Nashville Sports Bar*, this sometimes-house-sometimes-trance club heaves at the weekend under the weight of a sexy, youthful crowd. American soldiers, expat teachers, scantily clad Korean girls and aspiring Eastern European models – a truer microcosm of Itaewon society would be hard to find. Fri & Sat entry W10,000.

Hongdae

The following places are marked on the "Hongdae" **map**, p.95, within staggering distance of two subway stations: Sangsu (exit one) or Hongdae (exit five).

BricXX This candlelit underground lair is a popular place to take a date, with reasonably priced cocktails and excellent food – try the falafel. The seating areas are draped with curtains; try to get there in time to nab a seat in the ultra-chilled area lined with oriental silk pillows.

Chin Chin 친친 What the country has been begging for for years: an upscale *makkeolli* bar. There are now a few of them around, but this remains the best, serving rice wine varieties from across the land in funky vases and goblets. The food's also pretty good, and despite being so close to the university, few of the customers are students.

Club Tool Some of the best electronica DJs in town descend on this extremely stylish dance club, though the size of the floor, coupled with the occasional frostiness of the door staff, means that it can feel rather empty at times: a place to go with a group rather than on your own. W20,000.

FF Both Fs stand for "funky", though you're more likely to see some good ol' rock at this highly popular live music venue. A great many of the bands are foreign, bringing their pals and staying on for the DJ sets afterwards, so it's a great place to make new friends. Entry is around

W11,000 while the bands are on, and free for the DJ sets.

Flower 꽃 There's no sign outside, so you'll have to put your ear to the door to see if anything's going on. Weekends, however, see the small floor crammed with music fans, here to see the owner – Seoul's funkiest *ajumma* – and friends performing live reggae.

M2 The area's top nightclub, and accordingly packed to the gills on weekends, *M2* manages to rope in the occasional top international DJ to spin some house. On weekends, you may be spending upwards of an hour waiting in line to get in. Entry W15,000, Fri & Sat W25,000.

Nabi 나비 This pleasing underground bar has finally brought the word "bohemian" to Hongdae's nightlife. Marked only by a small sign on the outside, it may feel as if you've entered another world once you're through the door – candles float on a small pond, arty folk sit on cushions passing the hookah around, and nobody feels as if they're in Seoul any more. Despite the secluded location, the secret is out, and it can get very crowded at weekends – if there's no floorspace, you'll just have to wait.

Oi Trendy, out-of-the-way bar whose cave-like multilevel drinking areas make it look like a set from the *Smurfs*. Mood lighting creates a discerning atmosphere rare in this student area.

Samgeori Pocha 삼거리포차 Though it's technically a restaurant (see p.109), this is an integral part of Hongdae's nightlife – after a dance or a drink, Koreans love to eat (and drink a little more), so you may well find yourself dragged along to this rustic-looking place, where raw fish and steaming broths are on the menu, and tables are littered with empty *soju* bottles.

Shain Independent music is hard to track down in Korea, particularly if it's local stuff you're after. However, this bar plays nothing but Korean indie, and is run by the lead singer of *Huckleberry Finn*, one of the country's first such bands. A fair number of the customers here are members of other ensembles, and rarely for a Seoul bar, *makkeolli* is available by the glass.

Tinpan A meat market, yes, but Hongdae's best. It's W10,000 on weekends to get into either of the two *Tinpans* that face each other across a night-club-filled road; drinks are cheap and the floors are packed with a largely young crowd dancing to generic hip-hop.

Vinyl Get takeaway cocktails from the window of this small bar, where you can get Pina Coladas and Sex on the Beach in what appear,

Gay and lesbian Seoul

Seoul's burgeoning **queer nightlife** scene has come on in leaps and bounds since 2000, when star actor **Hong Seok-cheon** came out of the closet – the first Korean celebrity to do so. He has since opened up a whole raft of gay-friendly bars and restaurants in **Itaewon**, which remains the best gay area for foreigners; the best are listed below and marked on the "Itaewon" map, p.94.

Seoul does have other **gay zones**; the area around Jongno 3-ga station has long been home to underground gay bars, and recent years have seen the scene becoming more and more open. Unfortunately, few venues are foreigner-friendly, though the *Starmoon* café attracts all sorts – it's in the ground floor of the tall *Fraser Suites* building (see the "Insadong" map, p.83). Additionally, the university district of **Sinchon** is popular with the local **lesbian** community, many of whom congregate of an evening in "Triangle Park", a patch of concrete near exit 1 of Sinchon subway station (take the first right).

Always Homme Homo Hill institution with charismatic bar staff and excellent drinks. Shares much of its clientele with *Queen*, just down the road.

My Bed Loungey bar run by Hong Seok-cheon, Korea's first openly gay celebrity (see above). Hong has created something of a pink industry in Itaewon, with half-a-dozen establishments to his name. You'll often find him upstairs from *My Bed* at *My Thai*, a restaurant entirely staffed with, as Hong puts it, "handsome young men".

Queen The most popular gay bar on Homo Hill, with inviting staff and comfortable chairs. On warm weekend nights, even these can't stop the crowd spilling out onto the street for a dance.

Trance A thriving transgender bar on the main Itaewon drag, hosting regular strip nights that most foreign visitors find hugely entertaining, whatever their sexual orientation.

at first glance, to be colostomy bags. Such ingenuity brings the price down – W4000 for a cocktail, or just W2000 for a slightly larger bag of beer.

Southern Seoul and Apgujeong

The following places are marked on the "Southern Seoul" **map**, p.98.

Club Eden Yeoksamdong ⓦwww.eden-club.co.kr. Sinnonhyeon station. Gangnam über-club that has, for years, been *the* place to see and be seen, having transcended the boundaries of generic house and hip-hop by roping in a slew of top DJs. Entry is usually W30,000, and you'll have to be dressed up. It's in the basement of the *Ritz-Carlton*.

Club Heaven Yeoksamdong. Yeoksam station. A slightly less salubrious (and, some would say, less stuck-up) version of *Club Eden*, but also regularly finds itself host to top-notch DJs. Entry usually W25,000 and up.

Lound Cheongdamdong; Apgujeong station. Under the same ownership as *Seventy Four* down the road (see p.110), this bar serves pricey cocktails (W20,000) that are regularly voted "best in Seoul" by the bloggers and magazine writers who get to cast such judgement. The ground level is for drinking and dining; heading upstairs will get you into a club-like space with cool iPhone drink menus, which enable you to place orders electronically.

Platoon/Kunsthalle Nonhyeondong; Apgujeong station. This quirky "creativity space" – part gallery, part exhibition hall, part design lab – is also an atmospheric spot to have a drink. They have a small range of international beers and wines, and good German food; if you visit on an event night you're likely to get one or two drinks for free.

Northern Seoul

Apart from the *Woo Bar*, the places listed below are marked on the "Northern Seoul" **map**, p.111.

Comfort Zone Daehangno; Hyehwa station. The best bar in the area by a country mile. Here you'll be able to chill out over cocktails in the curtain-filled upstairs lounge, pop downstairs for a beer and a game of darts, or have a quiet chat on the outdoor veranda. Turn left out of exit four of Hyewha subway and walk along the road until you come to *Burger King*; it's down the alley to the left.

Dan Vie Daehangno; Hyehwa station. Tucked into a basement next door to *Comfort Zone*, this bar has a curious mix of decorative styles – some areas are cordoned off with dangling beads or shower curtains, others have space-station-style swivel chairs, and movies are projected onto the far wall.

Woo Bar Gwanjangdong; Gwangnaru station; see "Seoul" map, pp.66–67. In the lobby of the futuristic *W* hotel, this is almost a rite of passage for young Seoulites with cash to flash. Simply breathing ultra-trendiness, it's not for everyone, but if egg-shaped chairs, UV-lit sofas and space-helmet-like DJ booths appeal, this is the place to head. Drinks are expensive, but the staff are way too cool to make a fuss about anyone who nurses one beer all night.

Cinema

Korean **cinema** has become the subject of growing worldwide attention and acclaim, but because almost no films are screened with English-language subtitles, it's probably best to hunt them down in your home country.

Wherever you find yourself in Seoul, you won't be too far from the nearest **cinema**. CVG and Megabox are the two major cinema chains; foreign films are shown in their original language with Korean subtitles. There are also a few **arthouse** establishments catering to foreigners; in all cases, tickets cost between W5000 and W 10,000. Note that it's also possible to watch movies in a **DVD-*bang*** – see p.96 for details.

Cinematheque Jongno 3-ga station; see "Insadong" map, p.83. Also going under the names of "Hollywood" and "Seoul Art Cinema", this sits on top of the Nakwon Arcade east of Insadonggil, and has a rolling calendar of themed events, some of which are based around foreign films.

Mirospace Sinmunno 2-ga; Gwanghwamun station; see "Business district" map, p.90. Interesting hundred-seat venue showing arty films, usually from abroad. For once, there's no popcorn on offer, and after the movie you can glide into the sleek adjoining bar.

Sangsangmadang Sangsu station; see "Hongdae" map, p.95. The basement of this arts complex (see p.122) has some arty English-language screenings, of which around half are from abroad. Interestingly, they try to show films whose themes match what's on show in the second-floor gallery. Tickets W7000.

Theatre and performance arts

Seoul's wide array of **traditional performances** and musicals are particularly popular with foreign travellers.

Battle B-Boy B-Boy Theater, Hongdae ⓦsjbboys.com; Hongdae station. See "Hongdae" map, p.95. B-Boy breakdancing is still enthralling the nation, and this long-running play tells the story of a dance romance with some pretty incredible routines. Sat 2pm & 6pm, Sun 2pm, Wed–Fri 8pm; W50,000.

Chongdong Theatre Near City Hall, on a quiet road near the western wall of Deoksugung ⓦwww.chongdong.com; City Hall station. See "Business district" map, p.90. The 80min traditional song and dance shows here are extremely popular. Performances (Tues–Sun; April–Sept 8pm; Oct–March 4pm; from W20,000) are in Korean, with English subtitles next to the stage. Also on offer are classes in the *janggu*, a Korean drum.

Jump Cinecore Theater ⓦwww.hijump.co.kr; Jongno 3-ga station. See "Palace district" map, p.79. Ever wondered what a family entirely made up of martial arts experts would be like? Experience all of the inevitable jumps and kicks in this musical. Tues–Sat 4pm & 8pm, Sun 3pm & 6pm; W40,000.

Korea House Chungmuro ⓦwww.koreahouse.or.kr; Chungmuro station. See "Business district" map, p.90. Highly polished traditional performances from some of the country's top artists, combined with some of Seoul's best food (see p.108): this is one of the city's most popular nights out. Wonderful shows include fan dances, *pansori* opera and the "farmers' dance". Take exit three from the subway station and walk up the side street. Performances daily 7pm & 8.50pm; W50,000.

Namsan Gugakdang Chungmuro; Chungmuro station. See "Business district" map, p.90. Anyone looking for a traditional Korean performance should make this their first stop. Part of the Namsangol complex (see p.93), its shows revolve around

Seoul festivals

As long as you're not in Seoul during the long, cold winter, you'll almost certainly be able to catch a **festival** of some kind. In addition to national festivals (see p.47) and the traditional parades and street performances taking place on Insadonggil (usually every Thursday, Friday and Saturday), there are a whole host of events. A selection is detailed below.

APRIL

International Women's Film Festival ⓦwffis.or.kr. A week-long succession of films that "see the world through women's eyes" (even if they were created by men).

MAY

Hi Seoul Festival ⓦhiseoulfest.org. With everything from choreographed firework displays and tea ceremonies to men walking across the Han River by tightrope, this ten-day-long celebration of the coming of summer also incorporates the Seoul World DJ festival. There's simply no better time to be in the city.

Jongmyo Daeje First Sun of the month. Korean kings performed their ancestral rites at the Jongmyo shrine for hundreds of years, a tradition that's been carried forward to this day; the event is necessarily sober but very interesting, and is followed by traditional court dances.

Seoul International Cartoon & Animation Festival Late May; ⓦwww.sicaf.or.kr. Koreans young and old are major cartoon addicts, but while most of the national fix is sated by Japanese fare, there's still a lot of local talent – *The Simpsons*, *Family Guy* and *Spongebob Squarepants* are among the shows inked and lined here. Screenings take place in several locations.

JUNE

Korean Queer Culture Festival ⓦwww.kqcf.org. Not exactly an event trumpeted by the local tourist authorities – in fact, not so long ago the police were still trying to ban *gugak*, an ancient style of Korean music, plus regular thematic events of song, music, dance or all three. Ticket prices vary but are usually around W30,000.

Nanta Nanta Theatre ⓦ www.nanta.co.kr; City Hall station. See "Business district" map, p.90. This madcap kitchen-based musical has gone down a storm since opening in 1997 (it's Korea's longest running show), with songs, circus tricks and all sorts of utensil drumming mixed with a nice line in audience participation. Performances Mon–Sat 4pm & 8pm, Sun 3pm & 6pm; W40,000.

Live music

Seoul has a few venues where you can hear more highbrow offerings such as **jazz** or **classical music**. In addition, a few of the Hongdae bars and clubs feature **live rock** and similar music; see pp.115–117 for details.

All That Jazz Itaewon ⓦ www.allthatjazz.kr; Itaewon station. See "Itaewon" map, p.94. An Itaewon institution, with an atmosphere that's fun, rather than stuffy, and frequent audience interaction – some spectators have ended up playing on stage with the band. Performances 7pm Sat & Sun, 8.30pm Mon–Fri; tickets usually W5000.

Once in a Blue Moon Sinsadong; Apgujeong station. See "Southern Seoul" map, p.98. Perhaps the most renowned of Seoul's many jazz bars, and certainly the closest approximation to a Western venue. The music runs the gamut of styles, played while customers dine on French or Mexican cuisine, and there are lengthy wine and cocktail lists. Performances 7.30pm; admission free.

Sejong Centre Gwanghwamun ⓦ www.sejongpac.or.kr; Gwanghwamun station. See "Palace district" map, p.79. Gigantic venue offering a truly diverse array of music: everything from traditional Korean *gugak* to concertos from world-famous pianists. There'll be something going on every night of the week; check the website for details.

it – this is a great way to see Korea crawling out of its Confucian shell. A fortnight-long programme includes a film festival, art exhibitions and the obligatory street parade.

JULY

Jisan Valley and Pentaport Rock Festivals ⓦ www.valleyrockfestival.com & ⓦ pentaportrock.com. Two competing European-style music festivals (think tents, mud and portaloos) which manage to rope in major international acts, though admittedly ones usually on the wane in their homelands. Both events stretch across three alcohol-fuelled nights, the revelry running non-stop.

AUGUST

Seoul Fringe Festival ⓦ www.seoulfringefestival.net. This fortnight-long platform for all things alternative is very popular with local students, and its semi-international nature means it appeals to overseas visitors too. Hongdae is usually the best place to be.

SEPTEMBER

Seoul Performing Arts Festival Late Sept/early Oct; ⓦ www.spaf.or.kr. This increasingly acclaimed event has seen performances from as far afield as Latvia and Israel, though its main aim is to showcase Korean talent. It takes place in various locations around Seoul over a three-week period.

OCTOBER

Seoul Drum Festival Early Oct; ⓦ www.drumfestival.org. The crashes and bangs of all things percussive ring out at this annual event, which takes place in the Gwanghwamun area.

Seoul Fashion Week ⓦ www.seoulfashionweek.org. Since it started in 2000, this has become Asia's largest fashion event, functioning as a great showcase for Seoul's up-and-coming designers.

Seoul Arts Centre Near Nambu bus terminal ⓦwww.sac.or.kr; Nambu Bus Terminal station. See "Southern Seoul" map, p.98. The home of Korea's national ballet and opera companies, as well as the symphony orchestra, there's always something interesting going on at this rambling complex.

Sports and activities

Seoul has a small but pleasing range of ways to keep sport nuts entertained, as well as simple exercise equipment on almost every mountainside, as well as in parks, and dotting the banks of the Hangang and other waterways.

Baseball

Seoul has two main professional teams: **LG Twins** and the **Doosan Bears**, long-time rivals who both play in Jamsil Baseball Stadium – take subway line 2 to Sports Complex station, exit five or six. Games take place most days from April to October, and tickets can cost as little as W3000. Avid players can get some practice at a number of **batting cages** dotted around the city, particularly in student areas; these cost just W1000 for a minute's worth of balls. One is marked on the "Insadong" map, p.83.

Football

If you want to watch some **K-League** action, catch FC Seoul at the World Cup Stadium (ⓦwww.fcseoul.com; weekends March–Oct; tickets from W10,000); every now and then foreigners can buy special tickets that include a free beer. Seongnam and Suwon, the two most dominant Korean teams, also play near Seoul; the atmosphere at all grounds is fun but they can be on the empty side, unless you're lucky enough to be around for a major international game (ⓦwww.fifa.com). Those who prefer to play rather than watch can try their luck with the highly competitive **foreigners' football league** (ⓦssflkorea.com); this has been in operation for a number of years, and most of the competing teams are based in Seoul, though as the standard is quite high you'll have to be a decent player to get a regular game.

Ice-skating

In winter you can **skate** outdoors at various points in the city: Seoul Plaza (see p.75) and Gwanghwamun Plaza (p.81) turn into a gigantic ice-rinks for the season (usually mid-Dec to Feb; 10am–10pm; W1000), though skaters are turfed off every fifteen minutes or so for surfacing. The ticket prices includes skate and helmet rental. There's also a year-round rink in Lotte World (p.101), which charges W13,000 for entry and skate rental (10am–9.30pm); far cheaper is the Olympic-size rink at Korea National University (2–6pm; W5000); it's within walking distance of Korea University subway station.

Swimming

Unless you're staying at a higher-end hotel or serviced apartment, you may find it tricky to get a swim in Seoul. There are **municipal pools** in most parts of the city; enquire at a tourist office (p.70) for your nearest option. In summer, a number of **outdoor pools** open up around the Hangang; most convenient are those on Yeouido; see p.100.

Taekwondo

There are a number of ways in which foreign visitors can have a go at the Korean martial art of **taekwondo**. **Training sessions** have in the past taken place at

Korean cuisine

For many visitors, Korea's food is one of the highlights of a trip. The country's distinctive cuisine gets surprisingly little coverage internationally, and each mealtime can feel like a voyage of discovery. Korean food was uniformly mild until the seventeenth century, when chillies arrived on the ships of Western traders. Nowadays, if you don't like, or have little experience of, spicy food, be warned that there's very little respite from it – most meals come with lashings of red-pepper paste (*gochujang*), and some take the heat to eye-watering extremes.

Dakgalbi – chicken *galbi* – in Chuncheon ▲

Galbi ▼

Galbi

Galbi is a carnivore's dream come true. Here, you get to play chef with a plate of raw meat commonly placed on a grill over **charcoal**, and a pair of scissors to slice it all up. As excess fat drips off the meat onto the briquettes it releases the occasional tongue of flame, which lends a genuine air of excitement to the meal.

In dedicated *galbi* restaurants the dish is usually eaten sitting on the floor, but many cheaper places have outdoor tables, and on warmer weekends Koreans even drag their own mini barbecue to a park or riverbank for an alfresco picnic. In all cases, it's traditionally washed down with a bottle or three of *soju* – Korea's answer to vodka.

Most restaurants serve **beef** (*so-galbi*), but some places offer pork too (*dwaeji-galbi*, or *samgyeopsal* for fattier belly roll), and always with a range of free **side dishes**, known as *banchan*. Ranging from three to well over twenty, these include the obligatory *gimchi*, as well as bowls of pulses, tofu, leek, potato and tiny fish, all lovingly prepared and replenished at no extra cost. A boiling bowl of egg broth and a tray of leaves are also usually thrown in for the group to share – *galbi* is not a meal to eat on your own – and each person is given a bowl of chopped-up greens and a pot of sesame oil.

In Confucian Korea, it's common for the "lowest" adult member of the party – usually the youngest female – to cook and dish out the meat. To eat it, first place a leaf or two from the tray onto your left hand, then with your chopsticks add a piece of meat, a smudge of soybean paste and a few morsels from the *banchan*; roll the leaf around to make a ball, and you're ready to go.

Gimchi

No country on earth is as closely entwined with its national dish as Korea is with its beloved **gimchi**: a spicy mix of fermented vegetables, which is served as a complimentary **side dish** at pretty much every restaurant in the land. Many traditionally minded families still ferment their own *gimchi* in distinctive earthenware jars, but home-made or not it's an important part of breakfast, lunch and dinner in most Korean homes. Lots of people even have a dedicated *gimchi* fridge, quartered off to separate the four main types. The two most common varieties are **baechu gimchi**, made with cabbage, and **ggakdugi gimchi**, which are cubes of radish in a red-pepper sauce, but there are others made with cucumber or other vegetables.

Although generally spicy in nature, bland types of *gimchi* certainly exist – some have no more kick than a mild vinaigrette. However, salt, garlic and a hearty dollop of **red-pepper paste** are almost mandatory in a good *gimchi*, though additional ingredients vary from home to home and restaurant to restaurant. Many of the best recipes are shrouded in secrecy and handed down through the generations, but some of the most popular components include onion, brine, ginger and fish paste. Needless to say, the effect on the breath can be dramatic, to say the least.

Fermented *gimchi* was once used as a means of maintaining vegetable intake through Korea's long, bitter winters, but even today the health benefits are proclaimed proudly by Koreans. Foreigners often have a tough time adjusting, but love it or loathe it, there are few better ways to endear yourself to the locals than by chowing down on a bowlful of *gimchi*.

▲ *Gimchi*

▼ Food stall, Seoul

Gomanaru restaurant, Gongju ▲

Royal cuisine, *Korea House* ▼

Bibimbap

Literally meaning "mixed rice", **bibimbap** consists of a bowl of rice topped with seasoned vegetables, red-pepper paste, minced beef and a fried egg. It was originally a religious dish derived from the five principal colours of Korean Buddhism – **red** for the paste, **yellow** for the egg yolk, **white** for the rice, **blue** for the meat and **green** for the vegetables – and is one of the easiest dishes to find in Korea. Some restaurants serve it in a heated stone bowl (*dolsot bibimbap*); those in the countryside may make it using only vegetables sourced from the surrounding mountains (*sanchae bibimbap*); and certain establishments in **Jeonju** have elevated the dish to an art form, serving it with a whole witches' cauldron of fascinating ingredients – including pine kernels, fern bracken and slices of jujube – and up to a dozen individual side dishes.

Ten top dining spots

- **Baru** Buddhist temple food, Seoul (p.107).
- **Korea House** Royal banquets, Seoul (p.108).
- **Abai Sundae** Noodle sausages and a ferry trip, Sokcho (p.152).
- **Jagalchi fish market** Busan (p.213).
- **Chungmu Gimbap** Hearty food by the harbour, Tongyeong (p.218).
- **Eel Alley** Stamina-giving eel dishes, Jinju (p.221).
- **Jongno Hoetjip** The best *bibimbap* in the land, Jeonju (p.257).
- **Gomanaru** Feasts of flowers and leaves, Gongju (p.277).
- **Haewa Dal Geurigo Seom** Fist-sized sea snails, Udo (p.308).
- **North Korea** Anywhere and anything, for sheer excitement value (p.327).

Gyeonghuigung palace (see p.91; W15,000 per session), but had been shelved at the time of writing; should they return, note that the 10.30am sessions are for basic moves, 1.30pm for self-defence and 3.30pm for "breaking techniques" (pine boards, not people). Whether these return or not, tourist information offices are the best places to ask about *taekwondo* action, including longer programmes: figure on around W50,000 per day. There are also occasional performances and tournaments at the home of Korea's national sport, **Kukkiwon** (Mon–Fri 9am–5pm; free), a hall near Gangnam station.

Shopping

Shopaholics will be quite at home in Seoul: the city has everything from trendy to traditional, markets to malls. High on the itinerary of many tourists are the colossal markets of **Dongdaemun** and **Namdaemun** (see p.92).

Clothing

There are **department stores** all over the city; the bustling streets of **Myeongdong** host department stores from the biggest nationwide chains – Migliore, Shinsaegae, Lotte and Galleria – and there are also luxury examples in Apgujeong. Perhaps more interesting are the city's **boutiques**; these are most numerous (and expensive) around Apgujeong, though there are cheaper versions of the same in Hongdae and Samcheongdong. Itaewon is also worth a mention for its excellent **tailored suits**, and last, but not least, are the colossal **markets** of Dongdaemun and Namdaemun (p.92), which feature an almost bewildering array of cheap and knock-off brand-name clothing.

Galleria Apgujeongno; Apgujeong station. See "Southern Seoul" map, p.98. Almost universally agreed to be the country's most exclusive department store, this is arranged in two buildings facing each other across a major road. The artistically designed west wing features a slew of local designers, while the even more expensive east wing is home to international mega-labels.

Gwangjang Market 광장시장 Jongno 5-ga station. See "Business district" map, p.90. Though most famed for its culinary offerings, this sprawling market has a truly excellent secondhand section, with all manner of zany shirts, coats and jackets imported from abroad. It's a little hard to find: hunt down the staircase on the western side of the market, and head for the second floor.

Hahn's Custom Tailoring Itaewondong Ⓔhanstailor@hotmail.com; Itaewon station. See "Itaewon" map, p.94. Get a perfectly tailored suit for around US$500. Staff speak excellent English, and will be pleased to discuss the particular style you're after.

Hamilton Shirts Itaewondong Ⓦwww.hs76.com; Itaewon station. See "Itaewon" map, p.94. Tailored shirts for less than you'd pay on your local high street: most shirts go for around US$40. The quality is amazingly high for the price. 10am–9.30pm.

Lee Geon Maan Gwanhundong; Anguk station. See "Insadong" map, p.83. Well-located store selling ties for men and handbags for women. Their unique selling point is an innovative use of *hangeul*, the Korean text conspicuous by its absence on most Korean clothing.

Shinsegae Myeongdong; Myeongdong station. See "Business district" map, p.90. Designed back in the 1930s as a branch of the Japanese Mitsukoshi chain, this was Korea's first department store. Goods from luxury clothing and jewellery brands can be found inside, while the exterior of the old wing is quite charming at night, and extremely striking around Christmas time.

Stori Samcheongdong Ⓦwww.storisac.com; Anguk station. See "Palace district" map, p.79. Made with distinctively Korean materials and patterns, Stori's handbags have gone down a storm in London and other European cities in recent years.

Suecomma Bonnie Cheongdamdong Ⓦwww.suecommabonnie.com; Apgujeong station. See "Southern Seoul" map, p.98. Superb ladies' footwear made by local diva Bonnie Lee, who designed shoes for Carrie and co in Sex and the City. There's a smaller branch off Samcheong-donggil (See "Palace district" map, p.79).

Arts, crafts and antiques

The best place to head for anything vaguely arty is **Insadonggil** and its side streets, which have numerous **craft** shops selling paints, brushes, calligraphy ink and handmade paper. There are also a few shops selling **antiques** here, though there are more of the same in Itaewon; these sell cases, cupboards, medicinal racks and the like, many in a distinctively oriental style. Proprietors often speak English, and can arrange international shipping.

Kwang Ju Yo Gahoedong ⓦwww.kwangjuyo.com; Anguk station. See "Palace district" map, p.79. Korea has been at the forefront of world pottery for centuries; celadon bowls and porcelain vases are among the items on offer at this charming store, while they also sell Andong *soju* (see p.45) in elaborate jars: perfect souvenirs.

Mono Collection Buamdong ⓦwww.monocollection.com. See "Northern Seoul" map, p.111. This tiny store sells Korean-styled fabrics including curtains, pillowcases and tablecloths. Given the slightly out-of-the-way location, it may be easier to pop into their booth in *Korea House* (see p.108), or the branch at Incheon International Airport.

Royal Antiques Itaewondong ⓦwww.royal-antique.com; Itaewon station. See "Itaewon" map, p.94. Not on "Antiques Alley" itself, but the best place to head if you're looking for a genuine Joseon-era piece of furniture. The friendly owners speak English.

Sangsangmadang Gahoedong; Sangsu station. See "Hongdae" map, p.95. Unbelievable though it may sound, Hongdae was once more famed for its art than its bars. Times have changed, but the university that the area is named after is still artistically focused. This arty complex features a gallery, café and cinema, while the ground floor sells small lifestyle goods designed by local students.

Ssamziegil Gwanhundong; Anguk station. See "Insadong" map, p.83. A wonderfully designed building whose spiral walkway plays host to countless small shops selling traditional clothing, handmade paper, jewellery and the like. There's also a rooftop market on weekends, selling all manner of quirky arts and crafts.

Books and music

Most of Seoul's larger **bookstores** have dedicated English-language sections stocked with novels, history books and language study guides for those studying Korean or teaching English. Three of these are directly accessible from subway stations – Youngpoong and Bandi & Luni from Jonggak (see the "Insadong" map, p.83), and Kyobo Bookstore from Gwanghwamun (see the "Palace district" map, p.79). These are also the best places in which to find mainstream **music**; fans of anything edgier should head to Purple Record in Hongdae (see the "Hongdae" map, p.95).

Cameras and electronic equipment

Technophiles have two main choices – one is Yongsan Electronics Mart, a multi-level giant rising up alongside the train and subway station of the same name, and the other Techno Mart, near Gangbyeon subway station on line 2. At both, many staff speak a little English (particularly Yongsan, thanks to its proximity to Itaewon). Prices are generally about twenty percent less than elsewhere in the land; this can rise to fifty percent for imported goods.

Listings

Airlines Aeroflot ⓣ02/551-0321; Air Canada ⓣ02/3788-0100; Air China ⓣ02/774-6886; Air France ⓣ02/3483-1033; All Nippon Airways ⓣ02/752-5500; American Airlines ⓣ02/319-3401; Asiana Airlines ⓣ02/1588-8000; Japan Airlines ⓣ02/757-1711; KLM ⓣ02/2011-5500; Korean Air ⓣ02/1588-2001; Qantas ⓣ02/777-6871; United Airlines ⓣ02/757-1691.

Airport information The information line for both Incheon Airport (Ⓦwww.airport.or.kr) and Gimpo Airport (Ⓦwww.airport.co.kr) is Ⓣ02/1577-2600.
Banks and exchange Banks will exchange foreign currency or travellers' cheques, while some have a "Global ATM" that can be used with cards from around the world. If you have a debit card it may be easier to head to a convenience store such as 7-Eleven or Mini Stop.
Car rental Prices run from around W60,000 per day. Hertz (Ⓣ02/797-8000) and Avis (Ⓣ02/1544-1600) both have desks at Incheon International Airport.
Embassies Australia Ⓣ02/2003-0100; Canada Ⓣ02/3455-6000; China Ⓣ02/738-1173; Ireland Ⓣ02/774-6455; New Zealand Ⓣ02/736-0341; Russia Ⓣ02/752-0630; South Africa Ⓣ02/792-4855; UK Ⓣ02/3210-5500; US Ⓣ02/397-4114.
Emergencies Call the tourist information line (see p.59) on Ⓣ1330 for the fastest possible foreign-language advice on emergencies. Staff at the top hotels will also be willing to provide assistance, even to non-guests. Emergency numbers are Ⓣ112 for the police and Ⓣ119 for ambulance and the fire brigade.
Hospitals and clinics To find an English-speaking doctor, or a clinic suited to your needs, call the Seoul Help Center's medical line on Ⓣ010/4769-8212.
Immigration There are immigration offices at both Incheon and Gimpo airports, as well as one in City Hall. Call Ⓣ02/2650-6212, or go to Ⓦwww.immigration.go.kr.
Internet access Found all over Seoul and costing W1000 per hour, with a one-hour minimum fee. There are free terminals in the main KTO tourist information centre south of Jonggak subway station (see p.70). Top-range hotels usually have LAN connections, charging up to W20,000 per day.
Left luggage Most subway, train and bus stations have storage lockers costing W1000 per day, though these are too small to accommodate suitcases or large backpacks. Some hotels offer left luggage facilities, and a couple of guesthouses are willing to put your bags somewhere safe while you travel around the country.
Lost property The national lost property hotline is Ⓣ02/2299-1282, but since staff are unlikely to speak English it may be best to go through the tourist information line on Ⓣ1330. There are also lost property offices in City Hall and Chungmuro subway stations, as well as the main train stations.
Post offices There's a post office in every neighbourhood, all of which can handle international mail – just ask for the nearest *ucheguk* (usually Mon–Fri 9am–5pm). The main office on Jongno Road is open to 8pm on weekdays; 6pm on weekends (Ⓣ02/3703-9011).
Ticket agencies The big bookstores (see opposite) have ticket booths, or go online at Ⓦwww.ticketlink.co.kr.

Travel details

Trains

The trains between the major cities listed below are the fastest, most direct services; on some routes there exist slower, cheaper trains.
Cheongnyangni station to: Andong (11 daily; 4hr–5hr 30min); Chuncheon (hourly; 2hr); Gangneung (10 daily; 6hr 45min); Wonju (9 daily; 1hr 45min–2hr).
Seoul station to: Busan (regularly; 2hr 40min); Cheonan (regularly; 40min); Daegu (regularly; 1hr 35min); Daejeon (regularly; 50min); Suwon (regularly; 30min).
Yongsan station to: Cheonan (regularly; 35min); Daejeon (regularly; 50min); Gwangju (regularly; 2hr 50min); Iksan (regularly; 1hr 45min); Jeonju (direct 3hr 30min, for faster trains change in Iksan); Mokpo (regularly; 3hr 10min); Suwon (regularly; 30min).

Buses

Dong-Seoul Terminal Express section to: Busan (10 daily; 4hr 30min); Cheongju (every 30min; 1hr 40min); Daegu (every 30min; 3hr 30min); Daejeon (every 25min; 1hr 50min); Gangneung (every 35min; 3hr 20min); Gwangju (every 30min; 3hr 50min); Jeonju (every 45min; 2hr 50min); Jinju (5 daily; 3hr 50min); Samcheok (9 daily; 3hr 40min).
Dong-Seoul Terminal Intercity section to: Andong (34 daily; 2hr 50min); Buan (5 daily; 4hr); Cheonan (49 daily; 1hr 20min); Chuncheon (every 15min; 1hr 30min); Gangneung (20 daily; 3hr 10min); Gongju (12 daily; 2hr 10min); Guinsa (20 daily; 3hr 30min); Gyeongju (18 daily; 4hr); Haeundae (14 daily; 6hr); Incheon (34 daily; 1hr 10min); Jeongdongjin (3 daily; 3hr 30min); Sokcho (every 20min; 3hr 30min); Songnisan

(12 daily; 3hr 30min); Taebaek (26 daily; 4hr 30min); Wonju (70 daily; 1hr 40min).
Express Terminal Gyeongbu section to: Busan (every 20min; 4hr 30min); Cheonan (every 10min; 1hr 10min); Daegu (every 20min; 3hr 30min); Daejeon (every 5min; 1hr 50min); Gongju (every 30min; 2hr 20min); Gyeongju (every 30min; 4hr 15min); Pohang (every 20min; 5hr); Tongyeong (11 daily; 5hr).
Express Terminal Honam section to: Daecheon (hourly; 2hr 10min); Gangneung (every 20min; 3hr 10min); Gwangju (every 5min; 3hr 55min); Jeonju (every 10min; 2hr 50min); Jinan (2 daily; 3hr 30min); Jindo (4 daily; 6hr 10min); Mokpo (every 25min; 4hr 20min); Samcheok (every 45min; 3hr 50min); Sokcho (every 30min; 4hr 10min); Suncheon (every 35min; 5hr); Wando (4 daily; 6hr); Wonju (every 15min; 1hr 30min); Yeosu (every 50min; 5hr 40min).
Nambu Terminal to: Anmyeondo (12 daily; 3hr); Buyeo (19 daily; 2hr 10min); Daecheon (6 daily; 2hr 10min); Gongju (every 25min; 1hr 30min); Jeonju (18 daily; 2hr 50min); Jinju (29 daily; 4hr); Mallipo (5 daily; 3hr); Muju (5 daily; 3hr 20min); Songnisan (3 daily; 3hr 30min); Tongyeong (13 daily; 4hr 30min).
Sinchon Terminal to: Ganghwa-eup (every 10min; 1hr 10min); Oepo (hourly, 2hr).

Flights

Gimpo to: Busan (every 30min; 1hr); Gwangju (7 daily; 50min); Jeju City (every 15min; 1hr 5min); Jinju (3 daily; 55min); Mokpo (1 daily; 55min); Pohang (4 daily; 50min); Ulsan (hourly; 55min); Yeosu (8 daily; 55min).

2

Gyeonggi and Gangwon

CHAPTER 2 Highlights

* **Suwon** Scramble up a UNESCO-listed fortress wall, visit a nearby folk village, or join what may be the world's only toilet tour. See p.129

* **West Sea islands** Clean air, homely villages and a thriving fishing industry are what make a visit to the islands worthwhile; all this and only a day-trip from Seoul. See p.137

* **The DMZ** Walk through a tunnel under the world's most heavily fortified border, or take a couple of steps into official North Korean territory in the eerie Joint Security Area. See p.140

* **Cheorwon** Just a few kilometres from the North Korean border, there's tension in the air and some interesting sights related to the neighbours across the way. See p.145

* **Seoraksan National Park** With its tall pines and naked rock, Koreans are in near-unanimous agreement that this is the most beautiful national park in the country. See p.155

* **Jeongdongjin** An American warship and a North Korean submarine lie side by side near this small village, just begging to be clambered around. See p.162

* **Rail-biking** Speed 7km down the train tracks on a specially adapted rail-bike, north of Jeongseon. See p.168

▲ Ulsanbawi, Seoraksan National Park

2

Gyeonggi and Gangwon

Gyeonggi and **Gangwon**, South Korea's northernmost provinces, couldn't be much further apart in character, despite both being bounded to the north by the **Demilitarized Zone**, often described as one of the most dangerous places on Earth. In the small northwestern corner of the country, Gyeonggi (officially known as Gyeonggi-do) is a busy rabble of eleven million people much cut up by roads and buzzing with industry. It encircles the two cities of Seoul and Incheon; though these are administratively separate, the combined urban mass of 24 million people – around half of the country's population – makes little Gyeonggi one of the world's most densely populated areas.

Seoul functions as the province's beating heart by providing work to the masses, though most of Gyeonggi's surrounding cities are commuter-filled nonentities, whose sights are few and far between. However, **Incheon** to the west of the capital and **Suwon** to the south merit a visit; the former was the first city in the country to be opened up to international trade, and remains Korea's most important link with the outside world thanks to its international airport and ferry terminals. The airport squats on an island just west of Incheon in the West Sea, which also contains myriad nearby **islands** of a more tranquil nature. Inland, the Gyeonggi countryside is home to one of the most interesting sights in the country: **Panmunjeom** is a village sandwiched in the demilitarized zone between North and South Korea, where it's even possible to step across the border in the renowned Joint Security Area.

By comparison, Gyeonggi's rugged next-door-neighbour Gangwon (or Gangwon-do) has managed to remain the country's most natural mainland province. A lofty range of mountains scores its eastern flank, mopping up national and provincial parks along the way; these include **Seoraksan**, a limestone-heavy mass of beautiful rocky crags and spires, and **Odaesan**, a similar but much less touristed national park just down the coast. Elsewhere around the province it's possible to **raft** down whitewater rivers, go skiing, laze on a selection of unspoilt **beaches**, or fire down a rural valley on a specially built rail-bike. Even Gangwon's cities are relaxed; **Gangneung** is home to a wonderful Confucian shrine; salty **Sokcho** on the east coast has enough on its periphery to keep you occupied for a few days; and **Chuncheon**, the region's capital, is unhurried enough to allow for some pleasant bike-riding.

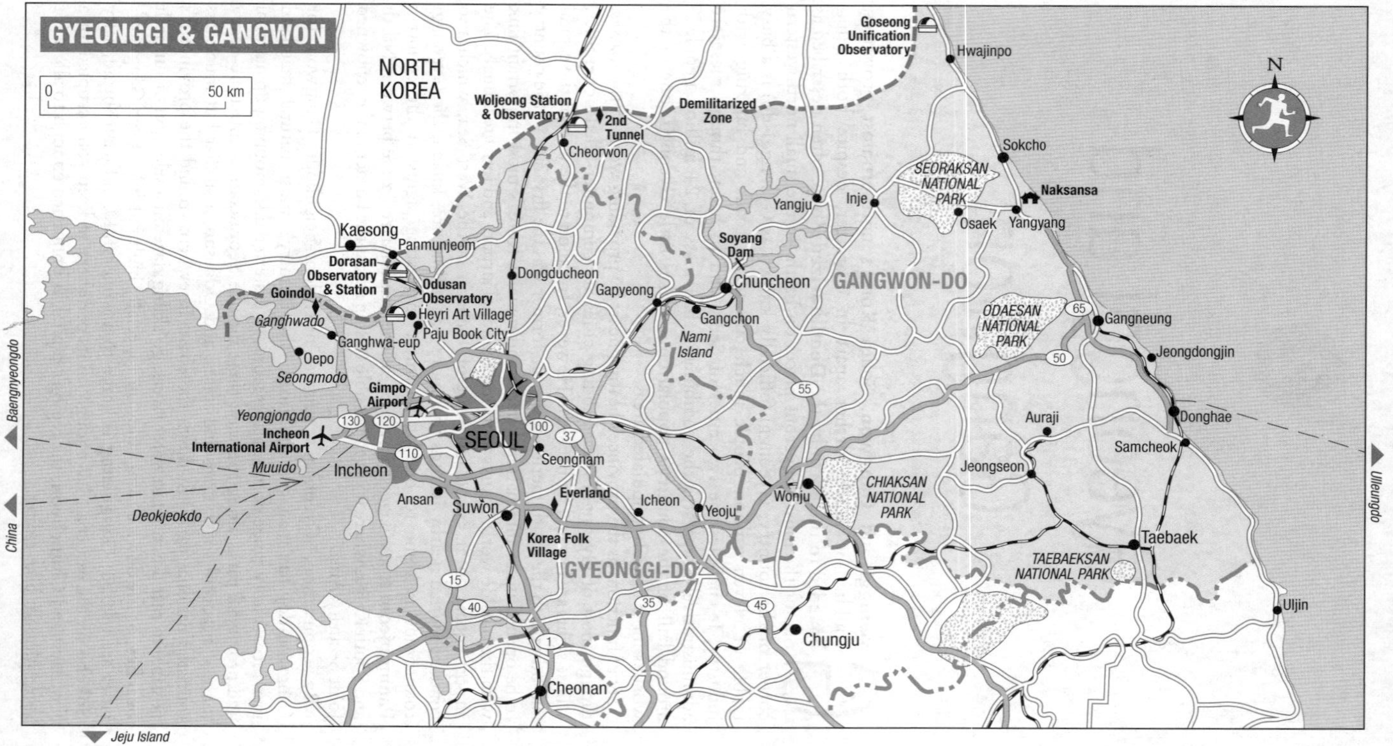

GYEONGGI & GANGWON

0 50 km

NORTH KOREA
Kaesong
Panmunjeom
Dorasan Observatory & Station
Odusan Observatory
Goindol
Ganghwado
Heyri Art Village
Paju Book City
Ganghwa-eup
Oepo
Seongmodo
Gimpo Airport
Yeongjongdo
Incheon International Airport
Muuido
Incheon
Deokjeokdo
Baengnyeongdo
China
Jeju Island
Woljeong Station & Observatory
2nd Tunnel
Cheorwon
Demilitarized Zone
Dongducheon
Gapyeong
Gangchon
Nami Island
Soyang Dam
Chuncheon
Yangju
Inje
SEOUL
Seongnam
Ansan
Suwon
Everland
Korea Folk Village
Icheon
Yeoju
Wonju
GYEONGGI-DO
GANGWON-DO
Chungju
Cheonan
Goseong Unification Observatory
Hwajinpo
Sokcho
SEORAKSAN NATIONAL PARK
Osaek
Naksansa
Yangyang
ODAESAN NATIONAL PARK
Gangneung
Jeongdongjin
Donghae
Samcheok
Auraji
Jeongseon
CHIAKSAN NATIONAL PARK
Taebaek
TAEBAEKSAN NATIONAL PARK
Uljin
Ulleungdo
N
130 120 110 100 37 55 50 65 15 40 35 45 1

Gyeonggi

Despite the presence of one of the world's biggest cities at its centre, **GYEONGGI** (경기) is a somewhat anonymous province. The long steel and concrete tentacles of Seoul stretch across the region, smothering the appeal of what must once have been a corner of commendable natural beauty. Because of this, travellers tend to bypass the area entirely on their way around the country, which is a shame because the bulky cities of **Suwon** and **Incheon** have some intriguing sights, and with both connected to Seoul by subway they make enjoyable day-trips from the capital. Suwon's main draw is the UNESCO-listed fortress, while Incheon is an important transport hub and sports the country's most thriving Chinatown.

A residue of traditional Korean life can be found off the mainland in the West Sea. Better known internationally as the Yellow Sea, it's home to a legion of **islands** from whose shores fishermen roll in and out with the tide as they have for generations. Some of the more notable isles are **Yeongjongdo**, home of Korea's main international airport and a rather scruffy place; **Deokjeokdo**, a laid-back and refreshingly unspoilt retreat from Seoul; and **Ganghwado**, an island within spitting distance of the North Korean border (not that you're allowed even to see North Korea from its army-controlled shores, let alone spit at it). Those who want to catch a glimpse of the neighbours should head to **Panmunjeom**, a village inside the **Demilitarized Zone** that separates North and South Korea. With security so tight, access is understandably subject to the conditions of the time, but most should be lucky enough to take a step across the world's most fortified border to what is technically **North Korean territory**. Alternatively you can make do with a view of the empty "Propaganda Village" on the opposite side of the DMZ, or a scramble through tunnels built by the North in readiness for an assault on Seoul.

Suwon and around

All but swallowed up by Seoul, **SUWON** (수원) is a city with an identity crisis. Despite a million-strong population, and an impressive history – best embodied by the **UNESCO-listed fortress** at its centre – it has had to resort to unconventional means to distance itself culturally from the capital, the best example being the dozens of individually commissioned **public toilets** that pepper the city (see p.130). Suwon, in fact, came close to usurping Seoul as Korea's seat of power following the construction of its fortress in the final years of the eighteenth century, but though the move was doomed to failure, Suwon grew in importance in a way that remains visible to this day – from the higher

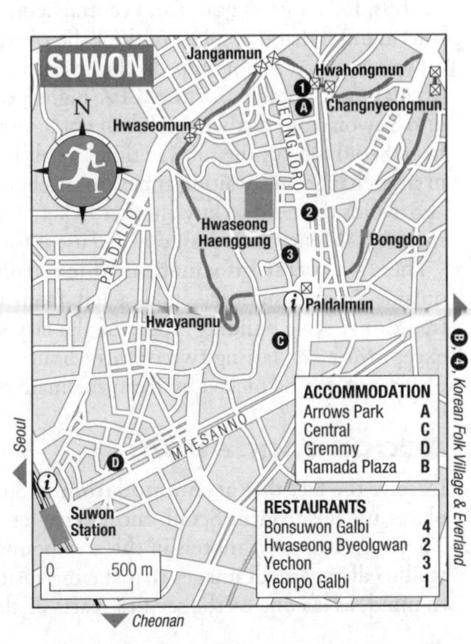

Mr Toilet

Bar its fortress, central Suwon carries precious little sightseeing potential, though one interesting facet is what may be the world's greatest concentration of public toilets – they all have names, and some are even marked on tourist maps. This concept was the brainchild of **Sim Jae-deok**, a man referred to, especially by himself, as "**Mr Toilet**". Apparently afflicted by something of a cloacal obsession (best evidenced by his house, custom-built to resemble a giant loo), Sim claims to have been born in a public restroom, but transcended these humble beginnings to become mayor of Suwon and a member of the national assembly. He then went on to create, and declare himself head of, the *other* WTO – the **World Toilet Organization**. Undoubtedly spurred on by his team's debatable findings that the average human being spends three years of their life on the toilet, Sim desired to improve his home city's facilities for the World Cup in 2002, commissioning dozens of individually designed public toilets – armed with the relevant pamphlet from the tourist office, it's even possible to fashion some kind of toilet tour. Features may include skylights, mountain views or piped classical music, though such refinement is sadly sullied, as it is all over Korea, by the baskets of used toilet paper discarded throne-side.

parts of the fortress wall, it's evident that this once-little settlement burst through its stone confines, eventually creating the noisy hotchpotch of buildings that now forms one of Korea's largest cities.

An hour away from central Seoul, Suwon is certainly an easy **day-trip** from the capital, though those who choose to stay will benefit from cheaper accommodation, and get the chance to enjoy some interesting nightlife. East of the centre lie **Everland** and the **Korean Folk Village**, two sites ideal for anyone travelling with children, though just as easily accessible from Seoul.

Arrival and information

Though **buses** run from Seoul to points all over Suwon, the most popular way for visitors to arrive is by rail, with the main station just within walking distance of the fortress. It's about an hour from central Seoul on the capital's **subway** line 1, though bear in mind that this splits south of the river, with many trains heading to Incheon. Suwon is also a major stop on the overland **train** line heading in or out of Seoul (though not, notably, for the KTX high-speed trains), meaning that those heading into Suwon from further south will not have to transit via the capital. Those heading from Seoul can cut the subway time in half by using this line, though after factoring in interchange and waiting times, most choose to stay on the subway, a move that also avoids the need to buy another ticket. Those who have a Seoul **transport card**, such as T-Money or Upass, can also use it for buses or subway trains in Suwon.

There's a useful **information office** (daily 7am–10pm; ⓣ031/228-4672) just outside Suwon station – take a left from the train exit, and look for a squat, traditional-style building; tours of the city start here at 10am and 2pm every day except Monday, lasting two or three hours and costing W8000. Buses to all places of interest can be picked up from the main road outside.

Accommodation

Despite the fact that **accommodation** in Suwon is markedly cheaper than similar places up the road in Seoul, most travellers visit on **day-trips** from the capital. There are troops of motels in the area bounded by the fortress wall, but you'd do well to disregard all images that staying inside a UNESCO-listed sight may bring to mind, as it's one of the seediest parts of the city. True budget-seekers can make use of the *Grand Sauna* (그랜드 사우나), an excellent *jjimjilbang* just off Rodeo Street, where for just W7000 you can clean off the city grime and put your head down in a dorm room for a night's rest.

Arrows Park Janganmun. Just inside the fortress gate, this motel's clean rooms make it a blessing in the surprisingly seamy area bounded by the fortress walls. The *Ruby* opposite has slightly inferior rooms at marginally lower prices. ❷

Hotel Central Gyodong ⓣ031/246-0011. In an excellent location for the fortress, as the name suggests, and not too run down for a Korean tourist hotel. Rooms are reasonably good value and have cable TV; a mini-buffet breakfast is also thrown in for free, but staff are unlikely to speak English, and the bar-filled street outside can get noisy at night. ❺

Motel Gremmy Maesanno ⓣ031/254-7557. Most Korean motels are a little "love-oriented", but at least this one is honest about it – racy pictures in the corridors, laid-on contraception and "special interest" videos to choose from in the lobby. It's obviously not for everyone, but rooms are large and clean; the more expensive ones have cavernous bathrooms. ❸

Ramada Plaza Umandong ⓣ031/230-0001, ⓦwww.ramadaplazasuwon.com. Suwon's best hotel, though in an uninteresting corner of the city, attracts well-heeled visitors – primarily Europeans on business – and offers all the comfort you'd expect of the chain. Some of the suites are truly stunning, and even standard rooms have been designed with care. ❼

Hwaseong fortress

Central Suwon has but one notable sight – **Hwaseong fortress** (화성; 24hr; free), whose gigantic walls wend their way around the city centre. Completed in 1796, the complex was built on the orders of **King Jeongjo**, one of the Joseon dynasty's most famous rulers, in order to house the remains of his father, **Prince Sado**. Sado never became king, and met an early end in Seoul's Changgyeonggung Palace at the hands of his own father, King Yeongjo (see p.88); it may have been the gravity of the situation that spurred Jeongjo's attempts to move the capital away from Seoul.

Several **buses** ply the route to Paldalmun, the usual fortress starting point (see below), from the train station, including #11, #13, #36 and #39, while the #300 heads there from the bus terminal.

The fortress

Towering almost 10m high for the bulk of its course, the **fortress wall** rises and falls in a 5.7km-long stretch, most of which is walkable, the various peaks and troughs marked by sentry posts and ornate entrance gates. From the higher vantage points you'll be able to soak up **superb views** of the city, but while there's also plenty to see from the wall itself, the interior is disappointing: other fortresses around the country – notably those at Gongju (p.275) and Buyeo (p.272) – have green, tranquil grounds with little inside save for trees, squirrels, pagodas and meandering paths, but Hwaseong's has had concrete poured into it, and is now a cityscape filled with restaurants, honking traffic and ropey motels. Even on the wall itself, it's hard to escape the noise, which is often punctuated by screaming aircraft from the nearby military base. Another complaint from visitors is that the wall looks too new, the result of copious restoration work, but as this slowly starts to "bed in", it will once again don thin veils of moss and ivy, achieving a look more proximate to the original appearance. Most visitors start their wall walk at **Paldalmun** (팔달문) – a gate at the lower end of the fortress, exuding a well-preserved magnificence now diluted by its position in the middle of a traffic-filled roundabout – before taking the steep, uphill path to Seonammun, the western gate.

Hwaseong Haenggung

In the centre of the area bounded by the fortress walls is **Hwaseong Haenggung** (화성행궁), once a government office, then a palace, and now a fine place to amble around; its pink walls are punctuated by the green lattice frames of windows and doors, which overlook dirt courtyards from where you can admire the fortress wall that looms above. There's a **martial arts display** (Tues–Sun 11am), and traditional **dance and music** performances take place at 2pm on Saturdays and Sundays from April to November.

Eating and drinking

Suwon is famous for a local variety of *galbi*, whereby the regular meat dish is given a salty seasoning. There's an excellent **food court** just above the main concourse of the train station, which serves hundreds of big dishes at surprisingly reasonable prices: there's no English-language menu, but plastic versions of the dishes on offer will help you make your choice; the cashier will then give you a numbered ticket and tell you which counter to collect from. You will more than likely find something appealing on **Rodeo Street**; the city's youth flocks here in the evening to take advantage of the copious cheap restaurants, and food segues into **drink** as the evening goes on.

Bonsuwon Galbi 본수원 갈비 Umandong. Around the back of *Hotel Central*, and therefore a little out of the way for those not staying there, is what may well be the best *galbi* restaurant in the city. The succulent meat doesn't come cheap, but is worth it for the chance to try Suwon's local take on Korea's most pyromanial eating experience.

Hwaseong Byeolgwan 화성 별관 Paldallo. Not far from the entrance to Haenggung, this presentable restaurant – though devoid of English-language menus – serves extremely cheap *bibimbap* and pork cutlet, as well as more expensive meat specials. The beef stew-like *ddukbaegi bulgogi* (뚝배기불고기) is great value at W7000. Look for the sign saying "Korean Royal Palace Cuisine".

Yechon 예촌 Paldalmun. Low-key, traditionally styled establishment serving savoury pancakes known as *jeon* (전) in many different styles (W7000–15,000), as well as superb *makkeolli* from Jeonju, a city in the southwest of the country.

Yeonpo Galbi 연포 갈비 Buksudong. In a quiet area just inside the fortress wall lies the best restaurant in the area. The *galbi* meat is rather expensive, but cheaper noodle dishes are available, and those who arrive before 3pm can get a huge *jeongsik* (set meal) for W15,000, which includes several small fish and vegetable dishes.

Korean Folk Village

This recreation of a traditional **Korean Folk Village** (한국민속촌; daily: March–Oct 9am–6.30pm; Nov–Feb 9am–5pm; W12,000) has become one of the most popular day-trips for foreign visitors to Seoul, its thatch-roofed houses and dirt paths evoking the sights, sounds and some of the more pleasant smells of a bygone time, when farming was the mainstay of the country. Its proximity to the capital makes this village by far the most-visited of the many such facilities dotted around the country, which tends to diminish the authenticity of the experience. Nevertheless, the riverbank setting and its old-fashioned buildings are impressive, though the emphasis is squarely on performance – shows of tightrope-walking and horseriding take place regularly throughout the day. Traditional wedding ceremonies provide a glimpse into Confucian society, with painstaking attention to detail including gifts of live chickens wrapped up in cloth like Egyptian mummies. Don't miss the **farmers' dance** (11am & 2.30pm; sometimes also 1.40pm), in which costumed performers prance around in highly distinctive ribbon-topped hats amid a cacophony of drums and crashes – quintessential Korea.

Free **shuttle buses** to the folk village leave from outside Suwon's tourist information office every half-hour from 10.30am to 2.30pm (30min; free with entry ticket), though the last one back to Suwon departs the village frustratingly early – usually 5pm. Regular city buses are available for those who want to stay a little longer. There are a few good **restaurants** on site, as well as an excellent tearoom.

Everland

Everland (daily, usually 9.30am–10pm; W30,000, discounts after 5pm; Ⓦeng.everland.com) is a colossal theme park that ranks as one of the most popular domestic tourist attractions in the country – male or female, young or old, it's hard to find a *hangukin* (Korean person) who hasn't taken this modern-day rite of passage. Most are here for the fairground rides, and the park has all that a rollercoaster connoisseur could possibly wish for. Other attractions include a **zoo** (which features a safari zone that can be toured by bus, jeep or even at night), a speedway track, a golf course, and the surprisingly good **Hoam Museum**, which contains a few excellent examples of Buddhist art, and some interesting French sculpture in an outdoor garden. The most popular part of the park, however, is **Caribbean Bay** (usually 9.30am–5pm, closes 7pm Sat & Sun; W30,000–65,000 depending upon season), with an indoor zone that's open year-round containing several pools, a sauna and a short river that you can float down on a tube, as well as massage machines and relaxation capsules. The **outdoor section** (same times June–Aug; W40,000–60,000) with its man-made beach is what really draws the summer crowds. It's no longer just the beach that's artificial – despite a fairly innocent beginning, when it was marketed squarely at family groups, this has become one of the most popular places for Korea's silicon crowd to show off their new curves. Off the beach, facilities include a water bobsleigh, which drops you the height of a ten-floor building in just ten seconds, and an artificial surfing facility.

Most locals usually drive to Everland, creating long queues on busy days, whereas foreign visitors tend to take the **bus**. These leave on the half-hour from outside the train station in Suwon, and take around an hour. Several routes head here from Seoul; one of the most frequent and useful runs from the Dong-Seoul bus terminal via Jamsil subway station (50min; W2200), and a second from just north of Gangnam subway station exit six, via Yangjae (40min; W1600).

Incheon

INCHEON (인천) is an important port and Korea's third most populous city. It's also home to the country's main international airport, though few foreign travellers see anything of the city itself, with the overwhelming majority preferring to race straight to Seoul on a limousine bus. However, in view of its colourful recent history, it's worth at least a day-trip from the capital. This was where Korea's "Hermit Kingdom" finally crawled out of self-imposed isolation in the late nineteenth century and opened itself up to international trade, an event that was spurred on by the Japanese following similar events in their own country (the "Meiji Restoration"). The city was also the landing site for **Douglas MacArthur** and his troops in a manoeuvre that turned the tide of the Korean War (see box, p.134).

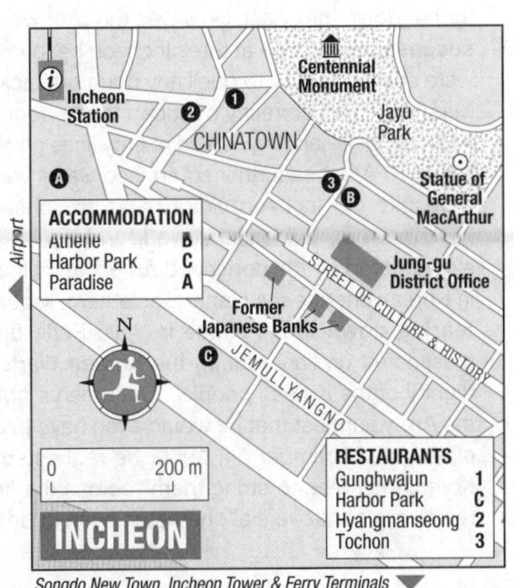

However, despite its obvious importance to Korea past and present, there's a palpable absence of civic pride, possibly due to the fact that Incheon is inextricably connected to the huge Seoul metropolis – the buildings simply don't stop on their long march from the capital. This may be about to change, however, as it has been chosen as the host of the **2014 Asian Games**, and is busily setting about smartening itself up in preparation for the event.

Incheon's various sights can easily be visited on a day-trip from Seoul, which is an hour away by subway. The most interesting part is **Jung-gu**, the country's only official Chinatown, a small but appealing area where you can rub shoulders with the Russian sailors and Filipino merchants who – after the Chinese – make up most of Incheon's sizeable foreign contingent. It sits below **Jayu Park**, where a statue of MacArthur gazes out over the sea. The only other area of note is **Songdo New Town**, an area being built on land reclaimed from the sea. At the time of writing this resembled a war zone (though with perfect roads, running buses and the odd hotel and apartment block), but by 2015 it should be more or less complete, and home to the **151 Incheon Tower**, set to be the world's second-tallest structure (a whopping 601m high) on completion.

General MacArthur and the Incheon landings

"We drew up a list of every natural and geographic handicap... Incheon had 'em all."

Commander Arlie G. Capps

On the morning of September 15, 1950, the most daring move of the **Korean War** was made, an event that was to alter the course of the conflict entirely, and now seen as one of the greatest military manoeuvres in history. At this point the Allied forces had been pushed by the North Korean People's Army into a small corner of the peninsula around Busan, but **General Douglas MacArthur** was convinced that a single decisive movement behind enemy lines could be enough to turn the tide.

MacArthur wanted to attempt an amphibious landing on the Incheon coast, but his plan was greeted with scepticism by many of his colleagues – both the South Korean and American armies were severely under-equipped (the latter only just recovering from the tolls of World War II), Incheon was heavily fortified, and its natural island-peppered defences and fast tides made it an even more dangerous choice.

The People's Army had simply not anticipated an attack on this scale in this area, reasoning that if one were to happen, it would take place at a more sensible location further down the coast. However, the plan went ahead and the Allied forces performed **successful landings** at three Incheon beaches, during which time North Korean forces were shelled heavily to quell any counterattacks. The city was taken with relative ease. MacArthur had correctly deduced that a poor movement of supplies was his enemy's Achilles heel – landing behind enemy lines gave Allied forces a chance to cut the supply line to KPA forces further south, and Seoul was duly retaken on 25 September.

Despite the Incheon victory and its consequences, MacArthur is not viewed by Koreans – or, indeed, the world in general – in an entirely positive light, feelings exacerbated by the continued American military presence in the country. While many in Korea venerate the General as a hero, repeated demonstrations have called for the **tearing down** of his statue in Jayu Park, denouncing him as a "war criminal who massacred civilians during the Korean War", and whose statue "greatly injures the dignity of the Korean people". Documents obtained after his eventual dismissal from the Army suggest that he would even have been willing to bring nuclear weapons into play – on December 24, 1950, he requested the shipment of 38 atomic bombs to Korea, intending to string them "across the neck of Manchuria". Douglas MacArthur remains a controversial character, even in death.

Also note that Incheon is the starting point for **international ferries** to a number of Chinese cities (see p.170), as well as a number of Korean islands in the **West Sea** (p.32).

Arrival and information

Importantly, there's no need to come to Incheon itself to get to and from the **international airport**, which is actually on an island west of the city proper and connected to the mainland by bridge: there are dedicated airport bus connections from Seoul and all over the country. To get to Incheon from the airport, you can use one of several limousine bus routes, or take city bus #306 to Incheon subway station. A second important point is that despite the city's size, there's **no train station**: it's best to take **subway line 1** from Seoul (1hr), though be sure that your train is bound for Incheon, as the line splits when leaving the capital. Outside Incheon subway station, the helpful **tourist information** office (daily 9am–6pm; ⓣ032/773-2225) usually has an English-speaker; further offices can be found in the ferry terminals.

International **ferries** dock at one of two terminals (see p.170 for details of which one to head to). Terminal 2 is the closer to the city centre, and is best accessed by taxi (W3000 from Incheon or Dong-Incheon subway stations). Terminal 1 is further out; a taxi will be less than W10,000, or buses #28 and #24 head the same way from Incheon and Dong-Incheon stations respectively. Right next to Terminal 1 is the Yeonan terminal, which caters for **domestic ferries** to almost all of the accessible islands in the Yellow Sea; details are given in the island accounts.

Accommodation

Incheon's proximity to Seoul means that most people choose to visit on a day-trip, but it's quite possible to spend a night here. There are a number of **motels** in and around Incheon and Dong-Incheon subway stations, as well as in Chinatown itself.

Athene Motel Songhakdong ⓣ032/772-5233. This hard-to-find gem of a motel is tucked away in a quiet area behind the Jung-gu district office, near *Tochon* restaurant (see p.136). Rooms and common areas have some nice floral touches, real and pictorial; combined with the pleasant drowsiness of the area, it's easy to put big-city bustle out of mind. ❷

Harbor Park Hotel Hangdong ⓣ032/770-9500, ⓦwww.harborparkhotel.com. The newest and best option in Jung-gu, with excellent service standards and great sea views. Unfortunately, standard rooms can be extremely small, so try to check a few if possible; suites, on the other hand, are generously sized. ❽

Paradise Hotel Hangdong 1-ga ⓣ032/762-5181, ⓦincheon.paradisehotel.co.kr. Though service can be a little ropey at times, and the crane-filled views may not appeal to some, this is the best hotel in the area. Despite being just a stone's throw from Incheon subway station, the hotel entrance is uphill and hard to reach, so you may prefer to take a cab. ❻

Chinatown

On exiting the gate at Incheon station, you'll immediately be confronted by the city's gentrified **Chinatown**, sitting across the main road and demarcated by the requisite oriental gate. Not so long ago, this area was dowdy and run-down, lent an unintentional air of authenticity with its cracked roads, rubble and grime; it has since been given a makeover, and is now a pleasant and surprisingly quiet area to walk around with a belly full of Chinese food.

Jayu Park

Uphill roads heading northeast from Chinatown lead to **Jayu Park** (자유 공원), also within easy walking distance of the subway station, and home to a statue of **General Douglas MacArthur**, staring proudly out over the seas that he conquered during the Korean War (see box, p.134). Also in the park is the Korean–American Centennial Monument, made up of eight black triangular shards that stretch up towards each other but never quite touch – feel free to make your own comparisons with the relationship between the two countries. Views from certain parts of the park expose Incheon's port, a colourful maze of cranes and container ships that provide a vivid reminder of the city's trade links with its neighbours across the seas.

The cultural district

South of Jayu Park lies a quiet but cosmopolitan part of town, where the streets are lined with Russian shops and sailor bars plastered with Cyrillic writing, as well as restaurants run by – and catering for – the city's Filipino community. From Chinatown, it's possible to take a pleasant, relatively traffic-free walk through Incheon's past on the way to Dong-Incheon station – pick up the *History through Modern Architecture* pamphlet from the tourist office, which will guide you directly to a road studded with distinctive **Japanese colonial buildings**. Surprisingly Western in appearance, three of these were originally banks, though two have now been turned into small **museums** (both Tues–Sun 9am–5pm; free), each worth popping into. The former 58th Bank of Japan offers interesting photo and video displays of life in colonial times, while the former 1st Bank down the road has a less interesting display of documents, flags and the like. Sitting in a small outdoor display area between the two, you'll find some fascinating pictures taken here in the 1890s, on what was then a quiet, dusty road almost entirely devoid of traffic, peopled with white-robed gents in horsehair hats – images of a Korea long gone.

However, one block to the north on a parallel road, the city has tried to evoke this bygone era on the slightly bizarre **Street of Culture and History**; the new wooden fronts added to the buildings are the only discernable things that constitute such a grand title, though they look decidedly pretty. Most of the businesses that received a facelift were simple shops such as confectioners, laundries and electrical stores, and surprisingly many are still going strong, the area yet to be inundated with arty cafés and the like.

Eating and drinking

Rarely for a Korean city, and perhaps uniquely for a Korean port, Incheon isn't renowned for its food, though the presence of a large and thriving **Chinatown** is a boon to visitors. Don't expect the food to be terribly authentic, since Koreans have their own take on Chinese cuisine. Top choices here, and available at every single restaurant, are sweet-and-sour pork (탕수육; *tansuyuk*), fried rice topped with a fried egg and black-bean paste (볶음밥; *beokkeumbap*), spicy seafood broth (짬뽕; *jjambbong*), and the undisputed number one: *jjajangmyeon* (자장면), noodles topped with black-bean paste.

Gonghwachun 공화춘 Bukseongdong. This is where Korea's *jjajangmyeon* fad started - it has been served here since the 1890s. W5000 will buy you a bowl, or you could try the sautéed shredded beef with green pepper (W20,000), and finish off your meal with fried, honey-dipped rice balls.

Harbor Park Hotel Hangdong. The buffet restaurant in this hotel (see p.135) is open to guests and non-guests alike, and dishes are superbly prepared; lunch is a steal at W18,000.

Hyangmanseong 향만성 Bukseongdong. Various Chinese dishes are on offer at this small but impressively authentic Chinatown institution, which has been operating for over forty years. They're proudest of the braised prawns in chilli sauce, but best value are the set deals, which start at around W20,000 per person (2 person minimum).

Tochon 토촌 Songhakdong. A wonderfully rustic lair, whose ground floor is surrounded on three sides by interconnected fish tanks. Fishy set meals go for W23,000 or more, though cheaper dishes are available, such as delicious mountain *bibimbap* for W7000.

The West Sea Islands

Gyeonggi's perforated western coast topples into the West Sea in an expanse of mud flats – the **tidal range** here is said to be the second biggest in the world after the Bay of Fundy in eastern Canada, though this is challenged by Britain's Bristol Channel. Whoever the silver medallist, the retreat of the tides is fantastic news for hunters of clams and other sea fare; it does, however, mean that beaches are in short supply. Fear not, Korean land rises again across the waves in the form of dozens of **islands**, almost all of which have remained pleasantly green and unspoilt; some also have excellent **beaches**. Life here is predominantly fishing-based and dawdles by at a snail's pace – a world away from Seoul and its environs, despite a few being close enough to be visited on a day-trip. Quite a number of these have next to no traffic, making them ideal places for a ride if you can find a bike to bring along.

Up the Gyeonggi coast from Incheon is **Ganghwado**, an island whose **dolmens** betray its ancient history. Just to the west is delightfully quiet **Seongmodo**, home to an enchanting temple. Ganghwa is connected to the mainland by bus, but there are other islands that can take hours to reach by ferry; two of these are **Deokjeokdo** and **Baengnyeongdo**, both beautiful and sufficiently far away from "regular" Korea to provide perfect escapes for those in need of a break. Swarms of less-visited islands are also there for the taking, if you're in an adventurous mood.

In case you haven't guessed already, the suffix **-do** (도) means "island" in Korean; accordingly, you may see signs for "Deokjeok Island" and so on.

Ganghwado

Unlike most Yellow Sea islands, **GANGHWADO** (강화도) is close enough to the mainland to be connected by road – buses run regularly from Sinchon bus terminal in Seoul via Gimpo, taking around ninety minutes to arrive in **Ganghwa-eup** (강화읍), the ugly main settlement; from here local buses dash to destinations across the island, though the place is so small that journeys rarely take more than thirty minutes. While this accessibility means that Ganghwa lacks the beauty of some of its more distant cousins, there's plenty to see. One look at a map should make clear the strategic importance of the island, which not only sits at the mouth of Seoul's main river, the Han, but whose northern flank is within a frisbee throw of the **North Korean border**. Would-be adventurers should note that this area is chock-full of military installations, and closed to the public.

Before the latest conflict, this unfortunate isle saw **battles** with Mongol, Manchu, French, American and Japanese forces, among others (see p.364). However, Ganghwado's foremost sights date from further back than even the earliest of these fisticuffs – a clutch of **dolmens** scattered around the northern part of the island, dating from the first century BC and now on UNESCO's World Heritage list.

The Yellow Sea

The West Sea is far better known abroad as the "**Yellow Sea**", a reference to the vast quantity of silt deposited into it by the Yellow River, which flows from the Chinese desert. Be warned that few Koreans will take kindly to this term, even though it's the accepted international name; there's nowhere near the intensity of debate that the East Sea/Sea of Japan on the other side of the country has inspired (see box on p.161 for more information), but those who want to stay on the better side of their Korean friends should refer to the body of water off the Gyeonggi coast as the "**West Sea**", or even better, the Korean name, Seohae (서해).

The dolmens

Misty remnants from bygone millennia, Ganghwa's **dolmens** are overground burial chambers consisting of flat capstones supported by three or more vertical megaliths. The Korean peninsula contains more than 30,000 of these ancient tombs – almost half of the world's total – and Ganghwado has one of the highest concentrations in the country. Most can only be reached by car or bike, though one is situated near a main road and accessible by bus. From Ganghwa-eup, take one of the buses bound for Changhu-ri, which depart every hour or so, and make sure that the driver knows where you want to go – ask to be dropped off at the main **Goindol** (24hr; free), a granite tomb which sits unobtrusively in a field as it has for centuries: a stone skeleton long divested of its original earth covering, with a large 5m by 7m capstone. The surrounding countryside is extremely beautiful, and you can combine a visit to the dolmen with a delightful walk. One of the best places to head to is the village of **Hajeom** (하점), not far to the west, where the roofs of some houses have been traditionally decorated with distinctive patterns. From the hills above Hajeom it's possible to view the North Korean bank of the Hangang, though sadly the propaganda that the North used to boom across the border from giant speakers can no longer be heard. Visual propaganda still remains, however, in the form of giant slogans best seen from the small mountain of **Bongcheonsan** (봉천산), a forty-minute walk north of Hajeon – the message visible across the border translates as "Yankees go home", a request that would doubtless be more effective were it not written in Korean.

The south and east coasts

To the south of the island is **Jeondeungsa** (전등사), a pretty temple dating from the fourth century – when Buddhism was just taking root on the peninsula – making it one of the oldest temples in the country. It was also the venue for the creation of the famed Tripitaka Koreana, eighty-thousand-plus blocks of carved Buddhist doctrine which now reside in Haeinsa temple near Daegu (see p.184). To reach the temple, take one of the half-hourly buses bound for Onsu-ri. About 5km west of Onsu is **Manisan** (마니산), the main peak of the island, which affords wonderful views of the surrounding islands.

Studding Ganghwado's east coast are three **fortresses** – Gwangseongbo (광성보), Deokjinjin (덕지진) and Chojijin (초지진) – which are best seen by making use of the bicycle lanes that run alongside the main road; otherwise, buses run every hour or so. Gwangseongbo (daily 9am–6pm; W1000) is the northernmost and most interesting of the three, and dates from the mid-seventeenth century; its strategic importance will be obvious to all visitors, as it peers out over the channel that separates Ganghwado from the mainland.

Oepo

The small settlement of **Oepo** (외포; pronounced "Way-paw") on the island's western coast is by far the most appealing place to stay; small and delightfully old-fashioned, it's a little like stepping into the Korea of the 1970s, before the country's "economic miracle" mopped up old traditions by the bucketload. There are no particular sights, so wandering around to soak up the atmosphere is the order of the day. There's an appealing little fish market near the dock, and restaurants all around it; you can even stay above one at the impossible-to-miss *Santa Lucia* (Ⓣ032/933 2141; ❷), the only building to take advantage of the village's views of Seongmodo, another island just across the water.

Seongmodo

Ferries (every 30min; 10min; W2000 return) run from Oepo's tiny terminal to **SEONGMODO** (석모도), across the water from Ganghwado; ornithophobes should note that large flocks of seagulls tend to circumnavigate the vessel for the entire journey, waiting to catch thrown crisps (and highly proficient at doing so). Buses (15min; W1000) meet the ferries and head to **Bomunsa** (보문사), a charming temple that constitutes the island's main sight. The complex is a five-minute uphill pant from the bus stop, with a small tearoom (9am–5pm) at its entrance; many choose to give their legs an extra workout by taking the mountain path behind the temple, which leads to a clutch of small grottoes that function as **Buddhist shrines** and boast wonderful sea views.

Ferries back to Ganghwado dry up at 8.30pm, but this is a wonderfully peaceful place to be stranded – there are **restaurants** and simple **accommodation** around both the temple and ferry terminal, as well as **bicycle hire** (W10,000/3hr) immediately off the ferry ramp for those with the muscle to pump up and down the island's hilly roads.

Deokjeokdo

Possibly the prettiest and most tranquil of the Yellow Sea isles, **DEOKJEOKDO** (덕적도) feels a world away from Seoul, though it's quite possible to visit from the capital on a day-trip. There's little in the way of sightseeing, and not much to do, but that's just the point – the island has a couple of stunning beaches and some gorgeous mountain trails, and makes a refreshing break from the hustle and bustle of the mainland. Around the ferry berth are a few shops, restaurants and *minbak*, while a bus meets the ferries and makes its way round to **Seopori Beach** (서포리 해수욕장) on the other, quieter side of the island – also home to a few *minbak*. Most who stay here for a day or two spend their time chatting to locals, lazing or throwing back beers on the beach, going fishing or taking the easy climb up to the island's main peak. Some adventurous souls make their way to **Soyado** (소야도), an island facing the ferry berth, and only a few minutes away if you can flag down a fishing boat. There's even less to do than on Seongmodo, though there are a couple of motels and *minbak* if you look hard enough, and you can rest assured you'll be one of very few foreigners to have overnighted on the island.

Three fast **ferries** (1hr; W21,900) run to Deokjeokdo from Incheon's Yeonan pier, departing at 9am, 9.30am & 2.30pm; slower ferries (2hr 30min; W12,100) leave at 8am from the same terminal.

Baengnyeongdo

Four hours' ferry-ride from Incheon is **BAENGNYEONGDO** (백령도), almost tickling the North Korean coastline and as such home to many military installations. In 2010 the **Cheonan**, a South Korean naval vessel, suspiciously sank just off the island, seriously damaging relations between the two Koreas; see p.369 for details. Baengnyeongdo literally means "White Wing Island", due to its apparent resemblance to an ibis taking flight, and although the reality is somewhat different you will find yourself gawping at Baengnyeongdo's spectacular **rock formations**, best seen from one of the tour boats that regularly depart the port. Some of the most popular are off Dumujin, to the west of the island, while at Sagot Beach the stone cliffs plunge diagonally into the sea.

The tranquil nature of these islands is sometimes diluted by swarms of summer visitors – it's best to visit on weekdays, or outside the warmest months. **Ferries** (3 daily; W57,400) head to Baengnyeongdo from Incheon's Yeonan pier, departing at 8am, 8.50am and 1pm; return sailings are at 8am, 1pm and 1.50pm. There's also simple **accommodation** on Baengnyeongdo, though given the island's distance from Incheon – and the recent military problems – it's best to organize this at a tourist information office before heading out.

The Demilitarized Zone

"The visit to the Joint Security Area at Panmunjeom will entail entry into a hostile area, and possible injury or death as a direct result of enemy action."

Disclaimer from form issued to visitors by United Nations Command

As the tour bus crawls out of Seoul and heads slowly north through the traffic, the seemingly endless urban jungle slowly diminishes in size before disappearing altogether. You're now well on the way to a place where the mists of the Cold War still linger on, and one that could still be ground zero for the Third World War – the **DEMILITARIZED ZONE**. More commonly referred to as "the DMZ", this no-man's-land is a 4km-wide buffer zone that came into being at the end of the Korean War in 1953. It sketches an unbroken spiky line across the peninsula from coast to coast, separating the two Koreas and their diametrically opposed ideologies. Although it sounds forbidding, it's actually possible to enter this zone, and take a few tentative steps into North Korean territory – thousands of civilians do so every month, though only as part of a **tightly controlled tour**. It's even home to two small communities, **Freedom Village** and **Propaganda Village** (see box, p.143). Elsewhere are a few platforms from which the curious can stare across the border, and a **tunnel** built by the North, which you can enter.

While most visitors content themselves with a packaged DMZ tour, there are more adventurous options available. The city of **Paju**, just southwest of Panmunjeom, has a few sights not at all related to North Korea – a small **arts village**, and a **publishing town** whose buildings are among the most adventurously designed in the land. To the east, and actually in Gangwon province, is the remote border town of **Cheorwon**, where anyone with their own transport – or just a little luck – will be able to take a free tour of the border. And, of course, you could go for broke and book a tour to Pyongyang in North Korea itself (p.340).

Some history

For the first year of the **Korean War** (1950–53), the tide of control yo-yoed back and forth across the peninsula (see p.365 for more details). Then in June 1951, General Ridgeway of the United Nations Command got word that the Korean People's Army (KPA) would "not be averse to" armistice talks. These talks took place in the city of Kaesong, now a major North Korean city (see p.349), but were soon shifted south to **Panmunjeom**, a tiny farming village that suddenly found itself the subject of international attention.

Ceasefire talks went ahead for two long years and often degenerated into venomous verbal battles littered with expletives. One of the most contentious issues was the repatriation of prisoners of war, and a breakthrough came in April 1953, when terms were agreed; exchanges took place on a bridge over the River Sachon, now referred to as the **Bridge of No Return**. "Operation Little Switch" came first, seeing the transfer of sick and injured prisoners (notably, six thousand returned to the North, while only a tenth of that number walked the other way); "Operation Big Switch" took place shortly afterwards, when the soldiers on both sides were asked to make a final choice over their preferred destination. Though no **peace treaty** was ever signed, representatives of the KPA, the United Nations Command (UNC) and the Chinese Peoples' Liberation Army put their names to an **armistice** on July 27, 1953; South Korean delegates refused to do so. The room where the signing took place was built specially for the occasion, and cobbled together at lightning speed by KPA personnel; it now forms part of most tours to North Korea (p.351).

An uneasy truce has prevailed since the end of the war – the longest military deadlock in history – and the DMZ is now something of a natural haven filled

The Axe Murder Incident

Relations between the two Koreas took a sharp nose-dive in 1976, when two American soldiers were killed by a pack of **axe-wielding North Koreans**. The cause of the trouble was a **poplar tree** which stood next to the Bridge of No Return: a UNC outpost stood next to the bridge, but its direct line of sight to the next Allied checkpoint was blocked by the leaves of the tree, so on August 18 a five-man American detail was dispatched to perform some trimming. Although the mission had apparently been agreed in advance with the North, sixteen soldiers from the KPA turned up and demanded that the trimming stop. Met with refusal, they launched a swift attack on the UNC troops using the axes the team had been using to prune the tree. The attack lasted less than a minute, but claimed the life of First Lieutenant Mark Barrett, as well as Captain Bonifas (who was apparently killed instantly with a single karate chop to the neck). North Korea denied responsibility for the incident, claiming that the initial attack had come from the Americans.

Three days later, the US launched **Operation Paul Bunyan**, a show of force that must go down as the largest tree-trimming exercise in history. A convoy of 24 UNC vehicles streamed towards the plant, carrying more than 800 men, some trained in *taekwondo*, and all armed to the teeth. These were backed up by attack helicopters, fighter planes and B-52 bombers, while an aircraft carrier had also been stationed just off the Korean shore. This carefully managed operation drew no response from the KPA, and the tree was successfully cut down.

with flora and fauna that's been left to regenerate and breed in relative isolation. However, there have been regular spats along the way. In the early 1960s a small number of disaffected American soldiers **defected** to the North, after somehow managing to make it across the DMZ alive (see p.375), while in 1968 the crew of the captured USS *Pueblo* (p.347) walked south over the Bridge of No Return after protracted negotiations. The most serious confrontation took place in 1976, when two American soldiers were killed in the **Axe Murder Incident** (see above), and in 1984, a young tour leader from the Soviet Union fled North Korea across the border triggering a short gun battle that left three soldiers dead.

Panmunjeom and the Joint Security Area

There's nowhere in the world quite like the **Joint Security Area** ("the JSA"), a settlement squatting in the middle of Earth's most heavily fortified frontier, and the only place in DMZ territory where visitors are permitted. Visits here will create a curious dichotomy of feelings: on one hand, you'll be in what was once memorably described by Bill Clinton as "the scariest place on Earth", but as well as soldiers, barbed wire and brutalist buildings you'll see trees, hear birdsong and smell fresh air. The village of **Panmunjeom** itself is actually in North Korean territory, and has dwindled to almost nothing since it became the venue for armistice talks in 1951. But such is the force of the name that you'll see it on promotional material for most **tours** that run to the area; these are, in fact, the only way to get in.

The JSA tour

Situated just over an hour from Seoul is **Camp Bonifas**, an American army base just outside the DMZ. Here you'll meet your guides – usually young infantry recruits whose sense of humour makes it easy to escape the seriousness of the situation – and be given a briefing session reminding you of the various dos and don'ts. Back on the bus look out for the white-marked stones pushed into the wire

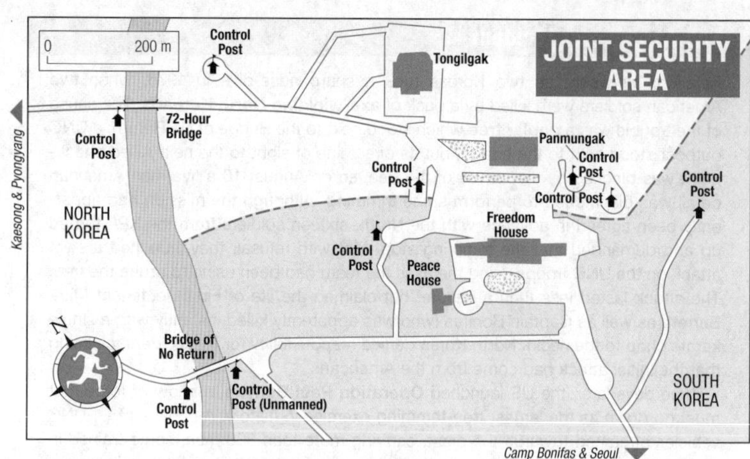

fence – these are detection devices that will fall out should anyone try to climb over. On both sides of the road you'll see hilltop points from where UNC forces keep a constant lookout across the border for any military build-up that would precede a large-scale attack.

Once inside the **JSA** itself, keep your fingers crossed that you'll be allowed to enter one of the three meeting rooms at the very centre of the complex, which offer some serious travel kudos – the chance to step into North Korea. The official Line of Control runs through the very centre of these cabins, the corners of which are guarded by South Korean soldiers, who are sometimes joined by their Northern counterparts, the enemy soldiers almost eyeball-to-eyeball. Note the microphones on the table inside the room – anything you say can be picked up by North Korean personnel. The rooms are closed to visitors when meetings are scheduled, which is just as well since some of them have descended into farce. One such fiasco occurred when members of one side – it's not clear which – brought a bigger flag than usual to a meeting. The others followed suit with an even larger banner, and the childish process continued until the flags were simply too large to take into the room; at this point, both sides agreed on a standard flag size.

From an outdoor **lookout point** near the cabins you can soak up views of the North, including the huge flag and shell-like buildings of "**Propaganda Village**" (see box opposite). You may also be able to make out the jamming towers it uses to keep out unwanted imperialist signals – check the reception on your phone. Closer to the lookout point, and actually within JSA territory, is the **Bridge of No Return**, the venue for POW exchange at the end of the Korean War (and also for James Bond in *Die Another Day* – though for obvious reasons it was filmed elsewhere).

On arriving back at Camp Bonifas you'll usually have time to pop into a gift shop, stocked with "I did the DMZ" T-shirts and a nice line in North Korean blueberry wine. Also in the area is a golf course once named by *Sports Illustrated* as the most dangerous on Earth, but there's only one hole (a par-three, for the record) and you won't be allowed to use it.

Practicalities

Almost all **tours** to the DMZ start and finish in Seoul, and there are a great number of outfits competing for your money. Note that some are much cheaper than others – these probably won't be heading to **the JSA**, the most interesting place in the DMZ, so do check to see if it's on the schedule. Most people go with the USO

"Freedom Village" and "Propaganda Village"

The DMZ is actually home to two small settlements, one on each side of the Line of Control. With the southern village rich and tidy and its northern counterpart empty and sinister, both can be viewed as a microcosm of the countries they belong to.

The southern village – referred to as "Freedom Village" by the US military, but actually called **Daeseongdong** – is a small farming community, but one out of limits to all but those living or working here. These are among the richest farmers in Korea: they pay no rent or tax, and DMZ produce fetches big bucks at markets around the country. Technically, residents have to spend 240 days of the year at home, but most commute here from their condos in Seoul to "punch in", and get hired hands to do the dirty work; if they're staying, they must be back in town by nightfall, and have their doors and windows locked and bolted by midnight. Women are allowed to marry into this tight society, but men are not; those who choose to raise their children here also benefit from a school that at the last count had eleven teachers and only eight students.

North of the Line of Control lies an odd collection of empty buildings referred to by American soldiers as "**Propaganda Village**". The purpose of its creation appears to have been to show citizens in the South the communist paradise that they're missing – a few dozen "villagers" arrive every morning by bus, spend the day taking part in wholesome activities and letting their children play games, then leave again in the evening. With the aid of binoculars, you'll be able to see that none of the buildings actually has any windows; lights turned on in the evening also seem to suggest that they're devoid of floors. Above the village flies a huge **North Korean flag**, one so large that it required a fifty-man detail to hoist, until the recent installation of a motor. It sits atop a 160m-high pole, the eventual victor in a bizarre game played out over a number of years by the two Koreas, each hell-bent on having the loftier flag. See opposite for details of yet another flag-centred battle.

(US$77; ⓣ02/724-7781, ⓦwww.uso.org/korea); tours should be booked at least four days in advance. You'll find pamphlets from other operators in your hotel lobby, and most operators speak enough English to accept a reservation by telephone; most notable are Young Il Tours (ⓣ02/730-1090, ⓦiloveseoultour.com), which adds a session of pistol shooting to the regular rounds (W105,000), and Panmunjom Travel Center (ⓣ02/771-5593, ⓦkoreadmztour.com), which offers a tour led by a North Korean defector (W77,000).

For all these tours you'll need to bring your **passport** along. Note that each comes with a number of **restrictions**, most imposed by the United Nations Command. Citizens of certain countries are not allowed into DMZ territory, including those from most nations in the Middle East, some in Africa, and communist territories such as Vietnam, Hong Kong and mainland China. An official dress code also applies (no flip-flops, ripped jeans, "clothing deemed faddish" or "shorts that expose the buttocks"), but in reality most things are OK. Also be warned that schedules can change in an instant, and that in certain areas **photography** is not allowed – you'll be told when to put your camera away. Lastly, remember that you'll be entering an extremely dangerous area – this is no place for fooling around or wandering off by yourself.

The Third Tunnel of Aggression

A short drive south of Panmunjeom is the **Third Tunnel of Aggression**, a sight that often forms part of day-tours to the DMZ. In 1974, a South Korean army patrol unit discovered a tunnel that had been burrowed under the DMZ in apparent preparation for a military attack from the North; tip-offs from North

Korean defectors and some strategic drilling soon led to the discovery of another two, and a fourth was found in 1990. North Korea has denied responsibility, claiming them to be coal mines (though they are strangely devoid of coal), but to be on the safe side the border area is now monitored from coast to coast by soldiers equipped with drills and sensors.

The third tunnel is the closest to Seoul, a city that would have been just a day's march away if the North's plan had succeeded. Regularly included in DMZ tour packages, it also gets the most visitors, though many emerge from the depths underwhelmed – it is, after all, a tunnel, even if you get to walk under **DMZ territory** up to the Line of Control that marks the actual border. On busy days it can become uncomfortably crowded – not a place for the claustrophobic. Before entering the tunnel, which runs up to 70m below the ground, visitors are usually ushered into a small theatre to be shown an **explanatory movie**. This is a ghastly but mercifully brief pro-unification shocker that gives no account at all of how the separation actually occurred, preferring instead to show the ground literally splitting to force a young girl from her family: Kim Jong-il himself would be proud of such nonsense.

Dorasan observatory and train station

South of the Third Tunnel is **Dorasan observatory**, from which visitors are able to stare at the North through binoculars – W500 is a cheap price to satisfy a bit of curiosity. This is also part of many tour schedules, but unlike the JSA you don't have to go on a guided tour. You can head instead by public transport to Dorasan station, at the end of the **Gyeonghui line**, a light-rail track which starts at Seoul station. This line continues to China, via Pyongyang: as one sign says, "it's not the last station from the South, but the first station toward the North". At the height of the inter-Korean freeze in 2007, a gleaming, modern station was built at Dorasan; in May of that year the first train in decades rumbled up the track to Kaesong in North Korea (another going in the opposite direction on the east coast line), while regular freight services got going that December. Relations between the two Koreas were extremely frosty at the time of writing and such connections had been cut, but there remains hope that this track will one day handle KTX services from Seoul to Pyongyang; in the meantime, there's a wall map showing which parts of the world Seoul will be connected to should the line ever see regular service, as well as a much-photographed sign pointing the way to Pyongyang.

To get to Dorasan, you'll first have to take the **train** to Imjingang, one station to the south, and around an hour from Seoul station. Here you'll have to go through security – bring your **passport**. There's a pretty little **park** and a few restaurants around Imjingang station, so it's possible to make a full or half-day of this trip.

Paju and around

Further south again is the satellite city of **Paju** (파주), which contains some of the most interesting sights in the border area; for once, some do not revolve around North Korea. Easiest to reach is **Paju Book City** (파주 출판도시 문화재단; Ⓦwww.pajubookcity.org), a publishing district filled with excellent **modern architecture** – quite a rarity in this land of sterile high-rise. There's no focus as such to the area, but strolling the quiet streets is rather pleasurable, and it's even possible to stay here at *Jijihyang* (Ⓣ031/955-0090; ❻), a stylish streamside hotel.

Similar architectural delights are on offer at **Heyri Art Valley** (헤이리문화예술마을), just 7km to the north; this artists' village is home to dozens of small galleries, and its countryside air is making it an increasingly popular day-trip for young, arty Seoulites. Sitting atop a hill just 1km west of Heyri is **Odusan observatory** (daily

9am–5pm; W3000), where you'll be able to peer across the border through binoculars, and buy alcoholic drinks from North Korea.

Practicalities

To **get to Heyri or the Book City**, take bus #2200 from exit 2 of Hapjeong subway station (50min; W1400); alternatively they're both within a W15,000 taxi ride of Daehwa subway station, the terminus of line 3. Buses to the observatory are irregular and tricky to find, so take a cab from either village; there won't be any taxis waiting when you exit, so check the return schedules at the observatory entrance and you'll be able to head back by bus.

Cheorwon

Were the two countries not still at each other's throats, you would be able to walk to **North Korea** from little **CHEORWON** (철원), the South's closest urban settlement to the North Korean border; note that unlike other sights in this section, it's actually in Gangwon province, not Gyeonggi. From Cheorwon, it's just about possible to take **free tours** of the **DMZ**, which given the town's remote location are far more relaxed than those on offer in Panmunjeom itself (see p.351). Driving around the area, you'll notice a substantial military presence, and checkpoints all over the place. It's not unusual to hear explosions either – training usually takes place once a week, more often if the North has been making similar noises. Be sure to look out for the large lumps of concrete suspended over the roads – their purpose is to block the path of North Korean military vehicles, should they ever arrive. Note that there are landmines and barbed wire around the border area, but you won't be allowed to venture anywhere dangerous.

Other than the free tour around the border sights, there are few actual sights in Cheorwon. However, before or after you take the tour be sure to head to nearby **Goseokjeong** (고석정), a rocky crag that pokes up through an extremely pretty section of the river that flows through Cheorwon. Buses head to this countryside location from all across the city; if you have time to kill before or after a tour, head to the riverbank – steps lead downhill from the small restaurant complex – where it's often possible to **hire a boat** for small trips (W9000 per group).

The North Korea tour

Though you can't step over the border, those wishing to get a sniff of North Korea can make use of a **free tour** laid on by the local authorities. Unfortunately it's only available to **those with their own car** – a guide comes with you in the vehicle – but it may be possible to join a ride with others taking the trip. However, the area is so quiet that it's quite common for nobody to turn up all day. Tours run from the **tourist information office** (near Goseokjeong, see p.145) four times a day (9.30am, 10.30am, 1pm & 2.30pm).

The tour is quite a thrill, and much cheaper than those operating from Seoul; guides will direct your route through beautiful countryside around the barbed wire, landmines and checkpoints to any of the official sights – there aren't many to choose from. The most popular stop is the **Second Tunnel of Aggression**, an excavated burrow discovered in 1975, and made by North Korea in apparent preparation for an attack on the South; wear decent footwear as the tunnel floor is rather wet. An armed guard – the bullets in whose gun are real – will escort you 150m under the DMZ itself to within a few hundred metres of official North Korean territory. Most then head to **Cheoluisamgak Observatory**, a short drive west of the tunnel, to peer at the North through a pair of binoculars (W500). Just outside the observatory is the disused **Woljeong-ri train station**, the last stop on the line that heads into the North. This is one of three main lines that headed across what is now the border prior to the division of the peninsula, and the carcass of one of the trains that used to ply the line is still on the tracks. The sign above the track reads "the train wants to go", but the rusty and crumbling vehicle is in no state to make requests; it'll be a long time before anything makes it down the line to Gagok, the first station on the other side of the DMZ.

On your way back to Cheorwon you'll spot plenty of **bombed out buildings** and landmine signs – the guide may allow you to stop your vehicle and get out to take a couple of pictures, but you won't be allowed anywhere near the buildings themselves.

Cheorwon practicalities

There are **buses** to Cheorwon from Seoul and several cities across Gangwon province. The city is frustratingly spread out, and you may arrive at either **Dongsong** (동송), the newer part of town, or **Gu-Cheorwon** (구철원), which is older and more atmospheric. There are plenty of motels and restaurants around both, but for a more relaxed **stay** head by bus or taxi (around W5000 from either station) to the countryside hamlet of **Goseokjeong**, from where the North Korean tours depart. These leave from the **tourist office**, which is large and pretty easy to spot in such rural climes; there are several restaurants to choose from in this area, and a couple of guesthouses too.

Gangwon

For Koreans, **GANGWON** (강원) exerts a magnetic pull. Enclosed by Gyeonggi to the west, Gyeongsang to the south, North Korea and the East Sea, it's a lush green land blessed with beaches, lakes and muscular peaks, whose rugged topography ensures that it remains the least-populated part of the country: despite being Korea's second largest province, it has a smaller population than many of its cities. Not that Gangwon is an undiscovered paradise – those in the know will direct you here, rather than to the more obvious tourist draw of Jeju Island. In summer, tour buses galore make a beeline for the region, especially the east coast beaches and the national parks, while skiers work their way around several resorts in the winter. Visitor numbers are still rising, thanks in part to a number of films and soap operas set in the province's more spectacular areas, which have roped in telly addicts from all over Asia (see box, p.150).

Chuncheon is Gangwon's capital and major city, but though it's an agreeable enough place most aren't visiting the province to sate urban pleasures. There are four **national parks** in the province, each differing in topography and popularity, and whose acknowledged champion, **Seoraksan**, contains some of the highest peaks in the land.

Beaches are even easier to come by – unlike Korea's indented, island-peppered southern and western coasts, Gangwon's eastern shore sketches a fairly straight line from the North Korean border to the Gyeongsang provinces, so you're never far away from a perfect sunrise. Neither are you likely to be far from a rushing blue river, a mountainside village, or lofty trees and peaks that recede into the distance – regular Korea can feel a world away.

Despite the natural attractions, Gangwon hasn't always been a paragon of serenity. Its historical boundaries actually extend far into North Korea, but since the end of the Korean War the province has been divided by the twin perimeters of the **Demilitarized Zone**. During the war, the mountainous terrain that for so long preserved Gangwon's tranquillity became a curse, with ferocious battles fought for strategically important peaks. Even today, the tension is palpable – much of the region's coast is fenced off to protect against attacks from the North, and even some of the most popular beaches are fringed with barbed wire and military installations – from the end of the Korean War until the signing of the armistice in 1953, all land above the 38th Parallel (which hits the coast at a point roughly halfway between Sokcho and Gangneung) came under **North Korean control**, and was eventually exchanged for an area almost equal in size north of Seoul. Tunnels under the DMZ were found in the 1970s, and a spy-filled North Korean submarine crashed on the Gangwon coast in 1996 (see p.164); the latter can still be seen, next to an old American warship, near the small village of **Jeongdongjin**.

Chuncheon and around

Despite its status as Gangwon's capital city, **CHUNCHEON** (춘천) remains small and relatively relaxed; in fact, it's the country's smallest provincial capital. Mountain-fringed and surrounded by artificial **lakes**, it boasts fresh air that's a welcome change for anyone who has been cooped up in a larger city. The main draw is the chance to sample *dakgalbi*, a famed local chicken dish (see box, p.148). Otherwise, Chuncheon is more of an "activity" destination, and there are a few good **bicycle** tracks.

Arrival and information

There are two kinds of **train** to Chuncheon from Seoul: the regular rail service from Cheongnyangni station, and the slower light-rail on the Gyeongchun line, officially part of Seoul's subway network. Express services on the main line may commence during the lifetime of this book, bringing the choice of trains to three. There are also **buses** from the capital's Dongseoul terminal and cities across Korea; you'll find a small **information booth** inside the bus terminal, which is fine for maps but little else. To get anywhere in town it's advisable to take a **taxi** (almost always less than W5000), as bus routes are too confusing and irregular for most travellers.

Accommodation

There's a line of reasonable, fairly new **motels** across the main road and downhill from the bus station; older places are dotted around the city's shopping district. As is often the way in provincial Korea, there's little real quality at the top end of the scale.

Chuncheon Bears Tourist Hotel Samcheondong ⓣ033/256-2525, ⓦwww.hotelbears.com. West of the centre and near the Jungdo ferries, Chuncheon's main tourist hotel has only been open since 1991, but is already in need of a serious revamp. There's a slightly Chinese feel to the place (and a restaurant in similar style), but some rooms have tranquil views of the lake. ❺

Grand Motel Okcheondong ⓣ033/243-5021 or 5022. The motel of choice for foreign backpackers can feel like a youth hostel at times, with helpful staff able to advise on the area. They even offer a free pick-up from the tourist office or bus station, but you won't be allowed to leave without signing the guestbook. The rooms are fine, and it's near Chuncheon's main shopping area. ❸

Motel If... Twigyedong ⓣ033/242-2154. Downhill from the bus terminal and on the opposite side of the road, this motel has funky rooms in a variety of styles. Some have internet access for a higher fee, and all have fantastic showers. ❸

The Town

The best place to **rent a bike** (W3000 per hour or W15,000 per day) is on the west side of town next to the **Ethiopian Veterans' Memorial Hall** (에티오피아 참전 기념관), a building that looks somewhat like a half-submerged Russian church. It's best to take a taxi here. From the memorial hall, a **cycleway** runs along the lake, though you may prefer to hunt down the nearby ferry dock, which has regular services to **Jungdo** (중도), a small island. Ferries run to Jungdo every half-hour, returning immediately (9am–6pm; W4300 return, bikes W1000 extra), and you'll be able to cycle around with no traffic to get in your way. In addition to the cycle tracks – some of which provide fantastic views of Chuncheon's surrounding mountains – you can also try your hand at rowing and waterskiing, though such mirth tends to restrict itself to weekends and holidays; at other times the island can be near-empty.

Two more small but pleasant islands lie further up the river – **Sangjungdo** (상중도) and **Wido** (위도). Next to the latter, which is connected to the city's northern flank by a bridge, is Chuncheon's colourful Puppet Theatre; each August, performers from Korea and abroad take part in a delightful **puppet festival** (Ⓦwww.cocobau.com). Other popular annual events include a **mime festival** (Ⓦwww.mimefestival.com), which takes place in May at venues across town.

Eating and drinking

Galbi's the word in Chuncheon; **dakgalbi**, to be precise (see below), and the shopping area in the city centre has a whole street of restaurants (Dakgalbi Golmok; 닭갈비골목) where you can sample this speciality. Another local favourite is *makguksu* (막국수) – cold buckwheat noodles with soup and hot pepper paste, and a bargain feed at about W3000 per bowl. There's only really one place to head for a **drink**, and that's the area around **Gangwon University** (강원대). Expats and locals alike often plan their night over a beer in front of the GS25 convenience store, with the former more often than not heading down the hill to the *Hard Rock Bar*.

Daewon Dakgalbi 대원 닭갈비 Onuidong. One of a number of similar places opposite the bus terminal, at the time of research this was serving the biggest portions of both *dakgalbi* and *makguksu* in the shortest time. It's straight across the footbridge from the terminal – look for the red sign.

Spoon Hyojadong. Stylish restaurant with mood music, latticed wood frames, and tatami mats to sit on. *Galbijjim* is the recommended dish, but simple meals such as *naengmyeon* noodles and *galbitang* are also available, at reasonable prices.

Umi Dakgalbi 우미 닭갈비 Dakgalbi Golmok. The most popular of a whole squadron of similar restaurants on the same street, this place is usually jam-packed; it may be hard to see what differentiates it from the rest, but bear in mind that when it comes to food, the Koreans are rarely wrong. It costs W8500 for a portion of the good stuff, and unlike many competitors they're willing to cater for single diners.

Dakgalbi

You may have sampled regular *galbi*, whereby you cook (or to be more precise, set fire to) meat at your own table. **Dakgalbi** (닭갈비) is a little different – it's made with chicken meat, rather than beef or pork, and is grilled in a wide pan so there's no visible flame action for regular *galbi* arsonists to enjoy. You'll find this dish pretty much anywhere in Korea, but for some reason Chuncheon gets the glory. Imagine throwing a **raw chicken kebab** into a hot metal tray to boil up with a load of veg – you get to do this at your table for around W8000 per portion. You usually need at least two people for a meal, and once you're nearly finished it's common, or perhaps obligatory, to throw some **rice or noodles** into the pan for a stomach-expanding second course.

Gangchon

Chuncheon's surrounding area is alluringly green and undulating, and well worth delving into. One of the most accessible places is the small town of **GANGCHON** (강촌), a pretty and (usually) tranquil place just west of Chuncheon. Although it has a national reputation as a student "MT" centre par excellence – **Membership Training** is a somewhat non-studious exercise that usually involves lots of drinking, singing and buzzing about on quad bikes – such revelry tends to confine itself to student holidays, and at other times it's a far more relaxing place to stay than Chuncheon for those who want a taste of inland Gangwon.

The major sight here is **Gugok-pokpo** (daily 8am–7pm; W1600), a tumbling waterfall surrounded by hills and trails that make for a rewarding few hours of exploration. It's 5km away from Gangchon down a highly picturesque valley studded with tiny houses, but the rural charm of this area is being diluted by the new train line being built through it. The journey from Gangchon to the falls is best made by bike on a cycle path that heads into the valley from town; roadside stalls in the village offer **cycle and scooter rental**, with bikes going for W2000 per hour or W10,000 per day, scooters for about six times that price, and quads for a little more again. To get to the falls from the train station, head into town and take the first right after the stream. Bus #50 heads there along the parallel road that runs down the stream's opposite bank.

Practicalities

Gangchon is one stop before Chuncheon on the **train** line, and two stops on the Gyeongchun **light-rail** line, from Seoul's Cheongnyangni station, and there are also regular **buses** from Chuncheon. The village has enough motels and restaurants to cater for the students during their holidays, and an excess for the rest of the year; one comfy **place to stay** is the *Good-Time Motel* (ⓣ033/261-4720; ❹) on the main road, which has large, clean rooms with big televisions. Cheaper and more rural *minbak* accommodation can be found in the valley linking the town with Gugok-pokpo; along this same road is *Lorellai*, a pleasant cabin-style **tearoom** and restaurant.

Nami Island

Further downstream from Gangchon is tiny **Nami Island** (남이섬), which has achieved international fame for being the scene of the main characters' first date and kiss on the hugely successful *Winter Sonata* soap opera (see box, p.150). The programme was most successful in Japan, and the island is often packed with Nipponese tourists, mostly middle-aged and female, some of whom bizarrely choose to sport **wigs** in an attempt to impersonate the male lead. Soap hysteria aside, you're likely to enjoy the island, which has plenty of paths lined with ginkgo and chestnut trees, maples and white birches that will make for a beautiful walk; you might even encounter the occasional **ostrich**. Unless you're on a tour bus ask at tourist offices in Chuncheon or Seoul (or Tokyo) for information – the easiest way to get here is by taxi from Gapyeong, a small city connected to Chuncheon by intercity bus, and also a stop on the train line.

Cheongpyeongsa

The gorgeous, man-made **Soyang Lake** (소양호) lies just east of Chuncheon, hemmed in at its western end by the huge **Soyang dam** (소양댐). It was once possible to rifle east towards Sokcho on fast ferries, but these services – among the most beautiful journeys that Korea has to offer – were cancelled in 2009; it would

Winter Sonata

Korean drama has recently enjoyed enormous popularity across Asia, with snow-filled **Winter Sonata** the biggest success to date. The story runs as follows: a boisterous girl named **Yujin** meets withdrawn **Junsang** on a bus. Despite being total opposites they fall in love and Yujin lends her gloves to her new man, who promises to give them back on New Year's Eve. He doesn't turn up, and Yujin hears that he died in a car accident on the way. Fast forward ten years to Yujin's engagement ceremony, when she thinks that she sees Junsang – now, for some reason, choosing to wear pink lipstick – through the crowd. She later finds out that it isn't Junsang but **Min-hyung**, a successful American architect. Yujin ends up working at the same company, and one further car crash later it transpires that unbeknown to Yujin not only is the man Junsang after all, but that he's Yujin's half-brother. As the pair part ways, Yujin hands him the blueprints for a beautiful house she'd designed as a farewell present. Of course, they're not related after all, and when Yujin returns to Korea from France three years later she finds out that Junsang is in fact the half-brother of her erstwhile fiancé. She then happens across the house that she once handed Junsang in blueprint form, finds him inside – now blind, just to heighten the tragedy – and they fall in love once more.

Junsang got hearts racing all over Asia, and **Bae Yong-jun**, the actor who played him, is now an international superstar whose face is plastered across all kinds of merchandise – just look at the socks on sale in Seoul's Myeongdong district. Nowhere was he more successful than in Japan, where he is now revered as *Yon-sama*, a title roughly equivalent to an English knighthood. Junsang also helped the stereotypically strong-but-sensitive Korean male replace the martial arts hero as Asia's role model, and Korean men now enjoy considerable demand from females across the continent.

be worth asking at a tourist office to see if they've resumed. The only ferries now leaving from the dam are those heading to **Cheongpyeongsa** (청평사; 24hr; W1300), a majestic temple that, until fairly recently, was only accessible by boat. The temple's appeal lies not in superb architecture or historical importance (though it's over a thousand years old, it was razed to the ground and rebuilt several times), but in the watery approach – ferries remain the easiest way of getting here – and even then, it's a fair walk from the ferry dock. Unfortunately, the secret is out, and the temple is now fronted by restaurants, snack stalls and *minbak* of a small tourist village.

Practicalities

To get to the dam, take **bus** #11 or #12 (40min; W1000) from outside Chuncheon's bus terminal; the **ferries** (15min; W5000) are then a short walk along the road. Once you arrive at Cheongpyeongsa dock, it's an easy half-hour walk to the temple.

Sokcho and around

As you head north along Korea's eastern coast, the appealingly ugly coastal city of **SOKCHO** (속초) is the country's last major settlement before the barbed wire of the DMZ. Despite its size, it still leans heavily on the fishing industry; all around you'll see racks of squid, hung out to dry in the sun like laundry. Brackish, decaying and a little over-large, it's a tough city to love, though repeated attempts have been made at sprucing it up a bit, particularly in the area around Expo Park,

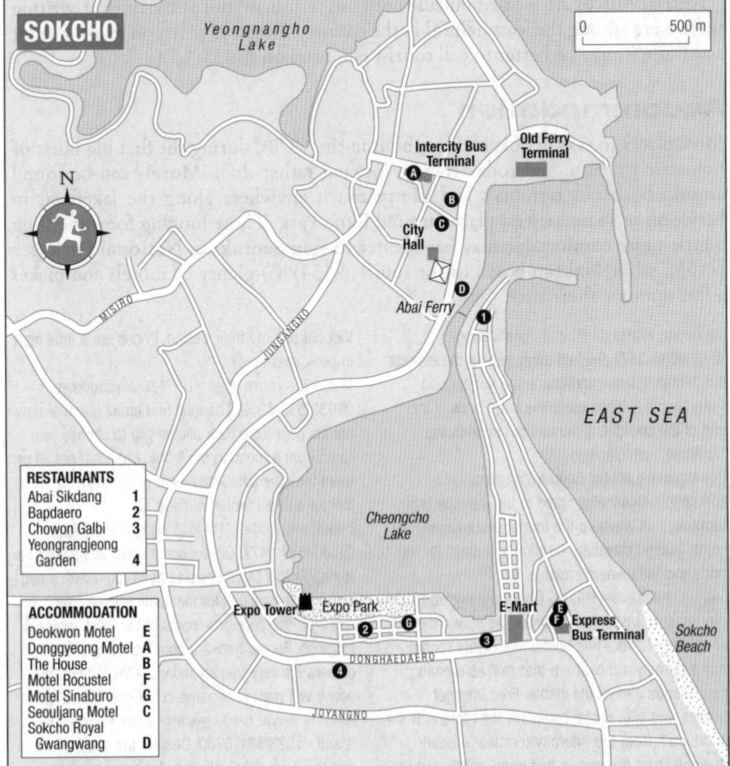

by adding walking trails and a small amusement park. Despite its faults, Sokcho receives more international visitors than any other city in Gangwon, though most of them are on their way to the wonderful crags of **Seoraksan National Park**, which lies within visible range to the west (see p.155). It's also possible to venture north to **Hwajinpo lagoon** for a look at some old presidential villas, or south to **Naksan Beach** and its resident temple. Sokcho's own sights are few and far between with only one a unique experience – the winch-ferry journey to tiny **Abai Island**. Both north and south of the city, the coast is littered with small packs of motels and restaurants, but though accessible by bus, their scattered positions mean that they're better visited with private transport.

Arrival and information

Sokcho curls around Cheongcho Lake in a C-shape, one loosely tied together in a very literal sense by the twin steel cables along which tiny ferry-platforms winch their way to Abai Island. To the north of the city is the **intercity bus terminal**, from which local buses aplenty trundle through the city centre to the **express bus terminal** in the south. Buses #7 and #7-1, from either terminal, continue on to Seoraksan National Park. Others head further down the coast to the local **airport** at Yangyang, but this has served no flights since 2008, and will likely be torn down before long.

Tourist offices are located outside both bus terminals, but at the time of writing these were among the least helpful in the country. Both can give you maps, but for assistance it may be better to call tourist enquiries on ⓣ033/1330.

Accommodation

Most places to stay in Sokcho were built in the 1970s, during the first big burst of domestic tourism, and today they're looking rather drab. **Motels** can be found around both bus terminals and pretty much anywhere along the lakefront in between, with the newest places around Expo Park. Those looking for something a little more comfortable may have better luck in **Seoraksan National Park** (see p.155), while **Naksan** beach to the south (p.154) has plenty of motels and makes a fun summer alternative.

Deokwon Motel 덕원 모텔 Joyangdong ⓣ033/635-3477. Tucked away behind the express bus terminal, this motel has some large, good-value rooms – try to score the large ones at the end of the corridor, if you can put up with the "romantic" circular beds. ❷

Donggyeong Motel Dongmyeongdong ⓣ033/631-6444. Right next to the intercity bus terminal, this is where the tourist office usually points budget travellers – rooms are great for the price and the owners amiable. ❷

The House Hostel Dongmyeongdong ⓣ033/633-3477. Under the stewardship of affable Mr. Yoo, this hostel has comfy rooms and a homely atmosphere that makes meeting new friends almost inevitable. Free internet access and bike rental complete the picture. It's a short walk from the intercity terminal – head downhill, turn the corner and keep an eye out to your right. Dorms W13,000, singles W20,000, doubles ❷

Motel Rocustel 모텔 로커스텔 Joyangdong ⓣ033/633-4959. You can't miss this pink jalopy of a building behind the express bus terminal. It's too brash for some, but has nice rooms with a bit of thought put into their design. Prices are a little high in peak season. ❹

Motel Sinaburo 모텔 시나부로 Joyangdong ⓣ033/636-5959. The best of a small patch of new motels near Expo Park allows you to choose your room from a menu in the lobby. Note that not all of them face the lake – maybe a good thing, as there's a small funfair outside. ❹

Seouljang Motel 시나브로 Dongmyeongdong ⓣ033/633-3477. Off-season it's just about possible to haggle this place down to get a room with a bed and private facilities for the same price as the sleep-on-the-floor box-rooms of the local *yeoinsuk* lodgings. Rooms here are comfy enough and the owners are very friendly indeed – the lady of the house will want your name in her guestbook. ❷

Sokcho Royal Gwangwang Hotel Facing Abai Island ⓣ033/631-8700. Despite the soulless lobby and the downright ugliness of the surrounding area, this hotel provides the comfiest possible stay in central Sokcho, which admittedly isn't saying much. Rooms are stylishly decorated and have wooden floors, with views of the city's port from the hotel's top levels. Ask about discounts off-season, when it can become quite a bargain. ❻

The City

There's little to see in Sokcho itself, and most of the attractions popular with visitors lie outside the city. One exception is tiny **Abai Island** (아바이 마을), the most brackish part of this salty city, and connected to it by road and winch-ferry. Seemingly transported here from a bygone era, Abai's warren of tight lanes is well worth a wander, and it's also famed for the peculiar dish *sundae*. The island is connected on its southern side to the express bus terminal road by an unnecessarily large bridge, and to the City Hall area by an incredibly cute ferry service. Little more than a platform attached to steel cables, it runs day and night along a winch line, the two operators using what look like giant tuning forks to haul the ferry across. It's quite a spectacle, and may well be the cheapest thrill you can get in Korea – just W200 per person. Near central Sokcho is **Expo Park**, a family area where bikes and mini-quads are available to rent; there's also a small amusement park and a viewing tower, the latter looking something like a space-age *hareubang*.

A twenty-minute walk north of the intercity bus terminal will bring you to **Yeongnangho** (영랑호), a tranquil lake set away from Sokcho's brine and bustle. From its eastern shore, you can see Ulsanbawi – Seoraksan's distinctive spiny rock ridge – reflected in the water. It's a great area for a **bike ride** – the nearest rental outlets are in the city centre (see "Lisitings", below). To get here by bus, take #1 or #1-1 from Sokcho's main road.

South of the city centre, and within walking distance of the express bus terminal, is **Sokcho beach** (속초 해수욕장); this small stretch of sand can get extremely busy in the summer, when you'll be able to rent out rubber rings or take a banana boat ride.

Eating

Like the accommodation, **restaurants** in Sokcho have a general air of decay about them; nonetheless, there are some decent places to eat. **Sundae** (순대) is the local speciality, but be warned that it has nothing to do with ice cream. It's actually a kind of sausage with various odds and ends stuffed into intestinal lining; like haggis, most people find the dish somehow tastes better than the sum of its parts. Though *sundae* is available all over Korea – mainly in markets – the squid variety (오징어 순대; *ojingeo sundae*) is an Abai speciality, and the island is the best and most atmospheric place in Sokcho to eat all varieties of the dish.

Abai Sikdang 아바이 식당 Abai Island. If you really fancy getting into the local groove and chowing down on stuffed intestine, this restaurant is the best place to try it. *Abai Sundae* – a local take on the dish – is a little expensive at W10,000, but it tastes superb; larger servings are available for those travelling in groups.

Bupdaero 법대로 Joyangdong. All you can eat for W5500 – if that doesn't tempt you, you're not hungry enough. Despite the low price and the canteen atmosphere, the (largely veggie-based) food is actually pretty good – just the treat for hungry hikers. Near the motels in Expo Park.

Chowon Galbi 초원 갈비 Joyangdong. Grilled pork ribs go for W8000 at this popular second-floor *galbi* joint, as well as rib-eye steak or amazingly cheap *naengmyeon* noodles. Head straight on from E-Mart, and look for the pig sticking its thumbs up.

Gimbap Cheonguk 김밥천국. This chain restaurant offers a long list of cheap, filling Korean specialities such as *gimbap*, *ramyeon* and *rabokki*, which are served up within minutes of your order. There are several branches on the main road, Jungangno.

Yeongrangjeong Garden 영랑정 가든 Joyangdong. Food in this mushroom-like building near Expo Park is expensive, but locals swear it's the best in town. The English-language menu has a list of succulent beef to barbecue from W26,000 per person, or there are cheaper noodle dishes.

Listings

Bike rental Bikes can be rented in Expo Park from underneath the large *hareubang*-like tower for W2000 per hour, or W8000 per day.

Car hire Several companies have offices outside the express bus terminal, including Avis and Juseong. Rates start at around W35,000 per day.

Hiking equipment There are numerous stores on the main road of the city centre, including Treksta and North Face, both conveniently located opposite City Hall.

Post office The main branch (Mon–Fri 9am–6pm) is located near the intercity bus terminal, just a short walk from City Hall.

Supermarkets There's an E-Mart a short walk north of the express bus terminal – come out of the main exit and head right down the main road, then right again at the next main junction.

Hwajinpo lagoon

Travelling north of Sokcho by road, tensions emanating from the area's proximity to North Korea become more and more apparent. Huge chunks of concrete sit suspended at the roadsides, ready to be dropped to block the path of any North Korean military vehicles that might one day come thundering along. Those with their own vehicle will be able to go all the way along to **Goseong unification observatory** at the border, but perhaps even more interesting is **Hwajinpo** (화진포), a stupendously beautiful **lagoon** en route. This was once used as a holiday escape by the Korean great and good – summer villas belonging to three prominent Korean politicians can be visited on the same ticket (daily 9am–5pm; W2000). **Kim Il-sung** (North Korea's creator, "Great Leader" and still the country's president despite his death in 1994; see p.337) had a base here before the area was given to the South after the Korean War. This building was destroyed, but a replica has been built in its place, and now contains a mildly interesting collection of photographs; two particular displays are titled "Ceaseless provocations and atrocities by North Korea" and "Nothing has changed at all" – hardly in the spirit of reconciliation. **Syngman Rhee** and **Lee Ki-boong** had villas here too; Rhee was President of South Korea from 1948 to 1960, when protests forced him to flee to Hawaii, at which point his deputy, Lee, killed himself shortly after shooting his parents. It's possible to walk between all three villas, but none is particularly interesting, and all could have been restored with far greater care; the beauty of the lagoon, however, makes a visit worthwhile, as does its sandy beach – white sands cordoned off by barbed wire and traps for North Korean frogmen (don't go swimming too far). There's also an aquarium in the area (same times; W1000).

Practicalities

To get to the lagoon, take the #1 or #1-1 **bus** from Sokcho and get off at Chodo (초도) stop; the lagoon is then a short walk down a side road. There are also plenty of *minbak* (❷) around the bus stop if you feel like **staying** the night in such bucolic environs.

Naksan beach and temple

Twelve kilometres south of Sokcho, and accessible on buses #9 and #9-1, is **Naksan Beach** (낙산 해수욕장), by far the longest along this stretch of coast. Almost unbearably popular in the summer, it's accordingly surrounded by hundreds of motels and seafood restaurants. Just north of the beach is **Naksansa** (낙산사; 24hr; free), a temple situated on the shore; it's highly photogenic, as you'd expect of a sea-facing temple, and worth noting that this combination is almost unique on the Korean peninsula. Naksansa is still undergoing restoration work after being ravaged by fire in 2005 – most of the complex looks a little *too* new, but you can still see charred tree trunks and stumps. A walk to the elegant white Goddess of Mercy statue at the top of the complex affords great views of the sea to the east and Seoraksan National Park to the west, with the gleaming teeth of Ulsanbawi particularly evident from here. The temple is breezy and open, with plenty of nooks and crannies to explore, particularly around the rocky shore area.

Practicalities

Accommodation rates in the area go up and down with the temperature, but motels get newer and cheaper as you move away from the beach and main access road. The only distinctive place is *Hotel Naksan Beach* (❼) near the temple entrance, but with its old, stuffy rooms and the faintly Soviet-era atmosphere of the lobby it represents poor value for money – you're better off at a decent motel on Naksan Beach. Their seawater **sauna**, however, is nicer than it sounds and can be used by non-guests for W6000.

Seoraksan National Park

Koreans gush about **SEORAKSAN NATIONAL PARK** (설악산 국립 공원), and with good reason. The nation's northernmost park, it contains some of the tallest peaks in the country, with mist-fringed bluffs of exposed crag that could have come straight from a Chinese painting. The name gains ambiguity in translation, but roughly translates as "Snow-cragged Mountains"; these bony peaks are pretty enough on a cloudy day, but in good weather they're set alight by the sun, bathed in spectacular hues during its rising and setting.

The park stretches around 40km from east to west and about the same from north to south, with the wide area crisscrossed with myriad **hiking trails**: the routes mentioned here are by no means exhaustive. Also bear in mind that some are closed off from time to time in rotation in order to protect the land: in peak season there can be literally queues of hikers stomping along the more popular routes, and this pressure takes its toll. The park offers several two-day hikes heading around **Daecheonbong**, its highest peak, but the focal point is undoubtedly **Ulsanbawi**, a beautiful spine of jagged rock to the north which resembles a stegosaur spine, the fossilized jaw of a giant crocodile, or a thousand other things depending on your angle, the time of day, and the weather. The time of year is important, too; Seoraksan is one of the highest parks in the country and, as a result, usually the first to display the reds, yellows and oranges of autumn.

Seoraksan can be roughly split into three main areas. **Outer Seorak,** the most accessible part of the park from Sokcho, is where most of the action takes place. **South Seorak** looms above the small spa town of Osaek, while to the west are the less crowded peaks of **Inner Seorak**.

Park accommodation

The bulk of Seoraksan's **accommodation** is situated a downhill walk from the Seorakdong entrance on the east of the park; there are a few classy hotels near the park gates, and a clutch of much cheaper motels around twenty minutes' walk back down the access road. It's also possible to stay at **Osaek**, the spa village at the southern end of the park; most of the *yeogwan* here pump **hot spring water** into the bedrooms, and some have communal hot spring baths that can be used by non-guests (W5000–10,000); rates vary from W35,000 in the winter to over W65,000 in summer and autumn. The top choice is *Green Yard*

Mountain shelters and camping in Seoraksan

If your hiking schedule necessitates an overnight stay in the mountains, you'll need to hunt down one of several basic **shelters**. These make for an atmospheric stay, and cost from W5000 to W7000 per night (an extra W1000 for blankets). While you're unlikely to be kicked out on a wet evening, to guarantee a place you'll have to book ahead on Korea's national park website (ⓦwww.knps.or.kr) or reserve through the Seoraksan park office (ⓣ033/636-7700). Unfortunately, you'll have to select the specific shelter in advance, which is a pain for those whose hike takes them longer than expected; most popular are the **Yangpok** and **Jungcheong** shelters, which generally allow for the most leeway. Sleeping at the peaks themselves is not allowed, though some intrepid hikers do so in their sleeping bags, waking sodden with dew in the midst of empty trails and wonderful views – just make sure you're well hidden. Rudimentary **camping facilities** are also available from W500 per tent at Seorakdong and Jangsudae. Book ahead in summer or on weekends in the autumn, when the leaves are turning and the trails are at their busiest.

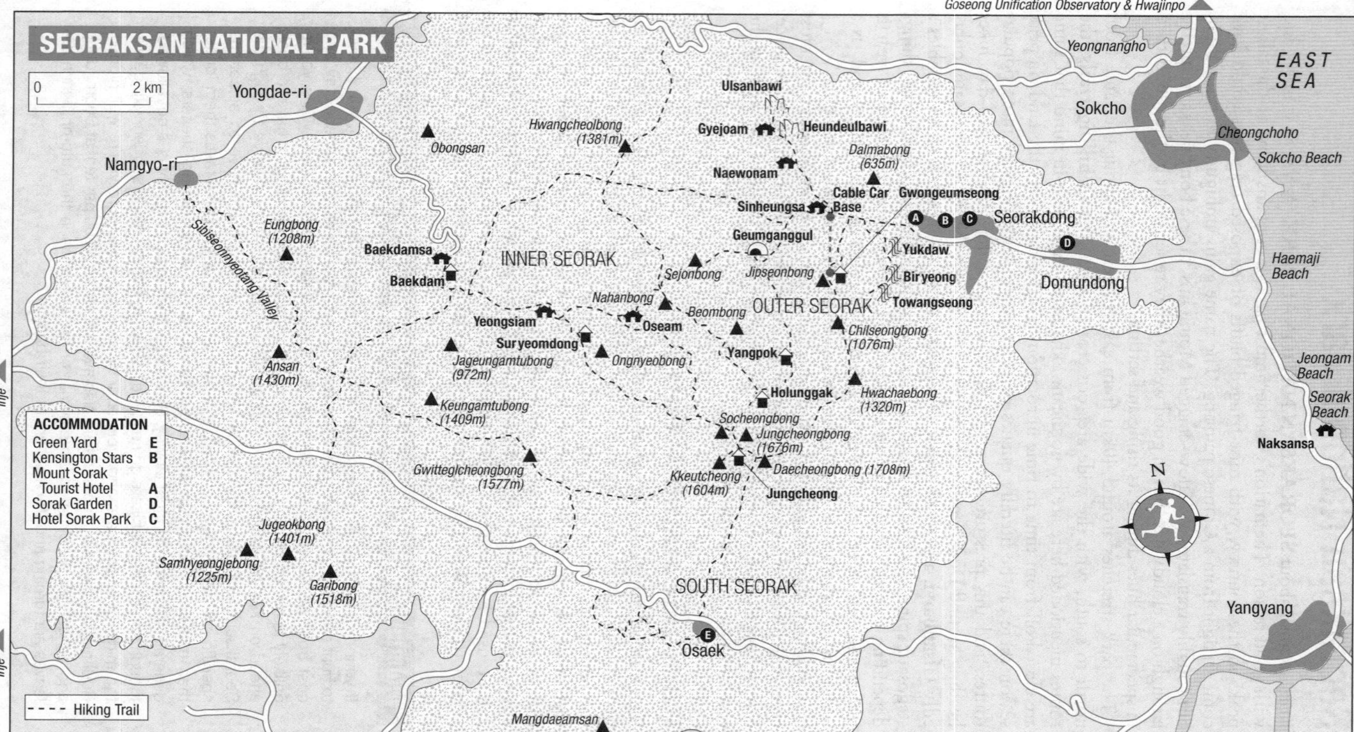
SEORAKSAN NATIONAL PARK
0
2 km
Goseong Unification Observatory & Hwajinpo
EAST SEA
Yeongnangho
Sokcho
Cheongchoho
Sokcho Beach
Haemaji Beach
Jeongam Beach
Seorak Beach
Naksansa
Yangyang
N
Yongdae-ri
Namgyo-ri
Obongsan
Hwangcheolbong (1381m)
Ulsanbawi
Gyejoam
Heundeulbawi
Naewonam
Dalmabong (635m)
Cable Car Base
Gwongeumseong
Sinheungsa
Seorakdong
Geumganggul
Domundong
Yukdaw
Biryeong
Towangseong
Jipseonbong
Sejonbong
OUTER SEORAK
INNER SEORAK
Eungbong (1208m)
Sibiseonnyeotang Valley
Baekdamsa
Baekdam
Nahanbong
Beombong
Yeongsiam
Oseam
Suryeomdong
Ongnyeobong
Yangpok
Chilseongbong (1076m)
Jageungamtubong (972m)
Ansan (1430m)
Holunggak
Hwachaebong (1320m)
Keungamtubong (1409m)
Socheongbong
Jungcheongbong (1676m)
Daecheongbong (1708m)
Kkeutcheong (1604m)
Jungcheong
Gwitteglcheongbong (1577m)
SOUTH SEORAK
Osaek
Jugeokbong (1401m)
Samhyeongjebong (1225m)
Garibong (1518m)
Mangdaeamsan
Inje
Inje
ACCOMMODATION
Green Yard E
Kensington Stars B
Mount Sorak Tourist Hotel A
Sorak Garden D
Hotel Sorak Park C
Hiking Trail

(Ⓣ033/672-8500; ⑤), a hotel with good-value rooms and a couple of restaurants. Simpler *minbak* accommodation (from W20,000 per room) is on offer at the village of **Yongdae-ri** on the park's northwest boundary.

All places listed below are in **Seorakdong**; note that prices from June to October tend to be far higher than at other times of year, especially on weekends.

Kensington Stars Hotel Ⓣ033/635-4001, Ⓦwww.kensington.co.kr. A favourite of visiting dignitaries, the *Kensington* has a genuinely English feel to it, with London buses parked up outside, suits of armour in the faux library, and mahogany everywhere. Built in 1971, it's managed to keep itself on form, with excellent rooms; hefty discounts can be enjoyed off-season, plus slightly smaller ones if you give breakfast a miss. ⑦

Mount Sorak Tourist Hotel Ⓣ033/636-7101 to 7105. Very simple rooms for the price, but you can chop the rack rate in half off-season. It's actually inside Seoraksan itself, and guests can enter the park for free, as the hotel's entrance road circumnavigates the park gates. ⑥

Sorak Garden Ⓣ033/636-7156. This motel lies, as the name suggests, in a leafy setting just off the main road in Seorakdong's main motel area. Rooms are simple, lino-floored and have TV; there's also a cheap restaurant in the lobby. ③

Hotel Sorak Park Ⓣ033/636-7711, Ⓦwww.hotelsorakpark.co.kr. Views of Seoraksan's peaks are particularly good from the balconies of this scrupulously clean hotel; from some rooms, you'll be able to see the sea at the same time. There are a few excellent restaurants, and free shuttle buses to Yangyang airport. ⑦

Outer Seorak

It's extremely easy to get from Sokcho to **Seorakdong** (설악동), the main Outer Seorak (외설악; *oe-seorak*) entrance – buses #7 and #7-1 (W950) leave often from the city's main road. The transition from the beaches and seafood restaurants of the coast to the peaks and pine lodges of the mountains can be surprisingly swift, sometimes taking as little as twenty minutes; on warm weekends and holidays, however, the access road can be blanketed by one huge traffic jam, and **delays** of over an hour are not uncommon before you're finally released outside the *Kensington Hotel*.

Just beyond the Seorakdong entrance is the entry terminal of a **cable car** (W5000 one-way, W8000 return), which whisks people up to the top of a nearby peak for some great views. From the base of the cable car lead three easy and rewarding two-hour round-trip hikes; everything is signposted in Korean and English, though it's prudent to nab a map from the park entrance (W1000).

The Heundeulbawi trail

The most popular trail heads to **Heundeulbawi** (흔들바위; literally "the rocking rock"). On the way you'll pass Sinheungsa, a modest temple-with-a-view founded in the seventh century but rebuilt several times since; this is home to a large bronze Buddha and some wonderfully detailed "Heavenly Kings", four painted guardians that watch over the temple. The trail then continues up to Gyejoam, a **cave hermitage** chiselled from the rock – this has for centuries been a place of meditation, but given the popularity of the trail you'll have to arrive very early to get any sense of serenity – from where it's a short distance to Heundeulbawi, a sixteen-ton boulder, which, despite its size, can be (and is, frequently) rocked to and fro by groups of people. Many visitors choose to stop here for a picnic, and there's also a small snack bar – it's hard to resist the sweet-smelling waffles on sale, though tea made from local fruits is a healthier option for those wishing to head beyond the rock, where the path becomes much steeper. An hour up this trail, which consists of metal stairways, vertigo-inducing bridge passes and more than eight hundred steps, is the summit of **Ulsanbawi** (울산바위), a highly distinctive 873m-high granite crag thrusting out of the surrounding pine trees. Legend has it that the large rock formation was once a living being that came from Ulsan, a city in southeast Korea. It heard one day that a new mountain range was being put together – the Geumgang mountains in present-day North Korea – which were to be the most beautiful on the whole peninsula. Finding on arrival that there was no more room for gargantuan masses of rock, Ulsanbawi headed back home, but fell asleep in the Seorak mountains and never woke up.

The Towangseong trail

From the cable-car base, a second popular hike heads southeast through a tight ravine, taking in a few **waterfalls** on the way – Yukdam, Biryeong and Towangseong. **Yukdam** is less a waterfall than a collection of tumbling cascades; hence its name, which means "Six Pools". The **Biryeong** fall further on is far taller, toppling almost forty metres down a cliff face. Almost an hour into the ravine, most hikers turn back here, but though it looks like the end of the line the last waterfall, **Towangseong**, is a further twenty-minute hike away.

The Geumganggul trail

A third walk – arguably the most pleasant in the whole park – heads west from Sinheungsa to the lofty cave of **Geumganggul** (금강굴). Just over half an hour's walk from the cable car, this grotto sits almost halfway up one of the many spires of rock that line the valley; it was created as a place of meditation, though the height of the cave and the commanding views it provides make it hard to truly relax.

Daecheongbong

From **Geumganggul**, many head back the way they came, but among the day-trippers you'll see people setting out for an assault on the park's highest peak, **Daecheongbong** (대청봉; 1708m), an otherworldly confusion of rock, and the third-highest peak in the country. From the cave it's a tough all-day hike, but it's possible to cut out some of the upward climb by taking a well-signed route from the top of the cable car. Either way, you'll probably need to spend the night at one of several **shelters** – see box, p.155 for details.

Osaek and South Seorak

Sitting pretty at the southern border of the national park, **Osaek** (오색) is a small village famed for the **hot spring waters** that course beneath its rolling hills. Osaek actually means "five colours", though this was a reference to the flowers fed by the nutritious springs, rather than the waters themselves. The subterranean bounty can be imbibed at several points in the village – the taste something close to an infusion made from flat lemonade and copper – or bathed in at the communal washrooms of numerous *yeogwan*, many of whose facilities are open to non-guests.

To get to Osaek, take one of the half-hourly **buses** from Sokcho's intercity bus terminal (W3500). From the village, it's possible to make an attempt on Daechongbong, which is just within day-hike territory – four hours up, three down.

Inner Seorak

If you want a quiet hike, this is the place for you. Further away from Sokcho than the Outer Seorak range, there is less to see at **Inner Seorak** (내설악; *nae-seorak*), and it receives a fraction of the visitors. The area is still accessible from Sokcho, although there are only a few buses a day; these head from the intercity bus terminal to within hiking distance of Baekdamsa, a temple in the northwestern side of the park, on the way passing Yongdae-ri, a small village that has *minbak* and restaurants for those who want to stay as close as possible to the mountains. **Inje**, a town just 15km west of the park, is another alternative base.

Ninety minutes' walk from Yongdae-ri, a route also plied by the occasional bus, is **Baekdamsa** (백담사), a temple with a curious history. It started life much further west in the seventh century, but a series of unexplained fires led to several changes of location, until the monks finally settled in Seoraksan surrounded by water – Baekdamsa actually means "The Temple of a Hundred Pools".

From here, there are a number of **hiking** options – one day-long trail heads to Seorakdong in the east of the park, while others converge on Daecheongbong; one of the most pleasant is a ridge route that runs from Daeseungnyeong, a peak lying around four hours' hike south of Baekdamsa. Daeseungnyeong can also be reached via the **Sibiseonnyeotang valley**, one of the prettiest routes in Inner Seorak, which heads southeast from Namgyo-ri, a village southwest of Yongdae-ri, and also connected to Sokcho by bus. Getting to Daecheongbong on either of these routes will certainly mean staying at a park shelter.

Gangneung and around

In terms of size and numbers, **GANGNEUNG** (강릉) is a big player in Gangwon terms – it's the biggest city on the northeastern coast and, like its provincial buddies Sokcho and Donghae, is spread thinly over a large area. Despite its relaxed atmosphere, staying overnight in Gangneung is not really recommended; nearby Jeongdongjin (p.162) is a far better option. That said, Gangneung makes a good base for hikers or temple-hunters heading to charming **Odaesan National Park**, and has a couple of sights of its own, including excellent **beaches**. If you're here in winter, you'll be able to make use of the superb facilities at **Yongpyeong Ski Resort**. However, if you can, try to time your visit around the fifth day of the fifth lunar moon – usually in May – when the riverside **Dano festival** is held. Events take place all over the country on this auspicious date, but the biggest is in Gangneung, a five-day event which has commemorated the "Double Fifth" with dancing and shamanist rituals for over four hundred years. The festival provides your best opportunity to see *ssireum*, a Korean version of wrestling often compared to sumo, but far more similar to the Mongolian practice.

The Town

Gangneung's main sight is **Ojukheon** (오죽헌; daily 9am–6pm; W2000), a network of floral paths and traditional buildings, and the birthplace of **Lee Yulgok**, also known as Yi-Yi, a member of the *yanbang* – Korea's Confucian elite – and one of its most famous scholars (see box, p.160). The complex is quite large, and much of it is paved, but there's a pleasant green picnic area surrounded by tall pines, as well as a patch of rare black bamboo to stroll through. Ojukheon is especially popular in the autumn, when its trees burst into a riot of flame. Rice fields surround the complex so it can be a little hard to know when to get off the bus (see p.160 for details) – be sure to tell the driver where you want to go. As you head east you come to **Gyeongpoho** (경포호; 24hr; free), a lake overlooked by an ornate pavilion, and the slightly bizarre **Chamsori Edison Gramophone Museum** (참소리 축음기 에디슨 박물관; daily 9am–5.30pm; W7000), which claims to be the largest gramophone museum in the world (those doubting the existence of any others should note that there's another in Jeongdongjin, just down the road). East again is **Gyeongpo beach** (경포 해수욕장), a long stretch of white sand that's one of the most popular beaches in the province; there's all kinds

Yi-Yi: star of the W5000 note

Lee Yulgok (1536–84), more commonly known by his pen name **Yi-Yi**, is one of the most prominent Confucian scholars in Korea's history, and once lived in the **Ojukheon** complex in Gangneung. A member of the country's *yangban* elite, he was apparently able to write with Chinese characters at the age of 3, and was composing poetry by the time he was 7 years old, much of it on pavilions surrounding the glassy lake at Gyeongpoho just down the road. At 19 he was taken to the hills to be educated in Buddhist doctrine, but abandoned this study to excel in **political circles**, rising through the ranks to hold several important posts, including Minister of Personnel and War. At one point, he advised the King to prepare an army of 100,000 to repel a potential **Japanese invasion** – the advice was ignored, and a huge attack came in 1592, just after Yi-Yi's death. His face is on one side of the **W5000 note**, while on the other is the famed "Insects and Plants", painting from his mother, **Sin Saimdang** (1504–51), who was a well-known poet and artist; you'll find her on the **W50,000 note**. Her selection, interestingly, managed to ruffle feathers with traditionalists and liberals alike – Confucian-thinking men were aghast that a woman should be on the front of Korea's most valuable note, while feminists were similarly distraught that this role model of "inferior" Confucian-era womanhood should be chosen ahead of more progressive ladies.

of water-based fun to be had in the summer, when it can be heaving with people. Well-informed locals prefer **Anmok beach** (안목 해수욕장), a more relaxed stretch of sand further south, which rarely fills up.

Practicalities

Gangneung is on Korea's **rail** network, but the coastal line service is sparse so it's usually more convenient to arrive by **bus**. The express and intercity terminals are joined at the hip in the west of the city, with a helpful **tourist information** centre outside (Ⓣ033/640-5129); another info booth can be found outside the train station. Most of the city's main sights lie on one **bus route** – pick up #202 from outside the train station or bus terminals, and make sure that the final destination is **Gyeongpo beach**, as some head elsewhere. On this route you can also disembark at Gyeongpoho and the Edison museum.

Spread-out Gangneung is a tad frustrating to get around – little **Jeongdongjin** (p.162), a seaside village just down the coast, is a far more pleasant place to stay. In Gangneung itself, half a dozen **motels** line the area behind the bus terminal and provide the city's most comfortable accommodation, if not the best located; *Equus* (Ⓣ033/643-0114; ④) is the pick of the bunch, with wood-panelled rooms, mood lighting and heavenly showers (most of which you can see into from the bedrooms). There are cheap places near the train station, but an abundance of pink lighting suggests that any prices quoted may be for more than just the room. One exception is the stylish *# Motel* (Ⓣ033/645-9692; ④), whose neon hash sign is just about visible from the station exit. The beach areas also have plenty of cheap accommodation options, as well as great **seafood** restaurants.

Odaesan National Park

A short ride to the west of Gangneung is **ODAESAN NATIONAL PARK** (오대산 국립 공원), markedly smooth and gentle compared with its jagged Gangwonese neighbours. Full of colour in the autumn, and with magnificent views from the stony peaks, it's relatively empty for a Korean national park as hikers tend to be sucked into the Seoraksan range a short way to the north.

Odaesan has **two main entrance points** – one in the pretty Sogeumgang area to the north of the park, and a south gate reached via the small town of Jinbu. Between the two are two temples and innumerable shrines, some of which are quite remote and receive next to no visitors – just the treat for adventurous hikers.

Sogeumgang (소금강; "Little Geumgang") is named after the spectacular range just over the border in North Korea. A maze of tumbling waterfalls, bare peaks and thickly forested slopes, Odaesan is more than a little similar to its renowned northern cousin, but substantially easier to get to. The south of the park contains two sumptuous **temples** – Woljeongsa and Sangwonsa. **Woljeongsa** (월정사) dates from 645, and contains an impressive octagonal nine-storey pagoda from the early Goryeo dynasty, adorned with wind chimes and striking a perfect balance with the thick fir trees surrounding the complex. It faces an ornate, and rare, kneeling Buddha. The complex as a whole addresses function rather than beauty, though in the main hall are two elaborate Buddhist paintings – most interesting is the one on the left, which features some hellish scenes of torture. Ten kilometres away through the pine trees is **Sangwonsa** (상원사), a complex containing what is believed to be Korea's oldest bronze bell, which dates from 725. Sangwonsa's appeal is its magical setting, facing a mountain ridge swathed with a largely deciduous wall of trees; in a country where pine-green reigns supreme, the blaze of colour that these create in the autumn is rather welcome. Both temples have little **tearooms** in which to rest.

A **hiking** trail leads from Sangwonsa to **Birobong**, the highest peak in the park at 1563m. Although the ascent can be made in less than two hours, it's steep and not an easy walk. Those who get to the top can continue along a ridge trail to Sangwangbong, or even attempt a U-shaped day-hike to Dongdaesan via Durobong – this walk is particularly tough on the legs. A waterfall-strewn day-hike heads up through Sogeumgang via Noinbong to Odaesan's spine road; unfortunately, this twisty thoroughfare sees no public transport, limiting onward movement from the park to hitchhiking or a lengthy walk.

Practicalities

Rather incredibly, there are no direct **buses** to Odaesan from Gangneung. Regular services head to **Jinbu** (진부), where you'll have to change, but onward connections to the park are infrequent – there's one every hour or so, though some only go as far as Woljeongsa. Don't worry about the misleading signs on the way – you'll know when to get off. There's a pleasantly low-key **minbak** area downhill

Victims of nautical nomenclature

The **victim mentality** drilled into Korean students during their history lessons is such that any perceived slant against the nation, no matter how slight, can turn into a serious issue that has the whole country boiling with rage. Anger is further magnified should the insult come from Korea's one time colonial masters, the **Japanese** – witness the case of the waters east of the Korean mainland, generally known across the world as the **"Sea of Japan"**. Koreans insist that this name is a symbol of Japan's imperial past, and youth hostel wall-maps around the world have had the name crossed out by *gimchi*-chomping Korean travellers and replaced with **"East Sea"**. Korean diplomats raised enough of a stink to take the issue to the United Nations, which tentatively sided with the Japanese, but left the topic open for further discussion. Although both terms have been used for centuries, neither is strictly correct – Korea controls a large portion of the waters, yet the sea lies plainly to Japan's west – so while this storm in a teacup continues to rage on, feel free to send your own suggestions of compromise to the UN: "Sea of Peaceful Diplomatic Negotiations", perhaps?

from the southern park entrance, with rooms in traditional houses going from W30,000. Further down again is the rather more comfortable *Odaesan Hotel* (℡033/330-5000; ❼). Inside the park itself, there's a tiny **shelter** between Woljeongsa and Sangwonsa, with the few rooms going for W30,000. There's also a **campsite** nearby; it costs up to W6000 per tent in July and August, but though it's free for the rest of the year the shower facilities will be unavailable. Sogeumgang also has a *minbak* area, as well as a campsite. **Hiking maps** can be bought for W1000 at the park entrances.

Yongpyeong ski resort

In Pyeongchang county, just west of Gangneung, is **YONGPYEONG** (용평; ⓦwww.yongpyong.co.kr), Korea's largest ski resort, also known as **Dragon Valley**. Facilities here are so good that Pyeongchang came within a whisker of being selected as the host of the 2010 **Winter Olympics**, but was usurped by Vancouver in the final ballot, and suffered defeat again to the Russian resort Sochi for the 2014 games.

The resort has all kinds of activities from snowboarding to sledding available in the winter and a mammoth **31 slopes** to choose from, accessed on fifteen ski lifts and gondolas. Prices depend on what time of day you'd like to ski – it's even possible (and cheapest) to do it at night under strong lights, but most go for the W71,000 lift-and-gondola pass, which will see you through morning and afternoon. Equipment is available to hire; renting skis and clothing will add around W51,000, though this too can rise or fall depending on your exact schedule. The *Dragon Valley Hotel* (call the resort on ℡033/335-5757; ❼) is the deluxe accommodation option on site, but there are many *yeogwan* and a **youth hostel** in the area too.

To get to Yongpyeong from Gangneung, take a **bus** from the intercity terminal to Hoenggye – there's one every ten or twenty minutes. From Hoenggye there are free shuttle buses during the ski season; at other times you can take a local bus. There are direct bus services to the resort from Gangneung and the capital's Dong-Seoul terminal. If you're looking for smaller, less-crowded ski resorts, go to Phoenix Park and Hyundae Sungwoo further down the Yeongdong highway, in the direction of Wonju.

Jeongdongjin

For those bored with temples, war museums and national parks, the area around **JEONGDONGJIN** (정동진) has some more unusual attractions which should float your boat, if you'll pardon the pun. Near this small, windswept coastal village lie two retired nautical vessels – an **American warship** from the Korean War, and an equally authentic **North Korean submarine**. From Gangneung, trains make the short trip down the coast, much of which is cordoned off with barbed wire, before stopping at what is apparently the world's closest train station to the sea. A short stretch of sand separates the track from the water, and it's here that Korean couples flock to hold hands and watch the sunrise – the area was featured in *Sandglass*, a romantic Korean soap opera (truly a truism, since all Korean soap operas are romantic).

Arrival

Jeongdongjin is best reached by **train**, though Gangwon's coastal line operates a frustratingly infrequent service so it pays to find out times in advance. Otherwise, it's accessible by **local bus** from Gangneung – #109 (40min) runs from the bus terminal, and #111, #112 and #113 from various stops around the city, passing Tongil Park on the way (30min).

Accommodation

The town trades on the romance dollar, with amorous couples arriving to hold hands and watch the sunset year-round, so there are plenty of **rooms** to choose from.

Full House Motel (No phone). The pick of the roadside motels near the train station, with en-suite facilities and pleasantly decorated rooms; make sure to get one with a sea view. ❷

Haslla Museum Hotel ⓣ033/644-9411, ⓦwww.haslla.kr. Forming part of the Haslla Art World complex just to the north of town (see below), this is without doubt the most distinctive hotel on the east coast. Each room has been individually, artistically designed; floor-to-ceiling windows provide wonderful sea views, and some rooms have their beds tucked away in gigantic wooden bowls – more comfortable than it may sound. Rack rates start at W300,000, though you can usually knock a fair chunk from this, and almost half on weekdays. ❽

Hyanggi 향기 호텔 ⓣ033/642-7512. Sitting in a prime location at the south end of the beach, this is a decent place to stay, but rooms are a little stuffy and rather overpriced. ❺

Sun Cruise Hotel ⓣ033/610-7000. You can't miss this place, perched as it is atop a cliff south of the station. It can be surprisingly cheap off-season (down to W70,000 for a double), and mercifully the nautical theme isn't carried through into its plain rooms. ❻

The Sun Cruise Hotel and around

There's not too much to see in the town itself, but the **Sun Cruise Hotel** is as much a tourist attraction as a place to stay. Designed to look like a boat, you really can't miss it – just look for the ship hanging precariously from a cliff. Although its souvenir shop is only on the ninth floor, the combined height of hotel and cliff means that you're a whopping 165m above sea level, and as you walk out of the shop onto the **viewing platform**, it's tempting to let your mind soar and imagine that you're up on the deck of the world's largest ship. One floor up is a revolving bar, where cocktails start at a reasonable W7000. Squatting a hundred metres from the hotel is another landlubbing ship, this one a **museum** containing old gramophones, phonographs, TVs and radios, as well as a floor dedicated to the inventions of one Thomas Edison. On the way back to the station, look out for the **giant egg-timer** – the sand inside takes exactly twelve months to fall through, and couples gather to watch it being turned over each New Year.

Haslla Art World

Around 2km north of Jeongdongjin is **Haslla Art World** (ⓦwww.haslla.kr), a superbly designed **contemporary art** complex ranged up a verdant hillside off the coast. There are a few indoor halls, one of which features what may well be the world's only **Cow Dung Art Gallery** (only a few of the sculpted dollops are real). However, the bulk of the installations lie outdoors: witness the metal spiders clambering up the hillside, or the much-photographed pair of adjoining chairs (again, Jeongdongjin is highly popular with couples) peering over the sea. The on-site "Sea Café" is an equally great place from which to watch the sunset, but perhaps best of all is the chance to stay in the wonderful **hotel** (see above). There are occasional **buses** along the coast, though taxis from Jeongdongjin barely cost any more.

Tongil Park

Jeongdongjin's resident warship and sub are permanently moored next to each other at **Tongil Park** (통일 공원; daily: March–Oct 9am–6pm; Nov–Feb

Espionage in the East Sea

Those who deem the Cold War long-finished should cast their minds back to September 1996. On the fourteenth, a submarine containing 26 **North Korean spies** arrived at Amin, on South Korea's Gangwon coast. Three disembarked, and made it back to the submarine after completing their surveillance mission on the Air Force base near Gangneung, but the waves were particularly strong that day and the sub came a cropper on the rocks. Eleven non-military crew members were killed by the soldiers, lest they leaked classified information to the South, and important documents were incinerated inside the vessel – the ceiling of the cabin in question is still charred with burnt North Korean spy material. The remaining fifteen soldiers attempted to return to the North overland, with their Southern counterparts understandably keen to stop them; the mission continued for 49 days, during which seventeen South Korean soldiers and civilians lost their lives. Thirteen of the spies were killed, one was captured, and the whereabouts of the last remains a mystery.

9am–5pm; W2000), 4km north of the village on the coast, and connected to Gangneung and Jeongdongjin by bus #11 (every 15min; W900). The ship saw action, having served in the Korean War, but the **submarine** has an even more interesting tale to tell, having made a dramatic final voyage – see the box above. It's hard to imagine that this small metal tube could hold a crew of thirty, as even with nobody else on board it's tough enough to navigate without bumping your head; faced with just one dark, cramped corridor, you're unlikely to be inside for long. By comparison, the US-made **warship** is 120m long, and it can take an hour or so to hunt down every nook and cranny; in the bridge you can play with the chunky steering equipment, twiddle knobs, check dials, and shoot imaginary torpedoes at your enemies. Though the ship is on dry land, nearby military installations and the waves crashing below can make it easy to let your imagination go wild, and if your karma is in credit there'll be fighter jets from the local Air Force base roaring overhead.

Eating

Jeongdongjin has no shortage of **restaurants**. Perhaps most fun for foreign visitors will be the chance to enjoy a **shellfish barbecue** (조개구이; *jogae gui*), which should cost from W35,000 for two people. One good place to head for this is the *Jeonmangdae Hoetjip* (전망대 횟집), just back towards the station from the *Hyanggi* hotel (see p.163). Also deserving of a mention is *Sseon Hansik*, a European-style white cottage on the main road near the train station; try the *sundubu* (순두부), a local speciality made from tofu in a spicy sauce – W20,000 for two people. Close by is *Café Sun*, serving **coffees** from around the world with great sea views, or cocktails when the sun has gone down.

Samcheok and around

Although **Donghae** (동해) is the largest city in the area after Gangneung, it's a little too cumbersome to be of much interest to travellers, other than those heading to the stunning East Sea island of Ulleungdo (see p.198), to which daily ferries run from March to October from a port next to Mukho train station. However, the beaches and caves of Donghae are well and truly trumped by more impressive versions around the smaller and more manageable town of

SAMCHEOK (삼척), just to the south, which makes a better base – far easier to navigate, and also close to interesting sights such as **Penis Park**, several secluded **beaches** and the gigantic cave of **Hwanseondonggul**.

Arrival and information

Samcheok is best approached by **bus**, as the train station is some distance from the centre and in any case carries a sparse service. The city's two bus terminals – express and intercity – lie almost side by side on the southern flank of a quadrilateral of roads that form the city centre; these are home to plenty of chain restaurants and high-street clothing stores, while much of the interior is taken up by an appealingly grimy market. Helpful staff at the **tourist information booth** just outside the express terminal are able to advise on accommodation and the ever-changing details of local transport.

Accommodation and eating

With the exception of *Hotel Palace*, all accommodation options listed below are in central Samcheok, and within easy walking distance of its **bus terminals**. For a more old-time coastal Gangwon atmosphere, adventurous travellers could do worse than head to the cheap guesthouses sprinkled around the **port area** east of town, an area whose restaurants and shops are almost entirely dedicated to fish, and home to something of an end-of-the-world atmosphere. **Samcheok beach** is also a pleasant place to stay, though prices at its various motels rise in summer.

Hanil Motel 한일 모텔 Namyangdong ⓣ033/574-8277. Right next to the bus terminal, this motel has reasonably large rooms, though the mattresses are a little hospital-like. The rosy silk wallpaper in the halls mercifully stops before it gets to the rooms. ❷

Jjimjilbang 찜질방 Jeongsangdong. For those willing to sleep on the floor of a darkened communal room, this is a budget option right next door to the *Moon Motel*; your W6000 entry fee pays for use of the pools and steam rooms, as well as the hire of a fetching set of matching T-shirt and shorts.

Moon Motel 문 모텔 Jeongsangdong ⓣ033/572-4436. The *Moon*, in a quiet part of town between the bus terminal and the river, has clean, comfy rooms that are remarkably stylish for a Korean motel. ❹

Hotel Palace Jeonghadong ⓣ033/575-7000. Way out of town on the coast, Samcheok's luxury option has several large restaurants and banquet halls; the cavernous rooms are linoleum-floored, making it feel a little like a well-tended Korean apartment. You can cut the rate in half off-season, or by even more if you don't require a sea view. ❼

Samil Yeoinsuk 삼일 여인숙 Namyangdong ⓣ033/573-2038. Take the small alley opposite the bus terminal's information booth to get to the *Samil*, which has *ondol*-heated rooms, as well as some with a bed for a few dollars more. All rooms have a TV and private bathroom, although you may have to ask for hot water, and even with heating the whole place may be a little too cold for comfort in the winter. ❶

The City

With Samcheok's main tourist draw – the colossal Hwanseon Cave – some way to the west, there's little to see in the city itself, though the **port area** to the east is worth a stroll. Here, it's common to see acres of squid hung out like laundry to dry in the sun, and there are more fish restaurants than you can count. Unfortunately, few buses head here from Samcheok centre, so taxis are usually the best way to go. A few kilometres north is **Samcheok Beach**, which attracts a young crowd in the summer; like many other beaches in the province, much of it is cordoned off with **barbed wire**. This makes it a rather interesting place to sunbathe; the wire is in place to prevent amphibious North Korean landings such as the one that occurred up the coast in Jeongdongjin in 1996 (see box opposite); also look out at night for the large spotlights used to keep an eye on the seas. Further south there are several more beaches, as well as Haesindang, a coastal park of **phallic sculpture**. Unfortunately, this once-beautiful coast is steadily being eroded, not so much by crashing seas as by the development of coastal highways.

Hwanseondonggul

Though Korea contains a fair number of navigable caves, **Hwanseondonggul** (환선동굴; daily: March–Oct 8am–5.30pm; Nov–Feb 8am–4.30pm; W4000), hiding away under a sumptuous range of hills west of Samcheok, is the one that can most justly be described as "cavernous" – the local tourist board claims that it's the **largest cave in Asia**. Superlatives aside, it's certainly a whopper – the system is over 6km long, featuring umpteen rooms and some subterranean water features. Hwanson's largest chamber measures 100m by 30m, its dimensions, shading and vaguely creepy atmosphere bringing to mind a Gothic cathedral. Only 1.6km is open to the public, most of which is traversed by platforms and staircases; be sure to bring suitable shoes and an extra layer of clothing, as it's damp and not very warm down there. Also bear in mind that the cave entrance is a rather steep half-hour trek from the ticket office, next to which are some examples of the area's traditional wooden mountain housing.

Bus #60 heads to the cave from Samcheok bus terminal (50min), though only five of the seven daily services allow you enough time to tour the cave. The latest is the 2.20pm service; the last bus back is at 7.30pm.

South to the beaches

The Gangwon coast continues on south of Samcheok, squeezing numerous **beaches** into a fairly short stretch along the way, although continued development of the coastal roads and the resulting increase in traffic means that in addition to the one in Samcheok only two are actually worth visiting – **Maengbang** and **Yonghwa**. The former is one of the largest in the area and its calm waters make it good for swimming. Surrounded by pine trees, it's usually quite peaceful as it's a twenty-minute walk from the nearest bus stop and *minbak* village. The beach at Yonghwa is smaller – only 200m in length – and much closer to the road, but equally attractive.

Penis Park

A little further on from Yonghwa beach is the rather curious **Penis Park** (해신당 공원; daily 9am–6pm; W3000); take the hourly #24 bus from Samcheok's terminal, though bear in mind that some maps and bus drivers refer to this area as **Sinnam**. Inside the park, paths are lined with **penis sculptures** of metal, stone and wood – one is lined with nails, several are carved into people-like shapes, and one metal ithyphallus is mounted on cannon wheels. While it may seem bizarre, the park owes its existence to one of the area's most intriguing **folk tales**, the story of a young bride-to-be who died by the shore in a violent storm. After this, her angry spirit chased the fish from the seas, depriving locals of their major source of income and sustenance. The only way around this, apparently, was to placate the newly dead's soul with carved wooden phalluses, which were driven into the beach – spirit thus satisfied, the fish returned in record numbers.

The main building's **folk exhibition** can be safely ignored, and is interesting only for a small display showing how local squid are lured to their deaths, and an almost comically bad simulation of a boat ride. It gets better in the **sculpture zone**, which has replicas of ancient pornographic statuary from Asia and beyond

– don't leave until you've checked out the Greek god's horny pose. Various **trails** make for a pleasant walk around the park – though one often made brisk by the seaside winds – with views of the sea crashing on to the crags below. You can go all the way down to the pebbly shore, which is certainly not safe for swimming thanks to the often fierce East Sea waves. A few *minbak* and stalls selling grilled fish from as little as W1000 can be found around the park's southern end.

Taebaeksan to Chiaksan

Heading west from the coast towards Gyeonggi-do and Seoul, you'll pass through some magnificent Gangwonese scenery, its carpet of rolling hills rising up to a couple of relatively untouristed **national parks**. The more easterly of the two, **Taebaeksan**, can be accessed from the relaxed city of **Taebaek**, while **Chiaksan** National Park lies east of **Wonju**, near the confluence of the Gangwon, Gyeonggi and Chungbuk borders.

Taebaek

The small, sedate city of **TAEBAEK** (태백) is one of the most typical of the Gangwonese interior. Surrounded by mountains and with little large-scale commerce to speak of, its elevation means the air is clean and fresh, and the climate is usually a little colder here than on the coast. It's mainly used as a transit point for the thoroughly enjoyable maze of hiking trails that is **Taebaeksan National Park**.

Practicalities

The **train** station, **bus** terminal and **information booth** (daily 9am–5pm; ⓣ033/550-2081) are all corralled around the same roundabout at the top of town, together with a range of cheap **places to stay**. You can't miss the *Aegis Motel* (ⓣ033/553-9980; ❹), with its white frame towering over the train station; rooms here are large and clean, though as the train line has some early morning services, it may not be ideal for light sleepers. Further down the road is the *Gardenjang Yeogwan* (가든장 여관; ❷), which has basic but adequate rooms, or roll out a futon on a heated floor at the *Bohye Yeoinsuk* (보혜 여인숙; ❶). For decent **food** you'll have to make your way into the city centre – walk down from the train station and turn right at the main road – where the two best places are *Chueokui Yeontanbul* (추억의 연탄불), which serves *samgyeopsal* with a great range of side dishes, and *Semi gipenmul* (샘이 깊은물), a traditionally styled drink'n'snack place on the second floor of a building opposite Hwangji pond.

Taebaeksan National Park

Within half-an-hour of Taebaek's bus terminal is the main entrance to **Taebaeksan National Park** (태백산 국립 공원), which is especially beautiful in winter months, and makes a much prettier place to stay than the city centre. The entrance is already 870m above sea level, and from here a pair of easy two-hour routes run to the twin peaks of Munsubong (1517m) and Cheonjedan (1561m), two of the highest in Korea. These are of particular importance to **shamanists**, as Taebaeksan is viewed as Korea's "motherly mountain" – ancient Korean kings were said to perform rituals here, and at the summits it's still common to see offerings left behind by hikers in honour of **Dangun**, the legendary founder of Korea (see Contexts, p.358). Cheonjedan plays host to a shamanist ceremony every year on October 3 – "National Foundation Day" in Korea, and a public holiday – as does the Dangun hall near the entrance. A rather less spiritual **coal museum** sprawls out just below the park entrance; the Taebaeksan area was once the heart of Korea's coal industry, and this museum charts its gradual decline. The top floor shows some interesting pictures of coal village life, and there are a couple of surprise simulations in store too.

Practicalities

The park is well signposted, but for peace of mind you can buy a **map** for W1000 at the entrance. Near the park entrance is a two-storey parade of buildings, with **restaurants** on the ground floor and **minbak** accommodation above. Nearby motels offer greater comfort, including *U-kin* (❸), whose attached restaurant allows you to eat in little private huts. Further downhill is a bunch of newer, homelier *minbak*, all charging around W25,000 per room.

The Jeongseon route

At **Mindungsan** (민둥산), 35km west of Taebaek, a spur splits from the main train line and barrels up north through an extremely picturesque valley, whose undulating hills and unspoilt scenery carry echoes of Shikoku in Japan. A single-carriage train plies this route, heading through Jeongseon to Auraji, though its modern swivel-chairs are somewhat incongruous with the surrounding bucolic scenery and the small, unassuming towns on route.

Situated 20km along this spur line, **JEONGSEON** (정선) is the only stop that could possibly be termed "touristy" – most of the valley's accommodation and restaurants can be found here, and there's a market on every date ending with a 2 or a 7, along with coinciding assorted cultural performances from April to November.

For the most enjoyable attraction on the route, you'll have to head 15km further to **AURAJI** (아우라지) at the end of the line: shuttle buses meet the trains and head further up the track to a now-disused station, from where you can cycle the 7km back down the train line to Auraji on a specially crafted **rail-bike** (W18,000 per pair). Its popularity means that it can be booked solid at weekends, though on slacker days curious foreigners may be given a free 100m dash – don't forget to brake. Also at the station is an odd burger-bar-cum-café in the shape of two fish.

Wonju

From Taebaek, trains head up and across a gorgeous succession of valleys and crests, and make a full 360-degree turn inside a mountain before arriving at **WONJU** (원주). Sadly, Wonju has next to nothing of tourist interest, other than its proximity to splendid **Chiaksan National Park**. Also within striking distance are several **ski resorts** – Oak Valley to the west, Hyundai Sungwoo to the east on the way to Gangneung, and Phoenix Park further along again. Other than Phoenix Park, these can be tricky to get to without your own transport – visit a tourist office for more info.

Wonju's **train** station and **bus** terminal are both in the city centre, a short cab ride (W3000) from each other. Arriving by bus is preferable, since the area is far more pleasant – the city's main red-light district starts just opposite the train station, and its motels are often put to questionable use. Hotels around the bus terminal are far better, if overpriced; best is the *Kingdom Motel* (Ⓣ033/748-6691; ❹), a green building across the road from the terminal's main exit. **Bus** #41 takes you to the main entrance of Chiaksan National Park; you can pick it up from a stop near the train station, to which you'll need another bus from the bus terminal. Also note that Wonju has a tiny **airport**, with a single daily service to Jeju the only feature on its departure boards. Bus #62 heads there every hour from the bus terminal and train station.

Chiaksan National Park

Visible from parts of Wonju are the principal ridges of **CHIAKSAN NATIONAL PARK** (치악산 국립 공원), the dozen or so 1000m-plus peaks rifling across the sky like a torn page, but despite its proximity to Seoul, and Wonju just to the west, the park is rarely overrun with visitors. This is partly due to the infrequency of public transport heading to the park – though several **buses** connect various park entrances to Wonju, only the #41 appears regularly, heading to the main entrance at the north of the park every half-hour or so; unless you find one of the others, you may have a tough job getting back without resorting to hitchhiking, a mission simplified by the fact that almost all cars heading from the park will be heading towards Wonju.

Near the main entrance is **Guryongsa** (구룡사), a small but well-formed temple complex dating from the dawn of Unified Silla rule in the mid-seventh century. From here a three-hour hiking route heads on via a small waterfall to **Birobong** (1288m), the park's highest peak, and continues along a ridge to Namdaebong, a slightly less lofty peak four hours or so to the south. From Birobong it's also possible to drop down past the lonely Ipseoksa temple to the Hwanggol entrance on the west of the park, though onward transport to Wonju is patchy at best.

Accommodation and eating

Outside the Guryeongsa entrance is one of the most pleasingly rural **minbak** villages of any Korean national park, entirely devoid of the neon signs, trinket shops and pumping grandmother techno that often sully park entrances; staying here is highly recommended if you're looking for a peaceful – if rustic – getaway. From the bus stop, go downhill and over the bridge crossing the stream – *minbak* dot the small valley for a few hundred metres. They're all very spartan and cost around W25,000 per room, so just choose one you like the look of. All should be able to cook you something, but for the local speciality, **gamja pajeon** (감자파전), a kind of savoury potato pancake eaten with soy sauce, you'll probably have to head up to the restaurants near the bus stop. At the bottom of the mountain is the excellent *Motel NYX* (Ⓣ033/732-4338; ④), a quirky place with great rooms.

Travel details

Flights

Wonju to: Jeju (daily; 1hr).

Trains

Chuncheon to: Gangchon (hourly; 20min); Seoul (hourly; 1hr 40min).
Gangneung to: Jeongdongjin (9 daily; 15min); Seoul (6 daily; 6hr 45min); Taebaek (6 daily; 2hr).
Jeongdongjin to: Gangneung (9 daily; 15min).
Suwon to: Seoul (regularly; 30min).
Taebaek to: Gangneung (6 daily; 2hr); Seoul (6 daily).
Wonju to: Andong (8 daily; 2hr 20min); Seoul (hourly; 1hr 20min).

Buses

Cheorwon to: Chuncheon (12 daily; 2hr 30min); Daejeon (2 daily; 3hr 30min), Seoul (regularly; 2hr).
Chuncheon to: Andong (1 daily; 2hr); Busan (14 daily; 6hr); Cheorwon (12 daily; 2hr 30min); Daegu (5 daily; 3hr 30min); Daejeon (7 daily; 2hr 50min); Gangneung (regularly; 3hr); Incheon (regularly; 2hr 30min); Jeonju (2 daily; 4hr 15min); Samcheok (10 daily; 4hr); Seoul (every 15min; 1hr 20min); Sokcho (frequently; 2hr); Suwon (regularly; 2hr 20min); Taebaek (1 daily; 5hr); Wonju (regularly; 1hr 30min).

Gangneung to: Busan (10 daily; 7hr); Cheonan (8 daily; 4hr); Cheongju (6 daily; 4hr); Chuncheong (regularly; 3hr); Chungju (regularly; 2hr 50min); Daegu (regularly; 5hr); Gwangju (6 daily; 5hr); Incheon (hourly; 4hr); Samcheok (regularly; 1hr); Seoul (regularly; 3hr 20min); Sokcho (regularly; 1hr 10min); Suwon (12 daily; 3hr 30min); Taebaek (regularly; 2hr 30min); Wonju (regularly; 2hr).
Incheon to: Andong (regularly; 4hr 10min); Busan (11 daily; 4hr 30min); Cheongju (regularly; 2hr); Chuncheon (regularly; 3hr); Daegu (hourly; 4hr 30min); Daejeon (regularly; 2hr 45min); Gangneung (hourly; 4hr); Gwangju (every 30min; 4hr); Jeonju (hourly; 3hr 10min); Mokpo (15 daily; 4hr 30min); Seoul (regularly; 1hr 10min); Sokcho (10 daily; 4hr 10min); Taebaek (3 daily; 4hr 25min); Wonju (regularly; 2hr); Yeosu (3 daily; 5hr 40min).
Samcheok to: Busan (10 daily; 5hr); Chuncheon (10 daily; 4hr); Daegu (regularly; 5hr); Gangneung (regularly; 1hr); Gyeongju (regularly; 5hr); Seoul (8 daily; 4hr 30min); Sokcho (9 daily; 3hr); Taebaek (regularly; 1hr 10min).
Sokcho to: Busan (10 daily; 7hr); Chuncheon (regularly; 2hr 30min); Daegu (10 daily; 4hr 30min); Gangneung (regularly; 1hr 10min); Gwangju (4 daily; 6hr); Samcheok (9 daily; 3hr); Seoul (regularly; 3hr 30min); Wonju (8 daily; 3hr 30min).
Suwon to: Busan (7 daily; 5hr); Daegu (14 daily; 3hr 30min); Daejeon (8 daily; 1hr 30min); Gwangju (regularly; 3hr 30min); Jeonju (12 daily; 2hr 40min); Mokpo (7 daily; 4hr 30min); Sokcho (8 daily; 4hr 30min).
Taebaek to: Andong (5 daily; 3hr); Busan (5 daily; 4hr 30min); Daegu (7 daily; 4hr 30min); Gangneung (regularly; 2hr 30min); Samcheok (regularly; 1hr 10min); Seoul (regularly; 3hr 30min).
Wonju to: Cheongju (regularly; 1hr 40min); Chuncheon (regularly; 1hr 10min); Chungju (regularly; 1hr 20min); Daegu (15 daily; 2hr 30min); Gangneung (regularly; 1hr 40min); Guinsa (6 daily; 2hr); Seoul (regularly; 1hr 30min); Sokcho (8 daily; 4hr).

Ferries

Of the many services to China, the route to Tianjin's port at Tanggu will put you closest to Beijing. Note that the Tuesday sailings arrive at a far more amenable hour than other departures.

Incheon International Terminal 1 to: Dalian (5pm Tues, Thurs & Sat; 16hr); Dandong (5pm Mon, Wed & Fri; 16hr); Qinhuangdao (7pm Mon, noon Fri; 23hr); Shidao (6pm Mon, Wed & Fri; 14hr); Yantai (6pm Tues, Thurs & Sat; 14hr); Yingkou (7pm Tues, noon Sat; 24hr).
Incheon International Terminal 2 to: Lianyungang (7pm Thurs, 3pm Sat; 24hr); Qingdao (5pm Tues, Thurs & Sat; 15hr); Tianjin (1pm Tues, 7pm Fri; 24hr); Weihai (7pm Mon, Wed & Sat; 14hr).
Incheon Yeonan Terminal to: Baengnyeongdo (3 daily; 4hr30min); Deokjeokdo (4 daily; 1hr–2hr 30min); Jeju City (Mon–Sat; 14hr).

3

Gyeongsang

CHAPTER 3 Highlights

* **Confucian academies** Two stunning Joseon-dynasty academies can be found in the Gyeongsang countryside – Oksan Seowon and Dosan Seowon. See p.196 & p.178
* **Folk villages** Savour a taste of Korean life long forgotten at Yangdong, a village near Gyeongju, and Hahoe, an equally gorgeous version near Andong. See p.197 & p.178
* **Gyeongju** Once the Silla kingdom's capital and now Korea's most laid-back city, Gyeongju has enough sights to fill at least a week. See p.185
* **The Underwater Tomb of King Munmu** Take an easy but enjoyable day-trip east of Gyeongju to two remote temples, before finishing at this unique coastal tomb. See p.196
* **Ulleungdo** This island's isolation out in the East Sea makes it the perfect place to see traditional life first-hand, or kick back and relax for a few days. See p.198
* **Busan** This smaller, more characterful version of Seoul has many sights including the Jagalchi Fish Market and Haeundae, the country's most popular beach. See p.204
* **Jirisan** Korea's largest national park – with its own resident population of bears – has umpteen lofty trails, including a three-day hike across the ridge. See p.221

▲ Burial mounds, Gyeongju

3

Gyeongsang

The surprisingly low number of travellers who choose to escape Seoul usually make a beeline to the **Gyeongsang provinces** (경상도) at the southeast of the country, and with good reason – a land of mountains and majesty, folklore and heroes, this area is home to some of the most wonderful sights that Korea has to offer. This was the base of the Silla kingdom that ruled for nearly a thousand years (see box below); though this came to an end a similar time-span ago, a horde of **jewellery**, **regal tombs** and wonderful **temples** provide present-day evidence of past wonders.

The Silla dynasty

In 69 BC a young Herod was learning how to talk, Julius Caesar was busying himself in Gaul and Spartacus was leading slave revolts against Rome. Legend has it that at this time, a strange light shone down from the East Asian sky onto a **horse** of pure white. The beast was sheltering an egg, from which hatched **Hyeokgeose**, who went on to be appointed king by local chiefs at the tender age of 13. He inaugurated the **Silla dynasty** (sometimes spelt "Shilla", and pronounced that way), which was to go through no fewer than 56 monarchs before collapsing in 935, leaving behind a rich legacy still visible today in the form of jewellery, pottery and temples. Many of the regal burial mounds can still be seen in and around **Gyeongju**, the Silla seat of power.

Though it was initially no more than a powerful city-state, successive leaders gradually expanded the Silla boundaries, consuming the smaller **Gaya kingdom** to the south and becoming a fully-fledged member of the **Three Kingdoms** that jostled for power on the Korean peninsula – Goguryeo in the north, Baekje to the west, and Silla in the east. Silla's **art and craft** flourished, Buddhism was adopted as the state religion, and as early as the sixth century a detailed social system was put into use – the *golpuljedo*, or "bone-rank system" – with lineage and status dictating what clothes people wore, who they could marry and where they could live, and placing strict limits on what they could achieve.

Perversely, given their geographical positions on the "wrong" sides of the peninsula, Baekje was allied to the Japanese and Silla to the Chinese Tang dynasty, and it was Chinese help that enabled Silla's **King Muyeol** to subjugate Baekje in 660 (see box, p.271). Muyeol died the year after, but his son, **King Munmu**, and promptly went one better, defeating Goguryeo in 668 to bring about a first-ever unified rule of the Korean peninsula. The resulting increase in power drove the state forward, though abuse of this new wealth was inevitable; pressure from the people, and an increase in the power of the nobility, gradually started to undermine the power of the kings from the late eighth century. Gyeongju was sacked in 927, and eight years later **King Gyeongsun** – by that time little more than a figurehead – finally handed over the reigns of power to **King Taejo**, bringing almost a millennium of Silla rule to a close, and kicking off the Goryeo dynasty.

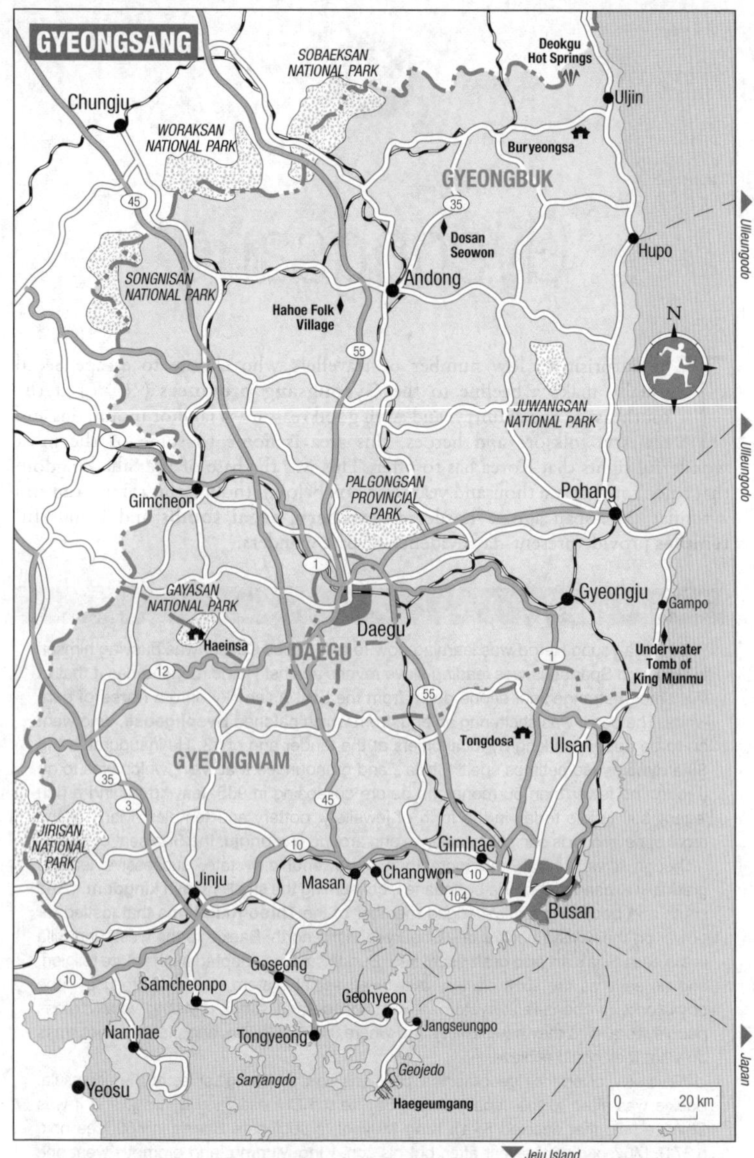

Though the Korean capital was transferred to Seoul following the collapse of the Silla dynasty, Gyeongsang has continued to exert influence on the running of the country. Since independence and the end of Japanese occupation, the majority of Korea's leaders have been Gyeongsang-born, with the resulting distribution of wealth and power making the area the country's most populated, and industrial, outside Greater Seoul. Despite this, Gyeongsang is well known for its beautiful countryside; **national parks** line the provincial borders, and the southern coast is surrounded by hundreds of stunning **islands**. Its richly traditional hinterland provides the biggest contrast to the rest of the country – here you may be lucky enough to see ancestral rites being performed, or beasts ploughing the fields, and villages of thatch-roofed houses.

Gyeongbuk

Covering one-fifth of the country, the largely rural province of **GYEONGBUK** (경북; "North Gyeongsang") is South Korea's largest, and one of the most popular with visitors. Here, age-old tradition lingers on to a degree unmatched anywhere else in Korea, with sights strewn around the area providing a chronological view into more than two thousand years of history. Wonderful **Gyeongju** was capital of the **Silla empire** from 57 BC to 935 AD, and is now a repository to the resulting treasures. The main sights here are the **regal tombs**, small hillocks that held the city's kings, queens and nobles; **Bulguksa**, one of the country's most revered temples; and **Namsan**, a holy mountain crisscrossed with paths, and studded with relics of Silla times. Traces of the **Joseon dynasty**, which ruled the peninsula from 1392 until its annexation by the Japanese in 1910, are also evident in a number of Confucian academies and traditional villages; both of which can be found around **Andong**, a small, peaceful city that's becoming ever more popular with foreigners. The years immediately preceding Korea's mass industrialization in the 1980s can be savoured on the scenic island of **Ulleungdo**, where fishing and farming traditions exist unadulterated by factory smoke or sky-high apartment blocks. Meanwhile, the saccharine delights of present-day Korea can be savoured in **Daegu**, the largest city in the region, and a fun place to hole up for a couple of days.

Andong and around

Surrounded by picturesque countryside and magical sights, **ANDONG** (안동) is deservedly one of the most popular draws in the region for foreign travellers. Whatever the Korean tourist booklets say about its history, don't go expecting a mini-Gyeongju – such a comparison is unfair and misguided, as there's little in the city itself. However, the wonderful sights on Andong's periphery mean that it has enough to be respected on its own terms. The centre is small, pleasant and unhurried, with the main sights located well out of town – **Dosan Seowon** to the north is a stunning Confucian academy dating from Joseon times, while to the west is **Hahoe Folk Village**, a rustic approximation of traditional Korean life. A similar village can be found nearer the centre, next to a rather absorbing **folklore museum**.

Arrival, information and orientation

Andong's **train** and **bus** stations are a few minutes' walk from each other, both on the same road to the south of the city centre. Outside the train station is an excellent **tourist information office**; staff are helpful and informative,

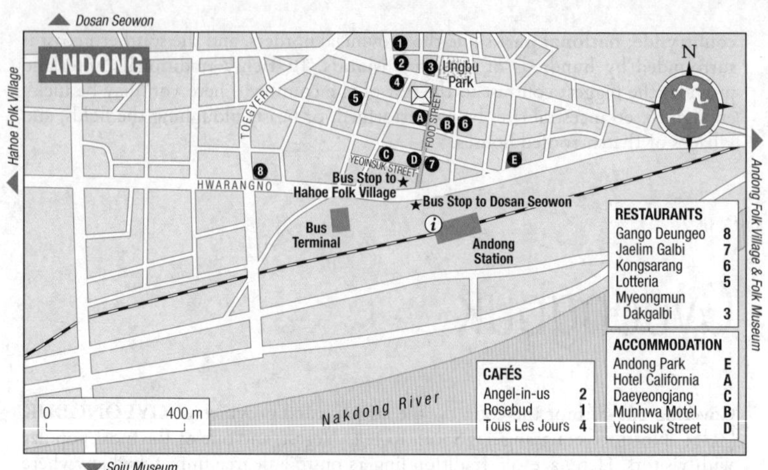

especially with regard to finding a place to stay, and there's usually an English-speaker on hand. Central Andong is extremely compact, but for the main sights both in Andong and its surrounding countryside, you're likely to need to use taxis or buses.

Accommodation

Andong's **accommodation** simply hasn't caught up with its increasing popularity as a tourist destination – if you're after any form of **luxury** you're advised to stay in Gyeongju and visit Andong on a tour or day-trip. Less picky souls should be able to find an acceptable place within walking distance of the train or bus stations; the **tourist information** office will even ring ahead to book a room if required.

Andong Park Unheungdong ⓣ054/853-1501. The only official hotel in town, though still pretty poor, despite recent renovations. Rooms are just about acceptable, however, and prices remain low. ❹

Hotel California Samsandong ⓣ054/854-0622. Surprisingly stylish for a motel – arty posters line the corridor walls, while rooms are just as flash, and come with great showers. It may be worth paying extra for the more expensive deluxe rooms, which are huge. It had temporarily closed for major renovations at the time of writing, and may well reopen with a new name, and in a higher price bracket. ❸

Daeyeongjang Yeogwan 대영장 여관 Samsandong. Rooms at this *yeogwan* on Yeoinsuk St (see below) have toilets and showers, comfy beds and windows, TVs and drinking water in the fridge – just like most motels, but cheaper at around W25,000. ❷

Munhwa Motel Dongbudong ⓣ054/857-7001. With powerful showers and mood lighting, this isn't a bad choice if the *California* is full. When demand is low, you'll be able to haggle the price down to near-*yeogwan* levels. ❸

Yeoinsuk Street Samsandong. Though extremely cheap at around W12,000 per person, all you'll get is a tiny linoleum room with a couple of blankets, and a TV if you're lucky. This said, there are few more authentically Korean places to stay. ❶

The City

For all the amazing sights around the city, there's not too much to see in Andong itself. The centre of the city, though relaxed, is for eating, drinking and sleeping in between excursions to the surrounding countryside, with a few attractions within a short taxi- or bus-ride. Just outside the main body of the city, and accessible on bus #3 – get off immediately after the river – is a small **folk village** (민속 마을; 24hr; free). With its buildings mere models, rather than functioning abodes, this is basically a heavily diluted version of the terrific folk village at Hahoe (see p.178), but it's worth a quick nose around, especially if the bus schedules from Andong to Hahoe or Dosan Seowon have left you with an hour or two to spare. If you have more time, you can stop at one of the **restaurants** at the top of the complex, a rustic bunch primarily occupied with the making and selling of *pajeon* – a fried savoury pancake made with a number of possible ingredients. Prefix *pajeon* with *haemul* for seafood (tentacles and things), *goju* for chilli pepper, *baechu* for cabbage or *buchu* for leek; all will cost around W5000, and are best washed down with *dongdongju*, a milky rice wine. After seeing the village, it's possible to cross the river on a zigzagging pedestrian bridge then catch the bus back to Andong from the other side of the road.

Don't leave without seeing the **Folk Museum** (민속 박물관; daily 9am–6pm; W1000) near the entrance to the complex, which is chock-full of interesting information about local culture and practices – including why Korean women give birth facing the south or east – and altogether more explanatory and less obsessed with cold, hard facts than most Korean museums. Look out for dioramas portraying village games – some of which still go on in the countryside on occasion – and some fascinating collections of clothing and headwear; on a good day, you may even walk out with a free scroll of calligraphy from an on-site artist.

Soju, of which Andong is home to a particularly strong variety, is the grog that oils Korea's wheels, and the town has a whole **museum** (소주 박물관; Mon–Sat 9am–5.30pm; free) dedicated to the stuff, a couple of kilometres to the south of town. Unfortunately, it isn't too interesting, but you're welcome to buy a bottle of the local variety that, at about 45 percent alcohol by volume, is nearly twice as strong as any other. Get there by taxi from the bus or train stations (W2500); stand on the opposite side of the main road.

Eating

A dedicated **food street** starts just opposite the train station – look for the gate with the mask – though the best restaurants are to be found away from this road. One interesting place to eat is the folk village east of the centre; see p.178 for more. The tourist booth outside the train station is an excellent source of information – they even have a cursory **restaurant map** for visiting foreigners. Of the various **cafés** *Rosebud* and *Angel-in-us* to the north of the centre are popular with the local youth, while just across the road is *Tous Les Jours*, a bakery good for a non-spicy breakfast.

Ilpum Gan-godeungeo 일품 간고등어 Unheungdong. An easy walk from the stations, here you can dine on salted mackerel, an Andong speciality. Ask for the *jeongsik* (정식) – a belly-filling set course featuring this plus an array of side dishes, yours for just W8000.

Jaerim Galbi 재림 갈비 Unheungdong. Though Andong has a dedicated Galbi Street, this is the best joint in town, and very popular with foreign tourists. Unlike most such restaurants, they're just about willing to cater for single diners – put on your biggest smile. Pork *galbi* is W7000 per portion, with marinated *bulgogi* a little more. The best meat, *hanu galbi*, costs a whacking W17,000 per portion, but is absolutely delicious.

Kongsarang 콩사랑 Dongbudong. A small restaurant with a stone-clad exterior, this is a good place to try simple Korean dishes such as *bibimbap* (mixed vegetables on rice) or *sundubu jjigae*, a spicy tofu broth, served with rice and vegetable side dishes. If you want to burn off calories afterwards, you can head across the road to the indoor driving range.

Lotteria This local burger joint has some interestingly Korean items on the menu, such as *galbi* or *bulgogi* burgers. More regular buns, fries and shakes are also available.

Myeongmun Dakgalbi 명문 닭갈비 Facing Ungbu Park. Just to the north of the city centre, this is the most popular place in town for *dakgalbi*, a delicious meal in which chicken meat and assorted vegetables are thrown into a hot pan to cook at the centre of your table.

Hahoe Folk Village

Korea has made many efforts to keep alive its pastoral traditions in the face of rapid economic growth; one particularly interesting example is its preserved **folk villages**. While some, such as the one near central Andong, exist purely for show others are functioning communities where life dawdles on at an intentionally slow pace, the residents surviving on a curious mix of home-grown vegetables, government subsidy and tourist-generated income. **Hahoe Folk Village** (하회 마을; 24hr; W2000) is one of the best and most popular in the country, a charming mesh of over a hundred **traditional countryside houses** nestling in the gentle embrace of an idle river. This charming mix of mud walls, thatched roofs and dusty trails is no mere tourist construct, but a village with a history stretching back centuries, and you'll be able to eat up at least a couple of hours exploring the paths, inspecting the buildings and relaxing by the river. The village's past is told on information boards outside the most important structures – seek out the Yangjin residence, for example, the oldest in the village, and built in a blend of Goryeo- and Joseon-era styles. The village can sometimes get a little busy with visitors, but it's easy to escape and find space – try the riverside at the far end of the village, past the church.

Some 2km outside the village, where the bus will likely set you down, the **Hahoe Mask Museum** (9am–6pm; W1000) features an absorbing collection of facewear from around the world. And every October Hahoe itself hosts an absorbing **mask dance festival** (Ⓦ www.maskdance.com).

Practicalities

Temptingly, there are a number of *minbak* at which you can **stay the night** in Hahoe, costing about W50,000 for a spartan room, and heated in colder months with the underfloor *ondol* system. The one upper-class option is *Rakkojae* (Ⓣ054/857-3410; ❼), a gorgeous complex affiliated to a similar establishment of the same name in Seoul (see p.74), and equipped with its own *jjimjilbang*. The tourist information office in Andong (see p.175) will be happy to book you into a guesthouse, and it's well worth staying to experience the village at night, when the vast majority of its visitors have gone home. Guesthouses serve light meals, which is handy since there are **no restaurants** in the village; there are, however, a couple of simple **grocery stores**.

Bus #46 runs to the village from Andong (8 daily; 40min). Day-trippers will be dropped off 2km from the complex and asked to buy a ticket; bus #46 continues merrily on into the village with genuine residents aboard, and visitors will have to take one of the regular **shuttle buses** (included with ticket price), even if they're staying the night.

Dosan Seowon

Dosan Seowon (도산 서원) is a Confucian academy, surrounded by some of the most gorgeous countryside that the area can offer. To get here take **bus** #67 from Andong – there are only a few per day, so check the return schedules at Andong's tourist information office. Not long after getting on you'll find yourself winding your way past rice paddies and some pleasantly unspoilt countryside, before ducking down to the academy's entrance (daily: March–Oct 9am–6pm; Nov–Feb 9am–5pm; W1500). From here it's a short walk to the complex itself; the wide **valley** to your right is simply stunning, the sound of rushing water from the stream occasionally augmented by the splutter of a faraway tractor.

The academy was established in 1574, in honour of Yi Hwang, a well-respected Confucian scholar also known as **Toegye** (see box opposite). It no longer functions as

Toegye, neo-Confucianist

Poet, scholar, all-round good guy and bearded star of the thousand-won note, **Toegye** (퇴계; 1501–70) is one of Korea's most revered historical characters. Born Yi Hwang, but better known by his pen name (pronounced Twegg-yeah), he exerted a major influence on the politics and social structure of his time. The country was then ruled by the **Joseon dynasty**, one of the most staunchly **Confucian** societies the world has ever known – each person was born with a predefined limit as to what they could aspire to in life, forever restricted by their genetics. The aristocracy oversaw a caste-like system that dictated what clothes people could wear, who they could marry, and what position they could hold, among other things.

Toegye was lucky enough to be born into privileged society. He excelled in his studies from a young age, and eventually passed the notoriously difficult governmental exams necessary for advancement to the higher official posts. Once there, he refused to rest on his laurels – he hunted down those he thought to be corrupt, and as a reward for his integrity was **exiled**, several times, from the capital. However, his intelligence made him a force to be reckoned with, and he set about introducing **neo-Confucian thought**, much of it borrowed from the Song dynasty in China; he advocated, for example, advancement based on achievement rather than heredity. After his death, the Confucian academy **Dosan Seowon** was built in his honour; it retains the contemplative spirit of the time, and of Toegye himself.

a place of study, but a refurbishment in the 1970s gave back the tranquillity of its original *raison d'être*: this was a highly important study place during the Joseon era, and the only one outside Seoul, for those who wished to pass the notoriously hard tests necessary for governmental officials. Opposite the main entrance, you may notice a little man-made hill topped by a **traditional-style shelter**; the stele underneath once marked an important spot for the government exams, with the original location somewhere towards the bottom of the lake that you pass on the bus in. As you enter the complex, beyond the flower gardens and up the steps are two libraries whose nameplates are said to have been carved by Toegye himself; the buildings were built on stilts to keep humidity to a minimum. Further on are structures that were used as living quarters, the main lecture hall, and a shrine to Toegye, though this last one is usually closed off. Passing back down under a cloak of maple – which flames roaring red in late autumn – you'll find an **exhibition hall** detailing the great man's life and times, as well as an astrolabe for measuring the movements of celestial bodies.

Beyond the academy are numerous other Toegye-related sights, all backed by **Cheongnyangsan**, a mountainous park. These scholarly sights are of more interest to Koreans than foreigners, but **Onhye**, Toegye's birth village, is a pretty place, and descendants of the don can still be found in one of his old abodes. A couple of daily buses on the #67 route continue past Dosan Seowon to Onhye and the park, but it's rather hard to do as a day-trip without your own transport. A number of **minbak** are located near the park entrance and in Dosan Seoburi, a small village just before the academy on the bus route from Andong.

Daegu and around

DAEGU (대구) is Korea's **fourth largest city** by population, and a major centre of business. The core of town is effectively one large shopping mall, the department stores supplemented by a lattice of streets devoted to particular products. Herbal Medicine Street is the best known, as the city has for centuries been a

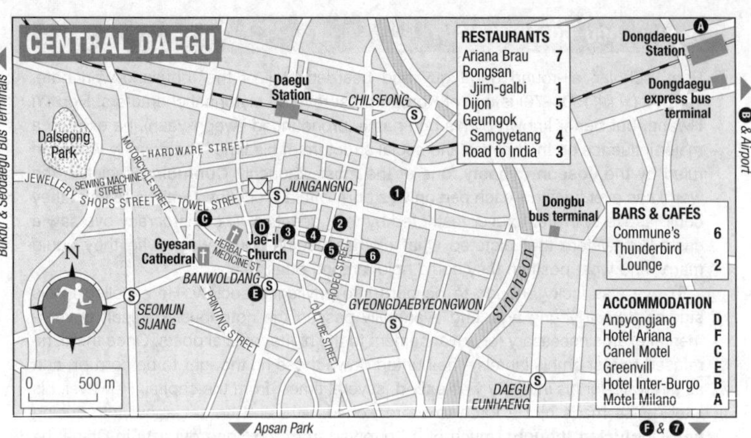

centre of **herbal medicine**, but you could also head to Steamed Rib Meat Street or Rice Cake Street if you're hungry, Shoe Street or Sock Street if your feet need clothing, or **Washing Machine Appliance Street** if, well, your washing machine needs maintenance.

For all this, it has to be said that Daegu as a city is not particularly attractive. However, in a country obsessed with appearance, it's hard to talk to a Korean about Daegu without being told how beautiful its women are; the city is based in a geological bowl, which makes for very hot summers, very cold winters and very delicious apples – this fruit that pops out of the surrounding countryside is said to keep the skin pimple-free, as well as providing the blanching effect that Korean girls crave. There are few notable sights in central Daegu, but it's a pleasant place to shop, or to catch up on your **partying** if you've been trawling the Gyeongsang countryside. Outside the city boundaries **Palgongsan** is a wonderful park to the north of town, while **Haeinsa** is one of Korea's best-known temples, and just a bus ride to the west.

Arrival

Daegu sprawls far and wide across the geological basin it calls home, which can make orientation more than a little tricky. Arriving by **bus** is particularly confusing, as there are **several terminals** across the city, though only a few of these are likely to be used by tourists. The Bukbu terminal and Seodaegu express terminal are frustratingly far (9km) to the northwest of the centre, as is the Seobu terminal to the southwest. The Dongbu terminal is marginally more central, but best is the **Dongdaegu express** (고속; *gosok*) **terminal,** which connects with trains and the subway system – to get here from other Korean cities you should head to their own *gosok* terminal. It's far better to arrive by **train** – Daegu station stares straight down at the main downtown area. For high-speed KTX services you'll have to head to Dongdaegu station, three stops to the east by subway. The city's **international airport** is a short bus or taxi ride east from Dongdaegu train station, and has a handful of connections to other Asian cities.

Information and getting around

Both train stations have **tourist information** booths, with English-speakers most likely at Dongdaegu (daily 9am–7pm; ⓣ053/939-0080). The stations are also

The Daegu subway fire

On February 18, 2003, a calamitous event took place under Daegu's downtown streets, one that was to have a heavy impact on the Korean psyche, and a terrible comedown after the spectacular success of the previous year's World Cup. The simple facts – around two hundred killed in a **subway fire** – do not even begin to tell the story, with failings before, during and after the event bringing about a national sense of shame, and a level of introspection previously unseen in a country accustomed to looking abroad for excuses.

A few months before the fire, a man named **Kim Dae-han** had suffered a stroke that left him partially paralysed. Ostracized by his family and friends, and losing his sanity, he decided to take his frustrations out on society. During a Tuesday morning rush-hour, he wandered into a subway train armed with gasoline-filled containers, which caught fire as the train pulled into Jungangno station. The fire spread rapidly through the carriages, owing to the lack of any fire-extinguishing apparatus on board; both the seats and the flooring produced toxic smoke as they burned. Kim managed to escape, along with many passengers from his train, but the poor safety procedures on the line meant that the driver arriving in the opposite direction was not informed of the problem, and pulled in to a plume of thick, toxic smoke. At this point the fire detection system kicked in and shut off power on the line, leaving both trains stranded. The driver of the second train told passengers to remain seated while he attempted to contact the station manager, and when finally put through was told to leave the train immediately. He duly scurried upstairs, but in his haste had removed the train's key, shutting off power to the doors, and effectively sealing the remaining passengers inside – death on a large scale was inevitable. The total count has never been fully established, as some bodies were burnt beyond all recognition.

The families of the victims, and the country as a whole, needed someone to blame. The arsonist was sentenced to life in prison, avoiding the death penalty on the grounds of mental instability; he died in jail soon afterwards. The incident raised some serious questions, primarily about **safety** being compromised by a thirst for profit, and the treatment of the **disabled** in Korean society – a baptism of fire for incoming president Roh Moo-hyun. Safety on Daegu's subway has since been significantly improved, and facilities for the disabled have improved across Korea. At least some good may be coming out of one of Korea's biggest modern-day disasters.

connected to the city's two-line **subway system**, which is cheap and efficient. As with all Korean cities, Daegu's **local bus** network is comprehensive, though likely to bewilder foreign tourists. If you're staying in the city for more than a couple of days you could use the Daegyong **travel card** (W2000), which gives slight discounts and avoids the need to rummage for change.

Accommodation

The information booths outside the train stations will be able to help you find a room – there are a few good **hotels**, **motels** aplenty can be found near both terminals, and there are some cheaper *yeogwan* within staggering distance of the nightlife area around Jungangno subway station. For those on a real budget, or just in need of a good scrub, there's *Greenvill*, a decent **jjimjilbang** (W8000) outside Banwoldang subway station, and another right outside Daegu Station.

Anpyongjang Yeogwan 안평장 여관 Jungangno area ⓣ053/424-0355. Cheap, cheerful and convenient for downtown, this *yeogwan* has decent enough en-suite rooms, though they occasionally rock to the sounds of a nearby *noraebang* singing room. Head to Jungangno subway station, and take the road opposite *Brannigan's*. ❷

Hotel Ariana Dusan Ogeori ⓣ053/765-7776, ⓦwww.ariana.co.kr. With clean, fresh and relatively spacious rooms, this Deurangil hotel is the city's best choice in this price range, but still overpriced unless you can land a discount; the "Deluxe" rooms are far bigger than the "Standard", and cost just a little more. There's a microbrewery on site in the German restaurant (see "Eating", below). ❻

Canel Motel 카넬 모텔 Namseongno ⓣ053/252-4466. Near the western end of Herbal Medicine Street, and, therefore, within walking distance of downtown, this motel will suffice for anyone on a tight budget. ❹

Hotel Inter-Burgo Manchondong ⓣ053/602-7114, ⓦhotel.inter-burgo.com. Though it may look like a leisure centre from outside, this is billed as Daegu's top hotel. It's overpriced and in an uninteresting part of town, though mercifully a short taxi ride from the airport or the train station. Book at the tourist office outside Dongdaegu station for big discounts. ❽

Motel Milano 모텔 밀라노 Dongdaegu Yeok-ap. A good choice near Dongdaegu train station, rising above its competitors by laying on free internet in many rooms. All the regular Korean motel conveniences are here, from the free can of coffee in the fridge to the shampoo in the bathroom. ❷

The City

Though the best sights are outside the city, Daegu's biggest draw is the variety of **shopping streets** that cover its centre. **Yasigolmok** (야시 골목) is a web of largely pedestrianized roads representing the city's modern heart – a collection of clothes shops, bars and cheap restaurants. To the west is the **Herbal Medicine Market** (한약 시장), which first got going in the 1650s. Markets like this used to be found all over the country but only a few remain, and today almost half of the country's buying and selling of medicinal herbage is undertaken on these streets. You'll find everything from fruits to roots, bark to bugs and lizard tails to deer antlers, with practitioners able to whip up combinations of weird and wonderful ingredients for a range of ailments; however, it must be said that the area isn't as picturesque as it may sound. On this street is the **Yangnyeongsi Exhibition Hall** (약령시 박물관; Mon–Sat 9am–5pm, Sun 10am–5pm; free), a mildly diverting display of medicinal ingredients and how they're used, though very little information is in English. Alongside is the **Je-il Church** (제일 교회), Daegu's first Christian place of worship, and the Gothic-style **Gyesan Cathedral** (계산 성당) is just around the corner. Nearby, **Daegu Hyanggyo** (대구 향교), a former Confucian academy, usually makes a pretty quiet spot for a wander.

Forming a western boundary to the specialist shopping street area is **Dalseong Park** (달성 공원), created on the site of what was apparently the oldest fortress in Korea; just around the corner from the entrance is a small **folk museum** (Tues–Sun daily 9am–5pm; free). Daegu has many other parks – the **National Debt Repayment Movement Park** near the city centre, is worth mentioning for the splendid name alone – but the only other one of note is **Apsan Park** (앞산 공원), a large green stretch to the south of the city; here you'll find plenty of temples and pavilions, a small exhibition on the Korean War, and a cable car that rises to a ridge and provides wonderful views of Daegu's sprawl.

Eating

There's a good, cheap **restaurant** around every corner in Daegu, and the rising number of expats means that the choice is becoming ever more cosmopolitan; Indian restaurants are becoming particularly popular. **Coffee** and morning snacks are far easier to hunt down in the Jungangno downtown area, as are Western joints such as *TGI Friday's* and *Brannigan's*.

Ariana Brau Dusan Ogeori. Fill up on bratwurst and sauerkraut at this German restaurant under the *Hotel Ariana*, and try a range of beers from the on-site microbrewery. Prices are a little high, so it's best to show up on Sat for the W17,000 buffet.

Dijon Gongpyeongdong. Terrific French restaurant that would surely go down well even in the trendier quarters of Seoul – indeed, the head chef once worked there at the *Millennium Hilton*. Their duck dishes are particularly sublime, and the quiet, romantic setting perfect for a date; figure on at least W30,000 for a meal and drinks. They also operate Into, an Italian restaurant next door.

Geumgok Samgyetang 금곡 삼계탕 Gongpyeongdong. *Samgyetang* is a soup containing a small chicken stuffed with rice and ginseng roots, which some foreign inductees find a little bland, and others delicious. This restaurant has a surprisingly un-Korean feel for such a dish, which is usually served in more traditional surroundings; still, it's the best place in the city to give it a try.

Jjim-galbi Street One of many cuisine-centred streets in the city, this is the best place to tuck into *jjim-galbi*, steamed rib meat that goes down particularly well with a few shots of *soju*. The oldest and most famous establishment here is Bongsan *Jjim-galbi* (봉산 찜갈비), which has been doling out the dish since the 1960s.

Road to India Gongpyeongdong. The first decent Indian restaurant to open up in central Daegu, with stylish decoration, cheerful staff and – far more importantly – a full roster of authentic curries. Look for the yellow sign.

Drinking

The downtown area has some great places to **drink**, most notably the *Thunderbird Lounge* (Thurs–Sat only), a chic, foreign-owned bar that revels in relative isolation a short walk from the main drag, and a great place to make new friends over a chilled Jagermeister or a microbrewed Alleykat pale ale. Nearby *Commune's*, which often plays music that's surprisingly underground for a Korean bar, also has live music at least once a week, and occasional quiz nights. In the same area is Rodeo Street, which holds all of the city's most popular **clubs** and lures local expats (and plenty of American soldiers) at weekends to dance until dawn – try *Frog* or *G2*.

Palgongsan Provincial Park

Just 20km north of Daegu, the land rises and folds, creating a peak-lined ridge and a series of valleys now studded with temples, hermitages and the odd carved Buddha. This area, **PALGONGSAN PROVINCIAL PARK** (팔공산 도립 공원), is an ideal setting for a day of relaxed hiking. Dating way back to 493, **Donghwasa** is the park's most famous temple, though a little over-hyped by the local authorities. Visitors are most likely to be impressed by a seated Buddha thought to date from the eighth century, and the gloriously intricate interior of the main hall. More modern is the mammoth **Tongil Buddha**, which stands next to some similarly outsized stone pagodas and lanterns. These uninspired creations were placed here in the hope that the two Koreas will one day become one – *tongil* means "reunification" – and though the religion-lite powers-that-be in Pyongyang are unlikely to approve of the Buddha, they're sure to be impressed by a liberal use of concrete rarely seen outside Communist societies.

Gatbawi (갓바위), another carved Buddha, occupies a lofty and far more natural setting, providing a view that's not quite top-of-the-world, but at least high enough to present Daegu in all its apartment block-filled glory. Situated up near the peak of Gwanbong (850m), it's around an hour's walk from the tourist village at the bottom of the trail. Many people make the journey on the 1st or 15th of the month to make a wish, as it is claimed that the Buddha will hear one from every visitor on these occasions. **Hikers** wanting to head from here to Donghwasa can do so without too much difficulty; a few hours should be enough to bring you to Yeombulbong (1121m), from where you can drop down the trail back to Donghwasa, stopping at Yeombulam, a hermitage on route. You could even take the cable car to or from an observation point near the hermitage – this runs from the tourist village beneath Donghwasa, and costs W3500 one way or W5500 return.

Palgongsan is fairly easy to get to by **bus**; from Dongdaegu station, #105 heads to Donghwasa and #104 to Gatbawi, each taking just under an hour to arrive. The **information booth** near Donghwasa has maps of the park; these should also be available at similar offices in Daegu.

Haeinsa

A bus ride away from Daegu, the secluded temple of **Haeinsa** (해인사) is part of Korea's holy trinity of "Jewel Temples" – the other two are Tongdosa (see p.198) and Songgwangsa (p.236), which represent the Buddha and Buddhist community respectively, while Haeinsa symbolizes the religion's teachings, or *dharma*. These doctrines have been carved onto more than eighty thousand wooden blocks, known as the **Tripitaka Koreana** (see box below), and remain visible through the vertical wooden rungs of the buildings that house them. Still in use today, Haeinsa's various buildings are pleasant enough; its location, however, is nothing short of spectacular: the path leading up to the main entrance, lined on both sides with colossal trees, is worth the trip alone, while the complex backs onto **Gayasan National Park** (가야산 국립 공원). Fame and beauty conspire to make the complex uncomfortably crowded at times, but few venture off the beaten track to enjoy the surrounding area. This is a shame, as a few hermitages can be found on the opposite side of the stream, and innumerable paths snake their way through the trees to peaks, farmland and secluded villages.

Practicalities

The temple sits just across the border in Gyeongnam; however, the easiest access is via Daegu. Regular direct buses head from the Seobu terminal, taking just over an hour to arrive; from the bus stop, it's a short but unnecessarily convoluted walk to the temple. There are, however, plenty of **places to stay** in the winding streets that surround the small terminal. The best rooms are on high at the *Haein Tourist Hotel* (Ⓣ055/933-2000; ❺); though it possesses the stained carpeting and slight chemical odour typical of official Korean tourist accommodation. The views, however, can be stunning, particularly on misty mornings. More interesting is the *Sanjangbyeoljang Yeogwan* (산장별장 여관; Ⓣ055/932-7245; ❷), with spartan rooms in a traditional-style building in keeping with its natural surroundings. You could even try to wangle a berth at **Haeinsa** itself – you'll have to be up early, but dawn at the temple is simply magical.

The Tripitaka Koreana

One of the most famous sights in the land, the eighty-thousand-plus wooden blocks of Buddhist doctrine known as the **Tripitaka Koreana** were first carved out in the eleventh century, over a 76-year period, in an attempt to curry the favour of the Buddha in a time of perpetual war. Though the originals were destroyed by rampaging Mongol hordes in the thirteenth century, the present set were carved shortly after that, and once again every possible measure was taken to please the Buddha. The best wood in the area was tracked down then soaked for three years in seawater before being cut to shape and boiled. The slabs then spent another three years being sheltered from sun and rain but exposed to wind, until they were finally ready for carving. Incredibly, not a single mistake has yet been found in over **fifty million** Chinese characters, a fact that led other countries to base their own Tripitaka on the Korean version. A superb feat of craft, patience and devotion, the outer spines of these blocks are still visible today at Haeinsa temple, and the set has been added to UNESCO's World Heritage List.

Gyeongju

A green jewel in Korea's tourist crown, **GYEONGJU** (경주) is a city that deserves a little more fame. Here you can walk among kings from a dynasty long expired and view the treasures accumulated during a millennium of imperial rule, while strolling around a city with infinitely more traditional sights than any other in the country. Strangely, much of Gyeongju's present charm is all down to a bit of good, old-fashioned dictatorship: in the 1970s and 1980s, authoritarian President **Park Chung-hee** managed to ensure that Korea's most traditional city stayed that way at a time when rapid economic progress was turning the country upside-down. He introduced height restrictions on structures built anywhere near historical remains – in other words, pretty much all of the centre – and passed a bill requiring almost everything static to have a traditional Korean-style roof. The rules have, sadly, not always been followed – spend as little time as possible in the mucky city centre – but the contrast with regular urban Korea remains quite palpable.

Chief among Gyeongju's sights are the dead kings' tombs, rounded grassy hills that you'll see all over town; it's even possible to enter one for a peek at the ornate way in which royalty were once buried. To the east of the centre there's **Anapji Pond**, a delightful place for an evening stroll under the stars, and a museum filled with assorted trinkets and fascinating gold paraphernalia from Silla times. Further east is **Bulguksa**, one of Korea's most famous temples; splendidly decorated, it's on the UNESCO World Heritage list, as is **Seokguram**, a grotto hovering above it on a mountain ridge. A less-visited mountain area is **Namsan** to the south of the centre, a wonderful park filled with trails and carved Buddha images.

Some history

The most interesting period of Gyeongju's lengthy history was during its near-millennium as capital of the **Silla kingdom** (see box, p.173). After so long as

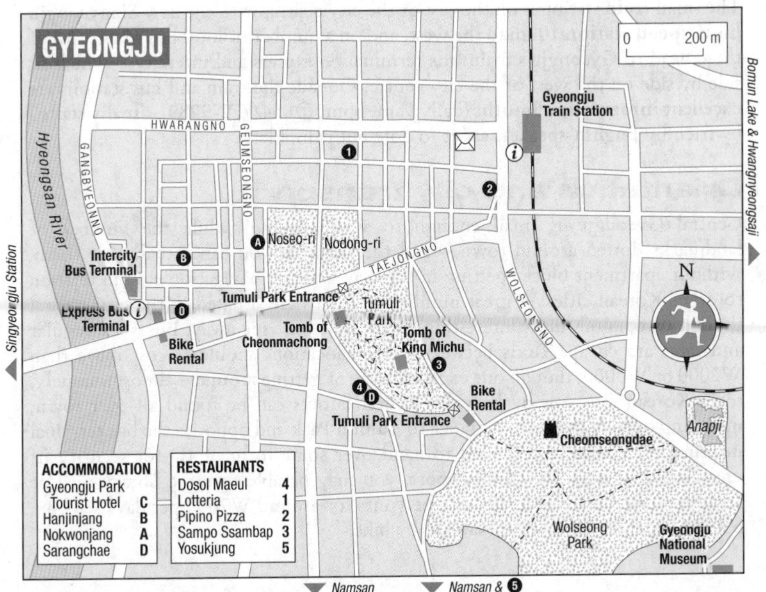

Gyeongju festivals

Throughout the year the city puts on many shows and events to please its guests. In warmer months, regular performances of traditional song and dance take place on **Bomun Lake** (see p.190) and around **Anapji Pond** (see p.189) at 8pm on Saturdays from April to October, but the biggest event by far is the three-day **Silla Cultural Festival**, in October, one of the best and most colourful in the land. On the menu are wrestling, archery, singing and dancing, and a parade in which a mock Silla king and queen are carried down the streets. Other events include the **Cherry Blossom Marathon**, held on the first Saturday of April, and a **Traditional Drink and Rice-Cake Festival** in late March, while on December 31 the New Year's crowd heads to King Munmu's seaside tomb (see p.196) to ring in the change of digits and enjoy the first sunrise of the year.

Korea's glamourpuss, the degree to which Gyeongju faded into the background is quite surprising – having relinquished its mantle of power, the city lived on for a while as a regional capital, but then fell into a **steep decline**. The Mongols rampaged through the city in the fourteenth century, the Japanese invasions a couple of hundred years later stripped away another few layers of beauty, and from a peak of over a million, Gyeongju's population fell to next to nothing.

Ironically, centuries after carrying countless spoils of war across the sea after their successful invasion, it was the Japanese who reopened Gyeongju's treasure-chest of history, during their occupation of the country in the early twentieth century. In went the diggers, and out came hundreds of thousands of relics, so that, even today, much visible evidence of the dynasty still remains around the city. Not all of this is above ground – excavations continue, and new discoveries are made every year.

Arrival and information

The small **train** station is on the east of the city centre, with the new Singyeongju **high-speed station** 10km to the west, and on a number of local bus routes. All of these head to Gyeongju's main **bus** terminals – express and intercity – which sit side by side on the west of the city centre. Outside the train and bus stations are excellent **information booths** (daily 9am–6pm; ⓣ054/772-9289), usually staffed by friendly English-speakers eager to dole out pamphlets.

Orientation and city transport

Central Gyeongju is small enough to **walk** around, while the number of landmarks dotted around town – and the fact that you can actually see them, without apartment blocks getting in the way – makes navigation easy in relation to other Korean cities. A great number of tombs are situated in the city centre, though Gyeongju's most interesting sights are a bus ride away. Buses are regular and fares are cheap. **Taxis** between central locations shouldn't cost more than W2000 or W3000, though one excellent way of getting around – almost uniquely, for a Korean city – is by **bicycle**. Rental outlets can be found all over town, including outside the main entrance to Tumuli Park and opposite the bus terminal information booth. You'll need to hand over some form of ID for security (if unwilling to part with your passport, you may be able to use a library card or something similar), and a bike will be yours for around W7000 per day. See box, p.192 for details on touring Namsan by bike.

Accommodation

For a city that trades so heavily on the tourist dollar, central Gyeongju's range of **accommodation** is a little poor. Its **five-stars** stand proud in a swanky collective around Bomun Lake, a short way east of the centre; all have the conveniences you'd expect, including LAN connections in the rooms, for which you'll pay an extortionate W20,000 or so per day. Rack rates can fall by up to fifty percent at quieter times of the year, but rooms are on the small side and lack character. Cheaper **motels** can be found together with some lower-end hotels near the bus terminals, though prices tend to be higher here than elsewhere in Korea. There are a couple of backpacker-oriented **guesthouses**, which generally provide free internet and cooking facilities, and common rooms in which to hang out with fellow travellers. Those on an even tighter budget should head left down the main road from the train station to the *yeoinsuk* area – these are guesthouses from days before Korea took off as an economic power, and possess nothing more than a few blankets, a TV and some toilet paper for use in a grubby shared toilet. They charge around W10,000 per night; if you're quoted anything higher than W20,000, it won't be just for the room.

Lastly, there's an interesting **farm stay** programme near Oksan Seowon, to the north of Gyeongju (p.196). There you may find yourself helping to plant rice, or roasting chestnuts around an open fire. Ask at one of Gyeongju's tourist information centres for details, or call ⓣ054/762-6148.

City centre

The places listed below are marked on the "Gyeongju" **map**, p.185.

Gyeongju Park Tourist Hotel Sincheondong ⓣ053/759-7002, ⓦwww.gjpark.com. Not a bad place to stay – cheaper than most official tourist hotels, and largely devoid of the regular scruffy floors – it has the faint air of a European hotel, and prices often drop as low as W50,000. The lobby contains a café and a small restaurant, and though the rooms are no bigger than those in the surrounding motels, all come with large TVs, and some provide free internet access. ❺

Hanjinjang Yeogwan Noseodong ⓣ054/771-4097, ⓦwww.hanjinkorea.wo.to. Grubby, hostel-like place that ropes in a surprising number of foreign guests. Standards of cleanliness are low, but it's a decent place to meet people, especially when evenings are warm enough to allow for a spot of drinking on the roof terrace. Dorms W17,500, doubles ❷

Nokwonjang Yeogwan Chukhyeop-ap ⓣ054/741-6277. In a quiet, relaxed area immediately to the west of the Noseo-ri tombs – look for the green building. Rooms are basic but perfectly acceptable, though the strange window constructions mess up what should really be a fine view of the tombs. ❷

Sarangchae Hwangnamdong ⓣ054/773-4868, ⓦwww.kjstay.com. Quite possibly the best guesthouse in the country, the *Sarangchae* throws friendly, informative management, free internet and cooking facilities and some friendly dogs into a gorgeously traditional courtyard setting. Book ahead though, as there are only a few rooms; also note that they're usually closed in December. ❷

Bomun Lake

The places listed below are marked on the "Gyeongju area" **map**, p.191.

Commodore Hotel Sinpyeongdong ⓣ054/745-7701. Rooms here are as tastefully designed as the lobby, with a choice of hill or lake views – the latter are best but marginally more expensive. There are a few good restaurants on site, as well as a lovely spa. ❼

Hotel Concorde Sinpyeongdong ⓣ054/745-7000. A slightly cheaper alternative to its flashy neighbours, rooms here are a little worn but still good value, and all come with balconies facing the lake. Service standards, however, are pretty poor. ❻

Gyeongju Hilton Sinpyeongdong ⓣ054/745-7788, ⓦwww.hilton.com. Possessing a slightly more international ambience than its neighbours, the *Hilton* has a swimming pool, gym, squash court and jogging track – and a Miró original in the lobby. ❽

Hotel Hyundai Sinpyeongdong ⓣ054/748-2233, ⓦwww.hyundaihotel.com. This hotel probably offers the best lake views in the area, though rooms with a hill view are a little cheaper. Rooms are pleasing, with some nice touches and relatively large bathrooms, and service is very good; there are also Italian, Chinese, Korean and Japanese restaurants to choose from, as well as a coffee shop that serves delectable pecan pie. 8

Bulguksa

Kolon Hotel Madong ⓣ054/746-9001, ⓦwww.kolonhotel.co.kr. See "Gyeongju area" map, p.191. Despite the unfortunate name, this is a quality place to stay, out of town and just down the road from Bulguksa, in a tree-surrounded setting that includes a nine-hole golf course. Rooms are a little dated, but views over the course and trees are lovely. Rooms are cheaper at weekends. 6

Tumuli Park

Gyeongju is often described by the Korean tourist board as an open-air museum, thanks to its large number of grassy regal, burial mounds. The tombs in question are known as **Tumuli**, which are prolific and impossible to miss. Right in the centre of town, the walled-off **Tumuli Park** (대릉원; daily 9am–10pm; W1500) contains over two dozen tombs. It's hard to imagine that this was until quite recently a functioning – though quiet – part of town, but in the 1970s the buildings were removed and the area beautified, creating a path- and tree-filled park that's wonderful for a stroll. Entrances are located at the east and north of the complex, but its most famous hump sits to the far west. Here lies **Cheonmachong** (천마총), the only tomb in Korea that you can actually enter. Its former inhabitant is not known for sure, but is believed to be a sixth- or seventh-century king whose many horse-related implements gave rise to the name – Cheonmachong means "Heavenly Horse Tomb". Excavated in 1973, it yielded over twelve thousand artefacts, which was the largest single haul in the country, and although many went to Gyeongju Museum, a few decorate the inner walls of the tomb. There's also a full-scale

What's green and lumpy?

Every culture has its own solutions for what to do with the deceased. Tibetan corpses are often left on a mountainside for vultures to carry away, certain Filipino societies place the departed in a coffin and pack it into a cliff, while the Yanomami of the Amazon rainforest choose to cremate their dead then eat the ashes with banana paste. Koreans have long preferred burial – a slightly more prosaic journey to the afterlife, for sure – and those who have travelled around the country a while will doubtless have seen the little green bumps that dot hills and mountains in the country's rural areas. Larger versions used to be a matter of course for Korean royalty.

Literally hundreds of **tombs** from the **Silla dynasty** can be found all over Gyeongju and its surrounding area. However, the identities of few of the tombs' occupants are known for sure – there were only 56 Silla kings, so it's clear that many were created for lesser royals, military leaders and other prominent members of society. Equally mysterious are the **interiors**, as the super-simple green parabolas give almost no hints as to their construction; however, a look inside **Cheonmacheong** in Tumuli Park should provide a few hints. Layers of gravel and stone make up the base of the tomb, with a wooden chamber placed in the centre to house the deceased – unlike a Pharaoh, he or she would not have supervised the construction, but as in Egypt they would have been buried with some of their favourite belongings. The chamber was then covered with large, rounded stones (these would eventually crush the chamber, after sufficient putrefaction of the wood), which in turn was covered with clay and dirt, and sown with grass.

Given the riches inside, surprisingly few of the tombs were plundered for their treasures – while such an endeavour would be long and rather conspicuous, that didn't stop thievery elsewhere in the country. Over the past century, many tombs have been carefully excavated, yielding thousands of artefacts, many of which are now on display in Gyeongju's National Museum.

mock-up of how the inhabitant was buried. Elsewhere in the complex is the large **tomb of King Michu**, who reigned from 262 to 284 and fought many battles to protect his empire from the neighbouring Baekje dynasty. According to legend, he even dispatched a ghost army from beyond the grave when his successor was losing one particular bout of fisticuffs; these phantoms disappeared during the resulting celebrations, leaving behind only the bamboo leaves that had infested the cavities of the enemy dead. For this reason, the tomb is often referred to as the "Tomb of the Bamboo Chief". One other tomb of note is the double-humped **Hwangnam Daechong**, which was almost certainly the resting place of a king and queen.

Noseo-ri and Nodong-ri

Across the main road, the tumuli continue, though less abundantly, into the city's main shopping district. Split by a road into two sections known as **Noseo-ri** (노서리) and **Nodong-ni** (노동리), these areas are not walled off, and are free to enter at any time of the day or night. Here lie some colossal mounds, as big as those you'll find in Tumuli Park – one, known as Bonghwangdae, is 22m high, with a 250m circumference. Although you're not allowed to climb onto the tombs, a faint path heading up this largest hump indicates that some find the temptation too great to ignore, and you'll usually find a couple of people seated here after the sun has gone down. Opposite, in Noseo-ri, is a monument dedicated to **Prince Gustav Adolf VI** of Sweden, who participated in the excavations here in 1926 before inheriting his country's throne.

Wolseong Park area

A short walk southeast of Tumuli Park will bring you to the pretty patch of greenery called **Wolseong Park** (월성 공원; 24hr; free), in and around which are some of the city's most popular sights. The paths that run through the park are pedestrianized, but you can also take a short horse-and-carriage ride around the area – you'll see them lined up opposite the main entrance to Tumuli Park. There are plenty of tombs around, though most Koreans make an eastward beeline to have their picture taken next to **Cheomseongdae** (첨성대; daily 9am–6pm; W500), an astronomical observation tower dating from the seventh century. Looking a little like a rook from a giant chessboard, its simplicity conceals a surprising depth of design: the twelve stones that make up the base represent either the months of the year or the signs of the Chinese zodiac, while the 27 circular layers were a nod to Queen Seondeok, ruler during the tower's construction and the 27th ruler of the Silla dynasty. Added to the two square levels on top and the base, this equals thirty, which is the number of days in a lunar month, while the total number of blocks equals the number of days in a year. Even more amazingly, the various gaps and points on the structure are said to correspond to the movements of certain celestial bodies.

South of Cheomseongdae and making up much of the park is **Banwolseong** (반월성), which was once a fortress; today only a few stones remain, though you're able to walk the tree-lined path that heads around the earthen wall. Down the northern fringe and across the road is **Anapji** (안압지; daily 8am–10pm; W1000), a pleasure garden constructed in 674 by the fantastically named **King Munmu** (see p.196). Numerous battles in the preceding decade had led to a first-ever unification of the Korean peninsula, after which Munmu built what was – and still remains – a tranquil, tree-filled area around a **lotus pond** whose shape roughly mirrored that of his kingdom. In an interesting twist of fate, this was where the empire also came to an end, being the scene of King Gyeongsun's handover of power to King Taejo, founder of the Goryeo dynasty. In the following centuries, the area fell into disrepair until 1975, when it received its first modern makeover. When the pond was dredged it revealed a few relics from Silla times. That few then grew to hundreds, then thousands – much of the bounty, including a whole barge, now sits in the National Museum just down the road. Relics were found in even greater numbers at **Hwangryongsaji** (황룡사지), a temple ruin a short walk to the north across the railroad tracks. The original was built here in the sixth century, then destroyed and rebuilt several times over before rampaging Mongol hordes finished it off for good in the thirteenth century. Apparently, it once contained a 70m-high wooden pagoda; support stones from this structure are still visible, and hint at its former size. **Bunhwangsa**, a short walk further north again, is an active temple; though small, it's worth a look around at what was once a large nine-storey stone pagoda (only three levels remain).

Gyeongju National Museum

Back on the perimeter of Wolseong Park, **Gyeongju National Museum** (경주 국립 박물관; Tues–Sun: April–Oct 9am–9pm; Nov–March 9am–6pm; free) is a repository of riches from the surrounding area, and with the exception of Seoul's National Museum (p.95), it's quite possibly the best in the country. The rooms run in chronological order from locally sourced stone tools and ancient pottery to modern times, via the Bronze Age. But it's the **Silla** bling that most are here to see. Beautifully crafted earrings, pendants and other paraphernalia in gold, silver and bronze were cast into spectacular shapes, often adorned with tiny golden discs or leaves. You'll also find pottery, golden antlers and some uncomfortable-looking spiked bronze shoes, but the undisputed star of the show, hidden away in its own private room, is a glorious golden sixth-century crown, intricately sculpted and boasting an array of dangling bean-shaped jades. Outside lies the **Emille Bell**, a veritable beast dating from 771. Known to Koreans as the Bell of King Seongdeok – in whose memory it was created – this is the largest existing bell in the country, and one of the biggest in the world; though estimates of its weight vary, even the smallest – nineteen tons – makes it a whopper by any standard. Legend surrounding the bell says that when it was first cast it failed to ring, only doing so once its constituent metal was melted back down and mixed with the body of a young girl. Her death-cry "Emille" (which rhymes with "simile") was a word for mother in the Silla dialect, and can apparently still be heard in the ring of the bell.

Bomun Lake

A few kilometres east of Wolseong Park, and on the bus route towards Bulguksa temple, you'll come to **Bomun Lake** (보문호). Surrounded by five-star hotels, it has become a venue of choice for the well heeled; largely devoid of the historical sights found elsewhere in the city, it's still a good place to head for a bit of easy fun. You can hire swan-shaped pedalos (30min; W5000) – the doyens of Korea's artificial waterways and bikes for the cycle-trails around the lake, while the **Sonjae Museum of Contemporary Art** (daily 10am–6pm; W3000) on the grounds of the *Hilton* provides higher-brow diversions. There are also regular cultural and musical performances at the Bomun Outdoor Performance Theater just down from the *Commodore Hotel* (generally July–Oct Thurs–Tues 8.30pm, Sat & Sun only in May & June). A number of **golf courses** can be found around the lake, ranging in size from nine to thirty-six holes.

Bulguksa and around

Sitting comfortably under the tree-lined wings of the surrounding mountains, **Bulguksa** (불국사; daily 7am–6pm; W4000) was built in 528 during the reign of King Beop-heung, under whose leadership Buddhism was adopted as the Silla

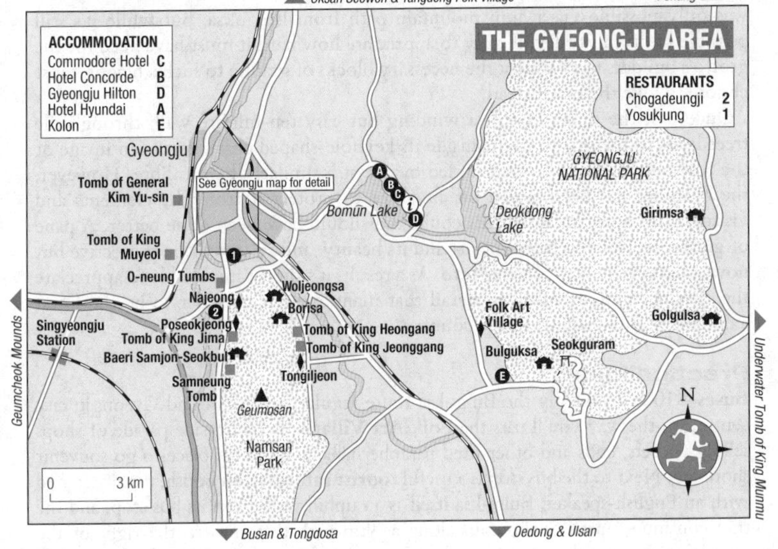

state religion. It was almost destroyed by the Japanese invasions in 1593 and, though it's hard to believe now, was left to rot until the 1970s, when dictatorial president Park Chung-hee ordered its reconstruction. It has subsequently been added to the UNESCO World Heritage list. As one of the most visited temples in the country, it can be thronged with people, many of whom combine their visit with a picnic on and around the path leading from the bus stop to the ticket office. Once through the gates, you'll walk a pretty path past a pond and over a bridge, before being confronted by the temple. Here **two staircases** lead to the upper level; these are officially "four bridges" rather than two flights of steps, leading followers from the worldly realm to that of the Buddha. Both are listed as national treasures, so you're not actually allowed to ascend them. Having entered the main courtyard, you'll be confronted by yet more treasures, this time two three-level **stone pagodas** from the Unified Silla period; one plain and one ornately decorated, representing Yin and Yang.

From the courtyard, it's best to stroll aimlessly and appreciate the views. The whole complex has been elaborately **painted**, but the artistry is particularly impressive in Daeungjeon, the main hall behind the pagodas, whose eaves are decorated both inside and out with striking patterns. At the top of the complex, another hall – Gwaneumjeon – looks down over Bulguksa's pleasing array of roof tiles; the steep staircase down causes problems for Korean girls in high heels, but there are other ways back. Making your way across the rear of the complex you'll come to Nahanjeon, a hall surrounded by bamboo and a cloak of maple leaves. Behind this lie small towers of stacked stones; you're welcome – expected – to add your own. The **tearoom** beneath the nearby trinket shop provides a useful rest stop.

Seokguram Grotto

After the temple, a visit to the Buddhist grotto of **Seokguram** (석굴암; same times as temple; W4000) may feel a little anti-climactic. However, the views from its lofty position alone justify the trip up, especially at sunrise. The East Sea is visible on a good day, and it is said that the statue was built to provide spiritual protection to the country from the Japanese across these waters. Until fairly recently, access was only possible via a 3km mountain path from Bulguksa, but while it's still possible to do this today, if only to appreciate how hard it must have been for the grotto's builders to transport the necessary blocks of granite to such a height, most choose to take the bus instead.

Once past the ticket booth, a winding but easy ten-minute walk through the trees leads to the grotto itself; inside its keyhole-shaped chamber sits an image of the Sakyamuni Buddha, surrounded by art of a similarly high calibre. However, the chamber has been sealed off in order to protect it from the elements and visitors, and unfortunately, this could and should have been done better. A pane of glass separates you from the art and its beauty, and an ugly little protective hut now stands in the way of the grotto. As a result, it's almost impossible to appreciate the elegance and attention to detail that many experts consider to be the finest example of Buddhist art in the country.

Practicalities

Buses #10 and #11 ply the Bulguksa route regularly from around Gyeongju city centre; on the way you'll pass the **Folk Art Village**, a countryside parade of shops selling tea sets, cups and other fired paraphernalia, and a great place to go souvenir shopping. Next to the bus stop is a useful **tourist information** booth, usually staffed with an English-speaker. Bulguksa itself is an uphill walk from its bus stop, and the trail continues up to Seokguram along a 3km path that runs to the right of the temple's ticket booth; you can judge for yourself how far it is by looking up at the horizon from the Bulguksa bus stop – that's the Seokguram ticket booth on top. However, most people take the **bus** – those going up leave Bulguksa at forty minutes past the hour, with the last at 5.20pm, and come back on the hour, the last at 6.20pm.

There are dozens of **restaurants** across from the Bulguksa bus stop, many of which have menus in English. The area also has a few **places to stay**, including one top-end hotel (the *Kolon*; see p.188), but these motels and guesthouses are generally the preserve of youth and family groups. Still, the quiet of the place at night is quite appealing.

Namsan Park

Central Gyeongju's ragtag assortment of buildings fades to the south, turning from urban to rural. Mercifully, development of this area is unlikely, as the city is

Touring Namsan by bike

For those with the inclination, and as long as the weather agrees, a **bike tour** around Namsan is one of the most enjoyable ways to spend a day in Gyeongju. To reach the mountain, come out of Tumuli Park and turn right at the main road; the tombs of Wolseong Park should be on your left, and a few tourist shops and restaurants to your right. Turn left at the T-junction and head over the bridge. When you reach the end of the road turn left to get to Namsan's eastern flank, or right for the west. For the **west side**, turn left after the golden Buddha and you'll be at the northeast corner of **O-neung**; the entrance is down the main road on the south side. After seeing the sights on the western flank, you can avoid the main road back by using the labyrinthine farm tracks that spread out between the road and the parallel river further back. On Namsan's **east side** a patchwork of fields provides more opportunities to get away from the main roads than on the west, and you can use your own initiative to hug Namsan's skirt of trees.

There are numerous places to **hire bikes** (W7000 per day) in Gyeongju; the most convenient is the outlet in the car park outside the main entrance to Tumuli Park.

hemmed in on its southern flank by **Namsan Park**, a small mountain area packed with trails and sights. New discoveries of ancient relics are made regularly, but even if you don't find yourself unearthing a piece of Silla jewellery, this is another of the city's must-sees. Roads run along the park's perimeter, giving access to a wealth of sights on both sides, while the interior is strewn with carved Buddhas and offers some fantastic hikes. Namsan is best tackled either by **bicycle** around its pleasantly traffic-free perimeter (see box opposite), or with a pair of hiking boots through its interior.

From Gyeongju, buses #500 to #508 run down the western side of the park, while #10 and #11 can be used for some of the sights on the eastern side.

The western flank

The first sight that you'll come to on the western flank is **O-neung** (오릉; daily: March–Oct 9am–6pm; Nov–Feb 9am–5pm; W500), which means "five tombs". The grassy area just inside the perimeter wall is popular with picnicking families in the summer, but if you make your way through the pines along one of the park's lovely paths you'll soon come to the tomb of Hyeokgeose (ruled 57 BC to 4 AD), the **first king** of the Silla dynasty. Little else is known about him, but a history this long deserves to be acknowledged with a little perspective: Hyeokgeose was born in 69 BC, the same year as Cleopatra – Hyeokgeose's hump has been around for a seriously long time. Nearby mounds contain three of his immediate successors – Namhae, Yuri and Pasa were the second, third and fifth Silla monarchs respectively – as well as Hyeokgeose's wife, **Alyeong**, who was apparently born as a dragon in a nearby well, and therefore suitably auspicious. The well can still be seen; just follow the signs. Hyeokgeose himself trumped his future wife's spectacular birth by hatching from an egg laid by a phantom horse; his birthplace is outside the park, just down the road at Najeong, but the site is badly neglected in comparison.

Heading south and across the main road you'll soon come across **Poseokjeong** (포석정; same times; W500), an uninteresting site, but one that's hugely popular with Korean tourists. Here once lay a villa in which Silla kings held regular banquets, but with the buildings long gone, you may wonder what all the fuss is about. The draw is actually a 6m-long water canal set within a loose perimeter of rocks – don't step inside – which was once used for royal **drinking games**: one member of the party would reel off a line of poetry, choose another guest to supply a suitable second line, and float a cup of wine down the watercourse. If the drink reached the challenger before he could think of a line, he had to drain the cup. Just across the way, and signposted from the Poseokjeong car park, is the **Tomb of King Jima**, who was the sixth Silla king, but now finds himself isolated among the trees. The neighbouring village of **Poseok** remains charming, and is worth a nose around. It's also home to some good, cheap **restaurants**, though the best is the tiny *Chogadeungji*, across the main road (see p.194).

Further down either the road or the footpath from Poseokjeong you'll find a couple of tiny temples housing a standing Buddha trio known as **Baeri Samjon-seokbul** (배리 삼존 석불; 24hr; free), which are said to date back to the early seventh century. This is a pretty area, and the starting point for a number of paths into Namsan's interior. At *Jungnim Nongjang*, a tiny farm-cum-**restaurant** south of the Buddhas, you can slurp *kalguksu* noodles under a flower-covered canopy. Continuing south you come to **Samneung** (삼릉; 24hr; free), a small, pretty complex containing three tombs. Here lies Adalla, the eighth Silla king (ruled 154–184 AD), next to Sindeok and Gyeongmyeong, the 53rd and 54th leaders, who ruled for just a few years each in the early tenth century as the empire struggled to its close.

The eastern flank and the interior

There's a little less to see on Namsan's eastern side, though cyclists will be able to get off the main road and head through some farm villages where it's hard to imagine that you're just a few kilometres short of Tumuli Park and its swarm of tourists. There are lots of little roads, but as long as you keep between the main road and the park it doesn't really matter where you head – small houses, trees, fields and drying laundry greet you at every turn. There are also a number of carved Buddhas, placed on Namsan's eastern side so that they may face the rising sun, though you'll need to trek a short way into the park to see them – the tourist office will have detailed **maps** of the area, and some guesthouses create their own.

One of the first Buddhas you'll reach on your way from Gyeongju is also the most accessible – follow signs for Woljeongsa temple – but the one uphill behind **Borisa** (보리사), the largest functioning temple on Namsan, is more interesting, dating from the eighth century and backed by richly detailed stonework. A path from here leads all the way to a viewing platform on the top of the mountain, after which you'll have a choice between heading west to Poseokjeon, south to the ruin-surrounded peak of Geumosan, or east to **Tongiljeon** (통일전). This "Palace of Reunification" (daily: March–Oct 9am–6pm; Nov–Feb 9am–5pm; W300) was constructed on the orders of Park Chung-hee in 1977, though with little apparent ambition – there's not much to see, but its secluded park-like location means that you may well find yourself alone. After climbing several large outdoor staircases, there's a sudden hush as you enter the topmost courtyard, the cream-coloured walls of which are lined with paintings depicting legends from Silla times. Those who've not yet had their fill of regal mounds can take one of two paths that push a short way into Namsan's pines just north of the palace; both lead to the tombs of Heongang and Jeonggang, two ninth-century kings who, in this isolated position, would doubtless appreciate the company. Beyond Tongiljeon you'll find a pond sporting a gorgeous pavilion; this area is dotted with rural temples that are historically unimportant, but pretty nonetheless.

Eating and drinking

Gyeongju is not known for its food, and unfortunately there's little of interest in the centre – the best food is served in the **five-star hotels** that surround Bomun Lake. One interesting feature is the simply incredible number of small bakeries selling *gyeongju-bbang* (경주빵), small, sweet cakes that are eagerly snapped up by Japanese tourists seeking their *omiyage* (near-compulsory edible travel souvenirs).

Chogadungji 초가둥지 Poseok; see "Gyeongju area" map, p.191. Little thatch-roofed bungalow-restaurant just off Namsan's western flank, and almost directly opposite the Tomb of King Jima. Here you can get a filling set meal (*jeongsik*) of veggies and fish for just W6000 – perfect if you're touring the mountain by bike.

Dosol Maeul 도솔 마을 Hwangnamdong. Near the *Sarangchae* guesthouse and very similar in appearance, here you can eat *pajeon* pancakes and quaff *dongdongju* – a milky Korean wine – by the bucketload in traditional rooms set around an equally rustic courtyard. A great place to kick back after a day's sightseeing.

Lotteria Hwangodong. Respite from Korean cuisine is available here in a sesame-seed bun. Though regular beef- or cheeseburgers are yours for the taking, those who want to impart at least a little local flavour to their meal can choose the *bulgogi* or *galbi* burgers instead.

Pipino Pizza Hwangodong ⓣ054/773-0987. While there are Western pizza chains in Gyeongju, *Pipino* offers a slightly more Korean experience for W10,000 and up. Toppings include vegetarian, sweet potato, *bulgogi* or "super special". If you speak Korean, or can find someone willing to translate, you can call for free delivery – perfect on a rainy day.

Sampo Ssambap 삼포 쌈밥 Hwangnamdong. Filled with assorted Korean bric-a-brac, this is the most atmospheric of a line of restaurants near the main entrance to Tumuli Park, all of which serve *ssambap* – a delicious, seemingly infinite array of mostly vegetable side dishes that make a fantastic way to fill your stomach for around W8000. Unlike most such restaurants, this one is willing to feed single travellers.

Yoseokjeong 요석정 Gyodong; see "Gyeongju area" map, p.191. A fabulous place for fabulous food, set around a traditional courtyard in a quiet area facing Namsan Park. There's no English menu, but good traditional food is guaranteed – set meals go from W30,000 to W100,000 per head, though there's a two-person minimum.

Listings

Banks Banks with exchange facilities include the Korea First Bank opposite the train station, and there are plenty of ATMs at 24hr convenience stores such as Family Mart or 7-Eleven.

Internet Some motels and all of the main backpacker guesthouses offer internet for free, or there are cafés available all over town which charge W1000 per hour – just look for the letters "PC", or ask for a "*pishi-bang*".

Martial arts Seonmudo courses are available at Golgulsa, a secluded temple to the east of Gyeongju – see below.

Post The main post office is opposite the train station (Mon–Fri 9am–5pm; ⓣ054/740-0114).

Around Gyeongju

An almost overwhelming number of sights litter the countryside around Gyeongju – those listed here make up just a fraction of the possibilities, so be sure to scour local maps and pamphlets for things that might be of particular interest to you. **Transport** to sights is not always regular – you may need to spend some time waiting for buses, so if possible, try to get the latest timetable from one of Gyeongju's tourist offices. While hitchhiking is never totally safe and can't be wholeheartedly recommended, you'll rarely get a better chance than on the run east to the **Underwater Tomb of King Munmu**, where the road is lightly trafficked and everyone is heading to or from Gyeongju. To the north of Gyeongju are **Oksan Seowon**, one of the country's best examples of a Joseon-era Confucian academy, and **Yangdong Folk Village**, a collection of traditional housing. To the west of the city and within cycling range are yet more regal tombs.

East of Gyeongju to the Underwater Tomb of King Munmu

On the way to see King Munmu and his watery grave, and easily combined as part of a day-trip, you'll pass a rural spur road leading to two out-of-the-way temples that inhabit a wonderfully unspoilt valley east of Gyeongju. **Golgulsa** (골굴사) is the nearer of the two, and famed as a centre of *seonmudo*, a Zen-based martial art. From the bus stop near the village of Andong-ni (#150, the same bus that heads to Munmu), it's just under 1km to the temple turn-off on the left. It's all uphill from here, with the track heading past a teahouse before rising into the small complex, from where it becomes even steeper. Backing the complex is a sixth-century Buddha, carved into a cliff navigable on some short but precipitous paths. Though now protected by a monstrous modern structure, a clamber up to the Buddha is essential for the picture-perfect **view** alone; there are barriers to stop you from going over the edge. Those of an even steelier disposition may like to stay at the temple for some martial arts practice; visit ⓦwww.golgulsa.com for more information.

Girimsa

Five kilometres further down the spur road is **Girimsa** (기림사; W3000), a temple that receives few visitors on account of its location. There are sometimes direct buses from Gyeongju – ask at the tourist office – but it's quite possible to make the long walk here from Golgulsa: allow at least an hour each way. The road sees little traffic, and the journey is its own reward, with farmland-backed views and the occasional man walking his pet bird of prey while the surrounding rice paddies reverberate to the sound of thousands of frogs. After such majestic countryside, the slightly drab grounds of the temple itself may come as something of a letdown, but it's a quiet place rarely overrun with visitors. Notable are a couple of statues of the Goddess of Mercy, and a centuries-old Bodhi tree.

The Underwater Tomb of King Munmu

Just off the coast east of Gyeongju is the **Underwater Tomb of King Munmu** (문무대왕 수중릉; 24hr; free). Though the name befits a good novel, and it's popular with Korean tourists, the actual signature of rocky crags may come as an anticlimax; it's worth the trip, however, not only to see the beauty of the surrounding countryside but also to feast on delicious fresh seafood.

The king's final resting place lies literally a stone's throw from the coast. In his lifetime, Munmu achieved the first unification of the Korean peninsula, reasoning that the power of his united forces would better repel any invasion from the Japanese. On his deathbed, and still clearly concerned by the Nipponese threat, he asked to have his ashes scattered on the offshore rocks, believing that he would then become a **sea dragon**, offering eternal protection to the country's coast. Just 1km inland you'll be able to make out two giant stone pagodas, 13m high, which mark the former site of **Gameunsa** (감은사; 24hr; free), a temple built on the orders of Munmu's son, Sinmun, in order to provide his sea-dragon father an inland retreat along the now-dry canal.

You may be lucky enough to witness one of the banana-heavy **shamanist ceremonies** that occasionally take place on the beach, honouring spirits of the local seas.

Practicalities

This area is easily accessed on **bus** #150 from Gyeongju – alight as soon as you hit the coast. Lining the beach are several **fish restaurants**, the best of which is *Saemteo Hoetjip*; dishes start at around W10,000 per person for *maeun-tang*, a fishy soup meal, or for *hoe-deopbap* – raw fish with rice. Those wanting less salty fare can head to the Chinese restaurant near the bus stop; the W4000 *beokkeumbap* – fried rice topped with black bean sauce and a fried egg – is particularly delicious. Although the area is an easy day-trip from Gyeongju, you could spend the night; there are a few **minbak** behind the fish restaurants, costing around W30,000 per night.

North of Gyeongju

After the Silla-era delights in and around Gyeongju, you can leap forward in time to the **Joseon dynasty** by making a trip 30km north of town to **Oksan Seowon** (옥산 서원), a Confucian school and shrine established in 1572 under the rule of King Seonjo. During this period Confucianism was the primary system of belief, particularly for the *yangban* aristocracy. However, most such places were closed in the 1870s at a time of social upheaval, and many were destroyed, making Oksan one of the oldest in the country, and quite possibly the most enjoyable to visit (though tiny Dosan Seowon near Andong gives it a run for its money, see p.178). It was dedicated to **Yi Eon-jeok** (1491–1533), a Confucian poet, **scholar** and all-round theological handyman who, while not as revered as his contemporaries Yi-Yi (see box, p.160) or Toegye (see box, p.179), certainly exerted an influence on neo-Confucian thought. Now restored, following years of neglect and the occasional fire, the complex still manages to put forward a gentle atmosphere in keeping with its original function as a place of study and reflection, helped by the stream bubbling away below, as well as the gorgeousness of the surrounding countryside and the surprisingly low number of visitors. It's also home to a copy of the **Samguk Sagi**, the only concise records of the Three Kingdoms period (albeit one that seems to be biased towards the Silla dynasty). To get to Oksan Seowon take **bus** #203 from Gyeongju; they leave very sporadically, so check the return schedule at the academy as soon as you arrive. For those with more time, there's a **motel** and a few *minbak* around the academy, and a few places to eat.

Just a short walk beyond Oksan Seowon is Yi Eon-jeok's former abode at **Dongnakdang**. Some of his descendants still live in the cramped compound, which appears be hiding under the skirt of a large tree, and is every bit as tranquil as the academy itself. Further ahead again are **Jonghyesa**, a temple famed for its curiously shaped pagoda, and **Dodeokam**, a tiny hermitage with a view balanced high up on the rocks. All are just about within walking distance of each other, though considering the rather poor bus connections from Gyeongju, it may be best to stay the night near Oksan Seowon.

Yangdong Folk Village

Korea has a number of **"folk villages"**, a product of Park Chung-hee's desire to keep alive rural traditions at a time when large-scale economic growth was smothering the nation in concrete. Usually they consist of a rural group of houses and associate buildings; some openly exist for show alone, while others are living, breathing communities whose denizens work the local fields, rewarded for their enforced deprivation of urban amenities with governmental subsidy. **Yangdong Folk Village** (양동 민속 마을), tucked into a countryside fold near the village of Angang-ni, is one of the best in the country, and home to some real history. Dating from the 1400s, this was once a thriving community of **yangban**, the aristocracy that ruled the country during the Joseon dynasty. Yi Eon-jeok, the great Confucian scholar to whom Oksan Seowon was dedicated, was born here in 1491; his life and the academy's history are relayed on information boards. As you walk around try to suspend belief and imagine yourself back in nineteenth-century Korea (though it probably smells much more pleasant now). Some buildings are permanently open, and you may even be lucky enough to be invited into a private house.

Several **buses** (presently #200, #208, #212 and #217, but these have been known to change) run from Gyeongju to a stop 2km from the village – a blessing in disguise, as it necessitates a short walk through the Gyeongsang countryside.

West of Gyeongju

The sights west of Gyeongju are quite scattered, making exploration a little tricky. For those not yet weary of dead Silla kings, a few **tomb complexes** lie a couple of kilometres beyond the River Hyeongsan, which runs along the western side of the city. The closest two are accessible **by bike** (see p.192 for rental information). The **tomb of King Muyeol** – who defeated the rival Baekje kingdom in 660 – lies just south of the bridge, though as the road is both a little too narrow and a little too busy for comfortable walking or cycling, it's best to head through the fields. Turn left down the bumpy riverside track immediately after the bridge, then down the first decent road that falls off to the right, and under the railway bridge.

Several kilometres further down this main road is the beguiling **Geumcheok** (금척) collection of tomb-mounds. Legend has it that Hyeokgeose, the first Silla king, once owned a golden stick (*geum-cheok*) that could restore the dead to life. However, the village got so overcrowded with Silla-dynasty undead that the townsfolk decided to bury the rod in a mound – forty decoy mounds were also raised in the area, and to this day nobody knows which one houses the stick.

A right-turn after the Hyeongsan bridge near Gyeongju will take you in the direction of the tomb of **General Kim Yu-sin**. Records in the *Samguk Sagi* (see p.197) state that in between his birth in 595 and his death in 673, he led the battles that defeated the Baekje and Goguryeo kingdoms, paving the way for Silla rule over the whole peninsula. The road leading here is quieter than those heading elsewhere from the bridge, but unfortunately for walkers and cyclists there are no real side-routes to make use of.

South of Gyeongju: Tongdosa

Well worth a visit if you are zooming between Gyeongju and Busan, **Tongdosa** (통도사) is one of Korea's three "Jewel Temples" (the others being Songgwansa and Haeinsa; see p.236 and p.184), and as such one of the most heralded in the land. It's a truly captivating place, especially around sunset, when its various buildings fall into a darkness amplified by their setting, shoehorned into a tight valley.

Part of the local **Jogye** sect, Tongdosa has been in existence since the mid-seventh century – long enough to pick up a few interesting quirks. Firstly, the candle is said to have stayed alight this whole time; easier to verify with your own eyes is the fact that there's no Buddha in the main hall. Rather, the main subject of veneration is a hall housing **sani**, a crystal-like substance said to be created inside the bodies of pure monks. Of course, it's not on public display. Lastly, take a look at the drum and bell tower: you'll see two of all four instruments (wooden fish, brass gong, drum and bell), rather than the more usual one. Despite its age, only the Daeungjeon hall withstood the Japanese attacks of the 1590s. However, most other buildings have been reconstructed with consumnate care, and look rather beautiful.

Practicalities

Tongdosa lies almost half-way between of Gyeongju and Busan, and is easily accessible by bus; there are even direct services from Seoul. However you arrive, you'll have to walk for around ten minutes from the bus station (known as Tongdosa but actually in the small town of **Jisan**) to the temple entrance, from where it's a further twenty-minute walk to the buildings along a gorgeous path, illuminated after sunset with picturesque stone lanterns. Those who wish to stay here will have no problems finding a **motel**, with their neon signs starting right outside the temple entrance. More suited to Tongdosa's air are a couple of superb restaurants, in the same place: *Sanchae Jeonmun* (산채 전문) serves huge *jeongsik* (정식) sets for just W7000 per head, as well as *sanchae bibimbap* (산채 비빔밥), made with roots, shoots and leaves from the mountains surrounding the temple.

Ulleungdo

With island groups dotted all around Korea's southern and western coasts, you may feel it prudent to forgo the three-hour ferry-ride to a small turret of land between Korea and Japan, and head instead to a closer isle. However, this would be a mistake – **ULLEUNGDO** (울릉도), covered in a rich, green cloak of trees and fringed with juniper, is refreshingly unspoilt and simply stunning. Its volcanic origin and the flora splashed around on its nutritious soils mark it out as a mini Jeju, but while increasingly popular with Korean travellers, Ulleungdo's isolation has kept it largely free from the ravages of mass tourism. Its armies of middle-aged Korean tourists are here mainly due to its proximity to **Dokdo**, an even smaller speck of land claimed by both Korea and Japan, and a focus of nationalistic

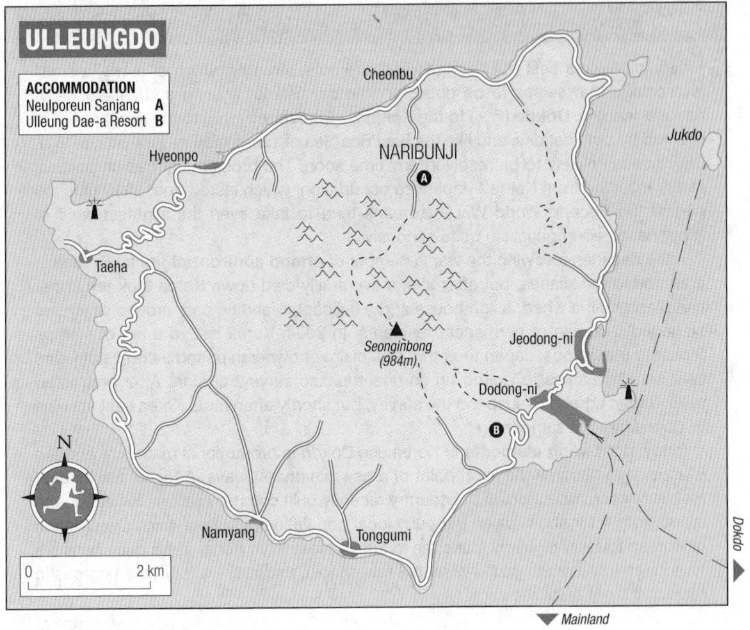

demonstrations (see box, p.200). With no Family Marts or five-star hotels, and just one bumpy main road tracing a vague parallel to the coast, the only time that the island's pulse seems to quicken is in the half-hour window surrounding ferry arrivals, when *ajummas* race around trying to draw tourists back to their *minbak* accommodation.

Few islands in Korea can provide as spectacular an arrival as Ulleungdo's main settlement, **Dodong-ni**, whose port makes a sudden appearance in a sumptuous pirate-like cove hidden and encircled by precipitous mountains, and squeezed in on both sides by the valley walls. Ulleungdo's second main settlement, **Jeodong-ni**, lies just up the coast, slightly smaller, but relatively open and rather different in character. These two villages, both an untidy but undeniably appealing mishmash of *minbak* and fish restaurants, give guests a taste of what the rest of the island is like. **Naribunji** is a farming area of tremendous beauty to the north of the island, whose flatness will come as a great surprise to those who've travelled the bumpy coastal road to get there. On the way, picturesque fishing settlements dot the coast, while there's some good **hiking** to be enjoyed around the rugged, volcanic peaks that rise up in the centre of the island, almost totally untouched by modern life.

Arriving by ferry

Due to the absence of an airport on the island, there's only one way to arrive – by **ferry**. At the time of writing, all services were using the port at the main settlement of Dodong-ni, but plans have long been afoot to make a larger terminal elsewhere on the island. Ferry schedules were also in a constant state of flux – most get here from **Pohang** (포항), a large but uninteresting city near Gyeongju on the mainland's eastern coast. Services leave each morning at 10.30am (W58,000; 3hr), returning at 4pm. The terminal at Pohang is a short taxi journey from the train station or either bus terminal. Fortunately, the ferry bay is one of the quieter, more pleasant areas in

Dokdo

Ninety kilometres east of Ulleungdo lies a remote, straggly bunch of rocks, a small archipelago that seems to be good for little bar fishing, fighting and assertions of national identity. **Dokdo** (독도) to the Koreans, **Takeshima** (竹島) to the Japanese, it is claimed by both nations, and like the East Sea/Sea of Japan dispute (see box, p.161), the issue is unlikely to be resolved any time soon. The problem centres on political rivalry resulting from Korea's Japanese occupation, which lasted from 1910 until the end of the Second World War – Koreans tend to take even the slightest whiff of Nipponese neo-imperialism quite seriously.

In the decades following the war, a number of **armed confrontations** took place in and around the islands, but after things eventually died down Korea took the upper hand, and built a wharf, a lighthouse and a helicopter-landing pad, around which are stationed a couple of permanent residents. In 2004, Korea issued a set of stamps featuring the islands; Japan took this as a claim of ownership, and a couple of years later sent two ships to Dokdo on an unauthorized survey mission. After protracted talks, Japan agreed to suspend the survey, but shortly afterwards Korea sent in ships to do exactly the same thing.

Today, **right-wing elements** in Korea use Dokdo in promotional materials, and the islands have become the focal point of a new nationalist wave. A few of the biggest mobile telecom operators in the country recently built communications towers on the island (totally for show, given the puny local population) and flag-waving ferry-loads of Korean tourists regularly make the journey across from Pohang. It's quite possible for foreign travellers to do likewise, but few choose to do so – without the bombastic fervour, it's not quite the same.

a generally ugly city; if you're unlikely to arrive in time for the ferry you can stay at one of several **motels** around the terminal, including *Joy-tel* and *N.Beach* (both ❹), both of which face a pleasant beach. There's also a 24-hour sauna in the *Pos Town* tower, where a night's sleep can be yours for just W6000. Alternatively it's possible, with an early start, to wake up in Gyeongju and make it to Pohang in time to catch the ferry – be sure to arrive at the terminal before 10am.

There's also an Ulleungdo service from the Mukho (묵호) terminal near **Donghae** (동해) in Gangwon province, but it's imperative to call the Korean tourist information line (Ⓣ054/1330) for the latest information, as you're unlikely to find an English-speaker at any of the relevant ports; tourist offices in Gyeongju will also be able to help.

Information and island transport

On Ulleungdo there's a small **tourist information** office just uphill from the ferry terminal – where the water stops, look to your left. Though you'll be lucky to find an English-speaker here, staff will be able to hunt down accommodation across the island, and arm you with the requisite maps and pamphlets. One very important thing to consider is **money** – those who have been travelling around Korea with their foreign bank card will have no luck in Ulleungdo, though a few banks here will be able to exchange foreign cash.

Getting around the island is also harder than you might expect – the coastal road runs in a "U" rather than a circle, ending in the northeast of the island, and just seven daily **buses** bump their way around, making it impossible to use them for more than a couple of sights per day. More convenient are the daily bus tours (W18,000; 4hr) leaving from the ferry terminal. Alternatively, it's possible to take one of the round-island **ferry tours** (W18,000; 2hr) which run six times a day in the summer, and twice a day at other times. Lastly, it's also possible to get around by **taxi**; haggling will start at around W100,000 for the day, though you'll likely be able to bash this down a tad.

Accommodation

Korea's developers must have a fear of long ferry-rides – Ulleungdo is almost entirely devoid of modern **accommodation**, bar one tourist hotel and a few overpriced motels in the main settlements, **Dodong-ni** and **Jeodong-ni**. There are also a few condos around the island, though these almost exclusively cater to well-off Koreans, and are in any case poor value. The most comfortable place to stay is just out of Dodong-ni at the *Ulleung Dae-a Resort* (☎054/791-8800; ⑥), which has small, stylish rooms and good sea views, but little going on around it.

The popularity of little Ulleungdo is such that almost every building in Dodong-ni seems to have **minbak** rooms, while such dwellings can also be found in Jeodong-ni and other settlements. You won't need to go hunting for offers, as elderly women will scream them at you on your walk up from the ferry. A fair price for a room sleeping two is usually around W30,000; don't be afraid to see a couple, or to play the *ajummas* off against each other – haggling is expected, maybe even mandatory. Heading around the island, there are a few tiny settlements where it's possible to stay, but the best by far is **Naribunji** in the north: there's a campsite here, as well as a few *minbak*; the best of these is the *Neulporeun Sanjang* (☎054/791-8181), which has rooms for around W30,000 per night, and doubles as a restaurant.

Dodong-ni

Seonginbong Motel ☎054/791-2677. Just up from the ferries on the right-hand side of the road, this is the best motel in the village, though the quality and accessibility mean that it's often packed with tour groups, and the price is accordingly a little high. ④

Skyhill Pension ☎054/791-1040. A good option, in relative isolation at the top of the village but still within walking distance of dozens of restaurants, this clean pension has cooking facilities in a communal area, and free videos in reception. ④

Ulleung Hotel ☎054/791-6611. This is the one official tourist hotel in the village, but not too overpriced, especially when the off-peak discounts kick in, and some of the more expensive rooms are colossal. Walking up from the ferries, keep on the right-hand side, and you'll eventually see the hotel up some stairs to your right. There's a good restaurant on the ground floor, and another – the *Eddiang* – underneath. ⑤

Jeodong-ni

Bideulgi Motel ☎054/791-7090. Located a block uphill from the main road that skirts the seafront, this motel has acceptable rooms; try to stay on the top floor for the best views. ②

Motel Jaeil ☎054/791-2637. Set back from the seafront, next to a small park visible from the waterfront, this is the best of Jeondong-ni's motley selection of accommodation. Rooms are surprisingly large and well appointed, and some have pretty sea or mountain views; there's also an attached sauna, in which you can take a scrub for a few thousand won. ②

Dodong-ni

Though still just a village in population terms, **DODONG-NI** (도동리) is the largest settlement on Ulleungdo and its main port, and as a result houses most of the island's overnight guests. However, despite the visitor numbers, it has remained surprisingly true to its old ways. The atmospheric village sits in a tight valley up from the ferry terminal, its few roads all heading uphill past a looping parade of *minbak*, small shops and raw fish restaurants. There are few sights as such, but many visitors find themselves heading to a **lighthouse** to the east of town, which can be reached on a number of routes; the most scenic is the half-hour walk around the jagged coast from the ferry terminal. You can walk a short way on the opposite side of the terminal, but all you'll find here – if you're lucky – are a couple of fish snack shacks.

If you head uphill from the ferries and stick to the left, you'll eventually come across a sign pointing to the **Dokdo Museum** (독도 박물관; daily 9am–6pm; free), which together with the adjacent historical museum form part of a small park. The former is the most interesting, as it details the Korean claim on Dokdo, a tiny scrawl of rock east of Ulleungdo (see box, p.200). Also in the park is a "healthy water" spring (the metallic taste presumably proof of some kind of goodness), while those who still have some energy after the climb can bounce off any remaining calories on the see-saw at the very top. The walk up is quite a slog, and most who make the climb are heading to the base of a **cable car** (W7000 return), ready to be whisked up a nearby peak to take in some wonderful views: on clear days, you may be able to see Dokdo across the seas.

Following any one of Dodong-ni's upward trails from the ferry terminal will bring you, after what may seem like a never-ending climb, to the island's main "coastal" road. Turn left from the village exit, then immediately right, and you'll find **Daewonsa** (대원사), a tiny temple that marks the beginning of most hikes into the interior (see box below).

Jeodong-ni

A short taxi-ride – or a half-hour walk – away from Dodong-ni is **JEODONG-NI** (저동리). Open-plan and spread out along a harbour, rather than wedged into a valley, it's something like a flattened version of its neighbour; while Dodong hasn't exactly been ravaged by tourism, here you'll see far fewer visitors, fewer *minbak*, and therefore an atmosphere more in keeping with the general nature of the island. It's the kind of place where you can idle away a fair few hours doing nothing at all. The **harbour** is a great place for a walk, full of fishing boats dangling dozens of high-wattage bulbs, used to lure squid to their doom. To its right-hand side is a ramshackle group of corrugated metal cabins dangling precariously from the hillside; from here there's a good view of the harbour, and the tall finger of stone that protrudes through its outer wall, called "**Candlestick Rock**", the village's defining landmark. You can take a stroll up to the rock, on the way to the harbour passing two **large concrete penguins** whose decidedly phallic appendages are used to load material onto waiting boats – if you can see one in action, it's likely to be the funniest moment of your stay

Around the island

You can explore the rest of Ulleungdo by ferry, bus or taxi (see p.200). There are a few small settlements dotted around the coast; all of the following offer simple guesthouse accommodation. **Tonggumi** (통구미) is a small, delightful village, and

Hiking

Wherever you are on the island, you're likely to see the sea on one side, and a group of verdant peaks hovering over you on the other. These unspoilt, richly forested slopes offer some wonderful **hiking** opportunities, and fortunately the walk up to the main summit, **Seonginbong** (984m), and back can be done in one day-trip. There are several paths into and around the interior, but the main access point is just north of Dodong-ni, near Daewonsa, a small temple. A spur-road just before the temple leads uphill to the right, marking the start of a clammy 4.1km walk to the top. From here, you can either turn back, or make your way further north to the opposite trailhead at Naribunji, 4.5km from the summit. Trails are well signposted, though as there's almost nothing en route, be sure to bring water and snacks.

a popular place to fish or dive (around W100,000 per person including wet-suit hire). A little further on, the similarly laid-back fishing village of **Namyang** (남양) has amazing views across the ocean from the slopes above. Within hiking distance of **Taeha** (태하), a port on the far northwestern cape of the island, are Seongha Shrine, some interesting rock formations, and a remote lighthouse. On Ulleungdo's northern coast, the twin harbour towns of **Hyeonpo** (현포) and **Cheonbu** (천부), like all the places here, are small and bursting with character; their secluded location on an already remote island means that few foreigners have ever made it this far.

To the north of the island lies a geographic anomaly – **Naribunji** (나리분지). This is the only flat space on Ulleungdo, a dreamy patchwork of fields entirely encircled by mountains. To get there, you'll have to get off the coastal road bus at Cheonbu, where a 4WD will be waiting to take passengers over the hill to Naribunji (W1000). Naribunji is a fantastic place to spend a day or two walking through fields, taking in the surrounding forest, or doing absolutely nothing. It's also a good start or finish point for a **hiking trip** up and over the mountain; you may notice cable-car wires heading up into the hills, but unfortunately this service is for the use of local military only.

Lastly, ferry tours (2 or 3 daily; W10,000) head from Dodong-ni to **Dokdo** (독도), a small, absolutely stunning island 4km northeast of Ulleungdo. The only form of access is a spiral staircase with one step for each day of the year; after panting your way to the top you'll come out at the island's one lofty "town" (population: 2), a perfect place for a walk and a picnic.

Eating

There are plenty of **restaurants** in Dodong-ni and Jeodong-ni, mostly centred around creatures culled from the sea, though less fishy things are available – the island's most famous edible product is, in fact, **pumpkin taffy**. Visitors used to Korea's open-all-hours culture will be in for a surprise, as even in Dodong-ni everywhere may be shut by 9pm. The most interesting places to eat in both main villages are the **raw fish outlets** – in good weather, a few cling limpet-like to the cliffs near Dodong-ni's ferry terminal, and there's an upper-floor parade above the one in Jeodong-ni. Selections at both depend on the season, the weather and the fortunes of local fishermen, but W10,000 per person should be enough for a belly full of fish; your food will be killed and sliced in front of you, and some of the hardier creatures will still be wriggling on the plate. There are more regular restaurants around, too, and anyone who has made it this far should know a few Korean dishes by now – a good thing, as English-language menus are rare. Alternatively, there's an Italian restaurant in Dodong-ni and a bakery next to the bus stop in Jeodong-ni.

99 Sikdang Dodong-ni. This friendly restaurant, in the very centre of the village, has whipped up quite an army of fans following appearances on Korean TV. Prices have stayed low, and there's an English menu of sorts, including spicy fish soup, steamed rice with mussels, and the house special – spicy grilled squid known as *ojingeo bulgogi*. All meals come with seasonal side dishes.

Eddiang Dodong-ni. Under the *Ulleung Hotel*, this homely place offers reasonably priced spaghetti, steak and pizza – the perfect respite from the ubiquitous fish restaurants.

Yakso Sutbul Garden Dodong-ni. Way up near the *Skyhill* at the top of Dodong-ni, this is a great place to tuck into filling *sanchae bibimbap* (산채 비빔밥) – mountain vegetables on rice – though most are here to barbecue beef or pork and throw it back with a few shots of *soju*. *Yakso jumulleok* (약소주물럭) is a popular choice; this is beef from cows raised on medicinal herbs and plants.

Gyeongnam

Korea's most southeastern province, **GYEONGNAM** (경남; "South Gyeongsang"), is as closely connected to the sea as its northern neighbour, Gyeongbuk, is to the land. The southern coast splinters off into an assortment of cliffs, peninsulas and **islands**, many of the latter preserved as the **Hallyeo Haesang National Park**. Here you can head by ferry to minute specks of land where life goes on as it has for decades, free of the smoke, noise and neon often hard to escape on the mainland. This greenery is not just confined to the province's shoreline – **Jirisan**, to the west, is the largest national park in the country. It's a real favourite among hikers, and not just for its size, or its beauty – a chain of **shelters** runs across the park's central spine, making multiday hikes a possibility. Despite these earthy features, Gyeongnam is no natural paradise. Nearly eight million people live in the area, making it the most densely populated part of the country outside Greater Seoul. Here lies Korea's second city, **Busan**, a fantastic place with good beaches, excellent nightlife, and a friendly, earthy nature.

Busan

There's an awful lot to like about **BUSAN** (부산), Korea's second city, which has emerged from the provincial shadows full of pep and character. By turns brackish, glamorous, clumsy and charismatic, it prides itself on simply being different from Seoul, and many travellers end up preferring it to the capital. The locals alone make it worth a visit: more characterful than those from the capital, Busanites talk almost as fast as their city moves, spouting provincial slang in a distinctive staccato that many foreigners initially mistake for Japanese.

Busan is not just Korea's second-biggest city, but the fifth-largest container **port** in the world – its salty fringes tumble away into a colourful, confetti-like jumble of corrugated containers. This connection to the sea is evident at two of Busan's most visited areas – **Haeundae**, a busy stretch of beach sprinkled with five-star hotels, and **Jagalchi Fish Market**, quite possibly the smelliest place on earth. There are plenty of temples and mountains to amble around, and you can shop till you drop at a variety of places from grimy markets to designer shopping malls. In the evenings, the setting sun throws the ships into cool silhouette on a sea of gold, and Busan's youth come out to paint the town red. While the nightlife here is second only to that in Seoul, for sheer verve there's no contest – Busan is the champion.

Some history

Even before it became the whirring economic dynamo that it is today, Busan played a pivotal role in the country's history. Though it was once part of the short-lived **Gaya kingdom** swallowed whole by the Silla dynasty (see box, p.173), it was at that time little more than a collection of fishing villages. In the fifteenth century it benefited from its proximity to Japan, when a trade treaty opened it up as a port to international trade – up until that point, most goods had been leaving the area as loot on pirate ships. This competitive advantage promptly swung around and hit Busan squarely in the face when the city was attacked by the Japanese in 1592; under the astute leadership of **Admiral Yi Sun-shin** (see box, p.232) damage was limited, but still devastating.

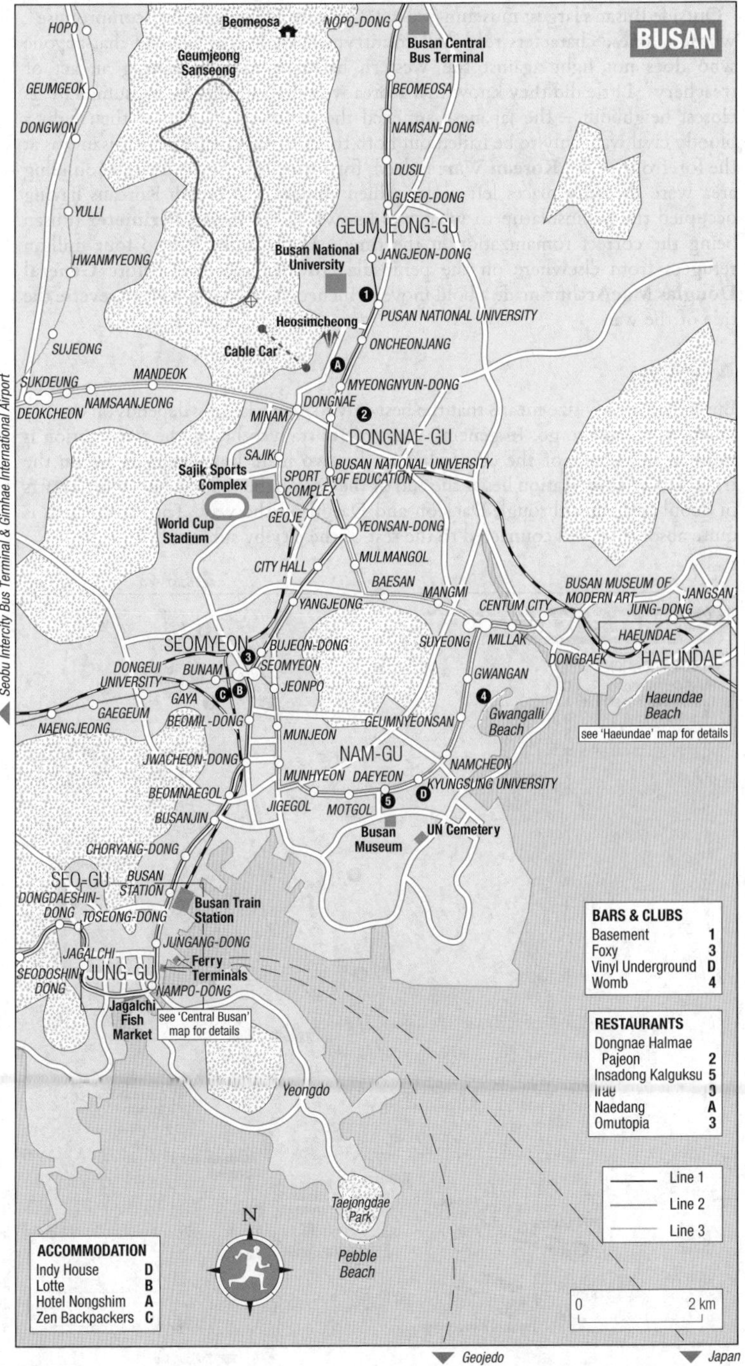
BUSAN
HOPO
Beomeosa
NOPO-DONG
Busan Central Bus Terminal
Geumjeong Sanseong
GEUMGEOK
BEOMEOSA
DONGWON
NAMSAN-DONG
DUSIL
GUSEO-DONG
YULLI
GEUMJEONG-GU
Busan National University
JANGJEON-DONG
HWANMYEONG
PUSAN NATIONAL UNIVERSITY
Heosimcheong
Cable Car
ONCHEONJANG
SUJEONG
MANDEOK
SUKDEUNG
MYEONGNYUN-DONG
NAMSAANJEONG
DEOKCHEON
DONGNAE
MINAM
DONGNAE-GU
SAJIK
Sajik Sports Complex
BUSAN NATIONAL UNIVERSITY OF EDUCATION
SPORT COMPLEX
World Cup Stadium
GEOJE
YEONSAN-DONG
CITY HALL
MULMANGOL
BAESAN
MANGMI
BUSAN MUSEUM OF MODERN ART
JANGSAN
YANGJEONG
CENTUM CITY
JUNG-DONG
SEOMYEON
BUJEON-DONG
SUYEONG
MILLAK
HAEUNDAE
DONGBAEK
DONGEUI UNIVERSITY
BUNAM
SEOMYEON
JEONPO
GWANGAN
GAYA
GAEGEUM
NAENGJEONG
BEOMIL-DONG
GEUMNYEONSAN
Gwangalli Beach
Haeundae Beach
see 'Haeundae' map for details
MUNJEON
NAM-GU
JWACHEON-DONG
NAMCHEON
MUNHYEON
DAEYEON
KYUNGSUNG UNIVERSITY
BEOMNAEGOL
JIGEGOL
MOTGOL
BUSANJIN
Busan Museum
UN Cemetery
CHORYANG-DONG
SEO-GU
BUSAN STATION
DONGDAESHIN-DONG
Busan Train Station
TOSEONG-DONG
JUNGANG-DONG
JAGALCHI
Ferry Terminals
SEODOSHIN DONG
JUNG-GU
NAMPO-DONG
Jagalchi Fish Market
see 'Central Busan' map for details
Yeongdo
Taejongdae Park
Pebble Beach
N
Seobu Intercity Bus Terminal & Gimhae International Airport
Geojedo
Japan
0
2 km
BARS & CLUBS
Basement 1
Foxy 3
Vinyl Underground D
Womb 4
RESTAURANTS
Dongnae Halmae Pajeon 2
Insadong Kalguksu 5
Irae 3
Naedang A
Omutopia 3
Line 1
Line 2
Line 3
ACCOMMODATION
Indy House D
Lotte B
Hotel Nongshim A
Zen Backpackers C

Outside Busan's largest museum (see p.210) is a stone "stele of anti-compromise", whose Chinese characters read "All countrymen are hereby warned that anyone who does not fight against the Western barbarians is committing an act of treachery". Little did they know that Korea would eventually be consumed by its closest neighbour – the Japanese annexed the peninsula in 1910 – then fight a bloody civil war, only to be bailed out both times by said barbarians. Busan was at the forefront of the **Korean War**; indeed, for a time, the city and its surrounding area were the only places left under Allied control, the North Koreans having occupied the peninsula up to what was known as the **Pusan Perimeter** (Pusan being the correct romanization at the time). At this point, up to four million refugees from elsewhere on the peninsula crowded the city, before **General Douglas MacArthur** made a bold move at Incheon (see box, p.134) to reverse the tide of the war.

Arrival

Busan's unwieldy size means that the best way to arrive largely depends on exactly where you want to go. In general, most prefer train to bus as the train station is right in the centre of the city, whereas the two main bus terminals are on the fringes. The **train** station lies at the end of the Gyeongbu railway line, which starts in Seoul and rifles through Daejeon and Daegu on the way. The station area is quite absorbing, and connected to the rest of the city by subway.

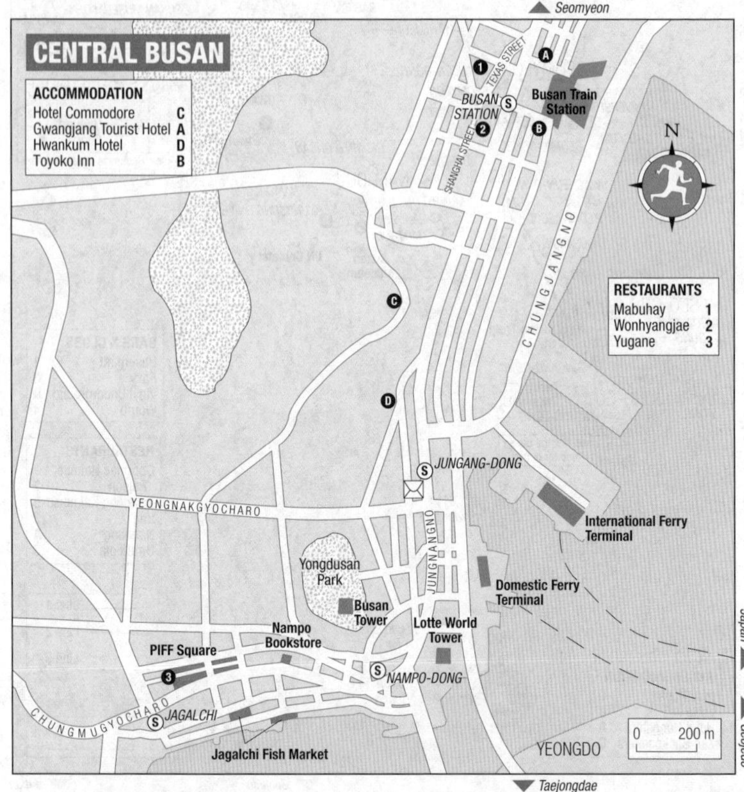

Arriving in Busan by **bus** is not really recommended, unless you're heading somewhere specific near either of the two main terminals. The so-called "central terminal" is way to the north on subway line 1 (Nogodan station), and is actually made up of two separate stations – one express and one intercity, with the latter often referred to as the Dongbu terminal. The Seobu terminal is way out west on line 2 (Sasang station). Those heading to Haeundae, far to the east of the city centre, may well be able to find a direct bus connection from locations around Seoul and the Gyeongsang region.

Gimhae airport lies in a flat estuary area around 15km west of the city centre. There are direct buses to the airport from most of the main cities in the Gyeongsang region, and local city buses link it to destinations around Busan. However, the most spectacular way to arrive into Busan is by sea. The city has two **ferry** terminals (one international, one domestic), both near Jungangdong subway station in the centre of town, just minutes from each other by foot. All international ferries head to Japan, with the Fukuoka connection especially popular with *hagwon* teachers on visa runs. There are also domestic connections to Jeju Island (see p.301), and Geojedo, a pretty island a short way to the west (p.216).

For more details on **leaving Busan by ferry**, see box, p.215.

Orientation and information

With buildings sprawling across the whole horizon, filling the gaps between the city's mountains and swamping some of the smaller hills entirely, Busan can be quite confusing for the first-time visitor. The de facto centre of the city, known as **Jung-gu**, is the area heading south from the train station down to Jagalchi Fish Market; on the way, you'll pass the ferry terminals, Busan Tower and Nampodong's maze of shops, cinemas, markets and restaurants. A short way north of the train station is trendy **Seomyeon**, a brand-name shopper's paradise, but also home to some of the earthiest restaurants, and excellent nightlife. A way east of here you'll find **Haeundae**, a fascinating beach area that's home to rich Koreans and five-star hotels, but still manages to retain much of its fishing village character.

For a city of such size, and with so many foreign visitors, Busan has a surprisingly poor network of **tourist information offices**. The most useful one is in the

Busan festivals

Busan hosts an incredible number of **festivals**, and many of them are quite incredibly bad – those dedicated to anchovy-rubbing or egg-rolling might sound comical, but they're really not worth the effort. However, there are a number of good ones – the most popular is PIFF, the **Pusan International Film Festival** (ⓦwww.piff.org), which takes place over a week or so each October. One of the biggest such events in Asia, it draws the cream of the continent's talent, and has recently expanded its scope to please non-mainstreamers too. Most of the action takes place around Nampodong and Haeundae, with the latter a great place to star-spot – you could even find yourself pitching ideas to a director over *soju*. Also interesting are the **Busan Biennale** (ⓦwww.busanbiennale.org), a festival of contemporary art that takes place on even-numbered years, though in seemingly random months, and the **International Rock Festival** (ⓦrockfestival.co.kr), which takes place in early August on Dadaepo Beach. The **Polar Bear Swim Contest** sees participants splash through the cold Haeundae waters each January, and is followed by the **Straw-Heap Burning Festival**, an event that does what it says, ostensibly to ward off evil. Worth mentioning for the name alone is the **Mass-Media Cutting-Edge Marine Fireworks Festival**, an event that sees things go bang over Gwangalli Beach each November.

train station (℡051/441-6565): you're unlikely to find any English-speakers at the offices in Haeundae and Seomyeon. Five-star hotels can come in very handy, but if you need some English-language information in a hurry, it's best to call ℡1330 (add an area code if using a mobile phone – Busan's is ℡051). There's also a special Foreigners' Service Centre in Choryangdong (℡051/441-3121).

Accommodation

Busan has plenty of choice at the **top end** of the accommodation range. The five-stars are almost all in **Haeundae**, the beach district far to the east of the centre that's by far the most interesting place to stay; here you'll also be able to find simple guesthouses that are dirt-cheap for most of the year, but raise their prices for the summer season. There are cheap **motels** all over the city; if you want to go out at night you're best basing yourself in Seomyeon or around the university drinking areas (see p.214), whereas sightseers should head for the cheap areas around the **train station** or **ferry terminal**. There are now a few **hostels** kicking around – more often than not, merely regular apartments kitted out for backpacker use. Those who really want to save cash can get a night's sleep for less than W10,000 in a *jjimjilbang* (see p.38); two of the most convenient are *Vesta*, east of the main hotel district in Haeundae, and *Nokju* in central Seomyeon.

Central Busan

The following places are marked on the "Central Busan" **map**, p.206.

Hotel Commodore Yeongjudong ℡051/466-9101. Visible from the port, this distinctive fusion of skyscraper and temple has acceptable rooms, and lies a short taxi ride from the main train station. The sliding windows are a nice feature, even more so given the views – Busan's crane-filled port on one side, and what passes for a Korean version of Naples on the other. However, many guests find the place as a whole a little overblown. ❻

Gwangjang Tourist Hotel Choryangdong ℡051/464-3141. This has all the drawbacks of the average Korean tourist hotel, but is far more honestly priced than most – even more surprising considering its proximity to the train station. The port views over the station may also please some. ❹

Hwangeum Motel 환금 모텔 Jungangdong ℡051/463-3851. The pick of a dirt-cheap bunch in the appealingly rustic area near the ferry terminal, with acceptable en-suite rooms, a rambling layout and likeable owners. Take exit 17 from Jungangdong subway station and turn left – the *Hwankum* is just under the staircase. ❶

Toyoko Inn Choryangdong ℡051/466-1045, ⓦwww.toyoko-inn.com. Japan's biggest business hotel chain has arrived in Busan, conveniently landing just a few steps from the train station. If you've stayed at a *Toyoko* before you'll know what to expect – small but perfectly clean rooms, near-total silence, free bathrobe and slippers, and a decent breakfast... like a little trip to the Land of the Rising Sun. ❺

Haeundae

The following places are marked on the "Haeundae" **map**, p.211.

Paradise Hotel ℡051/749-2111, ⓦwww.paradisehotel.co.kr. With widescreen TVs in the rooms, stylish lighting in the corridors and W6,000,000 suites, the *Paradise* has been carefully designed in a refreshingly modern style. It's a busy place with all manner of bars and restaurants, and there's even a boutique mall, while the pine-fringed outdoor pool stays open year-round and has views over the beach – an absolute must. Try to stay in the newer main building, and book online for the best deals. ❽

Seacloud Hotel ℡051/933-1000, ⓦwww.seacloudhotel.com. Benefiting from a relaxed ambience hard to come by in Haeundae's other big hitters, this smart-but-friendly business-oriented hotel is home to a healthy number of long-term guests. There are substantial discounts in colder months, while in summer an outdoor pool opens up. If you're in Busan for a while monthly rental is a good bet, starting at W2,400,000. ❽

Sunset ℡051/730-9900, ⓦwww.sunsethotel.or.kr. Stylish, hotel-like rooms at prices more proximate to a motel; the only thing lacking is decent service. Prices often drop below W100,000 during the week; book online for discounts. ❺

The Westin Chosun ℡051/749-7428, ⓦwww.westin.com. This Haeundae landmark provides great views of the beach, which comes to an abrupt end here. Though perfectly acceptable, rooms are surprisingly drab compared with the sleek lobby area, which includes an oh-so-trendy beach-facing bar, as well as an Irish "pub" that pulls a mean Guinness. Reserve through the website for the cheapest deals. ⑨

Other areas

The following places are marked on the "Busan" **map**, p.205.

Indy House Daeyeondong ⓣ070/8615-6442, ⓦindybusan.com. Charming hostel with a great location: equidistant from Jung-gu and Haeundae, and also within walking distance of a beach. Indy, the quirky owner, will even pick you up from the subway station (Kyungsung Univ.) with some advance warning. Dorms W20,000, doubles ④

Lotte Hotel Seomyeon ⓣ051/810-1000, ⓦwww.lottehotel.co.kr. Located in trendy Seomyeon, the small rooms and mall-like atmosphere found here are typical of the chain, which caters almost exclusively to shopaholics from Korea and other East Asian countries; service is good, however, and the place is huge – there's even an attached shopping mall. ⑧

Hotel Nongshim Oncheondong ⓣ051/550-2100, ⓦwww.hotelnongshim.com. Rooms are modest for the price, though you're paying for the hotel's proximity to Heosimcheong, the mammoth hot springs complex next door (p.212). Hefty discounts are usually available from the rack rate. ⑧

Zen Backpackers Seomyeon ⓣ010/8722-1530, ⓦwww.zenbackpackers.com. Highly popular hostel, handily located near the nexus of two subway lines in Seomyeon. The whole place has been quite superbly decorated, and the colourful private rooms are particularly appealing. Dorms W22,000, doubles ④

Downtown

The city's **downtown** spreads south from the train station to Jagalchi Fish Market. This area, often referred to as Jung-gu, is dripping with character but rather run-down, though large-scale construction work means that this is likely to change in the near future: the local powers-that-be are officially aiming for something like a Sydney-style harbour area. One interesting development here is the **Lotte World Tower**, which could be the start of a mushrooming series of super-tall skyscrapers – scheduled for completion in 2015 after years of delays, it's expected to rise to 510m in height, surely high enough to put it into the world's top ten for a few months at least. Traffic around here can be intense, though you can escape this – or inclement weather – by using the **underground walkway** that follows the subway line all the way from Jungangdong station to Nampodong, one stop down the line, a route studded all the way with cheap shopping stalls and snack bars.

Heading across the main road from Busan train station, you'll come to **Shanghai Street**, a pedestrianized "Chinatown" road filled with restaurants, and marked with the oriental gates you'll find in all such areas. This joins **Texas Street**, which has yet more places to eat – predominantly Russian and Filipino – but it's not all about the food. This area rivals Haeundae for the title of most cosmopolitan part of the city, though has an entirely different air: whereas Haeundae draws in beach bums and the convention crowd, here you may find yourself rubbing shoulders with Russian sailors, American soldiers, Filipino restaurateurs and lost tourists, and it is a great place to people-watch.

Yongdusan Park and Nampodong

Until the completion of the Lotte, you'll have to make do with **Busan Tower** (부산 타워; daily 9am–10pm; W5000), a comparatively puny structure, though one still affording **excellent views** of Busan's boat-filled surroundings. This long-standing city landmark is now crying out for renovation. The tower is the crowning glory of **Yongdusan Park** (용두산 공원), a popular area for walkers. The top of the park is already high enough for good views – take an early morning walk to the top, buy some instant *ramyeon* from the convenience store and watch the sun break through the mist. There's also an **aquarium** (same hours) near the base of the tower, and accessible on the same ticket, but this is hardly worth a visit, especially as all the fish you could ever want to see (or eat) are just down the road at Jagalchi Fish Market (see box, p.213). This lies south of the park in **Nampodong** (남포동), one of the city's main shopping and dining areas. Less modern than other parts of Busan, but catching up fast, its alleys and markets are good for an aimless wander.

Yeongdo

Facing Jagalchi Fish Market in downtown Busan is **Yeongdo** (영도); although it's technically an island, its double-bridge connection to Nampodong makes it feel more like a peninsula. There's not much to see here, but a walk around **Taejongdae** (태종대), a pretty park at the far end of the island, is worthwhile. A number of bus routes head from Busan's main centres to the entrance, including #88 from Seomyeon, via the train station and ferry terminals, and #30 from Nampodong. From here, regular train-shaped shuttle buses run to **Pebble Beach**, a rocky outcrop at the very end of the island, but as roads are otherwise empty it makes an appealing walk, particularly at sunset, when the sun sets over the mainland peninsula west of Yeongdo, casting the ships into silhouette on a golden sea.

Busan Museum and the UN Cemetery

In **Nam-gu** (남구), a district between Busan Station and Haeundae, lie a couple of sights relating to Korea's fascinating history. A short walk south of Daeyeon subway station, **Busan Museum** (부산 박물관; daily 9am–6pm; W500) charts the local area's history and its remains from the Neolithic era to the present day; exhibits include a **gilt-bronze crown** once worn by a Silla king, and a **standing Bodhisattva** of similar age and material. More recent history is generally presented in diorama form, with one of the more compelling displays showing Busan Station in the 1920s; the building has, of course, changed somewhat. Unfortunately, the more modern part of the exhibit leaves a rather bad taste in the mouth, stemming from the sad inevitability of the museum's choice to focus on the Japanese occupation rather than the Korean War. In the museum, there's just a single wall commemorating the tens of thousands of foreign troops who died here when Korean fought Korean; a pattern repeated all over the country – in classrooms as well as museums – but particularly galling here since many of the fallen are lying just outside in the **UN Cemetery**. Here you'll find over two thousand dead soldiers from Britain, Turkey, Canada, Australia, the Netherlands, France, the USA, New Zealand, South Africa and Norway; many more, of course, were never found, and those from Belgium, Ethiopia, Colombia, Thailand, Greece, India and the Philippines, as well as the vast majority of Americans, were repatriated. A photographic exhibition on site provides a small, mute tribute, and the grounds are welcoming and pretty.

Haeundae

On the eastern side of Busan, and about 25 minutes away by subway, **HAEUNDAE** (해운대) is without a doubt the most popular **beach** in Korea. Whether it's the best or not is open to question – in the summer it draws in families, teens and bronzed beach bums by the bucketload, though at only 2km in length, space here is tighter than a Brazilian's Speedos, while the sand gradually becomes a composite of cigarette butts, firework ash and other debris. Like it or not, it's an interesting place – Haeundae is not just the name of the beach, but also its surrounding area, one that attracts all sorts throughout the year. The **Pusan Film Festival**, one of the biggest in Asia, rolls into town each October with a cast of directors, actors, wannabes and hangers-on; the super-fit come to splash and dash out a **triathlon** course each October; hungry Koreans come to chow down on **raw fish** and throw back a few bottles of *soju* from the comfort of a plastic chair; affluent expats, trendy locals and the international convention crowd populate the many luxury

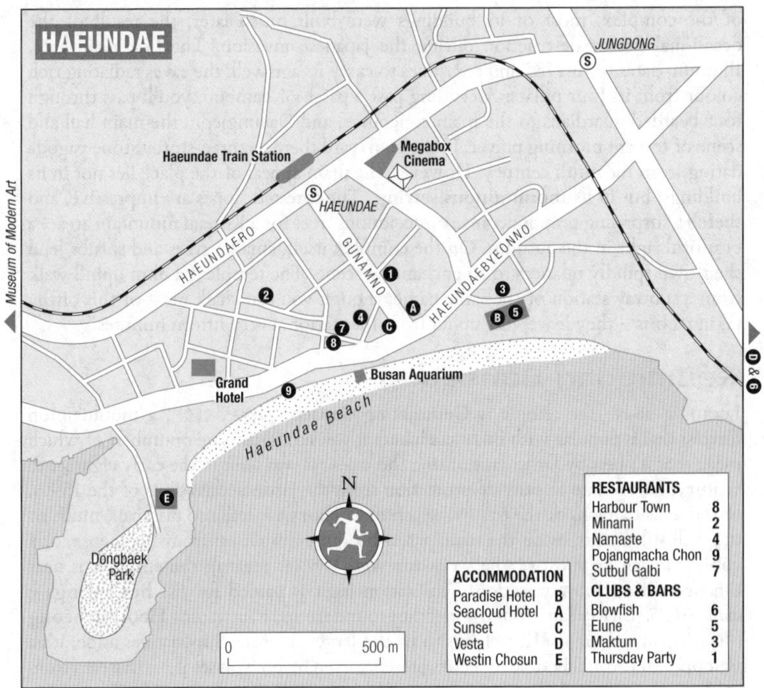

apartments and **five-star hotels**, while youngsters come from all over the country to spend a starry night on the beach. If you catch it at the right time, Haeundae can be quite magical.

The beach

The **beach** itself is good for swimming; tubes and boats are also available to rent, and the purchase of puny, multiround fireworks is near compulsory. There are also a couple of sights by the shore: on the beach is **Busan Aquarium** (Mon–Fri 10am–8pm, Sat & Sun 9am–10pm; W17,000), where three million litres of water host up to thirty thousand fish. Penguins and crocodiles are also on the complex, plus a touch pool for the kids. There's an underwater tunnel for those who want to see fish from below, or you can pay an extra W5000 to ride a glass-bottomed boat and see them from above instead. At the end of the beach, past a clutch of raw fish stalls and behind the *Westin Chosun*, there's **Dongbaek Park**, a pleasant place for a stroll, skate or bike-ride, while one subway station away from Haeundae is the **Busan Museum of Modern Art** (Ⓦwww.busanmoma.org; Tues–Sun 10am–8pm; free), an excellent gallery that keeps its exhibitions fresh; get off at the station of the same name – the gallery is signposted from exit five.

Beomeosa

A half-hour subway ride to the north of central Busan, you'll find one of the best sights in the city. The temple of **Beomeosa** (범어사), dating from 678, occupies a spectacular setting high above town and is a popular choice for foreigners looking to **templestay** (see Ⓦeng.templestay.com for details of programmes). Despite the age of the complex, most of its buildings were built much later, the result of the occasional fire or destruction during the Japanese invasion. The first main gate, Iljumun, dates from 1781 and continues to carry its age well, the eaves radiating rich colour from its four pillars. Ascending past a patch of bamboo, you'll pass through four bearded guardians to the main concourse, and Daeungjeon, the main hall and scene of fervent morning prayer. In the courtyard there's a three-storey stone pagoda dating from the ninth century. However, the main appeal of the place lies not in its buildings, but in its **mountainous setting.** The forested slopes are impressive, and there's a surprising preponderance of deciduous trees for a Korean mountain area – a beautiful sight in the autumn. On the complex itself, smaller trees and shrubs lend their own spindly nuances to an enchanting scene. The temple is a 3km uphill walk from a subway station of the same name, though you can chalk most of this off by taking a **bus** – they leave, just uphill from the station, every fifteen minutes.

Geumjeong Sanseong

Looming above the temple is **Geumjeong Sanseong** (금정산성), a mountaintop fortress that is popular with Busanese hikers at weekends, the sheer numbers of which mean that it's best by far to visit during the week. It was built in the early eighteenth century, far too late to provide protection from the Japanese invasions of the 1590s, or the repeat attacks of the following century. Though it fell into disrepair, much of the wall still stands, as do the main gates. It's quite a walk up from Beomeosa, or a **cable car** can do most of the work for you (W5000 return); the entrance is near Oncheonchang subway station. The station itself is named for the **hot springs** – *oncheon* (온천) in Korean – found under the ground around it, including **Heosimcheong** (허심청), an indoor spa that claims to be the largest in Asia. Superlatives aside, it's a whopper, and you'll be able to feel its presence even before you see it, with steam from subterranean waters billowing up through grates and pipes all around. The **spa** is a great place for a wash (5.30am–9pm; W7900), but note that naked foreigners tend to attract a lot of stares, even if the pool areas are segregated by gender. Also try to get any tranquil spa images out of your mind – Korean *oncheon* lack the style and sophistication of Japanese *onsen*. However, the facilities are generally excellent, with massage treatments, internet access, TV viewing areas and a small restaurant.

Eating

Busan's **cosmopolitan** nature is reflected in its culinary options. One of the most interesting eating areas is opposite the **train station** – no five-star paradise, but rather a motley crew of snack bars catering to sailors and assorted night-crawlers. Here, "Shanghai Street" provides a wealth of safe but relatively expensive **Chinese** restaurants, before merging effortlessly into "Texas Street", home to a lower-key choice of outlets; despite the American name, the most appealing food here lies in the cheap, cheerful **Filipino** snack-halls. The area running from the station to Jagalchi Fish Market is uninspired, though Korean staples are easy to track down, while the student areas (see "Nightlife") are predictably cheap – take your pick from innumerable **meat houses** or *izakaya*-style **Japanese** restaurant-bars. If you're looking for something a little classier head to one of the five-star hotels around **Haeundae** beach.

Central Busan

The following places are marked on the "Central Busan" **map**, p.206.

Jagalchi Market Nampodong. One of Busan's foremost attractions – see box opposite.

Mabuhay Texas Street. The pick of the Busan station area's many Filipino restaurants (*Amby's* down the road is a worthy runner-up), serving decent-sized portions of calamari, *adobo* chicken and the like for around W10,000.

Jagalchi fish market

Every single person in Korea knows about **Jagalchi** (자갈치 시장; daily 8am–10pm), the largest and most popular **fish market** in the country. It has been used as a set in numerous movies and dramas, and is atmospheric in a wonderfully salty kind of way. Mid-October is the best time to visit, since this is when the **Jagalchi festival** is held, offering a rare shot at hands-on fish preparation and a whole slew of freebies to munch.

Most of the dishes here will be utterly confusing to the average Westerner; easiest on both brain and palate are the fried slabs of tuna (참치; *chamchi*) served at the **outdoor stalls** (W5000 for four). The truly brave should make their way to the large **indoor market** for some raw seafood action. Its ground floor, swimming with seawater, is a truly hectic place full of tanks and baskets and thousands of fish. This is a place for buying, not eating, but whatever you purchase can be prepared (for a fee, of course) by chefs on the restaurant-like upstairs floor; alternatively, you can order a mixed set for around W15,000 per person. Here are few of the items you may well see on your plate, both in Jagalchi and at harbours, beaches and fish markets around the land:

Chamchi 참치 Tuna
Gaebul 개불 Sea worm
Galchi 갈치 Hairtail
Godeungeo 고등어 Mackerel
Gwang-eo 광어 Flatfish
Hoe-deop-bap 회덮밥 Sashimi on rice
Jangeo 장어 Eel
Kijogae 키조개 Pen shell
Meongge 멍게 Sea squirt
Ojingeo 오징어 Squid
Sannakji 산낙지 Baby octopus

Wonhyangjae 원향재 Shanghai Street. This Chinese restaurant is one of several good options on this interesting road near Busan Station. Meals are fairly pricey by Korean standards – figure on at least W15,000 per head – though simple rice and noodle dishes are delicious and cheap.

Yugane 유가네 Nampodong. If you don't fancy raw fish, you could do worse than heading to this large, fresh hall, full to the brim in the evenings with the young, hungry and budget-conscious. Staff will do the necessary chopping and mixing on your table – meat and fried rice are yours for around W4000, or chicken *galbi* for W5500, and unlike most places that serve the latter, single diners are welcome. There are branches around the city, including one in Seomyeon.

Haeundae

The following places are marked on the "Haeundae" **map**, p.211.

Harbour Town A perfect fallback for those who can't stand Korean food, or at least need a short holiday from it, this large complex houses a *Starbucks*, an *Outback Steakhouse* and a *TGI Friday's*, as well as *Ganga*, a worthy Indian restaurant.

Minami 미나미 Set back a couple of streets from the beach behind the *Grand Hotel* is this approximation of a Japanese *izakaya*, where you can throw back fish, beer and *sake* till morning. The place really comes to life during the film festival, when it often becomes a mingling place for the movie crowd.

Namaste Underground restaurant serving delectable Indian food. All of the main curry styles are on the menu, with most costing W12,000–15,000 per portion. The tandoori dishes are particularly recommended, as is the rare chance to try ginseng lassi.

Pojangmacha Chon 포장마차촌 A quintessential Korean dining experience – raw fish and assorted seafood served up by an equally salty *ajumma*. Look for the tarpaulin-covered stands sheltering tanks of fish, and prepare your stomach – some of your prey may still be moving. Happily, all have English-language menus.

Sutbul Galbi 숯불 갈비 On the fifth floor of a large building, and with good views of sea and beach, this *galbi* restaurant is open around the clock. Portions cost W6000 per diner, with a two-person minimum.

Seomyeon

The following places are marked on the "Busan" **map**, p.205.

Iraejinjok 이래진족 Bucheondong. Highly popular, though the Korean-only menu is almost entirely centred around *jok-bal*, which translates as "cow foot" (look out for the stylized hoof on the exterior) with a medium-sized portion big enough to feed two. This restaurant can become rather boisterous of an evening – there can be few better places to get a handle on the distinctive Busanese dialect.

Omutopia Bucheondong. *Omurice* is a Japanese attempt at culinary fusion now popular in Korea, whereby something like a portion of rice is wrapped in something resembling an omelette, then usually covered in tomato ketchup. Here, mercifully, you'll be able to try other sauces and side-servings, starting at around W5000 per meal.

Other areas

The following places are marked on the "Busan" **map**, p.205.

Dongnae Halmae Pajeon 동래 할매 파전 Bokchundong. Way off the beaten tourist track is this fascinating restaurant – despite the modern interior, it has nearly a century of history behind it, and the food is excellent. People come for the eponymous *pajeon*, a local version of the Korean pancake, and quite possibly the best example of the dish in the country. The restaurant is near the *Dongnae Gucheon* district office, within a W2000 taxi-ride of Dongnae subway station.

Insadong Kalguksu 인사동 칼국수 Daeyeondong. Near the museum entrance – on the right-hand side of the road heading back to Daeyeon subway station – and well worth hunting down, this friendly, family-run restaurant often has some amazingly cheap deals; though no information is in English, the pictures on the wall come in useful. Usually good value are the *shabu-shabu* sets – a boiling bowl of delicious meat broth, supplemented by excellent side dishes.

Naedang 내당 Oncheondong. Next door to the *Nongshim Hotel* (p.209) is one of the city's finest restaurants. Though the interior isn't as pretty as the building's traditional outer styling might suggest, the food is prepared with an attention to detail hard to come by in the Gyeongsang provinces, and more similar to that found in Jeolla-do – sets start at around W80,000 per person, with the fried sea bream and broiled beef especially tasty.

Nightlife

Busan has an excellent and varied **nightlife scene**, spread in uneven clumps across various parts of the city – a single evening can see you sipping *soju* over raw fish at sunset, rubbing shoulders with Russian sailors near the train station, throwing back beer with students in one of the university areas, then dancing all night at a beachside hip-hop club. To do this, however, you'd be spending plenty of money on taxi fares – best to simply pick an area and root down for the night.

The two main student areas – **Busan National University** to the north, and **Kyungsung University** west of Haeundae – are among the most interesting places to go out, and certainly the cheapest. Weekdays can be tame, but on weekends the partying goes on until the wee hours. The same can be said for the two beach areas – **Haeundae** and **Gwangalli** – which cater to a more upmarket crowd, and throw a couple of clubs and cocktail bars into the mix; there's also the option of buying some cans at a convenience store and drinking on the beach. Central Busan is markedly less interesting: **Seomyeon** has a few clubs, though these can be full of soldiers, with fights breaking out on a regular basis, while the bars around **Busan station** tend to be populated with Russian prostitutes and men in the market for them.

Haeundae and around

The following places are marked on the "Haeundae" **map**, p.211.

Blowfish Songjeong. A genuine surfer bar – the only one in Korea – next to Songjeong beach, a relatively quiet stretch of sand a few clicks north of Haeundae. To get here, first take the subway to Jangsang at the end of the line, then grab a cab (W3000).

Elune Haeundae. Electro-techno club in the bowels of the *Paradise Hotel* (p.208). It's a loungey affair, with comfy sofas on which to sup your cocktails (W7000) before hitting the dancefloor. Entry W10,000 weeknights, W20,000 weekends, more after 11pm.

Maktum Haeundae. Rather pretentious for a middling hip-hop club, but still worth a peek if you're in Haeundae and in need of a dance. Entry W15,000 or so; more on party nights.

Thursday Party Haeundae. You'll find branches of this Busanese bar-chain all over the city; cheap beer and clever choices of location mean that most of them are busy every night. The Haeundae branch is a particularly fun place to be on weekends.

Leaving Busan by ferry

Even though there's plenty to see inside it, **leaving Busan** can be one of the most rewarding experiences of your stay – it's as easy as getting on a **ferry**. Domestic departures invariably head west, so try to get a seat on the right-hand side of the vessel; this will ensure you have sweeping views of the sloping rows of tightly crammed buildings that prompt some to compare Busan to Naples.

While ferries to Japan quickly find themselves in open sea, domestic **routes** take you past Jagalchi fish market, and a whole armada of ships, cranes, buoys and bays, all backed by an undulating mess of grimy buildings. The city soon fades away, waves pounding instead against cliffs that fall into the sea in ice-creamy diagonal bands of yellow and purple – evidence that Busan once rode high above the waters, before being toppled down to sea level by the drift of plates. Lighthouses poke up from the crags like lonely crayons, backed all the way to your destination by a hurried scrawl of mountain scenery.

Other areas

The following places are marked on the "Busan" **map**, p.205.

Basement Busan National University. This underground lair has, for many a year, been by far the most popular bar in the Busan National University area. Drinks are cheap, staff are super-friendly, and there are regular theme and live music nights.

Foxy Seomyeon. Two-floor hip-hop venue that's as good a place as any to shake your thing in Busan. Weekend entry fees are around W10,000, and the place is usually pumping until *very* late.

Vinyl Underground Kyungsung University. Vibrant, stylish, student-friendly bar that's back to its best after a few slow years. Hosts occasional movie nights, live music and other events.

Womb Gwangalli. Basement venue that puts on huge weekend parties, with a pleasant variety to musical proceedings. They often rope in top Korean DJs, as well as a smattering from abroad.

Listings

Books Nampo Bookstore, across the main road from the Jagalchi fish market, has a good selection of books covering Korean language and culture, as well as the usual Rowlings and Grishams.

Cinemas Four large multiscreens stand almost eyeball-to-eyeball on PIFF Square in Nampodong. When PIFF rolls into town in October there are also showings at the big cinemas in Haeundae.

Embassies and consulates China, 1418 Uidong ⓣ051/743-7984; Japan, 1147-11 Choryangdong ⓣ051/465-5101; Russia, 10F Korea Exchange Bank BD, 89-1 Jungangdong 4-ga ⓣ051/441-1104.

Hospitals Pusan National University Hospital, 10 1-ga, Amidong (ⓣ051/254-0171), is most likely to offer English-language help or try the more central Maryknoll Hospital, 4-ga Daecheongdong (ⓣ051/465-8801).

Post The largest post office is just south of Jungangdong subway station on the main road (Mon–Fri 9am–8pm, Sat 9am–6pm), but there are smaller branches in every city suburb.

Sport Despite being the country's second-largest city, Busan's sporting teams usually fail to make waves in their national leagues. Busan I'Park is the city's football team, and plays in red-and-white-quartered shirts at the Asiad Stadium. The Lotte Giants are one of the best-known baseball teams in Korea, and you can catch them (and their manically noisy supporters) at the Sajik Baseball Stadium.

The South Sea coast and islands

Gyeongnam's south coast is surrounded by squadrons of islands. One of these, **Geojedo**, is the second largest in the country; despite a heavy amount of industrialization, it retains some worthwhile sights, particulary rocky **Haegeumgang**, a coastal formation best viewed by boat. Dozens of other islands have been placed under the protective banner of **Hallyeo Haesang**, one of only three national marine parks in the country; these are best accessed from **Tongyeong**, a coastal city whose square harbour must rank as one of Korea's most scenic.

Geojedo

Just an hour by ferry from Busan, but also connected to the mainland by road, is **GEOJEDO** (거제도); measuring 40km by 25km, this is Korea's second-largest island, and a craggy paradox of stone and steel. Here can be found large tracks of forest and some of the most impressive **coastal scenery** in the land, but while the island is famed for its natural vistas, parts of it have been shattered by industry – around a third of the world's container ships are built here in the two mammoth **shipyards** that now define the island, and provide much of its employment. The main centre of population is **Gohyeon**, tucked in to the north and sheltered from the South Sea. Other sights include **Haegeumgang**, where a simply gorgeous rock formation – quite possibly the most beautiful on the whole Korean coast – rises from the sea just offshore, and **Oedo**, a tiny, flower-covered island that's incredibly popular with Korean tourists.

Arrival and island transport

Thanks to the mammoth bridge to Tongyeong, Geojedo is easily accessible by **bus** from many mainland destinations – Gohyeon has by far the best connections, and its bus terminal is surrounded by motels and restaurants. The best way to arrive, however, is by **ferry** from Busan – regular ferries depart the city's domestic Yeonan terminal for several Geoje destinations; most head to Gohyeon or **Jangseungpo** (장승포), a small fishing village on the east of the island. One-way rides cost around W17,000, and take just over or under an hour, depending on which Geoje port you use. Wherever you land, regular **local buses** speed between the island's major centres. Ten **ferries** a day do the three-hour circuit to Oedo from Jangsuengpo, costing W17,000 on weekdays and W19,000 on weekends, when it can be hard to get a ticket. You'll get ninety minutes on the island – more than enough – and a pass saying which ferry you have to return on. Ferries also depart from Haegeumgang, and sometimes from Tongyeong.

Accommodation and eating

There are **places to stay** all over Geojedo, but for convenience, most make do with Jangseungpo or Gohyeon. Near **Jangseungpo**, *Hotel Art* (Ⓣ055/682-0075; ❺) is the best and most prominent place to stay, with some rooms overlooking the harbour – it's part of a large, Guggenheim-esque complex visible from the harbour, which contains a modern art gallery (free) on the sixth floor. Cheaper rooms can be found at the *Sky* and *Sun Park* motels (both ❸), painted in mint and peach tones respectively, and both visible from the main road.

Gohyeon is busier and less appealing; an easy walk from the bus terminal lie a few cheap motels. Culinary choices are similarly insipid, but near the bus terminal there's *Gimbap-gwa Spaghetti*, a cheap respite from all things fishy. **Haegeumgang** is a wonderful area to stay, with the village containing several *minbak* and a *yeogwan* (both ❷).

Gohyeon

During the Korean War, Geojedo was the base of one of the allied forces' main **prisoner of war camps**, which kept Chinese and North Korean captives almost as far as possible from the wavering line of control. The largest of several such bases was in **Gohyeon** (고현), now the island's biggest town and main travel hub. The freshly spruced-up **Prisoner of War Camp Museum** (daily 9am–6pm; W3000) recreates part of the original camp. Despite being diorama-heavy, the open-air display is surprisingly diverting for a Korean historical exhibition, right from the introductory escalator-based greeting from Mao, MacArthur, Kim and their cardboard comrades. Simulated gunfire, explosions and revolutionary music crackle around the squat buildings and dirt tracks, much of which are cordoned off by barbed wire, but the effect is spoilt somewhat – in Korean fashion – by the new flyover swooping above the complex. There's little information in English, but some of the exhibits speak for themselves – keep an eye out for the video footage of what life was like in the camp. The museum is just about within walking distance of Gohyeon bus terminal, but poorly signed – a taxi won't cost more than a couple of thousand won.

Haegeumgang and Oedo

The Geumgang Mountains in North Korea are rightly revered as the most beautiful on the peninsula, a Chinese painting come to life where tree-fringed scoops of sculpted rock rise through the mist. Similar sights – far smaller, but infinitely more accessible – are on offer at **Haegeumgang** (해금강) off the south coast of Geojedo – *hae* means sea – where the precipitous crags lift their skinny fists like antennas through the waters rather than the North Korean hinterland. Topped with a sprinkling of camellia and highly photogenic, Haegeumgang can also be seen from dry land – a network of trails web out from a nearby village, heading to a viewing point that's perfect for a picnic, but becomes yet more majestic under the light of the moon. However, as the peaks lie a few hundred metres offshore, they're most commonly viewed by boat on the way to **OEDO** (외도; pronounced "way-dough"), an island possessing a different kind of beauty. The brainchild of a couple of botanists from Seoul, it has been almost entirely covered with flowers, and is now one of the most popular sights in the country for **Korean tourists**, pulling in a couple of million each year. Though the flowers are beautiful, it's one of those experiences that appeals to Koreans far more than it does to foreign visitors, and the island's tight paths can get uncomfortably crowded – don't dare to go against the current.

Tongyeong

Straddling the neck of the Geosong peninsula, affable **TONGYEONG** (통영) occupies a special place in Korean hearts as the base from which **Admiral Yi Sung-Shin** orchestrated some of his greatest victories against the invading Japanese (see box, p.232). The town is now a laid-back place concentrating as much on its present as its past, with enough diversions to keep visitors occupied for a day, after which you may care to head off to the emerald confetti of islands that surround it (see p.218).

Arrival, information and accommodation

Although there's no train station, Tongyeong is a local transport hub, with regular **ferries** heading to the surrounding islands in all seasons. Most popular are the forty-minute trip to the twin peaks of Saryangdo and the half-hour hop to Jeseungdang (both 8 daily), and there's a twice-daily summer service to Jeju Island (see p.301). Tongyeong's **bus** station, inconveniently hidden in the northern suburbs, offers regular services to most cities in Korea, including half-hourly connections to Busan and Daegu. The station has a **tourist office**, though your chances of finding an English-speaking member of staff are slim.

Accommodation can be found around the bus station, but by far the most pleasant place to stay is the harbour. Standing out like a sore thumb is the *Napoli Motel* (ⓣ055/646-0202; ④), one of the tallest buildings around, and a little overpriced, but nice enough. Visible from the harbour is the *Geumjeongjang Motel* (❷), which though cheaper, and with similar views, may be a little seedy for some. More motels, *yeogwan* and cheap-as-chips *yeoinsuk* line the busier sides of the harbour, together with an acceptable *jjimjilbang*.

The Town

Tongyeong's four-sided **harbour** – known as Ganguan – forms the focal point of the city, and is where you'll be able to see, and taste, the city's pride and joy – **chungmu gimbap** (see below). The **promenade** lining its western flank can be a relaxing place to drink on warm evenings, the piped Bossa Nova augmented by the gentle lapping of moored fishing boats. The north bank forms the base of a small hill, with a maze of houses, tiny lanes and drainage channels snaking their way to the top.

A steep five-minute walk from the harbour brings you to **Sebyeonggwan** (세병관), a huge single-floor house built in 1605 as the headquarters of the Admiralty, and one of the oldest wooden structures in the country. Its lack of walls, windows or doors makes it almost unrecognizable as a house, but in the summer the giant roof, balanced on top of fifty carved wooden columns, provides welcome shade for *gimbap*-munching tourists. Just down the road lies the **Folklore and History Museum** (Tues–Sun 9am–5pm; free), which concentrates on Tongyeong's military triumphs but also features interesting local crafts and costumes. East of the harbour, Nammangsan hill is home to an excellent international **modern sculpture park** (24hr; free) and a statue of Lee Sun-shin (see p.232). The bearded Admiral Yi stands with his back to the art, fixing a patriotic gaze at the island-peppered scene of his victories.

Tongyeong is the proud host of a genuinely international summer **music festival**, a feast of modern and classical tunes. And for those who prefer muscles to music, Korea's number one **triathlon** sees competitors splash, dash and cycle through the city each June.

Eating

For food, there's only one recommendation – get your teeth around the city's famed **chungmu gimbap** (충무 김밥). These are small rice rolls with radish *gimchi* and chillied squid, and though available in specialist *gimbap* restaurants across the land they taste infinitely better here. The western side of the harbour is almost entirely occupied by tiny restaurants, each serving this local speciality on old newspaper – most outlets have pictures of female proprietors present and past on their nameboards; as a general rule of thumb, the older the *ajumma*, the more rustic the restaurant, and the better the food.

Islands of the South Sea

An almost innumerable number of islands radiate out into the South Sea like emerald stepping-stones. Much of this area is protected as the **HALLYEO HAESANG NATIONAL PARK** (한려 해상 국립 공원) and, as in other island groups around the country, offers a look into the heart of traditional Korean life. Here ports and villages have changed little for generations, places inextricably connected to their surrounding waters where the busy urban realities of modern Korea are little more than memory.

Mainland Tongyeong is the area's main transport hub, and from here you can hop to dozens of islands by ferry. **Mireukdo** (미륵도) is immediately opposite the ferry terminal, but is built up and a little too industrial, and in any case connected to Tongyeong by bridge. Just 20km to the west of Tongyeong, the twin-peaked island of **Saryangdo** (사량도) is far more serene, and popular with young travellers in the summer on account of some good beaches; at these times, many choose to camp under the stars, but there are *minbak* available. **Hansando** (한산도) is even closer to Tongyeong, and was once home to Admiral Yi's main naval base; nowadays it's best known for Jeseungdang, a large shrine. Just off its northeastern flank is the relaxed island of **Bijindo** (비진도), whose long, east-facing beach is a wonderful place to watch the sunrise over a smattering of small islets. Further afield, **Yeonhwado** (연화도) is home to a remote temple, as well as the *Yongmeori* – needles of rock protruding from the eastern cape. These are just a few possibilities – allow yourself a few days, armed with a map of the area, and forget about the mainland for a while. Many of the islands have simple *minbak* accommodation, but as banking facilities are all but nonexistent it's essential to bring the necessary funds along from the mainland.

Jinju

A small city typical of Korea's southern coast, but rather more akin to laid-back Jeolla than busy Gyeongsang in feel, **JINJU** (진주) is worth dropping into on account of its superb **fortress** alone – this was the scene of one of the most famous suicides in Korean history (see box, p.220), an event commemorated by an annual weekend **festival** at the end of May.

Here you can walk for hours along pretty paths, gaze over the river from traditional pavilions and pop into the odd temple. The beauty of Jinju is that all you need is within easy walking distance – the fortress is close to the intercity bus terminal, and surrounded by places to stay and eat. Unlike most towns in the region, the city is famed for its food, and a clutch of excellent **eel restaurants** can be found outside the fortress entrance. Jinju even has its own take on *bibimbap* – a popular dish across the nation, but prepared here with consummate attention – and a few restaurants still serving ostrich meat. The city also makes a good base for nearby national park of **Jirisan** (see p.221), one of the most popular in the country.

Arrival and information

With the **train** line seeing few daily services, and the domestic **airport** 20km away and similarly quiet, most of Jinju's visitors arrive by **bus**. The express terminal is to the south of town, past the train station, but the intercity terminal is well located in the thick of things, just north of the Nam River and within walking

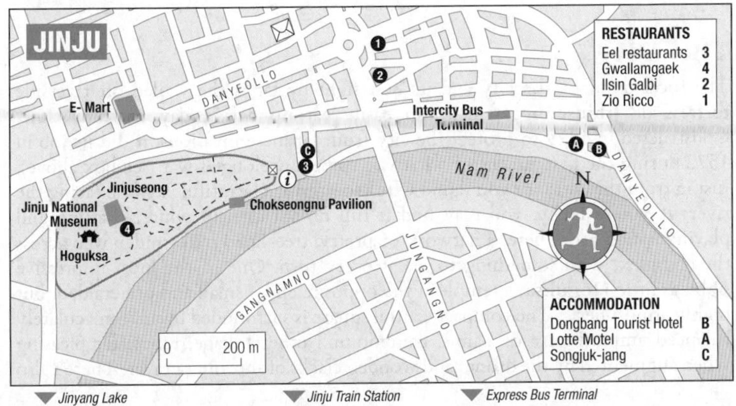

The Japanese attacks on Jinju

Jinju's fortress received its first serious test in October of 1592, during the first attacks of what was to be a prolonged Japanese invasion. Like Admiral Yi along the coast in Yeosu (see p.232), **General Kim Si-min** held fort despite being heavily outnumbered, with records claiming that 30,000 Japanese soldiers were seen off by just 3800 local troops. The following June, the Japanese returned in greater numbers, with up to 100,000 soldiers eager to obliterate the shame of their previous defeat, and it is estimated that 70,000 Koreans were killed during a week-long siege. Every tragedy needs a hero – or, in this case, a heroine – and this time a local girl named **Nongae**, one of several girls selected to "entertain" the Japanese top-dogs after their victory, stepped into the breach. After using her charms to lure Japanese general Keyamura to what should have been a suspiciously lofty position on the riverside cliff, she jumped to her death, bringing the general down with her. A **festival** commemorating Nongae's patriotic valour takes place in the fortress each May, while General Kim's memory lives on in statue form at the centre of the fortress.

distance of the fortress. There's a small **tourist information** booth outside the main fortress entrance, where staff can usually do little more than hand out maps, or perhaps shed some light on the bullfights that the city occasionally hosts.

Accommodation

While there are **places to stay** all over the city, there's little point in basing yourself anywhere other than the strip running from the bus station to the fortress, which is dotted with cheap motels and *yeogwan*. There are also a few crusty *yeoinsuk* lying around, which are extremely cheap at just W10,000 per room, but the room is all you'll get, with nothing inside but a couple of blankets, a TV, and some toilet roll for use in the communal washrooms – not quite the *Ritz*, but a quintessentially Korean experience.

Dongbang Tourist Hotel Okbongdong ⓣ055/743-0131. Better than the average Korean tourist hotel, though this really isn't saying much, and rooms are heavily overpriced. The river-facing location, however, is a plus. ⑥

Lotte Motel Okbongdong ⓣ055/741-4888. Just down the road from the *Dongbang*, but much cheaper. Rooms here are smallish but spotless, and come with fetching his 'n' hers nightgowns; some also have pleasing river views. ③

Songjuk-jang Jeongmun-ap. A cheap, interesting place run by a gaggle of *ajummas*-to-be, opposite the main entrance of the fort and down a side street. Rooms have their own toilet, which means that they're fine for the price. ②

The City

The focal point of the city and its best sight by far is the walled-off riverside fortress of **Jinjuseong**, which can easily eat up half a day of your time. Constructed in 1379 to protect the city from Japanese invasions, it did its job in 1572 during the first attacks of what was to be a prolonged war (see box above). Just in from the entrance you'll find **Chokseongnu**, a beautiful pavilion facing the river; if you're lucky, you may find it full of old men in white, chatting and playing *baduk*. From here, a network of pretty, tree-lined trails spider-web across the complex, with something to see at every turn. One of the most impressive sights is little **Hoguksa**, a temple at the opposite end – small and unheralded, but highly atmospheric. The compact central square is surrounded by an immaculately balanced amphitheatre of palms, bamboo and other foliage, especially pleasing when augmented by the drones and wooden clacks of morning prayer. There's also a large **museum** on site (Tues–Fri 9am–6pm, Sat & Sun 9am–7pm; W1000), which has been built in an unnecessarily modern style, at odds with its surroundings. However, it is good on history, with an inevitable focus on the 1592 Japanese invasions, several battles from which are depicted on folding screens.

Near the fortress you'll find several restaurants specializing in **eel** (see "Eating", below) as well as Insadong-gil, a street lined with **antique shops**. The Nam River is dammed a short distance upstream, with Jinyangho, the resulting **lake**, a popular place with Korean couples; here you'll also find an amusement park, and a small zoo. The river itself comes alive during an annual **lantern festival** at the beginning of October; this usually coincides with one of Korea's only **bullfighting** events, though you may be cheered to hear that the bulls fight each other, and don't die in front of a baying crowd.

Eating

Jinju's **food** is good, even by Korean standards. **Jeollanese** influence has clearly crept across the provincial border – meals are often served with a copious array of **side dishes**, and there's even a local version of that Jeonju favourite, the *bibimbap*. Surprisingly few Jinjuites will be able to point you to a restaurant serving this delectable dish, though one can be found fairly close to the fortress entrance. Even harder to find are the few restaurants still serving **ostrich** meat, a Jinju speciality, but on the decline – one, *Tajobaelli*, is a short taxi ride from the fortress area.

Eel restaurants Outside the main gate to the fortress lies a parade of restaurants, all devoted to the same dish – eel. There's precious little to choose between them in terms of price or quality, and all have English-language menus; the *Yujeong* has made the most effort in terms of decoration, but *Gangnaru* may overshadow it on the taste front. At all places, river eel costs around W15,000, with sea eel a couple of thousand won cheaper.

Gwallamgaek Sikdang Jinjuseong. Actually located inside the fort itself, and, therefore, a perfect place to fall back and fill up if you're spending a while here. Noodle dishes are cheap at W3000, but the *bibimbap* is better value at W5000.

Ilsin Galbi Dongseongdong. Though most come for the *galbi*, it would be a shame to turn down the fantastic local speciality, which is one of the most delicious dishes available in the province – Jinju *bibimbap*. Extremely similar to the Jeonju style, but half the price at just W5000, meticulous care goes into the meal and its accompanying side dishes. *Doenjang jjigae*, a *miso*-style stew, is also a bargain at just W3000. The restaurant is on a small alley near the bus station and a little hard to find – it's just in front of the *Dongbo Motel*, which is somewhat easier to track down.

Zio Ricco This Italian restaurant is a *gimchi*-free refuge for Jinju's small expat community, with its proximity to the bus station and fortress also making it a good choice for tourists. Pasta forms the bulk of the menu, and is inevitably served with the sweet pickles that Koreans must assume to be a regular side dish in Italy.

Jirisan National Park

Korea's largest national park, **JIRISAN** (지리산 국립 공원), pulls in hikers from all over the country, attracted by the dozen peaks measuring over 1000m in height, which includes Cheonwangbong, the South Korean mainland's highest. It has also found fame for its **resident bear population**; a park camera spotted an Asiatic Black Bear wandering around in 2002, almost two decades after the last confirmed Korean sighting. The bear group was located and placed under protection, and continue to breed successfully. Although you're extremely unlikely to see them, it lends the park's various twists and turns an extra dash of excitement – nowhere else in Korea will you be fretting over the sound of a broken twig. Jirisan is one of the only national parks in the country with an

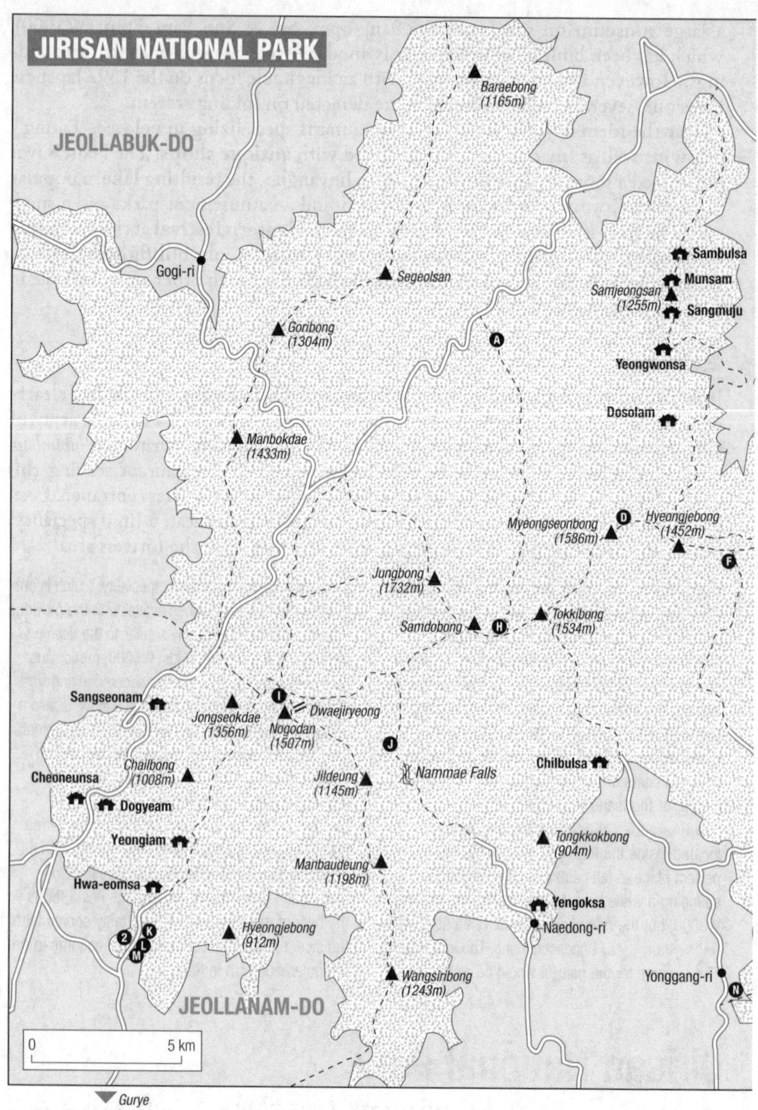

organized system of overnight **shelters** – there are few more atmospheric places to fall asleep in this corner of Korea. This makes **multiday hikes** an exciting possibility; one popular route heads across the main spine of the park from east to west, and takes three days to walk. There are large peaks all the way along this central ridge, from which numerous picturesque valleys drop down to the fields and foothills below. It's impossible to detail all of the possible hikes and sights in the park, better instead to arm yourself with the park map (available at park entrances and nearby tourist offices for W1000) and find your own lofty piece of paradise.

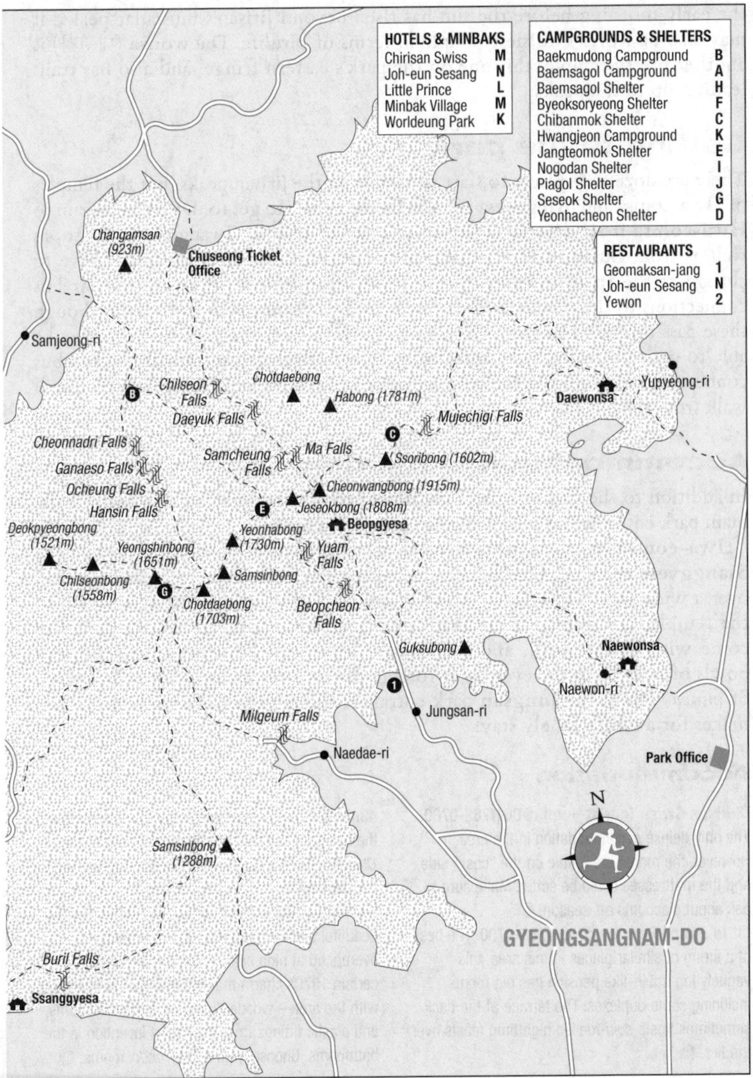

HOTELS & MINBAKS
Chirisan Swiss M
Joh-eun Sesang N
Little Prince L
Minbak Village M
Worldeung Park K

CAMPGROUNDS & SHELTERS
Baekmudong Campground B
Baemsagol Campground A
Baemsagol Shelter H
Byeoksoryeong Shelter F
Chibanmok Shelter C
Hwangjeon Campground K
Jangteomok Shelter E
Nogodan Shelter I
Piagol Shelter J
Seseok Shelter G
Yeonhacheon Shelter D

RESTAURANTS
Geomaksan-jang 1
Joh-eun Sesang N
Yewon 2

The park actually sprawls across three provinces, with its most popular access point – the temple of **Hwa-eomsa** – on the west of the park, and actually located across the provincial border in Jeonnam. The eastern side of Jirisan, in Gyeongnam province, lacks such a focal point – there are dozens of entrances, but though none are particularly popular or easy to get to, this usually makes for a quieter visit than you'd get at other national parks. One of the most popular trails is up from **Ssanggyesa** (쌍계사), a beautifully located temple at the south of the park. There's little of historical note here, bar a stone tablet apparently dating from 887, but the surroundings are delightful, particularly in the early morning before the sun has risen beyond Jirisan's muscular peaks; it may also be Korea's noisiest temple in terms of birdlife. **Daewonsa** (대원사) is another pretty temple, this one on the park's eastern fringe, and also has trails leading up to the peaks.

Getting to the park

There are dozens of places to start an assault on the Jirisan peaks, but the temples of Hwa-eomsa and Ssanggyesa are usually the easiest to get to. Direct buses run to **Hwa-eomsa** from the major Jeollanese cities of Jeonju, Gwangju and Yeosu, as well as from Busan in Gyeongsang province. From other cities, you'll have to change at the small town of Gurye (구례), from where there are regular bus connections to the temple. Direct buses head to **Ssanggyesa** from Jinju, though these pass through Hadong (하동), a small town nearer the park that you may be able to get to directly from other cities. The village of **Jungsan-ni** also has bus connections to Jinju, but the park entrance is a frustratingly long (20min) uphill walk from the bus stop.

Accommodation and eating

In addition to the shelters, there are **places to stay** and **eat** outside both of the main park entrances, as well as a smattering of campsites.

Hwa-eomsa has the most extensive accommodation possibilities, while the **Ssanggyesa** entrance, bucolic and open-plan, has *minbak* and restaurants spread over a wide area. The rustic *Joh-eun Sesang* (좋은세상; ❶), on the access path to the temple, is a family home that caters for both needs; rooms are basic but come with private bath, and the owners have been known to whip up free bowls of *ramyeon* in the evening if foreign guests look hungry. There's a clutch of *minbak* (❷) at the **Jungsan** park entrance, though the isolation of the place makes for a rather lonely stay.

Accommodation

Chirisan Swiss Tourist Hotel ☎061/783-0700. The only deluxe accommodation in the area. However, the rooms are a little on the "cosy" side, and the mattresses could be softer. Make sure to ask about discounts off-season. ❺

Little Prince Pension ☎061/783-4700. The best of a string of similar places in this area, this vaguely log-cabin-like pension has big rooms, including some duplexes. The terrace at the back sometimes hosts *soju*-fuelled nighttime feasts over the fire. ❹

Minbak Village There are plenty of *minbak* around the bus stop, but the nicer ones are close to the *Chirisan Swiss* a couple of hundred metres down the road. ❷

Worldeung Park Hotel ☎061/782-0082. Not a beautiful place by any means, and woefully overpriced at high season, but this hotel has a certain 1970s charm that is somewhat in keeping with the area – wooden furniture in the bedrooms, and plastic fittings from the age of invention in the bathrooms. Choose from bed or *ondol* rooms. ❹

Eating

Hwa-eomsa has the area's best restaurant – friendly *Yewon* (예원), which serves colossal, utterly delicious set meals (*sanchae jeongsik*; 산채 정식) of roots, shoots and mountain vegetables for W8000. The best place to eat near the **Jungsan** bus stop is at *Geomoksan-jang* (거목산장), where a friendly man with his own unique English dialect serves some pretty good *pajeon* pancakes – just the treat after a long hike.

If you're on a multiday hike you may be able to buy basic provisions in some park shelters, but while water is easier to find, it's advisable to bring your own food.

Hiking Jirisan National Park

A few of Jirisan's hundreds of routes are particularly popular. The biggest is the **26km-long trail** heading along the east–west main spine of the park. The hike connects **Nogodan**, a 1507m-high peak in the west, best accessed from Hwa-eomsa, and **Cheonwangbong** (1915m) in the east, the highest peak on the South Korean mainland and the second highest in the country. This trail takes most people three days to walk, with a couple of overnight stays at the **shelters** sprinkled along the way; there are eight of these on the spine, costing from W5000 to W7000 per person, and all are marked on the map. The westernmost shelter, at **Nogodan**, is very often full due to its proximity to a bus stop: to guarantee a place at any of the shelters you're asked to reserve a berth in advance through Korea's national park website (ⓦenglish.knps.or.kr). This can prove frustrating, as it's hard to tell where you will run out of daylight or energy on your hike, but reserving beds at Samdobong and Seseok should give you enough leeway whether you're heading east or west.

Numerous valleys head up to the park's main spine, and most make for excellent day-hikes. One of the most popular runs from **Jungsan-ni** (중산리), a village connected to Jinju by bus, up to the principal peak of Cheonwangbong and back again, though many choose to continue north and emerge out of the park at Chuseong, down a valley lined with small waterfalls. Others start at the temples of Daewonsa and Ssanggyesa, which are a little far away from the spine for a day-trip, so you'd have to overnight at a shelter.

Hwa-eomsa

Even if you're not up for a hike, the temple of **HWA-EOMSA** (화엄사), locked in Jirisan's muscular embrace, is a highly worthy detour. It lies a kilometre-plus uphill walk from the bus stop just outside the park entrance – an early morning visit is recommended, as you'll avoid any school groups and, hopefully, be able to see the sun rise over the peaks. At the entrance to Hwa-eomsa, the **temple guardians** are worth a look – the three regular bulgy-eyed fellows are joined by a serene buck-toothed figure strumming an instrument with huge fingers. Inside the complex are two **pagodas**; the western one is the more interesting, carved in Silla times with Buddhist figures that remain visible to this day. Nearby is a **stone lantern** that is – if you believe the Korean tourist authorities – the largest such sculpture in the world, an oversized beast emblazoned with cloud and lotus motifs, stretching over 6m from the ground. Subtler in its approach is the neighbouring stone pagoda, its main block balanced on the heads of four smug-looking lions. You'll see that some of the buildings around the complex are painted while some remain bare; attempts were made at repainting the whole lot, but these were quashed by a lack of funds and the deteriorating wood. **Gakhwangjeon** (각황전) is a particularly appealing hall. Looking all the better for its lack of renovation, its largely bare wooden structure forms a delicious contrast with the huge pictures that hang inside – a rhapsody in red. If you're after solitude, head behind the heart of the complex to **Gu-am** (구암). This hermitage is not as old or pretty as the buildings in the main complex, but filled as it is with vegetable plots, birdsong and mossy paths, and almost no signs of modern life, it's quite enchanting. Unfortunately, a large new hall was under construction at the time of writing, its size and location looking sure to puncture the temple's tranquil air.

From the Hwa-eomsa bus stop you can hike up to **Nogodan peak** (노고단; 1507m; around 3hr), or save time and energy by taking a connecting bus most of the way up. Times are infrequent but there's one roughly every hour from 7am to 6pm – check at the small **information centre** near the bus stop. If you do take the bus, the remaining distance to the top is an easy walk of an hour or so – leave enough time if catching the last bus down.

Travel details

Flights

Note that Busan and Daegu also have a range of international connections.

Busan (Gimhae airport) to: Jeju (every 20min; 50min); Seoul (every 30min; 55min).

Daegu to: Jeju (7 daily; 1hr).

Jinju (Sacheon airport) to: Jeju (4 weekly; 45min); Seoul (2 daily; 1hr).

Trains

The trains between the major cities listed below are the fastest, most direct services.

Andong to: Gyeongju (3 daily; 2hr); Seoul (9 daily; 4hr); Wonju (9 daily; 2hr 20min).

Busan to: Daegu (regularly; 45min); Daejeon (regularly; 1hr 40min); Gyeongju (regularly; 30min); Seoul (regularly; 2hr 40min).

Daegu to: Busan (regularly; 45min); Daejeon (regularly; 45min); Gyeongju (hourly; 1hr 20min); Pohang (hourly; 1hr 45min); Seoul (regularly; 1hr 35min).

Gyeongju to: Andong (3 daily; 2hr); Busan (regularly; 30min); Daegu (hourly; 1hr 20min); Pohang (hourly; 40min).

Buses

The connections listed below are the fastest, most direct services available.

Andong to: Busan (regularly; 3hr); Chuncheon (1 daily; 2hr); Daegu (regularly; 1hr); Daejeon (14 daily; 2hr 10min); Gwangju (2 daily; 3hr); Gyeongju (12 daily; 3hr); Pohang (regularly; 40min); Seoul (regularly; 3hr); Taebaek (3 daily; 3hr); Tongyeong (5 daily; 3hr); Wonju (regularly; 3hr); Yeongju (regularly; 1hr).

Busan Central bus terminal to: Andong (regularly; 3hr); Chuncheon (14 daily; 6hr); Daegu (regularly; 1hr 20min); Daejeon (regularly; 3hr 10min); Gangneung (10 daily; 7hr); Gwangju (regularly; 3hr 40min); Gyeongju (regularly; 50min); Incheon (11 daily; 4hr 30min); Jeonju (12 daily; 3hr 35min); Jinju (regularly; 2hr); Pohang (every 10min; 1hr 30min); Samcheok (3 daily; 4hr 30min); Seoul (regularly; 4hr 30min); Sokcho (8 daily; 7hr 30min); Yeosu (13 daily; 3hr 40min).

Busan Seobu terminal to: Gwangju (regularly; 3hr 30min); Jinju (regularly; 1hr 30min); Mokpo (7 daily; 5hr 40min); Ssanggyesa (3 daily; 2hr); Tongyeong (regularly; 2hr); Wando (5 daily; 6hr 40min).

Daegu Express terminal to: Andong (9 daily; 1hr 20min); Busan (every 50min; 1hr 40min); Daejeon (regularly; 2hr 20min); Gwangju (every 40min; 3hr 20min); Gyeongju (regularly; 50min); Incheon (10 daily; 4hr 30min); Jeonju (every 1hr 20min; 3hr 30min); Jinju (hourly; 2hr 10min); Seoul (regularly; 3hr 50min); Sokcho (3 daily; 4hr).

Daegu Dongbu terminal to: Gangneung (regularly; 5hr); Gyeongju (regularly; 50min); Pohang (regularly; 1hr 20min); Samcheok (11 daily; 6hr 30min); Sokcho (8 daily; 7hr).

Daegu Seobu terminal to: Busan (8 daily; 1hr 50min); Gyeongju (19 daily; 1hr 10min); Haeinsa (regularly; 1hr 30min); Jinju (regularly; 1hr 40min); Pohang (regularly; 1hr 30min); Tongyeong (regularly; 2hr 40min); Yeosu (7 daily; 4hr).

Daegu Bukbu terminal to: Andong (regularly; 1hr 30min); Gangneung (9 daily; 4hr); Guinsa (1 daily; 4hr); Muju (3 daily; 3hr 30min).

Geojedo to: Busan (regularly; 3hr 20min); Jinju (every 30min; 2hr 50min); Seoul (6 daily; 6hr); Tongyeong (regularly; 40min).

Gyeongju to: Andong (12 daily; 3hr); Busan (regularly; 50min); Daegu (regularly; 50min); Daejeon (regularly; 2hr 40min); Gangneung (16 daily; 5hr 30min); Gwangju (2 daily; 3hr 30min); Incheon (every 50min; 5hr 30min); Jinju (6 daily; 2hr 30min); Seoul (regularly; 4hr 15min); Sokcho (2 daily; 8hr).

Jinju to: Busan (regularly; 1hr 30min); Daegu (regularly; 2hr); Daejeon (hourly; 2hr); Daewonsa (hourly; 1hr 10min); Gwangju (2 daily; 2hr 40min); Haeinsa (3 daily; 2hr 20min); Seoul (every 30min; 3hr 35min); Suncheon (15 daily; 1hr 30min); Tongyeong (regularly; 1hr 30min); Yeosu (3 daily; 2hr 20min).

Tongyeong to: Busan (regularly; 2hr); Daegu (regularly; 2hr 40min); Daejeon (regularly; 2hr 40min); Geojedo (regularly; 40min); Gwangju (3 daily; 2hr 30min); Haegeumgang (2 daily; 1hr 30min); Jinju (regularly; 1hr 30min); Seoul (regularly; 4hr 10min).

Ferries

Busan International Terminal to: Fukuoka (several daily; 3–15hr); Shimonoseki (daily; 14hr).

Busan Domestic Terminal to: Gohyeon (5 daily; 1hr); Jangseungpo (7 daily; 45min); Jeju Island (7pm daily except Sun; 11hr).

Pohang to: Ulleungdo (10.30am daily; 3hr).

Jeolla

CHINA
N
NORTH KOREA
DMZ
EAST SEA (SEA OF JAPAN)
WEST SEA (YELLOW SEA)
SOUTH KOREA
JAPAN
0 50 km

CHAPTER 4

Highlights

* **Hyangiram** A tiny hermitage hanging onto cliffs south of Yeosu, and the best place in the country in which to see in the New Year. See p.234

* **Mokpo** This characterful seaside city is the best jumping-off point for excursions to the emerald isles of the West Sea. See p.239

* **Naejangsan** The circular mountain ridge within this national park looks stunning in autumn, and is the best place in the land to enjoy the season. See p.249

* **Byeonsanbando** Look out across the sea from the peaks of this peninsular national park, then descend to the coast at low tide to see some terrific cliff formations. See p.251

* **Jeonju's hanok village** There are all sorts of traditional sights and activities to pursue in this wonderful area of *hanok* housing. See p.254

* **Food** Jeollanese cuisine offers the best ingredients and more side dishes, and is best exemplified by Jeonju's take on *bibimbap*. See p.257

* **Tapsa** This cute temple, nestling in between the "horse-ear" peaks of Maisan Provincial Park, is surrounded by gravity-defying towers of hand-stacked rock. See p.259

▲ Craft shop in Jeonju's *hanok* village

Jeolla

If you're after top-notch food, craggy coastlines, vistas of undulating green fields, and islands on which no foreigner has ever set foot, go no further. Jeju Island has its rock formations and palm trees, and Gangwon-do pulls in nature-lovers by the truckload, but it's the **Jeolla provinces** (전라도) where you'll find the essence of Korea at its most potent – a somewhat ironic contention since the Jeollanese have long played the role of the renegade. Here, the national inferiority complex that many foreigners diagnose in the Korean psyche is compounded by a regional one: this is the most put-upon part of a much put-upon country. Although the differences between Jeolla and the rest of the country are being diluted daily, they're still strong enough to help make it the most distinctive and absorbing part of the mainland.

The Korean coast dissolves into thousands of **islands**, the majority of which lie sprinkled like confetti in Jeollanese waters. Some such as Hongdo and Geomundo are popular holiday resorts, while others lie in wave-smashed obscurity, their inhabitants hauling their living from the sea and preserving a lifestyle little changed in decades. The few foreign visitors who make it this far find that the best way to enjoy the area is to pick a ferry at random, and simply go with the flow.

In addition, **Jeollanese cuisine** is the envy of the nation – pride of place on the regional menu goes to *Jeonju bibimbap*, a local take on one of Korea's favourite dishes (see box, p.257). Jeolla's culinary reputation arises from its status as one of Korea's main food-producing areas, with shimmering emerald rice paddies vying for space in and around the national parks. The **Jeollanese people** themselves are also pretty special – fiercely proud of their homeland, with a devotion born from decades of social and economic repression. Speaking a dialect sometimes incomprehensible to other Koreans, they revel in their outsider status, and make a credible claim to be the friendliest people in the country.

Most of the islands trace a protective arc around **Jeonnam** (전남), a province whose name translates as "South Jeolla". On the map, this region bears a strong resemblance to Greece, and the similarities don't end there; the region is littered with ports and a constellation of islands, their surrounding waters bursting with seafood. Low-rise buildings snake up from the shores to the hills, and some towns are seemingly populated entirely with salty old pensioners. **Yeosu** and **Mokpo** are relatively small, unhurried cities exuding a worn, brackish charm, while further inland is the region's capital and largest city, **Gwangju**, a young, trendy metropolis with a reputation for art and political activism.

The same can be said for likeable **Jeonju**, capital of **Jeonbuk** (전북; "North Jeolla") province to the north and one of the most inviting cities in the land; its **hanok district** of traditional buildings is a particular highlight. Green and gorgeous, Jeonbuk is also home to four excellent **national parks**, where most of

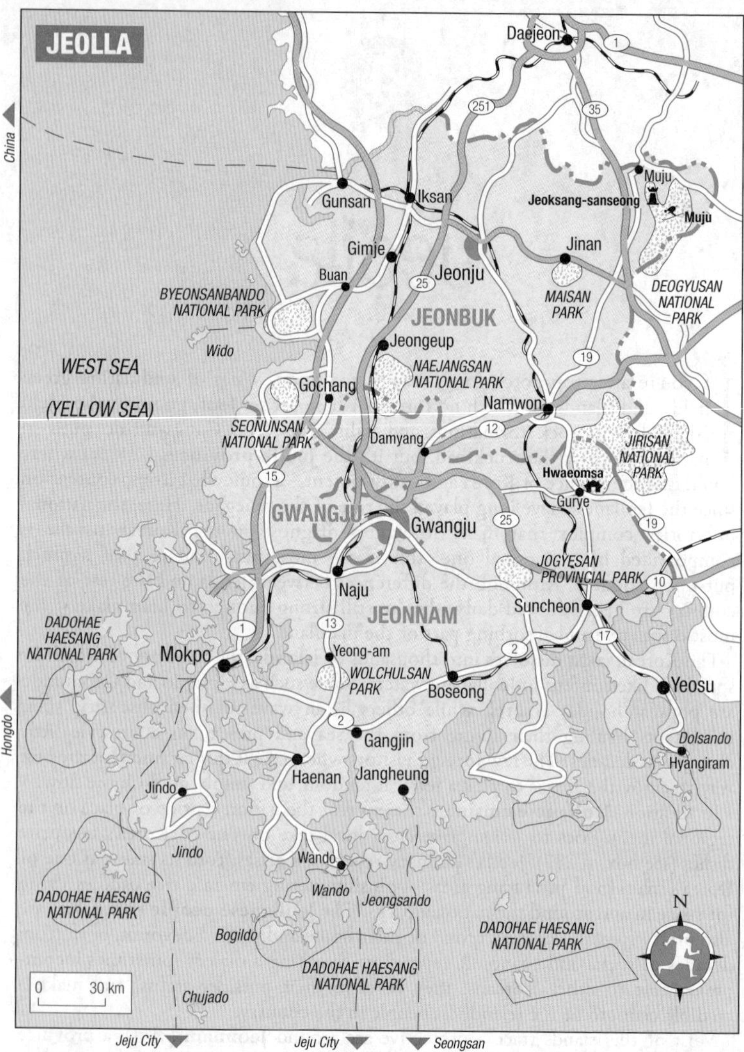

the province's visitors head; in addition, the arresting "horse-ear" mountains of **Maisan Provincial Park** accentuate the appeal of Tapsa, a glorious temple that sits in between its distinctive twin peaks.

Some history

Jeolla's gripe with the rest of the country is largely political. Despite its status as the **birthplace** of the Joseon dynasty that ruled Korea from 1392 until its annexation by the Japanese in 1910, most of the country's leaders since independence in 1945 have hailed from the southeastern Gyeongsang provinces. Seeking to undermine their Jeollanese opposition, the central government deliberately withheld funding for the region, leaving its cities in relative decay while the country as a whole reaped the benefits of the "economic miracle". Political discord reached its nadir in 1980, when the city of Gwangju was the unfortunate location of a **massacre** which left hundreds of civilians dead (see p.245). National democratic reform was gradually fostered in the following years, culminating in the election of Jeolla native and eventual Nobel Peace Prize laureate **Kim Dae-jung**. Kim attempted to claw his home province's living standards up to scratch with a series of big-money projects, notably in the form of highway connections to the rest of the country once so conspicuous by their absence. Despite these advances, with the exception of Gwangju and Jeonju, Jeolla's urban centres are still among the poorest places in Korea.

Yeosu and around

Charming in an offbeat way, **YEOSU** (여수) is by far the most appealing city on Jeonnam's south coast. Ferries once sailed from here to Jeju, but though these have been discontinued there's more than enough here to eat up a whole day of sightseeing. It's beautifully set in a ring of emerald islands, so the wonderful views over the South Sea alone would justify a trip down the narrow peninsula. Though parts of the coast remain rugged and pristine, the area around Yeosu has been heavily industrialized, especially the gigantic factory district to the city's north, and consequently many of Yeosu's few foreign visitors are here on business. However, in 2012 Yeosu plays host to an international **Expo**, an event that could put the city firmly, and deservedly, back on the tourist map.

Despite Yeosu's sprawling size, many of its most interesting sights are just about within walking distance of each other in and around the city centre. These include **Odongdo**, a bamboo-and-pine island popular with families, and a replica of Admiral Yi's famed **turtle ship**. Beyond the city limits are the black-sand beach of **Manseongni**, and **Hyangiram**, a magical hermitage at the end of the Yeosu peninsula.

Arrival and information

The new **airport** lies around 20km to the north – take a bus from the city's main bus terminal – and has flights to and from Seoul and Jeju Island. **Buses** and **trains**

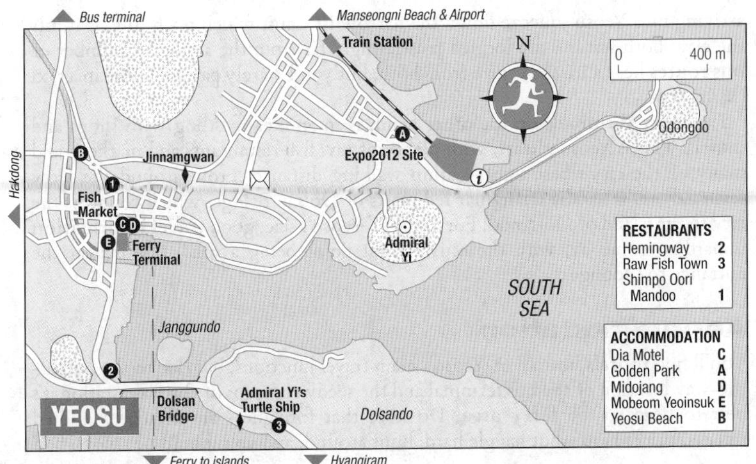

Admiral Yi, conqueror of the seas

"...it seems, in truth, no exaggeration to assert that from first to last he never made a mistake, for his work was so complete under each variety of circumstances as to defy criticism."

Admiral George Alexander Ballard, *The Influence of the Sea on the Political History of Japan*

Were he not born during the Joseon dynasty, a period in which a nervous Korea largely shielded itself from the outside world, it is likely that **Admiral Yi Sun-shin** (이순신; 1545–98) would today be ranked alongside Napoleon and Horatio Nelson as one of the greatest generals of all time. A Korean national hero, you'll see his face on the W100 coin, and **statues** of the great man dot the country's shores. The two most pertinent are at Yeosu, where he was headquartered, and Tongyeong (then known as Chungmu; see p.217), the site of his most famous victory.

Yi Sun-shin was both a beneficiary and a victim of circumstance. A year after his first major posting as Naval Commander of Jeolla in 1591, there began a six-year wave of **Japanese invasions**. Although the Nipponese were setting their sights on an eventual assault on China, Korea had the misfortune to be in the way and loyal to the Chinese emperor, and 150,000 troops laid siege to the country. Admiral Yi achieved a string of well-orchestrated victories, spearheaded by his famed **turtle ships**, vessels topped with iron spikes that were adept at navigating the island-dotted waters with ease.

Despite his triumphs, the admiral fell victim to a Japanese spy and the workings of the Korean political system. A double agent persuaded a high-ranking Korean General that the Japanese would attack in a suspiciously treacherous area; seeing through the plan, Admiral Yi refused the General's orders, and as a result was stripped of his duties and sent to Seoul for torture. His successor, Won Gyeun, was far less successful, and within months had been killed by the Japanese after managing to lose the whole Korean fleet, bar twelve warships. Yi was hastily **reinstated**, and after hunting down the remaining ships managed to repel a Japanese armada ten times more numerous. Peppering the enemy's vessels with cannonballs and flaming arrows, Yi waited for the tide to change and rammed the tightly packed enemy ships into one another. Heroic to the last, Yi was killed by a stray bullet as the Japanese retreated from what was to be the final battle of the war, apparently using his final gasps to insist that his death be kept secret until victory had been assured.

arriving into Yeosu squeeze down the narrow isthmus, which opens out as it hits the city; both stations are located frustratingly far from the action. A number of **bus routes** head into the centre from both, but you'll barely pay any more in a taxi (W4000 or so).

The **ferry terminal**, on the other hand, is in an area bristling with shops and motels. This is Yeosu's heart, with plenty of raw fish restaurants and markets, and many of the city's best sights within walking distance. From around the ferry terminal you'll see the triangular red masts of Dolsan Bridge, which connects the city to the island of Dolsando. For a city of Yeosu's size, good **travel information** is hard to come by, with the only decent point being a small booth near the entrance to Odongdo.

Accommodation

You'll find **motels** near all of Yeosu's main travel junctions, but due to the out-of-the-way location of the bus terminal and the seedy environs of the train station it's best to head to the **ferry area**. Do note that foreigners are regularly quoted inflated prices here – but haggle hard, hunt around, and you should be able to find a room for W30,000 or less. Those aiming even lower on the price scale – or just in need of a good wash after spending time on the Jeonnam coast – should head to the *jjimjilbang* on the shore near Admiral Yi's turtle ship, on the way to Hyangiram, which offers excellent sea views from some of its pool rooms. Lastly, a few new **top-end** options should have opened up by the time Expo 2012 kicks off.

Daia Motel 다이아 모텔 Gyodong ⓣ061/663-3347. Near the ferry terminal, this motel is just down the road from the *Midojang*, but the rooms are slightly plusher, and the prices accordingly higher. ❸

Golden Park Hotel Sujeondong ⓣ061/665-400. Poky *ondol* rooms make this more of a motel than a hotel, though it's a good option on the entrance road to Odongdo, and is also within walking distance of the train station. ❸

Midojang 미도장 Gyodong. This downtown motel, within a few minutes' walk of the ferry terminal, has perfectly acceptable rooms with private facilities. The owners offer slight discounts to foreigners. ❷

Mobeom Yeoinsuk 모범 여인숙 Ferry terminal area ⓣ061/663-4897. Just one of a clutch of *yeoinsuk* in a pleasantly brackish area opposite the ferry terminal, this is a friendly, family-run place with dirt-cheap rooms. ❶

Yeosu Beach Hotel Chungmudong ⓣ061/663-2011. Yeosu's best hotel has cosy rooms with great showers, and is just a short walk from the main shopping area. A popular choice with Korean honeymooners (though less so since the ferries to Jeju stopped), it has a decent on-site restaurant and café, and offers airport pick-up. Ask about discounts off-season – usually around thirty percent. ❻

The City

For many visitors the real joys of Yeosu can be found wandering around the city's many **fish markets**. However, the centre is home to a cache of interesting, unassuming sights. In the very centre of town, and just ten minutes' walk northeast of the ferry terminal, is **Jinnamgwan** (진남관), a pavilion once used as a guesthouse by the Korean navy. The site had previously been a command post of national hero **Admiral Yi** (see box opposite), but a guesthouse was built here in 1599, a year after his death, and replaced by the current structure in 1718. At 54m long and 14m high it's the country's largest single-storey wooden structure. In front of the guesthouse is a stone man – initially one of a group of seven – that was used as a decoy in the 1592–98 Japanese invasions. Just below the pavilion is a small **museum** (Tues–Sun 9am–6pm; free) detailing the area's maritime fisticuffs.

A statue of Admiral Yi stands to the east of the city centre, on a hill overlooking the small island of **Odongdo** (오동도; daily 9am–6pm; W1600). Essentially a botanical garden, it's crisscrossed by a deliciously scented network of pine- and bamboo-lined paths, and has become a popular picnicking destination for local families. A 700m-long causeway connects it to the mainland, and if you don't feel like walking you can hop on the bus – resembling a train – for a small fee. The island's paths snake up to a lighthouse, the view from which gives a far clearer rendition of Yeosu's surroundings than can be had from Jinnamgwan in the city centre. In the summer, kids love to cool off in the fountain by the docks on the northern shore – the water show comes on every twenty minutes or so. A number of **boat tours** operate from Odongdo – operators are unlikely to speak English, so these are best arranged through the tourist information centre outside the main entrance; routes include cruises across the harbour to Dolsan Bridge, and a longer haul to Hyangiram (p.234) and back. At the time of writing, the island was off-limits thanks to construction work on the new **Expo 2012 site**. This is set to feature all sorts of futuristic pavilions, as well as a digital gallery and a "Sky Tower"; see ⓦwww.expo2012.or.kr for more information.

To the south and across Dolsan Bridge is a replica of **Admiral Yi's turtle ship** (daily 8am–6pm; W1200), a small, rounded vessel with a wooden dragon head at the front. Such boats spearheaded the battles against the Japanese in the sixteenth century, and were so-called because they were tough to attack from the top, due to the iron roof covered with spiked metal. Inside the replica is a modern-day regiment of mannequins; the exterior is decidedly more interesting.

Eating and drinking

Yeosu's **restaurants** are surprisingly poor by Jeolla standards. If you're feeling brave, and have a decent command of Korean seafood menus, you will find that the canalside **fish market** north of the ferry terminal has a wealth of choice, as does **Raw Fish Town** – a parade of restaurants near Admiral Yi's turtle ship. Prices at the latter aren't cheap, and establishments cater for groups rather than solo travellers – large spreads are the order of the day (figure on paying W30,000 or more for a meal). Alternatively there's *Hemingway* (헤밍웨이), near Dolsan Bridge, which serves passable steak and pork cutlet dishes with splendid views back over the city. The shopping area has a lot of grimy Korean fast food dens but *Sinpo Woori Mandoo* (신포 우리 만두) stands out, and has an English-language picture menu to boot.

The downtown area is quiet even on weekend evenings, although on a warm night it's hard to beat a bottle of beer or *makkeolli* on the harbour front – take your pick from a number of convenience stores. For a **night out** you're much better off heading to the new area west of the centre called **Hakdong** (학동), though it's over half an hour away by bus, and expensive to reach by taxi. Here, the expat-friendly bars *Elle Lui* and *Lost Shepherd Girl* (also known as *LSG*) continue to get good reviews.

Manseongni

Around 4km north up the coast from Yeosu's train station, you'll find *minbak* and raw fish restaurants aplenty at **Manseongni** (만성리), which is revered as the only **black sand** beach on the Korean mainland – in truth, this volcanic material is actually rather grey in appearance. Mid-April is said to be the time of year when the beach "opens its eyes", and people flock to bury themselves in the allegedly nutritious sand, an experience somewhat akin to being a cigarette butt for the day. Other sights of note lie on the mess of islands south of Yeosu.

Dadohae Haesang National Park

South of the city centre, the mainland soon melts into a host of **islands**, many of which lie under the protective umbrella of **Dadohae Haesang National Park** (다도해 해상 국립 공원). Many can be accessed from Yeosu's ferry terminal, and as with Jeolla's other island archipelagos, these are best explored with no set plan. **Dolsando** (돌산도), connected to the mainland by road, is the most visited and most famed for **Hyangiram**, a hermitage dangling over the crashing seas (see below). Further south are **Geumodo** (금오도), a rural island fringed by rugged cliffs and rock faces, and **Geomundo** (거문도), far from Yeosu – and briefly occupied by Britain during the 1880s, during an ill-planned stab at colonizing Korea's southern coast – but now an increasingly popular holiday destination. From Geomundo you can take a tour boat around the assorted spires of rock that make up **Baekdo** (백도), a protected archipelago containing a number of impressive formations.

Hyangiram

Clinging to the cliffs at the southeastern end of Dolsando is the magical hermitage of **Hyangiram** (향일암; daily pre-dawn to 8pm; W2000), an eastward-facing favourite of sunrise seekers and a popular place to ring in the New Year. Behind Hyangiram is a collection of angular boulders which – according to local monks – resembles an oriental folding screen, and is soaked with camellia blossom in the spring. To get to Hyangiram, take a local bus from Yeosu's city centre – #111 also runs directly from the train station and Odongdo. Although the trip can take around an hour, on a bumpy, winding course, the journey costs just W1000. Outside the hermitage is a small town of **motels** and **restaurants** – *Hwangtobang* (ⓣ061/644-4353; ❷), near the entrance, offers both of these as well as a café, though other motels have better sea views.

Yeosu to Mokpo

The large coastal cities of Yeosu and Mokpo are connected by road, though in the summer it's possible to travel between them by ferry – a beautiful journey that jets passengers past whole teams of islands. Travelling overland, you'll pass **Jogyesan**, a provincial park home to two gorgeous temples; the tea plantation at **Boseong**; and the bald crags of **Wolchulsan National Park**, just outside Mokpo. Also in the Mokpo area are a couple of charming islands – **Jindo**, famed for its indigenous breed of dog, and **Wando**, home to a curious "miracle".

Jogyesan Provincial Park

The small but pretty **JOGYESAN PROVINCIAL PARK** is flanked by two splendid temples, **Seonamsa** and **Songgwangsa**. If you get up early enough, it's possible to see both temples in a single day, taking either the hiking trail that runs between them or one of the buses that heads the long way around the park. The park and its temples are accessible by bus from **SUNCHEON** (순천), an otherwise uninteresting city that's easy to get to by bus, and occasionally train, from elsewhere in the area.

Practicalities

The simplest way to get to the park is on one of the **tour buses** that leave from outside Suncheon's train station every day at 9.50am. As well as Seonamsa temple, tours take in a film set on which historical dramas are regularly shot, and the interesting **Nagan folk village**, set within authentic Jeoson fortress walls and a pleasingly rural place to stay. On weekends, another tour bus leaves at 9.40am, though it goes to Songgwangsa temple, rather than Seonamsa.

To get to the park on **public transport**, take bus #1 from central Suncheon to Seonamsa, or #111 to Songgwangsa. Both buses take an hour or so, and if moving between the two you'll save a lot of time by transferring at Seopyeong-maeul, a small village near Seonamsa, where the bus routes split. Also note that there are occasional buses to Songgwangsa from Gwangju. The paucity of buses to the park means that you may have to overnight in Suncheon; if so, head for the district of **Yeonhyangdong** (연향동), which has plenty of motels and restaurants.

There are also low-key **accommodation** and **restaurant** facilities at both entrances to the park; *minbak* offer the most authentic Korean experience, but for a little more comfort try *Saejogyesan-jang* (새조계산장; ⓣ061/751-9200; ❷) outside the Seonamsa entrance. The restaurants outside Songgwangsa are in traditionally styled buildings; *Suncheon Sikdang* (순천 식당) deserves a mention, if only for the charming way in which its name has been spelled out in Korean. As in many Korean rural areas, *sanchae bibimbap* (산채 비빔밥) is a favoured dish, and is made with local ingredients.

Seonamsa

Seonamsa (서남사), on the park's eastern side, is the closer temple of the two to Suncheon. On the way in from the ticket booth you'll pass Seungsongyo, an old rock bridge; its semicircular lower arch makes a full disc when reflected in the river below: slide down to the water to get the best view. There has been a temple here since 861 – the dawn of the Unified Silla period – but having fallen victim to fire several times, the present buildings are considerably more modern. The temple is apparently too poor to afford a full-scale refurbishment, but provides a pleasant visit as a result, despite the fact that a couple of the once-meditative ponds have been carelessly lined with concrete. Its entrance gate is ageing gracefully, though the dragon heads are a more recent addition – the original smaller, stealthier-looking ones can be found in the small museum inside. Notably, the temple eschews the usual four heavenly guardians at the entrance, relying instead on the surrounding mountains for protection, which look especially imposing on a rainy day. The main hall in the central courtyard is also unconventional, with its blocked central entrance symbolically allowing only Buddhist knowledge through, and not even accessible to high-ranking monks – this is said to represent the egalitarian principles of the temple. The hall was apparently built without nails, and at the back contains a long coffin-like box which holds a large picture of the Buddha that was once unfurled during times of drought, to bring rain to the crops. A smaller version of this picture hangs over the box. Around the complex are a number of small paths, one leading to a pair of majestic stone turtles; the one on the right-hand side is crowned by an almost Moorish clutch of twisting dragons. Another path fires west across the park to Songgwangsa, a four-hour walk, more if you scale Janggunbong (885m), the main peak, on the way.

Songgwangsa

To the west of the park is **Songgwangsa** (송광사), viewed by Koreans as one of the most important temples in the country, and is one of the **"Three Jewels"** of Korean Buddhism – the others are Tongdosa (see p.198) and Haeinsa (p.184). Large, well maintained and often full of devotees, it may disappoint those who've already appreciated the earthier delights of Seonamsa. The temple is accessed on a peculiar bridge-cum-pavilion, beyond which can be found the four guardians that were conspicuously absent at Seonamsa. Within the complex is Seungbojeon, a hall filled with 1250 individually sculpted figurines, the painstaking attention to detail echoed in the paintwork of the main hall; colourful and highly intricate patterns spread like a rash down the pillars, surrounding a trio of Buddha statues representing the past, present and future. Unfortunately, the Hall of National Teachers is closed to the public – perhaps to protect its gold-fringed ceiling.

Boseong

The town of **BOSEONG** (보성) is famed for the **tea plantations** that surround it; visitors flock here during warmer months to take pictures of the thousands of tea trees that line the slopes. They may not be as busy or as verdant as those in Sri Lanka or Laos, for example, but they're still a magnificent sight, particularly when sepia-tinged on early summer evenings. Pluckers comb the well-manicured rows at all times of year, though spring is the main harvest season, and if you're lucky you may be able to see the day's take being processed in the on-site factory. **Green tea** (녹차; *nok-cha*) rode the crest of the "healthy living" wave that swept the country in the early 2000s, and here you can imbibe the leaf in more ways than you could ever have imagined. A couple of on-site restaurants serve up green tea chicken cutlet, green tea *bibimbap* and green tea with seafood on rice, as well as a variety of dishes featuring pork from pigs raised on a green tea diet. There's also a café serving *nok-cha* ice cream and snacks – if you've never tried a *nok-cha* latte, you'll never get a better opportunity (though, admittedly, it's on sale at pretty much every café up to the North Korean border).

Daehan Dawon (대한 다원; daily: summer 5am–8pm; winter 8am–6pm; W1600) is the main plantation; to get here on public transport you'll first need to head to Boseong itself. From there, head coastward on one of the half-hourly buses to Yulpo, and get off at the tea plantation – let the driver know where you're going. Further up the same road are a few less-visited plantations that can be entered for free, one of which stretches down to a cute village by the water's edge.

Wolchulsan National Park

A short bus-ride east of Mokpo, **WOLCHULSAN NATIONAL PARK** (월출산 국립 공원) is the smallest of Korea's national parks and one of its least visited – the lack of historic temples and its difficult access are a blessing in disguise. Set within the achingly gorgeous Jeollanese countryside, Wolchulsan's jumble of mazy rocks rises to more than 800m above sea level, casting jagged shadows over the rice paddies.

Just five buses a day make the fifteen-minute trip to the main entrance at Cheonhwangsaji from the small town of **Yeong-am**; alternatively, it's an affordable taxi ride, or an easy walk. Yeong-am itself is well connected to Mokpo and Yeosu by bus. From here a short but steep hiking trail heads up to **Cheonhwangbong** (809m), the park's main peak; along the way, you'll have to traverse the "Cloud Bridge", a steel structure slung between two peaks – not for vertigo sufferers. Views from here, or the peak itself, are magnificent, and with an early enough start it's possible to make the tough hike to **Dogapsa** (도갑사), an uninteresting temple on the other side of the park, while heeding the "no shamanism" warning signs along the way. There's no public transport to or from the temple, but a forty-minute walk south – all downhill – will bring you to **Gurim** (구림), a small village outside the park, on the main road between Mokpo and Yeong-am. A couple of kilometres south of Gurim is the **Yeongam Pottery Centre** (daily 9am–6pm; free). Due to the properties of the local soil, this whole area was Korea's main ceramics hub throughout the Three Kingdoms period, and local artisans enjoyed trade with similarly minded folk in China and Japan. Sadly, the centre is as dull as the clay itself, though the on-site shop is good for souvenirs; you may get a chance to throw your own pot for a small fee, and there's a decidedly brutalist sculpture outside the main entrance which would look at home in Pyongyang (were it not for the South Korean flag). The downhill walk from Gurim to the centre is much more interesting – the town remains an important base for pottery production, and accordingly many of its houses have eschewed modern-day metals for beautiful, **traditional tiled roofs**. There are few concessions to modern life here.

Wando

Dangling off Korea's southwestern tip is a motley bunch of more than a hundred islands. The hub of this group and the most popular is **WANDO** (완도), owing to its connections to the mainland by bus and Jeju Island by sea. Wando also has plenty of diversions in its own right – a journey away from **Wando-eup** (완도읍), the main town, will give you a glimpse of Jeolla's pleasing rural underbelly. Regular buses run from here to **Gugyedeung** (구계등), a small, rocky beach in the coastal village of Jeongdo-ri, and to **Cheonghaejin** (청해진), a stone park looking over a tiny islet which, despite its unassuming pastoral mix of farms and mud walls, was once important enough to send trade ships to China.

Accommodation

In Wando-eup itself, most of the action is centred around the bus station, but the area around the main ferry terminal makes a quieter and more pleasant place **to stay**; *Naju Yeoinsuk* (나주 여인숙; ❶) has the cheapest rooms around, while *Hilltop Motel* (❷) just behind it is for those who prefer to sleep on a bed rather than *ondol* flooring. Overlooking the sea between the two terminals is the pale yellow *Dubai Motel* (Ⓣ061/553-0688; ❷), whose rooms are excellent value.

Eating

There's a fish market next to the ferry terminal, and plenty of **restaurants** serving both raw and cooked food. For something other than seafood, head a short way along the coast to *Jjajjaru* (짜짜루), a Chinese restaurant offering huge two-person courses that could feed three or four.

Islands around Wando

Heading further afield, you'll be spoilt for choice, with even the tiniest inhabited islands served by ferry from Wando-eup. **Maps** of the islands are available from the ferry terminal, where almost all services depart, with a few leaving from *Je-il Mudu* pier, a short walk to the north.

At the time of writing, **Cheongsando** (청산도) was the island most visited by local tourists, mainly due to the fact that it was the scene of *Spring Waltz*, a popular drama series. Naturally spring is the busiest time of year here – and quite beautiful, with the island's fields bursting with flowers. More beautiful is pine-clad **Bogildo** (보길도), a well-kept secret accessible via a ferry terminal on the west of Wando island – free hourly shuttle-buses make the pretty twenty-minute journey from the bus terminal in Wando-eup. In the centre of tadpole-shaped Bogildo is a lake whose craggy tail, stretching east, has a couple of popular beaches.

Jindo

As the coast curls northwest towards Mokpo, the bewildering array of islands shows no sign of letting up. **JINDO** (진도), one of the most popular, is connected to the Korean mainland by road, but every year in early March the tides retreat to create a 3km-long land-bridge to a speck of land off the island's eastern shore, a phenomenon that Koreans often compare to Moses' parting of the Red Sea – this concept holds considerable appeal in an increasingly Christian country, and "**Moses' Miracle**" persuades Koreans to don wellies and dash across in their tens of thousands. For the best dates to see this ask at any tourist board in the area, or call the national information line on Ⓣ1330 (see p.59). Visible throughout the year is the secluded temple of **Ssanggyesa** (쌍계사), which is best accessed by hourly bus (W1000) or taxi (W7000 from the bus terminal); if you're choosing the latter option, arrange a pick-up time with your driver, or at least hang onto his business card.

Jindu is also famed for the Jindo-gae, a white breed of **dog** with a distinctive curved tail; unique to the island, this species has been officially classified as National Natural Treasure #53. The mutts can be seen in their pens at a **research centre** – fifteen minutes' walk from the bus terminal – which occasionally hosts short and unappealing dog shows, as well as a canine beauty pageant each autumn.

The island is accessible from Mokpo by both **bus** and **ferry**, with free shuttle buses from the terminal to the relevant stretch of coast during the annual parting of the seas.

Mokpo

The Korean peninsula has thousands of **islands** on its fringes, but the seas around the coastal city of **MOKPO** (목포) have by far the most concentrated number. Though many of these are merely bluffs of barnacled rock poking out above the West Sea (also known as the Yellow Sea; see p.137), dozens are accessible by **ferry** from Mokpo; beautiful in an ugly kind of way, this curious city gives the impression that it would happily be an island if it could.

Korea's southwestern train line ends quite visibly in Mokpo city centre. The highway from the centre of the country does likewise with less fuss, but was not completed until fairly recently. For much of the 1970s and 1980s, public funding also ran out before it hit southern Jeolla – poor transport connections to the rest of the country are just one example of the way this area was neglected by the central government. For much of this time, the main opposition party was based in Mokpo, and funding was deliberately cut in an attempt to marginalize the city, which was once among the most populous and powerful in the land. Though the balance is now being addressed with a series of large projects, much of the city is still run-down, and Mokpo is probably the **poorest** urban centre in the country. Some Koreans say that taxi drivers are a good indicator of the wealth of the cities, and here cabbies have a habit of beeping at pedestrians in the hope that they want a lift, occasionally swinging around for a second go. Things are changing, however, especially in the new district of Hadang, which was built on land reclaimed from the sea, but it'll be a while before Mokpo's saline charms are eroded.

Arrival and information

Mokpo is not the easiest Korean city in which to get your bearings. The most logical way to arrive is by **train**, as the main station is right next to a busy shopping area in the centre of the city; **buses** terminate some way to the north, just W5000 by taxi to the centre, to which several city bus routes also head (15min; W900). The most useful of these is #1, which passes both the bus and the train stations on

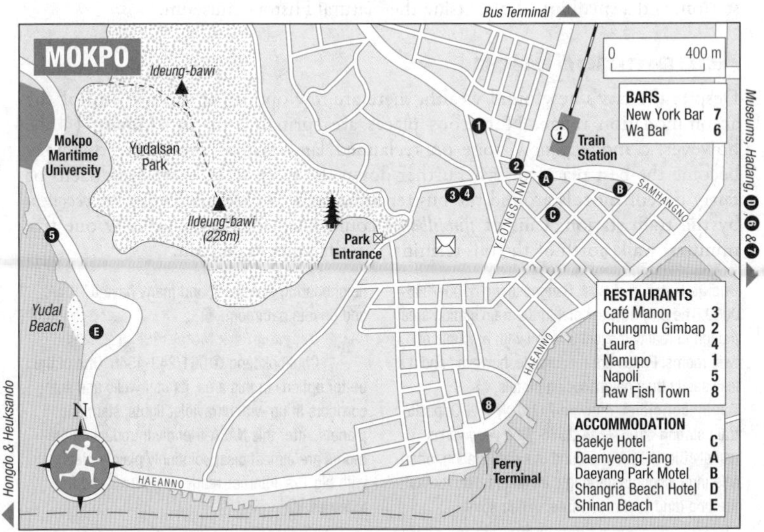

Formula 1 comes to Mokpo

In 2010, the **Formula 1** circus finally came to Korea, with the inaugural Grand Prix taking place at a brand-new track just east of Mokpo. The first hosting of this event was fraught with problems: the track was only given its safety certificate days before the race, spectator enclosures were hastily put together, and there were only three acceptable hotels in the whole of Mokpo. Most fans, and even some VIPs, were forced to stay at **love hotels** – one BBC journalist returned to her room to find that it had been used in her absence (a used contraceptive on the floor providing the evidence).

Race day itself was also memorable for the wrong reasons. **Traffic jams** resulting from poor access to the track meant that thousands of spectators arrived late – and in some cases, not at all. **Rain** didn't help matters, with the newly built track stubbornly refusing to drain; concerns about driver safety led to the race being delayed for over an hour, and at one point the embarrassing possibility of cancelling the event entirely was raised. In the end, the clouds parted, and after several notable drivers had spun off the slippery track Spanish driver **Fernando Alonso** emerged victorious.

Some, inevitably, questioned the wisdom of hosting the Korean Grand Prix in this out-of-the-way corner of the country – the simple truth was that Jeonnam province had made the most generous offer to the F1 powers. Despite these inauspicious beginnings, F1 is likely here to stay, and the lessons learned by local authorities will eventually make Mokpo one of the more comfortable stops on the motor racing calendar.

its way to the huge new **ferry terminal** on the city's southern shore, a lavishly funded structure standing incongruously in an area of apparent decay, and as such one of the most telling symbols of modern Mokpo. There are services to and from many islands in the West Sea (see p.242), as well as Jeju Island (p.301), and occasionally Yeosu (p.232).

Although things should improve as the city grows, **tourist information** has never been one of Mokpo's strong points; there's a near-useless booth in the train station, and a small info-hut outside the Natural History museum.

Accommodation

Despite the city's newfound wealth, there are few options at the **top end** of the accommodation range. Numerous places are springing up in **Hadang** (하당), however, a modern new zone on reclaimed land east of the centre that may become the best place to stay. Further down the price scale, there are dozens of fairly decent **motels** around the bus terminal, and an older collection of *yeogwan* by the train station. Fans of *jjimjilbangs* could head for the brand-new one five minutes' walk north of the bus terminal, on the same main road.

Baekje Hotel 백제 호텔 Sangnakdong ⓣ061/245-0080. The only official hotel in the train station area, though in reality it's just a motel with a couple of twin rooms. Prices are reasonable, however, and it's less seedy than neighbouring motels. ❹

Daemyeongjang Yeogwan 대명장 여관 Opposite train station ⓣ061/244-2576. This *yeogwan* is usually the cheapest around the train station, often offering discounts for single travellers. The rooms are fine (and cockroach-free, unlike some neighbouring *yeogwan*), and many have a TV, a/c and private bathroom. ❶

Daeyang Park Motel 대양 파크 모텔 Chukbokdong ⓣ061/243-4540. One of the better options in this area, its stairwells and some corridors lit up with ultraviolet lights, stars and planets. After this NASA-friendly introduction the rooms are almost disappointingly plain – clean, with big TVs, internet-ready computers and free toiletries. ❸

Shangria Beach Hotel Hadang ⓣ061/285-0100. Large hotel by the water in the new Hadang district, a taxi ride east of central Mokpo. Rooms are large and well kitted out, and though the prices can be a little high (off-season discounts notwithstanding) it's Mokpo's only decent option in this price range. ❼

Shinan Beach Hotel Seongsandong ⓣ061/243-3399. Cut off from the city centre by the mountains and with views of the sea, this was for decades Mokpo's only tourist hotel. Nowadays its stylings feel more than a little dated, and continued neglect may well kill it off before long. ❼

Yudalsan and around

Mokpo is a city of dubious charms that the short-term visitor may be unable to appreciate. Its main draw lies outside the city with the mind-boggling number of **islands** accessible by ferry (see p.242). Many of these are visible from the peaks of **Yudalsan** (유달산; daily 8am–6pm; W700), a small hill-park within walking distance of the city centre and train station. It's a popular place, with troupes of hikers stomping their way up a maze of trails, past manicured gardens and a sculpture park, towards **Ildeung-bawi**, the park's main peak. After the slog to the top – a twenty-minute climb of 228m – you'll be rewarded with a **spectacular view**: a sea filled to the horizon with a swarm of emerald islands, some large enough to be inhabited, others just specks of rock. Similar views can be had from Yudalsan's second-highest peak, **Ideung-bawi**, just along the ridge past a large, precariously balanced boulder.

Between the peaks, a trail runs west to a small **beach**. The water is not suitable for swimming, but hour-long **ferry cruises** run regularly to nearby islands from outside the nearby *Shinan Beach Hotel*. These tours offer delightful views of the islands that surround Mokpo, but bear in mind that the regular ferry routes from the city's main terminal are cheaper, longer, and offer a greater opportunity to observe island life.

The museum district

A handful of museums lie to the east of the centre, accessible on bus #111, but better approached by taxi. The most popular of this modern collective is the **Maritime Museum** (문화예술회관; Tues–Fri 9am–6pm, Sat & Sun 9am–7pm; W600), whose prime exhibits are the remains of a ship sunk near Wando in the eleventh century – the oldest such find in the country. Preserved from looting by its sunken location, celadon bowls and other relics scavenged from the vessel are on display, alongside a mock-up of how the ship may have once looked. Across the road is the large, breezy and modern **Pottery Museum** (남농기념관; same times; free), which contains almost nothing of interest. Along the road, and marginally more compelling, is the **Natural History Museum** (자연사 박물관; same times; W3000), home to an artily arranged butterfly exhibit, as well as a collection of dinosaur skeletons that is sure to perk up any sleepy youngster. Accessible on the same ticket, the building next door contains rather more highbrow sights, including calligraphy and paintings from **Sochi**, a famed nineteenth-century artist from the local area. Sochi was a protégé of Chusa, one of the country's most revered calligraphers (see p.299). More works from this talented duo and their contemporaries are on display, as are modern works by Oh Sung-oo, a Korean impressionist who painted modern takes of oriental clichés.

Eating, drinking and nightlife

You can't walk for five minutes in downtown Mokpo without passing a dozen **restaurants** serving cheap, delicious food. The area west of the train station is packed with all kinds of options, from cheap-as-chips snack bars to swanky *galbi* dens – note, though that the **museum area** has next to no places to eat. For a **caffeine** fix or a green tea latte, there are stacks of cafés both in Hadang and the train station area; the best in the latter is *Café Manon* on the access road to Yudalsan, a friendly escape filled with old turntables, gramophones and the like.

Hadang is the best place to head for a **night out**. On one particularly alcohol-fuelled street, *Wa Bar* and the *New York Bar* fight it out for the expat dollar, with the latter putting on a dance party every last Friday of the month. Alternatively, ask at one of the many **convenience stores** for a bottle of Mokpo *makkeolli*, a delicious local version of the drink.

Restaurants

Unless otherwise stated, the establishments listed below are in and around Mokpo's main shopping quarter, which lies between Yudalsan and the train station.

Chungmu Gimbap 충무 김밥 Downtown. This small chain serves up cheap but passable versions of the dish it's named after – spicy octopus with *gimchi* and laver-rolled rice, a speciality of Tongyeong in Gyeongsang province – plus the regular chain dishes.

Laura Cheuk-hudong. Just down the road from *Café Manon* (see above), this well-designed restaurant serves Korean versions of Western dishes at reasonable prices, including delicious smoked chicken.

Namupo 나무포 Downtown. Head here for the juiciest *galbi* in town, right in the city centre to boot. There's a variety of meat styles on the illustrated, English-language menu, though the dish of choice is the aromatic *Namupo galbi*.

Napoli Jukgyudong. Steaks and seafood fried rice are among the dishes on offer at this two-storey restaurant on the waterfront near Yudal Beach, on the western side of Yudalsan. Sadly, the pretty sea views aren't always matched by the dishes.

Raw Fish Town The main road opposite the ferry terminal is alive with raw fish outlets. English-language menus are nonexistent, but a simple solution is at hand – the fish are still alive outside each restaurant in glass tanks, so just point at what you want and agree a price. Alternatively, go for a mixed sashimi platter (모듬회; modeum-hoe), which will work out at about W20,000 per head.

West Sea islands

Looking west from Mokpo's Yudalsan peaks, you'll find a sea filled to the horizon with an assortment of **islands** – there are up to three thousand off Jeolla, and though many of these are merely bumps of rock that yo-yo in and out of the surf with the tide, hundreds are large enough to support fishing communities. The quantity is so vast, indeed, that it's easier to trailblaze here than in some less-developed Asian countries – many of the islands' inhabitants have never seen a foreigner, and it's hard to find a more quintessentially Korean experience.

Much of the area is under the umbrella of **Dadohae Haesang National Park**, which stretches offshore from Mokpo to Yeosu. The two most popular islands in the park are **Hongdo**, which rises steeply from the West Sea, and neighbouring **Heuksando**, a miniature archipelago of more than a hundred islets of rock. Further down the coast are **Jindo**, which owes its popularity to the local tide's annual parting of the sea, and **Wando**, connected to the mainland by road, but surrounded by an island constellation of its own.

All of the following islands are accessible from the **ferry terminal** in central Mokpo (see p.240); service at the tourist information office here is hit-and-miss, but at the very least you'll be able to pick up a map of the islands (the one named "Shinan Travel" was best at the time of writing) and an up-to-date ferry schedule.

Around Mokpo

The key to enjoying the islands around Mokpo is to kick back like the locals and do your own thing – just pick up a map, select an island at random, and make your way there; if you stop somewhere nice along the way, stay there instead. The **islanders** are among the friendliest people in Korea – some travellers have found themselves stuck on an island with no restaurants or accommodation, only to be taken in by a local family. These islands are not cut out for tourism and possess very few facilities, particularly in terms of banking – so be sure to take along enough **money** for your stay. It's also a good idea to bring a **bike** and/or **hiking boots**, as the natural surroundings mean that you're bound to be spending a lot of time outdoors.

One of the most pleasing ferry circuits connects come of Mokpo's closest island neighbours – a round-trip will take around two hours, and there are several ferries per day. The only island that sees any tourists whatsoever is **Oedaldo** (외달도), which has a decent range of accommodation and restaurants. Only a few kilometres from the mainland, though hidden by other islands, little **Dallido** (달리도; home to just 104 families) offers some of the best walking opportunities. Beyond these lie a pack of much **larger islands**, accessible on several ferry routes from Mokpo (Korean-only maps are available at the ferry terminal). Most of these will have beaches and hills to climb.

Hongdo and Heuksando

Lying on their own, well clear of the emerald constellations that surround Mokpo, and more than 100km west of the mainland, are this oddly matched pair of islands. Furthest-flung is **Hongdo** (홍도), whose slightly peculiar rock colouration gave rise to its name, which means "Red Island". Those who make it this far are less likely to be interested in its pigment than its spectacular shape. Spanning around 6km from north to south, the island rises sheer from the waters of the West Sea to almost 380m above sea level, with valleys slicing through the deep expanses of dense forest as though pared by a gigantic knife. It may seem like a hikers' paradise, but much of the island is protected, which means that most views of the rock formations will have to be from a boat. **Tours** (2hr 30min; W15,000) run from the tiny village where the ferry docks, one of only two on an island whose population barely exceeds five hundred; most trips go around the rocky spires of **Goyerido** (고예리도), a beautiful formation poking out of the sea just north of Hongdo.

In contrast to Hongdo's chunk of steep terrain, **Heuksando** (흑산도) is a jagged collection of isles that's fully open for hiking. There are some great trails, with the most westerly ones highly recommended at sunset, when Hongdo is thrown into silhouette on the West Sea; most people head to the 227m-high peak of Sangnabong. Ferries usually dock at Yeri, Heuksando's main village, from where **boat tours** (2hr 30min; W15,000) of the dramatic coast are available, though some choose to hire a taxi (W60,000 for around 3hr) to see the island's interior.

Practicalities

Both islands are accessed by **ferry** from the terminal in Mokpo, almost always on the same services; four daily services head to Heuksando (1hr 45min; W31,300), with two of these continuing on to Hongdo (2hr 15min; W38,300). Extra services are laid on in the height of summer, when thousands of tourists descend on the islands, and ferries are packed to the gills: it's advisable to book tickets in advance through a tourist information office (even those in Seoul will be able to help). Both islands have collections of *yeogwan* (❸), and if you're coming during the summer holidays, you are advised to book your accommodation prior to arrival through the tourist offices in Mokpo or Gwangju.

Gwangju and around

The gleaming, busy face of "new Jeolla", **GWANGJU** (광주) is the region's most populous city by far. Once a centre of political activism, and arguably remaining so today, it's still associated, for most Koreans, with the brutal **massacre** that took place here in 1980. The event devastated the city but highlighted the faults of the then-government, thereby ushering in a more democratic era. Other than a **cemetery** for those who perished in the struggle, on the city outskirts, there's little of note to see in Gwangju itself, except perhaps the shop-and-dine area in its centre. Largely pedestrianized, this is one of the busiest and best such zones in the country – not only the best place in which to sample Jeollanese cuisine but also a great spot to observe why Gwangjuites are deemed to be among the most fashionable folk on the peninsula. Also in this area is "**Art Street**", a warren of studios and the figurehead of Gwangju's dynamic **art scene**. Although most funding is now thrown at contemporary projects, the city's rich artistic legacy stems in part from the work of **Uijae**, one of the country's most famed twentieth-century painters and a worthy poet to boot. A museum dedicated to the great man sits on his former patch – a building and tea plantation on the slopes of **Mudeungsan Park**, which forms a natural eastern border to the city.

Arrival

Despite the substantial funds thrown at it by the city government, Gwangju's public transport network is poor for a Korean city. A brand-new **subway** line

The Gwangju massacre

"At 10.30 in the morning about a thousand Special Forces troops were brought in. They repeated the same actions as the day before, beating, stabbing and mutilating unarmed civilians, including children, young girls and aged grandmothers... Several sources tell of soldiers stabbing or cutting off the breasts of naked girls; one murdered student was found disembowelled, another with an X carved in his back... And so it continues, horror piled upon horror."

Simon Winchester, *Korea*

Away from the bustle of Gwangju, in what may at first appear to be a field of contorted tea trees, lie those who took part in a 1980 **uprising** against the government, an event which resulted in a brutal **massacre** of civilians. The number that died is still not known for sure, and was exaggerated by both parties involved at the time; the official line says just over two hundred, but some estimates put it at over two thousand. Comparisons with the **Tiananmen** massacre in China are inevitable, an event better known to the Western world despite what some historians argue may have been a similar death toll. While Beijing keeps a tight lid on its nasty secret, Koreans flock to Gwangju each May to pay tribute to those who died.

In an intricate web of corruption, apparent Communist plots and a presidential assassination, trouble had been brewing for some time before **General Chun Doo-hwan** staged a **military coup** in December 1979. Chun had been part of a team given the responsibility of investigating the assassination of President Kim Jae-kyu, but used the event as a springboard towards his own leadership of the country. On May 17, 1980, he declared martial law in order to quash **student protests** against his rule. Similar revolts had seen the back of a few previous Korean leaders (notably Syngman Rhee, the country's first president); fearing the same fate, Chun authorized a ruthless show of force that left many dead. Reprisal demonstrations started up across the city; the MBC television station was burnt down, with protestors aggrieved at being portrayed as Communist hooligans by the state-run operator. Hundreds of thousands of civilians grouped together, mimicking the tactics of previous protests on Jeju Island by attacking and seizing weapons from police stations. With transport connections to the city blocked, the government were able to retreat and pool their resources for the inevitable crackdown. This came on May 27, when troops attacked by land and air, retaking the city in less than two hours. After having the protest leaders executed, General Chun resigned from the Army in August, stepping shortly afterwards into presidential office. His leadership, though further tainted by continued erosions of civil rights, oversaw an economic boom; an export-hungry world remained relatively quiet on the matter.

Also sentenced to death, though eventually spared, was **Kim Dae-jung**. An opposition leader and fierce critic of the goings-on, he was charged with inciting the revolt, and spent much of the decade under house arrest. Chun, after seeing out his term in 1987, passed the country's leadership to his partner-in-crime during the massacre, Roh Tae-woo. Demonstrations soon whipped up once more, though in an unexpectedly conciliatory response, Roh chose to release many political prisoners, including Kim Dae-jung. The murky world of Korean politics gradually became more transparent, culminating in charges of corruption and treason being levelled at Chun and Roh. Both were pardoned in 1997 by Kim Dae-jung, about to be elected president himself, in what was generally regarded as a gesture intended to draw a line under the troubles.

runs through the centre from east to west, but for some reason doesn't connect with the **train** station or **bus** terminal (both of which are fairly central); this is particularly odd considering that the latter, a mall-style structure that serves both express and intercity buses, is also new. Getting from the **bus terminal** to other points in the city is tough – the area is full of traffic, and the bus stops on the busy main road outside are blocked by cars and taxis waiting for passengers. Those who wish to take a **local bus** often have to run out into the traffic – that's if they manage to see their bus coming. Add to that a confusing series of bus numbers and you have a recipe for chaos. Alighting from the **train** station is far simpler and more convenient.

The **airport**, just over 6km west of the centre, is served by a couple of short-haul international services; this actually *is* a stop on the subway line, while a taxi to the centre should cost less than W10,000.

Orientation and information

Gwangju is far too unwieldy to be covered on foot so you'll have to rely on the subway (W900 per ride), buses (W1000) or taxis to get around. The majority of the sights are on the city's perimeter, and all are easily accessible on public transport. Most tourists base themselves around **Geumnamno** (금남로), the major downtown artery, near the May 18th Democratic Plaza in Gwangju's main shopping district.

On the same road is a **tourist information centre** (daily 9am–6pm; ⓣ062/226-1050), which sits almost directly opposite the homely **Gwangju International Center**, an excellent source of local information, with a selection of secondhand English language books and films. The centre puts on Korean-language classes for expats, and also stocks the excellent monthly *Gwangju News* – one of the best expat **magazines** in the country, it's very useful for visitors, too.

Accommodation

Gwangju's **accommodation** is relatively poor by the standards of major Korean cities, and hasn't kept pace with the city's other advances. There are a couple of decent options at the higher end of the price range, and motels can be found in groups around the train and bus stations, as well as the city centre. The bus station area isn't a great option, as not only is it a convoluted walk from the station to the motels, but the establishments are even more brazenly "love"-based than elsewhere in the country – those around Geumnamno are far more appealing. There's an excellent *jjimjilbang* (W8000 for a night) atop the Migliore department store.

Geumsujang Hotel 금수장 Mudeungno ⓣ062/525-2111. Quite possibly Korea's cheapest "proper" tourist hotel, a ten-minute walk east of the train station. Rooms are surprisingly large and well appointed for the price, and the on-site restaurant serves gigantic traditional banquets (see p.248). ④

Kwang Ju Grand Hotel Bullodong ⓣ062/224-6111. Though the rooms are large, they're dated, and the whole hotel is in dire need of a refit. Facilities include a sauna, nightclub and restaurant, but rates are poor value, even with the free trip back to the 1970s thrown in. ⑤

Hotel Palace Hwanggeumdong ⓣ062/222-2525. Smallish, immaculate rooms in the centre of the city, and much better value than the more expensive hotels in the area. There's a funky café on the ground floor, as well as free internet and sauna facilities, but it's slightly hard to find in the middle of a bank of clubs and restaurants. ④

Ramada Plaza Bullodong ⓣ062/2717-7000, ⓦwww.ramadagwangju.com. Gwangju's top hotel by far, located in the Hadang "New Town" area, and walkable from Sangmu subway station. The whole complex is superbly designed – if the swish lobby doesn't blow you away, then check out the stunning suites (particularly the "Spa Corner"). In addition, prices are very fair – the cheapest rooms often dip below W180,000. ⑦

Sharp Motel Bullodong ⓣ062/228-2929. Clean if slightly musty rooms, and half the price of the official tourist hotels in the area. There are free videos to rent, a surprisingly large proportion of which are not sexual in nature. ②

On the art trail in Gwangju

Outside Seoul, Gwangju is by far Korea's most artistically inclined city. Much of this can be ascribed to the fact that it's the largest city in Jeolla, which during the 1970s and 1980s was a hotbed of political activism (see p.230); the gruesome massacre of 1980 (see box, p.245) saw raw emotion splashed onto many a piece of canvas. Regional tensions have long since subsided, meaning that present-day Jeollanese have a little less to say, but it's still worth taking a stroll through some of the city's many galleries.

The best place to go hunting is a narrow road in the city centre, affectionately known as **Art Street**. This is a funky collection of shops and studios selling art materials and works by local artists. There are similar streets in other Korean cities, but this one is larger, much more accessible and forms an active part of the city's life. Traditional art styles remain dominant but they're complemented – and sometimes sent up – by a more contemporary set. A few arty cafés and restaurants can be found in or just off the road, though as this area is also Gwangju's centre of after-school education, the discussions you'll hear are more likely to be about pop than Picasso. Near the eastern end of Art Street is the contemporary **Kunsthalle Gwangju** gallery (Ⓦwww.kunsthalle-gwangju.com), a regional offshoot of the facility in Seoul (see p.117), and similarly fashioned entirely from shipping containers. It's a temporary facility, filling the vacuum left by delays to the still-under-construction **Asian Culture Complex**, set for completion on an adjoining plot in 2014.

More traditional in nature is the work of Ho Baeknyon (1891–1977). Better known by his pen name **Uijae**, he was an important painter-poet-calligrapher, and in uniting those fine arts was likely one of the main catalysts behind Gwangju's dynamic art scene. His old house and tea plantation, as well as a **museum** (Tues–Sun 10am–5pm; W1000) dedicated to his work, stand on the slopes of **Mudeungsan** (무등산), a pleasant park bordering Gwangju on its eastern side, and easily accessible by bus from the city centre (#49 from the train station, #09 from the bus station). The most interesting piece on show is a ten-picture **folding screen**, whose images are said to represent the world's rainbow of personal characteristics: are you bamboo-, blossom- or orchid-like in temperament?

Lastly, those visiting in the autumn of even-numbered years will be able to attend the **Gwangju Biennale** (Ⓦgb.or.kr), the biggest and most important art festival in the land. Most of the action takes place at a huge dedicated hall north of the train station, and there's so much to see that even a full day is unlikely to be enough.

The museum district

Apart from its art spaces, Gwangju's only genuine tourist sights are the **museums** lying on the northern fringe of the city, around the Honam Expressway. The **National Museum** (광주 박물관; Tues–Fri 9am–6pm, Sat & Sun to 7pm; free) is set in a typically oversized, quasi-traditional building, a grubby place despite its relative youth. The most interesting rooms are those devoted to **Yuan-dynasty ceramics** scavenged from a Chinese trading boat, sunk off the Jeolla coast in the fourteenth century on its way to Japan, which lay undiscovered until 1975. Yuan-dynasty artisans were renowned across East Asia for their celadon pottery, and many of the pieces on display can be traced to **Jingdezhen**, China's most famous centre of ceramic production. Despite their centuries underwater, most pieces are in pretty good condition, a testament to the procedures of the time. Another section is devoted to items scavenged from a Korean wreck found nearby in 1983, though these pieces lack the gentle balance of their Middle Kingdom counterparts. Through a tunnel under the expressway is the less interesting **Gwangju Folk Museum** (same hours; W1000), a diorama-centric look at Jeollanese costumes and customs from as far back as the Three Kingdoms period. You can reach the museums on city buses #16, #19 and #26.

Eating and drinking

The Jeollanese pride themselves on their **food**, and as in other cities in the region, Gwangju cuisine is excellent. The areas around the bus terminal and train stations can be largely avoided; other than the *Geumsujang*, all the establishments listed below are **downtown**, near the May 18th Democratic Plaza. This area is also home to *Speakeasy*, the city's main expat bar; this is an excellent place to meet people and hosts regular live music.

Cheongwon Momil 청원 모밀 Bullodong. Opposite the Migliore department store, this little restaurant has been serving cheap noodles since 1960, making it almost Jurassic in Korean terms. The spicy buckwheat noodles (*bibim momil*) are particularly good (W3500).

Deung Chon 등촌 Chungjangno. In a side street behind the downtown tourist information centre, this is by far the most popular restaurant with Gwangju's expats, in no small part thanks to the presence of English-speaking staff. *Shabu-shabu* is the dish of choice (W10,000 per person), though noodles and fried rice are available too.

Geumsujang 금수장 Mudeungno. Gigantic banquet meals known as *hanjeongsik* are a Gwangju speciality, but places serving these traditional feasts tend to be hard to get to. This is the exception, located in the *Geumsujang Hotel* (see p.246); W100,000 will buy a set meal for two that could easily feed three.

Minsokchon 민속촌 Honamdong. Twinned with *Moojinjoo* across the road, this meat restaurant serves delicious *galbi* in a pleasant atmosphere; perhaps most distinctive is the *ddeok-galbi* (떡갈비), a famous Gwangju dish made from minced meat that's something like a barbecued burger.

Moojinjoo 무진주 Bullodong. Set on several stylish levels, this adventurous restaurant is the most aesthetically pleasing in the city. Unfortunately the menu is full of strange dishes and in Korean only, so take a local with you to get the most out of it; recommended dishes are *modeum bosam*, pork slices with a variety of succulent vegetable side dishes, or *yeongyang dolsotbap*, an energy-giving rice dish.

Red Mango Chungjangno. This chain serving low-fat iced yoghurt rode the crest of the healthy living wave that swept across the country in recent times. Its star is fading a little now but with a variety of toppings to choose from you're still in for a tasty snack.

Listings

Books The large bookshop in the bus terminal has a wide selection of English-language books and magazines, as well as an array of English-teaching materials.

Cinema The Migliore department store has a cinema with several screens.

Hospital Chonnam University hospital lies between the KT building and the river (☎062/220-6902). For English-language medical information, dial ☎119 from any public phone.

Post office There's a post office in every district (usually Mon–Fri 9am–5pm). Those in the bus terminal and just west of the May 18th Democratic Plaza are most convenient for visitors.

Shopping Gwangju is awash with department stores, including Migliore in the downtown area, and Shinsaegae near the bus terminal. The funky shops of Clothes Street can also be found near Migliore.

Spectator sports Gwangju Sangmu is the only military football team in Korea's top division, and plays at the World Cup Stadium to the south of the city. Players are sourced from men taking their two-year compulsory military service.

May 18th National Cemetery

One of Gwangju's most important sights, the **May 18th National Cemetery** (국립 5.18 묘지; daily 8am–5pm; free), lies in rolling countryside around forty minutes north of the city centre by bus. This is the resting place of those killed in the **1980 massacre** (see p.245); the thousands of participants who survived also have the right to be buried here. Though Gwangju has many sights related to this

Hiking in Korea

If you're wondering what keeps Koreans in such great shape, here's your answer – hiking. The activity is so popular that it thoroughly eclipses *taekwondo*, the national sport, and there are more than enough national parks to satisfy everyone from keen amateurs to experienced climbers. The parks tend to be busy year-round with a steady trail of locals enjoying a day out, but there are also areas of seclusion where you'll be able to hike in delightful tranquillity.

Hiking in Jeju ▲

Ulleungdo ▼

Jeju's coastal path ▼

Where to go

Wherever you are in the country, you're always within walking distance of a hiking trail. There are no fewer than **seventeen national parks** on the mainland – their names all end with the suffix "-san", which means mountain or mountains – and these are supplemented by an even greater number of lesser parks, mountains and hills. For a list of Korea's most popular hikes, see the box overleaf. Alternatively, you can escape the hustle and bustle of the mainland entirely and head to one of the four thousand or so islands surrounding the coast. **Jeju** is the largest – and deservedly most popular, with its own pretty offshore island, **Udo** – while gorgeous little **Ulleungdo** sits alone in the East Sea, and literally hundreds more can be accessed by ferry from the main hubs of Mokpo, Incheon and Tongyeong. Many are tiny specks of land where fishing is the only way of life, and time passes at a snail's pace; tantalizingly, some have never played host to a foreign visitor.

What to do

Hiking in Korea is extremely **easy**. English-language **maps** are available at all park offices, trails are well marked with dual-language signs, and each national park has a cluster of accommodation and restaurants outside its main entrance. Some are mini-towns bursting with neon signs and karaoke rooms, which dilutes the experience somewhat, but a Korean hike is not complete unless it's finished off with a good **meal**: *pajeon* is the most popular post-hike dish, a kind of savoury pancake made with mountain vegetables, while a creamy rice-wine named *dongdongju* is the drink of choice. Deceptively mild, it can pack a punch, especially the next morning.

What to see

It must be said that none of Korea's parks is huge, and there's very little fauna to see; since all parks are likely to be teeming with budding hikers, you're unlikely to get lost, either. However, they're usually awash with natural spectacles such as gorgeous peaks and **waterfalls**, and sprinkled with functioning **temples** and hermitages – some spectacular feasts of intricate architecture and colourful paintwork, others remote hideaways where the monks contemplate existence in near solitude. The beauty of hiking in Korea is not knowing what you will see on the way; the occasional holy grotto, **fortress** wall or hillside-carved Buddha make it easy to weave a spot of sightseeing into a good walk.

▲ Seoraksan National Park

▼ Wolchulsan National Park

When to visit

Despite the wealth of choice available, many of Korea's trails contrive to be packed to the gills, especially during **holidays** and warm **weekends**, when the parks are full with locals enjoying a day out. Many families bring along sizeable picnics to enjoy on their way to the peaks, and lone travellers may be invited to join in – Koreans hate to see people on their own. Special mention must be made of the fascinating **ajumma** brigade: Korean grandmothers are little short of indestructible, and these elderly women rock up to mountain ranges in huge, bubble-permed packs of up to fifty. Wearing fishing jackets identical but for the choice of red or blue, they laugh, shout and sing all the way up, then all the way down again, and put many a Westerner to shame with their strength and energy. You know when you've been *ajumma*-ed.

Udo ▲

Ulsanbawi, Seoraksan National Park ▼

Popular hikes

▶▶ **Day-trips from the city** With so much of the country covered by mountains, it's possible to see any Korean city from the vantage point of its surrounding peaks. Even Seoul has a national park. **Bukhansan** (see p.102) is the world's most visited, though occasionally offers surprising serenity.

▶▶ **Multi-day hikes** Only a couple of parks have shelters where you can stay the night. **Jirisan** (see p.221) is the largest in the country, and features a three-day, 26km-long spine route, and a small bear population. **Seoraksan** (see p.155) is not quite as expansive, but is considered the most beautiful in the country, with great clumps of rock peeking out from the pines like giant skulls; waking up on its misty peaks provides a top-of-the-world feeling.

▶▶ **Scaling peaks** South Korea's highest peak is on Jeju Island. The 1950m-high extinct volcanic cone of **Hallasan** (see p.320) dominates the island, but is surprisingly easy to climb, as long as Jeju's fickle weather agrees. The highest mountain on the whole peninsula is **Paekdusan** (2744m) on the Chinese-North Korean border (see p.353); its sumptuously blue crater lake, ringed by jagged peaks, is a font of myth and legend.

▶▶ **Getting away from it all** Hiking is so popular in Korea that some trails resemble supermarket queues, but there are a few splendid ways to get away from it all. **Taebaeksan** (p.167) has long been a Shamanist place of worship, while the small park of **Wolchulsan** (p.237) sees few visitors dash across the vertigo-inducing bridge that connects two of its peaks. Though popular on account of its enormous bronze Buddha, **Songnisan** (see p.286) has a tiny, secluded guesthouse; when the sun goes down, you'll be alone with nature, a trickling stream and a bowl of creamy *dongdongju*.

event, some even forming part of a rather macabre tour detailed in the official tourist literature, this is the least morbid and most factual. An overlarge oval of walkways and sculpture, the **visitor centre** is more of a testament to concrete than to the lives of the demonstrators, though it's worth a visit for the **photograph exhibition hall** – there are some astonishing pictures on display, and the tension of the time is painfully palpable. Be warned that many are rather graphic, though the worst have mercifully been cordoned off into a section of their own. The cemetery itself is a badly signed five-minute walk away. To get here by **bus**, at the time of writing it was best to take #518 – but check before setting out.

Western Jeonbuk: the national parks

You're spoilt for choice for **national parks** in the western half of **Jeonbuk province** – there are three, and each offers plenty of outdoor activities. **Naejangsan** lies closest to Jeonju, and is famed for its riot of colour in the autumn. **Seonunsan**, near the Jeonnam border, is Korea's big draw for rock-climbers, while on the coast is **Byeonsanbando**, a rural peninsula park that's also the scene of a controversial land reclamation project. Note that these parks are all to the south of the province; there's also **Deogyusan** east of Jeonju (see p.259).

Naejangsan National Park

NAEJANGSAN NATIONAL PARK (내장산 국립 공원) is one of Korea's most popular parks, with its ring of peaks flaring up like a gas ring in the autumn. Maple trees are the stars of the show in this annual incandescence, with squads of elm, ash and hornbeam adding their hues to the mix. The many trails and peaks across the park keep hikers happy year-round, though most visitors head to the amphitheatre-shaped mountain circle in the northeast, where the nearby village has plenty of accommodation and places to eat. The area's topography allows for two **hiking routes**: a short temple loop around the interior, and a far more punishing circuit around the almost circular ridge.

The **temple route** takes in three sights, and should take less than two hours. A pleasant, maple-lined path takes you from the entrance to **Naejangsa**, an unremarkable but pretty temple whose complex is dotted with informative English-language signs. Heading further up the valley you'll come to isolated **Wonjeogam**, a tiny hermitage home to a couple of monks and an abnormally large golden statue, before the trail swings back along the mountain face towards **Baengnyeonam**, another hermitage that marks the final sight on this route. Built in 632, the structure has been destroyed and rebuilt several times since then, and enjoys the most arresting setting of the three – bamboo stalks in a grove behind the main building point up towards the sheer rock crags of Naejangsan's main ridge, while in the other direction is the awesome view of a distant pavilion nestling beneath the peaks.

There are eight main peaks on the **ridge route**, and it's possible to scale them all on a calf-burning 13.8km day hike, but most visitors content themselves with a shorter trip up and down – wherever you are on this circular route, you won't be far from a path heading back towards Naejangsa in the centre, and it's even possible to take a **cable car** up to a restaurant (usually pumping with loud *ajumma* music) within a short hike of the southern ridge.

Practicalities

The park lies almost directly between Gwangju and Jeonju, and there are occasional direct **buses** from both cities. Otherwise you'll have to transfer in

Jeongeup (정읍), a small town well serviced by bus and train, and around thirty minutes from Naejangsan by bus. Once you've alighted at Naejangsan's main bus stop, getting to the park can be a little confusing; buses usually drop off outside the Family Mart, and from here you should turn left and follow the road. It's a fair walk to the entrance, but cheap shuttle buses run through the day, and it's also possible to pedal the route on a rented bike. The park's **information office** (daily 9am–5pm) is around five minutes' walk up the road from the Family Mart, and usually staffed with an English-speaker. Almost directly opposite is the *Swegobil Motel* (ⓣ063/538-8122; ❹), which is consistently decent, though prices are a little high. Connected to this is *Gwangju-daegwal Sikdang*, a restaurant that serves delicious mountain fare, and, handily, is next to the information office for when you need help with the menu. If you're looking for something more rustic, on the other side of the Family Mart is a small, friendly village of family homes, many of which lease out *minbak* rooms from W25,000 or so.

Seonunsan National Park

SEONUNSAN NATIONAL PARK (선운산 국립 공원) has more than a few aces hidden up its leafy sleeves. It offers some of the country's best **rock-climbing** and a few enjoyable hikes; these may not be as well signed as others in Korea, but some may find this liberating. A streamside path, lined with stalls selling delicious mountain berry juice in the summer and autumn, heads straight from the main entrance to **Seonunsa** (선운사), a dusty collection of buildings, stupas and the like that appear to have been thrown together with little care. It's quite possibly the least satisfying temple complex in the province, and the small hermitages strewn around the park are of more interest.

Once past the temple, you'll have a diverse range of trails to choose from. **Hikers** should head for the hills; the peaks are puny by Korean standards, rarely reaching above 400m, but this makes for some easy day-hikes, and you may be rewarded with occasional views of the West Sea. For more hardcore thrills, continue further on the temple path, across the river; hidden a ten-minute hike behind a small restaurant is a spectacular **rock-climbing** course. This is a tough route and should not be attempted alone or without equipment – see ⓦwww.koreaontherocks.com for climb details, and to contact the few Koreans (and expats) au fait with holds, conglomerates and juggy overhangs. Back towards the entrance, an underused side path heads along the temple wall and up a gorgeous valley lined with rows of tea trees and a few rustic dwellings. You'll soon come across a small, beautiful farming village, where one house offers *minbak* accommodation (❶); if you don't mind sharing a bathroom and sleeping on the floor, it's the best place to stay in the area. A motley collection of poor **hotels** lies outside the park entrance, including the over-expensive *Sun Un San* (ⓣ063/561-3377; ❺) and the dilapidated *Dongbaek* (ⓣ063/562-1560; ❸) – it's far better to stay elsewhere. There's also a small **tourist information** booth near the park bus stop.

Seonunsan is a day-trip from Jeonju or Gwangju, though access to the park is usually via **Gochang** (고창), the closest town and connected to it by regular buses. On the way back to Gochang, some bus drivers may be willing to drop you off within walking distance of a **dolmen site** (*Gochang goindol*; 고창 고인돌). Similar to the burial mounds found on Ganghwado (see p.137), this collection of ancient rocks is one of the few Korean sites saved for posterity by **UNESCO World Heritage**, and may be one of the least-visited places on their list. However, it's worth the effort of getting to if you've time, patience and a love of the countryside.

Byeonsanbando National Park

In addition to the usual mix of peaks and temples found in Korea's parks, **BYEONSANBANDO NATIONAL PARK** (변산반도 국립 공원) throws in some wonderful sea views. Best accessed by bus #100 (W1500; 30min) or taxi (W20,000) from the town of **Buan** (부안), the park is spread around a small, rural **peninsula** on the west coast from which it takes its name (*bando* literally means "half-island"). However, it's in the process of being hauled towards the mainland on its northern side with the aid of a 33km causeway, a development that will yield thousands of hectares of new farmland, but has caused one hell of a stink with Korean environmental groups (see box, p.252).

Chaesokgang and around

Heading west by bus from the end of the dam, you'll pass a couple of nice beaches before arriving at the unusual rock formations of **Chaesokgang** (채석강; daily 9am–6pm; W1600). You have to time it right to get the most out of the place – for much of the day it's just a bunch of pretty cliffs, but the surrender of the tide reveals page-like leaves of rock piled up like rusty banknotes, and teeming with crabs and other oceanic fauna.

Chaesokgang is served by four buses an hour from Buan, though its entrance is badly signed – from the bus stop (the last stop on the route) head back along the road for 100m or so, then turn left through an area of motels and fish restaurants. Near the port south of the cliffs is a ferry terminal, which has services to, and occasionally beyond, the island of **Wido** (위도), though this too has provided cause for environmental concern, and was at one point slated for the storage of nuclear waste.

The southern peninsula

The charming southern side of the peninsula offers more trails and temples. The temple complex of **Naesosa** (내소사) is more notable for its rural, mountain-backed

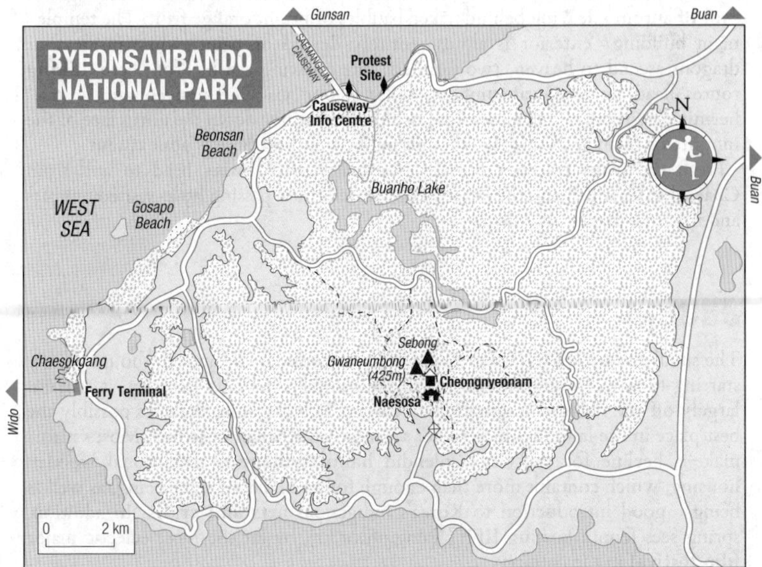

When I was a boy, all this was waves...

To the north of Byeonsanbando National Park lies a bizarre sight. Sketching a long line between sea and sky is a 33km-long **traffic-bearing causeway** that stretches all the way north to Gunsan. Prior to construction, more than 40,000 hectares east of this concrete snake were part of the West Sea, but are now slowly being converted into rice fields, a change large enough to be clearly visible on maps of the country.

Understandably, this mammoth project ruffled feathers in Korea's largely toothless **environmental lobby**, which was concerned about the effect of the loss of the area's mud flats on the local fish and bird populations, and asked why a country with a shrinking population needed so many new rice fields; Korea has long been forced to subsidize rice to prevent cheaper imports from destroying an important national industry. One interesting protest, dubbed "Three Steps, One Bow", saw demonstrators making a two-month, 300km pilgrimage to Seoul, taking three steps at a time before prostrating themselves on the ground. The protest failed to meet its goals, and the project should be completed by 2012; the main **protest site** near Buan – an area of large wooden poles, carved with anguished faces, rising from the sand of the former shore – may well have been drowned by then.

On the southern end of the causeway is the project's **information centre**; there's almost no information in English, but the staff will be willing to play you an unintentionally hilarious English-language DVD, in which a cute cartoon hostess communicates the benefits of the dam: "The blue ocean and the endless embankment!" she screams in introduction, before a token foreigner dreamily declares that it (presumably the dam, though he's looking at the sky) must be the most beautiful place he's ever seen. Though Kim Jong-il may have produced less balanced pieces of film, few could better the parody.

setting than any of its buildings, and is the most accessible place from which to start a hike. Persimmon trees surround the entrance (from where it's a short walk to the temple and its adjacent *minbak* village); these shed their leaves at the slightest sniff of autumn, leaving behind naked baubles of bright orange fruit. The temple's main building's exterior is almost entirely devoid of paint, while inside four dragons ascend to heaven, two headless, one gnawing a fish. From here, **hiking** routes head up to Gwaneumbong (425m), one via Cheongnyeonam, a small hermitage with great sea views. It's possible to continue down the north face of the mountains to an artificial lake, though public transport here is nonexistent.

From the main entrance outside Naesosa, hourly **buses** head to and from Chaesokgang and Buan, the latter a convoluted route passing little-visited temples and innumerable small villages.

Jeonju

The small city of **JEONJU** (전주) is a place of considerable appeal; though finally starting to attract domestic tourists in the numbers it richly deserves, it remains largely off the radar of international visitors. This is ironic, since it's possibly the best place in the land in which to get a handle on **Korean customs**. Most visitors make a beeline for the city's splendid **hanok village** of traditional wooden housing, which contains more than enough for a full day of sightseeing, as well as being a good introduction to Korea's indigenous **arts and crafts**. In addition, spring sees Jeonju hosting JIFF (Ⓦeng.jiff.or.kr), by far the most eclectic major **film festival** in the country.

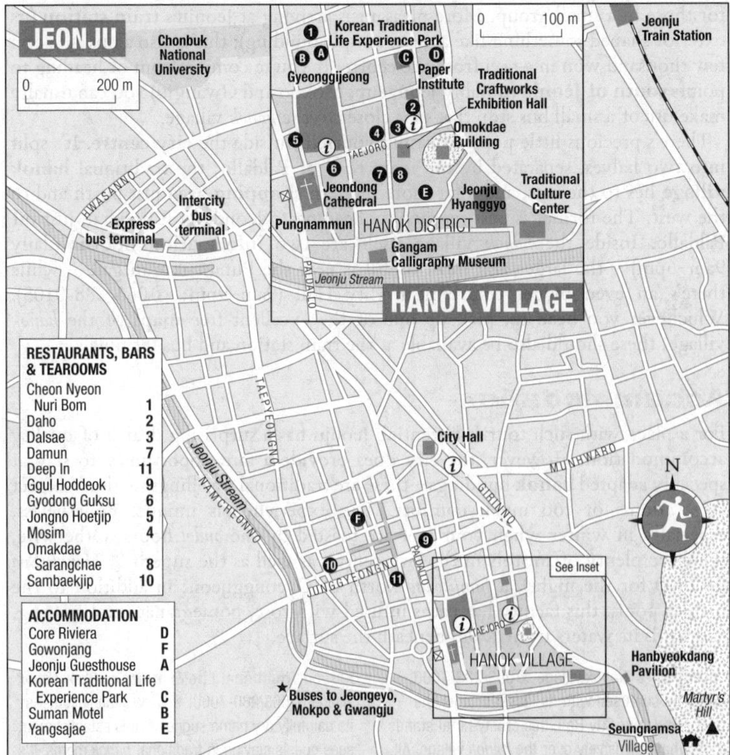

However, it's **food** that Koreans most readily associate with Jeonju. Many of the differences are too subtle to be noticed by foreigners – and in the cheapest places, nonexistent – but you're likely to find a greater and more lovingly prepared number of *banchan* (반찬; side dishes) here, and a slightly greater emphasis on herbal seasoning than on the somewhat less cultivated tastebud-tinglers of salt and red pepper paste. Particularly notable is the city's take on the tasty Korean staple, **bibimbap** (see box, p.257). The only downside is that Korean food just won't taste as good when you've moved on elsewhere.

Jeonju's ginkgo-lined streets help to create an ambience notably relaxed for a Korean city, but this disguises a hidden historical pedigree – this unassuming city marked the beginning of one of the longest lines of kings that the world has seen. It was here in the fourteenth century that the first kings of the **Joseon kingdom** were born, and the dynasty went on to rule Korea for over five centuries. Overlooked as the dynastic capital in favour of Seoul, today's Jeonju is not brimming with historical riches, but it has its charms, and is well worth a visit.

Arrival, information and orientation

Bus passengers are disgorged at one of two crusty terminals – one express, one intercity – in a messy area to the north of the city centre. Plenty of buses run into town from the main road a short walk to the east. However, it's far easier to go by taxi, which is unlikely to cost more than W3000, and may even work out cheaper for those in a small group. More pleasant is arriving at Jeonju's **train station** (its exterior shaped something like a giant temple building); this is also a bus ride or a few thousand won in a taxi from the centre. If you're coming from or heading to points **south of Jeonju** (notably Jeongeup, Mokpo and Gwangju) you can usually make use of a small bus stop that's far closer to the *hanok* village.

There's precious little point in basing yourself outside the **city centre**. It's split into two halves, separated by the main road of Paldallo; the traditional **hanok village** lies to the east, and a far more modern **shopping area** just north and to the west. The former is best reached by heading to Jeondong Cathedral, just off Paldallo. Inside the *hanok* village itself are two **information booths** (daily 9am–6pm) – the larger and most useful is near the Pungnammun gate – while there's an even bigger centre near City Hall (9am–9pm; ⓣ063/288-0105). Whichever you head to, pick up one of the excellent free **maps** of the *hanok* village; these should also be available at the train station and bus terminals.

Accommodation

For a place with such tourist potential, Jeonju has a surprising dearth of quality accommodation. However, the city does provide a rare opportunity to stay at specially adapted **hanok** buildings – these are traditional dwellings, so don't expect large rooms or too much comfort. The experience is unique, nonetheless, especially in winter when your feet are toasted by the *ondol* floors. Otherwise, there are plenty of **motels** in the city centre, as well as the superb *Hanok Spa* (W7000 for the night), a *jjimjilbang* north of Gyeonggijeon; in addition to the regular pools, this facility has baths infused with rose, pomegranate and ginseng, and hauls its waters from 170m beneath the surface.

Core Riviera *Hanok* village ⓣ063/232-7000. Not to be confused with its lesser brother the *Core Hotel* near City Hall, this crusty hotel stands somewhat obtrusively over the *hanok* village. All rooms are carpeted and homely, but poor value for the price – make sure you get one with a westward view over the traditional area below. Unfortunately, it's the only higher-end option in Jeonju. ❻

Gowonjang 고원장 Jungangdong ⓣ063/286-3211. One of a string of motels opposite the CGV cinema in the town centre, and usually the easiest to haggle down in price. Rooms are decent enough, and most have private facilities and cable TV. ❷

Jeonju Guesthouse Gyeongwondong ⓣ063/286-8886. Charming hostel, conveniently located just north of the *hanok* village. The English-speaking owner is a priceless source of local information, and although the bedrooms are a tiny bit stuffy the large common area is a great place to meet new friends. Dorms W19,000, twins ❹

Korean Traditional Life Experience Park *Hanok* village ⓣ063/280-7000, ⓦwww.jjhanok.com. As its painfully dry name suggests, this establishment sees guests staying in traditional *hanok* rooms. It's highly popular with Korean tourists, so try to book at least a week in advance. Non-guests can watch traditional music and dance performances each Sat at 8pm in the delightful courtyard. ❹

Suman Motel 수만 모텔 Gyeongwondong 2-ga ⓣ063/231-7770. Though a little soulless with its yellow linoleum rooms, this motel is as close as you'll get to Gyeonggijeon – a beautiful shrine in the *hanok* village – and is also within an easy walk of the shopping quarter. ❷

Yangsajae 양사재 *Hanok* village ⓣ063/282-4959, ⓦwww.jeonjutour.co.kr. One of the *hanok* district's traditional dwellings, this is smaller and less polished than others, and provides a more authentic experience. Its setting in the more rustic southern half of the district also helps, and although the rooms are tiny they're pleasant and *ondol*-heated. ❹

The hanok village

Jeonju's main attraction is undoubtedly its splendid **hanok village** (한옥 마을), a city-centre thatch of largely **traditional housing**. Highlights include a cathedral, an ancient shrine and a former Confucian academy, as well as museums for calligraphy, paper and wine; almost all sights are free, and there's enough to keep you busy for a full day. The best way to enjoy it is simply to turn up and wander around – whether it be a museum, a traditional restaurant or a photogenic house, there's something to see around every corner. There are no opening times or entry fees to the area and it remains a functioning part of the city, one that's particularly beautiful at night when most of the tourists have gone. The area has a distinct **north–south divide** – the north is far more polished and home to an ever-increasing number of bars and cafés, while the southern section is a pleasingly authentic and untouched slice of old Korea, with locals meandering up and down the narrow lanes as they have for decades. Musical **pansori** performances are frequent, and you may even be able to participate in traditional activities such as lantern-making or calligraphy.

The best place to get your bearings is **Taejoro**, a road that bisects the *hanok* village. Lightly trafficked and studded with small lights that glow at night, it has two **information offices** that can provide you with maps of the area. The eastern office offers free bike rental, though you'll probably have to get there early to nab one.

Pungnammun and Jeondong Cathedral

Most visitors start by heading to a sight just outside the village, across the main road that marks its western boundary. Here lies **Pungnammun** (풍남문; 24hr;

Traditional arts and crafts in the hanok village

Near the eastern end of Taejoro, the road bisecting the *hanok* **village**, you'll find the **Traditional Craftworks Exhibition Hall** (Tues–Sun: March–Oct 10am–7pm; Nov–Feb 10am–6pm; free), a traditionally styled wooden structure which holds crafts created by Jeonju artisans – a great place to hunt for souvenirs. If you're lucky you may get to see one of the traditional song and dance shows that are occasionally held just outside the complex – there's a list of performance times on the *hanok* **village** map. North of Taejoro, exhibits in the **Traditional Wine Museum** (Tues–Sun: June–Aug 9am–7pm; Sept–May 9am–6pm; free) aren't terribly interesting, but the beauty of the *hanok* building – and the fact that free tipples are occasionally handed out – make it worth a quick peek. Of more interest is the **Korean Paper Institute** (same times; free), where beautiful examples of products made with **handmade paper** (한지; *hanji*) are on display, many available to buy; if you ask nicely, you may even be able to try your hand at making a kite or lantern.

South of Taejoro, and overlooking the stream that marks the *hanok* village's southern boundary, is the **Gangam Calligraphy Museum** (10am–5pm; free); stored inside are wonderful examples of writing from some of Korea's best-known calligraphers. Artistic beauty of a different kind can be found a five-minute walk east along the streamside road, at the **Traditional Culture Center**, which puts on *pansori* shows (see box, p.258) every Friday at 7.30pm (W5000). The mournful singing and sparse drum-raps are well complemented by the old fashioned beauty of the building, the performers are usually of an extremely high standard, and the shows are not over-long, making this an absolute must-see. Other nights see similar performances, though of slightly lower quality. Other programmes run by the centre include a free **tea ceremony** course every third Thursday (10.30am–noon), and irregular cheap lessons (W5000–10,000) in cooking, **fan-making**, traditional music and the like; consult a tourist office for details.

Lastly, there are a few interesting **craft shops** in the *hanok* village. Abo sells **jewellery** made in a vaguely dynastic style, and the earrings, bangles and bracelets are all reasonably priced. Practically next door, Midang (Ⓦwww.mi-dang.net) sells beautiful **silks** and **traditional attire** made with a contemporary twist. On the other side of the road, you'll find a few decent **pottery shops**.

free), an ornate city gate whose present structure dates from 1768, but was originally built in the late fourteenth century as part of Jeonju's city wall. Now surrounded by a circle of rather ugly modern buildings, it holds a gruesome secret – this is where the heads of martyred Christians were displayed after purges in 1801 (see below). Inside the village, on the southern side of **Taejoro**, **Jeondong Cathedral** (전동성당) looks almost European with its brown brick walls and soaring spire. It was one of the first cathedrals to be built in Korea, and remains an active place of worship.

Gyeonggijeon

Almost directly opposite the cathedral is **Gyeonggijeon** (경기전; daily 9am–6pm; free), a park-like shrine area full of ornate buildings and beautiful trees – quite a sight in the autumn. It was built in 1410 to preserve a portrait of **King Taejo**, first leader of the famed Joseon dynasty and native of Jeonju, who had died two years previously after arguably the most productive reign in Korea's long regal history (see p.68). The portrait shows Taejo resplendent in an embroidered robe, against a pale yellow background, and sits proudly in a hall to the rear of the complex. It's surrounded by other members of his family, who were only officially made royals after Taejo's death, a move that gave posthumous legality to his bringing down of the Goryeo dynasty (see p.362).

Jeonju Hyanggyo

Near the southeastern corner of the *hanok* village is **Jeonju Hyanggyo** (전주 향교; opening hours vary; free), a former Confucian academy. Present here since 1603, and still housing a few of the original buildings, it sees surprisingly few visitors – a very good thing, as you'll appreciate more its contemplative *raison d'être*. Most notable are a number of large ginkgo trees, a couple of which – incredibly – actually predate the complex; with a majesty all of their own, these alone make a trip to this *hyanggyo* worthwhile.

Hanbyeokdang and around

A place for poets and contemplation, **Hanbyeokdang** (한벽당; free) is a pavilion dangling off a rock face across the road from the *hanok* village's southeast corner; one can only speculate on how beautiful the view must have been when this was built in 1404, before the main road arrived. From here continue south along the river, where the scene is further diluted by the overlarge (and uninteresting) Nature Ecological Museum – how ironic. Before long, however, you'll be rewarded with a **picturesque village**, whose paths snake between walls of rock and up the hill to the pine forest behind. The atmosphere here is something special, especially considering its proximity to the city centre; all the more surprising, then, that this little hamlet may have been the true **birthplace** of Joseon-era Korea – local rumours suggest that this was the source of the dynasty's first royals. Nowadays it's home to **Seungamsa** (승암사), a simple, deserted but intricately painted temple.

Martyrs Hill

It's possible to access **Martyrs Hill** behind the village via a path starting a little further down the river. The martyrs in question include Yi Hang-geom, killed in 1801 along with six of his family for his religious beliefs; his head was displayed on Pungnamun (p.255) in the city centre to show the populace what happened to Catholics. A thirty-minute slog will take you to his tomb, from where you can follow a number of paths back to the city, many of which are studded with yet more delightfully secluded temples and hermitages.

Eating and drinking

Jeonju has a national reputation as a city of culinary excellence and visitors should not leave without trying the city's wonderful **bibimbap** (see box below). There exist a number of excellent traditional restaurants in the *hanok* village, together with some rustic **tearooms** and an ever-growing number of **cafés**. The places to eat around the bus and train stations are surprisingly poor.

Cheon Nyeon Nuri Bom Gyeongwondong. Just north of Gyeonggijeon, this is a thoroughly noble restaurant – the volunteer staff are all female retirees, and all the food is free. You are, however, obliged to pay for the alcohol: it's W15,000 for a bowl of *dongdongju* rice-wine. After that, you're free to tuck into the superb Korean food on offer – you may well get a different dish each time you raise your hand. Wonderful.

Damun 茶門 *Hanok* village. With simple, traditionally styled rooms arrayed around a charming dirt courtyard, this is a highly atmospheric slice of old Korea. Filling set meals (한식; *hansik*) go for W10,000 per person (minimum two). It's a little tricky to hunt down – look for the Chinese-language sign.

Gyodong Guksu 교동 국수 *Hanok* village. There are just two items on the menu at this tiny place – you can have your noodles in a spicy sauce for W4000, or a marginally blander soup for W3000. Cheap but delicious, and a great place to fall into after a day in the *hanok* village.

Jongno Hoegwan 종로 회관 *Hanok* village. Not the most atmospheric restaurant serving up genuine Jeonju *bibimbap*, but the location next to Gyeonggijeon is pretty impressive, as is the dish itself. For W10,000 you get the meal and a mouthwatering array of side dishes – the mushrooms, in particular, are nothing short of heavenly.

Jungang-shijang Hoddeok 중앙시장 호떡 Pungnamdong. The name of this little booth is as much of a mouthful as the gloopy sugar-and-rice pancakes on sale for just W700 each – *hoddeok* (호떡; pronounced a little like "hot dog") are extremely popular winter snacks, and on a cold evening are hard to beat.

Omokdae Sarangchae 오목대 사랑채 *Hanok* village. Yet more traditional food is on offer at this smartly designed restaurant, which sits just south of the Traditional Craftworks Exhibition Hall; it's particularly recommended in the evening, when the interior is bathed in a soft glow. Jeonju *bibimbap* is available for W9000.

Sambaekjip 삼백집 Jungangdong. On the fringe of the shopping quarter, and for decades an extremely popular place with lunching Koreans, this restaurant is famed for its *kongnamul gukbap* (콩나물 국밥) – a rice-and-veg dish cooked in a hot stone pot. Try the *moju* (모주), a hot, spicy drink.

Cafés and tearooms

Daho 다호 *Hanok* village. One of the most picturesque tearooms in the area, where you sit in tatami-matted rooms around a courtyard. The teas are excellent, particularly the ginger variety.

Jeonju bibimbap

Jeonju's most famous dish is, without doubt, its **bibimbap** (전주 비빔밥). Regular *bibimbap* – a mixture of vegetables served on a bed of rice, with a fried egg and meat on top – is available across the country (see the *Korean cuisine* colour section), but in Jeonju they've picked up the formula and run with it. Recipes vary from place to place, but the ingredients are always well chosen and may include anything from pine kernels to bluebell roots or fern bracken in addition to the usual leaves and bean sprouts. In addition, your meal will invariably be surrounded by up to twenty free side dishes, made with just as much care, and an even greater variety of ingredients. Beware, however, of restaurants that claim to serve authentic Jeonju *bibimbap* – many places, particularly around the train station and bus terminals, will simply give you a regular version of the dish (though genuinely made in Jeonju, and thereby circumnavigating Korea's already weak product description laws). One way to sort Jeonju wheat from Jeonju chaff is the price – for the real deal, you shouldn't be paying less than W8000, but even at double this price it's likely to be money well spent.

Pansori

Usually marketed to foreigners as "Korean opera", **pansori** (판소리) performances are a modern-day derivative of the country's shamanist past. Songs and incantations chanted to fend off evil spirits or ensure a good harvest slowly mutated over the years into ritualized presentations; the themes evolved, too, with tales of love and despair replacing requests to spirits unseen.

A good *pansori* may go on for hours, but each segment will be performed by a cast of just two – a female singer (소리꾼; *sorikkun*) and a male percussionist (고수; *gosu*). The *sorikkun* holds aloft a paper fan, which she folds, unfolds and waves about to emphasize lyrics or a change of scene. While the *gosu* drums out his minimalist finger taps on the *janggo*, he gives his singer words – or, more commonly, grunts – of encouragement known as *chuimsae*, to which the audience are expected to add their own. The most common are "*chalhanda!*" and "*olshi-gu*!", which are roughly equivalent to "you're doing good!" and "hm!", a grunt acknowledging appreciation, usually delivered with a refined nod. Just follow the Korean lead, and enjoy the show.

Dalsae 달새 *Hanok* village. The extravagant full name of this tearoom (meaning "Moon-birds think only of the Moon") is bigger than the building itself – there are just four tables. But the menu has been translated into English of a sort, and the teas are top-notch.

Mosim 모심 *Hanok* village. Two-floor, wi-fi-friendly café whose innards have seemingly been fashioned entirely from pine. The coffee is good, and the chunky muffins beg to be eaten.

Nightlife

There are countless places to **drink** or dance the night away in the **student zones** around the universities, but the one outside Chonbuk National University is generally regarded as the best. The *Deep In* bar is very popular with expats and visitors alike, but due to its location just south of the shopping quarter – a ghost town at night – it's a little hit and miss, and can be empty during the week. A little further west is the *E-um Bar*; owned by the same people as the Traditional Wine Museum (see p.255), this also serves as a gallery of sorts, with rotating monthly exhibitions of painting or photography.

Finally, Jeonju is one of the best places in the land for the milky rice-wine known as **makkeolli**. You'll find over a dozen varieties on sale in convenience stores around the city (though usually only one or two per location); *Myeongga makkeolli* (명가 막걸리) is one recommended brand. Alternatively, you can buy connoisseur brands from *Myeongin Jeontong Juryu* (명인전통주류), a small stall opposite *Mosim* café.

East of Jeonju

With few urban areas to speak of, it's bucolic countryside all the way east of Jeonju. Easily accessible on a day-trip from the provincial capital are the wonderful twin peaks of **Maisan Provincial Park**. Between these lies **Tapsa**, one of Korea's most distinctive temples, surrounded by otherworldly spires of stacked rock that, though built without bonding agents and attacked by regular typhoons and snowstorms, continue to stand tall. Pushing on further east you'll soon hit the slopes of **Deogyusan National Park**, home to the popular ski resort **Muju**.

Maisan Provincial Park

Korea's pine-clad mountain ranges tend to look rather similar to each other. One exception is tiny **MAISAN PROVINCIAL PARK** (마이산 도립 공원), or "horse-ear Mountains", so-named after two of its peaks. It's easy to reach Maisan by bus on a day-trip from Jeonju, via the small town of **Jinan** (진안). The park is within walking distance of Jinan's decaying bus terminal, but most opt for taking a taxi along the lake to the main entrance north of the park – the fifteen-minute trip should cost around W4000, though many drivers will try to get you to go to the more distant Tapsa entrance for around three times that price. At the northern entrance are restaurants and a couple of places to stay, and from here steep flights of energy-sapping stairs take you between the horses' ears and over the scalp, where you'll probably need a rest. Unfortunately it's not possible to climb the peaks, which were closed for regeneration at the time of writing; the path up the western ear is due to reopen in 2014. Despite the threat of heavy fines and the fact that hikers stand out like a sore thumb, people still flout the rule.

If you continue between the peaks, you'll soon come to Unsusa, a dainty temple surrounded by flowers in warmer months, while further down the mountain is the highly popular temple of **Tapsa** (탑사), Maisan's real gem, which sits in a surreal clasp of stacked rock. Mildly Gaudíesque in appearance, the near-hundred-strong towers were the work of one monk, Yi Kap-myong (1860–1957), who apparently used no adhesive in their construction, even though some are over 10m high.

Muju and Deogyusan National Park

Locked into the northeast of Jeonbuk province is **Deogyusan National Park** (덕유산 국립 공원), whose lofty yet gentle terrain rises up south of **Muju ski resort**, then spills down in an undulating series of valleys. Both park and resort can be reached on regular buses via Muju town itself along a typically relaxed slice of rural Jeolla – the 19km drive in from the west is astonishingly beautiful. Buses continue past the resort on to Gucheondong, the main entrance to Deogyusan; there are also free hourly shuttle buses linking this entrance with the ski resort.

Muju ski resort

Despite being one of the warmest and most southerly ski resorts in Korea, **MUJU** (무주; ⓦwww.mujuresort.com) is one of the peninsula's most popular, and attracts hordes of skiers throughout the winter, a season artificially elongated with the aid of some hefty snow machines. Less bulky ski equipment is available for hire, and whether you're a ski veteran or an absolute beginner, you'll have more than twenty slopes to choose from. It's also possible to sled or go cross-country skiing, or take part in non-snow related activities from golf and paintball to bungee-jumping and bike-rides. There's plenty of fun to be had in **warmer months** too, which is actually a great time of year to go – accommodation prices plunge, and there's great hiking on the hills that would otherwise be covered with snow and skiiers.

Practicalities

It'll cost a pretty penny to stay next to the slopes. The cushy *Hotel Tirol* (ⓣ063/320-7617; ❼), right next to the ski runs and resembling an Austrian cabin, is absurdly expensive during the peak winter season, and far from cheap at other times. Things are much less expensive down the hill in the area's main **motel** district; few establishments are worthy of special mention, and it will always pay to shop around, but the best are on and around Baebang-gil, near the main road at the bottom. The oldest of these is the grandly titled *Uri-duri Neorang-narang Condo Pension Muju* (☎063/322-3425 or 6; ❹), a rambling light-brick complex with large rooms, and a steal off-season (though they can get a little grubby during these times). Below the *Hotel Tirol* is **Carnival Street**, a collection of overpriced **restaurants** and cafés whose wintry, quasi-Austrian atmosphere can make a refreshing change if you've been in Korea for a while. Otherwise there's *Mujunori*, near the top end of the village on the way to the resort, which deserves a shout for its adventurous decor and succulent *galbi*.

The rest of the park

A popular hike – one that almost every visitor to Deogyusan follows – links Muju ski resort with the main park entrance at Gucheondong. Though it's not especially taxing, much of the upward slog can be chalked off by **cable car** from the resort, which whisks passengers up the 1520m peak of Seolcheon-bong. From here it's a 6.2km hike back down to the ski area, or a longer, more beautiful one along a trail riddled with rocks, small waterfalls and pools to the Gucheondong park entrance.

In another section of the park is the fortress **Jeoksang Sanseong** (적상 산성), located near the bus route from Muju town to the resort and park, though sadly not directly on any public transport routes. Unless you hitch, you'll have to walk from the nearest bus stop, which is in the village of Bukchang-ri – let your driver know where you want to get off – from where the fortress is an hour's signposted walk away.

Practicalities

Motels and **restaurants** line the stream in Gucheondong, a village-like area below the park entrance, and much smaller and quieter than the similar district below Muju ski resort. The most pleasant places to stay are on the western side of the water; the best-priced is the *Shilla Motel* (☎063/322-0663; ❸), whose friendly owners give occasional discounts to foreigners. Across the creek are two neighbouring restaurants which, bizarrely, both go under the name *Jeonju Sikdang*: the one at the end of the row is marginally less amicable, but is the only establishment along here that has views of the park, rather than the road. *Minbak* line the main road all the way from the Muju resort turnoff and, unless you're camping, represent the cheapest accommodation any time of year – especially important during ski season, when the hotels and motels still manage to stay full despite some hardcore price-hikes. There's also a **campsite** near the park entrance (from W3000 per tent).

Travel details

Flights

Gwangju to: Jeju (8 daily; 45min); Seoul (7 daily; 50min).
Mokpo (Muan airport) to: Jeju (2 weekly; 45min).
Yeosu to: Jeju (2 weekly; 45min); Seoul (8 daily; 55min).

Trains

Gwangju to: Daejeon (hourly; 1hr 45min); Seoul (regularly; 2hr 50min).
Jeonju to: Daejeon (hourly; 1hr 30min); Iksan for transfer to KTX high-speed trains (hourly; 20min); Seoul (11 daily; 3hr 30min); Suncheon (hourly; 30min); Yeosu (hourly; 2hr).
Mokpo to: Busan (3 daily; 7hr 25min); Iksan (regularly; 1hr 25min); Jinju (3 daily; 4hr 35min); Seoul (regularly; 3hr).
Suncheon to: Jeonju (hourly; 1hr 30min); Yeosu (hourly; 35min).
Yeosu to: Jeonju (hourly; 2hr); Seoul (11 daily; 5hr 10min); Suncheon (hourly; 35min).

Buses

Gwangju to: Busan (every 30min; 3hr 40min); Chuncheon (4 daily; 5hr); Daegu (every 40min; 3hr 40min); Daejeon (every 20min; 2hr 50min); Gurye (every 30min; 1hr 30min); Gyeongju (2 daily; 3hr 30min); Incheon (hourly; 3hr 40min); Jeonju (every 30min; 1hr 40min); Jindo (every 40min; 2hr 50min); Jinju (3 daily; 2hr); Mokpo (every 30min; 1hr 30min); Naejangsan (5 daily; 1hr 30min); Seonunsan (8 daily; 1hr 40min); Seoul (every 5min; 3hr 55min); Sokcho (4 daily; 6hr); Wando (every 40min; 2hr 40min); Yeosu (regularly; 2hr).
Jeonju to: Buan (every 10min; 1hr 20min); Busan (11 daily; 3hr 35min); Daegu (hourly; 3hr 30min); Daejeon (every 20min; 1hr 20min); Gurye (regularly; 2hr); Gwangju (every 30min; 1hr 40min); Jeongeup (every 10min; 1hr); Jinan (regularly; 50min); Jinju (regularly; 3hr 30min); Mokpo (regularly; 3hr); Muju (regularly; 2hr 30min); Seoul (every 10min; 2hr 50min); Suncheon (11 daily; 2hr 20min); Yeosu (11 daily; 4hr).
Jindo to: Busan (2 daily; 6hr 30min); Gwangju (regularly; 2hr 30min); Mokpo (regularly; 1hr 10min); Seoul (4 daily; 5hr).
Mokpo to: Busan (9 daily; 5hr); Gwangju (regularly; 1hr 30min); Jeonju (regularly; 3hr); Jindo (regularly; 1hr 10min); Seoul (regularly; 5hr 20min); Wando (7 daily; 2hr); Yeosu (every 40min; 3hr 30min).
Muju to: Daejeon (regularly; 1hr 30min); Gwangju (regularly; 3hr 40min); Jeonju (regularly; 2hr); Seoul (5 daily; 2hr 40min).
Suncheon to: Busan (regularly; 3hr); Gwangju (every 20min; 1hr 30min); Gurye (regularly; 1hr); Jeonju (11 daily; 2hr 20min); Jinju (regularly; 1hr 30min); Mokpo (regularly; 2hr 50min); Seoul (6 daily; 5hr); Yeosu (every 5min; 50min).
Wando to: Gwangju (regularly; 2hr 40min); Mokpo (every 50min; 2hr); Seoul (4 daily; 6hr).
Yeosu to: Busan (hourly; 3hr 40min); Gwangju (regularly; 2hr); Jeonju (11 daily; 4hr); Mokpo (every 40min; 3hr 30min); Seoul (regularly; 5hr 40min).

Ferries

Mokpo to: Heuksando (4 daily; 1hr 45min); Hongdo (2 daily; 2hr 15min); Jeju City (4 daily; 3hr 10min–4hr 30min).

5

Chungcheong

5 CHUNGCHEONG

CHAPTER 5 Highlights

* **Boryeong mud festival** Get dirty on the beach at the most enjoyable festival on the Korean calendar. See p.267
* **West Sea islands** Take a ferry to these tiny, beach-pocked isles, home to fishing communities and a relaxed way of life hard to find on the mainland. See p.269
* **Buyeo and Gongju** Head to the former capitals of the Baekje dynasty to feast your eyes on their regal riches. See p.272 & p.274
* **Independence Hall of Korea** Delve into the nationalistic side of the Korean psyche at this huge testament to the country's survival of Japanese occupation. See p.285
* **Beopjusa Temple** Gaze in awe at the world's tallest bronze Buddha, before taking a hike in the surrounding national park. See p.287
* **Danyang** Take a midnight stroll, *makkeolli* in hand, along this tiny town's lakeside promenade. See p.288
* **Guinsa** Clamber around the snakelike alleyways of what may well be Korea's most distinctive temple. See p.291

▲ Guinsa

5

Chungcheong

Of South Korea's principal regions, **Chungcheong** (충청) is the least visited by foreign travellers, most of whom choose to rush through it on buses and trains to Gyeongju or Busan in the southeast, or over it on planes to Jeju-do. But to do so is to bypass the heart of the country, a thrillingly rural mishmash of rice paddies, **ginseng** fields (see box, p.267), national parks and unhurried **islands**. One less obvious Chungcheong attraction is the local populace – the Chungcheongese are noted throughout Korea for their **relaxed nature**. Here you'll get less pressure at the markets, or perhaps even notice a delay of a second or two when the traffic lights change before being deafened by a cacophony of car horns. The region's main cities are noticeably laid-back by Korean standards, and Chungcheongese themselves, particularly those living in the countryside, speak at a markedly slower pace than other Koreans (see box, p.277 for one folk tale).

Today split into two provinces, Chungcheong was named in the fourteenth century by fusing the names of Chungju and Cheongju, then its two major cities – they're still around today, but of little interest to travellers (Cheongju did, however, produce the world's first book; see p.287). To the west lies **Chungnam** (충남), a province whose name somewhat confusingly translates as "South Chungcheong". Its western edge is washed by the West Sea, and has a few good beaches – the strip of white sand in **Daecheon** is one of the busiest in the country, with the summer revelry hitting its zenith each July at an immensely popular **mud festival**. Off this coast are a number of accessible **islands** – tiny squads of rock stretch far beyond the horizon into the West Sea, and sustain fishing communities that provide a glimpse into pre-karaoke Korean life. Heading inland instead, the pleasures take a turn for the traditional: the small cities of **Buyeo** and **Gongju** fuctioned as capitals of the **Baekje dynasty** (18 BC–660 AD; see box, p.271) just as the Roman Empire was collapsing, yet each still boasts a superb wealth of dynastic sights. Both are home to fortresses, regal tombs and museums filled with gleaming jewellery of the period, which went on to have a profound influence on Japanese craft. As you head further east, the land becomes ever more mountainous. Anyone hiking across the spine of **Songnisan national park** will find a couple of gorgeous temples on the way, and on dropping down will be able to grab a bus to **Daejeon**, Chungcheong's largest city. North of Daejeon, and actually part of Seoul's sprawling subway network, is **Cheonan**, which is home to the country's largest, and possibly most revealing, museum.

Heading east instead will bring you to the province of **Chungbuk** (충북; "North Chungcheong"). As Korea's only landlocked province, this could be said to represent the heart of the country, a predominantly rural patchwork of fields and peaks, with three national parks within its borders. **Songnisan** is deservedly the

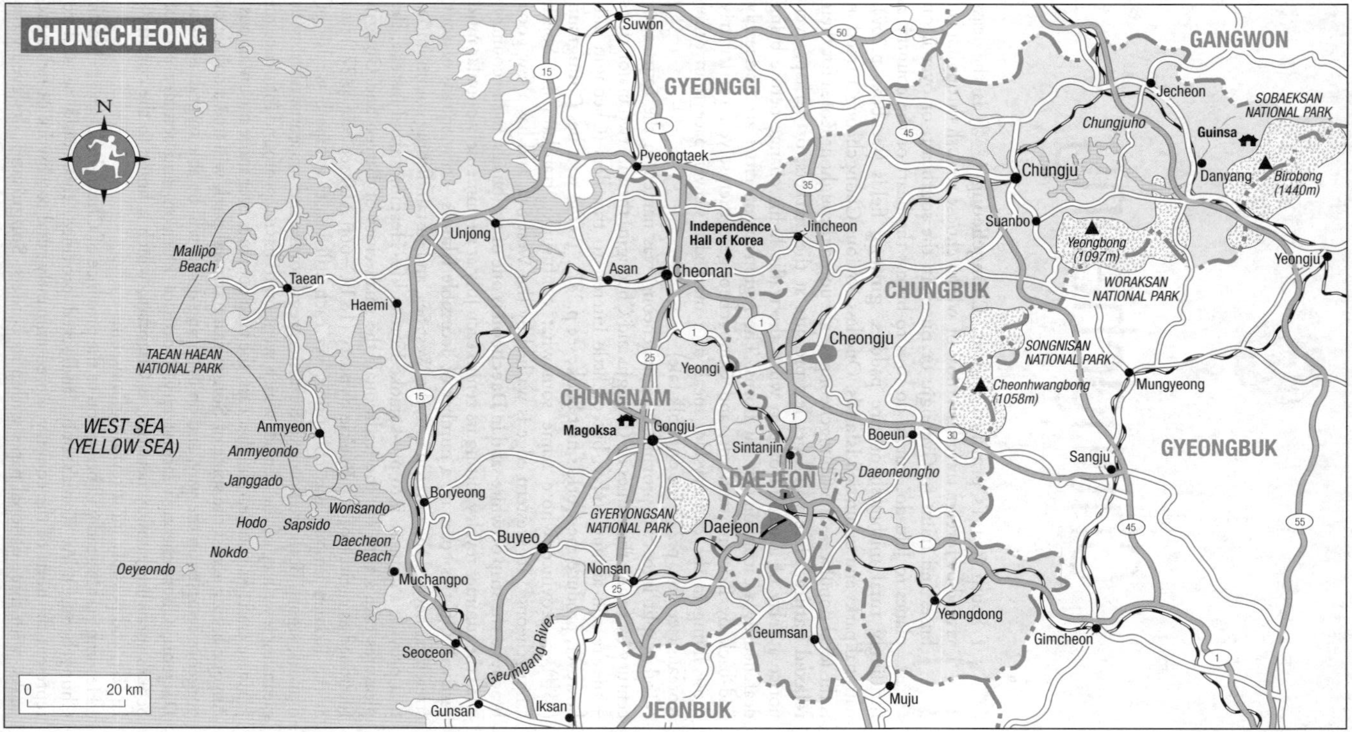

CHUNGCHEONG

GANGWON
GYEONGGI
CHUNGBUK
CHUNGNAM
DAEJEON
GYEONGBUK
JEONBUK
WEST SEA
(YELLOW SEA)
N
0 20 km

Suwon
Pyeongtaek
Unjong
Asan
Cheonan
Independence
Hall of Korea
Jincheon
Chungju
Chungjuho
Jecheon
Guinsa
Danyang
Birobong
(1440m)
SOBAEKSAN
NATIONAL PARK
Suanbo
Yeongbong
(1097m)
WORAKSAN
NATIONAL PARK
Yeongju
Cheongju
SONGNISAN
NATIONAL PARK
Cheonhwangbong
(1058m)
Mungyeong
Boeun
Sangju
Yeongi
Sintanjin
Daeoneongho
Daejeon
GYERYONGSAN
NATIONAL PARK
Magoksa
Gongju
Buyeo
Nonsan
Geumsan
Yeongdong
Gimcheon
Muju
Iksan
Gunsan
Geumgang River
Seoceon
Muchangpo
Daecheon
Beach
Boryeong
Haemi
Taean
Mallipo
Beach
TAEAN HAEAN
NATIONAL PARK
Anmyeon
Anmyeondo
Janggado
Wonsando
Hodo
Sapsido
Nokdo
Oeyeondo
1
4
15
25
30
35
45
50
55

The cure-all root

For centuries, perhaps even millennia, the **ginseng root** has been used in Asia for its medicinal qualities, particularly its ability to retain or restore the body's **Yin-Yang** balance; for a time, it was valued more highly by weight than gold. Even today, Korean ginseng is much sought after on the global market, due to the country's ideal climatic conditions; known locally as **insam** (인삼), much of it is grown in the Chungcheong provinces under slanted nets of black plastic. The roots take anything up to six years to mature, and suck up so much nutrition from the soil that, once harvested, no more ginseng can be planted in the same field for over a decade.

The **health benefits** of ginseng have been much debated in recent years, and most of the evidence in favour of the root is anecdotal rather than scientific. There are, nonetheless, hordes of admirers, and ginseng's stock rose further when it rode the crest of the "healthy living" wave that swept across Korea just after the turn of the millennium. Today it's possible to get your fix in pills, capsules, jellies, chewing gum or boiled sweets, as well as the more traditional tea or by eating the root raw. As the purported benefits depend on the dosage and type of ginseng used (red or white), it's best to consult a practitioner of oriental medicines, but one safe – and delicious – dish is **samgyetang** (삼계탕), a tasty and extremely healthy soup made with a ginseng-stuffed chicken, available for around W8000 across the land. Or for a slightly quirky drink, try mixing a sachet of ginseng granules and a spoon of brown sugar into hot milk – your very own **ginseng latte**.

most popular, and has a number of good day-hikes emanating from Beopjusa, a highly picturesque temple near the park's main entrance. **Sobaeksan** is less visited but just as appealing to hikers; it surrounds the lakeside resort town of **Danyang**, which makes a comfortable base for exploring the caves, fortresses and sprawling temple of **Guinsa** on the province's eastern flank.

Coastal Chungnam

Within easy reach of Seoul, Chungnam's coast is a popular place for anyone seeking to escape the capital for a bit of summer fun. Inevitably, the main attractions are the **beaches**, with the white stretches of **Mallipo** and **Daecheon** the most visited; the latter's annual **mud festival** is one of the wildest and busiest events on the peninsula. It's a short ferry trip from the mainland bustle to the more traditional offshore **islands**, a sleepy crew strung out beyond the horizon and almost entirely dependent on fishing.

Daecheon beach

Long, wide and handsome, **DAECHEON BEACH** (대천 해수욕장) is by far the most popular on Korea's western coast, hauling in a predominantly young crowd. In the summer this 3km-long stretch of white sand becomes a sea of people, having fun in the water by day, then drinking and letting off fireworks until the early hours. The revelry reaches its crescendo each July with the **Boryeong mud festival**, a week-long event that seems to rope in (and sully) almost every expat in the country. Mud, mud and more mud – wrestle or slide around in it, throw it at your friends or smear it all over yourself, then take lots and lots of pictures – this is one of the most enjoyable festivals on the calendar (see Ⓦwww.mudfestival.or.kr for more details). At other times you can still sample the brown stuff at the

Mud House (머드 하우스; 8am–6pm; W4000 after W1000 foreigner discount), the most distinctive building on the beachfront, where mud massages cost from W25,000. The ticket gets you entry to an on-site **sauna**, at which you can bathe in a **mud pool** or even paint yourself with the stuff; all manner of mud-based cosmetics are on sale at reception, including mud shampoo, soap and body cream. In summer, rent banana boats, jet-skis and large rubber tubes, or even a **quad bike** to ride up and down the prom.

Nine kilometres south of the beach is **Muchangpo** (무창포), a settlement that becomes popular for a few days every month when the tides retreat to reveal a path linking the beach with a small nearby island, an event inevitably termed "**Moses' Miracle**"; the sight of a line of people seemingly walking across water is quite something. For advice on the tides phone the tourist information line on ⓣ041/1330.

Arrival and information

Getting to Daecheon beach can be a little tricky. It's just 15km from the town of **Boryeong** (보령), and the two places have been known to trade names on occasion – hence the "Boryeong" Mud Festival. Coming from elsewhere in Korea, you'll arrive in Boryeong, whose **train** station (known as Daecheon) and **bus** station (this time Boryeong) are right next to each other. From both stations there are buses to the beach every half-hour or so (15min; W1800); get off as soon as you make a right at the *Legrand Beach Hotel*. Alternatively, the beach is less than W10,000 by **taxi** from either station. The bus route finishes at Daecheon harbour, at the northern end of the beach; you'll have to go here to take a ferry to one of the nearby islands.

There's an **information booth** near the mud centre where staff can reserve accommodation both in Daecheon and – helpfully – on the offshore islands, but you'd be lucky to find an English-speaker here; a map and some controlled mime should be enough to land you a booking.

Accommodation

Although there's very little at the top end of the scale, **motels** and *minbak* are everywhere, and even at the peak of summer you can usually find a bed without too much difficulty; prices can go through the roof on summer weekends and holidays, though with time, patience and a few words with the ubiquitous *ajummas*, you should find a bare-bones room for W30,000. Travellers and locals alike often save money by cramming as many people as possible into a room, or staying out all night on the beach with a few drinks. Lastly, there's a small **campground** with shower facilities behind the mud centre, which costs W5000 per tent in July and August, but is free to use at other times. The options listed below are all between the bus stop and the mud centre.

Legrand Beach Hotel ⓣ041/931-1020. The only higher-end option in the area, although rooms are vastly overpriced for what they are. Equally poor value is the near-decrepit on-site water park, tickets to which cost around W25,000. ❼

Moktobang Motel ⓣ041/931-7172. Easy to spot on account of its distinctive oriental roof, with wood-panelled and quite pleasing rooms all with en-suite facilities. ❹

Motel Coconuts ⓣ041/934-6595. Homely, family-run motel with cheerily decorated en-suite rooms, decent showers and cable TV. Be careful not to trip on the kids' toys in the lobby. ❹

Eating

Daecheon's culinary scene is simple – fish, fish and more fish. The seafront is lined with **seafood restaurants** and the competition is fierce – locals here are fond of literally dragging customers in. Best on the promenade is *Hwanghae* (황해), whose blue-ball outdoor lights are easy to spot at night. Most places display their still-alive goods in outdoor tanks; among the myriad options are eel, blue crabs, razor clams and sea cucumbers. Another speciality is *Jogae-gui* (조개구이), a shellfish barbecue that costs from around W15,000 per person; there's usually a two-person minimum for this or any other meal, meaning that solo travellers may have to subsist on *Hoe-deopbap* (회덮밥), chunks of raw fish with spicy sauce served on a bed of rice and leaves (usually W10,000). A more rustic patch of restaurants can be found near **Daecheon harbour**; these are quite atmospheric, especially in the evenings when the ramshackle buildings, bare hanging bulbs and coursing sea water may make you feel as though you've been shunted back in time a couple of decades. For anything other than fish you may have to rely on **snack stalls** or instant noodles from one of the convenience stores; the latter are also the source of most of the alcohol consumed in Daecheon, though there are plenty of old-fashioned **bars** lining the seafront.

West Sea islands

From Daecheon harbour, a string of tiny islands stretches beyond the horizon into what Koreans term the **West Sea**, a body of water known internationally as the Yellow Sea (see p.137). From their distant shores, the mainland is either a lazy murmur on the horizon or altogether out of sight, making this a perfect place to kick back and take it easy. **Beaches** and **seafood** restaurants are the main draw, but it's also a joy to sample the unhurried island lifestyle that remains unaffected by the changes that swept through the mainland on its course to First World status; these islands therefore, provide the truest remnants of pre-industrial Korean life. Fishing boats judder into the docks where the sailors gut and prepare their haul with startling efficiency; it's sometimes possible to buy fish directly from them. Restaurants on the islands are usually rickety, family-run affairs serving simple Korean staples.

Island practicalities

Ferries connect the islands in two main circuits, though with so few sailings, you won't be able to see more than one or two islands in a day. For **circuit one**, there are two sailings daily from Daecheon (8.10am & 3pm; 40min to Hodo, 20min more to Nokdo and a further 30min to Oeyeondo, from where return ferries leave at 10am & 4.40pm). **Circuit two** is accessible from either Daecheon or Anmyeondo. At least three sailings per day head around this loop; those leaving Daecheon at 7.30am and 12.50pm head clockwise, arriving first at Sapsido, while the 4pm ferry heads in the opposite direction, stopping first at Anmyeondo.

Remember to bring enough money for your stay, as most of the isles lack **banks** – the majority have mini-markets, but these can be hard to find as they tend to double as family homes. All islands have *minbak* **accommodation**, though don't expect anything too fancy – the rooms will be small and bare, and you'll probably have to sleep on a blanket on the floor. Prices start at W20,000 per night, and increase in summer.

Circuit one

This circuit fires 53km out to sea, terminating at the weatherbeaten island group Oeyeondo, before heading back to the mainland on the same route; as the ferries are for foot passengers only, the islands they visit are **quieter** than those on loop two.

The first stop is **Hodo** (호도), which attracts visitors for its beaches without the fuss of those on the mainland; the island's best beach is a curl of white sand just a short walk from the ferry dock and is great for swimming. Around the terminal are plenty of *minbak* rooms – pretty much every dwelling in the village will accept visitors, though there are only around sixty on the whole island. Try to track down Mr Choi at *Gwangcheon Minbak* (광천 민박); he's the proud owner of the only land vehicle on Hodo (a beat-up 4WD) and can be persuaded to give free nighttime rides through the forest or a splash across the mudflats if the tide is out – tremendous fun. Next stop is **Nokdo** (녹도), the smallest island of the three and home to some superb hill trails. Unlike on the other islands, the hillside town and its accommodation options are a fair walk from the ferry dock – everyone will be going the same way, so you should be able to hitch a lift without too much bother. The ferries make their final stop at **Oeyeondo** (외연도), a well-weathered family of thickly forested specks of land. This has the busiest port on the loop, with walking trails heading up to the island's twin peaks, as well as a tiny beach that's good for sunsets.

Circuit two

This is a proper loop, with ferries heading both ways around a circle that starts and ends in Daecheon. These boats can accommodate vehicles, meaning that the islands here are busier than on circuit one; however, the salty and remote appeal remains. All have *minbak* accommodation from around W20,000 (more in summer).

As you head clockwise, the first port of call is **Sapsido** (삽시도), the most popular island in the whole area (and pronounced "sap-shi-do"). Its shores are dotted with craggy rock formations, some with a hair-like covering of juniper or pine, while the island's interior is crisscrossed with networks of dirt tracks – it's possible to walk from one end to the other in under an hour. Depending on the tides, ferries will call at one of two ports – there are *minbak* aplenty around each, and both have decent beaches within walking distance, but make sure that you know which one to go to when you're leaving the island. Next stop is **Janggodo** (장고도), whose name derives from its contours, which are said to be similar to the Korea *janggo* drum (though it's actually shaped more like a banana). Home to some stupendous rock formations, it's popular with families and, thanks to some particularly good beaches, the trendier elements of the Korean beach set. Local buses wait at the northern terminal (there are two) to take passengers to the *minbak* area (it's a little far to walk). It's then a short hop across a strait usually filled with fishing nets to little **Godaedo** (고대도), an island renowned for its seafood; thus the pungent aroma that can often be smelt from the ferry. Depending on the ferry and the tides, you may also stop at **Wonsando** (원산도) and **Hyojado** (효자도) on your way back to Daecheon, but one certain stop is **Anmyeondo** (안면도); the largest island in the group, and the only one connected to the mainland by road. It also constitutes the most accessible part of **Taean Haean National Park** (태안해안 국립 공원). White sand beaches fill the coves that dot Anmyeondo's west coast, many of them only accessible by footpath from a small road that skirts the shore between **Anmyeon** (안면), the main settlement and transport hub, and **Yeongmok** (영목), a port village at the southern cape that receives ferries from Daecheon and other West Sea islands. Connecting the two are buses that meet the ferries and run approximately once an hour.

The Baekje capitals

Gongju and **Bueyo** are two small settlements in Chungnam that were, for a time, capitals of the **Baekje dynasty** which controlled much of the Korean peninsula's southwestern area during the **Three Kingdoms** period (see box below). Once known as Ungjin, **Gongju** became the second capital of the realm in 475, when it was moved from Wiryeseong (now known as Seoul), but held the seat of power for only 63 years before it was passed to **Buyeo**, a day's march to the southwest. Buyeo (then named Sabi) lasted a little longer until the dynasty was choked off in 660 by the powerful Silla empire to the east, which went on to unify the peninsula. Today, these three cities form an uneven historical triangle, weighed down on one side by Gyeongju's incomparable wealth of riches. Although the old Silla capital sees by far the most foreign tourists, the Baekje pair's less heralded sights can easily fill a weekend. Many of these echo those of the Silla capital – green grassy mounds where royalty were buried, imposing fortresses, lofty pavilions and ornate **regal jewellery**. Unabashedly excessive, yet at the same time achieving an ornate simplicity, Baekje jewellery attained an international reputation and went on to exert an influence on the Japanese craft of jewellery-making; some well-preserved examples in both cities can be found at their **museums**, which are two of Korea's best. Additionally, the **Baekje Culture Festival** takes place each September, with

The Baekje dynasty

The **Baekje dynasty** was one of Korea's famed **Three Kingdoms** – Goguryeo and Silla being the other two – and controlled much of southwestern Korea for almost seven hundred years. The *Samguk Sagi*, Korea's only real historical account of the peninsula in these times, claims that Baekje was a product of sibling rivalry – it was founded in 18 BC by Onjo, whose father had kick-started the Goguryeo dynasty less than twenty years beforehand, in present-day North Korea; seeing the reins of power passed on to his elder brother Yuri, Onjo promptly moved south and set up his own kingdom.

Strangely, given its position facing China on the western side of the Korean peninsula, Baekje was more closely allied with the kingdom of Wa in Japan – at least one Baekje king was born across the East Sea – and it became a conduit for art, religion and customs from the Asian mainland. This fact is perhaps best embodied by the Baekje artefacts displayed in the museums in Buyeo (p.273) and Gongju (p.276), which contain lacquer boxes, pottery and folding screens not dissimilar to the craftwork that Japan is now famed for.

Though the exact location of the first Baekje capitals is unclear, it's certain that Gongju and Buyeo were its last two seats of power. Gongju, then known as Ungjin, was **capital** from 475 to 538; during this period the aforementioned Three Kingdoms were jostling for power, and while Baekje leaders formed an uneasy alliance with their Silla counterparts the large fortress of Gongsanseong (see p.275) was built to protect the city from Goguryeo attacks. The capital was transferred to **Sabi** – present-day Buyeo – which also received a fortress-shaped upgrade (see p.272). However, it was here that the Baekje kingdom finally ground to a halt in 660, succumbing to the Silla forces that, following their crushing of Goguryeo shortly afterwards, went on to rule the whole peninsula.

Though local rebellions briefly brought Baekje back to power in the years leading up to the disintegration of Unified Silla, it was finally stamped out by the nascent Goryeo dynasty in 935. Despite the many centuries that have elapsed since, much evidence of Baekje times can still be seen today in the form of the regal burial mounds found in Gongju and Buyeo.

colourful parades and traditional performances in both Buyeo and Gongju; see Ⓦwww.baekje.org for more.

The two cities remain off the radar of most international travellers, and most who visit do so on day-trips from Seoul. Much of this can be attributed to the fact that there's next to no higher-end **accommodation** in either city, though a resort has recently opened up just outside Buyeo. Though unheralded even by Koreans, the cities' unassuming **restaurants** are a different story altogether – though extremely earthy, the food on offer here is some of the best and most traditional in the land, and an extremely well-preserved secret.

Buyeo

The smaller and sleepier of the Baekje duo, **BUYEO** (부여) is nonetheless worth a visit. The Baekje seat of power was transferred here from Gongju in 538, and saw six kings come and go before the abrupt termination of the dynasty in 660, when General Gyebaek led his five thousand men into one last battle against a Silla-Chinese coalition ten times that size. Knowing that his resistance would prove futile, the general killed his wife and children before heading into combat, preferring to see them dead than condemn them to slavery. Legend has it that thousands of the town's women threw themselves off a riverside cliff when the battle had been lost, drowning both themselves and the Baekje dynasty. Today, this cliff and the large, verdant **fortress** surrounding it are the town's biggest draw, along with an excellent **museum**.

Arrival and information

Buses arrive at a tiny station in the centre of town; from here most major sights – as well as the majority of motels and restaurants – are within walking distance, though it's easy to hunt down a cab if necessary. Buyeo's main street runs between two roundabouts – Boganso Rotary to the north, and Guncheon Rotary 1km to the south. By the latter is a statue of General Gyebaek, while next to the fortress entrance (east of the northern roundabout) is a **tourist information office** (daily 9am–6pm; Ⓣ041/830-2523), where you'll usually find an English-speaker.

Accommodation

As long as you're not too fussy, **accommodation** is easy to find in Buyeo, and a high-end resort finally opened up just outside the city in 2010. Try to avoid the area around the bus terminal, which contains some rather insalubrious places to stay.

Baekje Hotel Ⓣ041/236-7979. Inconveniently located a short taxi-ride from the bus terminal, this is the only official tourist accommodation in central Buyeo. Rooms are a little drab but fairly priced, and there's a small café-bar on site. ❺

Lotte Resort Ⓣ041/939-1000, Ⓦwww.lottebuyeoresort.com. Superbly designed resort hotel, whose pleasing, twin-horseshoe-shaped exterior is best described as "neo-Baekje". Although service is patchy, it has some of the best-value rooms in the land, with five-star facilities for just W120,000. It's located a W7000 taxi ride from central Buyeo, next to Baekje Cultural Land. ❻

Motel VIP Ⓣ041/832-3700. Near Boganso Rotary, with the best rooms in central Buyeo. Though this admittedly isn't saying much, the place is spotless, with mood lighting in the rooms and piped music in the corridors. ❸

Sky Motel Ⓣ041/835-3331. Slightly cheaper than the *VIP*, this motel's rooms are clean, airy and agreeably furnished; some have internet, for which you'll pay about W5000 more. Look for the building with the stone-clad exterior. ❷

Busosan

Buyeo's centre is dominated by its large fortress. **Busosan** (부소산; March–Oct 7am–7pm; Nov–Feb 8am–5pm; W2000) lacks the perimeter wall of Gongju's

Gongsanseong, but with its position perched high over the Baengman River, plus a greater variety of trees and a thoroughly enjoyable network of trails, many visitors find this one even more beautiful. It also has history on its side, as this is where the great Baekje dynasty came to an end after almost seven centuries of rule.

On entering the fortress, you'll happen upon one of the many **pavilions** that dot the grounds, though the scattered nature of the trails mean that it's neither easy nor advisable to see them all. Yeonggillu is nearest the entrance and has a particularly pleasant and natural setting; it's also where kings brought local nobility for regular sunrise meetings, presided over by a pair of snakelike wooden dragons that remain today. Paths wind up to Sajaru, the highest point in the fortress and originally built as a moon-viewing platform. The path continues on to the cliff top of **Nakhwa-am**; from here, it is said, three thousand wives and daughters jumped to their deaths after General Gyebaek's defeat by the Silla-Chinese coalition, choosing suicide over probable rape and servitude. This tragic act gave Nakhwa-am its name – **Falling Flowers Rock** – and has been the subject of countless TV epics. Down by the river is **Goransa**, a small temple backed by a spring that once provided water to the Baekje kings on account of its purported health benefits – servants had to prove that they'd climbed all the way here by serving the water with a distinctive leaf that only grew on a nearby plant. The spring water is said to make you three years younger for every glass you drink. The best way to finish a trip to the fortress is to take a **ferry ride** from a launch downhill from the spring. These sail a short way down the river to a **sculpture park** and some of the town's best restaurants; in summer there's a ferry every half-hour or so (W3000 one-way), but the service can be annoyingly infrequent in winter.

Around the city

Heading south of Busosan's main entrance, you might want to swing by **Jeongnimsaji** (정림사지; daily: March–Oct 7am–7pm; Nov–Feb 8am–5pm; W1000), a small but pretty site where a temple once stood. Several buildings here have been recreated, and you'll also find a five-storey stone pagoda – one of only three survivors from Baekje times – and a seated stone Buddha dating back to the Goryeo era.

Of more interest is **Buyeo National Museum** (부여 국립 박물관; Tues–Fri 9am–6pm, Sat & Sun 9am–7pm; free), a large but slightly out-of-the-way place east of the city-centre statue of General Gyebaek. As with other "national" museums in Korea, it focuses exclusively on artefacts found in its local area; here there's an understandable emphasis on Baekje riches. Some rooms examine Buyeo's gradual shift from the Stone to the Bronze Age with a selection of pots and chopping implements, but inside a room devoted to Baekje treasures is the museum's pride and joy – a **bronze incense burner** that has become the town symbol. Elaborate animal figurines cover the outer shell of this 0.6m-high egg-shaped sculpture, which sits on a base of twisted dragons; it's considered one of the most beautiful Baekje articles ever discovered, displaying the dynasty's love of form, detail and restrained opulence.

A short walk south of General Gyebaek's statue is **Gungnamji** (궁남지), a beautiful lotus pond with a pavilion at its centre, and surrounded by a circle of willow trees; outside this weepy perimeter lie acres of lotus paddies, making this peaceful idyll feel as if it's in the middle of the countryside. To the east of town is a cluster of seven **Baekje tombs** (백제 왕릉); their history is relayed in a small information centre, though none of the former occupants are known for sure. A taxi from central Buyeo shouldn't cost much more than W3000.

Baekje Cultural Land

Across the river from Busosan, **Baekje Cultural Land** (daily 9am–5pm; W9000) opened in 2010, a large new facility intending to showcase the city's dynastic history. Despite these noble intentions, it comes across as something of a rush-job, but it's still just about worth the trek from central Buyeo (around W7000 by taxi). Near the entrance there's an overlarge **museum** with absolutely nothing of historical interest inside, its curators choosing instead to bring ancient Baekje to life with a succession of cheesy dioramas. Just behind this brutal structure is a **mock-Baekje palace**, which is at least a little more in keeping with dynastic times; however, on closer inspection its reproduction buildings reveal themselves to be rather poorly painted, and the incessant piped music parping from innumerable speakers ruins the atmosphere somewhat. Best, perhaps, is the **recreation of Wiryeseong**, the first Baekje capital (which was actually inside present-day Seoul; see p.66). Here you'll find a clutch of thatch-roofed buildings, separated by dirt paths. Hunt around and you'll find a small booth selling seafood pancakes (해물 파전; *haemul pajeon*), drinks and simple snacks; other restaurants outside the complex include an excellent option inside the adjacent *Lotte Resort* (see p.272).

Eating

Food in Buyeo has similarities in style, content and quality with the cuisine of Jeolla province – expect plenty of **side dishes**, and more use of **herbs** and **natural seasoning** than is usual in typical Korean food. One fascinating place is ★ *Minsokgwan* (민속관), a traditionally styled restaurant with a courtyard full of old Korea paraphernalia, and tables and chairs inside fashioned from tree trunks. The *naengmyeon* (냉면) – buckwheat noodles served in a cold, spicy soup – are good for cooling off in the summer, or try the home-made *gimchi*-tofu mix (두부김치). It's on the road heading from Busosan to the ferry dock, and perhaps best accessed by taxi; if you go looking yourself, keep an eye out for a Chinese-language sign with a pair of stone turtles straining their necks towards it. Otherwise, try ★ *Baekjeae-jip* (백제의집), on the main road just outside the fortress entrance; here you can have a gigantic set meal of leaves, duck meat (or beef, though duck is a local speciality) and innumerable side dishes, for around W10,000 per person.

Gongju

Presided over by the large fortress of Gongsanseong, small, sleepy **GONGJU** (공주) is one of the most charming cities in the land, and deserving of a little more fame. It's also the best place in which to see relics from the Baekje dynasty that it ruled as capital in the fifth and sixth centuries: **King Muryeong**, its most famous inhabitant, lay here undisturbed for over 1400 years, after which his tomb yielded thousands of pieces of jewellery that provided a hitherto unattainable insight into the splendid craft of the Baekje people. Largely devoid of the bustle, clutter and chain stores found in most Korean cities, and with a number of wonderful sights, Gongju is worthy of at least a day of your time.

Arrival, information and city transport

Gongju is divided by the Geumgang River, with its small but spick-and-span new **bus terminal** just off the north bank. There are direct buses here from cities and towns across the Chungcheong provinces, as well as Seoul and other major Korean cities. The small **local bus terminal** near the fortress serves Gongju's periphery. The main **tourist information** centre (Ⓣ041/856-7700; daily 9am–6pm; winter 9am–5pm), under Gongsanseong, usually has helpful, English-speaking staff.

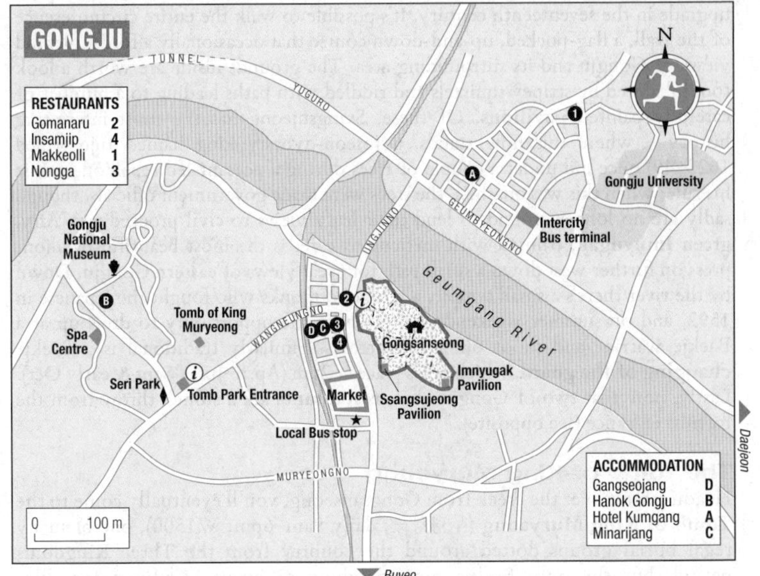

Gongju's small size means that it's possible to **walk** between all of the sights listed here, with Gongsanseong a beautiful fifteen-minute walk from the terminal, along the river and over the bridge. **Taxis** are also cheap, with W4000 enough to get you anywhere in town.

Accommodation

Gongju's poor range of **accommodation** is no doubt the main reason why the city has failed to attract international tourists, bar the occasional busloads of Japanese day-trippers from Seoul. **Motels** are centred in two areas: north of the river, to the west of the bus terminal, is a bunch of new establishments (including a couple of cheesy replica "castles", looking over the Geumgang at a real one), while a group of older cheapies lie south of the river across the road from Gongsanseong. The latter is a quainter and more atmospheric area, and slightly closer to the sights, but the newer rooms are far more comfortable.

Gangseojang 강서장 ⓣ041/853-8323. This red-brick, creekside *yeogwan* is the best option south of the river, and has decent-enough rooms; ask for the one with a computer terminal and free internet. Nearby, and also acceptable, is the similarly priced *Minarijang*. ❷

Hanok Gongju ⓣ041/840-2763. A fairly decent recreation of a Baekje-era village (complete with café and convenience store), its wooden *hanok* buildings heated from beneath by burning wood. Rooms are spartan, for sure, but the location is relaxing, and the experience somewhat unique. ❺

Hotel Kumgang ⓣ041/852-1071. The only official "hotel" in town, though in reality just a less-seedy-than-average motel with a few twin rooms to augment the doubles. However, it has friendly staff, spacious bathrooms, internet-ready computer terminals in most rooms and a moderately priced bar-restaurant on the second floor, and should suffice for all but the fussiest travellers. ❸

Gongsanseong

For centuries, Gongju's focal point has been the hilltop fortress of **Gongsanseong** (공산성; daily 9am–6pm; winter 9am–5pm; W1500), whose 2.6km-long **perimeter wall** was built from local mud in Baekje times, before receiving a stone upgrade in the seventeenth century. It's possible to walk the entire circumference of the wall, a flag-pocked, up-and-down course that occasionally affords splendid views of Gongju and its surrounding area. The grounds inside are worth a look too, inhabited by stripey squirrels and riddled with paths leading to a number of carefully painted **pavilions**. Of these, Ssangsujeong has the most interesting history – where this now stands, a Joseon-dynasty king named Injo (ruled 1623–49) once hid under a couple of trees during a peasant-led rebellion against his rule; when this was quashed, the trees were made government officials, though sadly are no longer around to lend their leafy views to civil proceedings. Airy, green **Imnyugak**, painted with meticulous care, is the most beautiful pavilion; press on further west down a small path for great views of eastern Gongju. Down by the river there's a small temple, a refuge to monks who fought the Japanese in 1592, and on summer weekends visitors have the opportunity to dress up as a Baekje warrior and shoot off a few arrows. Similarly traditional is a Baekje **changing of the guard**, which takes place at 2pm (April–June, Sept & early Oct). Lastly, note that two of Gongju's best **restaurants** are a stone's throw from the fortress entrance (see opposite).

The tomb of King Muryeong

Heading west over the creek from Gongsanseong, you'll eventually come to the **Tomb of King Muryeong** (무령왕릉; daily 9am–6pm; W1500), one of many regal burial groups dotted around the country from the Three Kingdoms period, but the only Baekje mound whose occupant is known for sure. Muryeong, who ruled for the first quarter of the sixth century, was credited with strengthening his kingdom by improving relations with those in China and Japan; some accounts suggest that the design of Japanese jewellery was influenced by gifts that he sent across. His gentle green burial mound was discovered by accident in 1971 during a civic construction project – after one-and-a-half millennia, Muryeong's tomb was the only one that hadn't been looted. All have now been sealed off for preservation – the fact that you can't peek inside is disappointing, but the sound of summer cicadas whirring in the trees, and the views of the rolling tomb mounds themselves, make for a pleasant stroll. A small exhibition hall contains replicas of Muryeong's tomb and the artefacts found within. Opposite the entrance is **Park Seri Park**, a tiny patch of land dedicated to female golfer **Seri Park**, Gongju's most famous citizen. Incidentally, another famous sporting Park also hails from Gongju – Major League pitcher **Park Chan-ho**.

Gongju National Museum

To see the actual riches retrieved from Muryeong's tomb head west to **Gongju National Museum** (공주 국립 박물관; Tues–Sun 9am–6pm; free), set in a quiet wooded area by the turn of the river. Much of the museum is devoted to jewellery, and an impressive collection of Baekje bling reveals the dynasty's penchant for gold, silver and bronze. Artefacts such as elaborate golden earrings show an impressive attention to detail, but manage to be dignified and restrained with their use of shape and texture. The highlight is the king's flame-like **golden headwear**, once worn like rabbit ears on the royal scalp, and now one of the most important symbols not just of Gongju, but of the Baekje dynasty itself. Elsewhere in the museum exhibits of wood and clay show the dynasty's history of trade with Japan and China.

Near the museum, you can relax at a small **hot spring** spa resort; the W5000 admission fee allows you entry to the pools and sauna facilities, and is a small price to pay to emerge clean and refreshed.

Eating and drinking

Food in Gongju is almost uniformly excellent, yet this wonderfully enjoyable facet of the city remains surprisingly off the radar, even for Korean tourists. The local specialities are **duck meat** (오리고기; *ori-gogi*), **chestnuts** (밤; *bam*) and **ginseng** (인삼; *insam*), and as in neighbouring Buyeo you'll find your table festooned with even more **side dishes** than the national norm (which is already a lot). Another dish that deserves a mention is dog-meat soup (보신탕; *bosintang*), which may appeal to adventurous travellers; you'll find plenty of places serving this dish around the local bus terminal. Two excellent **restaurants**, catering for more regular tastes, can be found near Gongsanseong; criminally, almost no places have a view over the river.

The area around **Gongju University** (공주대), north of the main bus terminal, has some interesting places to **drink**, with the bar called *Makkeolli* a focal point; open until late and busiest during term-time, the full version of its name translates as something like "W10,000 can make you happy", and the deceptively smooth rice wine certainly proves this point. Convenience stores, as well as the restaurants listed below, sell bottles of **chestnut makkeolli** (밤 막걸리; W1800 in a shop, W5000 in a restaurant), a particularly creamy and delicious local take on the drink.

Gomanaru 고마나루 This unassuming restaurant is, quite simply, one of Korea's most enjoyable places to eat. Here W10,000 per head (minimum two) will buy a huge *ssam-bap* (쌈밥), which features a tableful of side dishes, and over a dozen kinds of leaves to eat them with. An extra W5000 will see the whole shebang covered with edible flowers – absolute heaven.

Insamjip 인삼의집 Although ginseng pops up in the side dishes at many Gongju restaurants, this place prides itself on the stuff: W5000 will get you a ginseng *bibimbap*, W6000 a *galbi-tang* (beef rib soup) infused with ginseng, and W7000 a full set meal where the "cure-all root" pops up in almost every dish.

Nongga 농가 Like *Gomanaru*, this restaurant may not look like much, but the food is nothing short of superb. Everything on the menu features chestnut in some way; you'll likely see the things being shelled by the charming local family who own the joint. W5000 will buy you a chestnut-and-seafood pancake (밤 해물파전), five huge chestnut dumplings (밤 만두) or much more besides – an almost embarassingly low price for such delectable food.

Magoksa

A beautiful 45-minute bus ride through the countryside west of Gongju is **Magoksa** (마곡사; daily 8am–6pm; W3000). The exact year of this temple's creation remains as mysterious as its remote, forested environs, but it's believed to date from the early 640s. It is now a principal temple of the **Jogye** order, the largest sect in Korean Buddhism. Although the most important buildings huddle together in a tight pack, rustic farmyard dwellings and auxiliary hermitages extend

Slow talk

When passing through rural Chungcheong, those who've been travelling around Korea for a while may notice something special about the way locals talk. The **pace of conversation** here is slower than in the rest of the land (particularly the staccato *patois* of Gyeongsang province), with some locals speaking in a drawl that can even have non-native students of the language rolling their eyes and looking at their watches in frustration. One folk tale, retold across the nation, describes a Chungcheongese town that was destroyed by a falling boulder: apparently it was spotted early enough, but locals were unable to elucidate their warnings in a speedy enough manner.

into nearby fields and forest, and can easily fill up a half-day of pleasant meandering if you're not temple-tired. The hushed vibe of the complex provides the main attraction, though a few of its buildings are worthy of attention. **Yeongsanjeon** (영산전) is a hall of a thousand individually crafted figurines, and has a nameplate said to have been written by King Sejo (ruled 1455–68), a Joseon-dynasty monarch perhaps best famed for putting his brother to the sword. At the top of the complex, **Daeungbojeon** (대웅보전) is a high point in more than one sense; the three golden statues in this main hall are backed by a large, highly detailed Buddhist painting, and look down on a sea of fish-scaled black roof tiles.

Practicalities

Magoksa can be reached on **buses** #7 and #18 from the small terminal near the fortress in Gongju. On the way from the bus stop to the temple you'll find a number of **motels** and **restaurants**, the best of which are the *Magok Motel* (마곡 모텔; ⓣ041/841-0047; ❸), pretty swanky considering the rural location, and *Gareung-binga* (가릉빈가) just down the hill, a restaurant-cum-teahouse that serenades diners with traditional piped music.

Gyeryongsan National Park

Despite its comparatively puny size relative to its Korean brethren, **GYERYONGSAN NATIONAL PARK** (계룡산 국립 공원) is a true delight, with herons flitting along the trickling streams, wild boar rifling through the woods and bizarre long net stinkhorn mushrooms – like regular mushrooms, but with a yellow honeycombed veil – found on the forest floors. It is said to have the most *gi* (기; life-force) of any national park in Korea, one of several factors that haul in 1.4 million people per year, making it the most visited national park in the

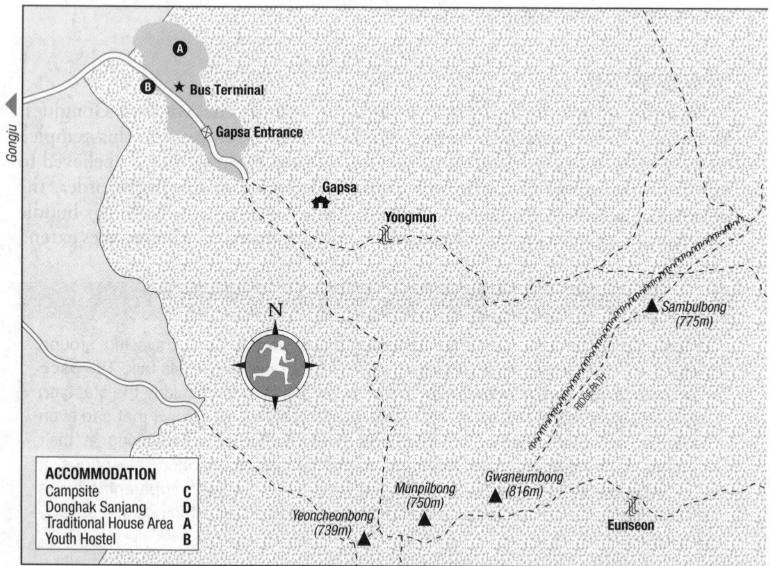

Chungcheong region. The main reasons for this are accessibility and manageability – it lies equidistant from Gongju to the west and Daejeon to the east, and easy day-hikes run up and over the central peaks, connecting **Gapsa** and **Donghaksa**, two sumptuous temples that flank the park, both of which date back over a thousand years.

Arrival and accommodation

To get to the Gapsa entrance, take **bus** #2 from Gongju's local bus terminal. Another #2 bus runs here from Daejeon's Yuseong terminal, meaning that – unbelievably – there are only two buses serving Gapsa, both of which have the same number. From Daejeon, **bus** #107 runs from Yuseong to the Donghaksa entrance every fifteen minutes or so.

The bulk of Gyeryongsan's **rooms (and restaurants)** are around the bus terminal below Donghaksa, but not all are of high quality; the Gapsa end is prettier and more relaxed. *Donghak Sanjang* (동학 산장; ⓣ042/825-4301; ❸) has average rooms but is right above the Donghaksa bus terminal and consequently one of the first to sell out. Nearby is a **campsite** (from W3000 per tent). Below Gapsa are some very rural *minbak* (❶), while on the other side of the car park is an achingly sweet village of **traditional houses** with simple rooms for rent – at night the cramped, yellow-lit alleyways create a scene that is redolent of a bygone era, and make for a truly atmospheric stay. Rooms go from W20,000, but hunt around to find the best and try to haggle the price down. There's also a **youth hostel** in the Gapsa area (ⓣ041/856-4666; dorms W15,000), which is as soulless as others around the country.

The temples

Gapsa (갑사) is the larger and more enchanting of the pair, its beauty enhanced further when surrounded by the fiery colours of autumn – maple and ginkgo trees

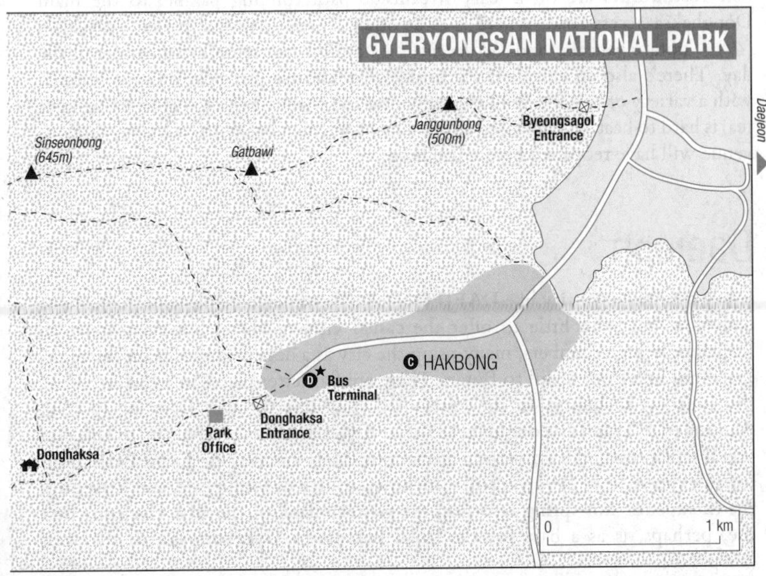

make a near-complete ring around the complex, and if you're here at the right time you'll be treated to a joyous snowfall of yellow and red. It was established in 420, during the dawn of Korean Buddhism, though needless to say no extant structures are of anything approaching this vintage.

On the other side of the park entirely, and connected to Gapsa with umpteen hiking trails (see below), **Donghaksa** (동학사) is best accessed from Daejeon and is said to look at its most beautiful in the spring. It has served as a college for Buddhist nuns since 724, and its various buildings exude an air of restraint (though some have, sadly, been renovated without much care).

Hiking across the park

Although the temples are pretty, most visitors to the park are actually here for the **hike** between them – two main routes scale the ridge and both should have you up and down within four hours, including rests; given the terrain, it's slightly easier to hike east to west if you have a choice. Heading in this direction, most people choose to take the path that runs up the east side of Donghaksa, which takes in a couple of ornate stone pagodas on its way to Gapsa. Others take a faster but more challenging route south of the temple, which heads up the 816m-high peak of Gwaneumbong; these two routes are connected by a beautiful **ridge path** that affords some excellent views. Whichever way you go, routes are well signposted in Korean and English, though the tracks can get uncomfortably busy at weekends; a less crowded (and much tougher) day-hike runs from Byeongsagol ticket booth – on the road north of the main eastern entrance to the park – to Gwaneumbong, taking in at least seven peaks before finally dropping down to Gapsa.

Eating

Local *ajummas* will go out of their way to lure you into their establishments. The best **restaurants** are on a leafy streamside path running parallel to the main Donghaksa access road, where – as at other Korean national parks – *gamjajeon* (감자전; potato pancake) and *dongdongju* (동동주; milky rice wine) are the order of the day. There's also an excellent streamside **teahouse** just below Gapsa temple, with a variety of teas for W4000 – in winter the bitter *saenggang-cha* (생강차; ginger tea) is hard to beat. It had closed at the time of writing, but with luck this gorgeous venue will have reopened before too long.

Daejeon

Every country has a city like **DAEJEON** (대전) – somewhere pleasant to go about daily life, but with little to offer the casual visitor. These, however, arrive in surprisingly high numbers, many using the city as a default stopover on the high-speed rail line from Seoul to Busan. There are far better places in which to break this journey, including on the lesser-used slow line through Danyang (p.288), Andong (p.175) and Gyeongju (p.185), but if you do choose to hole up in Daejeon you'll find a few mildly diverting attractions. Most vaunted are **Expo Park**, built for an exposition in 1993 yet still somehow a source of local pride, and **Yuseong**, the therapeutic hot-spring resort on the western flank of the city. Daejeon's best use, perhaps, is as a base for the small but pretty **Gyeryongsan** to the west (see p.278).

Arrival and information

Daejeon has excellent **bus** connections to every major city in the country, though arrivals are often hampered by the city's incessant traffic. Rather confusingly, there are three main bus terminals: buses from most Chungcheong destinations arrive at the Seobu terminal to the south of the city, while the other two – the express (*gosok*) terminal and the intercity Dongbu terminal – sit across the road from each other to the northeast. The city also has two **train** stations: Daejeon station is right in the centre and sits on the Seoul–Busan line, while Seodaejeon station is a W3000 taxi-ride away to the west, sitting on a line that splits off north of Daejeon for Gwangju and Mokpo. Daejeon station has an excellent **tourist information office** on the upstairs departure level (daily 9am–6pm; Ⓣ042/221-1905), which can help out with accommodation or bus routes; there's a slightly less useful one outside the express bus terminal.

City transport

The city's size and the amount of traffic makes getting around frustrating. The **city bus** network is comprehensive but complicated, with hundreds of routes – two of the most useful are #841, which connects Daejeon station to all three bus terminals, and #107, which runs from the express terminal via Yuseong to Gyeryongsan (see p.278). Given the traffic it may be better to head from Daejeon station to Yuseong by **subway**, on the line that bisects the city, running past Dunsandong's bars on the way; tickets come in the form of cute blue plastic tokens, and cost W900.

Accommodation

Finding a **place to stay** shouldn't be too much trouble, though don't expect much in the centre – the higher-end lodgings are all way out west in **Yuseong**, the default base for the city's many business visitors. Many of these squat over **hot springs**, the mineral-heavy waters coursing up into bathrooms and communal steam rooms; non-guests can usually use the latter for a fee (W6000–25,000). The city centre's main **motel** areas are notoriously sleazy, particularly the one surrounding the bus terminals. Pickings are even slimmer in Eunhaengdong, the area west of the main train station, but if you come out of the main exit and turn right onto the side street before the main road, you'll come across a warren of near-identical **yeoinsuk** – bare rooms with communal showers and squat toilets set around courtyards, but dirt-cheap at W10,000.

Bijou Motel Eunhaengdong ⓣ042/254-6603. Across the main road from the train station (to the right of the T-junction as seen from the exit), this is an acceptable lower-end choice, with clean and cheerily decorated en-suite rooms. ❸

Carib Theme Motel Yuseong ⓣ042/823-8800. Just around from the *Legend*, this is one of the best cheap sleeps in Yuseong. Ask to see a few rooms – some have internet, some are carpeted, and some even trump the upmarket hotels with steam saunas. ❸

Legend Yuseong ⓣ042/822-4000, ⓦwww.legendhotel.co.kr. The cheapest and friendliest of Yuseong's top hotels, the stylish *Legend* gives five-star service at four-star prices. Rooms are decked out in relaxing tones, and there's an on-site restaurant and spa. ❼

Motel Bobos Express Bus Terminal area. The zone around the main bus terminals is awash with sleazy motels, and this is no exception, but rooms here are the cushiest in the area. ❸

Hotel Riviera Yuseong ⓣ042/823-2111, ⓦwww.hotelriviera.co.kr. The plushest hotel in the city features Japanese and Chinese restaurants, as well as a stylish lounge bar, and is large enough to seem quiet most of the time. The rooms have been pleasantly decorated and have internet, though not all have bathtubs. ❼

Around the Gapcheon

On the northern fringe of the city, just past the Gapcheon River (officially a stream, but fairly wide), you'll find Daejeon's official draw, **Expo Park** (엑스포 공원; Tues–Sun 9am–6pm; W3000), along with a clutch of surrounding sights. Built for the city's Expo '93 World's Fair, the park's buildings were designed almost a decade in advance of the festival itself; they already looked dated by the time the party rolled into town, and do so to an even greater degree today. While it won't appeal to everyone, this urban dystopia has its own unique appeal, particularly when allied to the fact that the park is almost totally empty other than on national holidays. Behind the park is **Kumdori Land** (daily 9am–7pm; W20,000), an amusement park named after the little yellow alien mascot of the Expo.

The banks of the Gapcheon come alive in the summer with picnickers, and the park-like area immediately south of the river, across the pedestrianized Expo Bridge, is a popular weekend hangout for local families. You can rent bikes for W3000 per hour from a booth just south of the bridge. Also here is **Hanbat Arboretum** (한밭 수목원; daily 9am–6pm; summer evenings until 9pm; free), a peaceful area containing some interesting tree life, and an excellent **modern art gallery** (Tues–Sun 10am–5pm; W2000). Further on is the **National Government Complex**, four large, sinister cuboids that would look quite at home in Pyongyang. While there's nothing to see inside, these are the most visible examples of Korea's recent attempts to shift its capital from Seoul to the Daejeon area, a move ditched – after considerable expense – following the discovery that it violated the national constitution.

Mountains

The best way to enjoy Daejeon is to head to the mountains that encircle the city. Budding hikers should make their way to **Bomunsan** (보문산), a 458m-high peak that marks the city's southern fringe. It's a simple, invigorating climb that provides fantastic views of Daejeon to the north and rolling mountainous countryside to the south. Avoid the abysmal zoo adjacent to the mountain, unless you want to see lonely seals, miserable penguins and what must be the world's saddest eagles. Also great for a climb is **Gyejoksan** (계족산), a similarly sized peak rising cone-like from a plateau to the northeast, and particularly popular when the weather looks like creating a good sunset. Both peaks take a couple of hours to get up and down, and signs point the way to secluded temples and hermitages. Gyejoksan also has a couple of sections of fortress wall from the Baekje era.

Several **bus** routes head to Bomunsan from Daejeon; most useful are the #724 from Daejeon station and the #113 from City Hall. Gyejoksan is also on a number of routes, including the #720 and #102; you're unlikely to have to wait for more than fifteen minutes for any of them.

Eating and drinking

Daejeon's culinary scene is unremarkable, but you should still eat well. There are a tremendous number of **restaurants** in the centre, within walking distance of Daejeon station; locals are particularly fond of Galbi Street, a whole row of establishments south of Jungangno subway station devoted to the dish. The restaurants near the express bus terminal are more tightly packed; this is a good place to find a healthy local favourite called *samgyetang* (삼계탕), a ginseng-infused chicken soup. Ten minutes' walk southwest of the terminals along Dongseoro, *Pungnyeon Samgyetang* (풍년 삼계탕) is the oldest and most famed establishment, though several places serve the same dish closer to the buses – figure on W8000 or more per head.

Eunhaengdong, the area around the train station, has a number of **bars** that are wildly popular with local expats. *J-Rock* is particularly recommended; it's within walking distance of Jungangno subway station – take exit four. Interest has shifted of late to the ever-growing "new downtown" area of Dunsandong, near City Hall; here you can puff on a hookah (W10,000) in ★ *Ethnic*, a faintly Arabic subterranean lair centred on a small pond.

Cheonan and around

After years in the shadows, **Cheonan** (천안) is a city on the up: now connected to Seoul by subway and high-speed train, its population has boomed in recent years, both with disaffected office workers from the capital and migrants from Asia who have been brought over to work on one of the many construction projects. The new **KTX line** has enabled commuters to work in Seoul while living in a cheaper, more manageable city, but despite the flashy new department stores and housing complexes, there's little here to detain travellers bar the superb **Arario Gallery** – instead, visitors mainly use Cheonan as a jumping-off point for the largest museum in the country, the fascinating **Independence Hall of Korea**.

Arrival and information

Cheonan's main **train** (including subway) and **bus** stations are a twenty-minute walk from each other in the city centre. Outside the former is a small **tourist**

information booth (daily 9am–5pm; ⓣ041/550-2445). The city is at the tail end of Seoul's subway line 1 – it's a fair couple of hours to central Seoul, and another to Soyosan at the northern end of the line. Regular trains take an hour from the capital.

High-speed **KTX** services, meanwhile, take just thirty minutes, but terminate at a dedicated station some way west, next to **Onyang**, a hot spring resort – you'll have to take the subway to central Cheonan.

Accommodation

Good **accommodation** is a little thin on the ground, but there are plenty of acceptable places to stay. The main **motel** cluster is near the bus terminal – turn left on exiting the building, cross to the opposite corner of the crossroads, and burrow into the side streets. There's also an extremely decent *jjimjilbang* in this area – turn left out of the bus station, go straight over the main road, and it'll be on your left.

Hotel California ⓣ041/566-3311. Good cheap option near the bus station. Rooms at this motel (it's manifestly not a hotel) are furnished with black tiles and dark wood, and you'll find a free can of beer waiting in the fridge. ❷

Hotel Metro ⓣ041/622-8211, ⓦwww.hotelmetro.co.kr. Visible from the train station exit, this is the best place in town (for what it's worth), though hugely overpriced. Its carpeted rooms are decent with vault-like doors, though bathroom goings-on can be sometimes too visible through the frosted glass that separates them from the bedrooms. ❻

Western Hotel ⓣ041/551-0606. Excellent-value motel (again, *not* a hotel) in the bus station area, offering free internet, soft drinks, snacks and international calls. ❸

The Arario Gallery

The only sight of note in central Cheonan is the excellent **Arario Gallery** (아라리오 갤러리; Tues–Sun 11am–7pm; W5000) next to the bus terminal, which is linked to the contemporary gallery in Seoul (see p.86), and makes a good pit stop en route to the independence hall. Outside the main entrance sits one of Damien Hirst's body-with-bits-exposed sculptures, alongside a tall tower of car axles that pokes fun at the city's ever-declining reputation as a mere transit hub; inside are two exhibition floors, both small but almost always brimming with high-quality modern art. The gallery has excellent connections to China (there's another Arario in Beijing's superlative 798 gallery-cum-warehouse complex), which means that it's often possible to catch glimpses of the burgeoning art scene across the West Sea. The gallery complex is also Cheonan's best place to eat – see "Eating and drinking", below for more.

Getting here from the bus station is a piece of cake – turn left outside the station exit, and you're there. From the train station it's a little trickier; a W3000 taxi ride will do the job, or you can walk it in about twenty minutes. Turn left on the main road running past the station, then after ten minutes or so take the second right at the five-way intersection.

Eating and drinking

Cheonan has a fair few decent **restaurants**, the best (and most accessible) of which are within the Arario complex, near the bus station. Here you'll find *Sodo*, a Japanese restaurant; the *Coffee Bean* café; and *All That Barbeque*, which focuses on Western-style barbecued meats rather than Korean. For the Korean variety, head directly across the main road from the bus station exit to *Bulgogi Brothers*, sibling establishment of the one in Seoul (see p.107). There are a few cheap eats around the train station, and mention must also be made of *hodugwaja* (호두과자),

small **nut cakes** that the city is famous for, and near-compulsory souvenirs for local tourists. They're on sale immediately outside the station exit from W2000. As for **nightlife**, the bus station area is full of bars with little to choose between them, but the hottest club is *St. 101*, home to a popular weekly hip-hop night (W5000 entry).

Independence Hall of Korea

Set in a wooded area east of Cheonan, Korea's largest museum, the **Independence Hall of Korea** (독립 기념관; Tues–Sun: March–Oct 9.30am–6pm; Nov–Feb 9.30am–5pm; free; Ⓦwww.independence.or.kr), is a concrete testament to the country's continued struggle for independence during its most troubled time, from 1910 to 1945, when it suffered the indignity of being **occupied by Japan**. Though this was a relatively short period, the effects were devastating (see box below), and despite the Korean government's initial appeal for locals not to be "filled with bitterness or resentment", the popularity of the place and the size of its seven large exhibition halls – each of which would probably function quite well as individual museums – show that the wounds are still sore. Scarcely an opportunity is missed to insert a derogatory adjective against the Japanese people and policies of the time, but this combination of vitriol and history makes the place an absorbing visit.

Each hall highlights different aspects of the occupation, with the most important displays labelled in English. However, many locals head straight for those detailing

Japanese occupation

If you've done any sightseeing in Korea, you'll no doubt have come across information boards telling you when, or how often, certain buildings were burnt down or destroyed by the Japanese. The two countries have been at loggerheads for centuries, but the 1910–45 **occupation period** caused most of the tension that can still be felt today. In this age of empire, Asian territory from Beijing to Borneo suffered systematic rape and torture at the hands of Japanese forces, but only Korea experienced a full-scale assault on its **national identity**. Koreans were forced to use Japanese names and money, books written in *hangeul* text were burnt and the Japanese language was taught in schools. These measures were merely the tip of the iceberg, and Japan's famed attention to detail meant that even the tall trees were chopped down: straight and strong, they were said to symbolize the Korean psyche, and they were replaced with willows which drifted with the wind in a manner more befitting the programme. The most contentious issue remains the use of over 100,000 **comfort women**, who were forced into slave-like prostitution to sate the sexual needs of Japanese soldiers.

The **atomic bombs** that brought about the end of the World War II also finished off the occupation of Korea, which slid rapidly into civil war. This post-occupation preoccupation kept both factions too busy to demand compensation or apologies from Japan – they were, in fact, never to arrive. While some countries have bent over backwards to highlight wartime misdeeds, Japan has been notoriously stubborn in this regard – its prime ministers have regularly paid respects at **Yasukuni**, a shrine to those who died serving the empire, but notably also to at least a dozen Class A war criminals, and school textbooks have increasingly glossed over the atrocities. This has led to repeated and continuing protests; surviving comfort women, having still not been compensated, hold weekly **demonstrations** outside the Japanese Embassy in Seoul (see p.85). Korea, for its part, has failed to debate successfully the role of **local collaborators** during the resistance, or to acknowledge fully in its own schoolbooks and museums the foreign influences that ended both the Japanese occupation and the Korean War.

Japanese brutality during the colonial period – "Torture done by Japan", a life-size display featuring some unfortunate mannequins, is one of the most popular exhibits, but there are also numerous photographs. Should you tire of the unrelenting indignation, the "Hall of National Heritage" is filled with less bombastic displays detailing traditional Korean life.

A number of city **buses** run to the museum from the bus and train stations in central Cheonan (all have three-digit numbers beginning with 4); the journey takes around half an hour. Ask for *Dongnip Ginyeom-gwan*, if you can get your tongue around it, and the driver will drop you off outside.

Songnisan National Park

SONGNISAN NATIONAL PARK (속리산 국립 공원) is justly one of the most popular parks in Korea, pratly due to its position in the centre of the country, but also thanks to its temple and the visually arresting **33m-high bronze Buddha**, the tallest such figure in the world. Songnisan's myriad trails are a joy to hike, the paths winding uphill alongside gentle streams to heady 1000m-high peaks, but though the park's name translates as "mountains far from the ordinary world", the area between the bus terminal and the main park entrance couldn't be more typical of a Korean tourist hotspot, with more souvenir shops, restaurants and karaoke rooms than you'd expect to find in the midst of such tranquil environs.

There are direct **bus** connections to Songnisan every twenty minutes or so from Cheongju, as well as regular services from Daejeon and the Dong-Seoul terminal in the capital. Buses stop just under 1km away from the park entrance itself, and their arrival is often delayed on summer weekends by the solid traffic running into the park.

Accommodation

The best **accommodation** in the area is at *Lake Hills* (ⓣ043/542-5281 or 2; ⓦwww.lakehills.co.kr; ❻), a hotel snuggled up next to the park entrance. Prices at this heavyweight champ of the Songnisan circuit pack a bit of a punch, but the rooms are just about worth it. Further down the price scale before you

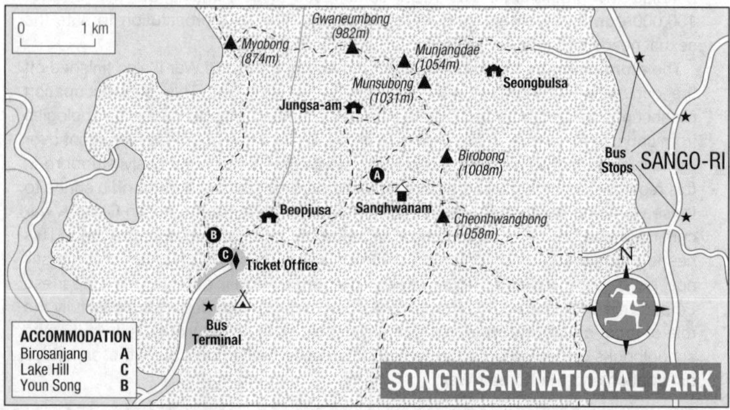

Jikji

To the west of Songnisan lies the city of **CHEONGJU** (청주), an uninteresting place with just one claim to fame: it witnessed the birth of **Jikji** (직지), the first-ever book produced with **movable metal type** rather than single-use page-blocks, and as such a direct ancestor of every newspaper, magazine or Catherine Cookson novel you've ever read. A guide to Seon Buddhism (better known as Zen in the West), *Jikji* was produced in 1377, thereby predating Germany's **Gutenberg Bible** by some 78 years; initially two books were made, but one was destroyed in a fire. The remaining copy was taken to Paris, apparently as an agreed form of compensation for the murder of French missionaries towards the end of the Joseon dynasty, and has now become Korea's equivalent of the Elgin Marbles – despite attempts at repatriation, it still lies in the Bibliothèque Nationale de France.

reach the ubiquitous *minbak* rooms – cheap, simple and often part of family homes, these go for around W30,000 per night – is *Youn Song* (Ⓣ043/542-1500, Ⓦwww.songnisanhotel.com; ❹), a cavernous hotel that's fair value for money. There's a fascinating budget option inside the park itself – the *Birosanjang* (Ⓣ043/543-4782; ❷) is essentially a *yeoinsuk* with a motel price tag, though the location is worth the extra cash – it hangs over a trickling stream, around which chipmunks, frogs and colourful moths pop by for regular visits. Despite the remote location, food is available, and occasionally the *dongdongju* flows well into the night. Remember to sign one of the guestbooks, which date back over thirty years (notable for the chance to see the word "groovy" used with no sense of irony).

Beopjusa

Inside the park, a short, shaded path leads to the park's main draw – the glorious temple **Beopjusa** (법주사). Entirely surrounded by pine and peaks, its name means – somewhat tautologically – "the temple where Buddhist teachings reside", and indeed it has been an active place of worship and religious study since built in 653. Standing with his back to the west (the direction of his death), the huge bronze Buddha statue stands atop an underground hall housing hundreds of figurines, including a rather splendid golden **goddess of compassion**. Back outside and facing the statue is **Palsangjeon** (팔상전), an unconventional five-storey building that, despite a rather squat appearance fostered by the shallow lattice windows, is also the tallest wooden structure in Korea. As with all Korean temple halls bearing this name, it contains eight painted murals depicting various stages from the life of the Buddha; however, this is likely to be the oldest such building in the land. Nearby are two elaborately decorated **stone lanterns**; two lions hold up the torch segment on one (though the flames have long been extinguished), while the other is adorned with four carved devas and a statue of a bodhisattva. This deity incarnate once held an incense burner until he was consumed by fire, presumably reaching nirvana during his show of determination.

Hiking Songnisan

Plenty of **hiking** opportunities lie beyond Beopjusa. The main target is the 1054m-high summit of Munjangdae, an easy three hours away from Beopjusa; locals often make a wish after their third visit to this peak. A short walk from here is the peak of **Birobong** (1008m). Geographically speaking, this can credibly claim to be the centre of the country, as rain falling here – depending on what face it lands on – will end up flowing down the Nakdong River to Busan in the south, running through Gongju on its way to the west coast, or pouring north into the Han River and exiting the mainland through Seoul. An easy ninety-minute ridge trail connects Munjangdae to **Cheonhwangbong**, the park's highest peak at 1058m; a further two-hour walk west will bring you back down to the main park entrance, or you can continue east towards Sango-ri in Gyongsang province.

Eating

Songnisan's **restaurants** are excellent; corn jelly (도토리묵; *dotorimuk*) is the official local speciality, but the *pajeon* (파전; a kind of savoury pancake) here are possibly the best in the country, and are usually slung back with a pot of *dongdongju* (동동주) rice wine. One good place to fill up is the family-run *Chanumul* (찬우물), an orangey building south of the main road.

Danyang and around

Home to a rarified and almost resort-like air, the sleepy town of **DANYANG** (단양) is, quite simply, one of the most relaxing places in Korea. There's little of the noise and clutter found in other urban areas, and life dawdles by at a snail's pace – quite appropriate, really, since **river snails** are a local delicacy. These are dredged from **Chungju Lake**, a river-like expanse that curls a C-shape around the town centre; traversable by ferry, this route is Korea's prettiest navigable inland waterway. Green, pine-covered ripples rise up from the lake – almost totally unspoilt, they make for a thoroughly enchanting backdrop. The loftiest converge at **Sobaeksan**, a pretty national park easily accessible from Danyang; on its cusp is **Guinsa**, one of the most distinctive temples in the whole of the land, and perhaps the highlight of the whole area.

Arrival and information

Danyang's **train** station is inconveniently located a few kilometres west of the centre; it's a W6000 taxi ride into town, or a forty-minute walk along the lakeside trail. The town's **bus terminal** is much more central, and can be found near the western end of the bridge crossing the lake. This building doubles as a **ferry terminal**, from where there are occasional ferries along the lake (see p.290). The town's **tourist office** stands in near-total isolation at the opposite end of the bridge (daily 9am–6pm; ⓣ043/422-1146); English-speaking staff are not always available, but with prior notice they can sometimes organize **paragliding** or **rafting** trips in the area.

Ondal

Anyone spending any time in Danyang is sure to catch occasional glimpses of **Ondal** (온달), the town mascot – you'll see him, and his huge eyebrows, on everything from restaurant signs to toilet doors. According to local legend, he was the town fool until wooing a **local princess** (perhaps using those eyebrows) to one of the town's caves for an underground tryst; after their subsequent marriage, Ondal became a soldier of such skill that he eventually found himself promoted to general, fighting fierce battles at the **fortress** up the hill. The extremely Korean moral of the story seems to be that anything is possible with a good woman at your side.

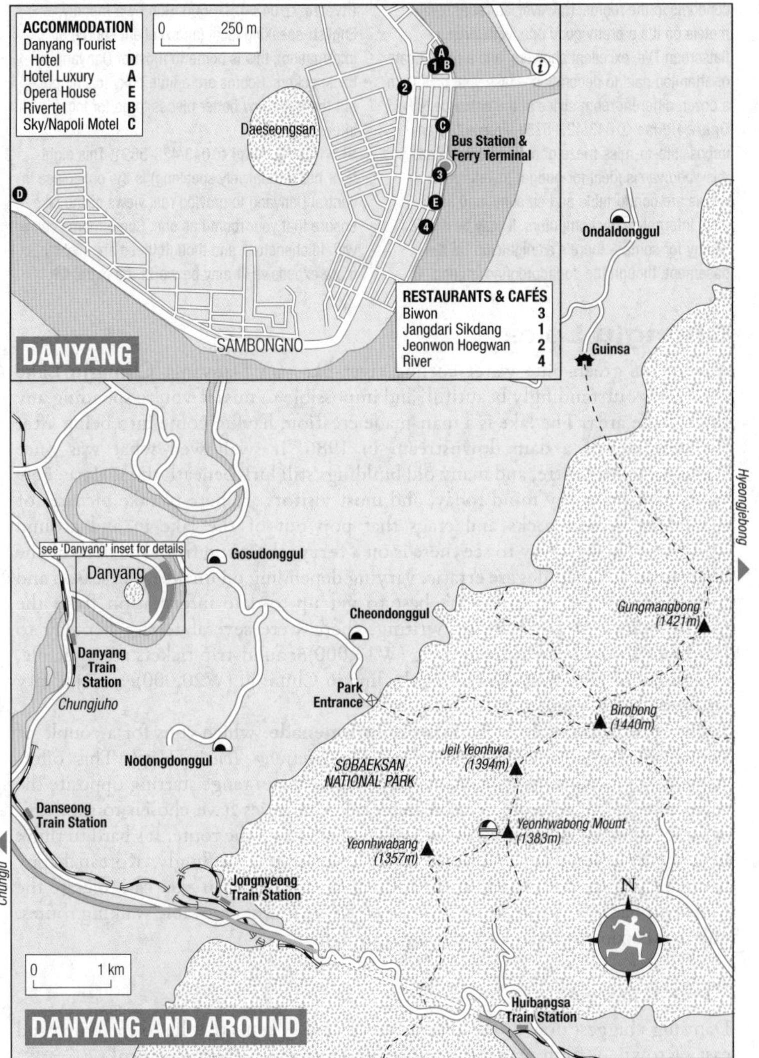

Accommodation

As with most of provincial Korea, there's next to nothing at the higher end of the **accommodation** scale. A few smart new motels have opened up around the bus station, though surprisingly few make use of the phenomenal lake view.

Danyang Tourist Hotel ⓣ043/423-9911, ⓦwww.danyanghotel.com. Away from the centre, and just across the river from the train station, this is an upmarket place with a sauna and the cushiest rooms in town. The prices are fair, though there's little of interest in the surrounding area. It was changing its name to *Edelweiss* at the time of writing. ❺

Hotel Luxury ⓣ043/421-9911. This is manifestly a love motel, not a hotel, as evidenced by the free condoms in the rooms. However, as far as love motels go it's a pretty good one, with large flatscreen TVs, excellent showers, and a great deal of attention paid to decoration – take your pick from a dozen different room styles at the entrance. ❹

Opera House ⓣ043/423-5751. Fronted by an impossible-to-miss frieze of naked Roman gods, this *yeogwan* is ideal for budget travellers. Its rooms are comfortable and en suite, and some have internet-ready computers. It may be a little seamy for some – there's a "nightclub" in the basement, though the soundproofing is good. ❷

Rivertel ⓣ043/421-5600. Run by a friendly, English-speaking local (an excellent source of information), this is home to most of Danyang's backpackers. Rooms are a little poky for the price, but there are few better places to go for local information. ❸

Sky/Napoli Motel ⓣ043/423-5891. This eight-floor beast (relatively speaking) is the only place in central Danyang to provide real views of the lake – ensure that your room has one. Some rooms come with kitchenettes, and though these are slightly more expensive, it may be worth the extra. ❹

Chungju Lake

A body of green-blue water curling river-like past Danyang, **Chungju Lake** (충주호) is outstandingly beautiful, and impossible to miss if you're spending any time in the area. The lake is a man-made creation, having come into being after the building of a dam downstream in 1986. It swallowed what was once Danyang town centre, and many old buildings still lurk beneath the surface. Few locals give these any mind today, and most visitors are here to take pictures of the oddly shaped rocks and crags that pop out of the lake in and around Danyang. The best way to see these is on a **ferry**; these run from the back of the bus terminal. Schedules are erratic, varying depending on finance, the season and the height of the water, so it's best to get up-to-date information from the tourist office. At the time of writing, there were several ferries per day to Janghoe (W8000) and Cheongpung (W13,000); round-trip tickets are available, or you could get off at the end of the line in Chungju (W20,000), a major city with good bus connections.

More easily accessible is the **lakeside promenade**, which runs for a couple of kilometres from the bus terminal to the *Danyang Tourist Hotel*. This offers staggeringly beautiful views of the unspoilt mountain range starting opposite the town centre, but for some reason the local authorities have chosen to spoil this natural beauty by putting up dozens of speakers along the route. It's hard to think of something less appropriate to the surroundings – bafflingly, Korean happy hardcore was on the playlist at the time of writing – but if you can tolerate the sonic bombardment you'll find this one of Korea's most enjoyable walking routes, one that becomes particularly romantic at night.

The caves

Danyang's biggest draw is the abundance of cave systems that lie to the north and east of town. Within walking distance of the centre is **Gosudonggul** (고수동굴; 9am–5pm; W4000); dating back millennia, this 1.7km-long grotto was discovered less than forty years ago. Underground, its honey-yellow stalagmites and stalactites ripple through the dim, damp tunnel, and are visible from metal walkways and staircases. Note, however, the cave is a popular stopover with families out for a weekend drive through the countryside, and can become uncomfortably crowded: visit on a weekday, if possible. To get to Gosudonggil from Danyang cross the bridge, pass the tourist office, and continue until you see the souvenir shops on the left-hand side. The road beyond forks to give access to two further caves, both only a couple of kilometres further away. **Cheondonggul** (천동굴) is highly beautiful, but its tight tunnels make it unsuitable for claustrophobes. **Nodongdonggul** (노동동굴) is a smaller, far less-visited version of Gosudonggul;

buses to this cave are extremely rare so it's better to take a taxi, which should only cost about W5000 one-way. One other cave system, **Ondaldonggul** (온달동굴), can be found on the way to the temple of Guinsa, and forms part of a slightly tacky theme park centred around **Ondal**, the town mascot (see box, p.288).

Eating

Danyang is famed for its **garlic**, which often fills the **market** in the town centre; there's even a festival related to the bulbs each July, which features a **Miss Garlic contest**. Don't miss the local dish, *maneul dolsotbap* (마늘 돌솥밥), in which four types of grain are served in a hot earthenware bowl speckled with chestnuts, dates, ginkgo nuts and other goodies. One good place for this is the rather sorry-looking *Jangdari Sikdang* (장다리 식당) behind the *Rivertel*, which serves the famous dish for W10,000. Another town speciality is *olgaengi haejangguk* (올갱이 해장국), a warming vegetable soup filled with tiny **river snails** from the lake outside. *Biwon* (비원), just across the road from the ferry terminal, is a good place for this dish (W7000). For a meat feast, head directly uphill from the bridge's western end; up and over the crossroads on the left-hand side is *Jeonwon Hoegwan* (전원 회관), a popular *galbi* den with large and plentiful side dishes. Do note that most restaurants in Danyang shut up by 9pm; exceptions include the pizza places on the main road, heading south from the crossroads. Lastly, caffeine addicts should make a morning dash to *River*, a homely little lakeside **café** just south of the ferry terminal.

Guinsa

Shoehorned into a tranquil valley northeast of Danyang is **GUINSA** (구인사; 24hr; free), one of Korea's more remarkable **temple** complexes. A great divider among Koreans, it's viewed by many as the most un-Korean temple, which is emphatically true – the colours and building styles are hard to find anywhere else in the country, and the usual elegant restraint of the traditional layouts has been replaced by a desire to show off. On the other hand, numbers alone bear witness to its importance – well over one thousand monks may reside here at any one time, and the kitchens can dish up food for twice that number on any given day. Guinsa is the headquarters of the Buddhist **Cheontae sect**; once the most powerful in the country, it declined to near-extinction by the 1940s, but was given a second lease of life in 1945 by Songwol Wongak, a monk who put his overseas studies to good use by creating an altogether different temple. Here, the usual black slate of Korean temple roofing has occasionally been eschewed for a glazed orange finish reminiscent of that in Beijing's Forbidden City, and some buildings show hints of Lhasa's Potala Palace with their use of height and vertical lines. Buildings swarm up the valley and connect in unlikely ways, with alleys and bridges crisscrossing like the dragons depicted around the complex; you'll often wander up a path, and

The Cheontae sect

Cheontae (천태) is a Buddhist sect whose Korean followers number almost two million, making it one of the biggest in the country. As with other Korean sects, the school descended from China, where it was created in the sixth century and known as Tiantai (天台). On crossing the West Sea the sect's beliefs were polished into a local form deemed more logical, consistent and holistic than its Chinese predecessor; after wrestling with competitors during Unified Silla rule, the school became fully established in the eleventh century.

on looking back discover three or four routes that could have brought you to the same place. Despite being infested with an almost plague-like number of dragonflies in late summer, it's one of the most scenic places in the country.

Entry to the main body of the complex is through the **Gate of Four Heavenly Kings**, from where you'll head up to the five-storey **law hall**; this is one of the largest such facilities in Korea, and like many other buildings on the complex is elaborate both in terms of painting and structural design. Inside you'll find a golden Shakyamuni Buddha and two attendants – tempting as it may be, you are not allowed to take photos in this building. Further along the maze of paths is a courtyard, sometimes barely visible under the masses of *gimchi* pots used for making dinner, which is cooked up in colossal kitchens and served in the huge **cafeteria** (11.30am–1.30pm; voluntary donation). Close by are several buildings which serve as **living quarters**; the one with the sheer vertical face is the newest and largest structure in the still-growing complex. Heading up alongside this on a wonderful pine-covered path you come to the **Great Teacher Hall**, the achingly gorgeous golden crown of the complex, and a gleaming shrine to its creator, whose statue stands proud at the centre of the hall. Continuing on the uphill path will bring you to his well-tended gravesite, while further on are the western slopes of **Sobaeksan National Park** (see below).

Practicalities

Guinsa is one of the most interesting places in Korea to embark on a **temple-stay** programme, though the sheer number of people here on a typical day will dash any thoughts of Zen (the sect is, in fact, opposed to the Seon school, which approximates Japanese Zen). It's not always possible and is best arranged through a tourist office; the nearest is in Danyang. Failing that, there are **minbak** at the foot of the complex (❶), as are plenty of **restaurants** if you miss lunch at the temple. On the way from the car park to the temple is a **bus stop**, which sees hourly buses to Danyang (the last one leaving the temple at 6pm), several every day to Seoul, and ever-changing connections to other Chungcheong cities.

Sobaeksan National Park

Far quieter than most Korean parks on account of its location, **SOBAEKSAN NATIONAL PARK** (소백산 국립 공원; 8am–6pm; free) is an unheralded delight. It is best visited at the end of spring (around May or June), when a carpet of royal **azalea blooms** paints much of the mountainside a riot of pink, but at any time of the year the views are impressive – the park is traversed by a relatively bare ridge heading in an admirably straight line from northeast to southwest, crossing numerous high peaks. A steep three-hour uphill path runs from the main entrance at Cheondong-ri to **Birobong**, the park's highest peak at 1440m. After reaching the ridge most head straight back down, but if you follow it along in either direction you will be rewarded with a succession of amazing views. Many opt to head northeast to Gungmangbong (1421m), an hour or so away, but only the hardcore continue all the way to Hyeongjebong. Southwest of Birobong are three peaks, confusingly all named Yeonhwabong; on the central crest, taking advantage of the park's clean air and lofty elevation, is Korea's main **astronomical observatory**, though unfortunately it is closed to visitors. From here it's possible to exit the park to the south through the Huibang park entrance, the two-hour walk mopping up small waterfalls and a secluded temple on the way.

Practicalities

The **Cheondong entrance** is close to Danyang – just beyond Cheondonggul cave – and is therefore best reached by taxi (W6000), though there are local buses every hour or so from the town's bus terminal. The park's other entrances aren't easily accessible without your own transport. The **Huibang entrance** is a 2km walk from Huibangsa train station (희방사); those travelling by rail from Danyang should note that the track at one point dives into the mountain, and makes a 360-degree turn before coming out again much further up.

Minbak rooms cluster by the Cheondong entrance; the price goes down and the quality up the further away you get from the entrance. However, the best rooms are about 1km down the road in *Carpe Diem* (ⓣ043/421-2155; ❺), a chic pension with a café and art gallery, whose rooms are filled with modern art and plastic fruit strewn about the place (and Marilyn Monroe at the entrance). Both park entrances have **camping grounds**, and park **maps** are available for the usual W1000.

Travel details

Flights

Cheongju to: Jeju (10 daily; 1hr).

Trains

Cheonan to: Daejeon (regularly; 20min); Seoul (regularly; 30min).
Daecheon to: Seoul (hourly; 2hr 30min).
Daejeon to: Busan (regularly; 1hr 40min); Cheonan (regularly; 20min); Daegu (regularly; 45min); Gwangju (regularly; 1hr 45min); Jeonju (hourly; 1hr 20min); Seoul (regularly; 50min).
Danyang to: Andong (7 daily; 1hr 20min); Seoul (7 daily; 2hr 30min).
Suwon to: Cheonan (regularly; 30min); Seoul (regularly; 35min).

Buses

Buyeo to: Cheongju (10 daily; 1hr 40min); Daecheon (11 daily; 1hr); Daejeon (regularly; 1hr 30min); Gongju (regularly; 1hr); Seoul (regularly; 3hr 30min).
Cheonan to: Cheongju (regularly; 50min); Daecheon (regularly; 2hr 40min); Daejeon (regularly; 1hr); Gongju (regularly; 1hr 10min); Jeonju (8 daily; 2hr 30min); Seoul (regularly; 1hr).
Cheongju to: Buyeo (10 daily; 1hr 40min); Daejeon (every 5min; 1hr); Gongju (regularly; 1hr); Seoul (regularly; 1hr 20min); Songnisan (regularly; 1hr 50min).
Daecheon to: Cheonan (regularly; 2hr 40min); Daejeon (regularly; 2hr 50min); Seoul (regularly; 2hr).
Daejeon Express terminal to: Busan (hourly; 3hr 10min); Cheonan (regularly; 1hr); Daegu (every 30min; 2hr 20min); Gwangju (every 30min; 2hr 30min); Gyeongju (4 daily; 2hr 40min); Jeonju (every 20min; 1hr 20min); Seoul (regularly; 1hr 50min).
Daejeon Dongbu terminal to: Andong (16 daily; 2hr 40min); Cheongju (every 10min; 1hr); Gongju (regularly; 1hr 10min); Muju (regularly; 1hr); Songnisan (regularly; 1hr 40min).
Daejeon Seobu terminal to: Buyeo (every 20min; 1hr 20min); Daecheon (regularly; 1hr 50min); Gongju (regularly; 1hr).
Danyang to: Busan (1 daily; 5hr); Cheongju (regularly; 3hr 30min); Guinsa (13 daily; 30min); Seoul (regularly; 2hr 10min).
Gongju to: Buyeo (regularly; 1hr); Cheonan (regularly; 1hr 10min); Daecheon (regularly; 1hr 40min); Daejeon (every 5min; 50min); Seoul (regularly; 1hr 20min).

6

Jeju Island

CHAPTER 6 Highlights

* **Udo by bike** There are few more enjoyable activities in all Korea than gunning around this tiny island's narrow lanes on a scooter. See p.307
* **Route 97** A rural day-trip along this road can see you take in a volcanic crater, a folk village and a culture museum, before finishing at the beach. See p.309
* **Seogwipo** Flanked by waterfalls, Jeju's second largest city is a relaxed base for tours of the sunny southern coast. See p.310
* **Teddy Bear Museum** The moon landings and the fall of the Berlin Wall are just some of the events to be given teddy treatment at this shrine to high kitsch. See p.314
* **Yakcheonsa** Turn up for the evening service at this remote temple for one of Jeju's most magical experiences. See p.315
* **Geumneung Stone Garden** See whole legions of *hareubang* – distinctive rock statues, and the number one symbol of Jeju. See p.319
* **Hallasan** Korea's highest point at 1950m, this mountain dominates the island and just begs to be climbed. See p.320

▲ *Hareubang* at Geumneung Stone Garden

Jeju Island

The mass of islands draping off Korea's southern coast fades into the Pacific, before coming to an enigmatic conclusion in the crater-pocked **JEJU ISLAND**, known locally as **Jejudo** (제주도). This tectonic pimple in the South Sea is the country's number-one holiday destination, particularly for Korean honeymooners, and it's easy to see why – the volcanic crags, innumerable beaches and colourful rural life draw comparisons with Hawaii and Bali, a fact not lost on the local tourist authorities. This very hype puts many foreign travellers off, but while the five-star hotels and tour buses can detract from Jeju's natural appeal, the island makes for a superb visit if taken on its own terms; indeed those who travel into Jeju's more remote areas may come away with the impression that little has changed here for decades. In many ways it's as if regular Korea has been given a makeover – splashes of tropical green fringe fields topped off with palm trees and tangerine groves, and while Jeju's **weather** may be breezier and damper than the mainland, its winter is eaten into by lengthier springs and autumns, allowing oranges, pineapples and dragon fruit to grow.

Around the island, you'll see evidence of a rich local culture quite distinct from the mainland, most notably in the form of the **hareubang** – these cute, grandfatherly statues of volcanic rock were made for reasons as yet unexplained, and pop up all over the island (see box, p.320). Similarly ubiquitous are the **batdam**, walls of hand-stacked volcanic rock that separate the farmers' fields: like the drystone walls found across Britain, these were built without any bonding agents, the resulting gaps letting through the strong winds that often whip the island. Jeju's distinctive **thatch-roofed houses** are also abundant, and the island even has a breed of miniature horse; these are of particular interest to Koreans due to the near-total dearth of equine activity on the mainland. Also unique to Jeju are the *haenyeo*, **female divers** who plunge without breathing apparatus into often treacherous waters in search of shellfish and sea urchins (see box, p.308). Although once a hard-as-nails embodiment of the island's matriarchal culture, their dwindling numbers mean that this occupation is in danger of petering out.

Jeju City is the largest settlement, and whether you arrive by plane or ferry, this will be your entry point. You'll find the greatest choice of accommodation and restaurants here, and most visitors choose to hole up in the city for the duration of their stay, as the rest of the island is within day-trip territory. Although there are a few sights in the city itself, getting out of town is essential if you're to make the most of your trip. On the east coast is **Seongsan**, a sumptuously rural hideaway crowned by **Ilchulbong**, a green caldera that translates as "Sunrise Peak"; ferries run from here to **Udo**, a tiny islet that somehow manages to be yet even more bucolic. Inland are the **Manjanggul lava tubes**, one of the longest such systems in the world, and **Sangumburi**, the largest and most accessible of Jeju's many craters.

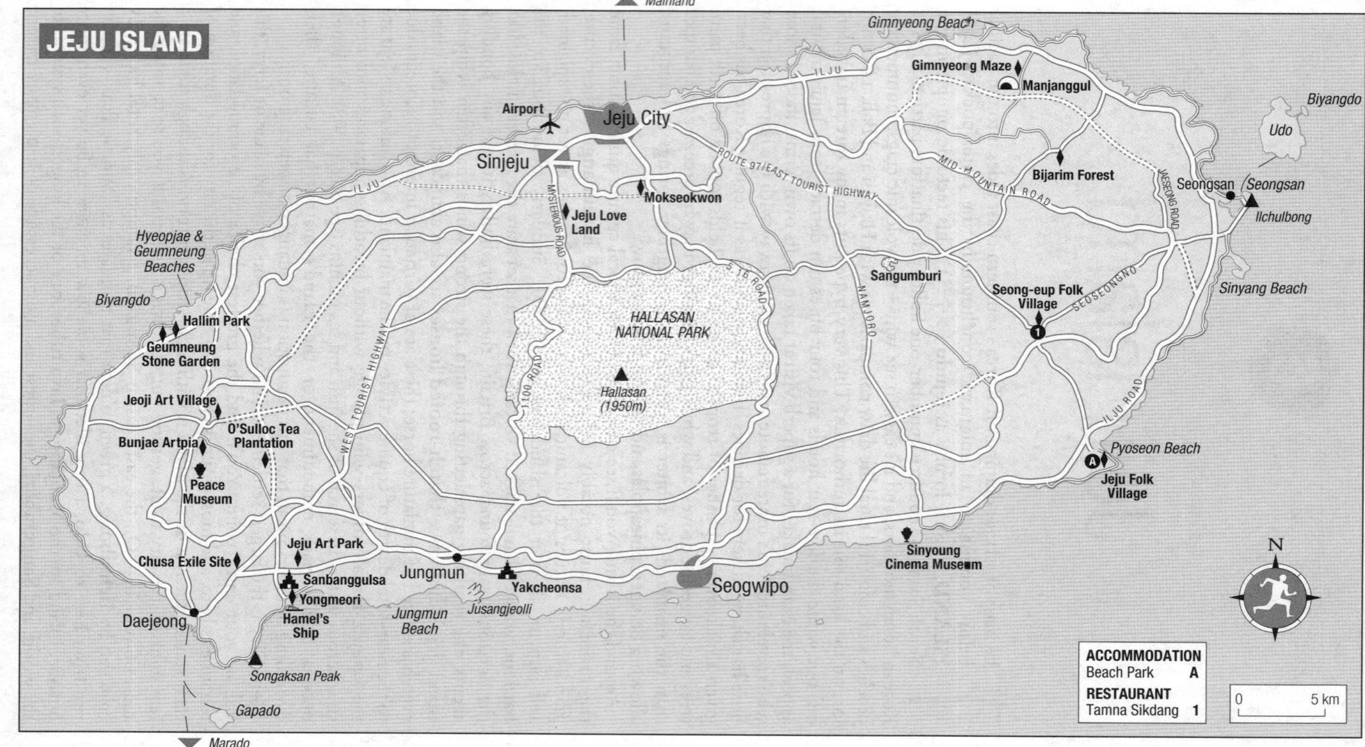
JEJU ISLAND
Mainland
Gimnyeong Beach
Gimnyeong Maze
Manjanggul
Biyangdo
Udo
Airport
Jeju City
Sinjeju
ILJU
ROUTE 97/EAST TOURIST HIGHWAY
MID-MOUNTAIN ROAD
Bijarim Forest
JAESEONG ROAD
Seongsan
Seongsan
Ilchulbong
Mokseokwon
MYSTERIOUS ROAD
Jeju Love Land
Hyeopjae & Geumneung Beaches
Biyangdo
5.16 ROAD
Sangumburi
Seong-eup Folk Village
SEOSEONGNO
Sinyang Beach
NAMJORO
Hallim Park
Geumneung Stone Garden
HALLASAN NATIONAL PARK
Hallasan (1950m)
1100 ROAD
WEST TOURIST HIGHWAY
Jeoji Art Village
O'Sulloc Tea Plantation
Bunjae Artpia
Peace Museum
ILJU ROAD
Pyoseon Beach
Jeju Folk Village
Sinyoung Cinema Museum
Jeju Art Park
Chusa Exile Site
Sanbanggulsa
Yongmeori
Hamel's Ship
Jungmun
Yakcheonsa
Seogwipo
Daejeong
Jungmun Beach
Jusangjeolli
Songaksan Peak
Gapado
Marado
N
ACCOMMODATION
Beach Park A
RESTAURANT
Tamna Sikdang 1
0 5 km

All roads eventually lead to **Seogwipo** on the south coast; this relaxed, waterfall-flanked city is Jeju's second-largest settlement, and sits next to the five-star resort of **Jungmun**. Sights in Jeju's west are a little harder to access, but this makes a trip all the more worthwhile – the countryside you'll have to plough through is some of the best on the island, with the fields yellow with rapeseed in spring, and carpeted from summer to autumn with the pink-white-purple tricolour of cosmos flowers. Those with an interest in calligraphy may want to seek out the remote former home of Chusa, one of the country's most famed exponents of the art. In the centre of the island is **Hallasan**, an extinct volcano and the country's highest point at 1950m, visible from much of the island, though often obscured by Jeju's fickle weather.

Jeju is one of the few places in Korea where renting a car or bicycle makes sense (see p.306 for listings). Outside Jeju City, roads are generally empty and the scenery is almost always stunning, particularly in the inland areas, where you'll find tiny communities, some of which will never have seen a foreigner. **Bicycle trips** around the perimeter of the island are becoming ever more popular, with riders usually taking four days to complete the circuit – Seongsan, Seogwipo and Daecheong make logical overnight stops.

Some history

Jejudo burst into being around two million years ago in a series of volcanic eruptions, but prior to an annexation by the mainland Goryeo dynasty in 1105 its history is sketchy and unknown. While the mainland was being ruled by the famed Three Kingdoms of Silla, Baekje and Goguryeo, Jeju was governed by the mysterious **Tamna kingdom**, though with no historical record of Tamna's founding, it is left to Jeju myth to fill in the gaps: according to legend, the three founders of the country – Go, Bu and Yang – rose from the ground at a spot now marked by **Samseonghyeol** shrine in Jeju City. On a hunting trip shortly after this curious birth, they found three maidens who had washed up on a nearby shore armed with grain and a few animals; the three fellows married the girls and using the material and livestock set up agricultural communities, each man kicking off his own clan. Descendants of these three families conduct twice-yearly – in spring and autumn – ceremonies to worship their ancestors.

More prosaically, the *Samguk Sagi* – Korea's main historical account of the Three Kingdoms period – states that Tamna in the fifth century became a tributary state to the Baekje kingdom on the mainland's southwest, then hurriedly switched allegiance before the rival Silla kingdom swallowed Baekje whole in 660. Silla itself was consumed in 918 by the Goryeo dynasty, which set about reining in the island province; Jeju gradually relinquished autonomy before a full takeover in 1105. The inevitable **Mongol** invasion came in the mid-thirteenth century, with the marauding Khaans controlling the island for almost a hundred years. The horses bred here to support Mongol attacks on Japan fostered a local tradition of horsemanship that continues to this day – Jeju is the only place in Korea with significant equine numbers – while the visitors also left an audible legacy in the Jejanese dialect.

In 1404, with Korea finally free of Mongol control, Jeju was eventually brought under control by an embryonic **Joseon dynasty**. Its location made it the ideal place for Seoul to exile radicals. Two of the most famed of these were **King Gwanghaegun**, the victim of a coup in 1623, and **Chusa**, an esteemed calligrapher whose exile site can be found on the west of the island (see p.318). It was just after this time that the West got its first reports about Korea, from **Hendrick Hamel**, a crewman on a Dutch trading ship that crashed off the Jeju coast in 1653 (see box, p.317).

With Jeju continually held at arm's length by the central government, a long-standing feeling of resentment against the mainland was a major factor in the **Jeju Massacre** of 1948. The Japanese occupation having recently ended with Japan's

Getting to Jeju

Jeju is accessible by **plane** from most mainland airports (usually around W85,000), as well as a fair few cities across eastern Asia; this has long been the preferred form of arrival for locals, and the resultant closure of ferry routes means that planes are generally the way to go for foreign travellers too.

Ferry schedules have long been in a state of flux, but at the time of writing there were a few daily fast (3hr; W50,000) and slow (5hr; W26,000) ferries to Jeju City from Mokpo, as well as overnight journeys every day bar Sunday from Busan (11hr; from W25,000) and Incheon (14hr; W50,000). A daily high-speed route (1hr 50min; W30,000) started up in 2010, linking Seongsan in east Jeju (p.306) with Jangheung on the mainland.

Whichever way you arrive, it's usually necessary to bring your **passport**.

surrender at the end of World War II, the Korean-American coalition sought now to tear out the country's Communist roots, which were strong on Jejudo. Jejanese guerrilla forces, provoked by regular brutality, staged a simultaneous attack on the island's police stations. A retaliation was inevitable, and the rebels and government forces continued to trade blows years after the official end of the **Korean War** in 1953, by which time this largely ignored conflict had resulted in up to thirty thousand deaths, the vast majority on the rebel side.

Things have since calmed down significantly. Jeju returned to its roots as a rural backwater with little bar fishing and farming to sustain its population, but its popularity with mainland tourists grew and grew after Korea's took off as an economic power, with the island becoming known for the *samda*, or three bounties – rock, wind and women. Recently tourist numbers have decreased slightly, with richer and more cosmopolitan Koreans increasingly choosing to spend their holidays abroad, though Jeju still remains the country's top holiday spot.

Jeju City

JEJU CITY (*jeju-shi*; 제주시) is the provincial capital and home to more than half of its population. Markedly relaxed and low-rise for a Korean city, and loomed over by the extinct volcanic cone of Hallasan, it has a few sights of its own to explore, though palm trees, beaches, tectonic peaks and rocky crags are just a bus-ride away, thus making it a convenient base for the vast majority of the island's visitors.

Jeju City was, according to local folklore, the place where the island's progenitors sprung out of the ground (you can still see the holes at **Samseonghyeol**), and while there are few concrete details of the city's history up until Joseon times, the traditional buildings of **Mokgwanaji**, a governmental office located near the present centre of the city, shows that it has long been a seat of regional power. Other interesting sights include **Yongduam** ("Dragon Head Rock"), a basalt formation rising from the often fierce sea, and **Jeju Hyanggyo**, a Confucian academy. There are also a couple of vaguely interesting **museums**, best reserved as shelter on one of Jeju's many rainy days. South of the centre along the **Mysterious Road**, where objects appear to roll uphill, is the entertainingly racy **Love Land**.

Arrival

Domestic flights from several mainland destinations arrive every few minutes, landing at the island's **airport** a few kilometres west of the city centre. Six **bus** routes make

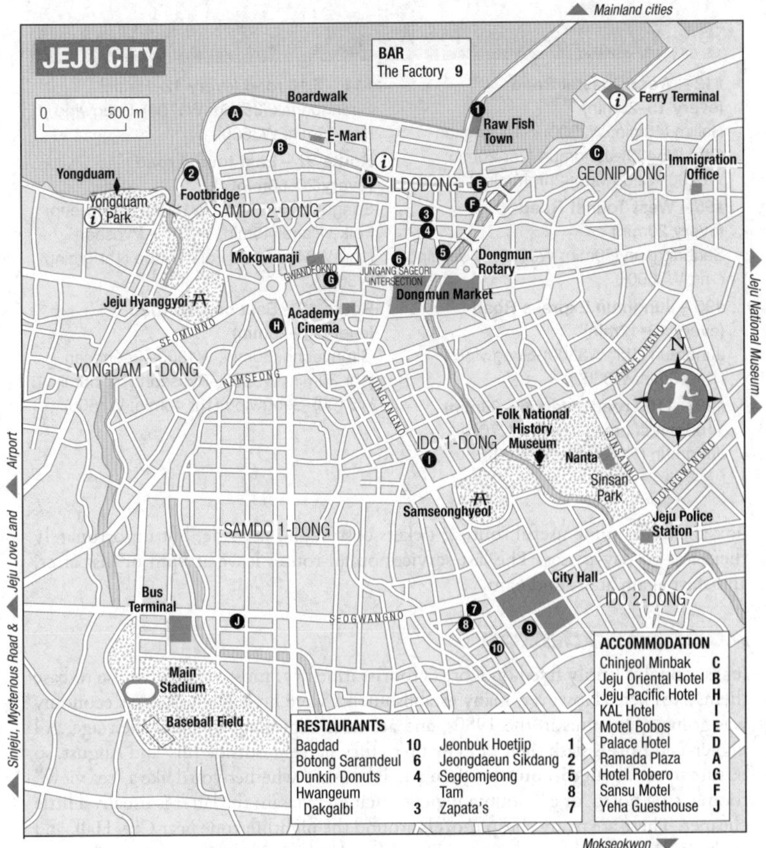

the short run to Gujeju, the city centre, the most useful of which is #100 (W850), which heads east every fifteen minutes or so to the bus terminal, then on to Dongmun Rotary in the city centre, or south to Sinjeju. Bus #600 runs at similar intervals to the top hotels in Jungmun (W3900) and Seogwipo (W5000), south of the island. At the eastern edge of the city is the **ferry terminal**, with connections from several mainland cities. A couple of companies use the **International Ferry Terminal**, 1km further east on the same road; despite the name there are no regular international connections, though cruise ships occasionally dock here. See box opposite for more details.

Information and city transport

There are, for some reason, two **tourist information** desks just metres apart from each other at the airport. At least one will be open from 8am to 10pm (Ⓣ064/742-8866), but both can supply you with English-language maps and pamphlets and help with anything from renting a car to booking a room. Another booth at the ferry terminal offers similar assistance (10am–8pm; Ⓣ064/758-7181). English-language help can also be accessed by phone on Ⓣ064/1330.

Jeju City is small and relaxed enough to allow for some walking, but in order to see everything you'll have to resort to taxis – these shouldn't cost more than W5000 for destinations within Gujeju – or one of the numerous **local buses** (see

Jeju bus routes

#12 – West Coastal Road (every 15–25min)
Hallim (40min; W2300)–Sanbangsan (2hr; W5400)–Jungmun (2hr 20min; W6200)–Seogwipo; 2hr 40min; W7300).

#95 – West Tourist Road (every 20min)
Sanbangsan (50min; W3500)–Moseulpo (1hr; W3600).

#95 – Jungmun Express Road (every 10–12min)
Jungmun (1hr; W3300)–Seogwipo (1hr 10min; W3600).

#99 – 1100 road (every 60–90min)
1100m rest area (40min; W2700)–Jungmun (1hr 20min; W5100).

#11 – 5.16 road (every 12–15min)
Seongpanak (35min; W1700)–Seogwipo (1hr 10min; W3600).

Route 97 – East tourist road (every 20–60min)
Sangumburi (25min; W1800)–Seong-eup Folk Village (45min; W2300)–Pyoseon (1hr; W3400)–Jeju Folk Village (1hr 5min; W3600).

Route 12 – East coastal road (every 15–25min)
Gimnyeong (50min; W1900)–Seongsan (1hr 30min; W3800)–Pyoseon (1hr 55min; W5100)–Seogwipo (1hr 40min; W7500).

box above for some useful routes); tickets cost W850 per ride, but unfortunately there are no day-passes. The last services on all routes leave at 9pm or just after, and start again at around 6am.

Accommodation

Jeju's capital is firmly fixed on Korea's tourist itinerary; most visitors choose to base themselves here. However, many establishments were built when Korea's economy was going great guns in the 1980s, and are now beginning to show their age. All higher-end **hotels** slash their rates by up to fifty percent outside July and August, so be sure to ask about **discounts**. Often you'll be asked whether you'd like a "sea view" room facing north, or a "mountain view" facing Hallasan; the latter is usually a little cheaper. There are many cheap **motels** around the nightlife zone near City Hall, and in the rustic canalside area between Dongmun market and the ferry terminal.

Chinjeol Minbak 친절 민박 Geonipdong ⓣ064/755-5132. One of the cheapest places to stay in the city, with friendly owners who usually try to lure foreign travellers emerging from the ferry terminal, just a short walk away. The atmosphere is pleasant and can feel like a youth hostel at times; try to get a room with a private toilet and TV. ❶

Jeju Oriental Hotel Samdodong ⓣ064/752-8222, ⓦwww.oriental.co.kr. Upper rooms have great sea views; few live up to the promise of the large reception area, but you'll be paying for the facilities anyway – a casino and four restaurants, internet in every room, and courteous staff. Serious competition from the new *Ramada Plaza* across the road means that discounts of fifty percent are not uncommon. ❼

Jeju Pacific Hotel Yongdamdong ⓣ064/758-2500. Set a bit away from things, though just a 10min walk from the sea, this hotel caters mainly to Japanese visitors, and is accordingly surrounded by sushi restaurants and karaoke rooms. All rooms have internet, and some offer views of Hallasan and the ocean from the same window. Rates are slashed off-season. ❼

KAL Hotel Idodong ⓣ064/724-2001, ⓦwww.kalhotel.co.kr. An immaculate hotel and Jeju's tallest building, with 21 floors; friendly, white-suited staff buzz about the place, though the rooms lack character and are small for the price. There's a funky cocktail bar on the top floor, though budget cuts mean that, sadly, it no longer revolves. ❽

Motel Bobos Ildodong ⓣ064/727-7200. Don't be put off by the rather dingy reception area – the wood-floored rooms here are large and airy, and you'll get a free coffee in the morning. The motel is also within walking distance of the ferry terminal and seaside promenade, as well as some of the city sights. ❸

Palace Hotel Samdodong ⓣ064/753-8811. One of several similar hotels on the waterfront, all of which are showing their age and provide rather austere rooms bettered by many motels. The on-site cocktail bar, sauna and two restaurants put it above the competition nearby. ⑤

Ramada Plaza Samdodong ⓣ064/729-8100, ⓦwww.ramadajeju.co.kr. A modern, cavernous hotel – it's even bigger than it appears from outside. Vertigo-inducing interior views, plush interiors and some of Jeju's best food make it the hotel of choice for those who can afford it, though the atmosphere may be a little mall-like, especially when it hosts conventions. ⑧

Hotel Robero Samdodong ⓣ064/757-7111, ⓦwww.roberohotel.com. The modern art strewn about the place fails to disguise the fact that a renovation is overdue, though the rooms themselves are cosy and as good as you'd expect at this price level. Criminally, few have decent views of pretty Mokgwanaji across the road. ⑤

Sansu Motel 산수 모텔 Geonipdong ⓣ064/757-1614. Clean rooms with cable TV and decent private facilities come at rock-bottom prices at this guesthouse run by a Korean-Mexican couple. Try to nab a room facing the stream; it's possible to swim here in summer. ②

Yeha Guesthouse Samdodong ⓣ064/724-5506, ⓦwww.yehaguesthouse.com. Finally, Jeju has a hostel! This friendly, immaculately clean place is a short walk from the bus terminal – an uninteresting part of town, but close to the best bars. Dorms W19,000, doubles ④

The City

The capital's sights aren't a patch on those found elsewhere on the island, but some are still worthy of a visit. Most famous are the "Dragon Head Rock" of **Yongduam** and the shrine at **Samseonghyeol**; Korean tourists are more or less obliged to pay both a visit and show photographic evidence to friends and family. Between these, in the very centre of town, lies the former seat of Jejanese government known as **Mokgwanaji**, a relaxing place to take a stroll around genteel oriental buildings. A day should be enough to visit all these places.

Near the seafront

Who'd have thought that basalt could be so romantic. The knobbly seaside formation of **Yongduam**, or "Dragon Head Rock" (용두암; 24hr; free), appears in the honeymoon albums of any Korean couple worth their salt – or, at least, the ones who don't celebrate their nuptials overseas – and is the defining symbol of the city. From the shore, and in a certain light, the crag does indeed resemble a dragon, though from the higher of two viewing platforms a similar formation to the right appears more deserving of the title. According to Jeju legend, these are the petrified remains of a regal servant who, after scouring Hallasan for magical mushrooms, was turned into a dragon by the offended mountain spirits. Strategically positioned lights illuminate the formation at night, and with fewer people around, this may be the best time to visit. On the way back east towards the city centre, you may be tempted to take one of the gorgeous paths that crisscross into and over tiny, tree-filled Hancheon creek, eventually leading to **Jeju Hyanggyo** (제주 향교), a Confucian shrine and school built at the dawn of the Joseon dynasty in the late fourteenth century. Though not quite as attractive as other such facilities around the country, this academy is still active, and hosts age-old ancestral rite ceremonies in spring and autumn.

In the centre of the city are the elegant, traditional buildings of **Mokgwanaji** (목관아지; daily 8am–7pm; W1500), a recently restored site that was Jeju's political and administrative centre during the Joseon dynasty; it's a relaxing place that makes for a satisfying meander. Honghwagak, to the back of the complex, was a military officials' office established in 1435 during the rule of King Sejong – the creator of *hangeul*, Korea's written text, featured on the W10,000 note – and since rebuilt and repaired countless times. The place also provides evidence that vice and nit-picking are far from new to Korean politics – several buildings once housed **concubines**, entertainment girls, and "female government slaves", while the pond-side banquet site near the site entrance was repossessed due to "noisy frogs".

There's an appealing walk along the **seafront promenade**, a few hundred metres north of Mokgwanaji, which curls around the *Ramada Plaza* hotel and east to a large bank of seafood restaurants that marks the beginning of the harbour. In bad weather the waves scud in to bash the rocks beneath the boardwalk, producing impressive jets of spray; sea breaks are in place, but you should exercise caution all the same.

Samseonghyeol

Jeju's spiritual home, **Samseonghyeol** (삼성혈; daily 8am–6.30pm; W2500), is a shrine that attracts a fair number of Korean tourists year-round. Local legend has it that the island was originally populated by Go, Bu and Yang, three local demigods that rose from the ground here (see p.299). The glorified divots are visible in a small, grassy enclosure at the centre of the park, though it's hard to spend more than a few seconds looking at what are, in effect, little more than holes in the ground. The pleasant wooded walking trails that line the complex will occupy more of your time, and there are a few buildings to peek into as well as an authentic *hareubang* outside the entrance.

The museums

Heading east along Samseongno you'll come to the **Folklore and Natural History Museum** (민속 자연사 박물관; daily 8.30am–6pm; W1100). Local animals in stuffed and skeletal form populate the first rooms, before the diorama overload of the folklore exhibition, where the ceremonies, dwellings and practices of old-time Jeju are brought to plastic life. Unless you're planning to visit the two folk villages on Route 97 (see p.309), there are few better ways to get a grip on the island's history.

A taxi-ride (W3000) further east is **Jeju National Museum** (제주 국립 박물관; Tues–Fri 9am–6pm, Sat & Sun 9am–7pm; W1000, free 1hr before closing). As with all other "national" museums around the country, it focuses almost exclusively on regional finds, but as this particular institution – despite its size – has surprisingly little to see, the free hour before closing time is enough for many visitors. Highlights include some early painted maps, a collection of celadon pottery dating from the twelfth century, and a small but excellent display of calligraphy – be sure to take a look at the original **Sehando**, a letter-cum-painting created by Chusa, one of Korea's most revered calligraphers (see p.318). The upper floor is not open so you'll have to make do with staring up at the sprawling stained-glass ceiling from the lobby.

South of the city

It may seem a little cheeky to have a dedicated rock-and-tree park on an island that's filled with little else, but **Mokseokwon** (목석원; daily 8am–9pm; winter 8am–8pm; W2000), just a few kilometres south of Jeju City, is a delightful place. Arty exhibits here, made from assorted pieces of stone and wood found around the island, provoke a range of feelings from triumph to contemplation. While none is astonishing individually, a lot of thought has gone into the park as a whole: on one side of the complex, a romantic story is played out in rock form; though cheesy, the contorted shapes of stones in love do their best to fire your imagination. The site is just a little too far south of the city to be overrun with visitors, but is easy to get to; bus #500 (25min) runs from various stops.

A few kilometres southwest of Jeju City, and best accessed by taxi, are a couple of intriguing sights. One short section of Route 99, christened the **Mysterious Road** (도깨비도로), has achieved national fame, and though no scheduled buses run to this notorious stretch of tarmac, there's always plenty of traffic – cars and tour buses, or indeed pencils, cans of beer or anything else capable of rolling down a hill, are said to roll upwards here. Needless to say, it's a visual illusion created by the angles of the road and the lay of the land. Some people think it looks convincing, while others wonder why people are staring with such wonder at objects rolling down a slight incline, but it makes for a surreal pit stop. Right next door is another place where the tourists themselves constitute part of the attraction – **Jeju Love Land** (제주 러브 랜드; daily 9am–midnight; W7000) is Korea's recent sexual revolution contextualized in a theme park. This odd collection of risqué sculpture, photography and art has been immensely popular with the Koreans, now free to have a good laugh at what, for so long, was high taboo. There are statues that you can be pictured kissing or otherwise engaging with, a gallery of sexual positions (in Korean text only, but the pictures need little explanation), several erotic water features, and what may be the most bizarre of Korea's many dioramas – a grunting plastic couple in a parked car. You may never be able to look at a *hareubang* in the same way, or see regal tombs as simple mounds of earth – maybe this park is the continuation of a long-running trend. **Taxis** cost around W10,000 from Jeju City; to get back, flag down another cab or ask around for a lift.

Eating, drinking and entertainment

Jeju prides itself on its **seafood**, and much of the city's seafront is taken up by fish restaurants. These congregate in groups, with two of the main clusters being the large, ferry-like complex at the eastern end of the seafront promenade, and another near Yongduam rock. There's plenty of non-fishy choice away from the water – the two best areas are the shopping district around Jungang Sagori, which contains some excellent chicken *galbi* restaurants, and the trendy **student** area west of City Hall. Most of the city's **drinking** takes place in this latter area; particularly recommended are *Bagdad* (see below) and *The Factory*, a good bar. Visitors also have a chance to see *Nanta*, a fun **musical** imported from Seoul (Tues–Sun W40,000).

Bagdad Idodong. Excellent curry house with Nepali chefs and a laid-back, loungey air – particularly as the restaurant segues into a *shisha* bar of an evening.

Botong Saramdeul 보통 사람들 Ildodong. Simple Korean mains go for W4000 and under at this friendly little lair, with daily specials bringing the price down further. Chicken cutlet is a good filler, and the cold buckwheat noodle dishes (*naeng-myeon*) provide relief from the summer heat. The restaurant can be hard to find – look for the pink sign.

Daejin Hoetjip 대진 횟집 Geonipdong. Located on the lower deck of the ferry-like "Raw Fish Town" complex, the *Daejin* has an English-language menu, and a decent choice for sushi experts. A huge W80,000 mixed sashimi meal could feed four, or try the delicious broiled sea bream with tofu for W10,000.

Dunkin Donuts Jungang Sagori. If you're sick to the stomach of Korean food, try these sugary antidotes from W700 per dose.

Hwanggeum Dakgalbi 황금 닭갈비 Near Dongmun Rotary. *Dakgalbi* is a raw chicken kebab cooked at your table in a hot metal tray, which is then boiled up with a load of veggies. It costs around W9000 per portion (there's usually a minimum of two people). When it's nearly finished, you should then add some rice, noodles (or both) to the scraps for yet another meal.

Jeongdaeun Sikdang 정다은 식당 Yongdamdong. Watch Jeju's air traffic glide over the sea at this fish restaurant, which occupies a great location at the tip of a small peninsula between Yongduam and the *Ramada Plaza*. Most dishes are for groups of three or four (W10,000–15,000 per person); solo diners may have to content themselves with the *Hoedeopbap* – raw fish in spicy sauce on a bed of rice.

Segeomjeong 세검정 Dongmun Rotary. Low, low prices mean that this meat restaurant is almost permanently full. The menu is little more than a list of flesh to barbecue, including *saeng galbi* and the saucier *yangnyeom galbi*.

Tap 탑 Geonipdong; look for the Chinese sign 塔. *Soju* flows freely into the early hours at this stylish, wood-panelled restaurant as students set fire to, then eat, a variety of meats. *Samgyeopsal* (pork belly) goes for W8000 per portion, with *gimchi* fried rice a cheap extra.

Zapata's Idodong. The tacos, burritos and quesadillas at this small Mexican restaurant go down well with travellers, and prices are good at W4000–9000 per portion. The owners seem to assume that foreigners can't handle spicy food, so you may have to ask for extra chilli.

Listings

Bike rental The Lespo Mart, just town-side of *Chinjeol Minbak* on the same side of the road, rents out decent bikes for W7000 per day; you'll need your passport to leave behind as security. *Yeha Guesthouse* rents out bikes (guests only) for W5000 per day.

Car rental Several companies at the city airport. Rates start at around W35,000 per day.

Cinema The Academy Cinema, in a large complex a short walk south of Mokgwanaji, is the best place to catch a film; tickets cost W7000.

Hiking equipment There are stores all over the city, especially in the shopping area around Jungang Sagori. Prices are higher than you might expect, but Treksta is a fairly safe choice.

Hospital The best place for foreigners is the Jeju University hospital (☎064/750-1234); call ☎119 in an emergency.

Internet In addition to the usual cafés dotted around the city there are also free booths in the ferry and bus terminals.

Motorbike rental Jeju Bike, near the bus station, has motorcycles and scooters to hire or sell, and an English-speaking owner (☎064/758-5296).

Post office Post offices across the island are open weekdays from 9am–5pm, with the central post office (☎064/758-8602), near Mokgwanaji, also open on Saturdays until 1pm.

Eastern Jeju

The eastern half of Jeju is wonderfully unspoilt – the coast is dotted with unhurried fishing villages, while inland you can see evidence of Jeju's turbulent creation in the form of lava tubes and volcanic craters. Buses to the region leave Jeju City with merciful swiftness, passing between the sea and lush green fields, the latter bordered by stacks of *batdam*. **Seongsan**, on the island's eastern tip, is the most attractive of Jeju's many small villages, crowned by the majestic caldera of **Ilchulbong**.

Just offshore is **Udo**, a bucolic island whose sedentary pace tempts many a visitor to hole up for a few days. A cluster of natural attractions can be found south of the port village of Gimnyeong, most notably **Manjanggul**, which are some of the world's longest underground lava tubes. Further south again, **Route 97** heads southeast from Jeju City across the island's interior, running past **Sangumburi**, a large, forested volcanic crater, and two rewarding **folk villages**: one a working community with a patchwork of traditional thatch-roofed houses, the other an open-air museum which – though devoid of inhabitants – provides a little more instruction on traditional Jeju life.

Seongsan

You're unlikely to be disappointed by **SEONGSAN** (성산), an endearing rural town with one very apparent tourist draw looming over it: **Ilchulbong** (일출봉), or "Sunrise Peak", is so named as it's the first place on the island to be lit up by the orange fires of dawn. The town can easily be visited as a day-trip from Jeju City but many visitors choose to spend a night here, beating the sun out of bed to clamber up the graceful, green slope to the rim of Ilchulbong's crown-shaped caldera (24hr; W2000). It's an especially popular place for Koreans to ring in the New Year – a small **festival** celebrates the changing of the digits. From the town it's a twenty-minute or so walk to the summit; a steep set of steps leads up to a 182m-high **viewing platform** at the top, and although the island's fickle weather and morning mists usually conspire to block the actual emergence of the sun from the sea, it's a splendid spot nonetheless. Powerful bulbs from local squid boats dot the nearby waters; as the morning light takes over, the caldera below reveals itself as beautifully verdant, its far side plunging sheer into the sea – unfortunately, it's not possible to hike around the rim. If you turn to face west, Seongsan is visible below, and the topography of the surrounding area – hard to judge from ground level – reveals itself.

Besides the conquest of Ilchulbong, there's little to do in Seongsan bar strolling around the neighbouring fields and tucking into a fish supper, though the waters off the coast do offer some fantastic diving opportunities. South of town is **Sinyang Beach**, where the water depth and incessant wind make it a good place to windsurf; equipment is available to rent.

Practicalities

Minbak and **fish restaurants** can be found in abundance, but anybody wanting higher-end accommodation, or meat not culled from the sea, may have a hard time. Simple rooms are easy to find – alternatively, hang around and wait for the *ajummas* to find you – and are split into two main areas: those peak-side of the main road, which tend to be tiny and bunched in tight clusters, or those in the fields facing Hallasan, which are generally located in family homes, and are slightly cleaner. A bit of haggling should see the prices drop to W15,000–20,000. Comfier rooms can be found at the *Condominium-style Minbak* (콘도형 민박; ⓣ064/784-8940; ❸), in a big blue building at the southern edge of town, above a ground-floor restaurant. Rooms here are adequate, and some have internet access; try to nab one with a balcony facing Ilchulbong. Sinyang beach, a few kilometres to the south, also has plenty of rooms for rent, though prices rise sharply during the summer holidays. Coffee and snacks are available from a 24-hour **convenience store** near the Ilchulbong ticket booth.

Sealife Scuba (ⓣ064/782-1150), near *Kondohyeong Minbak*, offers spectacular **diving** trips for around W150,000 per person, equipment included.

Udo

Visible from Ilchulbong is **UDO** (우도), a rural speck of land whose stacked-stone walls and rich grassy hills give it the air of a Scottish isle transported to warmer climes. Occasionally, the nomenclature of Korea's various peaks and stony bits reaches near-Dadaist extremes; "Cow Island" is one of the best examples, its contours apparently resembling the shape of resting cattle. This sparsely populated dollop of land is a wonderful place to hole up for a few days, and one of the best places to spot two of Jeju's big draws – the stone walls (밭담; *batdam*) that line the island's fields and narrow roads, and the **haenyeo**, female divers long famed for their endurance (see box, p.308).

Other than these – and the diving grannies are almost impossible to spot these days – there are very few tourist sights on Udo. Those that do exist can be accessed on the **tour buses** (W5000) that meet the ferries. Usually under the direction of charismatic local drivers, they first stop at a black-sand beach for half an hour or so, which allows just enough time to scamper up the hill to the lighthouse for amazing views that show just how rural Udo really is. The buses stop at a small natural history **museum** (Tues–Sun 9am–5pm, W2000, free entry with bus ticket) – whose second floor is home to some interesting *haenyeo* paraphernalia – and continue past Sanhosa beach before returning to the ferry terminal.

Arrival and getting around

Udo is reached on regular **ferries** (W5500 return) from Seongsan port, which is within walking distance of the town itself. These dock at one of two terminals, so on arrival it may come in handy to note what time the ferries return; if you're staying the night, your accommodation will advise on which terminal to head to.

Tour buses are the easiest way to get around (see above), but infinitely more enjoyable are the **scooters** (W10,000/2hr) and **buggies** (double that) available for

Jeju's diving grannies

It may be hard to believe in a place that once was, and in many ways still is, the most Confucian country on earth, but for a time areas of Jeju had **matriarchal** social systems. This role reversal is said to have begun in the nineteenth century as a form of tax evasion, when male divers found a loophole in the law that exempted them from tax if their wives did the work. So were born the **haenyeo** (해녀), literally "**sea women**"; while their husbands cared for the kids and did the shopping, the females often became the breadwinners, diving without breathing apparatus for minutes at a time in search of shellfish and sea urchins. With women traditionally seen as inferior, this curious emancipation offended the country's leaders, who sent delegates from Seoul in an attempt to ban the practice. It didn't help matters that the *haenyeo* performed their duties clad only in loose white cotton, and it was made illegal for men to lay eyes on them as they worked.

Today, the *haenyeo* are one of Jeju's most famous sights. Folk songs have been written about them, their statues dot the shores, and one can buy postcards, mugs and plates decorated with dripping sea sirens rising from the sea. This romantic vision, however, is not entirely current; the old costumes have now given way to black wetsuits, and the *haenyeo* have grown older: even tougher than your average *ajumma*, many have continued to dive into their 70s. Modern life is depleting their numbers – there are easier ways to make money now, and few families are willing to encourage their daughters into what is still a dangerous profession. The figures peaked in the 1950s at around thirty thousand, but at the last count there were just a few hundred practising divers, the majority aged over 50. Before long, the tradition may well become one of Jeju's hard-to-believe myths.

rent outside both ferry terminals. Udo is so small that it's hard to get lost, and most simply fire around the island's near-empty lanes until it's time to return their vehicle. Don't worry if you're a bit late – this is Udo, after all.

Accommodation and eating

Minbak are readily available, though the rural ambience comes at a slightly higher price than you'd pay in Seongsan; prices are around W30,000 per night. The only truly notable one is *Deungmeoeul* (등머울; ☎064/784-3878; ☎ Mobile 011/341-3604; ❹), which is actually located on an even smaller island, connected to Udo by a small bridge. This is tiny **Biyangdo** (비양도), formerly an important *haenyeo* hangout but now down to a population of just two – a friendly couple who run the *minbak*, speak a little English, and will collect you from the ferry terminal if you give them a call. Back across the bridge is Udo's best **restaurant**, *Haewa Dal Geurigo Seom* (해와달 그리고 섬), which specializes in colossal, fist-sized sea snails called *sora* (소라; W20,000 per portion). You'll find other restaurants near the ferry terminals and above the black-sand beach.

Manjanggul

A short way east of Jeju City, a group of natural attractions provide an enjoyable day-trip. Foremost among them is **Manjanggul** (만장굴; daily: April–Oct 9am–6pm; Nov–March 9am–5pm; W2000), a long underground cave formed by pyroclastic flows. Underwater eruptions millions of years ago caused channels of surface lava to crust over or burrow into the soft ground, resulting in subterranean tunnels of flowing lava. Once the flow finally stopped, these so-called "**lava tubes**" remained. Stretching for at least 9km beneath the fields and forests south of the small port of Gimnyeong, Manjanggul is one of the longest such systems in the world, though only 1km or so is open to the public. This dingy and damp "tube" contains a number of hardened, lava features including balls, bridges and an 8m-high pillar at the end of the course.

Buses run south past the cave to **Bijarim Forest** (비자림숲), a family-friendly network of trails and tall trees. Heading the other way, north of the cave and maze, small but busy **Gimnyeong Beach** has the area's greatest concentration of restaurants and accommodation, and is accessible on the buses that run along the coastal road.

Route 97

With a volcanic crater to see and two folk villages to explore, rural **Route 97** – also known as the East Tourist Road – is a delightful way to cut through Jeju's interior. All three attractions can be visited on a day-trip from Jeju City, or as part of a journey between the capital and Seogwipo on the south coast, though it pays to start reasonably early.

Sangumburi

Heading south from Jeju City on Route 97, the first place worth stopping is **Sangumburi** (산굼부리; daily 9am–7pm; W3000), one of Jeju's many **volcanic craters**; possibly its most impressive, certainly its most accessible, though currently the only one you have to pay to visit. Hole lovers should note that this particular type is known as a Marr crater, as it was produced by an explosion in a generally flat area. One can only imagine how big an explosion it must have been – the crater, 2km in circumference and 132m deep, is larger than Hallasan's (see p.320). A short climb to the top affords sweeping views of some very unspoilt Jejanese terrain; peaks rise in all directions, with Hallasan 20km to the southwest, though not always visible. The two obvious temptations are to walk into or around the rim, but you must refrain from doing so in order to protect the crater's wildlife – deer and badgers are among the species that live in Sangumburi. Consequently there's not an awful lot to do here, though there's a small art gallery on site. Buses (W1800) take around 25 minutes to get here from the terminal in Jeju City; note that most East Tourist Road buses miss Sangumburi, with only one an hour coming here. If you're continuing south the next bus will arrive approximately an hour after your arrival – stand on the main road to flag it down, but keep an eye out, as it'll come by in a flash.

Seong-eup Folk Village

A twenty-minute bus ride south of Sangumburi brings you to dusty **Seong-eup Folk Village** (성읍 민속 마을), a functioning community living in traditional Jeju-style housing, where you're free to wander among the thatch-roofed houses at will; the residents, given financial assistance by the government, are long used to curious visitors nosing around their yards. Here you'll see life carrying on as if nothing had changed in decades – farmers going about their business and children playing while crops sway in the breeze. Most visitors spend a couple of pleasant hours here, and if you're lucky you'll run into one of the few English-speaking villagers, who act as guides.

Though there's nowhere to stay, there are a few **restaurants** around the village; best is *Tamna Sikdang* (탐라 식당), who serve tasty set meals of black pork and side dishes (*heukdwaeji jeongsik*; 흑돼지 정식) for W8000 per head, and make their own *makkeolli*. **Buses** to the village take around 45min from Jeju City, and almost all continue on to Jeju Folk Village.

Jeju Folk Village and around

Route 97 buses terminate near the coast at the **Jeju Folk Village** (제주 민속 마을; daily: April–Sept 8.30am–6pm; Oct–March 8.30am–5pm; W6000). This coastal

Jeju traditions

Essentially a frozen piece of the past, Seong-eup Folk Village is a wonderful place to get a handle on Jeju's ancient **traditional practices**, but you'll see evidence of these age-old activities all over the island. Many locals still wear *galot* (갈옷), comfy Jejanese **costumes** of apricot-dyed cotton or hemp; these are available to buy in Seong-eup, though you'll also find them for sale outside most Jeju sights. Local homes are separated from each other with *batdam* (밭담), gorgeous **walls** of hand-stacked volcanic rock built with no adhesive whatsoever – ironically, this actually affords protection against Jeju's occasionally vicious winds, which whip straight through the gaps. The homes themselves are also traditional in nature, with **thatched roofs** and near-identical gates consisting of three wooden bars, poked through holes in two stone side-columns. This is a quaint local **communication system** known as *jeongnang* (정낭), unique to Jeju and still used today – when all bars are up, the owner of the house is not home, one bar up means that they'll be back soon, and if all three are down, you're free to walk on in. Some houses still have a traditional open-air Jeju **toilet** in their yard; these were located above the pig enclosures so that the family hogs could transform human waste into their own, which could then be used as fertiliser. Needless to say, no locals now use these toilets – traditional, for sure, but some things are best left in the past.

clutch of traditional Jeju buildings may be artificial, but provides an excellent complement to the Seong-eup village to its north. Information boards explain the layout and structures of the buildings, as well as telling you what the townsfolk used to get up to before selling tea and baggy orange pants to tourists. The differences between dwellings on different parts of the island are subtle but interesting – the island's southerners, for example, entwined ropes outside their door with red peppers if a boy had been born into their house. However, the buildings may all start to look a little samey without the help of an English-language **audio guide** (W2000; available from a hidden office behind the ticket booth). There's a cluster of **restaurants** near the exit, though for accommodation you'll have to take a short walk to the nearby coastal town of **Pyoseon**. The best place to stay is the *Beach Park Motel* (Ⓣ064/7877-9556; ❷), on the junction of Route 12 and the folk village access road, which has decent new rooms, though few face the large beach that sits across the road. **Buses** from Pyoseon to Seogwipo run from a road a few blocks further uphill – ask for directions. En route, near the town of Namwon, is the **Sinyoung Cinema Museum** (Tues–Sun 9am–6.30pm; W6000), set in a highly distinctive building whose whitewashed walls and coastal setting carry faint Mediterranean echoes. Its contents are mildly diverting – old projectors and the like – though perhaps most appealing are the surrounding gardens.

Seogwipo

The charming town of **SEOGWIPO** (서귀포) sits sunny-side-up on Jeju's fair southern coast: whereas days in Jeju City and on the northern coast are curtailed when the sun drops beneath Hallasan's lofty horizon, the south coast has no such impediment. Evidence of this extra light can be seen in the tangerine groves that start just outside the city and are famed across Korea. Though the real attraction here is the chance to kick back and unwind, there are a few things to see and do – gorgeous waterfalls flank the city, while water-based activities range from diving to submarine tours.

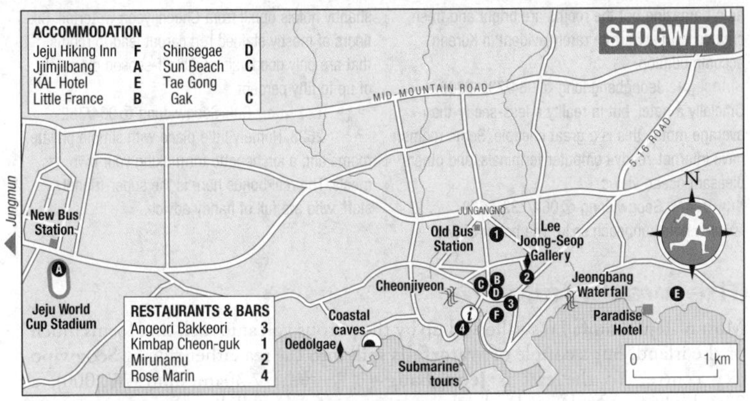

Arrival, information and tours

There are several **bus** routes across the island from Jeju City (see box, p.302), all stopping in Seogwipo's new bus station, inconveniently located several kilometres east of the city centre, near the World Cup Stadium. Buses on routes heading east of Hallasan usually make a stop by the old station in central Seogwipo – get off when the driver tells you to.

The main **tourist office** (daily 9am–6pm; ⓣ064/732-1330) is at the entrance to Cheonjiyeon, a waterfall just west of the centre. Follow the stream out towards the sea, on the same side as the ticket booth, and before long you'll come to the launch point for a **submarine tour** (every 45min; W50,000). The subs dive down to 35m, allowing glimpses of colourful coral and marine life, including octopus, clownfish and the less familiar "stripey footballer". You could also take a **boat trip** around the coast and offshore islets; check with the tourist office for details. **Diving** around the same islands is also popular; Big Blue, a German-run operation (ⓣ064/733-1733; ⓦwww.bigblue33.co.kr), offers a range of courses starting at W95,000 per person. Several places **rent motorbikes** (from around W30,000 per day); your accommodation will have pamphlets directing you to the nearest.

Accommodation

Seogwipo has a range of accommodation to suit all budgets. However, since the closure of the wonderful old *Paradise Hotel* (two years ago and counting at the time of writing, though with plans to reopen at some point), the city's higher-end **hotels** are poor value. There are better pickings further down the price scale, as well as plenty of motels; **camping** by Oedolgae rock is another possibility, or for a cheap and slightly bizarre place to stay, there's a **jjimjilbang** (W8000) in the World Cup Stadium to the west of the city.

Jeju Hiking Inn Seogwidong ⓣ064/763-2380. This quasi-hostel gets mixed reviews, thanks to often smelly corridors and the incredible number of mosquitos that haunt the free internet room in summer. However, the rooms are comfy enough, with passable bathrooms, and you can rent bicycles for W10,000 per day. ❷

KAL Hotel Topyeongdong ⓣ064/733-2001, ⓦwww.kalhotel.co.kr. As with its sister hotel in Jeju City, this is a very businesslike tower that stands proudly over its surroundings. It's immaculate – a little too clinical for some – and the grounds are beautiful. There's also a tennis court, a jogging track, and various on-site restaurants and cafés. ❼

Little France Seogwidong ⓣ064/732-4552, ⓦwww.littlefrancehotel.co.kr. Vaguely European in feel, this chic hotel is a real find. Views aren't amazing but the rooms are bright and fresh, created with a warmth rarely evident in Korean accommodation. ❺

Shinsegae Jeongbangdong ⓣ064/732-5800. Officially a hotel, but in reality a less-seedy-than-average motel, this is a great cheapie. Some rooms have internet-ready computer terminals, and others pleasant ocean views. ❹

Sun Beach Seogwidong ⓣ064/732-5678, ⓦwww.hotelsunbeach.co.kr. The better of two shabby hotels uphill from Cheonjiyeon waterfall. Six floors of mostly stained red carpet lead to rooms that are only good value with off-season discounts of up to fifty percent. ❻

Tae Gong Gak Seogwidong ⓣ064/762-2623. Homely little place with simple private rooms and a kitchenette for making your own meals. The real bonus here is the super-friendly staff, who are full of handy advice. ❸

The waterfalls

Most of Jeju's rainfall is swallowed up by the porous volcanic rock that forms much of the island, but a couple of **waterfalls** spill into the sea either side of Seogwipo city centre. To the east is **Jeongbang** (정방 폭포; 7.30am–6pm; W2000), a 23m-high cascade claimed to be the only one in Asia to fall directly into the ocean. Unique or not, once you've clambered down to ground level it's an impressive sight, especially when streams are swollen by the summer monsoon, at which time it's impossible to get close without being drenched by spray. Look for some Chinese characters on the right-hand side of the falls – their meaning is explained by an unintentionally comical English-language cartoon in an otherwise dull exhibition hall above the falls.

The western fall, **Cheonjiyeon** (천지연 폭포; daily: April–Oct 8am–11pm; Nov–March 8am–10pm; W2000), is shorter but wider than Jeongbang, and sits at the end of a pleasant gorge that leads from the ticket office, downhill from the city centre: take the path starting opposite *Jeju Hiking Inn*. Many prefer to visit at night, when there are fewer visitors and the paths up to the gorge are bathed in dim light.

Other sights

In the centre is an interesting **gallery** (이중섭 미술관; Tues–Sun: July–Sept 9am–8pm; Oct–June 9am–6pm; W1000) devoted to the works of **Lee Joong-seop** (1916–56), who used to live in what are now the gallery's grounds. During the Korean War, he made a number of pictures on **silver paper** from cigarette boxes, which now take centre stage in a small but impressive collection of local modern art. Many of Lee's pieces echo the gradual breakdown of his private life, which culminated in his early demise. Just down the road from the gallery is *Mirunamu*, Seogwipo's most characterful café (see opposite).

West of the city centre is the "Lonely Rock" of **Oedolgae** (외돌개). This stone pinnacle jutting out of the sea just off the coast is an impressive sight at sunset, when locals fish by the waters and the column is bathed in radiant hues. **Buses** (#200 and #300) run here from the city centre, but a taxi shouldn't cost more than W4000. **Camping** is possible along the network of trails that lead through the pines from the bus stop to the rock, below a shop-cum-café with an outdoor seating area.

Eating and drinking

A number of appealing **restaurants**, some with great views, line the sides of the estuary leading up to Cheonjiyeon, though the greatest concentration can be found south of the Jungjeongno-Jungangno junction. *Kimbap Cheon-guk* (김밥천국) by this crossroads dishes out simple but consistent Korean staples at low prices, but a better recommendation is *Angeori Bakkeori* (안거리밖거리), which serves colossal set meals for W7000 – a small price to pay for a table near-covered with delectable (and largely vegetarian) side dishes. Up the road from this restaurant you'll find *Mirunamu* (미루나무), a wonderful **café** run by a local writer; some evenings, they screen films on one of the walls. Equally atmospheric, but in a totally different way, is *Rose Marin*, a curious **bar** by the sea; you have to buy your drinks from a convenience store-like booth, then take them outside to a seating area festooned with scuba gear, surfboards and goodness-knows-what. They sometimes serve a local version of **makkeolli** made with Jeju oranges (*gamgyul*; 감귤); if not, pop down the road to the convenience store.

Jungmun

Korea's most **exclusive resort** curls along a beautiful beach west of Seogwipo, a place where expense-account tourists come from the mainland and abroad to play a few rounds of golf, shop for designer bags or relax in five-star pools in between business conventions. However, to write off **JUNGMUN** (중문) on account of this would be a mistake – the surrounding area has the island's greatest and most varied concentration of sights, accessible on any budget, and can even credibly claim to possess the most distinctive temple, gallery and museum of Korea's inexhaustible collection – all this shoehorned amid beaches, gardens and waterfalls.

Limousine bus #600 (every 15min; 50min; W3900) runs directly from the airport to outside the top hotels listed below. There are also a few routes here from Jeju City's bus terminal, see the box on p.302 for details.

Accommodation and eating

Jungmun's **accommodation** caters almost exclusively to the well-heeled, especially in the resort area, where the *Hyatt*, *Shilla* and *Lotte* all have presidential suites for the über-rich with rack rates of W5,000,000. More affordable rooms are, of course, available, and standards are among the highest in the country, but travellers on very low budgets are advised to stay in nearby Seogwipo. The big-shot lodgings jostle for space along **Jungmun Beach**, while there are a few poor-value motels outside the resort on the main road. At this price level, it's hardly surprising that most guests eat at their hotel, though there are a few **restaurants** at the top of the resort, near the Teddy Bear Museum.

Hana Jungmun Resort, next to the *Shilla* ⓣ064/738-7001. Primarily for conventioneers, this hotel gives guests scant attention for the price – which drops considerably outside summer. ❻

Hyatt Regency Jungmun Resort ⓣ064/733-1234, ⓦwww.hyattcheju.com. The most relaxed of the three major hotels, whose attention to detail is much as you'd expect of this chain; a leaf-filled atrium leads to ample, muted-tone rooms, and the on-site bars and restaurants are top-notch. A health club, spa and nine-hole putting green can also be found on site, and there's a walking trail down to the beach. ❽

Lotte Jungmun Resort ⓣ064/731-1000, ⓦwww.lottehotel.com. The *Lotte* prides itself on being the "finest resort hotel in the world", but can be a little overblown for some. Aimed squarely at designer handbag-toting guests from Japan and Hong Kong, the busy interior resembles a shopping mall, with the outside a theme park where every evening is celebrated with a Vegas-style volcano show; though the rooms are excellent, the outside bustle can often be hard to escape. ❾

The Shilla Jungmun Resort ⓣ064/738-4466, ⓦwww.shilla.net/jeju. Immaculately designed, *the Shilla* is the hotel of choice for Western tourists. Soft music tinkles through the lobby and plush corridors, and it's a big place – though it may look low-rise from the outside, there are seven large floors and 429 soothing rooms. ❾

The Suites Jungmun Resort ⓣ064/738-3800, ⓦwww.suites.co.kr. This hotel is less busy and more minimalist in style than its nearby competition, but the lack of clutter and less starchy attitude of the staff may come as something of a relief. Hefty discounts can usually be clawed from the rack rate. ❼

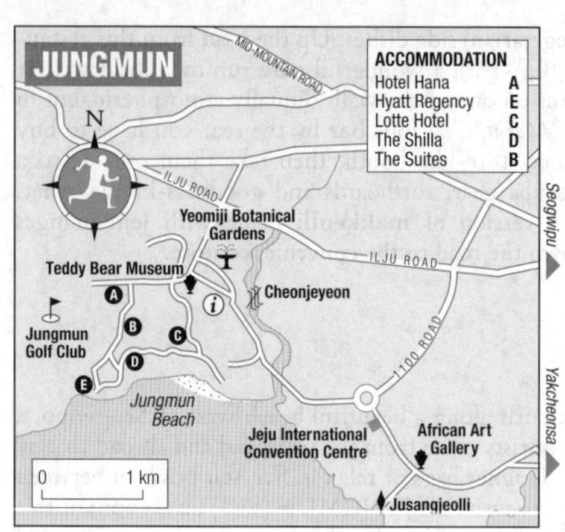

The resort

Although it may sound like the epitome of Jeju tack, the **Teddy Bear Museum** (테디베어 박물관; daily: summer 9am–7pm; winter 9am–6pm; W6000) impresses even its most sceptical visitors. The main building is filled with floors of bears, but the diorama room is the museum highlight, with furry depictions of historical events – one for every decade of the twentieth century. Moving backwards in time, you'll see teddies bashing down the Berlin Wall and fighting in World War II. Then following on from the battle, what appears to be a roller-skating teddy Hitler races into view, though he's soon revealed to be a teddy Charlie Chaplin. Other delights include a teddy Elvis, a "Teddycotta" Army, and a vision of what teddies may be up to in the year 2050, as well as a shop (no prizes for guessing what's on sale here) and garden.

A short walk east of the museum you can stretch your legs on the paths around **Cheonjeyeon** (천제연; daily 8am–6pm; W2500), a string of three small **waterfalls** (not to be confused with the similar-sounding Cheonjiyeon falls in Seogwipo). Note the seven white nymphs painted onto the vermilion humpback bridge – these fairies were said to bathe in the falls in the moonlight; a performance in their honour is put on by the falls every May. The uppermost fall gushes into a pool of almost unnatural sapphire, from where paths head through subtropical flora. More leafy things can be found nearby at **Yeomiji botanical gardens** (여미지 식물원; daily 8.30am–6pm; W6000), an expansive collection of themed gardens presided over by a gigantic greenhouse.

Summer crowds throng to **Jungmun Beach** (중문 해수욕장), which many deem the best in Korea. Despite its popularity, however, the waves rolling in from the Pacific can often be fierce, and this short stretch of sand claims at least one victim a year. Every August it's the starting point for the Ironman Korea Triathlon when competitors thrash out a few kilometres in the ocean, followed by a 180km bike ride across the island, and a 42km marathon for dessert.

East of the resort

East of the beach, waves smash against the hexagonal basalt columns of **Jusangjeolli** (주상절리; daily 10am–6pm; W2000), which rise in angular beauty from the sea in formations similar to the Giant's Causeway in Ireland. These strange creations were created when lava from one of Jeju's many volcanic explosions came in contact with sea water, and can be viewed from a loop platform that runs along the coast. The columns are about 2km from the resort – just about within walking distance, or a short taxi ride away – and can be combined with a visit to the **African Art Gallery** (아프리카 미술 박물관; daily 9am–7pm; W6000) a stone's throw away. This was the brainchild of Mr Han, a traveller and interior designer who developed his collection into a museum. The collection was moved in 2004 from Seoul to a larger and more interesting building – a large faux-dirt structure peppered with logs on the outside, built to resemble the world's largest adobe building, the spectacular Grand Mosque in Djenné, Mali. Inside there's an interesting display of African photography on the ground floor, while the upper levels are mostly filled with sub-Saharan carved wood. Make sure your visit coincides with one of the entertaining **musical performances** (Tues–Sun 11.30am, 2.30pm & 5.30pm); the groups are usually from the musical hotbeds of Ghana, Nigeria and Senegal.

Yakcheonsa temple

A few kilometres east of Jungmun, and best reached by taxi or bike, is the stunning temple of **Yakcheonsa** (약천사; 24hr; free). Built in the 1990s, what it lacks in historical value it more than makes up for with its main building, a feast of intricate decoration despite its colossal size – the cavernous four-storey main hall is claimed to be the biggest in Asia, and is one of the most impressive in the country. The huge golden Buddha at the centre is best viewed from the encircling upper levels, which are themselves crowded with thousands of Buddhist figurines. Yet more (over five hundred, and all individually crafted) can be found in an exterior hall to the front of the complex; most are jovial (cheer up, no. 184) and many are individually interesting – take a look at no. 145's disturbing party trick, if you can find him. The best time to visit is 7pm on a summer evening, when worshipping locals **chant** under the interior glow with their backs to the sunset. Insect and bird calls add extra resonance to the bell rings that mark the beginning of the service, while squid boats out at sea shine like fallen stars on the horizon.

The best way to get to Yakcheonsa is by rented **scooter**, since it's not on any bus routes, and those taking a **taxi** to the temple will likely have to pay the driver to stick around if they want a ride back. Failing that, it's a beautiful half-hour **walk** on quiet farmland roads from the nearest bus stops – the route is a little circuitous, so you'll have to ask for directions, but basically the main road is to the north (ie away from the sea), and the temple nearer the small coastal road to the south. Few pedestrians use these paths, so the local farmers occasionally neglect to chain up their dogs; an attack is unlikely, and crouching to pick up a rock (real or imaginary) should be enough to scare away any that come too close.

Western Jeju

Jeju's western side, though strikingly beautiful, is somewhat wilder and less hospitable than east of Hallasan, with its sights generally harder to reach – if you have no **transport** you may have to resort to the occasional spot of hitchhiking. However, this remoteness is very much part of the appeal, and those who've been drawn to the island by promises of empty roads, bucolic villages and unspoilt terrain should look no further – to many, this is quintessential Jeju.

The sights are grouped into three main clusters; it's possible to complete any of these within a day, even after factoring in transport to and from Jeju City (commuting from Seogwipo is also possible, but will require a little extra patience).

Jeju's windswept southwestern corner boasts a collection of sights, three of them within walking distance of each other around the mountain of Sangbangsan and accessible on a single ticket. **Sangbanggulsa** is a temple hewn out of the peak itself, which looks down on **Yongmeori**, a jagged and highly photogenic coastline pounded mercilessly by waves; adjacent to this sits a replica of a Dutch vessel which came a cropper near these crags. In the distance lie the wind- and wave-punished islets of **Gapado** and **Marado**, the latter being Korea's southernmost point.

Just north of Sangbangsan are a couple of arty attractions – contemporary fans may appreciate the large outdoor **sculpture park**, while traditionalists should head to the former exile site of **Chusa**, one of Korea's foremost calligraphers. Further inland, in a remote area hard to penetrate without your own transport but well worth the effort, are a **tea plantation**, a **bonsai park** and the underground tunnels and rusty munitions of a **peace museum**.

Sanbangsan and around

Jeju's far southwest is one of its most scenic locales, presided over by the mountain of **SANBANGSAN** (산방산), which rises crown-like from the surrounding terrain. According to local folklore, this mountain once lay in what is now Hallasan's crater area, and was blasted to the edge of the island when the mountain erupted. Although the sharp cliffs that separate Sanbangsan's lower regions from its tree-flecked summit would make rock climbers go weak at the knees, the mountain has long been considered holy, and the highest you're allowed to go is the cave temple of **Sanbanggulsa** (산방굴사), about halfway up (there are, however, some challenging rock trails lower down). The holy grotto (daily 8.30am–7pm; W2500), created by a monk in Goryeo times, is bare but for a Buddha on its rear wall, while fresh, drinkable mountain water drips unceasingly from the ceiling near the entrance; slow as the flow is, try to catch the drops directly in one of the plastic cups provided, as the pool that they land in is hardly ever cleaned. The cave constitutes one of Jeju's official "ten grand sights", but after sweating up the hundreds of steps that lead here you're more likely to be impressed by the superlative view of the ocean and the area's surrounding communities than the cave itself. This view is partially obscured by some ugly metal mesh at the top of the grotto opening, which provides important protection from falling rocks, a fact hammered home by several large indentations.

From Sanbangsan's slopes you should be able to make out what appears to be a marooned **ship** just inland from the coast. This is a replica of a Dutch trading ship that crashed off Jeju's shores in 1653, with important consequences for Korea and its relationship with the West – see box opposite. An account of the ship and her crew's story is provided in an **exhibition** inside the vessel (same times as Sanbanggulsa, and accessible on the same ticket); some of this has, rather tenuously, been devoted to a more recent Dutch connection – South Korea's 2002 World Cup manager Guus Hiddink. In case you're wondering, the statue fighting the dinosaur outside the ship is also Guus, even if it does look more like Bill Clinton.

Yongmeori

The dramatic, wind-swept cliffs of **Yongmeori** (용머리) stretch into the sea just past the ship, and are accessible on the same ticket (same times too). A fissure-filled walkway curls around the rocks, but be warned that it may be closed if the waves are coming in with a lot of force: the seas in this unsheltered corner of Jeju are notoriously unpredictable, so don't venture too near the edge. The rock formations are stunning, their beauty somehow heightened by the strong winds that usually race in from the South Sea, and once around the outermost tip the contrast between the golden horizontal strata of the cliffside and the vertical grey crags of Sanbangsan becomes apparent. Keep an eye out for naturally made water paths that surge through the rock, where small fish peek out and dash between the crevices. *Ajummas* sometimes set up stalls along here to sell freshly caught fish. The community settled along this stretch of the coast is **HWASUN** (화순), situated at what would be an idyllic place were it not for

A peek inside the "Hermit Kingdom"

In 1653 a **Dutch trading ship** bound for Nagasaki in Japan encountered a fierce typhoon south of the Korean peninsula and ran aground on the tiny island of **Gapado**. Just half of its crew of 64 survived the shipwreck, but despite their obvious status as victims rather than aggressors, they had entered the **"Hermit Kingdom"** and found themselves treated with scant respect – Joseon-era Korea was a highly isolationist land, whose policy (one rarely triggered) was to bar any foreigners who washed ashore from returning to their homeland. Forced into servitude, they made repeated attempts to escape, but it was not until 1666 that a group of eight managed to flee to Japan from Yeosu, a port city in what is now Jeonnam province. Unfortunately, they found Japan little more welcoming, but one year later a second escape took them back to the Netherlands. The accounts of survivor **Hendrick Hamel** became a bestseller in his homeland, and gave the West its first real portrayal of the Korean peninsula; English-language copies of *Hamel's Journal: A Description of the Kingdom of Korea 1653–1666* have been published, but are hard to track down.

the ugly power station that was built by the shore to supply much of Jeju's energy. If this blight wasn't enough, now the depth of the bay (and its convenient location, as far as possible from Pyongyang) has attracted the **South Korean navy**, which plans to move a number of destroyers into a purpose-built naval port by 2020. The residents' regular protests are doing little to block a deal apparently set in stone, which makes a mockery of Jeju's designation as the "Island of World Peace". For now, though, nearby **Hwasun beach** is a scenic place to relax.

Offshore lie the islets of **GAPADO** (가파도) and **MARADO** (마라도), home to tiny communities of just a few dozen people who somehow manage to eke out a living from land and sea. Low-lying **Gapado** was the unlikely conduit for the West's first contact with Korea, as it was where Hamel's ship ran aground. **Marado** is smaller, loftier and more popular, attracting fans of geographical extremities who come to stand at Korea's southernmost speck of land. The place recently achieved national fame in a popular TV commercial in which a parachutist floated onto the island asking who had ordered the *jjajang-myeon*, a Chinese noodle dish; now an essential part of any Korean tourist's visit, the island's restaurants serve little else. From the ferry, you may notice caves in the cliffs – these were military storage cavities made by the Japanese during their occupation of Korea, in anticipation of American attacks on strategically important Jeju.

Practicalities

Despite sharing the same coast as Seogwipo, this southwestern region is much more easily visited from Jeju City; **buses** run every 20 minutes from the island's capital (W3500), usually arriving at Sanbangsan within an hour. A similarly frequent bus runs along the coast, though this takes more than twice as long to arrive. Those seeking to travel from Seogwipo or Jungmun may have to change once or twice but services are frustratingly irregular; the drivers should be able to drop you off in the right places. If you fancy the "remote Jeju" experience, you may wish to **stay the night**, and there are a few acceptable places in the area; one such, nestling between Sanbangsan and the sea (and easy to find), is *Ocean House Jeju* (❹), a wood cabin with cooking facilities in every room.

Twice-daily **ferries** to Gapado and Marado run from Daejeong harbour, which can be reached via West Coastal Road buses from Jeju City. However, a number of factors can wreak havoc on the schedule so call Ⓣ064/794-3500 to check if it's running, or pop into any tourist information booth on the island. Ferries also run to Marado from Songaksan on Jeju; there are currently four per day, though again it's wise to call for up-to-date information (Ⓣ064/794-6661).

Jeju Art Park

A few kilometres north of Sangbangsan – off Route 95 – is **Jeju Art Park** (제주 조각 공원; daily 8am–7.30pm; W4500), a large, open-air exhibition of contemporary sculpture from around the world. If you can imagine Copenhagen's Little Mermaid having a garden party with a bunch of oddly shaped friends, you're on the right track, but though metal sculptures are the predominant features around the park's grassy confines, there are several themed areas too, as well as a couple of indoor painting exhibitions. Fairly regular **buses** run to a stop near the park from Jeju City.

Chusa's exile site

Those wanting to make a day of it can try to track down the **exile site** of a calligrapher named **Chusa Jeokgeori** (추사 적거리; daily 9am–6pm; W500), which sits a couple of kilometres west in the midst of some of Jeju's most beautiful farmland. Kim Chun-hee, better known by his pen name, was exiled here in 1840 for his involvement in a political plot. Like a naughty boy sent to his room to consider his actions, he took to drawing on the walls, eventually honing his brush-strokes to such a degree that he is now revered as one of Korea's greatest artists and calligraphers. A letter-cum-painting named **Sehando** is his most famous piece, though the one on display is a replica, the original having been moved to Jeju National Museum (p.304). The exhibition room is small with few actual articles, and there's no English-language information. After you've seen the art you can wander around the nearby traditional buildings that Chusa once called home. While there's little here to detain any but ardent devotees of his work, the surrounding area – particularly that leading up to the distinctive mountain to the south – contains some achingly bucolic farming communities, a timeless land where elderly ladies sow grain, beasts plough the fields and mainland Korea feels a lifetime away.

It's possible to **stay** just a few hundred metres from Chusa's exile site at the excellent *Island Guesthouse* (mobile Ⓣ010/2509-8662), a surprisingly fresh hostel (dorms W20,000) with one double room (❺). It's almost literally in the middle of nowhere, which is what many Jeju travellers are looking for, but it'll be hard to find by yourself; staff will be willing to meet you at the nearest bus stop if you phone ahead.

O'Sulloc tea plantation and around

As you head further north the countryside feels ever more remote; covered with the purples, pinks and whites of cosmos bloom from summer to autumn, this is Jeju at its rural best. It's a fantastic area to explore by bicycle, but without wheels of some kind it can be tough to get around. Somewhat paradoxically, Jeju's lack of traffic means that it's the best place in Korea to hitchhike – even though there are few vehicles on the road, you'd be unfortunate to have more than two or three turn you down. That said, there are one or two busy areas, and tour buses descend en masse to the open plan **O'Sulloc tea plantation** (오설록 차 재배단지), which is a pleasant pit stop for groups touring the west of the island. A café in the **visitor centre** (daily: April–Sept 10am–6pm; Oct–March 10am–5pm; free) serves a stash of green-tea-related goods: try *nok-cha* tiramisu, cookies, ice cream – or even have a cup of tea – before visiting the viewing deck on the top level. The big building on view is the factory itself, one of two that the company uses to make the nation's favourite tea (though to keep costs down, much of it is now grown in China). The real attraction here is the opportunity to walk through the **tea fields**. If you've been to Boseong in Jeolla (p.236) you'll know what to expect, though the fields here are flatter, and despite the plantation's popularity with Korean tourists, a little walk will find you alone among the leaves.

Bunjae Artpia

Greenery of a tinier kind can be found at the **Bunjae Artpia** (분재 아트피아; daily 8.30am–6pm; W7000), a highly picturesque bonsai garden that's hard to reach on public transport. Not so long ago the site on which the park now sits was wild, uncultivated land; nowadays, thanks primarily to the efforts of a lone botanist, this site claims to be the largest bonsai exhibition in the world. Though the English language uses the Japanese word, bonsai culture actually originated in China, where it was known as *penjing*, and hit Korea (known here as *bunjae*), before finally making it to Japan. There's lots of English information (and Russian too) to read as you take a sweet-smelling walk around the gentle mounds of earth that make up the complex. A five-hundred-year-old juniper stands in tiny pride as the star of the show, a mushroom-shaped mini-tree with a two-tone trunk – the light wood is dead, the dark still going strong. A more dynamic exhibit is a Korean elm that has wedged open the rock beside it, in a manner similar to the Angkor temple of Ta Prohm in Cambodia. You can buy capsules of fish food to feed the **koi carp** that swim in a nearby pond, some of which are more than twenty years old. For food, there's a **buffet** in the dining room (11am–2pm; W6500), or try the delicious red snapper set menu in the afternoon (2.30–5pm; W8000).

The Peace Museum

Tucked away in countryside near the tea plantation is the **Peace Museum** (평화 박물관; daily 8.30am–6pm; W5000), one of many such places in Korea. Like the others, it's entirely devoted to Japan's occupation of the Korean peninsula, and not so peaceful at all when groups of school kids are having nationalistic rhetoric barked at them through megaphones. If you're lucky enough to avoid these, you'll be rewarded with a modest but absorbing exhibition set in an extremely tranquil area. Deeming Jeju a strategically important hub between China, Korea and the Japanese mainland, Japanese forces established headquarters on the site of the museum during their occupation of Korea, and at one point planned to station up to seventy thousand soldiers on the island. Korean slaves were used to dig the 2km of **tunnels** that still snake underfoot, some of which are open to the public – cool, squat and dark, they're not for claustrophobes. There are relics from the occupation period on show in the main building (guns, grenades and the like), where staff will be pleased to show you an English-language film. This contains interviews with survivors from the camp, and explains the site with a refreshing lack of vitriol, though as there are a few gory pictures, it's not really for kids. Across the road is a **botanical garden** (daily 9am–5pm; W1000), which is a great place to reward your endeavours, with a cup of herbal tea, for getting this far.

The northwestern coast

Hareubang are all over Jeju – and Korea, in fact – so you may question the need to gather together a whole park full of them. However, **Geumneung Stone Garden** (금릉 석물원; daily 8am–7pm; W1000) is an absorbing sight nonetheless, since it houses Jeju's famed stone grandfathers in substantial numbers. Many of these are in the regular *hareubang* shape, though most have been pushed and pulled into unconventional forms by young local artists. Big, small, wonky or squat, they make for some great photo opportunities, as do the statues with Buddhist and local themes. Abandon hope all ye who enter the **Hell Path** – a crying child points the way to a narrow, snaking trail of ghoulish stone misshapes that, in true hellish fashion, seems to go on without end. There's also a collection of small *hareubang*

Grandfathers of rock

What is it with Pacific islands and **statues**? The *moai* of Easter Island are the most famous, but similar relics have been found on Fiji, Tahiti, Hawaii and Okinawa, among other places. Jeju's own version is the *dolhareubang*, or **"stone grandfather"**. Commonly abbreviated to **hareubang** (하르방), they can be found all over Korea – nowadays usually outside fish restaurants wishing to drum up custom. Bulgy-eyed and often cheery, they differ from their Polynesian counterparts by being quite expressive. Their hands rest on their tummies as if full of food; those with left above right are said to be military, as opposed to the more scholarly right-above-left brigade.

Like the *moai*, the origin and purpose of the statues remain shrouded in mystery, though it seems likely that they were placed at village entrances as a means of protection. Another theory, and one supported by their extremely **phallic appearance**, is that they served as sources of fertility – today, miniature versions are sold to women who are having trouble getting pregnant, as well as tourists wanting a souvenir of their trip to Jeju.

Today, only a few dozen **authentic** *hareubang* remain; the most accessible can be found in Jeju City, at the entrance to the Folklore and Natural History Museum, and outside Samseonghyeol.

presented to – and presumably given back by – some of Jeju's most famous international guests.

If you're travelling with children or your time on Jeju is short, a visit to **Hallim Park** (한림 공원; daily 8.30am–6pm; W6000) is worthwhile as it groups some of Jeju's principal attractions into one easy-to-swallow site. Caves, stone sculptures, traditional Jeju houses or bonsai gardens – they're all here. Two good **beaches** (Hyeopjae and Geumneung) stretch from the park entrance, the palm trees and shallow, turquoise water lending the scene an almost Caribbean air. Across the sea is the beautiful nearby islet of **BIYANGDO** (비양도), accessible by ferry. **Minbak** accommodation is plentiful in this area, and there's also a fragrant camping ground among the pine trees; the *Hallim Geumneung Motel* (ⓣ064/796-0015; ⑤) offers spacious and well-appointed rooms, some with a decent view of the beach. Regular **buses** head down the West Coastal Road from Jeju City (see box, p.302).

Hallasan National Park

Arriving by ferry on a clear day, you can see the whole of Jeju tapering slowly to Mount Halla, known locally as **HALLASAN** (한라산), a dormant volcano at the centre of the island, and Korea's highest point at 1950m. Blanketed with pink azalea in the spring, and snow in the winter, the centre of the island has long been a **national park**, with four well-trodden hikes heading to Hallasan's crater, a grassy bowl pocked with grey volcanic rocks, and home to a couple of small lakes. As long as the weather cooperates, a climb up Hallasan is one of the main goals for adventurous visitors from the mainland. The **four main routes**, starting from the north and heading clockwise, are Gwanamsa, Seongpanak, Yeongsil and Eorimok.

Hiking Hallasan

Jeju's porous volcanic rock means that Hallasan's climbing trails provide more grip than your average Korean national park, even in wet weather. Though the climb is not a terribly difficult walk, hikers should take certain **precautions** if attempting to reach the summit. In order to stop lots of feet stomping indelible

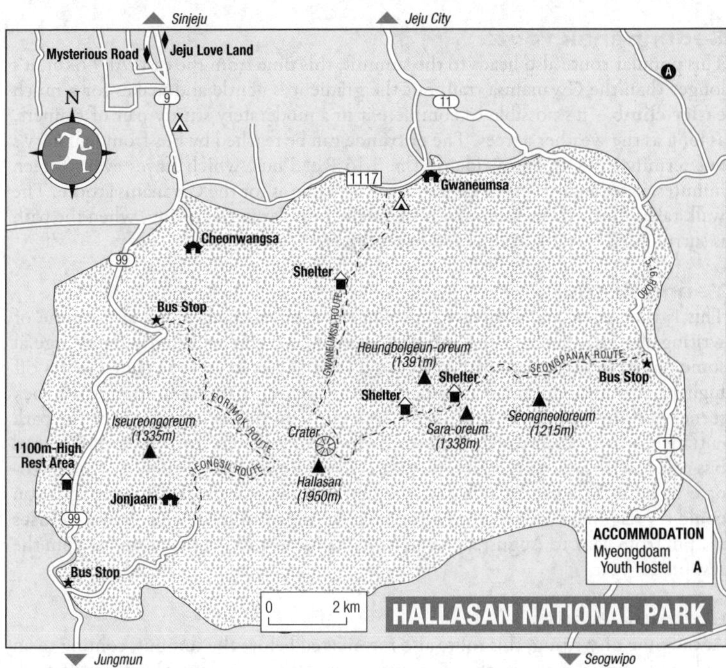

lines into the mountain, trail sections – or even whole routes – are regularly **closed off**; your first point of call should be one of Jeju's many tourist offices, or telephone the tourist information line on ⓣ 064/1330 for up-to-date information. To make sure that everyone gets down in time, routes may close earlier than expected, sometimes even at 9am. This also reduces the chance of getting wet, which becomes increasingly high towards evening as the air cools – bear in mind, though, that even a sunny morning may degenerate rapidly into thick fog and zero visibility at higher elevations; **bad weather** is the number one cause of most failed attempts to the summit. Even if you avoid the rain, strong winds can bite – bring at least a few layers of decent clothing. Also remember to bring enough **water** – Halla's rock absorbs most of the rainwater, so there are very few springs on the trails. With the longer walks some energy-giving **snacks** are a must; cooking and camping are prohibited, though the usual snack shops can be found at the trailheads.

Gwanamsa route

This route, heading to the peak from the north, is the best if you'd like to tackle the peak without the crowds. This path is longer, more challenging and **less accessible** than others – there are no public buses here, and though it's only an 11km taxi ride from Jeju City, you may have to pay almost double for the trip, as the driver will have next to no chance of picking someone up for the return leg. The most important advice is to get to the entrance early – it opens at 6am (5am in the summer) but is already closed at 10am between May and August, and 9am at other times. From here, most hikers take around four hours to walk the 8.3km to the summit, but as there are a lot of steps on this route, many opt to use it for their **downhill** run. Initially, it's easy going, but things soon get steeper. The park's only **campsite** is near the start of the trail – book from one of Jeju's tourist offices.

Seongpanak route

This popular route also heads to the summit, this time from the east. At 9.6km, it's longer than the Gwanamsa trail, but the gradient is gentle and makes for a much **easier climb** – it's possible to complete it in a moderately sturdy pair of trainers, as long as the weather agrees. The **entrance** can be reached by bus from Jeju City's bus terminal; it's a 35min ride on the 5.16 Road bus, which leaves every fifteen minutes or so, and the entrance hours are the same as for the Gwanamsa route. The walk takes four to five hours and is especially popular in the spring, when the path is surrounded by pink azaleas and other flowers.

Yeongsil route

This is the easiest and **shortest** route up the mountain, although at the time of writing the final burst to the **summit** was closed – this will no doubt change at some point, so ask at a tourist office for advice. The picturesque course starts off higher up the mountain than other routes, heading past some impressive rock scenery on the way to the top. There's currently no **public transport** to the park entrance, and it's a fair walk uphill from the "Yeongsil" bus stop on the 1100 Road bus route, with annoyingly irregular buses every hour or so – get hold of an up-to-date schedule at a tourist office or the Jeju City bus terminal. Alternatively you could try flagging down a car heading up from the main road. The entrance **closes** at 2pm from May to August, at noon from November to February, and at 1pm the rest of the year.

Eorimok route

At the time of writing, this route also terminated before the summit, coming to an end at the same point as the **Yeongsil** route. It's a **moderately difficult** trail, approaching the park from the northwest; the 1100 Road buses (see above) take half an hour to get from Jeju City to the park entrance, which has the same opening hours as Yeongsil. Passing through lush forest at the beginning before heading into bamboo, it's a three-hour walk to the end of the course. Many Koreans believe this to be the most beautiful of the park's paths.

Travel details

Ferries

Daejeong to: Gapado (2 daily; 15min); Marado (3 daily; 30min).
Jeju City to: Busan (daily except Sun; 11hr); Incheon (daily except Sun; 14hr); Mokpo (4 daily; 3hr 10min–4hr 30min).
Sanseong to: Jangheung (daily; 1hr 50min); Udo (hourly; 10min).

Buses

Jeju is not connected to the mainland by road, but a number of bus routes spread out across the island from Jeju City; see the box on p.302 for details.

Flights

Jeju City to: Busan Gimhae (hourly; 55min); Cheongju (hourly; 1hr); Daegu (8 daily; 50min); Gwangju (8 daily; 45min); Incheon (4 weekly; 1hr 5min); Jinju (2 weekly; 50min); Seoul Gimpo (every 15min; 1hr 5min); Ulsan (2–7 weekly; 1hr); Wonju (daily; 1hr 10min); Yeosu (2 weekly; 45min).

North Korea Basics

North Korea Basics

Getting there

First things first: yes, it is possible to enter North Korea. However, you can't just pop in on a whim, and those permitted entry will only be able to visit government-approved sights, and even then only in the company of a local guide. The process is often lengthy and never cheap, but it can be surprisingly simple: a travel agency usually does all the hard work with visas, permits and suchlike. The price of your tour will include pretty much everything: transport (most commonly a flight from Beijing to Pyongyang and an overnight train back out, as well as all internal travel), accommodation, meals and entry fees. Citizens of certain countries – most pertinently the US and Israel – will find their opportunities limited, but are occasionally allowed in.

Note that you can actually enter the country **from South Korea**, if only for a minute or two: some of the DMZ tours from Seoul allow you to take a few highly guarded steps across the border in the Joint Security Area (see p.351). Though extremely enjoyable, this doesn't offer a true taste of the DPRK – for this, you'll just have to head to Pyongyang.

From China

While several routes into North Korea exist – there's even a direct train from Moscow – almost all Western travellers start their journey in **Beijing**. From here you can either take a flight on Air Koryo, or an overnight train; which one you use will depend on your tour operator, and the cost will be factored into your tour price. Most tour groups fly into Pyongyang and take the train out, the latter leg giving a warts-and-all view of the North Korean countryside. Don't be too trigger-happy on the camera, however: some tourists have got into trouble after being reported as spies by local farmers (see p.332 for more on photography restrictions).

The **flight** (around 2hr from Beijing to Pyongyang) can be interesting to say the least, since most of Air Koryo's fleet are Soviet relics from the 1970s and 1980s. The airline has actually been **banned from flying** into the EU, and in 2007 was the only carrier worldwide to be given a one-star seal of disapproval by Skytrax.

Train journeys take around 24 hours from Beijing, though with the permission of your tour company you'll also be able to get on in Dandong, a Chinese city near the North Korean border; from here it's only a seven-hour trip to Pyongyang. Carriages are split into four-bed berths, with foreigners usually grouped together in the same carriage. There's also a restaurant car. Note that if crossing the border by train, the **toilets** are often locked for hours – go before you reach Dandong on the way to North Korea, and before arriving at Sinuiju, a city just a few kilometres from the Chinese border, on the way out. At Sinuiju station, those able to escape the guards' attention may be able to take a quick look out over the town square.

Customs inspections are usually thorough, whether at the airport or at Sinuiju, so expect to be questioned (see box, p.326 for information on what not to bring).

Tours and packages

A surprising number of travel operators offer **tours** into North Korea (see p.326 for a few of the best), most lasting for four to seven days. All visit the same core of Pyongyang-based sights, though some of the more expensive head to locations around the country. Group tours are cheapest – the size of the party can be anything from four to forty – but some also offer **individual packages**. These may sound appealing, but ironically you get more freedom on group trips – it's simply a lot harder for the two guides to keep tabs on twenty people than one or two, so those on group tours get a bit more leeway when walking around, such

How to get deported

Be careful when **packing your bags** for North Korea – with your trip likely to cost a pretty penny, it would be a shame to have to end it at **customs control**. In addition to the regular contraband – drugs, weapons, pornography and the like – you should be careful about taking in electronic equipment. Most cameras are fine (lenses larger than 150mm are not allowed), though video recorders may be confiscated on entry, as will any **mobile phones** or other communications equipment – these will be given back to you as you leave.

Beware of taking anything that's very obviously American or South Korean – while K-pop on your music player is unlikely to be picked up, any clothing emblazoned with the stars and stripes surely will. Literature deemed to be of a subversive nature (which may include this guidebook) will also be frowned upon.

as more picture-taking opportunities, the occasional chance to wander off by yourself for a few minutes, and less official spiel. Many is the tale of woe from an individual traveller who has been marched around the same sights as group tourists, had no foreign company to bounce ideas, questions or frustrations off, and paid twice the price for the privilege.

While all tours are pretty dear, it's possible to save a lot of money by going through a **Chinese operator** in Beijing; the drawbacks are that these tours are hard to arrange, conducted in Mandarin only, and tend to revolve more around food than sightseeing.

To travel with the following operators, try to apply at least four weeks in advance.

Tour operators

Explore Nelson House, 55 Victoria Rd, Farnborough GU14 7PA, UK ⓣ0870/333 4001, ⓦwww.explore.co.uk. This UK-based operator offers occasional twelve-day tours from London, which include four nights in Pyongyang, two at other DPRK destinations and a few in Beijing, from the curious price of £2527 per person, including flights.

Koryo Tours Near Yashow Market, Sanlitun, Beijing, China ⓣ010/6416 7544, ⓦwww.koryogroup.com. This company takes more than half of the DPRK's foreign tourists, and its success is fully deserved – the tours are the best-informed and most enjoyable. So good are Nick Bonner's contacts within North Korea that he's been allowed to co-produce three documentaries in this highly secretive nation: see p.375 for more. All tours head off from Beijing, and range from four nights (€1190) to seven days (from €1690). Individual tours are available, as are visits to cities and sights inaccessible to any other company.

Regent Holidays Froomsgate House, Rupert St, Bristol, UK ⓣ0845/277 3317, ⓦwww.regent-holidays.co.uk. This agency has more than two decades of experience of sending travellers to North Korea and other far-out destinations. A standard tour gives seven nights in the DPRK for £1295, while "long weekend" trips cost £895.

Young Pioneers ⓦdprk.youngpioneertours.com. Operating from the Chinese city of Xi'an, this group offers the cheapest visits to the DPRK but cannot be recommended, since their tours are poorly organized and have been known to descend into farce. It's hard to give an estimate of tour prices, since they seem to be made up on the spot.

Getting around

Once inside North Korea you'll have precious little say in your day-to-day travels – all transportation requirements will be arranged before you set foot inside the country, the cost factored in as part of the tour price, and you'll be obliged to stick to the schedule.

Most travel is done by **tour bus** if you're in a group, and **taxi** on independent tours, both within Pyongyang and for most trips to nearby destinations. You'll notice that the roads are quiet in the capital, and almost deserted outside. Contrary to popular belief, the countryside around the highways hasn't been overhauled to present a false face to foreign tourists, and you'll see a great deal of poverty. The main highways themselves, however, are almost exclusively for foreign tour groups and military vehicles – they pass small villages, but there are almost no exits (hardly surprising given that almost no rural civilians own a car). There's a **subway system** in Pyongyang, which figures on most tour schedules – see p.347 – though the city's trams and buses are off-limits on all but the most expensive tours. **Internal flights** also exist, and those heading to Paekdusan or other more remote locations will find themselves taking one.

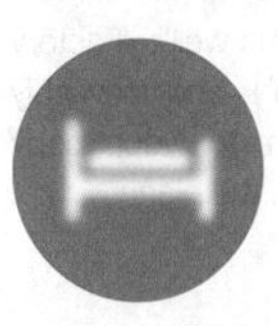

Accommodation, food and drink

As with transportation, all of your accommodation and dining requirements will be taken care of and paid for prior to your arrival. While the country has occasional – and often severe – problems sourcing food, and leans heavily on the outside world for aid, try not to feel too guilty about eating here: the money you're paying is more than enough to cover what you eat, and at least part of it will be used to help feed the locals.

Most travellers spend every night of their tour in **Pyongyang**, where there are a few excellent hotels – see p.342 – but some tours include a night or two outside the capital; the two most common provincial bases are **Kaesong**, near the DMZ (p.349), and **Paekdusan**, a mountain straddling the Chinese border (p.353).

The quality of your own **food** will vary according to financial, political and climatic conditions, but most visitors emerge well fed. If you have special dietary requirements you should make them clear to your tour company on application. Local **specialities** include *naengmyeon* (a buckwheat noodle dish similar to Japanese *soba*, but served in a spicy cold soup) and barbecued duck.

There's more choice with local **drink**, as it's one of the only things that you'll have to pay for once inside the country; many travellers buy a few bottles of grog to take home (perhaps more for the bragging rights than the taste). Local hooches include some curious mushroom, ginseng and berry concoctions, and the **beers** are great value at around €0.50 per bottle – Taedonggang is the most popular, but try to hunt down Ryongsong, which has a distinctive hoppy taste.

The media

While locals subsist on the Nodong Shinmun ("Workers' Daily"), North Korea also produces a surprising amount of English-language printed material, and is more than happy to offload it on foreign visitors.

In addition to the **books** written by Kim Jong-il – he's said to have authored well over a thousand, and many have been translated into various languages for foreign consumption – there are a few interesting **newspapers** and periodicals, some of which may be dropped into your lap on the flight from Beijing. Once you get to your hotel, you'll be able to tune into **KCTV**, the state television channel – for locals, this is off-air for much of the day, but foreign visitors get a full 24 hours of looped North Korean news and period drama. The latter is mainly made up of patriotic heroes refusing to capitulate to foreign forces, the themes a mix of Japanese occupation period, Korean War times, and not much else. In addition, there's Ⓦwww.kcna.co.jp, the official news website of the DPRK; the near-daily stories (some real, some not) of South Korean unrest against American military presence bring to mind the news reports about Eurasian and Eastasian activity in Orwell's *Nineteen Eighty-Four*.

Titles to look out for include *Korea Pictorial* a colourful, glosssy A3 monthly – with the word "Korea" on the front – that focuses more on photography than reportage, though some stories are rather absorbing. *Korea Today* is a smaller, far wordier version, with a songsheet reading of the "Song of General Kim Il-sung" on the inside cover. The articles are rather insipid, but for the odd gem. The weekly newspaper, the *Pyongyang Times*, is not always easy to find inside the country, though its stories are fascinating ("School performs well"; "Factory increases shoe production"), and inevitably Kims-obsessed. Hang on to your copy should you be given one on the plane.

Festivals

There's only one event on the North Korean travel calendar, but what an event it is. The Mass Games (see box, p.341) must count as one of the world's great spectacles, but contrary to popular belief, this colourful feast of song and dance is not aimed at tourists – almost all of the spectators are North Korean, and almost all citizens aim to see it at least once in their life: a kind of Juche rite of passage (see box, p.346 for more on Juche).

The timing of the games has been erratic of late, but the authorities are trying to make it a yearly celebration in **July and August**. Festival season normally lasts three or four weeks, with, usually, a performance every evening, lasting around ninety minutes, with tickets costing €50.

Special events are held on important anniversaries, and the 100th anniversary of the birth of Kim Il-sung in April 2012 promises to be one hell of a bash, perhaps the biggest ever seen in the DPRK – apply for your trip well in advance.

Culture and etiquette

The first rule when travelling through North Korea is this: do not disrespect the Kims. Disobeying could lead to dramatic consequences, but the sheer madness of the place makes acquiescence a hard line to toe – it's difficult not to pass comment on something that's likely to run contrary to your own upbringing. While the propaganda stuffed down your throat may be hard to stomach, it's unwise to react to it – asking questions or making accusations is not going to change the way that anybody thinks, much less the running of the country, and can only lead to trouble.

You'd be foolish to travel to North Korea with the intention of creating a stink, even after your visit: while a critical blog or travel article will not be of any danger to its author, the North Korean guides tarnished by association may get into a lot of trouble, and travel agencies have been known to lose their licences.

Good behaviour is required in private as well as public places – rumours abound of hotel rooms being **bugged**, and these cannot be wholly discounted; it's also claimed that some in the *Koryo* have hidden cameras. Even seemingly innocent activity is not above suspicion – there's one oft-quoted tale of a traveller who got into serious trouble after stubbing out his cigarette on a newspaper, inadvertently desecrating the holy face of Kim Jong-il.

However frightening all of this may seem, the vast majority of travellers encounter no problems whatsoever, and most have a fantastic time. Simply do as you're told, don't go running off, don't take pictures when you've been told not to, and keep any frustrations bottled up until you're back in Beijing. The local **guides** are usually amiable folk; getting into their good books at the beginning of the tour by behaving yourself and asking permission to take pictures is likely to result in your gaining greater leeway as you make your way around. Neither should you fear the local North Korean people, who end up being the highlight of many a journey. Repeated contact with Western tour groups has convinced many Pyongyangers that foreigners are not to be feared; acting in a courteous manner will continue the trend.

It's also a good idea to bring **gifts**, not just for your guides and driver but for the locals who you're likely to run into along the way. Make sure that they're appropriate – nothing overtly capitalist, American or South Korean in origin. Western cigarettes go down well with local men and postcards from home with everyone, while balloons and small toys are always popular with children; try to ask a parent's permission before handing anything over.

Shopping

While staunchly anti-capitalist North Korea isn't exactly renowned for its shopping possibilities, there are a number of interesting things to buy, most of which are impossible to get anywhere else, and make fantastic souvenirs.

The race to stock up on as much North Korean material as possible often starts on the plane – wet-wipe packets, tissues, cutlery sleeves and even sick bags can be sold for a quick buck on the internet, though most people choose to hang on to these little mementoes. You may also be handed propaganda-filled North Korean periodicals during your flight – see p.328.

The larger tourist hotels have shops in which you can buy local goods. Among the more appealing buys are **pin-badges**, which come in a variety of styles from the North Korean national flag to commemorations of judo events; **postcards**, which render the beautiful DPRK both photographically and in socialist realist style; and a range of **alcoholic drinks**, usually including beer, mulberry wine and some acrid mushroom concoctions. Of interest to some are the **tailored suits** made in the *Yanggakdo* hotel. Most customers are looking for Kim Jong-il's distinctive buttoned-up-to-the-collar chic, affectionately known to DPRK veterans as the "Kim-suit". Prices vary – and on big occasions the tailors are booked solid – but for just over €100 you can usually get a made-to-measure bargain. Unfortunately, the sale to foreigners of one of the other great DPRK purchases – **socialist realist prints** and paintings – was recently made illegal, ostensibly because the espoused Juche philosophy is for North Korean consumption only. Those still interested can contact Koryo Tours in Beijing (see p.326), who should be able to point you in the right direction.

You're likely to be shown around a few shops on your travels around Pyongyang. The **stamp shop** is a popular stop that will delight philatelists and novices alike. If you're staying in the *Koryo* and ask your guide nicely you may even be able to pop there on your own, as it's just down the road from the hotel's main entrance. There's also the **foreign-language bookshop**, which stocks translated works from the pens of Kim & Kim, as well as a range of absorbing booklets about the country and a few of its more minor heroes. In Pyongyang there are also a couple of department stores, which feature on the occasional tour.

Travel essentials

Children's North Korea

It's quite possible to travel to North Korea with **children**, but there are two points to consider. First, the sight-packed days can be hard even on adults – you'll spend a lot of time in a tour bus or taxi, and yet more standing at sights while being bombarded with the greatness of the Kims. Second, there are precious few facilities for children, either in the hotels or around the country – bring everything that your child will need. That said, every housing block in Pyongyang has a small playground area; while tightly planned group tours are unlikely to squeeze this in, independent tours should be able to work a quick play into the schedule.

Communications

It's possible to make **international calls** or send **faxes** from all major hotels, but the prices are guaranteed to be high – unless you're happy with paying €15 for a minute-long telephone call or €20 for a one-sheet fax, it's best to assume that you'll be incommunicado with the outside world for the duration of your stay in North Korea. Also note that your mobile phone will be confiscated on arrival (see p.326); even were that not the case, it wouldn't work anyway thanks to interference devices placed around the border (you'll even experience this if visiting Panmunjeom from South Korea).

In the major hotels you'll find a computer terminal, from which you can send **emails**; this can only be done on the hotel's account, and it's not possible to receive replies. Also bear in mind that whatever you say or send is likely to be monitored. This also applies to **post**, which will be read and understood, whatever the language; anything that seems cryptic will be thrown away, and may also be used as evidence of espionage.

Costs and money

All accommodation and transport will be included in your tour fee, as well as two or three meals per day, but for drinks, snacks and souvenirs you'll have to use hard currency, as there are no ATMs or banks accessible to foreigners. Most prices for tourist goods are quoted in **euros**, though American dollars and Chinese yuan are just as widely accepted. Those in North Korea for the Mass Games (see p.341) will have to pay €50 for a ticket, which is quite a bargain for such a stupendous event.

The official currency of the DPRK is the **North Korean won**, but you're unlikely to have much contact with it as foreigners aren't allowed to use local money. There was a time when the won was pegged at 2.16 to the dollar, a fiscally ridiculous nod to Kim Jong-il's birthday on February 16, but this policy was abandoned in 2001.

Note that it's illegal to export **North Korean currency** out of the country – if you do manage to get hold of some, keep your cache of cash well hidden when leaving. The easiest approach is to ask at your hotel reception; usually they won't mind if you say that you're collecting money from around the world. The notes that they dole out are suspiciously clean, but while they make for good souvenirs they're nothing like the dirty, tattered, falling-to-bits rags that ordinary North Koreans use; to get your hands on one of these, you'll have to use a bit of initiative. One good source are the tiny ice-cream stands that you'll see around Pyongyang in warmer months – you don't have any local money, the ice-cream women only have local change and will be glad for foreign currency, so everyone's a winner. As long as your guide doesn't notice, you should be able to walk away with a fistful of genuine notes.

Tipping is not a Korean custom, but will obviously be appreciated in a country as poor as this. A representative from most tour groups will usually pass the hat around on your final day, then split the pooled money between the various guides and drivers, who are not well paid despite their regular contact with foreigners – North Korean convention tends to reward work on the basis of danger, so guiding tourists is not high on the list. In larger groups, €5 per person usually adds up to a sizeable donation, while those travelling individually are advised to give around €20 to each guide and driver.

Entry requirements

Everyone needs a **visa** to enter North Korea, and though the process of obtaining one is lengthy, as long as you've got money and make your plans a couple of months in advance you should find it pretty easy to get in. Those from the "wrong countries" (ie US and Israel) are allowed in occasionally, most often during the Mass Games period – ask one of the travel agencies listed on p.326 for the latest details. **Journalists** can also find it hard to get in, though again it's not impossible – it's the travel agency's responsibility to vet applicants, so if you say that you're a circus freak and they believe you, you're in. Many try to avoid fraud by asking for signed confirmation from your employer.

Your visa is organized prior to arrival by the travel agency and forms part of your tour price. Unless you do your own visa application in a country that has diplomatic relations with the DPRK, it will come on a slip of paper (not as an insert in your passport) that you'll only possess for a short time on entry to North Korea. You won't receive a stamp, so there'll be no evidence of your visit in your passport.

It's wise to have **travel insurance** wherever you go, and North Korea is no exception. Most travel policies cover North Korea, but do check by making a quick call to your company; if they won't cover you, find one that will.

Photography

In terms of pictures per traveller, North Korea must be one of the most photographed nations on earth, a hugely ironic fact given that most of it is closed off, and even official sights are subject to **photographic restriction**. This is a nation where even the mundane is incredible, and even on the shortest trips some visitors end up with over a thousand images.

Some of the photographic **rules** are those that apply worldwide: don't take pictures of military installations or soldiers (unless you're in the DMZ, where it is almost expected), and ask permission if taking any photographs of people. Others are a little harder to guess, many of them surrounding **the Kims** – if you're taking a picture of a statue, mural or painting of the great men, try to get the whole body into your shot, as anything else may be viewed as disrespectful. (This can be quite a feat at the huge bronze statue of Kim Il-sung at Mansudae; see p.344). It's also risky to photograph anything that might be taken as a **criticism of the country**: a picture of a peasant sitting by the roadside could be construed as a deliberate attempt to smear North Korea's stellar reputation (something which may also see you hauled in and accused of being a spy). In practice, though, these rules are hard to police, and customs officials simply can't sift through each and every picture.

Travellers with disabilities

Travellers with **disabilities** can travel to North Korea, but there are next to no access facilities laid on for wheelchairs, and there are far easier countries to visit. It's interesting to note that disabled locals are highly revered in North Korea, a country where brave resistance is the theme of most songs, films and TV dramas; many women, indeed, consider it their duty to marry injured soldiers.

7

North Korea

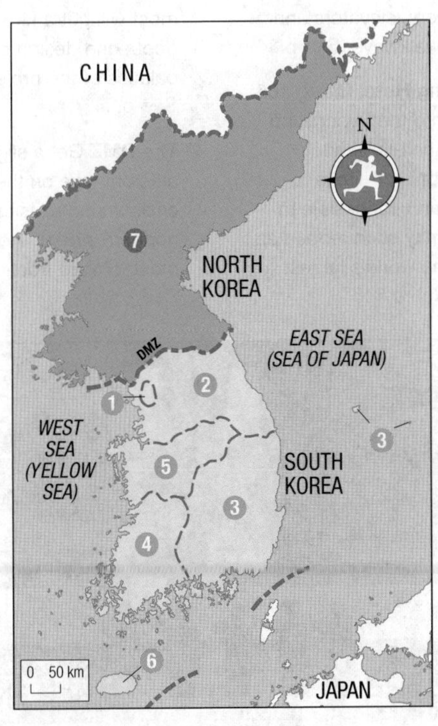

CHAPTER 7 Highlights

* **The Mass Games** Unquestionably one of the most spectacular events you'll ever see – try to time your visit to coincide with it if at all possible. See p.341

* **Kumsusan Memorial Palace** Pay a visit to the father of the nation, who lies in state beyond a labyrinthine warren of corridors, elevators and moving walkways. See p.342

* **Ryugyong Hotel** Rising 105 stories into the Pyongyang sky, this half-finished mammoth is off-limits to tourists and impossible to miss; it may soon reopen as one of the world's largest hotels. See p.343

* **Monumental Pyongyang** The largest granite tower in the world and a colossal bronze effigy of the "Great Leader" are just a few of the capital's larger-than-life sights. See p.344

* **Pyongyang subway** Though only two stations are usually accessible to foreigners, most will get a kick out of the depth and design of these palaces of the proletariat. See p.347

* **The DMZ** Get a slightly different take on the Korean crisis during a visit to the northern side of the world's most fortified frontier. See p.351

▲ Mansudae grand monument

North Korea

Espionage, famine and nuclear brinkmanship; perpetrator-in-chief of an international axis of evil; a rigidly controlled population under the shadowy rule of a president long deceased... you've heard it all before, but North Korea's dubious charms make it the Holy Grail for hard-bitten travellers. A trip to this tightly controlled Communist society is only possible as part of an expensive package, but a high proportion of those fortunate and intrepid enough to visit rank it as their most interesting travel experience.

North Korea is officially known as the **Democratic People's Republic of Korea**, or the DPRK. However, real democracy is thin on the ground, and comparisons with the police state in Orwell's *Nineteen Eighty-Four* are impossible to avoid: in addition to a regime that acts as a single source of information, residents of Pyongyang, and many other cities, do indeed wake up to government-sent messages and songs broadcast through speakers in their apartments, which can be turned down but never off – the fact that this is often the cue for callisthenic exercises further strengthens associations with the book. (Messages are also often relayed into many South Korean apartments, though these tend to be about garbage disposal and missing children, and the speakers can be turned off.) Other Big Brother similarities include verified claims that the country is crawling with

Busting myths

A lot has been said and written about the current situation in North Korea, much of it true. These crazy truths, however, make it awfully easy to paint **rumours**, assumptions and hearsay as cast-iron fact. Political falsehoods have been detailed by excellent authors such as Cumings, Winchester and Oberdorfer, who take both sides' views into account (see p.380 for some recommended reading), but a few of the more straightforward rumours can be easily debunked.

The first great untruth to put to bed is that North Koreans are somehow **evil**; whatever their leader's state of mind, remember that the large majority of the population have no choice whatsoever in the running of the country or even their own lives, much less than other populations that have found themselves under authoritarian rule. Another myth is that you'll be escorted around by a **gun-wielding soldier**; it's true that you'll have guides with you whenever you're outside the hotel, but they're generally very nice people and it's occasionally possible to slip away for a few minutes.

Sometimes even the myths are myths. The tale of Kim Jong-il hitting **eleven holes in one** on his first-ever round of golf is bandied about in the West as evidence of mindless indoctrination; the so-called rumour itself is actually unheard of in North Korea.

informants, each seeking to further his or her own existence by denouncing friends, neighbours or even family for such crimes as letting their portrait of the Great Leader gather dust, singing unenthusiastically during a march, or simply being related to the wrong person. Also true is the rumour that locals have to wear a **pin-badge** portraying at least one of the leaders – **Kim Il-sung**, the country's inaugurator and "Great Leader", and the "Dear Leader", his eldest son **Kim Jong-il**. Interestingly, Kim Il-sung remains the country's official president, despite having died in 1994. Both Kims are revered almost as gods, by a people with precious little choice in the matter.

For all this, North Korea exerts a **unique appeal** for those willing and able to visit. Whether you're looking out over Pyongyang's oddly barren cityscape or eating a bowl of rice in your hotel restaurant, the simple fact that you're in one of the world's most inaccessible countries will bring an epic feel to everything you do. It's also important to note the human aspect of the North Korean machine. Behind the Kims and their carefully managed stage curtain live real people leading real lives, under severe financial, nutritional, political and personal restrictions unimaginable in the West. Thousands upon thousands have found conditions so bad that they've risked imprisonment or even death to escape North Korea's state-imposed straightjacket. All the more surprising, then, that it's often the locals who provide the highlight of a visit to the DPRK – many, especially in Pyongyang, are extremely happy to see foreign visitors, and you're likely to meet at least a couple of people on your way around, whether it's sharing an outdoor *galbi* meal with a local family, chatting with the staff at your hotel, or saluting back to a marching gaggle of schoolchildren. This fascinating society functions in front of an equally absorbing backdrop of brutalist architecture, bronze statues, red stars and colossal murals, a scene just as distinctive for its lack of traffic, advertising or Western influence.

A visit to North Korea will confirm some of the things you've heard about the country, while destroying other preconceptions. One guarantee is that you'll leave with more questions than answers.

Some history

The Democratic Republic of Korea was created in 1948 as a result of global shifts in power following the Japanese defeat in World War II and the **Korean War** that followed (see p.365). The Korean War, which ended in 1953, left much of the DPRK in tatters; led by **Kim Il-sung**, a young, ambitious resistance fighter from Japanese annexation days, the DPRK busied itself with efforts to haul its standard of life and productive capacity back to prewar levels. Kim himself purged his "democratic" party of any policies or people that he deemed a threat to his leadership, fostering a personality cult that lasts to this day. Before long, he was being referred to by his people as *Suryong*, meaning "Great Leader", and *Tongji*, a somewhat paradoxical term describing a higher class of comrade (in North Korea, some comrades are evidently more equal than others). He also did away with the elements of Marxist, Leninist or Maoist thought that did not appeal to him, preferring instead to follow "**Juche**", a Korean brand of Communism that focused on national self-sufficiency (see box, p.346). For a time, his policies were not without success – levels of education, healthcare, employment and production went up, and North Korea's development was second only to Japan's in East Asia. Its GDP-per-head rate actually remained above that of South Korea until the mid-1970s.

The **American threat** never went away, and North Koreans were constantly drilled to expect an attack at any time. The US Army had, in fact, reneged on a 1953 armistice agreement by reintroducing **nuclear weapons** into South Korea, and went against an international pact by threatening to use such arms against a country that did not possess any; North Korea duly got to work on a reactor of their own at Yongbyon.

There were regular skirmishes both around the **DMZ** and beyond, including an attack on the USS *Pueblo* in 1968 (see p.347), assassination attempts on Kim Il-sung and South Korean president Park Chung-hee around the same time, and the famed "Axe Murder Incident" that took place in the Joint Security Area in 1976 (p.144). During the 1970s at least three tunnels were discovered heading under the DMZ (see p.143 & p.145), which undetected could have seen KPA forces in Seoul within hours.

Decline to crisis

Then came the inevitable **decline** – Juche was simply not malleable enough as a concept to cope with external prodding or poor internal decision-making. Having developed into a pariah state without parallel, North Korea was forced to rely on the help of fellow Communist states – the Soviet Union and China, which was busy solving problems of its own under the leadership of Chairman Mao. The economy ground almost to a halt during the 1970s, while in the face of an

Nuclear brinkmanship

Say this about North Korea's leaders: they may be Stalinist fanatics, they may be terrorists, they may be building nuclear bombs, but they are not without subtlety. They have mastered the art of dangling Washington on a string.

David Sanger, *New York Times*, March 20, 1994

Since the opening of a reactor at **Yongbyon** in 1987, North Korea has kept the outside world guessing as to its **nuclear capabilities**, playing a continued game of bluff and brinkmanship to achieve its aims of self-preservation and eventual reunification with the South. The folding of the Soviet Union in 1991 choked off much of the DPRK's energy supply; with few resources of their own, increasing importance was placed on nuclear energy, but the refusal to allow international inspectors in strengthened rumours that they were also using the facilities to create weapons-grade plutonium. **Hans Blix** and his crew at the International Atomic Energy Agency (IAEA) were finally permitted entry in 1992, but were refused access to two suspected waste disposal sites, which would have provided strong evidence about whether processed plutonium was being created or not; Blix was, however, shown around a couple of huge underground facilities that no one on the outside even knew about. North Korea was unhappy with the sharing of information between American intelligence (the CIA) and the independent IAEA, but after threatening to withdraw from the **Nuclear Nonproliferation Treaty** (NPT) they agreed in 1994 to freeze their programme in exchange for fuel. This only happened after an election within the White House – Bill Clinton was more willing to compromise than his predecessor George Bush Senior. North Korea continued to do itself no favours, at one point launching a missile into the Sea of Japan in 1993 (though this was actually a failed attempt at launching a satellite, it was seen by many as practice for a future attack).

The second part of the crisis erupted more suddenly. In 2002, after making veiled threats about a possible resumption of their nuclear programme, North Korea abruptly booted out IAEA inspectors. Coming at the start of the war in Afghanistan, the timing was risky to say the least, but Pyongyang skated even closer to the line by admitting not only to having **nuclear devices** (and claiming that it did not know how to dismantle them), but also to being willing to sell them on the world market. All of these were bargaining ploys aimed at getting George W. Bush's administration to follow the "Sunshine Policy" pursued by Clinton and Kim Dae-jung. Regular six-party talks between China, Russia, Japan, the US and the two Koreas achieved little, and in 2006 North Korea conducted its **first nuclear test**, and sent another missile into the Sea of Japan. North Korea had shown it had yet another card up its sleeve, and talks continued with greater candour. In July 2007 Pyongyang finally announced that it was shutting down its Yongbyon reactor in exchange for aid, and its permanent disability was confirmed by international inspectors two months later.

American-South Korean threat that never diminished, military spending remained high. It was around this time that **Kim Jong-il** was being groomed as the next leader of the DPRK – the Communist world's first dynastic succession.

During the 1990s North Korea experienced alienation, famine, nuclear threats and the death of its beloved leader. The break-up of the **Soviet Union** in 1991 nullified North Korea's greatest source of funds, and a country officially extolling self-sufficiency increasingly found itself unable to feed its own people. Despite the **nuclear crisis** with the US (see box above) the DPRK was making a few tentative moves towards peace with the South; indeed, it was just after examining accommodation facilities prepared for the first-ever North-South presidential summit that Kim Il-sung suffered a heart attack and died. This day in July 1994 was followed by a long period of intense public mourning – hundreds of thousands attended his funeral, in Pyongyang, and millions more paid their respects around the country – after which came a terrible **famine**, a period known as the "Arduous March". Despite being dead, Kim Il-sung was elected "Eternal President", though his son, Kim Jong-il, eventually assumed most of the duties that require the authorization of a living body, and was made Supreme Commander of the army.

The Sunshine Policy

The year 1998 brought great changes to North-South relations. **Kim Dae-jung** was elected president of South Korea, and immediately started his "**Sunshine Policy**" of reconciliation with the North, which aimed for integration without absorption (assimilation having been the main goal of both sides up until this point). With US president **Bill Clinton** echoing these desires in the White House, all three sides seemed to be pulling the same way for the first time since the Korean War. The two Kims held a historic Pyongyang summit in 2000, the same year in which Kim Dae-jung was awarded the Nobel Peace Prize. The southern premier revealed to the Western media that Kim Jong-il actually wanted the American army to remain in the South (to keep the peace on the peninsula, as well as for protection from powerful China and an ever more militarist Japan), as long as Washington accepted North Korea as a state and pursued reconciliation over confrontation. Clinton was actually set for a summit of his own in Pyongyang, but the election of **George W. Bush** in 2000 put paid to that. Bush undid many of the inroads that had been made, and antagonized the DPRK, famously labelling it part of an "Axis of Evil" in 2002.

The **second nuclear crisis**, in 2002 (see box oppsite), brought about a surprise admission from the North – Japanese prime minister **Junichiro Koizumi** went across for a summit expecting to be forced into saying sorry for Japanese atrocities during occupation. Instead it was Kim Jong-il who did the apologizing, astonishingly admitting to a long-suspected series of **kidnappings** on the Japanese coast in the late 1970s and early 1980s, ostensibly as a rather convoluted way of teaching his secret service personnel Japanese. Though the number of abductions was probably higher, Kim admitted to having taken thirteen people, of whom eight had died; one of the survivors had married **Charles Robert Jenkins**, an American defector from the post-Korean War period. The belief that more hostages were unaccounted for – and possibly still alive – made it impossible for Koizumi to continue his policy of engagement with the DPRK.

In 2002 **Roh Moo-hyun** was elected South Korean president, and adhered to the precepts of the Sunshine Policy. While the course under his tenure was far from smooth – the US and the DPRK continued to make things difficult for each other, South Korean youth turned massively **against reunification**, and Roh himself suffered impeachment for an unrelated issue – there was some movement, however, notably the symbolic reopening of train lines across the DMZ in 2007.

Return to crisis

In 2008, a South Korean tourist was **killed** after entering a high-security area on a visit to the Geumgang mountains. Seoul suspended these cross-border trips, choking off a much-needed source of income for Pyongyang, who eventually confiscated all South Korean-owned property in the area. Tension remained high until 2010, when two catastrophic incidents brought inter-Korean relations to a postwar low (see box, p.369). First came the **sinking of the Cheonan**, a South Korean naval vessel; this was followed later in the year by the shelling of the West Sea island of **Yeonpyeongdo**, and retaliatory attacks by the South. At the time of writing, the situation remained extremely tense, with full-on military confrontation a distinct possibility.

Pyongyang

The North Korean capital of **PYONGYANG** (평양) could credibly claim to be the most unsettling city on the face of the earth. This city of empty streets, lined with huge grey monuments and buildings, and studded with bronze statues and murals in honour of its idolized leaders, is a strange concrete and marble experiment in socialist realism. It stands as a showcase of North Korean might, with its skyscrapers and wide boulevards giving a faint echo of Le Corbusier's visions of utilitarian urban utopia: every street, rooftop, doorway and windowsill has been designed in keeping with a single grand vision. On closer inspection, however, you'll notice that the buildings are dirty and crumbling, and the people under very apparent control.

Pyongyang's near three million inhabitants live a relatively privileged existence. Life here is far better than in the countryside, though you'll still see signs of poverty: power cuts are commonplace, and each evening the city tumbles into a quiet darkness hard to fathom in a capital city. There's also next to no visible commerce – the city is entirely devoid of the billboards and flashy lights commonplace in a metropolis of this size; instead socialist realist murals form the only advertising, and vie for attention with the Communist slogans screamed in red from the tallest buildings. You'll be taken by bus around a selection of officially sanctioned sights. These include **Kumsusan Memorial Palace**, where the body of Kim Il-sung lies in state, and **Mansudae**, his colossal statue; the distinctive granite **Juche Tower** overlooking the Taedong River; and the **Pyongyang metro**, one of the world's most intriguingly secretive subway systems. Pyongyang is also the venue for the amazing **Mass Games** (see box opposite), which take place at the May Day Stadium. However, all sights aside, whether you're simply eating at a restaurant or relaxing in your hotel, Pyongyang is always fascinating.

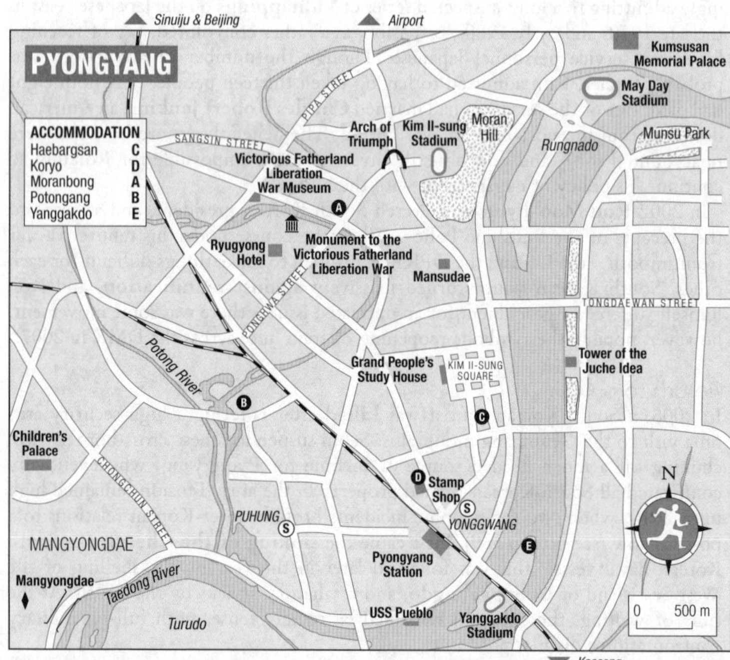

The Mass Games

The spectacular **Mass Games** are among the world's must-see events. Also known as the "Arirang Games", they take place in Pyongyang's 150,000-seater **May Day Stadium** – though this is always full to bursting, unbelievably there are always more performers than there are spectators. Wildly popular with foreign tourists, the show is actually created for local consumption – this is a propaganda exercise extraordinaire, one used by the West as evidence of a rigidly controlled population in thrall to the Kim dynasty.

Even the warm-up will fill you with wonder, awe and trepidation. Your entry to the stadium is serenaded by upwards of twenty thousand schoolchildren; filling the opposite stand, they scream out in perfect unison while flashing up the names of their schools on large **coloured flipbooks**, effectively forming human pixels on a giant TV screen that remains an ever-changing backdrop throughout the show. The performers themselves come out in wave after wave, relaying stories about the hardships under Japanese occupation, the **creation of the DPRK**, and the bravery in the face of American aggression, as well as less bombastic parables about farming life or how to be safe at the seaside. Among the cast will be thousands-strong teams of *chosonbok*-wearing dancers, ball-hurling schoolkids and miniskirt-wearing female "soldiers" wielding rifles and swords, their every move choreographed to a colourful perfection. The form of the displays changes – military-style marches give way to performances of gymnastics or traditional dance, and the cast are at one point illuminated in brilliant blue, forming a rippling sea. Visitors are often left speechless – you'll just have to see for yourself. See p.328 for more details.

Arrival and information

Most visitors to Pyongyang are here to start a guided excursion, so whether you **arrive** by plane or train – your only two options – a bus or private car will be waiting, ready to whisk you to your hotel. The twenty-minute journey from the airport to central Pyongyang is a fascinating one for first-time visitors, displaying an impoverishment that the authorities have made surprisingly little effort to conceal. The road is in good condition but usually empty, save for occasional pedestrians on their way to or from work, and the countryside rather barren. Those disembarking at the far more central train station will have to settle for urban views. Given the tightness of the average itinerary, you're likely to visit at least one sight before checking in at your hotel.

There's no tourist **information** office in North Korea, but your **guide** will be on hand to answer any questions. Most topics are fine, but asking anything that could be construed as disparaging of the regime could land you or your host in hot water. The guides are usually amiable, though at some sights you'll be in the hands of specialists employed to bark out nationalistic vitriol (which, you'll notice, increases in force and volume when either of the Kims are mentioned).

City transport

Getting around the city is usually as simple as waking up in time to catch your tour bus (those left behind will be stuck in the hotel until their group returns). Pyongyang's crammed **public buses** and **trams** are for locals only, and your guides would think you crazy to want to use them when you already have paid-for private transport, but if you have any say in your schedule be sure to ask for a ride on the **Pyongyang subway** – see p.347. The buses themselves are pretty photogenic, many of the Hungarian relics from the 1950s; look out for the stars on their sides, as each one represents fifty thousand accident-free kilometres.

Traffic ladies

While Pyongyang does have a few traffic lights dotted around its rather empty streets, these eat up energy in a country not blessed with a surplus of power – step forward the **traffic ladies**. Chosen for their beauty by the powers-that-be, and evidently well schooled, they direct the traffic with super-fast precision, in the middle of some of the busier intersections, and sport distinctive blue (sometimes white) jackets, hats and skirts, as well as regulation white socks. The traffic ladies are rather popular with some visitors, and one or two tour groups have persuaded their guides to stop by for a brief photo-shoot.

Accommodation

There are fewer than a dozen hotels in Pyongyang designated for foreigners, and which one you end up at will be organized in advance by your tour operator. Most groups stay at Pyongyang's **top hotels**, the *Koryo* and *Yanggakdo*; there's little between them in terms of service and quality. Both provide a memorable experience and are tourist draws in their own right, which is a good thing, considering the amount of time you'll be spending there – in the evening, when your daily schedule is completed, there's not really anywhere else to go. Note that the colossal *Ryugyong* (see opposite) was under development at the time of writing.

Haebangsan This is the cheapest hotel for foreigners, and a recent renovation has made it a perfectly acceptable place to stay – at least in warmer months, since 24-hour running water is not guaranteed. Another drawback is a near-total lack of atmosphere or on-site activities.

Koryo Hotel The salmon-pink twin towers of the *Koryo* sit on a main thoroughfare, making for a much better appreciation of local life than is possible in the *Yanggakdo*. Rooms at this forty-storey hotel are well kept and the on-site restaurants passable, while the ground-floor mini-market – stocked with foreign drinks, biscuits and other comestibles – is the best place in the city to sate Western sugar cravings. If you are on an independent tour you can request trips to nearby restaurants or the Swiss co-venture bakery-cum-café across the road.

Moranbong A boutique hotel in Pyongyang – whatever next? There are just twelve rooms here, and the fitness centre and pool exude an atmosphere rather contrary to the rest of the country. However, it's popular with diplomats and as such a little hard to book.

Potonggang Just west of central Pyongyang, in a dull part of town, the *Potonggang* is the only hotel to feed a couple of American TV channels into the rooms. Despite the acceptable facilities, few Westerners end up staying here; if you do, you'll find it hard to miss the huge Kim mural in the lobby.

Yanggakdo This 47-storey hotel sits on an islet in the Taedong, and commands superb views of both the river and the city from its clean, spacious rooms. The isolated location means that you'll be able to wander around outside without provoking the ire of guides or guards, though to be honest there's precious little to do. The on-site restaurants are excellent, with one that revolves slowly at the top of the tower, which is a great place for a nightcap. The ground-floor bar brews its own beer, which is quite delicious after a hard day slogging around sights. Also on site are a bowling alley, a karaoke room and a tailor.

Kumsusan Memorial Palace

The huge **Kumsusan Memorial Palace** is a North Korean cathedral, labyrinth, palace and Mecca all rolled into one, and the single most important place in the country. It's here that the body of **Kim Il-sung** lies in state, though only invitees are allowed to see it – you'll witness a lot of high-ranking military proudly wearing their medals and stripes. The official residence of Kim Il-sung until his death in 1994, it was transformed into his final resting place under the orders of his son and heir, Kim Jong-il. While perceived disrespect to the Great Leader isn't advisable anywhere in the country, it will not be tolerated here – be on your best behaviour, dress smartly and keep any conversation hushed.

The walk around the palace and past Kim Il-sung is a long, slow experience, one that usually takes well over an hour. **Security** is understandably tight – you'll be searched at the entrance and told to leave cameras, coats and bags at reception. Then starts the long haul through corridor after marble corridor, some of which are hundreds of metres long; thankfully, moving walkways are in place, but stand on them, rather than walk – it's an experience to be savoured, and you're likely to see several locals, even the butchest of soldiers, in tears. One room is filled with reliefs and friezes of the Korean people mourning the loss of their leader; here you'll be handed an mp3 guide, complete with earphones, for an **English-language lecture**, one delivered in a posh, quavering voice and as bombastic as they come – "just as the sun burns itself to give light and heat to the universe, so did President Kim Il-sung devote himself wholeheartedly to the Juche cause". Be prepared for this: Kumsusan is *not* the place in which to be struck by a fit of the giggles.

After accessing an upper floor by elevator, your proximity to **Kim's body** will be heralded by a piped rendition of the "Song of General Kim Il-sung", composed after his death. Absolute silence is expected as visitors pass into the main room, bathed in a dim red light. A queue circles around the illuminated body – follow the North Korean lead, and take a deep bow on each side.

The world's largest shell

The Ministry of Truth – Minitrue, in Newspeak – was startlingly different from any other object in sight. It was an enormous pyramidal structure of glittering white concrete, soaring up, terrace after terrace, three hundred metres into the air... the Ministry of Truth contained, it was said, three thousand rooms above ground level, and corresponding ramifications below.

George Orwell *Nineteen Eighty-Four*

It's somewhat ironic that North Korea's most distinctive building seems to have had its design lifted from the pages of *Ninteen Eighty-Four*, a book banned across the country. In a Pyongyang skyline dominated by rectangular apartment blocks, the **Ryugyong Hotel** is the undisputed king of the hill – a bizarre triangular fusion of Dracula's castle and the Empire State building. Despite the fact that it sticks out like a sore and rather weathered thumb, a whole generation of locals have viewed it as a taboo subject – this was something that couldn't be painted over with the regular whitewash of propaganda.

Construction of the pyramidal 105-floor structure started in 1987, a mammoth project intended to showcase North Korean might. The central peak was to be topped with a revolving restaurant, while the two lower cones may have held smaller versions of the same. For a time, Pyongyang was one of only three cities in the world that could boast a hundred-storey-plus building, the others being New York and Chicago. Kim Il-sung had expected the *Ryugyong* to become one of the world's most admired hotels, its near-3000 rooms filled with awestruck tourists. But no sooner had the concrete casing been completed than the (largely French) funding fell through, and the project was put on indefinite hold. It was left empty, a mere skeleton devoid of electricity, carpeting and windows.

Work only recommenced in earnest in 2008. By 2010, the crane that had maintained a lonely, sixteen-year vigil atop the structure had disappeared, and most of the naked exterior had finally been covered with tinted windows. It's scheduled to reopen for Kim Il-sung's 100th birthday bash in 2012 (as, it seems, is everything else in the land), but for now you're not allowed to enter its immediate area – those who have the Victorious Fatherland Liberation War Square on their schedules will get quite near. This is one of the city's largest ongoing projects, so it seems that before too long the world's largest shell will become one of its most distinctive places to stay.

After paying your respects, you'll be ushered through more corridors. In one room are Kim's many medals, prizes, doctorates and awards – note that a few of the universities on his dozens of diplomas have never existed. Then it's past a wall-map of the world showing the countries that Kim visited, and the train carriage and car that he did some of his travelling in. After collecting your things you'll usually be allowed out onto the main square for a much-needed stroll.

Mansudae Grand Monument

At **Mansudae**, west of the river, a huge **bronze statue** of Kim Il-sung stands in triumph, backed by a mural of Mount Paekdu – spiritual home of the Korean nation, see p.353 – and lifting a benevolent arm to his people. Unlike the mausoleum, this is not actually a memorial, but was cast when Kim was still alive: a sixtieth birthday present to himself, paid for by the people and monies donated by the Chinese government (Beijing was said to be unhappy with the unnecessary extravagance of the original gold coating, and it was soon removed). So important is the statue that, despite its size – a full 20m – it's given a thorough scrub at least once a week. The respect given by North Korean visitors to the statue is also expected of foreigners: each individual, or every second or third person if it's a large tour party, will have to **lay flowers** at the divine metal feet (these will be bought on the walk towards the monument, and you may be asked to chip in). Each group must also line up and perform a simultaneous bow – stay down for at least a few seconds. Note that taking any pictures that might be deemed "offensive", which includes those cutting part of the statue off or pretending to support Kim as you might the Leaning Tower of Pisa, may result in your camera being confiscated.

Sloping up from the monument is **Moran Hill**, a small park crisscrossed with pleasant paths, and used by city-dwellers as a place to kick back and relax. While there's nothing specific to see, those who visit on a busy day will get a chance to see North Korean life at first hand – this is one of the best places in the country to make a few temporary friends. A simple smile, wave or greeting (in Korean, preferably) has seen travellers invited to scoff *bulgogi* at a picnic or dance along to traditional tunes with a clutch of chuckling grannies.

The Arch of Triumph

The huge white granite **Arch of Triumph**, at the bottom of Moran Hill, is on almost every tourist itinerary; you may even be taken here before checking in to your hotel. Modelled on the Arc de Triomphe in Paris, but deliberately built a little higher than its French counterpart, it's the largest such structure in the world. The arch was completed in 1982 to commemorate Korea's resistance to Japan, whose occupation ended in 1945. Despite the fact that it was actually Soviet forces that liberated the city, the on-site guide will tell you that **Kim Il-sung** did all the hard work. Though these erroneous contentions are absorbing, if you're part of a larger group you may prefer to sidestep the spiel for a stroll around the area. Just a minute's walk away, and easily visible from the arch, is a tremendous **mural** of the Great Leader receiving the adulation of his public, while set further back is the 100,000-seater **Kim Il-sung Stadium**; don't venture too close to the latter unless you want to receive reprimanding whistles from folk in uniforms. There's also a small **theme park** nearby, which features on some itineraries; a recent overhaul, replete with imported equipment, has made this one of the city's most enjoyable attractions.

Kim Il-sung Square and around

West of the Taedong River is **Kim Il-sung Square**, a huge paved area where the sense of space is heightened by its near-total lack of people. First-time visitors may also get a sense of *déjà vu* – it's in all the stock North Korean footage of goose-stepping soldiers that is shown whenever the country is in the news (incidentally this act is far from a daily event, and not even an annual one – it's only performed on important military anniversaries). State propaganda peers down into the square from all sides in the form of oversized pictures and slogans. The message on the party headquarters on the north side of the square reads "Long live the Democratic People's Republic of Choson!" Others say "With the Revolutionary Spirit of Paekdu Mountain!" and "Follow the Three Revolutionary Flags!" – the red flags in question read "history", "skill" and "culture", and are being reared away from by Chollima, a winged horse of Korean legend. Visible to the east across the river is the soaring flame-like tip of the Juche Tower (see below). At the west of the square is the **Grand People's Study House**, effectively an oversized library and one of the few buildings in the city to be built with anything approaching a traditional style – a little ironic, considering its status as a vault of rewritten history. This isn't on all tour itineraries, but anyone given the chance to enter will doubtless be impressed by the super-modern filing system.

Tower of the Juche Idea

While the Mansudae Grand Monument was Kim Il-sung's 60th birthday gift to himself, the **Tower of the Juche Idea** is what he unwrapped when he turned 70 in

A resident's view of life in Pyongyang

"We in Pyongyang are pretty lucky – life here is much better than in the countryside. As elsewhere, our apartments are provided to us by the government, and we don't pay rent. Most people have a TV and a refrigerator, some have a washing machine, and quite a few now have a computer; these are usually secondhand units from Europe or China. Actually, kids have been getting into chatting on the internet, but it's not possible to contact people outside the country, and sometimes the whole network goes down for weeks or even years at a time, the same as for our mobile telephones. We all hate it when that happens.

"I guess our educational system is pretty similar to other countries. We have club activities after lessons, usually sports, and we can study foreign languages at school – English is the most popular, followed by Russian. One thing people won't get outside our country is teachings on the 'Three Revolutions': these are ideology – that's the most important one – culture and technology. Kim Jong-il says that technology is important if we are to progress, so lots of people want to study it at university now. Kim Il-sung University is the biggest, with maybe twelve thousand students, but there are other ones around the country; the one in Wonsan, for example, is pretty famous for economics. Military service is compulsory for boys, who have to do three years, and girls can join as volunteers.

"In my free time I like to listen to music, and sing it too, of course. Like lots of people I go to a sports club – football, basketball and fishing are popular, but I like volleyball more, so that's what I do. It's also pretty common to rent movies; we can get American films from the rental store as well as local ones, but nothing really political. Men like to drink beer – they get five litres per month from the government in vouchers, and often go to the bar straight after work. This makes them drunk before they come home for dinner, which makes a lot of our women really angry."

Anon

The Juche idea

A local take on Marxist-Leninist theory, **Juche** is the official state ideology of the DPRK, and a system that informs the decision-making of each and every one of its inhabitants. Though Kim Il-sung claims the credit for its invention, the basic precepts were formed by *yangban* scholars in the early twentieth century, created as a means of asserting Korean identity during the Japanese occupation. The basic principle is one of **self-reliance** – both nation and individual are intended to be responsible for their own destiny. Kim Il-sung introduced Juche as the official ideology in the early 1970s, and the doctrines were put to paper in 1982 by his son Kim Jong-il in a book entitled *On the Juche Idea*. Foreign-language editions are available at hotels in Pyongyang, though the core principle of the treatise is as follows:

...man is a social being with independence, creativity and consciousness, which are his social attributes formed and developed in the course of social life and through the historic process of development; these essential qualities enable man to take a position and play a role as master of the world.

As one local puts it, "Juche is more centred around human benefit than material gain relative to the theories of Marx or Lenin. There's no time for asking why we don't have something, or excusing yourself because of this absence... if the state doesn't provide something, make it yourself!" In spite of this apparent confidence, there are some pretty serious flaws and contradictions evident in the DPRK's pursuit of its own creed – the country preaches self-reliance but has long been heavily dependent on the international community for aid, and though Juche Man is said to be free to make his own decisions, **democracy** remains little more than a component part of the state's official title.

Despite the all-too-apparent failings of North Korea's interpretation of the theory, Juche managed to sow seeds abroad – Pol Pot and Ceaucescu borrowed heavily from the philosophy, though neither achieved much success, a lesson for Kim Jong-il, perhaps.

1982, a giant, 150m-high candle topped with a 20m red flame, rising up from its site on the banks of the Taedong River. Named after the North Korean take on Communist theory (see box above) it's the tallest granite tower in the world, and one of the few points of light in Pyongyang's dim night sky. A kind of socialist version of Cheomseongdae in the South (see p.189), but without the astrological capabilities, it is made out of 25,550 granite slabs – one for each day of Kim's 70 years.

It's possible to take a **lift** to the torch-level for stupendous views over Pyongyang. You could choose to stay behind, citing a fear of heights, for a guide-free walk around the area: the two guides will have to go up with your group, leaving you alone to wander the riverside park; given the slug-like speed of the lift, this may be some time.

The Children's Palace

Behind their strained faces, you sense all the concentration that goes into playing the music, and especially into trying to keep up those Miss World smiles...It's all so cold and sad. I could cry.

Guy Delisle, *Pyongyang*

The **Children's Palace** showcases the impressive talents of some of the most gifted youths in the country – you'll be escorted from room to room, taking in displays of everything from volleyball and gymnastics to embroidery and song. For some visitors, this by-product of Kim Il-sung's contention that "children are the treasure of the nation" is a sweet and pleasant part of the tour, for others the atmosphere can be more than a little depressing – while there's no denying the abilities of the young performers, it's hard to dispel the level of intensity required in their training. At the end of the tour is an impressive but brutally regimental **performance** of song and dance in the large auditorium, showcasing North Korean expertise to foreign guests, but many leave wondering what the country would be like if similar efforts were put into more productive educational pursuits.

Pyongyang subway

Many visitors find it incredible that a country as poor as North Korea has something as decadent as a functioning **subway system** (Ⓦwww.pyongyang-metro.com), one that even has two lines; in fact, there are likely to be several more for government-only use, though details are kept well under wraps. Only two of the sixteen known stations – **Puhung** and **Yonggwang** – are open to foreign visitors (though *Koryo Tours*, p.326, has access rights for a full six), a fact that has led some reporters to declare that no more exist. Some even claim that North Korean passengers on the line are nothing more than actors who shuffle onto the trains, only to reappear minutes later on the other platform, but a visit of your own should put paid to these notions.

The first thing you'll notice is the length of the escalator; Pyongyang has some of the world's **deepest** subway platforms, said to be reinforced and deep enough to provide protection to the Pyongyang masses in the event of a military attack. Marble-floored, with sculpted columns and bathed in the dim glow of low-wattage chandelier lights, these platforms look surprisingly opulent, and are backed by large socialist realist mosaics. The trains themselves are a mix of Chinese rejects and relics of the Berlin U-Bahn, the latter evident in the occasional bit of ageing German graffiti; all feature the obligatory Kim pictures in each carriage.

The journey between stations doesn't last long, but will give you the chance to make a little contact with the locals. Photos of the subway or the boards that mark it from the outside – "*ji*" (지) in Korean text, short for *jihacheol* – go down particularly well with South Koreans, most of whom are totally unaware that such a facility exists in the North.

USS Pueblo

A piece of history floating on the Taedong River, the **USS Pueblo** would count as a Pyongyang must-see were it not for the fact that you'll probably have to see it anyway. On January 23, 1968, this small American research ship was boarded and captured by KPA forces in the East Sea – whether it was in North Korean or international waters at the time depends on whom you ask. The reasons for the attack, in which one crew member was killed, also vary from one side to the other – the North Koreans made accusations of espionage, the Americans contend that Stalin wanted an on-board encryptor – as do accounts of what happened to the 83 captured crew during their enforced stay in the DPRK; the misty cloak of propaganda makes it hard to verify tales of torture, but they're equally difficult to reject. What's known for sure is that Pyongyang spent months waiting for an **apology** which the Americans deferred for months, and it was only on December 23 that the crew finally crossed to safety over Panmunjom's "Bridge of No Return" (p.140).

You'll be ushered into the ship, part of which has been converted into a tiny cinema, and shown a short **documentary**. This is fascinating, and states the North Korean position on the matter in no ambiguous terms, showing how well the prisoners were kept, then reprimanding these "brazen-faced American aggressors" for failing to turn around to salute their captors on crossing at Panmunjom. A uniformed "soldier" will then escort you through the rest of the ship, pointing out bullet holes and the like, before escorting you back onto dry land.

The museums

North Korean tours once revolved around Pyongyang's surprisingly large number of **museums**. Tour companies have mercifully wised up to the fact that most travellers would prefer simply to stroll down a city street than be bombarded with hours of national triumph and foreign aggression, and consequently the average number of museum visits has been pared down to two or three. There are few better windows into the "official" national mentality, or what's taught at school across the land.

If you have any say in your schedule, make sure that it includes a visit to the **Victorious Fatherland Liberation War Museum**. Right from the huge, cheery mural at the entrance, you'll be subjected to the most fervent America-bashing that you're likely to hear in North Korea; the terms "aggressors", "imperialists" and "imperialist aggressors" are used avidly. You'll be escorted through rooms filled with photos and documents relating to atrocities said to have been inflicted on Korea by the Americans, many of which were apparently seized after the liberation of Seoul during the Korean War. The important bits on the documents are underlined, which helps to steer the eye away from some suspiciously shoddy English – however obvious forgeries may be (and there are some), don't be tempted to point it out, and just treat it as part of the game. The tour then continues to the basement, which is full of war machinery including several bullet-ravaged planes, a torpedo ship and some captured guns and trucks. Of most interest is a **helicopter** shot down over North Korean territory; next to the vehicle's carcass is an extraordinary photograph of the pilot surrendering next to his dead buddy. From here you then move on to the **panorama room**, where the scenery slowly revolves around a central platform. This depiction of a battle in the Daejeon area is spectacular, having been rendered on an apparently seamless 15m x 132m length of canvas.

Mangyongdae

A visit to **Mangyongdae** – the purported **birthplace** of Kim Il-sung on April 15, 1912 – is almost guaranteed to feature on your itinerary. Despite the lack of things to see, the park-like area is pretty in a dull sort of way, and kept as modest as possible, its wooden buildings surrounded by greenery and meandering paths providing a nod to Kim's peasant upbringing. You'll likely be offered spring water from the on-site well, which supposedly gets visitors "into the revolutionary spirit of things". The nearby funfair is marginally more interesting, and features a coconut shy where you can hurl projectiles at targets dressed up as American and Japanese soldiers.

Eating and drinking

As with accommodation, all your **dining** requirements will be sorted out in advance. North Koreans seem to think that foreigners will only enjoy their meal if they're rotating slowly – both the *Koryo* and *Yanggakdo* hotels have revolving **restaurants**. Contrary to many reports, others *do* exist in Pyongyang; in fact, there's one on almost every block, but many are camouflaged by their lack of signage and rather hard to spot (the locals know where to go and almost all are off-limits to outsiders, so there's no need for a sign). The best places, however, are closed to all but foreigners and the party elite, and you'll probably eat at a different one on each day of your stay.

Two of the most popular restaurants are *Pyongyang Best Barbecued Duck*, which serves this and not much else, and the *Chongnyu*, which specializes in Korean hotpot. Those staying at the *Koryo* should ask to be taken to *Pyolmori*, a nearby café-cum-bakery part-owned by a Swiss group – in addition to tasty snacks, they serve what's undoubtedly the best coffee in the country.

You usually have breakfast in your hotel, and on some days will also have lunch or dinner there. Both the volume and the quality of food will depend on the prevailing food situation at the time of your visit – experienced diplomats suggest that the fare seems to improve when big groups or important folk are in town. Lastly, those visiting in warmer months may spot ladies selling **ice cream** from tiny booths. There's usually only one variety – a creamy stick-bar called an Eskimo – but the real appeal for many is the opportunity to get some North Korean money as change (see p.331).

Drinking can be one of Pyongyang's most unexpected delights – while you won't exactly be painting the town red, many travellers stagger to bed from the hotel bar absolutely sozzled every single night of their stay (and then have to get up at 7am to catch the tour bus). The *Koryo* and *Yanggakdo* are both topped with revolving restaurants, which become bars of an evening – perfect for a nightcap with a view of Pyongyang's galaxy of faint lights. The *Yanggakdo* has a nightclub, as well as a ground-floor bar churning out draught beer and stout from an on-site microbrewery.

Other sights in the DPRK

Most of the country is closed off to foreign visitors, but even the shortest tour itinerary is likely to contain at least one sight outside Pyongyang. The most common trip is to **Panmunjom** in the DMZ, via **Kaesong**, the closest city to the border, but there are other popular excursions to **Paekdusan**, the mythical birthplace of the Korean nation and its highest peak, and the wonderful "Diamond Mountains" of **Kumgangsan** near the South Korean border. If you do venture further than Pyongyang, you'll witness poverty-stricken North Korea at first hand – in the capital there's little to remind you of its Third World status, but outside things are extremely different, and this is only the poverty you're allowed to see. You'll also notice a notable change in the locals' reaction to your presence: whereas a smile or wave may be reciprocated in Pyongyang, elsewhere you may invoke trepidation.

Kaesong

Other than Pyongyang, **KAESONG** (개성) is usually the only North Korean city that foreign travellers get to see. From the capital, it's an easy ninety-minute trip south along the traffic-free **Reunification Highway**; the road actually continues all the way to Seoul, just 80km away, though it's blocked by the DMZ a few kilometres south of Kaesong. Its proximity to the border means the surrounding area is armed to bursting and crawling with soldiers, and it's hardly surprising that Kaesong's long-suffering citizens often come across as a little edgy. The city itself is drab and grimy in comparison with Pyongyang, but offers a far more accurate reflection of "typical" North Korean life.

Despite the palpable tension, Kaesong – romanized as "Gaeseong" in the South – is actually a place of considerable history: this was once the capital of the **Goryeo dynasty**, which ruled over the peninsula from 936 to 1392, though thanks to wholesale destruction in the Korean War, you'll see precious little evidence of this today. One exception is **Sonjuk Bridge**, which was built in the early thirteenth century; it was here that an eponymous Goryeo loyalist was assassinated as his dynasty fell. The one sight guaranteed to catch the eye is somewhat

Special excursions

This section details a few of the most common DPRK sights outside Pyongyang. All regularly feature on tour itineraries, but new areas are opened up from time to time – this is largely thanks to *Koryo Tours* (see p.326), who take a hugely proactive stance in these regards.

Haeju A great side-trip for history buffs: the city is home to a huge pavilion erected in 1500, while the surrounding area is home to a Goryeo-dynasty mountain fortress and a Joseon-era Confucian academy. It's possible to stay the night here.

Hamheung Major east coast city, only opened to tourism in 2010 – your presence will cause quite a stir. It's visually interesting, with lots of buildings designed by East German architects, while attractions include factory tours and trips to local farms.

Kumgangsan Just north of the DMZ, and within a ninety-minute drive of Wonsan, this has long been regarded as the most beautiful mountain range on the peninsula. It was once open to South Korean tourists, but for now the only way in is from the North. You'll be able to take in a few beautiful lakes – one of these, Sijungho, has a guesthouse whose spa offers mud treatments.

Nampo A major city just 45 minutes west of Pyongyang by bus. Sights are low-key, but interesting in their own way – most visitors get shown around the 8km-long West Sea Barrage, the steelworks and a couple of factories. Ask for a trip to the hot springs resort.

Wonsan A large port city – visitors usually get shown around the docks, though more interesting is the chance to swim in the sea at Songdowon Beach, just down the coast. On the way to or from Pyongyang (a four-hour drive) you may be able to stop at the gorgeous Ulim waterfalls – ask permission for a dip, if it's warm.

more modern – a huge **statue of Kim Il-sung**. One of the most prominent such statues in the country, and even visible from the Reunification Highway on the way to Panmunjom, it's illuminated at night come what may owing to its own generator, which enables it to surf the crest of any power shortages that afflict the rest of the city.

There are a few officially sanctioned sights in Kaesong's surrounding countryside. West of the city on the road to Pyongyang is the tomb of the unfortunately named **Wang Kon**, the first leader of Goryeo and the man responsible for moving the dynasty's capital to Kaesong, his home town. In the South, he's more commonly known as King Taejo, and his decorated grass-mound tomb is similar to those that can be found in Seoul (see p.99). Further west is another tomb, this one belonging to **Wang Jon**. Also known as King Kongmin, he ruled (1351–74) during Mongol domination of the continent; in keeping with the traditions of the time, he married a Mongol princess and was buried alongside her – the tiger statues surrounding the tomb represent the Goryeo dynasty, while the sheep are a nod to the Mongol influence. North of Wang Kon's tomb is **Pakyon**, a forest waterfall whose surroundings include a fortress gate and a beautiful temple.

Groups heading to or from Panmunjom often have a **lunch** stop in Kaesong; the unnamed restaurant favoured by most tour leaders lays on a superb spread, apportioned into little golden bowls. It's also possible to **stay** in Kaesong, which is an interesting add-on to many tours – the *Kaesong Folk Hotel* is a parade of traditional rooms running off a courtyard, the complex dotted with swaying trees and bisected by a peaceful stream. Rooms are basic, and sometimes fall victim to power outages, but it's a unique experience with an entirely different vibe from the big hotels in Pyongyang.

Panmunjom

Do I hate Americans? Not really – I don't like the policies of their government or military, but that's no reason to hate the people. Our Dear Leader himself has American friends – have you heard of Billy Graham? We don't have many Americans on this tour, but I always make a special effort to please them; in fact, I stay in touch with a couple as pen-pals. One of my dreams is that Korea will reunify, and then I can meet them again, either here or in their own country.

North Korean soldier, Joint Security Area

The village of **PANMUNJOM** (판문점) sits bang in the middle of the **Demilitarized Zone** that separates North and South Korea (see p.140 for more information on how it can be reached from the South, where it's referred to as Panmunjeom). You'll see much the same from the North, but with the propaganda reversed – all of a sudden it was the US Army that started the Korean War and Kim Il-sung who won it. Interestingly, many visitors note that the cant is just as strong on the American side (though usually more balanced).

The route to Panmunjom follows the Reunification Highway from Kaesong. Your first stop will be at the **KPA guardpost**, which sits just outside the northern barrier of the DMZ; the southern flank and the democracy beyond are just 4km away, though it feels far further than that. Here you'll see a wonderful hand-painted picture of a boy and girl from each side savouring unification, but for some reason the guards aren't keen on people taking photos of it. After being given a short presentation of the site by a local soldier, it's back onto your bus for the ride to the DMZ itself – note the huge slabs of concrete at the sides of the road, ready to be dropped to block the way of any invading tanks (this same system is in place on the other side). A short way into the DMZ is the **Armistice Hall**, which was cobbled together at incredible speed by North Korean soldiers to provide a suitable venue for the signing of the Korean Armistice Agreement, a document which brought about a ceasefire to the Korean War on July 27, 1953. Tucked away in a corner is what is said to be the weapon from the famed "Axe Murder Incident", an incident for which North Korea claims little responsibility (see p.141).

From the Armistice Hall you are taken to the **Joint Security Area** (see p.141), where Panmun Hall – which, whatever the American soldiers on the other side might say, is a real, multilevel building of more than a couple of metres in depth – looks across the border at a South Korean building of similar size. You may even see a few tourists being escorted around. From here, you're taken into one of the halls that straddle the official line of control, and are permitted to take a few heavily guarded steps into South Korean territory. The whole experience is bizarre, but fascinating, and an oddly tranquil place, despite its status as one of the world's most dangerous border points.

Many of the same **DMZ rules** apply, whichever side you're coming from – dress smartly, refrain from gesticulating to the other side, and don't go off on your own. It's possible to pop briefly across the official border, but it almost goes without saying that you won't be allowed to go any further. If you time it right, you could even hit the border from both sides within a few days, and stand in almost exactly the same square metre without having had any hope of crossing immediately to the other side: such is the nature of the Korean conflict.

Kumgangsan

Before partition, the **KUMGANGSAN** (금강산) mountain range – which sits just north of the DMZ on Korea's east coast – was widely considered to be the most beautiful on the peninsula. The DPRK's relative inaccessibility has ensured that this remains the case. Spectacular crags and spires of rock tower over a skirt of

The Hyundai Asan scandal

In 1998 a section of the Kumgangsan mountains in North Korea was bought on a long-term lease by **Hyundai Asan**, a wing of the gigantic Hyundai corporation which was in charge of various cross-border business ventures. Its head, **Chung Mong-hun** – the son of tycoon Chung Ju-yung, Hyundai's founder – found himself accused of illegally shifting hundreds of millions of dollars to Kim Jong-il's coffers. The secret payments centred around the first summit between the leaders of North and South Korea, which took place in 2000 and eventually landed the South Korean president, Kim Dae-jung, the Nobel Peace Prize; it didn't help that the North seemed to be using at least some of these funds to recommence work on their Yongbyon nuclear reactors. Chung Mong-hun was eventually indicted in what became known as the "Cash-for-summit" scandal; disgraced and heading for prison, he leapt to his death from his high-level office on August 4, 2003.

pine-clad foothills, its pristine lakes and waterfalls adding to a richly forested beauty rivalled only by Seoraksan just across the border (see p.155). There are said to be more than twelve thousand pinnacles, though the principal peak is Birobong, which rises to 1638m above sea level.

Kumgangsan can be visited as part of a North Korean tour, and was indeed once visitable on **a trip from South Korea** (where it's spelt "Geumgangsan", but pronounced the same); the area could almost be viewed as the "Republic of Hyundai", having been leased for controlled tourism by the South Korean business behemoth (see box above), but at the time of writing their properties north of the border had been confiscated, and tours put on indefinite hold.

Myohyangsan

Many North Korean tours include a visit to **MYOHYANGSAN** (묘향산), a pristine area of hills, lakes and waterfalls around 150km north of Pyongyang. Though it's about as close as the DPRK comes to a mountain resort, the reason to come here isn't to walk the delightful hiking trails, but to visit the **International Friendship Exhibition** – a colossal display showing the array of presents given to the Kims by overseas well-wishers. After the exhibition you're likely to be taken to see **Pohyonsa**, an eleventh-century temple just a short walk away, and **Ryongmun** or **Paengryong**, two stalactite-filled limestone caves that burrow for a number of kilometres under the surrounding mountains.

Should your schedule allow for an **overnight stay**, you're likely to find yourself at the pyramidal *Hyangsan Hotel*; this is currently the best hotel in the country, with an on-site health complex and stupendous pool, as well as the obligatory top-floor revolving restaurant.

The International Friendship Exhibition

The halls of the **International Friendship Exhibition** burrow deep into a mountainside – insurance against any nuclear attacks that come the DPRK's way. Indeed, such is the emphasis on preservation that you'll be forced to don a pair of comically oversized slippers before you enter the halls. The combination of highly polished granite floors and friction-lite footwear makes it incredibly tempting to take off down the corridors like a speed skater, but this would be looked on as a sign of immense disrespect and is therefore cautioned against. Inside the exhibition hall, gifts numbering 200,000 and rising have been arranged in order of country of origin, the evident intention being to convince visitors that Kim Sr and Kim Jr command immense respect all over the world

– of course, this is not the place to air any painful truths. Mercifully, you won't have to see all of the presents, though even the officially edited highlights can become a drag.

The first rooms you come to are those dedicated to **Kim Il-sung**. For a time, gifts were pouring in from all over the Communist world, including a limousine from Stalin and an armoured train carriage from Chairman Mao. There are also a number of medals, tea sets, pots, cutlery and military arms, as well as more incongruous offerings such as fishing rods and a refrigerator. Next you'll be ushered into a room featuring a life-size **wax statue** of the great man; local visitors bestow on this exhibit all the respect they would on Kim himself, and you'll be required to bow in front of the figure – with piped music echoing all over the room it's a truly surreal experience. The **Kim Jong-il** rooms are less stacked with goodies, and instead feature heavily corporate treats and electronic gadgets. Perhaps most interesting is the **basketball** donated by former American Secretary of State Madeleine Albright, signed by Michael Jordan, of whom Kim is apparently a big fan; on receiving the ball he was said to have been eager to get outside for a quick jam.

Paekdusan

The highest peak on the Korean peninsula at 2744m, the extinct volcano of **PAEKDUSAN** (백두산) straddles the border between North Korea and China, and is the source of the Tuman and Amnok rivers (Tumen and Yalu in Mandarin) that separate the countries. Within its caldera is a vibrant blue **crater lake** surrounded by a ring of jagged peaks; it's a beguiling place steeped in myth and legend. This was said to be the landing point for **Dangun**, the divine creator of Korea, after his journey from heaven in 2333 BC (see p.358); more recently, it was also the apparent birthplace of **Kim Jong-il**, an event said to have been accompanied by flying white horses, rainbows and the emergence of a new star in the sky. Records seem to suggest that he was born in Soviet Siberia, but who needs history when the myth is so expressive. In fact, "new" history is discovered here from time to time in the form of slogans etched into the mountain's trees, apparently carved during Kim Il-sung's time here as a resistance fighter, and somehow always in keeping with the political beliefs prevailing at their time of discovery. Emblazoned on one of the slopes surrounding the crater lake is the slogan, "Mount Paekdu, sacred mountain of the revolution".

Even with so much historical significance, it's the natural beauty of the place that attracts foreign visitors to Paekdusan. The ring of mountains is cloaked with lush forest, with some pines rising up to over 50m, and bears, wolves, boar and deer inhabiting the area; it's even home to a small population of **Siberian tigers**, though you're highly unlikely to see any. As long as the weather holds – and at this height, it often doesn't – you may be able to climb to the top of the Korean peninsula by taking a hike to **Jong Il peak**. A cable car also whisks guests down to the lakeside, where you can have a splash in the inviting waters in warmer months.

With Paekdusan being a place of such importance, every person in the country is expected to make the pilgrimage at some point; the journey is usually paid for in full by the government, even though it's well over a day by train from Pyongyang. Foreign tourists wishing to visit must take a **chartered flight** from Pyongyang, and then a car the rest of the way, though due to weather conditions the journey from the capital is usually only possible during warmer months. It's also possible to visit from the Chinese side, as thousands of South Koreans do each year (see box, p.354).

North Korea from the outside

If budgetary constraints or possession of the wrong kind of passport make a trip to North Korea impossible, there are a number of ways to peer into the country from outside.

From South Korea

The two Koreas share a 250km-long border, and though the area around the Demilitarized Zone that separates them is largely off-limits, there are a number of vantage points from which you can look across. **DMZ tours from Seoul** are highly popular (see p.142). Itineraries vary, but can include views of the North from an observatory, a trip inside tunnels dug by North Koreans in preparation for an attack on Seoul, as well as the chance to step onto **DPRK territory** in the Joint Security Area. While these excursions are good value, you can visit a similar observatory and tunnel for free on a guided tour from the remote town of **Cheorwon** (p.145), and there's another observatory just north of **Sokcho** on the east coast (p.151). It has, in the past, been possible to take an expensive tour across the border to the gorgeous mountains of **Kumgangsan**, but these trips were cancelled with the deterioration of inter-Korean relations in 2008; ask at a tourist office to see if they've been resumed.

From China

Two Chinese provinces border North Korea. Over one million ethnic Koreans live in Jilin (a city as well as a province) and another 250,000 in Liaoning – the latter even contains an autonomous Korean prefecture, where the mix of Communism and poverty make some towns fairly similar in feel to the DPRK.

The large city of **Dandong** is right on the North Korean border, with only the Yalu River ("Amnok" in Korean) separating it from Sinuiju on the other side; those entering North Korea by train will pass through Dandong, and some choose to stop off on their return leg. The two cities offer a rather incredible contrast, with the tall, neon-seared skyscrapers on the Chinese side overlooking poor, low-rise Sinuiju across the water. On Dandong's riverside promenade you'll be able to buy (mostly counterfeit) North Korean banknotes and pin-badges, and protruding from this is the Old Yalu bridge, which comes to an abrupt halt in the middle of the river, its North Korean half having been dismantled. From the promenade, you can also take a boat trip to within a single metre of the North Korean shore, and get just as close from Tiger Mountain, 25km east of the city and the easternmost section of China's Great Wall. Although jumping across for a quick picture may appear tempting, note that one foreign traveller foolish enough to do this spent months in a DPRK *gulag* after being snatched by hidden guards.

With the mountain and its crater lake straddling the border, it's also possible to visit **Paekdusan** (p.353) from the Chinese side, a trip highly popular with South Koreans. The simplest approach is to join a tour from Jilin city; this will include all accommodation, entrance fees and transport, though it's possible to chalk much of the distance off on an overnight train from Beijing to Baihe, a village close to the mountain.

Contexts

Contexts

History

With its two-millennium-long chain of **unbroken regal rule** interspersed by regular fisticuffs, the Korean peninsula offers plenty for history buffs to get their teeth into. The country's early beginnings are shrouded in mystery, though events have been well documented since before the birth of Christ, a period when Korea's famed **Three Kingdoms** were springing into existence. Replacing Gojoseon – the first known Korean kingdom – these were **Silla**, **Goguryeo** and **Baekje**, three states that jostled for peninsular power for centuries, seeing off other nascent fiefdoms while dealing with the Chinese and Japanese states of the time. Even today, tangible evidence of all three kingdoms can still be seen. It was Silla that eventually prevailed, emerging victorious from a series of battles to bring the peninsula under **unified control**. Infighting and poor governance led to its demise, the slack taken up by the **Goryeo** dynasty, which lasted for almost five hundred years before folding and being replaced by **Joseon** rule. This was to last even longer, but was snuffed out by the Japanese at a time of global turmoil, bringing to an end Korea's succession of well over one hundred kings. World War II ended **Japanese annexation**, after which Korea was split in two in the face of the looming Cold War. There then followed the brutal **Korean War**, and in 1953 the Communist north and the capitalist south went their separate ways, each writing their own historical versions of the time, and in the case of North Korea, slewing historical events even prior to partition. The war was never technically brought to an end, and its resolution – either peaceable, or by force – will add the next chapter to Korea's long history.

The beginnings

Remains of *homo erectus* show that the Korean peninsula may have been home to hominids for more than half a million years. The first evidence of habitation can be found in several clusters of Neanderthal sites dating from the Middle Paleolithic period (roughly 100,000–40,000 BC). The assortment of hand axes, scrapers and other tools made of stone and bone hauled from the complexes suggest a **hunter-gatherer** existence, while fish bones, nut shells and burnt rice provide further windows on the Korean caveman diet; the presence of carved tigers,

Korea's major historical eras

Gojoseon	c.2333 BC to c.109 BC
Three Kingdoms	c.57 BC to 668 AD
Silla	c.57 BC to 668 AD
Goguryeo	c.37 BC to 668 AD
Baekje	c.18 BC to 660 AD
Unified Silla	668–935
Goryeo	918–1392
Joseon	1392–1910
Japanese colonial period	1910–45
Republic of Korea (South)	1945 to present day
Democratic People's Republic of Korea (North)	1945 to present day

leopards and bears on animal bones, as well as drawings, also shows that artistic endeavour on the peninsula goes back a long way. **Neolithic** sites (8000–3000 BC) are far more numerous than those from the Paleolithic era, and in these were found thousands of remnants from the peninsula's transition from the Stone to the Bronze Age. In addition to the use of metal tools, from 7000 BC **pottery** was being produced with distinctive comb-toothed patterns (*jeulmun*) similar to those found in Mongolia and Manchuria. Fired earth also came to play a part in death rituals, a fact made evident by small, shell-like "jars" into which the broken bodies were placed together with personal belongings; these were then lowered into a pit and covered with earth. An even more distinctive style of burial was to develop, with some tombs covered with large stone slabs known as **dolmen** ("*goindol*" in Korean). Korea is home to over thirty thousand burial mounds. Three of the most important sites – Gochang and Hwasun in the Jeolla provinces, and Ganghwado, west of Incheon – are UNESCO World Heritage sites.

Gojoseon

The peninsula's first kingdom was known as Joseon, though is today usually referred to as **Gojoseon** (고조선; "Old Joseon") in an effort to distinguish it from the later Joseon period (1392–1910). Its origins are obscure to say the least; most experts agree that it got going in 2333 BC under the leadership of **Dangun**, who has since become the subject of one of Korea's most cherished myths (see box below). Joseon initially functioned as a loose federation of fiefdoms covering not only parts of the Korean peninsula, but large swathes of Manchuria too. By 500 BC it had become a single, highly organized dominion, even drawing praise from Confucius and other Chinese sages. Accounts of the fall of Joseon are also rather vague, but large parts of its Manchurian population were squeezed onto the Korean peninsula during the Chinese **Warring States Period** (470–221 BC), and it seems likely to have fallen victim to a nascent Han dynasty in 109 BC. Joseon's historical name lives on: North Korea continues to refer to its land as such (and South Korea as Namjoseon, or "South Joseon"), while many South Korean tourist brochures use "The Land of Morning Calm" – a literal translation of the term – as a national motto.

The legend of Dangun

The Korean peninsula has played host to some of the world's longest-running monarchies, and such regal durability has made for comprehensive records. However, much of what's known about the years preceding the Three Kingdoms period remains obscure, and Korea has resorted to mythology to fill in the gaps of its creation – primarily the legend of **Dangun**.

The story begins with **Hwanin**, the "Lord of Heaven", whose son **Hwanung** desired to live as a mortal being on Earth. Hwanin set his son down on Mount Paekdu (located in present-day North Korea) together with an army of three thousand disciples. Hwanung and his tribe took charge of the locals, and fostered celestial ideals of law, art and social structure. Two of his pets – a bear and a tiger – prayed to Hwanung that they be made human, just as he had been; they were each given twenty cloves of garlic and a bundle of mugwort, and told to survive on noting else for a hundred days, before being sent to a cave. The tiger failed the challenge, but the bear prevailed, and on being made human soon bore Hwanung's child, Dangun, who went on to found **Joseon** in 2333 BC.

In 1993 North Korean officials announced that they had found Dangun's tomb in a location close to Pyongyang; unfortunately, they've been unwilling to share this evidence with the rest of the world.

The Three Kingdoms period

By 109 BC, after the fall of Gojoseon, power on the peninsula was decentralized to half-a-dozen fiefdoms, the most powerful of which – **Silla**, **Goguryeo** and **Baekje** – went on to become known as the Three Kingdoms. Though exact details regarding their beginnings are just as sketchy as those surrounding Gojoseon – two of the inaugurators are said to have hatched from eggs – this period saw the first definitive drawing of borders in Korean history, although it must be noted that none of them became fully-fledged kingdoms for a couple of centuries, each existing initially as a loose confederation of fiefdoms. Several of those jostling for power after Gojoseon's demise are not included under the Three Kingdoms banner; most notably, these include the states of **Gaya**, which was absorbed by Silla, and **Buyeo**, parts of which were incorporated by Goguryeo and Baekje. The kingdom of **Tamna**, isolated on Jeju Island, also came under Baekje control.

Territorial borders shifted continuously as all three kingdoms jostled for power, and a number of fortresses went up across the land, many of which can still be seen today. Outside forces were occasionally roped in to help; interestingly, Baekje was closely aligned with Japan for much of its time, while Silla sided with the Chinese Tang dynasty, despite their positions on the "wrong" sides of the peninsula. Because of these close ties with China and Japan, Korea acted as a conduit for a number of customs imported from the continent: Chinese characters came to be used with the Korean language and the import and gradual flourishing of **Buddhism** saw temples popping up all over the peninsula. However, it was **Confucianism**, another Chinese import, that provided the social building blocks, with a number of educational academies supplying the *yangban* scholars at the head of the aristocracy. Great advances were made in the arts, particularly with regard to jewellery and pottery; wonderful relics of the time have been discovered in their thousands from the grassy hill-tombs of dead kings and other formerly sacred sites. After **centuries of warring** that saw the kingdoms continually changing allegiance to each other and to Chinese and Japanese dynasties, matters finally came to a head in the mid-seventh century. In 660, supplemented by Tang forces from China, Silla **triumphed in battle** against Baekje, whose people leapt to their death from a cliff in the city of Buyeo. Muyeol died just a year later, but within a decade his son King Munmu defeated Goguryeo, setting the scene for a first-ever **unified rule** on the peninsula.

Goguryeo

The kingdom of **Goguryeo** (고구려) covered the whole of present-day North Korea, a large chunk of Chinese Manchuria and much of what is now Gangwon-do in the South, making it by far the largest of the Three Kingdoms by territory. Because of its location, the majority of Goguryeo's relics are a little harder to come by today than those from the Baekje or Silla kingdoms, and the history even more vague; most guesses place the inauguration of the first Goguryeo king, Dongmyeong, at 37 BC. At this point Goguryeo was still paying tax and tribute to China, but when the **Han dynasty** started to weaken in the third century, Goguryeo advanced and occupied swathes of territory; they eventually came to rule over an area (much of which is now in the Chinese region of Dongbei) almost three times the size of the present-day Korean peninsula. Baekje and Silla forces mounted sporadic attacks from the south, and the Chinese Tang invaded from the north, squeezing Goguryeo towards the Tuman and Anmok rivers that mark North Korea's present boundary. The Tang also provided pressure from the south by allying with the Silla dynasty, and when this **Tang-Silla coalition** defeated Baekje in 660, the fall of Goguryeo was inevitable; it was finally snuffed out in 668.

Baekje

The **Baekje** (백제) dynasty, which controlled the southwest, was created as the result of great movements of people on the western side of the Korean peninsula. **Buyeo**, a smaller state not considered one of the Three Kingdoms, was pushed southward by the nascent kingdom of Goguryeo, and some elements decided to coalesce around a new leader – **Onjo**, the son of Dongmyeong, the first king of Goguryeo. Jealous of his brother's inheritance of that kingdom, Onjo proclaimed his own dynasty in 18 BC. Baekje is notable for its production of fine jewellery, which exhibited more restraint than that found in the other kingdoms, a fact often attributed to the dynasty's relatively early adoption of Buddhism as a state religion. Evidence of Baekje's close relationship with the **Japanese kingdom of Wa** can still be seen today – the lacquered boxes, folding screens, immaculate earthenware and intricate jewellery of Japan are said to derive from the influence of Baekje artisans. Unfortunately for Baekje, the Wa did not provide such protection as the Chinese Tang dynasty gave Silla, and much of its later history was spent conceding territory to Goguryeo. The capital shifted south from a location near present-day Seoul to Ungjin (now known as Gongju), then south again to Sabi (now Buyeo); after one final battle, fought in 660 against a Tang-Silla coalition, Baekje's small remaining population chose death over dishonour, and committed suicide from Sabi's riverside fortress.

Silla

Although it held the smallest territory of the Three Kingdoms, in the southeast, and was for centuries the most peaceable, it was the **Silla** (신라) dynasty that defeated Baekje and Goguryeo to rule over the whole peninsula. Unlike its competitors, it only had one dynastic capital – Gyeongju – and many of the riches accumulated in almost a millennium of power (including over two hundred years as the capital of the whole peninsula) can still be seen today.

Silla's first king – Hyeokgeose – was crowned in 57 BC, but it was not until the sixth century AD that things got interesting. At this time, Silla accepted Buddhism as its state religion (the last of the Three Kingdoms to do so), and created a Confucian "bone rank" system in which people's lives were governed largely by heredity: Buddhism was used to sate spiritual needs, and Confucianism as a regulator of society. Following threats from the Japanese kingdom of Wa, they also began a rapid build-up of military strength; under the rule of King Jinheung (540–76) they absorbed the neighbouring **Gaya** confederacy, and started to nibble away at the other neighbouring kingdoms. Initially they sided with Baekje to attack Goguryeo, a dynasty already weakened by internal strife and pressure from the Chinese Tang to the north; a century later, Silla turned the tables on Baekje by allying with the **Tang**, then used the same alliance to finish off Goguryeo to the north and bring the Korean peninsula under unified rule.

Unified Silla

Following the quickfire defeats of its two competitor kingdoms in the 660s, the **Silla dynasty** gave rise to the Korean peninsula's first ever unification, keeping Gyeongju as the seat of power. This was, however, no easy matter: small pockets of Baekje and Goguryeo resistance lingered on, and a new (perhaps necessarily) nationalistic fervour developed by the king meant that the Chinese Tang – allies previously so crucial to Silla – had to be driven out, an action that also sent a strong "stay away" message to would-be Japanese invaders. Silla also had to contend with **Balhae** to the north; this large but unwieldy successor state to Goguryeo claimed back much of that kingdom's former territory, and set about establishing favourable relationships with nearby groups to the north.Once the dust had settled, the Chinese officially accepted the dynasty in exchange for regular tributes paid to Tang emperors; King Seongdeok (ruled 702–37) did much of the work, convincing the Tang that his kingdom would be much more useful as an ally than as a rival. Silla set about cultivating a peninsular **sense of identity**, and the pooling of ideas and talent saw the eighth century become a high-water mark of artistic development, particularly in metalwork and earthenware. This time also saw temple design reach elaborate heights, particularly at Bulguksa, built near Gyeongju in 751. Rulers stuck to a rigidly Confucian "bone rank" system, which placed strict limits on what an individual could achieve in life, based almost entirely on their genetic background. Though it largely succeeded in keeping the proletariat quiet, this highly centralized system was to lead to Silla's demise.

Decline and fall

The late eighth century and most of the ninth were characterized by **corruption and in-fighting** at the highest levels of Silla society. Kings' reigns tended to be brief and bloody – the years from 836 to 839 alone saw five kings on the throne, the result of power struggles, murder and enforced suicide. Tales of regal immorality trickled down to the peasant class, leading to a number of **rebellions**; these increased in size and number as regal power over the countryside waned, eventually enveloping Silla in a state of perpetual civil war. With the Silla king reduced to little more than a figurehead, the former kingdoms of Baekje and Goguryeo were resurrected (now known as "**Hubaekje**" and "**Taebong**" respectively). Silla shrunk back beyond its Three Kingdoms-era borders, and after a power struggle Taebong took control of the peninsula; in 935 at Gyeongju's Anapji Pond, King Gyeongsun ceded control of his empire in a peaceful transfer of power to Taebong leader **Wang Geon**, who went on to become Taejo, the first king of the Goryeo dynasty.

The Goryeo dynasty

Having grown from a mini-kingdom known as Taebong, one of the many battling for power following the collapse of Silla control, it was the name of the Goryeo (고려) dynasty that eventually gave rise to the English term "Korea". It began life in 918 under the rule of **Taejo**, a powerful leader who needed less than two decades to bring the whole peninsula under his control. One of his daughters was to marry Gyeongsun, the last king of Silla, and Taejo himself to wed a Silla queen, two telling examples of the new king's desire to cultivate a sense of national unity; he was even known to give positions of authority to known enemies. Relations with China and Japan were good, and the kingdom became ever more prosperous.

Following the fall of Silla, Taejo moved the national capital to his home town, Kaesong, a city in present-day North Korea. He and successive leaders also changed some of the bureaucratic systems that had contributed to Silla's downfall: power was centralized in the king but devolved to the furthest reaches of his domain, and even those without aristocratic backgrounds could, in theory, reach lofty governmental positions via a system of state-run examinations. Despite the Confucian social system, **Buddhism** continued to function as the state religion: the *Tripitaka Koreana* – a set of more than eithty thousand wooden blocks carved with doctrine – was completed in 1251, and now resides in

Haeinsa temple. This was not the only remarkable example of Goryeo ingenuity: 1377 saw the creation of *Jikji*, the world's first book printed with movable metal type (now in Paris, and the subject of a tug-of-war with the French government), and repeated refinements in the pottery industry saw Korean produce attain a level of quality only bettered in China. In fact, despite great efforts, some **pottery techniques** perfected in Goryeo times remain a mystery today, perhaps never to be replicated.

The wars

Though the Goryeo borders as set out by King Taejo are almost identical to those that surround the Korean peninsula today, they were witness to numerous skirmishes and invasions. Notable among these were the **Khitan Wars** of the tenth and eleventh centuries, fought against proto-Mongol groups of the Chinese Liao dynasty. The Khitan had defeated Balhae just before the fall of Silla, and were attempting to gain control over the whole of China as well as the Korean peninsula, but three great invasions failed to take Goryeo territory, and a peace treaty was eventually signed. Two centuries later came the **Mongol hordes**; the Korean peninsula was part of the Eurasian landmass, and therefore a target for the great Khaans. Under the rule of Ögedei Khaan, the first invasion came in 1231, but it was not until the sixth campaign – which ended in 1248 – that Goryeo finally became a vassal state, a series of forced marriages effectively making its leaders part of the Mongol royal family. This lasted almost a century, before **King Gongmin** took advantage of a weakening Chinese–Mongol Yuan dynasty (founded by Kublai Khaan) to regain independence.

The Mongol annexation came at a great human cost, one echoed in a gradual worsening of Goryeo's economy and social structure. Gongmin made an attempt at reform, purging the top ranks of those he felt to be pro-Mongol, but this instilled fear of yet more change into the *yangban* elite: in conjunction with a series of decidedly non-Confucian love-triangles and affairs with young boys, this was to lead to his murder. His young and unprepared successor, King U, was pushed into battle with the Chinese Ming dynasty; Joseon's General **Yi Seong-gye** led the charge, but fearful of losing his soldiers he stopped at the border and returned to Seoul, forcing the abdication of the king, and putting U's young son Chang on the throne. The General decided that he was not yet happy with the arrangement, and had both U and Chang executed (the latter just 8 years old at the time); after one more failed attempt at putting the right puppet king on the throne, he decided to take the mantle himself, and in 1392 declared himself King Taejo, the first leader of the Joseon dynasty.

The Joseon dynasty

The **Joseon era** (조선시대) started off much the same as the Goryeo dynasty had almost five centuries beforehand, with a militaristic king named **Taejo** on the throne, a name that translates as "The Grand Ancestor". Joseon was to last even longer, with a full 27 kings ruling from 1392 until the Japanese annexation in 1910. Taejo moved the capital from Kaesong to **Seoul**, and immediately set about entrenching his power with a series of mammoth projects; the first few years of his reign saw the wonderful palace of Gyeongbokgung, the ancestral shrines of Jongmyo and a gate-studded city wall go up. His vision was quite astonishing – the chosen capital and its palace and shrine remain to this day, together with sections of the wall. More grand palaces would go up in due course, with another four at some point home to the royal throne. From the start of the dynasty, Buddhism declined in power, and **Confucianism** permeated society yet further in its stead. Joseon's social system became even more hierarchical in nature, with the king and other royalty at the top, and the hereditary **yangban** class of scholars and aristocrats just beneath, then various levels of employment towards the servants and slaves at the bottom of the pile. All of these social strata were governed by heredity, but the *yangban* became ever more powerful as the dynasty progressed, gradually starting to undermine the power of the king. They were viewed as a world apart by the commoners, and placed great emphasis on study and the arts. Only the *yangban* had access to such education as could foster literacy in a country that wrote with Chinese characters. In the 1440s **King Sejong** (reigned 1418–50) devised **Hangeul**, a new and simple local script that all classes could read and write; the *yangban* were not fond of this, and it was banned at the beginning of the sixteeth century, lying largely dormant until beached by waves of nationalist sentiment created by the end of Japanese annexation in 1945.

The Japanese invasions

In 1592, under the command of feared warlord **Hideyoshi**, Japan set out to conquer the Ming dynasty, with China a stepping stone towards possible domination of the whole Asian continent. The Korean peninsula had the misfortune to be both in the way and loyal to the Ming, and after King Seonjo refused to allow Japanese troops safe passage, Hideyoshi mustered all his military's power and unloaded the lot at Korea. After two relatively peaceable centuries, the Joseon dynasty was ill-prepared for such an assault, and within a month the Japanese had eaten up most of the peninsula; the advance was halted with forces from a Ming dynasty keen to defend its territory. By the time of the second main wave of attacks in 1597, Korean **Admiral Yi Sun-shin** had been able to better prepare Korea's southern coastline, now protected by a number of fortresses. The Japanese found themselves losing battle after battle, undone by Admiral Yi's "**turtle ships**", vessels proclaimed by Koreans as the world's first armoured warships.

The "Hermit Kingdom"

The Japanese attacks – together with the dynastic transfer from Ming to Qing in China in the 1640s, which led to Joseon becoming a vassal state forced to spend substantial sums paying tribute to the emperors in Beijing – prompted Korea to turn inwards; it became known as the "**Hermit Kingdom**", one of which outsiders knew little, and saw even less. One exception was a Dutch ship which crashed off Jeju Island in 1653 en route to Japan; the survivors were kept prisoner for thirteen years but finally managed to escape; the accounts of **Hendrick Hamel** provided the western world with one of its first windows into isolationist Korea.

The Dutch prisoners had entered a land in which corruption and factionalism were rife, one that achieved little social or economic stability until the rule of **King Yeongjo** (1724–76), who authorized a purge of crooked officials. In 1767, inside the grounds of Changgyeonggung palace, he forced Sado – his son and the country's crown prince – into a rice basket, locked the flap and left him inside to starve rather than let the country fall into his hands. Sado's son **Jeongjo** came to the throne on Yeongjo's death in 1776; he went on to become one of the most revered of Korea's kings, instigating top-to-bottom reform to wrench power from the *yangban* elite, and allowing for the creation of a small middle class. The lot of the poor man gradually improved.

The end of isolation

Following Japan's **opening up** to foreign trade in the 1860s (the "Meiji Restoration"), Korea found itself under pressure to do likewise, not just from the Japanese but from the United States and the more powerful European countries – warships were sent from around the globe to ensure agreement. Much of the activity occurred on and around the island of Ganghwado, just west of Seoul: the French occupied the isle but failed with advances on the mainland in 1866, their battle fought partly as retaliation for the murder of several of their missionaries in Korea. Five years later, and in the same location, the Americans also attempted to prise the country open to trade; though they failed, the third bout of gunboat diplomacy – this time by the Japanese in 1876 – resulted in the Treaty of Ganghwa, which dragged Korea into the global marketplace on unfair terms. From this point to the present day, Korea would be a ship largely steered along by foreign powers.

Through means both political and economic, the Japanese underwent a gradual strengthening of their position in Korea. Local resentment boiled over into occasional riots and protests, and peaked in 1895 after the Japanese-orchestrated **murder of Empress Myeongseong** – "Queen Min", to the Japanese – in Gyeongbokgung palace. After this event, **King Gojong** (reigned 1863–1910) fled to the Russian embassy for protection; in 1897, when things had quietened down sufficiently, he moved into the nearby palace of Deoksugung, there to set up the short-lived **Empire of Korea**, a toothless administration under almost full Japanese control. In 1902 Japan forged an alliance with the British Empire, recognizing British interests in China in return for British acknowledgment of Japanese interests in Korea. Sensing shifts in power, Russia at this point began moving its rooks into Korea, though they ran into the Japanese on the way. To avoid confrontation, Japan suggested that the two countries carve Korea up along the **38th parallel**, a line roughly bisecting the peninsula. Russia refused to accept, the two fought the Russo-Japanese War in 1904–05, and after its surprise victory Japan was in a position to occupy the peninsula outright. They were given tacit permission to do so in 1905 by US Secretary of State and President-to-be William Taft, who agreed in a secret meeting to accept Japanese domination of Korea if Japan would accept the American occupation of the Philippines. Korea became a Japanese protectorate that year, and Japan gradually ratcheted up its power on the peninsula before a final **outright annexation** in 1910. Joseon's kings had next to no say in the running of the country during its last quarter-century under dynastic succession, and it was with a whimper that the book closed on Korea's near two thousand years of unbroken regal rule.

The Japanese occupation

After the signing of the Annexation Treaty in 1910, the Japanese wasted no time in putting themselves in all the top posts in politics, banking, law and industry with their own personnel; despite the fact that they never represented more than four percent of the peninsular population, they came to control almost every sphere of its workings. Korea was but part of the Empire of Japan's dream of **continental hegemony**, and being the nearest stepping stone to the motherland, it was also the most heavily trampled on. While the Japanese went on to occupy most of Southeast Asia and large swathes of China, only in Korea did they have the time and leverage necessary to attempt a total annihilation of **national identity**. Some of the most powerful insults to national pride were hammered home early. The royal palace of **Gyeongbokgung** had all the Confucian principles observed in its construction shattered by the placing of a modern Japanese structure in its first holy courtyard, while nearby **Changgyeonggung** suddenly found itself home to a decidedly unroyal theme park and zoo. Korean currency, clothing and even the language itself were placed under ever stricter control, and thousands of local "**comfort women**" were forced into sexual slavery. Korean productivity grew, but much of this was also for Japan's benefit – within ten years, more than half of the country's rice was being sent across the sea.

The local populace, unsurprisingly, objected to this enforced servitude. In 1919, the **March 1st Movement** saw millions of Koreans take to the streets in a series of non-violent nationwide protests. A declaration of independence was read out in Seoul's Tapgol Park, an act followed by processions through the streets and the singing of the Korean national anthem. The Japanese police attempted to suppress the revolt through force; around seven thousand died in the months of resistance demonstrations that followed. The result, however, was a marked change of Japanese policy towards Korea, with Saito Makoto (the Admiral in charge of quelling the chaos) agreeing to lift the bans on Korean radio, printed matter and the creation of organizations, and promoting harmony rather than pushing the militarist line. The pendulum swung back towards oppression on the approach to World War II – in the late 1930s, Japan began forcing Koreans to worship at Shinto shrines, speak in Japanese, and even adopt a Japanese name (a practice known as *soshi-kaimei*), all helped by local **collaborators** (*chinilpa*). Thousands of these went across to Japan, but though many were there to do business and strengthen imperial ties, most were simply squeezed out of Korea by Japanese land confiscations.

The end of annexation

Throughout the remainder of the occupation period, the Korean government-in-exile had been forced ever further west from China's eastern seaboard, eventually landing near the Tibetan plateau in the Sichuanese city of Chongqing. Modern Korean museums and history books extol the achievements of what was, in reality, a largely toothless group. In doing this they gloss over the fundamental reason for Korea's independence: the American A-bombs that fell on Hiroshima and Nagasaki, thereby ending both World War II and the Empire of Japan itself. With Tokyo busy elsewhere, Seoul was little affected by the war: the main change in city life was the conscription of tens of thousands of Korean men, many of whom never returned. An even greater number of Koreans had moved to Japan prior to the war. Some, of course, were collaborators fearful of reprisals should they head home, but the majority were simply squeezed out of their impoverished homeland by Japanese land confiscations. Many of these Korean families remain in Japan today, and are referred to there as "Zainichi Koreans".

The Korean War

Known to many as the "**Forgotten War**", sandwiched as it was between World War II and the war in Vietnam, the Korean conflict was one of the twentieth century's greatest tragedies. The impoverished peninsula had already been pushed to the back of the global mind during World War II; the land was under Japanese control, but the Allied forces had developed no plans for its future should the war be won. In fact, at the close of the war American Secretary of State Edward Stettinius had to be told in a meeting where Korea actually was. It was only when the **Soviet Union** sent troops into Korea in 1945 that consideration was given to

Korea's postwar life. During an emergency meeting on August 10, 1945, officials and high-rankers (including eventual Secretary of State Dean Rusk) with no in-depth knowledge of the peninsula sat with a map and a pencil, and scratched a line across the 38th parallel – a simple solution, but one that was to have grave repercussions for Korea.

The build-up to war

With World War II rapidly developing into the **Cold War**, Soviet forces occupied the northern half of the peninsula, Americans the south. Both countries imposed their own social, political and economic norms on the Koreans under their control, thereby creating two de facto states that refused to recognize each other, the two diametrically opposed in ideology. The **Republic of Korea** (now more commonly referred to as "South Korea") declared independence on August 15, 1948, exactly three years after liberation from the Japanese, and the **Democratic People's Republic of Korea** (now better known as "North Korea") followed suit just over three weeks later. The US installed a leader favourable to them, selecting **Syngman Rhee** (ironically born in what is now North Korea), who had degrees from American universities. Stalin chose the much younger **Kim Il-sung**, who like Rhee had been in exile for much of the Japanese occupation. The foreign forces withdrew, and the two Koreas were left to their own devices, each hellbent on unifying the peninsula by absorbing the opposing half; inevitably, locals were forced into a polarization of opinion, one that split friends and even families apart. Kim wanted to wade into war immediately, and Stalin turned down two requests for approval of such an action. The third time, for reasons that remain open to conjecture, he gave the nod.

War breaks out

Nobody knows for sure exactly how the Korean War started. Or, rather, everyone does: the other side attacked first. The South Korean line is that on June 25, 1950, troops from the northern **Korean People's Army** (KPA) burst across the 38th parallel, then little more than a roll of tape. The DPRK itself claims that it was the south that started the war, and indeed both sides had started smaller conflicts along the line on several occasions, but declassified Soviet information shows that the main battle was kicked off by the north. With the southern forces substantially ill-equipped in comparison, Seoul fell just three days later, but they were soon aided by a sixteen-nation coalition fighting under the **United Nations** banner – the vast majority of troops were from the United States, but additional forces arrived from Britain, Canada, Australia, the Philippines, Turkey, the Netherlands, France, New Zealand, Thailand, Ethiopia, Greece, Colombia, Belgium, South Africa and Luxembourg; other countries provided non-combative support.

Within three months, the KPA had hemmed the United Nations Command (UNC) into the far southeast of the country, behind a short line of control that became known as the **Pusan Perimeter**, a boundary surrounding the (now re-romanized) city of Busan. Though the KPA held most of the peninsula, American general Douglas MacArthur identified a weak logistical spine and poor supply lines as their Achilles heel, and ordered amphibious landings behind enemy lines at **Incheon**, just west of Seoul, in an attempt to cut off Northern supplies. The ambitious plan worked to perfection, and UNC forces pushed north way beyond the 38th parallel, reaching sections of the Chinese border within six weeks. At this stage, with the battle seemingly won, the **Chinese** entered the fight and ordered almost a million troops into North Korea; with their help, the KPA were able to push back past the 38th parallel. The UNC made one more thrust north in early 1951, and after six months the two sides ended up pretty much where they started. The lines of the conflict settled around the 38th parallel, near what was to become the **Demilitarized Zone**, but the fighting did not end for well over two years, until the signing of an armistice agreement on July 27, 1953. North Korea, China and the United Nations Command signed the document, but South Korea refused to do likewise, meaning that the war is still technically being fought today.

A land in ruins

In effect, both sides lost the Korean War, as neither had achieved the aims espoused at the outset. Seoul had fallen four times – twice to each side – and Korea's population was literally decimated, with over three million killed, wounded or missing over the course of the war; to this can be added around half a million UNC troops, and what may well be over a million Chinese. Had the war been "contained" and brought to an end when the line of control stabilized in early 1951, these figures would have been far lower. The war split thousands of families; in addition to the confusion created by a front line that yo-yoed up and down the land, people were forced to switch sides to avoid starvation or torture, or to stay in contact with family members. Though the course of the battle and its aftermath were fairly straightforward, propaganda clouded many of the more basic details, and the war was largely forgotten by the West. For all the coverage of Vietnam, few know that a far greater amount of **napalm** fell on North Korea, a much more "suitable" target for the material thanks to its greater number of large urban areas; also kept quiet is how close **nuclear weapons** were to being used in the conflict. After the war, General MacArthur was quoted as saying that he "would have dropped between thirty and fifty atomic bombs... strung across the neck of Manchuria." Since the end of the war there have been innumerable accounts of atrocities committed by both sides, many detailing beatings, torture and the unlawful murder of prisoners of war, others documenting the slaughter of entire villages. Korea lay in ruins, yet two countries were slowly able to emerge from the ashes.

To the present day

Considering its state after the war, South Korea's transformation is nothing short of astonishing. A rapid phase of industrialization, one often referred to as the "**Economic Miracle**" in the west, saw it become one of Asia's most ferocious financial tigers, and Seoul morph from battle-scarred wasteland into one of the world's largest and most dynamic cities. The country's GDP-per-head shot up from under US$100 in 1963 to almost US$30,000 in 2010. Thanks in large part to the bullishness of large conglomerates (known as *jaebeol)* such as Samsung, Hyundai and LG, it now sits proudly on the cusp of the world's ten most powerful economies. And, since flinging off its autocratic straightjacket in the 1980s, it developed sufficiently to be selected to host some of the world's most high-profile events – the **Olympics** in 1988, soccer's **World Cup** in 2002 and the G20 Summit in 2010.

The following information refers to South Korean history after the Korean War. For details on North Korean events and information on North-South relations since the conflict, see pp.337–339.

Problematic beginnings

The **postwar period** proved extremely difficult for South Korea: cities had been laid to waste and families torn apart, accusations and recriminations were rife, and everyone knew that hostilities with the North could resume at any moment. American-educated **Syngman Rhee**, who had been selected as president before the war, ruled in an increasingly autocratic manner, making constitutional amendments to stay in power and purging parliament of anyone opposed to his policies. In 1960 disgruntled students led the **April 19 Movement** against his rule, and after being toppled in a coup he was forced into exile, choosing Hawaii as his new home. One dictator was swiftly replaced with another: Yun Bo-seon came to office as a puppet of military general **Park Chung-hee**, who then swiftly engineered a coup and took the presidency himself in 1962. To an even greater degree than Rhee before him, Park's name became synonymous with corruption, dictatorship and the flouting of human rights – thousands were jailed merely for daring to criticize his rule. To his credit, Park introduced the economic reforms that allowed his country to push forward – until the mid-1970s, the South Korean economy actually lagged behind that of North Korea – and the country made great advances in automotive, electronic, heavy and chemical industries. This was, however, achieved at a cost, since Korean tradition largely went out of the window in favour of bare economic progress. These policies were a major factor behind the **loss of Korea's traditional buildings**: Seoul has almost none left. Park's authoritarian rule continued to ruffle feathers around the country, and the danger from the North had far from subsided – Park was the subject, and Seoul the scene, of two failed **assassination** attempts by North Korean agents. It was, however, members of his own intelligence service who gunned him down in 1979, claiming that he was "an insurmountable obstacle to democratic reform". Those responsible were hanged the following year. Park's eventual successor, **Chun Doo-hwan**, was also from the southeast of the country, and the resultant Seoul–Gyeongsang tangent of power saw those parts of the country developing rapidly, while others languished far behind. The arrest of liberal southwestern politician **Kim Dae-jung**, as well as the botched trials following the assassination of Park Chung-hee, was a catalyst for mass uprisings across the land, though mainly concentrated in Jeju Island and the Jeolla provinces. These culminated in the **Gwangju Massacre** of May 1980, where over two hundred civilians died after their protest was crushed by the military.

The Olympic legacy

Incredibly, just one year after the massacre, Seoul was given the rights to host the **1988 Summer Olympics**: some estimates say the death count at Gwangju was similar to the Tiananmen Square massacre, but it's hard to imagine Beijing being granted a similar honour the year after those events. Although the Olympic plan had been Park Chung-hee's, Chun Doo-hwan followed it through in an apparent attempt to seek international recognition. Though he may have regarded the 1981 Olympic vote as a tacit global nod of acceptance, the strategy backfired when the country was thrust into the spotlight. Partly as a result of this increased attention, Korea's first free elections were held in 1987, with **Roh Tae-woo** taking the helm. During the same period Korean conglomerates, known as the *jaebeol*, were spreading their financial arms around the world. Korea's aggressive, debt-funded expansion only worsened the effect of the Asian Currency Crisis on the country in 1997.

In 1998, once-condemned liberal activist Kim Dae-jung completed a remarkable turnaround by being appointed president himself. The first South Korean leader to favour a peaceable reunification of the peninsula, he wasted no time in kicking off his **"Sunshine Policy"** of reconciliation with the north; some minor industrial projects were outsourced across the border, and new Seoul-funded factories were built around the city of Kaesong, just north of the DMZ. In 2000, after an historic Pyongyang summit with North Korean leader Kim Jong-il, he was awarded the **Nobel Peace Prize**.

Into the twenty-first century

South Korea's international reputation was further enhanced by the hugely successful co-hosting of the **2002 World Cup** with Japan. However, that same year a series of incidents gave rise to something of an anti-American (and, by extension, anti-Western) sentiment: most significant was the accidental killing of two local schoolgirls by an American armoured vehicle, which led to large protests against the US military presence (one that has declined, bit by bit, ever since). Late that year, **Roh Moo-hyun** was elected president on a slightly anti-American ticket; however, the fact that he sent Korean troops to Iraq so soon after taking office in early 2003 made him instantly unpopular, and he committed suicide in 2009, following a bribery scandal. Roh's presidency coincided with **Lee Myung-bak**'s tenure as mayor of Seoul. In 2003, Lee announced plans to gentrify the **Cheonggyecheon** creek in the capital; the burden on local taxpayers made this a deeply unpopular project, though it has come to be loved by the public since. Lee was elected president in 2008, but as with Roh before him, there were almost immediate protests against his rule, this time thanks to a beef trade agreement made with the USA. Fears that mad cow disease would be imported to this beef-loving land resulted in mass protests around the city, and **rioting** around the land; in Seoul, one man died after setting fire to himself in protest. However, these political protests were small-fry compared to the North Korean attacks of 2010; see box below.

The sinking of the Cheonan, and the Yeonpyeongdo attacks

On March 26, 2010, the **Cheonan**, a South Korean naval vessel, sank in the waters off Baengnyeongdo, killing 46 of its crew of just over one hundred, and claiming the life of one rescue worker. With the incident taking place in waters so close to the North Korean border, there was immediate worldwide suspicion that Pyongyang was behind the attack; Seoul refused to be drawn however, choosing instead to wait for the results of a full investigation. South Korean **conspiracy theorists** initially pointed fingers at an American submarine that had "gone missing", though such rumours were hurriedly put to bed when the sub resurfaced a few days later on the other side of the world. One rumour that refused to go away was that the attack may have been an internal show of force from **Kim Jong-un**, who was at the time being groomed for leadership in North Korea. It was suggested that Kim may have used the incident to prove himself to the country's military leadership, who were known to be unhappy with a dynastic transfer of power from his father, Kim Jong-il. Two months after the incident, an international team found that the *Cheonan* was sunk by a torpedo, most likely fired by a North Korean vessel.

Pyongyang continues to deny responsibility for the sinking of the *Cheonan*, but the attacks of 23 November, 2010 were more directly attributable to North Korea. Almost two hundred shells and rockets were fired from North Korea's southern coast at the South Korean island of **Yeonpyeongdo**, in response to Seoul's refusal to halt a military training exercise in nearby waters. The northern shelling appeared to be indiscriminate, killing two civilians and two soldiers from the South, which responded in kind with howitzers of its own. This was one of the most serious cross-border incidents since the Korean War, and many southerners formerly sympathetic to the North were suddenly favouring a powerful military response to any future attacks. At the time of writing, the situation remained tense.

Religion

Korea has a long and fascinating religious history, one that has informed local life to the present day. Strewn with temples, the country is most closely identified with **Buddhism**, though **Christianity** actually has a greater number of followers. The rise of the latter is particularly interesting when laid over Korea's largely **Confucian** mindset, which is often diametrically opposed to Christian ideals and beliefs – priests and pastors preach equality at Sunday service, but outside church relative age still governs many forms of social interaction, and women remain inferior to men.

Buddhism

Buddhism is a religion deriving from the teachings of the Buddha – also known as the Siddhartha Gautama or Sakyamuni, he lived in India sometime between the fourth and sixth centuries BC. Although there are two main schools of thought and several smaller ones, Buddhist philosophy revolves around the precept that karma, rebirth and suffering are intrinsic elements of existence, but that the cycle of birth and death can be escaped on what is known as the "Noble Eightfold Path" to nirvana.

An import from China (which had in turn imported it from the Indian subcontinent), Buddhism arrived in Korea at the beginning of the Three Kingdoms period. **Goguryeo** and **Baekje** adopted it at around the same time, in the last decades of the fourth century: Goguryeo king Sosurim accepted Buddhism almost as soon as the first Chinese monks touched down in 372, while Baekje king Chimnyu adopted it after taking the throne in 384. The **Silla** kings were less impressed by the creed, but a major change in regal thought occurred in 527 after an interesting episode involving an official who had decided to switch to Buddhism. He was to be beheaded for his beliefs, and with his final few gasps swore to the king that his blood would not be red, but a milky white; his promise was true, and the king soon chose Buddhism as his state religion.

Even in China, Buddhism was at this point in something of an embryonic phase, and Korean monks took the opportunity to develop the **Mahayana** style by ironing out what they saw to be inconsistencies in the doctrine. Disagreements followed, leading to the creation of several **sects**, of which the **Jogye** order is by far the largest, covering about ninety percent of Korea's Buddhists; other notable sects include **Seon**, largely known in the west as Zen, the Japanese translation, and **Cheontae**, which is better known under its Chinese name of Tiantai.

Ornate **temples** sprang up all over the peninsula during the **Unified Silla** period but, though Buddhism remained the state religion throughout the **Goryeo** era, the rise of Confucianism squeezed it during **Joseon** times. Monks were treated with scant respect and temples were largely removed from the main cities (thus there are relatively few in Seoul, the Joseon capital), but though the religion was repressed, it never came close to evaporating entirely. Further troubles were to come during the **Japanese occupation period**, during the latter years of which many Koreans were forced to worship at Shinto shrines. Mercifully, although many of the temples that weren't closed by the Japanese were burnt down in the Korean War that followed the Japanese occupation, reconstruction programmes have been so comprehensive that in most Korean cities, you will seldom be more than a walk away from an active temple.

Temples

Korea's many **temples** are some of the most visually appealing places in the country. Most run along a similar design scheme: on entry to the temple complex you'll pass through the *iljumun* (일주문), or "first gate", then the *cheonwangmun* (천왕문). The latter almost always contains **four large guardians**, two menacing figures towering on each side of the dividing walkway; these control the four heavens and provide guidance to those with a righteous heart. The central building of a Korean temple is the **main hall**, or *daeungjeon* (대웅전). Initially, it was only Sakyamuni – the historical Buddha – who was enshrined here, but this was soon flanked on left and right by bodhisattvas (a term for those who have reached nirvana). Most of these halls have doors at the front, which are usually only for elder monks; novices (and visiting foreigners) use side-entrances. Among the many other halls that you may find on the complex are the *daejeokgwangjeon* (대적광전), the hall of the Vairocana Buddha; *gwaneumjeon* (관음전), a hall for the Bodhisattva of Compassion; *geungnakjeon* (극락전), the Nirvana Hall and home to the celestial Amitabha Buddha; *mireukjeon* (미륵전), the hall of the future Maitreya Buddha; and *nahanjeon* (나한전), the hall of disciples. Some also feature the *palsangjeon* (팔상전), a hall featuring **eight paintings** detailing the life of the Sakyamuni Buddha, though these are more often found on the outside of another hall.

Somewhere in the complex you'll find the *beomjonggak* (범종각), a "**bell pavilion**" containing instruments to awaken the four sentient beings – a drum for land animals, a wooden fish for the water-borne, a bronze gong for creatures of the air, and a large bell for monks who have slept in. The bell itself can sometimes weigh upwards of twenty tonnes, and the best will have an information board telling you how far away it can be heard if you were to strike it lightly with your fist. Needless to say, you shouldn't test these contentions.

Confucianism

Like Buddhism, **Confucian thought** made its way across the sea from China – the exact date remains a mystery, but it seems that it first spread to Korea at the beginning of the Three Kingdoms era. Although Confucianism can't be classified as a religion – there's no central figure of worship, or concept of an afterlife – it is used a means of self-cultivation, and a guide to "proper" conduct, particularly the showing of respect for those higher up the social hierarchy. For centuries it co-existed with the state religion, informing not only political thought but also national ethics, and in many ways it still governs the Korean way of life today. Central to the concept are the **Five Moral Disciplines** of human-to-human conduct, namely ruler to subject, father to son, husband to wife, elder to younger and friend to friend.

During the Three Kingdoms period, the concepts of filial piety began to permeate Korean life, with adherence to the rules gradually taking the form of ceremonial rites. In the Silla kingdom there developed a "bone rank" system used to segregate social strata, one that was to increase in rigidity until the Joseon era. This was essentially a caste system, one that governed almost every sphere of local life – each "level" of society would have strict limits placed on what they could achieve, the size of their dwelling, who they could marry and even what colours they were allowed to wear.

At the dawn of the Joseon dynasty in 1392, King Taejo had the **Jongmyo shrines** built in central Seoul, and for centuries afterwards, ruling kings would venerate their ancestors here in regular ceremonies. At this time, Confucianism truly took hold, with numerous academies (*hyanggyo*) built around the country at which students from the elite *yangban* classes would wade through wave after wave of punishing examinations on their way to senior governmental posts. Buddhism had been on the decline for some time with Confucian scholars arguing that making appeals to gods unseen had a detrimental effect on the national psyche, and that building ornate temples absorbed funds too readily. Some, in fact, began to clamour for the burning of those temples, as well as the murder of monks. As with other beliefs, some followers violated the core principles for their own ends and, despite the birth of great neo-Confucian philosophers such as **Yi-Yi** and **Toegye**, enforced slavery and servitude meant that the lot of those at the lower caste levels changed little over the centuries.

Confucianism today

It's often said that Korea remains the **most Confucian** of all the world's societies. In addition to several remaining academies and shrines – there's one of the latter at Inwangsan, just west of Gyeongbokgung – colourful ancestral ceremonies take place each year at Jongmyo in Seoul. Its impact on everyday life is also clear: on getting to know a local, you'll generally be asked a series of questions both direct and indirect (particularly with regard to age, marriage, education and employment), the answers to which will be used to file you into conceptual pigeonholes. Though foreigners are treated somewhat differently, this is the main reason why locals see nothing wrong in barging strangers out of the way on the street or showing no mercy on the road – no introduction has been made, and without knowledge of the "proper" behaviour in such a situation no moves are made towards showing respect. Among those who do know each other, it's easy to find **Confucian traits** – women are still seen as inferior to men (their salary continues to lag far behind, and they're usually expected to quit their job on having a child, never to return to the workplace); the boss or highest earner will usually pay after a group meal; family values remain high; and paper qualifications from reputable universities carry more weight than actual intelligence. Also notable is **bungsu**, a concept that involves the moving of ancestral grave sites. Perhaps the most high-profile examples of corpse-shifting have been before general elections. After Kim Dae-jung lost the elections in 1987 and 1992, he decided to move the graves of his ancestors to more auspicious locations, and he duly won the next election in 1998. All that said, Confucian ideas are slowly being eroded as Westernization continues to encroach, particularly as the number of Christians continues to grow.

Christianity

Practised by well over a quarter of the population, **Christianity** is now Korea's leading religion by number of worshippers, having surpassed Buddhism at the start of the twenty-first century. Surprisingly, the religion has been on the peninsula since the end of the eighteenth century, having been brought across the waters by missionaries from various European empires. At the time, the Confucian *yangban* in charge were fearful of change, hardly surprising considering how far apart the fundamental beliefs of the two creeds are. Christianity's refusal to perform ancestral rites eventually led to its repression, and hundreds of Christians were **martyred** in the 1870s and 1880s. A number of French missionaries were also murdered in this period, before Korea was forcefully opened up for trade. The numbers of Christians have been growing ever since, the majority now belonging to the Presbyterian, Catholic or Methodist churches.

Village practices

Mountain rites

By far the most common form of spirit worship in Korea, the *sansinje* remains a part of annual village festivals all across the country. The Dano festival in Gangneung – the biggest traditional event in the land – actually starts off with one of these in honour of General Kim Yu-sin, spearhead of the Silla campaigns that resulted in the unification of the country. Near Samcheok, just down the way, groups head to the hills for shamanistic *gut* ceremonies and animal exorcisms.

Rites to sea spirits

Though these rites are held at points all along Korea's coastline, they are most numerous in Gangwon province on the east, particularly around the city of Gangneung. The spirit is often the ghost of a local female who perished tragically, often without having married (see "Phallicism" below); when finally placated by ceremonies and sacrifices, she becomes a patron of the village in question. One popular Gangwon tale regards a man who was prompted in a dream to rescue a travelling woman from a nearby islet; all he found on arrival was a basket containing the woman's portrait, and after carrying it home his village was blessed with a bumper crop. Villagers continue to pay respects to this day.

Rites to tree spirits

Korea has many trees dating back five centuries or more, so it's understandable that many local Korean myths – including the Tangun legend, which details Korea's creation – include a sacred tree somewhere along the way. Trees of such repute are treated with enormous respect, as even to snap a twig is said to invoke a punishment of some kind from the spirit that lives within.

Rites to rock spirits

As you make your way around Korea, you'll see English-language pamphlets pointing you towards rocks that are said to resemble turtles, tigers, sea dragons and the like. While some require an almost superhuman stretch of the imagination, many of these are still the subject of regular ceremonies for the spirits that are said to reside within the rock. You'll also see man-made stone mounds in and around certain temples, most notably wonderful Tapsa in Maisan Provincial Park, which is surrounded by spires of rock that were all stacked by just one man.

Jangseung

Having long served a range of purposes from protector to boundary marker, these carved wooden sticks may have jovial faces or snarling mouths full of blocky, painted teeth. You'll see the real things at the entrance to traditional villages – and replicas outside traditional restaurants.

Phallicism

Anyone who has seen the mysterious but rather phallic *hareubang* statues on beautiful Jeju Island will know that willy worship has long been popular in Korea. This usually takes the form of fertility rites, but the reasoning for some ceremonies is not so predictable: on a village south of Samcheok in Gangwon province once lived a young bride-to-be who was swept from the shore in a powerful storm. Her enraged spirit chased the fish from the seas until it was placated by a carved wooden penis; hundreds of the things now rise from the ground in a nearby park.

Churches tend to be monstrous concrete edifices (many of them sporting rather frightening red neon crosses), and some are huge, with room for thousands of worshippers. In fact, Seoul's mini-island of Yeouido officially has the largest church in the world, with 170 pastors and over 100,000 registered deacons.

Film

For all of its efforts in finance, electronics and promoting its food and tradition, it's Korea's film industry that has had the most success in pushing the country as a global brand. While Korean horror flicks have developed an international cult following, and a number of esteemed directors have set international film festivals abuzz, special mention must also be made of the locally produced TV **dramas** that have caught on like wildfire across Asia. Like many of the movies, these are highly melodramatic offerings that don't seek to play on the heartstrings so much as power-chord the merry hell out of them. All of these form part of the **Hallyeo movement**, a "New Wave" of Korean production that has been in motion since cinematic restrictions were lifted in the 1980s.

The beginnings

Film was first introduced to Korea at the very end of the **nineteenth century**; in 1899, just after making Korea's first-ever telephone call, King Gojong was shown a short documentary about the country put together by American traveller Burton Holmes, and Seoul's first cinema was opened shortly afterwards. Unfortunately, few examples from the prewar **silent era** have made it onto the international market; Korean produce was also scaled down, and at one point cut off entirely, during the Japanese occupation (1910–45). After **World War II**, and the end of annexation, there followed a short burst of films – many of which, understandably, had freedom as a central concept – but this was brought to an abrupt halt by the outbreak of the **Korean War** in 1950.

After the Korean War

Following the war, the film industries of the two Koreas developed separately; leaders on both sides saw movies as a hugely useful **propaganda tool**, and made immediate efforts to revive local cinema – see opposite for the continuation of the North Korean story. In the south, President Syngman Rhee conferred tax-exempt status on moviemakers, who got busy with works looking back at the misery of wartime and the occupation, and forward to a rosy future for non-Communist Korea. By the end of the 1950s, annual movie output had reached triple figures, the most popular being watched by millions, but the accession of **Park Chung-hee** to president in 1961 brought an end to what passed for cinematic freedom. In addition to the censorship and hard-fisted control over local produce, foreign films were vetted for approval and placed under a strict quota system, elements of which remained until 2006. As Park's rule grew ever more dictatorial, he inaugurated a short-lived era of **"governmental policy" films**; these were hugely unpopular, and cinema attendance dropped sharply. After Park's death, democratization and the gradual relaxation of restrictions gave rise to the Hallyeo movement.

The Hallyeo "New Wave"

Throughout the periods of governmental suppression, a clutch of talented directors were forced to keep their best ideas under wraps, or else be very clever about putting them forward. With the loosening of the lid in the 1980s, the highest skilled came to the fore and finally gave Korea exposure in the West; foremost among these was **Im Kwon-taek**, a maverick who shrugged off his role as a creator of commercial quota-fillers to unleash striking new works on the world. The South Korean government continued to provide funding for films until the 1999 release of *Swiri*, the country's first fully independent film. Since then the industry has reached an ever-greater international audience, and a number of Korean directors such as **Kim Ki-duk** and **Park Chan-wook** are now globally acclaimed.

The country's **dramas** have arguably been even more successful than its movies, though with an appeal largely limited to the Asian continent. Foremost among these was *Winter Sonata*, a series that received an almost religious following in Japan (see p.150).

North Korean cinema

Cinema is big business in **North Korea** – Kim Jong-il was pouring funds into the industry for decades before he became leader of the country, and in 1978 even went so far as to organize the kidnapping of **Shin Sang-ok** – a prominent South Korean director – in an effort to improve the quality of local produce. North Korea produces some of the world's most distinctive films; unfortunately, this niche in global cinema has remained almost entirely unexplored by the outside world. A few films have started to trickle onto the **international market**; to buy,

Dan Gordon's documentaries

The DPRK has kept a tight lid on foreign production within the country, but after years of cajoling British director Daniel Gordon was allowed in to shoot a documentary about survivors of the country's 1966 football team. Together with his two follow-up efforts, they provide excellent windows into contemporary North Korean society.

The Game of Their Lives (2002)

In 1966 North Korea's football team had gone into the World Cup Finals in England as rank underdogs, but a stirring victory over Italy sent them through to the quarter-finals, where they lost 5–3 in an amazing game against Portugal; incredibly, they were 3–0 up at one point and heading for the semi-finals. The team returned home as international heroes, but little more was heard of them until the screening of this revealing documentary.

A State of Mind (2004)

On the surface, this is a documentary about two young girls training for the Arirang Mass Games in Pyongyang, but it amounts to a first-ever stab at a genuine portrayal of the average life of today's North Koreans. It was evidently a success: after the film was shown on DPRK state TV, locals complained that it was "dull", having merely filmed them going about their daily lives; little did they know how compelling such reportage is to the average foreign viewer.

Crossing The Line (2006)

James Joseph Dresnok is a movie-maker's delight, but this fascinating documentary is the world's only peek inside the mind of "Comrade Joe", one of four American soldiers known to have defected to North Korea after the Korean War. With a candour that shows a genuine love of his new country, Dresnok tells of his journey from a troubled adolescence to old age in Pyongyang, including his crossing of the treacherous DMZ, a failed attempt at escape, and his stint as a star on the North Korean silver screen.

go to Ⓦwww.north-korea-books.com. The themes stick rigidly to brave North Korean resistance during the Korean War and the Japanese occupation, depicting Americans as unspeakably evil and South Koreans as their puppets. Highlights include *Nameless Heroes* (a twenty-part series produced at immense cost while the country was gripped by famine), *Sea of Blood*, *Duty of a Generation*, *We Love Our Soldiers* and the surprisingly comical *Family Basketball Team*.

Kim Ki-duk

3-Iron (2004) Korean movies about eccentric loners are ten a penny. Here, the protagonist is a delivery boy who breaks into and then polishes up the houses that he knows to be empty. When he happens across one that's still home to a lonely girl, the couple begin a strange kind of silent relationship. Superbly acted, and an interesting take on the traditional love story.

Bad Guy (2001) A sadomasochistic thread runs through Kim Ki-duk's films, evident in *Bad Guy*, where a mute thug falls in love with a young beauty and tricks her into becoming a prostitute. This disturbing study of small-time gangsters and sexual slavery tells painful truths about Korean society, and though clichéd is absorbing in more than a voyeuristic sense.

Samaritan Girl (2004) A storyline that's less explicit and far deeper than its premise may suggest. Two teenage girls looking to save up for a trip to Europe enter the murky world of prostitution, one sleeping with the clients, the other managing the affairs while keeping an eye out for the cops. Inevitably, things don't quite go according to plan.

Spring, Summer, Fall, Winter... and Spring (2003) With just one set – a monastery in the middle of a remote lake – and a small cast, Kim Ki-duk somehow spins together a necessarily slow but undeniably beautiful allegory of human nature, one that relays the life of a boy nurtured to manhood by a reclusive monk.

The Isle (2001) In the middle of a lake, a mute woman rents out small floating huts to men looking to escape city life for a while, sometimes selling herself to them, sometimes murdering them. This was the film that pushed Kim Ki-duk's unique style onto the world stage, a dark love story with a couple of nasty surprises.

War and history

Chihwaseon (2002) Sometimes going under the title *Painted Fire*, this beautifully shot tale of Jang Seung-eop – a nineteenth-century Seoulite painter best known by his pen name Owon – won the Best Director award at Cannes for Im Kwon-taek, a maverick who had been around for decades but was previously ignored on the international stage.

Joint Security Area (2000) Any Korean film about the DMZ is worth a look, as is anything by acclaimed director Park Chan-wook. Here, two North Korean soldiers are killed in the DMZ; like *Memento* (which,

In these lists, the symbol ✯ indicates a movie that is particularly recommended.

Park Chan-wook's "Vengeance Trilogy"

Sympathy for Mr Vengeance (2002)
Acclaimed director Park Chan-wook kicked off a trio of films about revenge with this tale of a deaf-mute man who hatches a plot to find a kidney for his ailing sister, inadvertently kicking off a series of revenge-fuelled murders.

Oldboy (2003)
Oldboy was the first Korean film to win big at Cannes, a dark and violent tale of a businessman mysteriously arrested after a night out, imprisoned for years then given three days to discover why he was put away and to hunt down those responsible. Though lead man Choi Min-sik has an unfortunate habit of looking like an actor, even when he's not acting, it's still riveting.

Sympathy for Lady Vengeance (2005)
A teenage girl gets framed and sent down for killing a young boy, and spends her time in jail plotting revenge. On her release she's offered a plate of metaphorically cleansing white tofu by a Christian group; the tofu ends up on the floor and our heroine sets about getting back at the man to blame for her imprisonment.

incidentally, came out the following year), the story plays backwards, revealing the lead-up piece by piece.

Shiri (1999) Also known as *Swiri*, this was a landmark film in Korean cinema, marking the dawn of a Hollywood style long suppressed by the government. The mix of explosions and loud music is not of as much interest to foreigners as it is to Koreans, but the plot – South Korean cops hunt down a North Korean sniper girl – is interesting enough. The girl was played by Yunjin Kim, who later found fame on the American TV series *Lost*.

Silmido (2003) Loosely based on events in the 1960s, which saw South Korean operatives receive secret training on the island of Silmido to assassinate North Korean leader Kim Il-sung. The film broke Korean box office records, and provides a fascinating depiction of the tensions of the time.

Taegukgi (2004) Though it suffers from occasional shoddy acting, and the sense of history is unconvincing, this is an enjoyable war film, following the fate of two brothers as they battle through the horrors and in-fighting of the Korean War.

The King and the Clown (2005) A period drama with homosexual undercurrents, this was an unexpected smash hit at the box office. Set during the reign of King Yeonsan – whose short rule began in 1494 – it tells of a pair of street entertainers who find themselves in Seoul's royal court. One of them fosters an ever-closer relationship with the king.

Welcome to Dongmakgol (2005) Too twee for some, but heart-warming to others and beautifully shot to boot, this tells of a motley assortment of American, South Korean and North Korean combatants from the Korean War who somehow end up in the same village, among people unaware not only of the conflict raging around them but of warfare in general.

Drama and horror

The Host (2006) The tranquil life of a riverside merchant is blown to smithereens when the formaldehyde disposed into the river by the American military creates a ferocious underwater creature. This comic thriller smashed box office records in Korea; the international reception was nowhere near as fervent, but it's worth a look nonetheless.

Secret Sunshine (2007) It's rare for government ministers to go into movie-making, but so successful was Lee Chang-dong's effort that his film even won an award at Cannes. Focused on a woman entering middle age, it's a well-delivered interpretation of human suffering.

A Tale of Two Sisters (2003) This chiller seeks to petrify viewers not with lashings of ultra-violence but with that which cannot be seen. An adaptation of a Joseon-era folk story, it keeps its audience guessing, and some will find it Korea's best take on the horror genre.

Thirst (2009) Winner of the Jury Prize at Cannes, this was director Park Chan-wook's follow-up to his hugely successful Vengeance Trilogy. It's a romantic horror in which a priest, in love with his friend's wife, turns into a vampire – an odd concept that shouldn't work, but somehow Park pulls it off.

Comedy

My Sassy Girl (2001) A mega-hit from Tokyo to Taipei, this tale doesn't add too much to the rom-com genre, but one scene was almost entirely responsible for a spate of high-school-themed club nights. It's worth watching, as is *My Tutor Friend*, a follow-up that hits most of the same buttons.

The President's Last Bang (2005) Korea has long been crying out for satire, particularly something to inject a little fun into its turgid political reportage, and this hits the nail squarely on the head (as demonstrated by the lawsuit that followed). It's based on a true story, namely the assassination of president Park Chung-hee in 1979; the portrayal of Park as something of a Japanese-sympathetic playboy certainly ruffled a few feathers.

Save the Green Planet! (2003) A social recluse and his tightrope-walker girlfriend endeavour to save the earth by hunting down the aliens that they believe to have infiltrated mankind; once captured, the extraterrestrials can only be destroyed by applying menthol rub to their groin and feet. Enough said.

Books

Despite Korea's long and interesting history, the East Asian sections in most bookshops largely focus on China and Japan. The majority of books that are devoted to Korea cover **North Korea** or the **Korean War**; far less biased than most newspaper or television reports, these are the best form of reportage about the world's most curious state and how it was created.

In the following lists, the symbol 犬 indicates a title that is particularly recommended.

History and society

Michael Breen *The Koreans: Who They Are, What They Want, Where Their Future Lies*. Although the four main sections of this book – society, history, economy and politics – may seem dry, the accounts are relayed with warmth and a pleasing depth of knowledge.

Bruce Cumings *Korea's Place in the Sun: A Modern History*. The Korean peninsula went through myriad changes in the twentieth century, and this weighty tome analyzes the effects of such disquiet on its population, showing that the South's seemingly smooth trajectory towards democracy and capitalism masked a great injury of the national psyche.

Kim Dong-uk *Palaces of Korea*. A photo-filled hardcover detailing not only the minutiae of Seoul's wonderful palaces, but how they vary in style and form from those found elsewhere in Asia.

Korean Cultural Heritage *Koreana*. A compendium of articles written about Korean culture, mainly with reference to religious and shamanistic practices. Much of the detail overlaps, but it's worth tracking down.

Keith Pratt *Everlasting Flower: A History of Korea*. This thoroughly readable book provides a chronicle of Korean goings-on from the very first kingdoms to the modern day, its text broken up with interesting illustrated features on the arts and customs prevalent at the time.

Rhee Won-sok *Korea Unmasked: In Search of the Country, the Society and the People*. The peculiarities of Korean society relayed in an easy-to-read comic strip. While it could be said that it makes light of some serious problems, it's an entertaining primer on the local psyche.

Simon Winchester *Korea: A Walk Through the Land of Miracles*. This highly entertaining book details Winchester's walk from southern Jeju to the North Korean border. Written in the 1980s, it's now an extremely dated snapshot of Korean society, it is amazing how much it has changed in such a short time.

Local literature

Cho Se-hui *The Dwarf*. Even miracles have a downside: Seoul's economy underwent a truly remarkable transformation in the 1970s, but at what cost to its people and culture? This weighty, tersely delivered novel uncovers the spiritual decline of Seoul's *nouveau riche*, via twelve interconnected stories; *A Dwarf Launches a Little Bell* is particularly recommended, and has been reprinted hundreds of times in Korea.

Park Wan-Suh *Who Ate Up All the Shinga?* A semi-autobiographical mother-daughter story from one of Korea's most highly acclaimed writers, set during the Korean War. Fans of Park should also check out *Sketch of the Fading Sun*, a collection of short stories.

Yi Munyeol *Our Twisted Hero*. This tale of psychological warfare at a Korean elementary school has a deceptively twee plotline, managing to explore the use and misuse of power while providing metaphorical parallels to Korean politics of the 1970s.

Young Ha Kim *Your Republic is Calling You* and *I Have the Right to Destroy Myself*. Two books from a man whose international reputation is growing by the year, his popularity and his existentialist tendencies marking him out as a potential Korean Murakami. The first book revolves around a North Korean spy torn between his homeland and the South, while the second, set in Seoul, is the dark tale of a refined thinker with suicidal tendencies.

North Korea and the Korean War

Jasper Becker *Rogue Regime: Kim Jong Il and the Looming Threat of North Korea*. Despite Becker's view of North Korea being thoroughly one-sided, it often lends itself to easy sensationalism. A meaty fleshing-out of how the Western world sees Kim Jong-il.

Erik Cornell *North Korea Under Communism – Report of a Special Envoy to Paradise*. Sweden was the first Western country to open up diplomatic connections to the DPRK, and Cornell spent three years as the head of its embassy in Pyongyang. His book is rather political, but provides a unique insight into life in North Korea.

Bruce Cumings *North Korea: Another Country*. The US-North Korean dispute is far more complex than Western media would have you imagine, and this book provides a revealing – if slightly hard to digest – glance at the flipside. Cumings' meticulous research is without parallel, and the accounts of American atrocities and cover-ups both in the "Forgotten War" and during the nuclear crisis offer plenty of food for thought.

Guy Delisle *Pyongyang*. A comic strip describing his time as a cartoonist in Pyongyang, Delisle's well-observed and frequently hilarious book is a North Korean rarity – one that tells it like it is, and doesn't seek to make political or ideological statements. His illustrations are eerily accurate. For anyone with even a passing interest in North Korea, this is a must-read.

Max Hastings *The Korean War*. A conflict is not quite a war until it has been given the treatment by acclaimed historian Max Hastings. With this, he has provided more than his usual mix of fascinating, balanced and well-researched material; the account of the stand of the Gloucesters on the Imjin is particularly absorbing.

Kang Chol-Hwan *The Aquariums of Pyongyang*. Having fled his homeland after spending time in a North Korean gulag, Kang's harrowing accounts of squalor, starvation and brutality represent one of the only windows into the world's most fenced-off social systems. He's not a natural author, however, and the confused sermonizing at the end rather dilutes the book's appeal.

Bradley K. Martin *Under the Loving Care of the Fatherly Leader*. Almost 900 pages long – 200 of which are references – this isn't one to carry around in your backpack, but for an in-depth look at the Kims and the perpetration of their personality cult, it's hard to beat.

Don Oberdorfer *The Two Koreas: A Contemporary History*. Lengthy, but engaging and surprisingly easy to read, this book traces the various events in postwar Korea, as well as examining how they were affected by the actions and policies of China, Russia, Japan and the US. You'd be hard pressed to find a book about North Korea more neutral in tone.

Recipe books

Cecilia Hae-Jin Lee *Eating Korean: From Barbecue to Kimchi, Recipes from My Home*. Easy-to-follow instructions for more than a hundred Korean dishes. The more predictable rice and noodle dishes are supplemented with side dishes, soups, teas and desserts.

Young Jin Song *Korean Cooking: Traditions, Ingredients, Flavours, Techniques, Recipes*. As the sweeping subtitle suggests, this is not so much a recipe book as an all-encompassing guide to Korean cuisine.

A–Z of contemporary Korea

A: Ajumma power

An **ajumma** is a Korean woman, though the term is something of a grey area: it encompasses old age and anything approaching it, but can also be used to describe a married female, or one with children. However, with women understandably reluctant to be tarred with the term, it's usually reserved for Korean grandmothers. In a country where women are still not regarded as equals, they've fought their way through war and poverty to provide a tough-as-nails embodiment of harder times, many regarding old age as a liberation of a kind from chauvinistic yokes. To do something with strength, purpose and resilience is to do it with "ajumma power". Almost every single old-age *ajumma* has the same hairstyle – a bubble-perm affectionately known as a *bbogeul-bbogeul* (pronounced "boggle-boggle"), and foreign women with even a slight natural curl to their hair may well be asked where they go to get it permed.

B: Burberry man

What's generally known as a "flasher" in English is referred to as a **Burberry man** in Korea. These gents – dressed in a three-quarter-length jacket and little else – hang around universities in order to expose themselves to female students, most commonly when large crowds are gathered in the front enclosures. They're surprisingly common – most Korean girls will have seen at least one, and many schools see a Burberry man show up regularly. Korea's love of conformity means that even these sex pests have a uniform of sorts: while the Burberry label is not essential, most of their jackets are brown, and for some reason knee-length grey socks seem almost mandatory.

C: Clones and couple-look

The subject of **cloning** has long been controversial, but in Korea questions of morality come with a tinge of scandal. In 2005 a team of scientists from Seoul National University created an Afghan Hound named "Snuppy" – a combination of "puppy" and the initials of the university – and the world's first cloned human embryo, both to tumultuous acclaim from the world scientific community. Shortly afterwards, the team leader – Dr Hwang Woo-suk – was revealed to have fabricated much of his evidence. Surrounded by inconsolable team members, Dr Hwang issued a profuse apology on live TV. While the human embryo had been bluffed, the dog was later found to be a bona fide clone.

Identical appearances are nothing new in Korea – newlyweds have long worn matching clothes for the duration of their honeymoon, a concept known as "**couple-look**". The preponderance of pinks and pastels shows which half of the pair usually makes the decisions, though it's becoming increasingly common for men to sport clothes that complement, rather than match, those of their bride. The best places to see the trend in action are Seoul's Myeongdong district, and the "honeymoon island" of Jeju.

D: Daeri-unjeon

In Korea, businessmen inevitably find themselves having to drink an awful lot as "social" job obligations, even if travelling with a car. To get round this situation Korea has **daeri-unjeon**, a network of drivers who drive both the customer and his car home, and who can be called from most bars; the telephone numbers usually end with 8282, digits whose pronunciation is almost identical to the Korean for "hurry, hurry!"

E: Eyelid surgery

In a country where appearance is not quite everything but pretty damn close, beauty is big business. The large and thriving plastic surgery industry sees women – and more than a few men – get all sorts from nose-jobs to a nip and tuck, but the most popular alteration by far is **eyelid surgery**. This involves the creation of a crease in the upper eyelid, the results being apparently more beautiful to Koreans, but distinctly non-oriental.

F: "Fan death"

"**Fan death**" is a truly curious phenomenon – whereas around the world people fall asleep with a fan or the air-conditioning left on, only in Korea does such folly regularly seem to result in fatalities. The reasons given include air currents starving the victim of air, reduced room temperatures inducing hypothermia, or even fan blades actually cutting the oxygen molecules in two. This is enough to convince most Koreans that the humble electric fan is an instrument to be feared – even broadsheet newspapers run fan-death stories, and the Korean government has issued warnings against using fans at night. Such beliefs are of much amusement to Korea's expat population (unless they find themselves sharing a room with a Korean in the summer).

G: Golf, gyopo and grandmother techno

Despite Korea's mountainous countryside and crowded, sprawling cities, **golf** has become one of the most popular sports in the country. Gongju's Seri Park is perhaps the best-known golfer, having won three of the four majors on the women's circuit and found her way onto the World Golf Hall of Fame; Grace Park and Jeong Jang have also won major titles. The men have fared less well, but K. J. Choi broke into the world's top 10 in 2007. Michelle Wie, a child prodigy dubbed the "female Tiger Woods" and competing in male events when barely into her teens, was born in Hawaii to Korean parents.

Wie is one of the most famous **gyopo**; this is a term used to refer to ethnic Koreans who live outside Korea, especially those who have become citizens of another country. Other famous *gyopo* include Yunjin Kim of *Lost* fame, Joe Hahn from nu-metal band Linkin Park; *ESPN* anchor Michael Kim; and Woody Allen's wife Soon-yi Previn. "Oddjob", the Korean villain of Bond fame, was actually played by a Japanese-American wrestler.

While modern K-pop has swept across continental Asia, there's another strain of music that you're just as likely to come across on your way around Korea: "Trot" songs – best described as a kind of **grandmother techno** – are fast-paced ballads, set to odd synthesized rhythms and crooned out in a semi-compulsory warble. The songs have changed over the years but the style has been around since the 1930s and remains hugely popular with Korea's older set, as anyone who's seen a clutch of grannies getting down to the beats will testify. However, *Trot* is not the sole preserve of the elderly, and is unlikely to go out of fashion any time soon – university students belt out hits in *noraebang*, while young artists such as Jang Yoon-jeong have scored big by crossing the genre with the ballads that younger Koreans tend to prefer. Ubiquitous cabaret shows mean that *Trot* is rarely off the TV, and highway service stations on long-distance bus routes are filled with *Trot* tapes – they make fantastic souvenirs.

H: Hompy and Harisu

Koreans don't tend to follow worldwide internet trends – they're usually one step ahead. Most Koreans have for years had a **hompy** (a Korean bastardization of the word "homepage"), onto which they load countless photographs, musings, journal entries, songs and any other digitizable part of their lives. Foreigners living in Korea will often be asked to create a local hompy by Korean friends – if you don't exist online, you don't exist at all – and some have found them a great way to expand their social network.

Harisu didn't need the internet to find fame, just a sex change. Born male, she underwent sexual reassignment surgery, and flew in the face of a conservative society to become the country's first celebrity transsexual; she was also one of the first in the queue to change gender when it became legal to do so. Harisu's big break was a cosmetics commercial, in which the camera focused on her Adam's apple; her fame and voice were enough to propel several albums into the chart, and she has appeared in a number of films.

I: Internet deaths

Koreans are famed for their use of computers, most notably the amount of time they spend playing online games. In fact, there is a growing backlash among the non-Korean gaming community: such is their domination that the country's gamers are accused of taking over international gaming sites and tournaments. They even hit the international headlines with occasional **internet deaths**: stories of gamers making mammoth stints (one was measured at 92 hours) at one of the ubiquitous PC bars have become less common since the government ordered tighter controls, but there's still the occasional death behind closed doors.

J: Jaebeol and jeonse

Korean business is dominated by a troupe of gigantic business conglomerates known as **jaebeol**. A few of these organizations have achieved fame around the world, though most foreigners probably wouldn't know that the company is Korean even if the name is familiar to them. Some of the largest and most renowned *jaebeol* include Samsung, LG, Hyundai, SK, Lotte, Daewoo and Kumho Asiana. Most are still family-controlled, leading to enormous riches for the man at the helm; their power was a driving force behind Korea's "Economic Miracle". Times have changed; after the Asian Financial Crisis and the resultant reforms, many chose (or were forced) to break up into smaller units.

Foreigners who choose to live in Korea full-time may well come into contact with **jeonse**, the country's unique system of property rental. Instead of paying a monthly rent, tenants slam down a huge "key money" deposit, which in most cases is over half of the property's value; the landlord earns off the interest, and refunds the deposit at the end of the contract. This is one reason why most Koreans live with their parents until marriage – youngsters are usually only able to pay the lump sum with family help. It's also quite risky – many families have lost everything after their landlord did a runner. This system is slowly giving way to a more international rental style, prompted in part by much lower interest rates.

L: Louis Vuitton

Though the numbers are gradually starting to decline, patterned brown handbags from French designer **Louis Vuitton** have long been standard issue on female Korean arms. However, high prices – and increased expertise of counterfeiting in China – force many to invest in a fake bag. Watch what happens if it starts to rain.

M: Missionaries and military service

Many visitors to Korea are surprised to learn that Buddhism, the state religion for centuries, has been surpassed as the most common religion by Christianity. Koreans assume most foreigners to be Christian, and some of the most actively religious will stop you in the street for a chat about joining their church – expats soon learn to steer clear of those approaching with a pamphlet or book. Korean Christianity made world news in 2007, when a group of 23 **missionaries** was abducted by the Taliban in Afghanistan; two were executed before a deal could be struck, and the rest had to suffer for over a month before their release.

South Korea still has compulsory **military service** for its young men. This was once 36 months, but is now around 24 months; it's likely to decrease further. Conscientious objectors will be jailed, but there are ways around the rule – many students manage to tie their service into university courses such as logistics and electronic engineering. Military service is also mandatory for men in North Korea, and women are actively encouraged to enrol as volunteers.

N: Nocheonnyeo

A **nocheonnyeo** is an "over-the-hill spinster", a woman who has gone past the perceived outer boundary of marriageable age; 30 has long been the feared number, though the Korean age-counting system (whereby children are born aged 1 and become 2 on the date of the next Lunar New Year) makes this 28 or 29 in international terms. While it remains much harder for a woman to marry after achieving *nocheonnyeo* status, societal shifts (notably an increase in divorce rates, and the slow decline of the resign-after-marriage path for females) mean that it's by no means impossible.

O: Ohmy News

In a country whose news output generally ranges from insipid to downright corrupt, **Ohmy News** has ruffled feathers by providing a much-needed independent voice. In operation since 2000, this online newspaper may not be written by journalists (their motto is "Every Citizen is a Reporter", and around eighty percent of their content comes from the public), but regular scoops have made them a big part of the news scene. They've even made a name for themselves abroad – the *New York Times* of March 6, 2003, ran with the headline "Online Newspaper Shakes Up Korean Politics", a reference to the popular belief that *Ohmy* influenced the outcome of the 2002 presidential election by prompting protests against the American army presence.

P: Private tutoring

With Korea's mix of generous salaries and relatively poor foreign language rates, there's a large and growing market for English teachers. Most head across – at least initially – to teach children at after-school **private tutoring** institutes known as *hagwon*. These are not just for English lessons – the huge pressures inherent in

Korea's educational system prompt an extremely high proportion of parents to push their kids into extra-curricular classes from ages as young as 5. In addition to language classes and "regular" school, the little mites may have violin lessons, computer training, art classes, dance groups and piano recitals crammed into their weekly schedule.

Q: Questionable English

Anyone spending time in Korea will note that expats employed as translators are having a good laugh. T-shirts splashed with **questionable English** are all over the place – "Skinny Bitch" got to be popular with young girls, though "Hey Guy! Lay Me" was a mercifully short-lived fad; some have more surreal slogans such as "Is Your Barn Insured?", and others simply have random cuttings from foreign newspapers. The mirth is not restricted to clothing – *Kiss* and *Asse* are two of the biggest brands of toilet paper, there's an energy drink called *Coolpis*, a bakery chain called *Gout*, children's clothing shops called *Hunt Kids* and *Baby Hunt*, and bars with such names as *Super Excellent Big Boy Club*. Some questionable names, however, are purely down to the Koreans. There are spelling mistakes galore: "crab" is spelt with a "p" on a surprising number of the country's menus, and a certain hamburger chain is often spelt "Bugger King" on English-language maps. There's also the legacy of football hero Ahn Jung-hwan, who celebrated his two goals in the 2002 World Cup by kissing then holding aloft his wedding ring; within days, hundreds of bars and restaurants across the land had changed their name to "Kiss Ring".

R: Red Devils

Having casually pinched their nickname from England's Manchester United, the South Korean national football team is often referred to as the "**Red Devils**", as are their main supporters' group. A noisy but friendly bunch, the latter were one of the highlights of the 2002 World Cup, an event half-hosted in Korea; wearing standard-issue red T-shirts, their chant of "*Dae-Han-Min-Guk!*" – the country's name in Korean – pushed the team on to the semi-finals of the competition. Most wore a T-shirt emblazoned with "Be The Reds!", perhaps the best-known example of "Konglish" (a hybrid of Korean and English which makes little sense in either language). The inventors of the logo initially neglected to copyright it, and it was eventually superseded by the official slogan of the supporters' club, the more grammatically correct "Reds Go Together".

S: Sexy bars and sogaeting

Sexy bars are one of Korea's many takes on the hostess theme. Drinks at these places are served by scantily clad women to male customers who are expected to pay not just for their own drinks, but for the expensive ones selected by the woman or women. Those who just want a beer or two will be tolerated, but it's rich, whisky-quaffing regulars who get preferential treatment. Though this doesn't always lead to sex – there are plenty of dedicated brothels around, and many customers head to sexy bars for nothing more than an ego-boosting chat – it does happen. This line of work has become popular with university students seeking to top up their funds, but many girls are trafficked in from Southeast Asia or former Soviet states, and have little more freedom than the Korean "comfort women" from the Japanese annexation period.

One thing a sexy bar certainly won't play host to is a blind date, or "**sogaeting**". Until recently, these were usually arranged by parents in anticipation of a happy marriage between friendly families, but in an increasingly liberal Korea *sogaeting* is now more common as a way for boys and girls to find their own partners.

T: Tongil and table gifts

After the cleaving apart of the Korean peninsula, both sides held a strong desire for reunification. "**Tongil**", the local word for the concept, forms part of the names of parks, monuments, roads, bars, restaurants, hairdressers and countless more besides, but its popularity has been noticeably declining among South Korean youth: in an all-pervasive manner of which the North would be quite proud, almost anyone born after 1980 will claim that the absorption of such a poor country would play havoc on their own economy, pointing to Germany's fiscal woes after the fall of the Berlin Wall.

A first birthday party is a pretty special event wherever you are in the world, but Korea has added its own distinctive twist to proceedings – **table gifts**. At some point in the occasion, the baby will be seated on or dangled over a table laid out with money, rice, thread and a pencil, and pushed to make a selection that, it is said, will influence their future path. Money speaks for itself, but the selection of rice is said to lead to a comfortable life, thread to a long one, and a pencil to a scholarly career. Of course, this is not enough to satisfy many modern parents, who throw contemporary choices such as golf balls, footballs, DVDs or microphones onto the table too, often giving their young one precious little choice in the selection. Also interesting are the parties thrown to celebrate the hundredth day of a child's life – in times of high infant mortality, this was when the child was said to have "made it", and the special day continues to be celebrated with a feast of colourful rice-cake.

U: Unconstitutional law and US forces

Koreans were, until recently, banned from marrying anyone of the same clan. This may have sounded like an extremely severe rule in a country with so few family names (around one-quarter of Koreans are named Kim, another fifteen percent Lee, and almost ten percent Park), but the ruling only in fact covered those who had both the same name and the same ancestral clan; some of these subdivisions, however, were over a million-strong in number. Same-clan marriages were termed incestuous, even if the pair were a dozen generations apart, but this law was found **unconstitutional** by the Korean court in 1997, and thousands have since taken advantage of this ruling.

US forces arrived back on Korean soil at the beginning of the Korean War in 1950, only years after leaving the area following Japan's defeat in World War II; they have remained on the peninsula ever since in their tens of thousands. Their presence is largely unpopular in Korea, with regular protests taking place in Seoul. Successive Korean leaders have been forced to walk a political tightrope, telling locals that the American presence would be scaled down, but simultaneously begging them to stay. The mini-cities of good-time girls that have developed outside the major bases would also be short of custom.

V: Vanity mirrors

Korean girls are famed throughout East Asia for being a little vain. A **vanity mirror** is an almost essential part of every girl's armament; these are used at what can be disturbingly regular intervals to make sure that every single eyelash is in perfect position, and are usually kept in outer pockets – for some, the inside of a handbag is just too far away. Many Korean girls now have mirrored screens on their mobile phones.

W: Westernization

Though it remains one of the most unique societies on earth, Korea certainly doesn't suffer from a lack of **Western influence**. The once-traditional *hanbok* suits and horsehair hats gave way decades ago to T-shirts and jeans, the former almost always adorned with an English-language logo or slogan. Innumerable Western words have entered the Korean lexicon, albeit altered to fit the local tongue; foreign fast-food chains are everywhere; and American shows such as *CSI*, *Lost* and *Prison Break* are among the most popular on TV.

X: Xenophobia

Koreans tend to make foreigners feel very welcome, but this friendliness conceals a rampant **xenophobia**. Korea remains one of the most homogenous societies on earth, and traces of the "Hermit Kingdom" remain, mainly thanks to history lessons that paint the motherland in virginal white while detailing every single injustice inflicted on her; most of the official ire is reserved for the Japanese, but anti-Americanism is also rife. It must be said that this very rarely results in anything approaching violence – Korea is simply seen as a world apart, where foreigners will always be viewed as such, even if they were born in Korea and speak the language fluently. People are likewise seen as nationals first and human beings second, which leads to some blanket stereotyping; the rationale for many local deeds will be "because I'm Korean". It also explains the surprise that many Koreans will show to Westerners able to use chopsticks – no matter how close you live to a Chinatown, it's simply not in your DNA.

Y: Yuhaeng and Yes!!

Yuhaeng is a Korean word meaning "in vogue" – and the compulsion to be in vogue has led to a recent fad for fancy underwear. After years of beige-coloured bras, Korean women (and their men, of course) needed something different, and one of the biggest and most innovative movers was **Yes!!**, a nationwide lingerie chain. One notable piece of marketing genius was seen on a bra-and-knickers set which had the word "No" plastered all over it; with the aid of glow-in-the-dark printing, this magically changed to "Yes!!" when the lights were off.

Z: Zodiac

Koreans are a superstitious bunch, and you'll see small tent-like fortune-telling booths in every city, most often attended by young couples looking for celestial approval of their relationship, or workers thinking about changing jobs. People's place in the **zodiac** may also be supplemented by palm-reading, teacup-gazing, craniology or Tarot cards.

Language

Language

Korean

The sole official tongue of both North and South Korea, the **Korean** language is used by upwards of seventy million people, making it by some estimates the eleventh most spoken in the world. A highly tricky language to pick up, much to the chagrin of linguists it remains stubbornly "unclassified" on the global language tree, its very origins something of a mystery. Some lump it in with the **Altaic** group (itself rather vague), which would put it on the same branch as Turkish and Mongolian, though many view it as a **language isolate**. Korean is therefore in the same boat as Japanese, its closest linguistic brother; both share a **subject-object-verb** syntax and similar grammar, though well over half of the Korean words themselves actually originate from China. Korea also used Chinese text for centuries, even after creating its own characters – known as **hangeul** – in the 1440s, but now almost exclusively uses the local system for everyday functions.

Native speakers of European languages will encounter some highly significant **grammatical differences**. Korean **nouns** remain unaffected whether they refer to singular or plural words; very little use is made of **articles**; and **verbs** do not change case according to who or what they're referring to – *gayo* can mean "I go", "he/she/it goes" or "we/they go", the meaning made clear by the context. Verbs do, however, alter depending on which **level of politeness** the speaker desires to use. The country's Confucian legacy is still evident, so the conversation will sound quite different depending on whether it's between a child and a mother, a boss and an employee, or even good friends of slightly different age. In general, it's pretty safe to stick to verbs with the polite – **yo** ending.

Korean characters

Many foreigners find Korean text, a scrawl of circles and Tetris shapes, surprisingly **easy to learn**. Koreans are immensely proud of *hangeul*, which they see as the world's most logical written system. While this is no great exaggeration, the efficiency also has a downside – user-friendly it may well be, but in reality *hangeul* is a very narrow system that cannot cope with sounds not found in the Korean language, a fact that partially explains the Korean people's generally poor pronunciation of foreign tongues. Koreans tend to assume that foreigners don't have the inclination or mental capability to decipher *hangeul*, so your efforts will not go unappreciated.

Hangeul

Korean characters are grouped into **syllabic boxes** of more-or-less equal size, and generally arranged left-to-right – if you see a line of text made up of eighteen of these character-chunks, it will have eighteen syllables when spoken. The way in which the **characters** fall into the boxes is rather unique and takes a bit of figuring out – some have two characters in the top half and one at the bottom (the top two are read left-to-right, followed by the bottom one, so 한 makes *han*), while others have two or three characters arranged vertically (these are read downwards, so 국 makes *guk*). Thus put together, we have 한국 – *hanguk*, meaning "Korea". The basic building blocks are listed below, though note that some of these symbols **change sounds** depending on whether they're at the beginning or end of a syllable or word (syllable-ending sounds are bracketed in the boxed text), and that "ng" is used as an initial null consonant for syllables that start with a vowel. Guides to pronouncing the **vowel clusters** are given in the next section; there also exist consonantal clusters, though these are beyond the scope of this book. For a short history of the text, see the box on p.8.

ㄱ	g (k)	ㅎ	h	ㅔ	e
ㄴ	n	ㅇ	ng	ㅐ	ae
ㄷ	d (t)	ㅏ	a	ㅖ	ye
ㄹ	r/l	ㅑ	ya	ㅒ	yae
ㅁ	m	ㅓ	eo	ㅟ	wi
ㅂ	b (p)	ㅕ	yeo	ㅞ	we
ㅅ	s (t)	ㅗ	o	ㅙ	wae
ㅈ	j (t)	ㅛ	yo	ㅘ	wa
ㅊ	ch (t)	ㅜ	u	ㅚ	oe
ㅋ	k	ㅠ	yu	ㅢ	ui
ㅌ	t	ㅡ	eu	ㅝ	wo
ㅍ	p	ㅣ	i		

Pronunciation

Pronouncing Korean words is a tough task – some sounds simply do not have English-language equivalents. You'll see from the *hangeul* box above that there's only one character for "l" and "r", with its actual sound some way in between the two – try saying both phonemes at the same time. The letters "k", "d", "b" and "j" are often written "k", "t", "p" and "ch", and are pronounced approximately half-way towards those Roman equivalents; unfortunately, the second set also have their place in the official system, and are usually referred to as **aspirated consonants**, accompanied as they are by a puff of air. Consonants are fairly easy to master – note that some are doubled up, and spoken more forcefully – but pronunciation guides to some of the tricky **vowels** and **dipthongs** are as follows (British English readings offer the closest equivalents):

a	as in "c**a**r"
ya	as in "Jan"
eo	as in "h**o**t"
yeo	as in "**yo**b"
o	pronounced "ore"
yo	pronounced "**yo**ur"
u	as in "**Jew**"
yu	pronounced "you"

eu	like the *e* in "bitten"; grimace and make a quick "uhh" sound of disgust
i	as in "p**ea**"
e	as in "b**e**d"
ae	as in "**ai**r"
ye	as in "**ye**t"
yae	as in "**yea**h"

Transliteratary troubles

Rendering the Korean language in Roman text is a battle that can never be won – a classic problem of square pegs and round holes. Numerous systems have been employed down the years, perhaps best exemplified in the Korean family name now usually romanized as "Lee": this has also been written as Rhee, Li, Ri, Lih, Rhi, Ree, Yi, Rii and more besides. Under the current system it would be "I", but the actual pronunciation is simply "ee" – it's amazing how much trouble a simple vowel can cause (especially when almost a fifth of the country has this name).

A Korean's age, schooling, family and even lifestyle influence the way that they'll romanize a given word, but official standards have long been in place. The **Yale** and **McCune-Reischauer** systems became widely accepted in the 1940s, and the latter is still much in evidence today; under its rules, aspirated consonants are marked with apostrophes, and certain vowels with breves. One problem – other than looking ugly – was that these punctuation markings are often neglected, even in language study books; though it remains the official system in North Korea, the South formulated its own system of **revised romanization** in 2000. While this is far from perfect, it's the official standard, and has been used throughout this book; exceptions include names of the many hotels, restaurants, universities and individuals who cling to the old ways. One other issue is the Korean syllable *shi*; this is now romanized as *si*, a rather ridiculous change since it takes Koreans years of language classes before they can pronounce the syllable without palatalizing it – "six" and "sister" will be pronounced "shix" and "shister". We've written it as *shi* in the language listings to help you achieve the correct pronunciation, but obeyed the official system in the rest of the book – Sinchon is pronounced "Shinchon", Sapsido "Sapshido", and so on.

Koreans find it hard to render **foreign words** in *hangeul* as there are many sounds that don't fit into the system – the difficulties with "l" and "r" sharing the same character being an obvious example – but even when parallels exist they are sometimes distorted. The letter "a" is usually written as an "e" or "ae" in an unsuccessful effort to Americanize the pronunciation – "hat", for example, will be pronounced "het" by the majority of the population.

wi	as in "**wi**ndow"
we	as in "**we**dding"
wae	as the beginning of "**whe**re"
wa	as in "**wa**g"
oe	as in the beginning of "**wa**y"
ui	no English equivalent; add an "ee" sound to *eu* above
wo	as in "**wa**d"

Useful words and phrases

Basics

Yes	*ye/ne*	예/네
No	*aniyo*	아니요
Please (asking for something)	*…juseyo*	…주세요
Excuse me	*shillye hamnida*	실례합니다
I'm sorry	*mian hamnida*	미안합니다

Thank you	*gamsa hamnida*	감사합니다
You're welcome	*gwaenchan-ayo*	괜찮아요
What?	*muot?*	무엇?
When?	*eonje?*	언제?
Where?	*eodi?*	어디?
Who?	*nugu?*	누구?
How?	*eotteokke?*	어떻게?
How much?	*eolma-eyo?*	얼마에요?
How many?	*myeokke-eyo?*	몇 개에요?
I want…	*…hago-shipeoyo*	…하고 싶어요
Please help me	*dowa-juseyo*	도와주세요

Communicating

I can't speak Korean	*jeo-neun hangugeo-reul mot haeyo*	저는 한국어를 못 해요
I can't read Korean	*jeo-neun hangugeo-reul mok ilgeoyo*	저는 한국어를 못 읽어요
Do you speak English?	*yeongeo halsu-isseoyo?*	영어 할 수 있어요?
Is there someone who can speak English?	*yeongeo-reul haljul a-neun bun isseoyo?*	영어를 할 줄 아는 분 있어요?
Can you please speak slowly?	*jom cheoncheonhi malhae jusilsu isseoyo?*	좀 천천히 말해 주실수 있어요?
Please say that again	*dashi han-beon mal haejuseyo*	다시 한번말 해주세요
I understand/I see	*alasseoyo*	알았어요
I (really) don't understand	*(jal) mollayo*	(잘) 몰라요
What does this mean?	*i-geot museun ddeushi-eyo?*	이것 무슨 뜻이에요?
How do you say (x) in Korean?	*(x) eul/reul hanguk-eoro eotteoke mal haeyo?*	(x) 을/를 한국어로 어떻게 말해요
Please write in English	*yeongeo-ro jegeo jushillaeyo*	영어로 적어 주실래요
Please wait (a moment)	*(jamggan) gidariseyo*	(잠깐) 기다리세요
Just a minute	*jamggan manyo*	잠깐 만요

Meetings and greetings

Hello; Good morning/ afternoon/evening	*annyeong haseyo*	안녕 하세요
Hello (polite)	*annyeong hashimnikka*	안녕 하십니까
How are you?	*jal jinaesseoyo?*	잘 지냈어요?
I'm fine	*jal jinaesseoyo/jo-ayo*	잘 지냈어요 / 좋아요
Nice to meet you	*bangapseumnida*	반갑습니다
Goodbye (when staying)	*annyeong-hi gaseyo*	안녕히 가세요
Goodbye (when leaving)	*annyeong-hi gyeseyo*	안녕히 계세요
What's your name?	*ireum-i eotteokke doeshimnikka?*	이름이 어떻게 되십니까?
My name is…	*ireum-i … imnida*	이름이… 입니다.
Where are you from?	*eodi-eso wasseoyo?*	어디에서 왔어요?
I'm from…	*…eso wasseoyo*	에서 왔어요

Korea	*han-guk*	한국
Britain	*yeong-guk*	영국
Ireland	*aillaendeu*	아일랜드
America	*mi-guk*	미국
Australia	*oseuteureillia/hoju*	오스트레일리아 / 호주
Canada	*kae-nada*	캐나다
New Zealand	*nyu jillaendeu*	뉴질랜드
South Africa	*nam apeurika*	남 아프리카
How old are you?	*myeot-sal ieyo?*	몇 살이에요?
I am (age)	*(age)-sal ieyo*	(age)살이에요
Do you like…?	*......jo-a haeyo?*	...좋아 해요?
I like…	*jo-a haeyo*	좋아 해요
I don't like…	*an jo-a haeyo*	안 좋아해요
Do you have (free) time?	*shigan isseoyo?*	시간 있어요?

Numbers

Rather confusingly, the Korean language has two separate number systems operating in parallel – a **native Korean** system, and a **Sino-Korean** system of Chinese origin – and you'll have to learn according to the situation which one to use. To tell the time, you'll actually need both – amazingly, minutes and hours run on different systems! The native Korean system only goes up to 99, and has been placed on the right-hand side of the readings in the list below. Dates and months use the Sino-Korean system alone, with *il* (sun) used as a suffix for days, and *wol* (moon) for months: June 7 is simply *yuk-wol chil-il*.

Zero	*yeong/gong*	영/공
One	*il/hana*	일/하나
Two	*i (pronounced "ee")/dul*	이/둘
Three	*sam/set*	삼/셋
Four	*sa/net*	사/넷
Five	*o/daseot*	오/다섯
Six	*yuk/yeoseot*	육/여섯
Seven	*chil/ilgop*	칠/일곱
Eight	*pal/yeodeol*	팔/여덟
Nine	*gu/ahop*	구/아홉
Ten	*shib/yeol*	십/열
Eleven	*shib-il/yeol-hana*	십일/열하나
Twelve	*shib-I/yeol-dul*	십이/열 둘
Twenty	*i-shib/seumul*	이십/스물
Thirty	*sam-shib/seoreun*	삼십/서른
One hundred	*baek*	백
Two hundred	*i-baek*	이백
Thousand	*cheon*	천
Ten thousand	*man*	만
One hundred thousand	*sim-man*	십만
One million	*baeng-man*	백만
One hundred million	*eok*	억

Time and dates

Now	*jigeum*	지금
Today	*o-neul*	오늘
Morning	*achim*	아침
Afternoon	*ohu*	오후
Evening	*jeonyok*	저녁
Night	*bam*	밤
Tomorrow	*nae-il*	내일
Yesterday	*eoje*	어제
Week	*ju*	주
Month	*wol/dal*	월/달
Year	*nyeon*	년

Monday	*wolyo-il*	월요일
Tuesday	*hwayo-il*	화요일
Wednesday	*suyo-il*	수요일
Thursday	*mogyo-il*	목요일
Friday	*geumyo-il*	금요일
Saturday	*toyo-il*	토요일
Sunday	*ilyo-il*	일요일

What time is it?	*myo-shi-eyo?*	몇시에요?
It's 10 o'clock	*yeol-shi-eyo*	열시에요
10.20	*yeol-shi i-shib-bun*	열시 이십분
10.30	*yeol-shi sam-shib-bun*	열시 삼십분
10.50	*yeol-shi o-ship-bun*	열시 오십분

Transport and travel

Aeroplane	*bihaenggi*	비행기
Airport	*gonghang*	공항
Bus	*beoseu*	버스
Express bus (terminal)	*gosok beoseu (teominal)*	고속 버스 (터미널)
Intercity bus (terminal)	*shi-oe beoseu (teominal)*	시외 버스 (터미널)
City bus	*shinae beoseu*	시내 버스
Airport bus	*gonghang beoseu*	공항 버스
City bus stop	*jeong-ryu-jang*	정류장
Train	*gicha*	기차

Train station	*yeok*	역
Subway	*jihacheol*	지하철
Ferry	*yeogaek-seon*	여객선
Ferry terminal	*yeogaek teominal*	여객 터미널
Left-luggage office	*jimbogwanso*	짐보관
Ticket office	*maepyoso*	매표소
Ticket	*pyo*	표
Platform	*seunggangjang*	승강장
Bicycle	*jajeon-geo*	자전거
Taxi	*taek-shi*	택시

Directions and general places

Where is (x)?	*-i/ga eodi-eyo?*	-이/가 어디에요?
Straight ahead	*jikjin*	직진
Left	*oen-jjok (pronounced "wen-chok")*	왼쪽
Right	*oreun-jjok*	오른쪽
Behind	*dwi-e*	뒤에
In front of	*ap-e*	앞에
North	*buk*	북
South	*nam*	남
East	*dong*	동
West	*seo*	서
Map	*maep/jido*	맵/지도
Entrance	*ip-gu*	입구

Exit	*chul-gu*	출구
Art gallery	*misulgwan*	미술관
Bank	*eunhaeng*	은행
Beach	*haebyeon*	해변
Department store	*baekhwajeom*	백화점
Embassy	*daesagwan*	대사관
Hot spring spa	*oncheon*	온천
Museum	*bangmulgwan*	박물관
Park	*gongwon*	공원
Sea	*haean/bada*	해안/바다
Temple	*Jeol/sachal*	절/사찰
Toilet	*hwajang-shil*	화장실
Tourist office	*gwan-gwang annaeso*	관광 안내소

Accommodation

Hotel	*hotel*	호텔
Motel	*motel*	모텔
Guesthouse	*yeogwan*	여관

Budget guesthouse	*yeoinsuk*	여인숙
Rented room	*minbak*	민박

Youth hostel	*yuseu hoseutel*	유스 호스텔
Korean-style room	*ondol-bang*	온돌방
Western-style room	*chimdae-bang*	침대방
Single room	*shinggeul chimdae*	싱글 침대
Double room	*deobeul chimdae*	더블 침대
Twin room	*chimdae dugae*	침대 두개
En-suite room	*yokshil-ddallin bang*	욕실 딸린방
Shower	*syaweo*	샤워
Bath	*yokjo*	욕조
Key	*ki*	키
Passport	*yeogwon*	여권
Do you have any vacancies?	*bang isseoyo?*	방 있어요?

I have a reservation	*jeo-neun yeyak haesseoyo*	저는 예약 했어요
I don't have a reservation	*jeo-neun yeyak anhaesseoyo*	저는 예약 안했어요
How much is the room?	*bang-i eolma -eyo?*	방이 얼마에요?
Does that include breakfast?	*gagyeok-e achim-shiksa poham-dwae isseoyo?*	가격에 아침식사 포함돼 있어요?
One/two/three nights	*haruppam/i-bak/sam-bak*	하룻밤/이박/삼박
One week	*il-ju-il*	일주일
May I see the room?	*bang jom bolsu-isseoyo?*	방 좀 볼수 있어요?

Shopping, money and banks

Bank	*eunhaeng*	은행
Foreign exchange	*woe-hwan*	외환
Won	*won*	원
Pounds	*pa-un-deu*	파운드
Dollars	*dalleo*	달러
Cash	*don*	돈
Travellers' cheque	*yeohaengja supyo*	여행자 수표표
How much is it?	*eolma-eyo?*	얼마에요?

It's too expensive	*neomu bissayo*	너무 비싸요
Please make it a little cheaper	*jom kkakka-juseyo*	좀 깎아주세요
Do you accept credit cards?	*keurediteu kadeu gyesan dwaeyo?*	크레디트 카드 계산 돼요?

Post and telephones

Post office	*uche-guk*	우체국
Envelope	*bongtu*	봉투
Letter	*pyeonji*	편지
Postcard	*yeopseo*	엽서
Stamp	*u-pyo*	우표
Airmail	*hanggong u-pyeon*	항공 우편
Surface mail	*seonbak u-pyeon*	선박 우편
Telephone	*jeon-hwa*	전화

Fax	*paekseu*	팩스
Telephone card	*jeonhwa kadeu*	전화카드
Internet café	*PC-bang*	피씨방
I would like to call...	*...hante jeonhwa hago-shipeoyo*	...한테 전화하고 싶어요
May I speak to...	*...jom baggwo juseyo*	...좀 바꿔 주세요
Hello?	*yeoboseyo?*	여보세요?

Health

Hospital	*byeongwon*	병원
Pharmacy	*yak-guk*	약국
Medicine	*yak*	약
Doctor	*uisa*	의사
Dentist	*chigwa-uisa*	치과의사
Diarrhoea	*seolsa*	설사
Nausea	*meseukkeo -um*	메스꺼움
Fever	*yeol*	열
Food poisoning	*shikjungdok*	식중독
Antibiotics	*hangsaengje*	항생제
Antiseptic	*sodok-yak*	소독약
Condom	*kondom*	콘돔
Penicillin	*penishillin*	페니실린
Tampons	*tampon*	탐폰
I'm ill	*jeo-neun apayo*	저는 아파요
I have a cold	*gamgi geoll-yeosseoyo*	감기 걸렸어요
I'm allergic to...	*...allereugi-ga isseoyo*	...알레르기가 있어요
It hurts here	*yeogi-ga apayo*	여기가 아파요
Please call a doctor	*uisa-reul bulleo juseyo*	의사를 불러 주세요

Food and drink

Places

Restaurant	*sikdang*	식당
Korean barbecue restaurant	*galbi-jip*	갈비집
Korean staples (fast food) restaurant	*gimbap-cheonguk*	김밥천국
Seafood restaurant	*hoet-jip*	횟집
Western-style restaurant	*reseutorang*	레스토랑
Italian restaurant	*itallian reseutorang*	이탈리안 레스토랑
Chinese restaurant	*jungguk-jip*	중국집
Japanese restaurant	*ilshik-jip*	일식집
Burger bar	*paeseuteu-pudeu-jeom*	패스트푸드점
Convenience store	*pyeonui-jeom*	편의점
Market	*shijang*	시장
Café	*kape*	카페
Bar	*ba/suljip*	바/술집
Club	*naiteu-keulleob*	나이트클럽
Expat bar	*woeguk-in ba* (*pronounced "way-guk-in ba"*)	외국인 바
Makkeolli bar	*makkeolli-jip*	막걸리집
Soju tent	*pojangmacha*	포장마차
Where's (a) ... ?	*...eodi isseoyo?*	...어디 있어요?

Ordering

Waiter/Waitress (lit. "Here!")	*yeogiyo!*	여기요!
How much is that?	*eolma-eyo?*	얼마에요?

I would like...	*...hago shipeoyo*	...하고 싶어요
May I have the bill?	*gyesanseo juseyo?*	계산서 주세요
I'm a vegetarian	*jeo-neun chaeshikju uija-eyo*	저는 채식주의자에요
Can I have this without meat?	*gogi bbaego haejushilsu isseoyo?*	고기 빼고 해주실수 있어요?
I can't eat spicy food	*maeun-geot mot meogeoyo*	매운 것 못 먹어요
Delicious!	*mashisseoyo!*	맛있어요!
Chopsticks	*jeot-garak*	젓가락
Fork	*po-keu*	포크
Knife	*nai-peu/kal*	나이프/칼
Spoon	*sut-garak*	숟가락
Menu	*menyu*	메뉴

Staple ingredients

Beef	*so-gogi*	소고기
Chicken	*dak-gogi*	닭고기
Duck meat	*ori-gogi*	오리고기
Gimchi	*gimchi*	김치
Fish	*saengsun/hoe (raw fish)*	생선/회
Ham	*haem*	햄
Meat	*gogi*	고기
Noodles	*myeon*	면
Pork	*dwaeji-gogi*	돼지고기
Red-pepper paste	*gochu-jang*	고추장
Rice	*bap*	밥
Rice-cake	*ddeok*	떡
Seaweed laver	*gim*	김
Shrimp	*sae-u*	새우
Squid	*ojing-eo*	오징어
Tuna	*chamchi*	참치
Vegetables	*yachae*	야채

Rice dishes

Bibimbap	*bibimbap*	비빔밥
Fried rice (usually with egg and vegetables)	*bokkeumbap*	볶음밥
...on rice	*deop-bap*	덮밥
Beef...	*bulgogi*	불고기
Curry...	*kare*	카레
Spicy squid...	*ojingeo*	오징어
Rice rolls	*gimbap*	김밥

Meat dishes

Barbecued ribs	*galbi*	갈비
Boiled beef rolls	*shabeu-shabeu*	샤브샤브
Dog-meat soup	*boshintang/yeongyangtang*	보신탕/영양탕

Marinaded beef	*bulgogi*	불고기
Pork belly slices	*samgyeopsal*	삼겹살
Spicy squid on rice	*ojingeo deop-bap*	오징어 덮밥
Steamed ribs	*galbi-jjim*	갈비찜

Stews and soups

Beef and noodle soup	*seolleong-tang*	설렁탕
Beef rib soup	*galbi-tang*	갈비탕
Cold buckwheat noodle soup	*naengmyeon*	냉면
Dumpling soup	*mandu-guk*	만두국
Gimchi broth	*gimchi jjigae*	김치 찌개
Ginseng-stuffed chicken soup	*samgye-tang*	삼계탕
Noodles with vegetables and meat	*makguksu*	막국수
Soybean broth (miso)	*doenjang jjigae*	된장 찌개
Spicy fish soup	*maeun-tang*	매운탕
Spicy noodle soup	*ramyeon*	라면
Spicy tofu soup	*sundubu*	순두부
Tuna broth	*chamchi jjigae*	참치 찌개

Snacks and Korean fast food

Battered flash-fried snacks (tempura)	*twigim*	튀김
Breaded pork cutlet	*donkkaseu*	돈까스
Dumplings	*mandu*	만두
Fried dumplings	*gun-mandu*	군만두
Rice wrapped in omelette	*omeuraiseu*	오므라이스
Rice-cake in red-pepper paste	*ddeokbokki*	떡볶이
Savoury pancake with vegetables	*pajeon*	파전
Steamed dumplings	*jjin-mandu*	찐만두
Stuffed sausage	*sundae*	순대

Seafood

Broiled fish	*saengseon-gu-i*	생선구이
Fried baby octopus	*nakji bokkeum*	낙지 볶음
Raw fish platter	*modeum-hoe*	모듬회
Sliced raw fish	*saengseon-hoe*	생선회
Spicy squid on rice	*ojingeo deop-bap*	오징어 덮밥

Western food

Bread	*bbang*	빵
Cereal	*shiri-eol*	시리얼
Cheese	*chi-jeu*	치즈

Chocolate	*chokollit*	초콜릿
Eggs	*gyeran*	계란
Fruit	*gwa-il*	과일
Pizza	*pija*	피자
Spaghetti	*seupageti*	스파게티
Steak	*seuteikeu*	스테이크

Tea

Black tea (lit. "red tea")	*hong-cha*	홍차
Chrysanthemum tea	*gukhwa-cha*	국화차
Cinnamon tea	*gyepi-cha*	계피차
Citron tea	*yuja-cha*	유자차
Five flavours tea	*omija-cha*	오미자차
Ginger tea	*saenggang -cha*	생강차
Ginseng tea	*insam-cha*	인삼차
Green tea	*nok-cha*	녹차
Honey ginseng tea	*ggulsam-cha*	꿀삼차
"Job's Tears" tea	*yulmu-cha*	율무차
Jujube tea	*daechu-cha*	대추차
Medicinal herb tea	*yak-cha*	약차
Plum tea	*maeshil-cha*	매실차
Wild herb tea	*ma-cha*	마차

Alcoholic drinks

Baekseju	*baekseju*	백세주
Beer	*maekju*	맥주
Blackberry wine	*bokbunja*	복분자
Bottled beer	*byeong maekju*	병 맥주
Cocktail	*kakteil*	칵테일
Dongdongju	*dongdongju*	동동주
Draught beer	*saeng maekju*	생맥주
Ginseng wine	*insamju*	인삼주
Makkeolli	*makkeolli*	막걸리
Plum brandy	*maeshilju*	매실주
Soju	*soju*	소주
Wine	*wain*	와인
Whicky	*wiseuki*	위스키

Other drinks

Coffee	*keopi*	커피
Orange juice	*orenji jyuseu*	오렌지쥬스
Fruit juice	*gwa-il jyuseu*	과일 쥬스
Milk	*uyu*	우유
Mineral water	*saengsu*	생수
Water	*mul*	물

Glossary

ajeossi an older or married man.

ajumma an older or married woman; see p.382.

-am hermitage.

anju bar snacks.

-bang room.

-bawi boulder or large rock.

-bong mountain peak. The highest peak in a park is often referred to as *ilchulbong* ("Number One Peak").

bongjak a highly distinctive style of Korean music, also known as "Grandmother techno", and much favoured by older generations; see p.383 for more.

buk- north.

buncheong a Korean style of pottery that became popular in Joseon times. The end product is often bluish-green.

celadon a Korean style of pottery (also common in China and Japan), used since the Three Kingdoms period but largely overtaken by *buncheong* in Joseon times. The end product is often pale green, with a cracked glaze.

cha tea.

-cheon stream or river of less than 100km in length.

Chuseok Korean Thanksgiving.

dae- big, large, great.

daeri-unjeon a network of taxi drivers without taxis; see p.383.

Dangun mythical founder of Korea.

DMZ the Demilitarized Zone that separates North and South Korea.

-do island.

-do province.

-dong city neighbourhood; part of a *–gu*.

dong- east.

dongdongju a milky rice wine much favoured by Korean students; very similar to *makkeolli*.

DPRK Democratic People's Republic of Korea.

-eup town.

-ga section of a major street.

-gang river of over 100km in length.

geobukseon the "turtle ships" as used by Admiral Yi in the late sixteenth century; see p.232.

-gil street.

-gu district of a city, subdivided into *–dong* neighbourhoods.

-gul cave.

-gun county.

-gung palace.

gwageo civil service examinations in the Joseon era.

Gyopo Koreans, or people of Korean descent, living overseas.

hae sea. Korea's East, West and South seas are referred to as *Donghae*, *Seohae* and *Namhae* respectively, though the international nomenclature of the first two (more readily referred to as the "Sea of Japan" and the "Yellow Sea" abroad) is a touchy subject with Koreans.

haenyeo diving ladies, a few of whom still live on Jeju Island (see p.308).

hagwon private academy for after-school study. Many expats in Korea are working at an English academy (*yeongeo hagwon*).

hallyu the "Korean New Wave" of pop culture, most specifically as regards cinema.

hanbok traditional Korean clothing.

-hang harbour.

hangeul the Korean alphabet.

hanja Chinese characters, which are still sometimes used in Korea.

hanji traditional handmade paper.

hanok a style of traditional, tile-roofed wooden housing.

hareubang the famed "grandfather statues" of Jeju Island (see p.320).

-ho lake; also used for those artificially created after the construction of a dam.

hof a Korean-style bar.

hompy personal homepage; see p.384.

insam ginseng.

jaebeol major Korean corporation; see p.384.

-jeon temple hall.

jeonse Korean system of property rental; see p.384.

jjimjilbang Korean spa-cum-sauna facilities, often used by families, youth groups and the occasional budget traveller.

Juche North Korea's state-sanctioned "religion", a take on Marxist-Leninist theory developed during the Japanese occupation period.

KNTO Korea National Tourism Organization.

KTX the fastest class of Korean train.

makkeolli a milky rice wine very similar to *dongdongju*.

minbak rented rooms in a private house or building, most commonly found near beaches and national park entrances.

mudang shamanist practitioner; usually female.

mugunghwa Korea's third-highest level of train, one below a *saemaeul*. Named after Korea's national flower, a variety of hibiscus; also known as the "Flower of Sharon", it arrives punctually each year.

-mun city or fortress gate.

-myo Confucian shrine.

nam- south.

-ni village; sometimes pronounced *–ri*.

-no large street; sometimes pronounced *–ro*.

nocheonnyeo an "over-the-hill" woman; see p.385.

noraebang a "singing room" often the venue of choice for the end of a night out.

oncheon hot spring bath or spa.

ondol traditional underfloor system of heating, made by wood fires underneath traditional buildings, but replaced with gas-fired systems in Korean apartments and modern houses.

pansori Korean opera derived from shamanistic songs, sung by female vocalists to minimalist musical accompaniment.

-pokpo waterfalls.

pyeong Korean unit of measurement equivalent to approximately 3.3 square metres; still commonly used to measure the floorspace of housing or offices.

Red Devils a nickname for the South Korean national football team, or their noisy supporters.

-ri village; sometimes pronounced *–ni.*

-ro large street; sometimes pronounced *–no.*

ROK Republic of Korea.

-sa temple.

Saemaeul Korea's second-highest level of train, one faster than a *mugunghwa* but slower than a KTX. Also the name of the "New Community Movement" inaugurated by Korean president Park Chung-hee in the 1970s.

-san mountain; often used to describe an entire range.

sanseong mountain fortress.

seo- west.

Seon Korean Buddhist sect proximate to Zen in Japan.

seonsaengnim title for a teacher, which goes before the family name, or before the given name in the case of most expat teachers in Korea. It's also used as a version of "Mister".

seowon Confucian academy, most prevalent in Joseon times

-si city, subdivided into *–gu* districts.

sijang market.

soju clear alcoholic drink (around 25 percent alcohol by volume) which is often compared to vodka, and usually cheaper than water at convenience stores.

ssireum a Korean wrestling style inevitably compared to sumo, but far more similar to Mongolian or Greco-Roman styles.

taekwondo Korean martial art; now practised around the world.

tap pagoda.

tongil unification, a highly important concept on the divided Korean peninsula.

tongmu "comrade", especially useful in Communist North Korea.

woeguk-in foreigner; pronounced "way-goog-in". *Woeguk-saram* is also used.

yangban the scholarly "upper class" in Joseon-era Korea.

yeogwan Korean form of accommodation, similar to a motel but privately run and almost always older.

yeoinsuk Korean accommodation, similar to a *yeogwan* but with communal toilets and showers.

Small print and
Index

A Rough Guide to Rough Guides

Published in 1982, the first Rough Guide – to Greece – was a student scheme that became a publishing phenomenon. Mark Ellingham, a recent graduate in English from Bristol University, had been travelling in Greece the previous summer and couldn't find the right guidebook. With a small group of friends he wrote his own guide, combining a highly contemporary, journalistic style with a thoroughly practical approach to travellers' needs.

The immediate success of the book spawned a series that rapidly covered dozens of destinations. And, in addition to impecunious backpackers, Rough Guides soon acquired a much broader and older readership that relished the guides' wit and inquisitiveness as much as their enthusiastic, critical approach and value-for-money ethos.

These days, Rough Guides include recommendations from shoestring to luxury and cover more than 200 destinations around the globe, including almost every country in the Americas and Europe, more than half of Africa and most of Asia and Australasia. Our ever-growing team of authors and photographers is spread all over the world, particularly in Europe, the US and Australia.

In the early 1990s, Rough Guides branched out of travel, with the publication of Rough Guides to World Music, Classical Music and the Internet. All three have become benchmark titles in their fields, spearheading the publication of a wide range of books under the Rough Guide name.

Including the travel series, Rough Guides now number more than 350 titles, covering: phrasebooks, waterproof maps, music guides from Opera to Heavy Metal, reference works as diverse as Conspiracy Theories and Shakespeare, and popular culture books from iPods to Poker. Rough Guides also produce a series of more than 120 World Music CDs in partnership with World Music Network.

Visit www.roughguides.com to see our latest publications.

Rough Guide credits

Text editor: Samantha Cook
Layout: Anita Singh
Cartography: Jasbir Sandhu
Picture editor: Rhiannon Furbear
Production: Rebecca Short
Proofreader: Stewart Wild
Korean proofreader: Min Woo Han
Cover design: Nicole Newman, Dan May
Photographers: Martin Richardson, Tim Draper
Editorial: **London** Andy Turner, Keith Drew, Edward Aves, Alice Park, Lucy White, Jo Kirby, James Smart, Natasha Foges, James Rice, Emma Beatson, Emma Gibbs, Kathryn Lane, Monica Woods, Mani Ramaswamy, Harry Wilson, Lucy Cowie, Alison Roberts, Lara Kavanagh, Eleanor Aldridge, Ian Blenkinsop, Charlotte Melville, Lorna North, Joe Staines, Matthew Milton, Tracy Hopkins; **Delhi** Madhavi Singh, Jalpreen Kaur Chhatwal, Dipika Dasgupta
Design & Pictures: **London** Scott Stickland, Dan May, Diana Jarvis, Mark Thomas, Nicole Newman; **Delhi** Umesh Aggarwal, Ajay Verma, Jessica Subramanian, Ankur Guha, Pradeep Thapliyal, Sachin Tanwar, Nikhil Agarwal, Sachin Gupta
Production: Liz Cherry, Louise Minihane, Erika Pepe
Cartography: **London** Ed Wright, Katie Lloyd-Jones; **Delhi** Rajesh Chhibber, Ashutosh Bharti, Rajesh Mishra, Animesh Pathak, Swati Handoo, Deshpal Dabas, Lokamata Sahu
Marketing, Publicity & roughguides.com: Liz Statham
Digital Travel Publisher: Peter Buckley
Reference Director: Andrew Lockett
Operations Coordinator: Becky Doyle
Operations Assistant: Johanna Wurm
Publishing Director (Travel): Clare Currie
Commercial Manager: Gino Magnotta
Managing Director: John Duhigg

Publishing information

This second edition published October 2011 by

Rough Guides Ltd,
80 Strand, London WC2R 0RL
11, Community Centre, Panchsheel Park, New Delhi 110017, India

Distributed by the Penguin Group

Penguin Books Ltd,
80 Strand, London WC2R 0RL

Penguin Group (USA)
375 Hudson Street, NY 10014, USA

Penguin Group (Australia)
250 Camberwell Road, Camberwell, Victoria 3124, Australia

Penguin Group (NZ)
67 Apollo Drive, Mairangi Bay, Auckland 1310, New Zealand

Rough Guides is represented in Canada by Tourmaline Editions Inc. 662 King Street West, Suite 304, Toronto, Ontario M5V 1M7

Cover concept by Peter Dyer.

Typeset in Bembo and Helvetica to an original design by Henry Iles.

Printed in Singapore

416pp includes index

A catalogue record for this book is available from the British Library

ISBN: 978-1-84836-890-3

The publishers and authors have done their best to ensure the accuracy and currency of all the information in **The Rough Guide to Korea**, however, they can accept no responsibility for any loss, injury, or inconvenience sustained by any traveller as a result of information or advice contained in the guide.

11 12 13 14 8 7 6 5 4 3 2

Help us update

We've gone to a lot of effort to ensure that the second edition of **The Rough Guide to Korea** is accurate and up-to-date. However, things change – places get "discovered", opening hours are notoriously fickle, restaurants and rooms raise prices or lower standards. If you feel we've got it wrong or left something out, we'd like to know, and if you can remember the address, the price, the hours, the phone number, so much the better.

Please send your comments with the subject line "**Rough Guide Korea Update**" to ⓔmail@uk.roughguides.com. We'll credit all contributions and send a copy of the next edition (or any other Rough Guide if you prefer) for the very best emails.

Find more travel information, connect with fellow travellers and book your trip on ⓦwww.roughguides.com

Acknowledgements

Norbert Paxton finds it hard to know where to start thanking those who helped make his latest trip around Korea so memorable. His Seoul *chingus* deserve much love: Michael Spavor, Jason Strother, Sora Kim and sister Nicole. Then there were Jeju travel buddies Weno Geerts and Chika Kimura, the Torro Rosso Grand Prix team in Mokpo, Juhee Jang in Gwangju, Boston Brian and Miri Park in Busan, two happy Welsh readers in Jeongdongjin, Simon for the northern stuff, reader HH Saffery for some useful tips and the various Seoul cafés in which much of the writing was conducted. Thanks also to Korea's wonderful restaurants, which kept Norbert's belly full.

Photo credits

All photos © Martin Richardson, Tim Draper/Rough Guides except the following:

Introduction

p.13 Socialist realist posters, Pyongyang © Tony Waltham/Robert Harding
p.14 Deogyusan National Park © Korea Tourism Organisation

Things not to miss

02 Udo beach © Korea Tourism Organisation
03 Secret garden, Changdeokgung Palace © Christophe Boisvieux/Robert Harding
05 Boryeong Mud Festival © Josh Kraemer/OnAsia
06 *Makkeolli* © Korea Tourism Organisation
09 Yakcheonsa © Martin Zatko
11 Flower *Ssambap* © Martin Zatko
14 Naejangsan © Korea Tourism Organisation
16 Buamdong © Korea Tourism Organisation
17 *Noraebang* © Korea Tourism Organisation
19 Gongsanseong © Korea Tourism Organisation
20 Jeongdongjin © Korea Tourism Organisation
21 Gyeongju, Royal Tomb of King Naemul of Silla © Steve Vidler/Superstock
22 A mural outside the Sinchon War Crimes Museum, North Korea © NK News/Getty Images
23 Nuclear imagery during the 2009 Arirang Mass Games, North Korea © NK News/Getty Images
24 Paekdusan © GTI
25 Subway station, Pyongyang, North Korea © AFP/Getty Images

Hiking in Korea colour section

Hiking in Jeju © Korea Tourism Organisation
Ulleungdo © Korea Tourism Organisation
Jeju's coastal path © Korea Tourism Organisation
Udo © Martin Zatko

Korean cuisine colour section

Namdaemun market, Seoul © Eurasia/Robert Harding
Galbi © Korea Tourism Organisation
Gomanaru restaurant, Gongju © Korea Tourism Organisation

Black and whites

p.334 Pyongyang, young female soldiers paying tribute to Kim Il-sung © Photononstop/Superstock

SMALL PRINT

Index

Map entries are in colour.

INDEX

I

J

K

L

M

INDEX

N

O

P

R

S

T

INDEX

U

V

W

Y

I INDEX

Map symbols

maps are listed in the full index using coloured text

Chapter division boundary	Museum
International boundary	Bus stop
Regional boundary	Point of interest
Motorway	Observatory
Major road	Monument
Minor road	Tourist office/information point
Pedestrianized street	Post office
Railway	Palace
Cable car	Arch
Footpath	Accommodation
River	Skiing
Ferry	Campsite
Wall/fortification	Border crossing
Gate	Tower
Bridge	Fortress
Cliff	Shrine
Mountain range	Buddhist temple
Mountain peak	Statue/memorial
Mountain pass	Temple
Rocks	Pagoda
Cave	Market
Waterfall	Building
Spring	Church
Mountain lodge	Stadium
Lighthouse	Park
Airport	Beach
Subway	

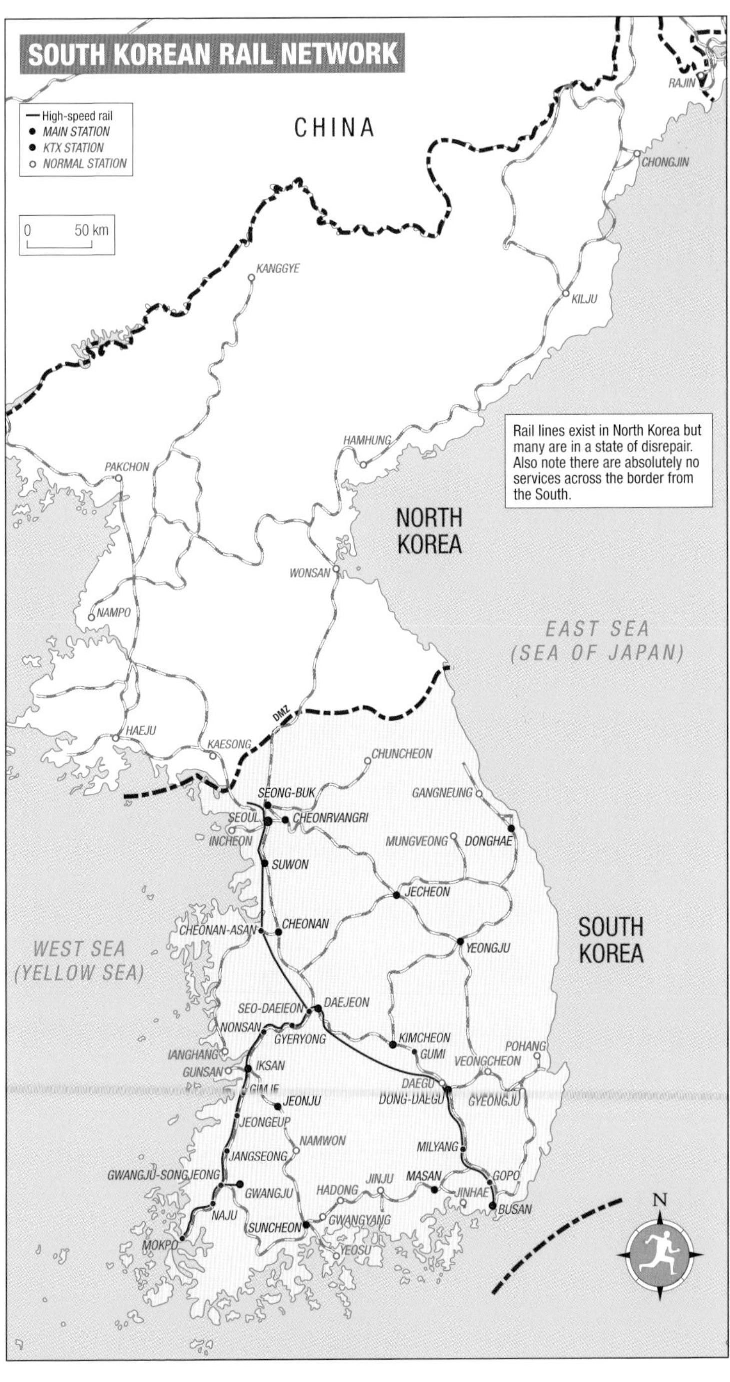
SOUTH KOREAN RAIL NETWORK
High-speed rail
MAIN STATION
KTX STATION
NORMAL STATION
0 50 km
CHINA
RAJIN
CHONGJIN
KANGGYE
KILJU
Rail lines exist in North Korea but many are in a state of disrepair. Also note there are absolutely no services across the border from the South.
HAMHUNG
PAKCHON
NORTH KOREA
WONSAN
NAMPO
EAST SEA (SEA OF JAPAN)
DMZ
HAEJU
KAESONG
CHUNCHEON
SEONG-BUK
GANGNEUNG
SEOUL
CHEONRVANGRI
INCHEON
MUNGVEONG
DONGHAE
SUWON
JECHEON
CHEONAN
CHEONAN-ASAN
SOUTH KOREA
WEST SEA (YELLOW SEA)
YEONGJU
SEO-DAEIEON
DAEJEON
NONSAN
GYERYONG
KIMCHEON
IANGHANG
GUMI
POHANG
VEONGCHEON
GUNSAN
IKSAN
DAEGU
DONG-DAEGU
GYEONGJU
JEONJU
JEONGEUP
NAMWON
MILYANG
JANGSEONG
GWANGJU-SONGJEONG
GWANGJU
HADONG
JINJU
MASAN
GOPO
JINHAE
BUSAN
NAJU
SUNCHEON
GWANGYANG
MOKPO
YEOSU
N

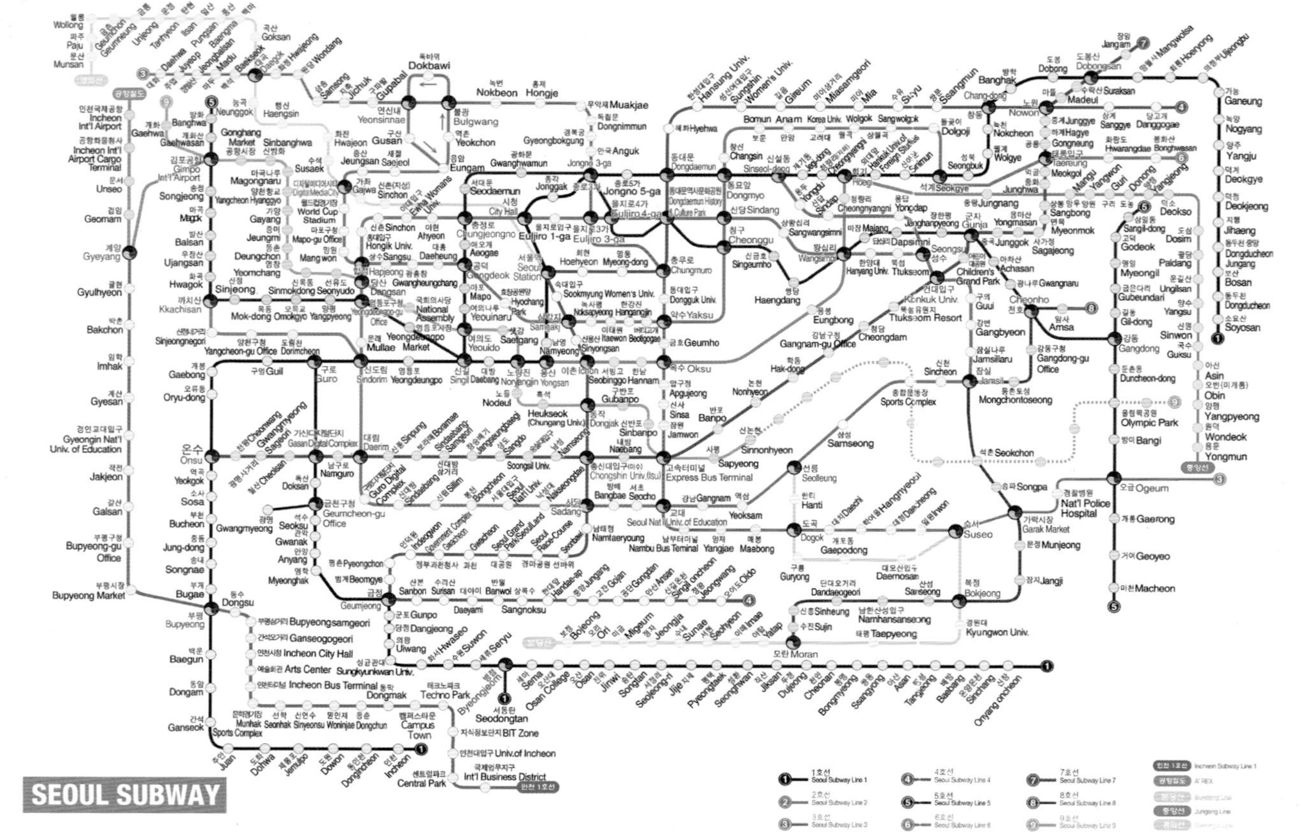
SEOUL SUBWAY
1호선 Seoul Subway Line 1
2호선 Seoul Subway Line 2
3호선 Seoul Subway Line 3
4호선 Seoul Subway Line 4
5호선 Seoul Subway Line 5
6호선 Seoul Subway Line 6
7호선 Seoul Subway Line 7
8호선 Seoul Subway Line 8
9호선 Seoul Subway Line 9
인천 1호선 Incheon Subway Line 1
공항철도
중앙선 Jungang Line